re Reference

Microsoft®

MICROSOFT® VISUAL J#™ .NET

John Sharp
Andy Longshaw
Peter Roxburgh

rosoft®
net™

PUBLISHED BY
Microsoft Press
A Division of Microsoft Corporation
One Microsoft Way
Redmond, Washington 98052-6399

Library of Congress Cataloging-in-Publication Data
Sharp, John, 1964-
Microsoft Visual J# .NET / John Sharp, Andy Longshaw, Peter Roxburgh.
p. cm.
Includes index.
ISBN 0-7356-1550-0
1. Microsoft Visual J++. 2. Java (Computer program language). 3. Microsoft .NET. I. Longshaw, Andy. II. Roxburgh, Peter. III. Title.

QA76.73.J38 S457 2002
005.2'768--dc21 2002071758

Printed and bound in the United States of America.

1 2 3 4 5 6 7 8 9 QWT 7 6 5 4 3 2

Distributed in Canada by H.B. Fenn and Company Ltd.

A CIP catalogue record for this book is available from the British Library.

Microsoft Press books are available through booksellers and distributors worldwide. For further information about international editions, contact your local Microsoft Corporation office or contact Microsoft Press International directly at fax (425) 936-7329. Visit our Web site at www.microsoft.com/mspress. Send comments to *mspinput@microsoft.com.*

Acquisitions Editor: Danielle Bird
Project Editor: Kathleen Atkins
Technical Editor: Marzena Makuta

Body Part No. X08-73257

Table of Contents

Introduction xvii

Part I **The Architecture of .NET**

1 The Challenge of *N*-Tier Development 3

Client/Server and *N*-Tier Architectures 4

Two-Tier Architecture 4

N-Tier Architecture 6

The Northwind Traders Example 8

Connectivity and Data Formats 12

Sockets 12

Remote Procedure Calls 14

Object RPCs 16

Remote Method Invocation 17

The Web 19

Data Access 21

Open Database Connectivity 21

Java Database Connectivity 22

ADO and ADO.NET 22

Nonfunctional Requirements 23

Security 23

Scalability and Availability 24

Integrity and Transactions 25

.NET Enterprise Servers 25

Java and .NET 26

Summary 27

2 Microsoft .NET 29

Compilers and Language Support 29

The Common Language Runtime 30

Cross-Language Development 40

Memory Management 45

Integrating Unmanaged Code into .NET Applications 50

Assemblies and Deployment 51

The Joy of DLLs: The Movie 51

.NET Assemblies 52

Private Assemblies 55

The Global Assembly Cache 56

Configuring an Application 60

The .NET Framework Class Library 65

Namespaces 67

.NET Remoting and the Web 69

The .NET Remoting Architecture 69

Remote Object Activation 71

ASP.NET 71

Web Services 72

.NET Security 73

Application Domains 74

Role-Based Security 76

Code Access Security 81

Summary 87

3 Java and the Common Language Runtime 89

Components and Java 91

JavaBeans 92

Components in .NET 98

Java, J#, and the .NET Framework 106

Packaging and Locating Classes 106

The Java Class Hierarchy 108

Other Issues 118

Migrating to J# 121

Metadata and Attributes 123

Reflection in .NET 124

Attributes 131

Enterprise Java 133

The Elements of J2EE 133

Comparing .NET to J2EE 139

The Java Pet Store 142

Summary 144

4 **Graphical User Interfaces** **145**
Desktop GUIs 146
Revisiting Java GUI Development 146
The Windows Forms Library 149
Porting Existing Java Applications 150
Porting AWT Applications to .NET 157
Writing a GUI Application Using the .NET Classes 159
Creating the Windows Form 160
Adding Controls to the Form 165
Handling Events 171
Using File Dialog Boxes 174
Working with the System Clipboard 178
Building and Running the Application 180
Summary 181

Part II Managing and Manipulating Data

5 **Processing XML** **185**
Using XML in a .NET Application 186
XML as a Data Format 186
Roles for XML 189
What Applications Need from XML Support 190
Processing XML Data 191
Support for XML in Visual J# and the .NET Framework 192
Single-Pass Processing of XML Documents 195
Parsing XML Documents Using the *XMLReader* Class 196
Processing XML Using an *XMLTextReader* Instance 197
Other Options for Reading and Navigation 205
Types and Namespaces 207
Exception Handling 208
Writing XML Documents Using the *XmlWriter* Class 209
Escaping and Copying When Writing 212
Validation and Entity Resolution 213
Validating XML Documents 213
Resolving Entities 218

Processing XML Documents in Memory 219
In-Memory Processing 219
Loading XML into the *XmlDocument* Class 221
Obtaining Information from a DOM Document 222
Treating a DOM Fragment as a Stream 227
Writing and Manipulating In-Memory XML Documents 227
Altering Content in a DOM Tree 227
Making Substantial Changes to XML Documents 228
Writing Out the DOM Tree 230
XML and Data 230
Links Between XML and ADO.NET Data 231
Viewing XML as Relational Data 232
Manipulating XML as Relational Data 233
Viewing Relational Data as XML 234
Summary 235
6 Transforming XML 237
Transforming XML in .NET Applications 238
The Need for Transformation 238
The XSLT Processing Model 240
Applying Transformations 244
.NET Support for XML Transformations 246
Applying Stylesheets to XML Documents 246
Simple Transformations Using *XslTransform* 247
Transformation Sources and Targets 248
Transforming a *DataSet* 250
Optimization and Partial Transformation 250
Searching and Navigating Using XPath 251
Optimizing XSLT Transformations 252
Partial Transformations 253
Parameterization and External Functionality 254
Passing in Parameters 254
Invoking External Functionality 258
Summary 263

7 ADO.NET 265

The ADO.NET Architecture 265

ADO.NET Components 266

DataSet Objects 268

Connections and Data Adapters 269

Connecting to a Data Store 270

Connecting to a Data Source (OLE DB and SQL) 270

Connections and Visual Studio .NET 272

Connection Pooling 273

Consuming Connection Events 273

Executing Commands Against a Data Store 274

Building Commands 275

Using Parameters in Statements 276

Invoking Stored Procedures 282

Retrieving a Single Record from a Data Source 283

Using a *DataReader* Object for Read-Only Data Retrieval 283

Using *DataSet* Objects for Data Access 285

Populating a *DataSet* Table from a Data Adapter 285

Navigating a Typed *DataSet* 288

Navigating an Untyped *DataSet* 291

Manipulating and Updating a Data Store from a Data Adapter 292

Defining Relationships and Constraints 296

Transaction Management 299

Working with XML and ADO.NET 301

Writing a *DataSet* as XML 301

Writing *DataRelation* Objects as XML 304

Inferring the *DataSet* Structure from XML 304

Summary 306

Part III Developing for the Enterprise

8 Multithreading with .NET 309

Threads and .NET 310

Application Domains and Threads 312

Creating Threads 312

Threads and Security 314
Passing Parameters to Threads 314
Thread States 315
Terminating Threads 318
Scheduling Threads 321
Threads and Unmanaged Code 323
Synchronization 325
Manual Synchronization 329
Automatic Synchronization 338
Static and Thread Data 341
Interthread Communication 343
Thread Notification 343
Timers 354
Thread Pooling 355
The *ThreadPool* Class 356
Asynchronous I/O 357
Summary 359

9 Basic Network Programming 361

Sockets Essentials 362
Connection-Oriented Sockets 363
Data Transmission Issues 380
Connectionless Sockets 382
Blocking and Nonblocking Sockets 387
Using Sockets Asynchronously 389
The *Poll* and *Select* Methods 389
Network Streams 391
Web Network Programming 393
Pluggable Protocols 394
Requesting and Receiving Data Using HTTP 396
Posting Data 399
Processing Requests Asynchronously 401
Using a *WebClient* Object 402
HTTP Connection Management and Pooling 403
Security over the Internet 405
Authentication and Authorization 405

Encryption 408

Summary 409

10 Serializing Objects 411

Serializing and Deserializing Data 412

Formatting Data 412

Deserialization 416

Versioning 417

Being Selective 422

Advanced Serialization 423

Customizing Serialization 423

Handling Object Graphs 427

XML Serialization 433

XML Formatting 433

Deserializing an XML Stream 441

Summary 445

11 .NET Remoting 447

The Common Language Runtime Remoting Architecture 447

Remote Objects 448

The .NET Remoting Model 451

The *ObjRef* Object and Proxies 457

Messages, Channels, and Channel Sinks 458

Programming with TCP Remoting 460

Server-Activated Object Remoting 461

Client-Activated Object Remoting 469

Managing Object Lifetimes and Leases 471

TCP Remoting Security 474

Remote Method Parameters 475

Remote Events 476

HTTP Remoting 480

Remoting Server Hosting 481

Hosting with IIS 483

HTTP Remoting Security 485

Customizing Remoting 486

One-Way Remoting 486

The *RemotingServices* Class 487
Tracking Handlers 489
Custom Channel Sinks and Channels 492
Summary 494

12 Using Message Queues 495

The Architecture of Message Queuing 3.0 496
Queues, Servers, and Active Directory 496
Transactional Message Queues 498
Managing Queues 498
System Queues 500
Message Delivery 501
Message Queuing Triggers 502
Programming Message Queues 502
Posting and Receiving Messages 502
Handling Messages 514
Managing Queues 520
Asynchronous Operations 525
Receiving Messages Asynchronously 525
Disconnected Queues 527
Requesting an Acknowledgment 530
Messaging in the Real World 532
Reliability and Transactions 532
Message Authentication and Encryption 537
Messaging over HTTP 540
Summary 540

Part IV Integrating with Windows

13 Integrating with Unmanaged Components 543

Managed and Unmanaged Code 544
Invoking Methods in Unmanaged DLLs 545
Using J/Direct 546
The Platform Invoke Service 551
Other P/Invoke Issues 567
Calling COM Components 571

Creating and Using an RCW 572
Sinking COM Events 577
Using COM Objects Without Type Libraries 580
Integrating .NET Components into COM 589
Designing .NET Components for COM Interop 589
Creating a COM Callable Wrapper 594
Testing the CCW 598
Interoperability with Other Technologies 600
The Real Solution: XML Web Services 602
Summary 603

14 Serviced Components and COM+ 605

Using an Existing COM+ Component 607
The FourthCoffee Components Revisited 608
Configuring the Fourth Coffee COM+ Application 608
Using the Fourth Coffee COM+ Application 612
Subscribing to a Loosely Coupled Event 613
Building a Serviced Component 621
Serviced Component Basics 622
Registering and Using the Serviced Component 629
Features of Serviced Components 633
Synchronization, Activities, and Context 633
Static Methods 637
Serviced Component Activation 638
Caching Shared State 645
More About Transactions 650
.NET and COM+ Security 655
Code Access Security Requirements 655
The .NET Role-Based Security Model 655
The COM+ Role-Based Security Model 656
Implementing COM+ Security from .NET 657
COM+ Imperative Security 660
Asynchronous Components 661
Creating a Queued Component 661
Supporting Loosely Coupled Events 662
Summary 665

15 Implementing Windows Services 667

Controlling a Windows Service 668

Displaying Service Information 668

Starting and Stopping a Service 673

Writing a Windows Service 675

The Structure of a Service Application 675

Understanding Installer Classes 680

Creating a New Installer 681

Adding a Service Description 685

Installing and Testing the Service 686

Uninstalling a Service 688

Summary 688

Part V Building Applications for the Web

16 ASP.NET: A Better ASP 691

Introducing ASP.NET 692

Browser-Based Web Applications 692

The ASP.NET Environment 693

The Basic ASP.NET Programming Model 695

HTML Forms and ASP Forms 700

ASP.NET Web Forms 705

The Server-Side Controls 708

The Code Behind the Page 710

Handling Events 714

Client-Side Validation 718

Migrating from ASP Pages 724

Language and Code 724

The User Interface 725

Pages, Controls, and Data 727

The *Page* Class 727

Common Controls 732

Creating Your Own Controls 735

Binding to Data 739

Building ASP.NET Web Applications 742

Web.config 742

Global.asax 743

Deploying an ASP.NET Application 745

Managing State 746

Error Handling 754

Security 760

Caching 764

Summary 768

17 Building a Web Service 769

An Overview of Web Services 769

What Is a Web Service? 769

Web Service Technologies 770

Web Services in .NET 774

Creating a Web Service 775

A Simple Web Service 775

Creating a Web Service Using Visual Studio .NET 781

Web Service Description and Data Types 784

Exposing a Web Service Interface 785

Invoking the Service 797

Passing Complex Data Types 799

Passing *DataSet* Objects 811

Passing XML Documents 814

Creating an XML Web Service Application 815

Web Services as ASP.NET Applications 816

Transactions and Web Services 826

Exposing Existing Applications as Web Services 828

Summary 830

18 Creating a Web Service Client 831

Web Service Clients 832

The Client View of a Web Service 832

Creating a Web Service Client Using Visual Studio .NET 834

Going Beyond the Simple Client Scenario 838

Other Client Types 859

Dynamic Discovery of Web Services 863

Discovering Services on a Server 863

Discovering Services Through UDDI 870

Summary 875

Acknowledgments

This is the second book I have written for Microsoft Press. In the acknowledgments in my first book (*Microsoft Visual C# .NET Step By Step*) I said I had not realized how much work was involved in authoring a book. When I set out on the long-running project that was this volume, I thought I had a better idea of the effort that would be required. Boy, was I ever wrong! The late nights, frustrations, tears, and ultimate feelings of elation were only the beginning—eventually I had to leave the night club, come home, and start writing. Suffice to say that without the unstinting efforts of my coauthor and friend Andy Longshaw, as well as my long-suffering project manager at Content Master, Suzanne Carlino, this book would never have made it. It would also be very remiss of me not to thank the editorial team at Microsoft Press for their sterling work and incredible patience with my usual collection of poor spellings, grammatical errors, and tendency to write stuff that would get me sued if left uncorrected! So, my heartfelt appreciation must also go to Marzena Makuta, Ina Chang, Kathleen Atkins, and Barbara Moreland at Microsoft Press, and Debi Mishra of the product group.

Finally, as ever, the last word must go to my family: to Diana who thinks I am insane but still loves me; to James, who keeps asking me when I am going to get a proper job; and to Frankie, who still gets all embarrassed when I walk her to school.

I nearly forgot. Up the Gills!

John Sharp
July 2002

John says all of the nice things in his acknowledgments, so I'd just like to reiterate his thanks to all of the people at Content Master and Microsoft who have made this book possible. I'd also like to thank John for his help in talking through issues and the incredible amount of in-depth knowledge he brings to bear on the issues that had me tearing my hair out. Alex Mackman, Simon Horrell and the VSJ champs also deserve a mention for their help in answering tricky .NET and J# questions. My contributions to this book have been made far better by my coworkers on the CSD project who have posed real-world questions and challenged me to answer them using the .NET Framework. Their

Ian, Anup, Dave S., Jon, Henry, Rachael, Dee, Barry, Richard R. and the rest of the team for their questions and opinions, and to Dave de Naeyer for having confidence in me. My sympathy as ever goes to my family who put up with the inevitable mood swings that accompany writing software that pushes at the boundaries of a platform so that you can see how things really work.

Andy Longshaw
July 2002

Introduction

Blaise Pascal, Ada Lovelace, Edna Cobol, and now John Sharp. What do we all have in common? Well, as it happens, not as much as my ego would like. It would be nice to think that Microsoft named Visual J# after me, but sadly that's not the case. It's just one of those strange coincidences that happens from time to time.

So, what is J# and why has Microsoft developed it? In some ways, it's easier to say what J# isn't. J# is not Java. J# is a programming language that uses Java syntax so that Java developers can build applications with the Microsoft .NET Framework. You'll find that you can recompile many existing Java classes using J# to generate executables that will run in the .NET common language runtime. J# is also a great language for developing new applications. It provides a path into .NET for Java and J++ developers who don't want to abandon the comfort of a familiar syntax.

This book describes how to build enterprise applications in a .NET environment using J# and Microsoft Visual Studio .NET. Building distributed systems is what .NET is designed to help you do. It offers a rich framework of classes that provide an infrastructure that you can extend to meet your own requirements. This book shows in detail how you can exploit the multitude of .NET features while programming in J#. As a result, you'll find a lot of information in this book about how .NET and the common language runtime work.

What doesn't this book do? This book will not teach you how to program in Java—we're assuming that you're familiar with the syntax and semantics of the Java language. Many of the concepts and ideas are presented in terms that a Java developer should understand, but where J# concepts are distinctly different we try to explain them more thoroughly.

Writing a book of this nature about an unreleased product is a challenging task. And a product that is not finished tends to change and mutate a little as it edges toward the release date. (If you have either of the publicly available beta releases, you should upgrade because significant changes have been made!) However, as always, we take full responsibility for any errors or inaccuracies in this book and would be delighted to hear about them so we can fix them.

P.S. Before anybody e-mails me, I know that COBOL was not named after Edna Cobol. She just happens to be my pet cat's psychotherapist and she agreed to waive her fees if I gave her a mention.

How This Book Is Organized

Part I, "The Architecture of .NET," provides technical information about .NET itself. Chapter 1 summarizes the challenges that distributed systems present. Chapter 2 describes the overall purpose and structure of the .NET platform. It introduces key concepts such as the .NET Framework, the just-in-time (JIT) compilers, and the relationship between .NET and other important technologies such as COM+. Chapter 3 covers the common language runtime in detail and describes the Microsoft Intermediate Language (MSIL) and the managed execution environment. It also discusses the component-oriented features of the common language runtime—attributes, properties, namespaces, delegates, and events—and shows you how they're mapped into the implementation of Java in J#. Chapter 4 compares the GUI libraries available in .NET to those of the Java Developers Kit.

Part II, "Managing and Manipulating Data," concentrates on processing data in J#. Chapter 5 examines the eXtensible Markup Language (XML) support available to J# and looks at how to produce and consume valid XML data. Chapter 6 shows you how to transform XML from one format to another using the XML Stylesheet Language for Transformations (XSLT) support built into .NET. Chapter 7 covers Microsoft ADO.NET. It shows you how to use ADO.NET to connect to a data source, issue queries, and perform updates and deletes in an efficient and scalable manner.

Part III, "Developing for the Enterprise," examines how to build multithreaded applications that span the local area network (LAN). Chapter 8 describes the .NET threading model and shows you how to exploit multiple threads with J#. Chapter 9 looks at the basic networking mechanisms available for communicating with other machines and platforms (such as UNIX) and covers the implementation of sockets in .NET. Chapter 10 describes the mechanisms .NET uses for marshaling objects between threads and processes. It looks at how serialization and deserialization work and compares XML to binary serialization. Chapter 11 examines the .NET Remoting architecture in detail, covering value and reference object remoting, channels, custom message sinks, handling remote events, activation models, security, and encryption. Chapter 12 shows you how to use Microsoft Message Queue (MSMQ) for implementing reliable, asynchronous messaging using J# and .NET.

Part IV, "Integrating with Windows," covers key topics related to building applications that use Microsoft Windows features and services. Chapter 13 looks at how to integrate legacy Java components, DLLs, and COM components into a J# application. It also shows you how to create COM callable components in J# that support early and late binding. Chapter 14 describes how to create a J# component that makes use of Component Services (COM+). It shows you how to create components that can use transactions to maintain data integrity. Chapter 15 shows you how to write Windows services in J#. It describes the structure and lifecycle of a service application and covers installation and security issues.

Part V, "Building Applications for the Web," shows you how to build J# applications that use the Internet to attain global reach. Chapter 16 describes how the ASP.NET model works and shows the structure of an ASP.NET application in J#. Chapter 17 describes how to build a Web service in J# and how to make services and components accessible over the Web. It also describes SOAP in detail and explains techniques for using a Web service as a facade for COM and other components. Chapter 18 shows you how to build a Web service client that's capable of invoking a Web service synchronously and asynchronously. It also describes dynamic Web service discovery and the use of Universal Description, Discovery, and Integration (UDDI).

System Requirements

The examples in this book have been built and tested using Windows XP Professional and Windows .NET Server (Beta 3). Apart from the examples in Chapter 15, the code will also run using Windows 2000 (SP2 recommended). Of course, you'll also need to have Visual Studio .NET and Visual J# .NET installed.

To run some samples, you will also need the following:

- Microsoft Internet Explorer 5.5 or later
- Internet Information Services (IIS)
- .NET Framework SDK, which installs with Microsoft Visual Studio .NET

Installing the Sample Files

The sample files can be downloaded from the Web site at *http://www.microsoft.com/mspress/books/<>.asp*. To download the sample files, simply click the "Companion Content" link in the More Information menu on the right side of the Web page. This will load the Companion Content page, which includes links for downloading the sample files.

Microsoft Press Support Information

Every effort has been made to ensure the accuracy of this book and the contents of the practice files Web site. If you do run into a problem, Microsoft Press provides corrections for its books through the World Wide Web at

http://www.microsoft.com/mspress/Support/

If you have comments, questions, or ideas regarding the presentation or use of this book you can send them to Microsoft using either of the following methods:

Postal Mail:

Microsoft Press
Attn: Microsoft Visual J# .NET (Core Reference) Editor
One Microsoft Way
Redmond, WA 98052-6399

E-mail:

MSPINPUT@MICROSOFT.COM

Please note that product support isn't offered through the preceding mail addresses.

John Sharp

Part I

The Architecture of .NET

1

The Challenge of *N*-Tier Development

These days, developers rarely build standalone, self-contained business applications that are intended to run on a single computer. It seems that all the applications being built are part of something bigger and comprise other bits and pieces. Of course, you need not know how these other components work. The code simply has to "talk" to them using well-defined interfaces. What's more, these components can be located almost anywhere on the planet. The developer's job is to build a system using these components and to make sure it works.

Integrating preexisting components into a functional, scalable, distributed structure that operates in a timely manner and makes the most efficient use of resources is actually what makes designing and building systems fun. With the right set of tools and a little logic, developers have been able to create ever more complex and elegant systems. This book is all about using one particularly cool set of tools that allow Java developers to create distributed applications: Microsoft Visual J# .NET.

Before we delve into J#, let's take a quick tour of the concepts and technologies that underlie modern distributed systems. This chapter will also describe a number of architectural and design challenges that the rest of the book will show you how to address using J# and Microsoft .NET, and it will generally get you in the mood for the topics covered in the rest of the book.

Client/Server and *N*-Tier Architectures

Distributed applications have come about through evolution rather than a revolution, albeit with occasional sudden leaps as new technology has become available. From the first hesitant decoupling of the desktop from the database server over a low-bandwidth network to the current situation in which the Internet predominates, the basic goal has remained the same—to access and process shared data in a timely and secure manner.

Two-Tier Architecture

The classic two-tier architecture is what many developers mean by *client/server*, although if you put two developers in a room and ask them for a definition of client/server, you'll most likely end up with three opinions.

Here's how we define the terms *client* and *server*:

- A client is a process that requests a service (such as access to a database).
- A server is a process (such as a database server) that provides a service.

Notice that these definitions are process-oriented. It is perfectly feasible for both the client process and the server process to be located on the same machine, although in many cases they will be distributed—that's the more common case, especially when a single server is handling requests from multiple clients. The usual example of this sort of architecture is the database management system (DBMS). Figure 1-1 depicts a typical database client/server system.

In this case, the services being provided are requests to retrieve data and requests to create, modify, or remove items from the database. The client application and the server communicate using an agreed-upon mechanism—for example, structured query language (SQL) over a common network protocol. The server interprets the SQL statement, processes it, and sends an appropriate response back to the client. If the server is serving multiple clients simultaneously (using multiple threads), it might need to ensure that concurrent requests do not conflict. For example, two clients might attempt to update the same data at the same time; the server should reschedule one client, making it wait until the other has performed its work and released the necessary resources.

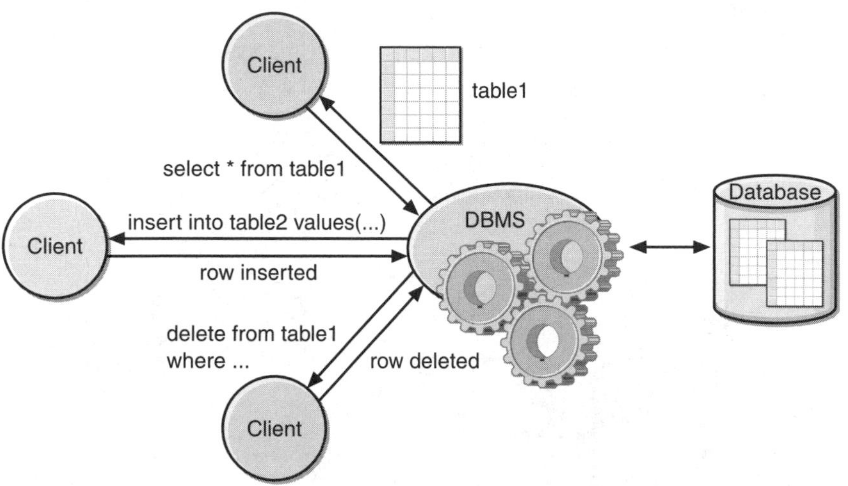

Figure 1-1 A database client/server system

All of this is transparent to the client, in theory. In practice, however, a client might notice the delays that occur while the server tries to work its way through the competing client requests. The database design, application code, and other tuning issues become paramount in ensuring that the system scales well.

Further complications can arise when a designer realizes that a server can also be a client, and vice-versa; in order to perform its service, a server might need to request services from other servers, which in turn might use further servers, and so on. In a distributed database (depicted in Figure 1-2), the DBMS might be configured to forward requests to access data in a particular table to another DBMS (using a linked SQL Server, for example).

Note One could conceivably end up in a situation in which the DBMS that is contacted directly by a client simply becomes a channel through which all requests for data are passed to one or more other DBMSs. The original DBMS will still perform a useful service and can enforce various security and integrity checks as the client requests or updates data, but it's not being very DBMS-like anymore.

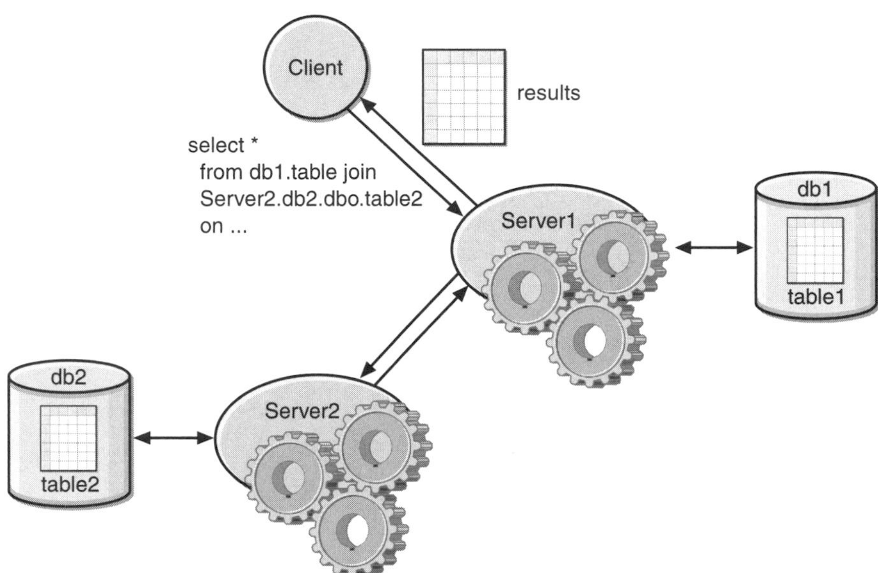

Figure 1-2 A distributed database (SQL Server)

N-Tier Architecture

N-tier systems (where *n* is 3 or more) require careful design and even more careful implementation. It is usual, but not mandatory, for each tier to contain components that perform well-defined roles. Different organizations give different names to each tier, reflecting the responsibilities of each tier. Examples of tiers from the Microsoft world include the User Services Tier, the Business Services Tier, and the Data Services Tier. The User Services Tier contains the presentation logic used for displaying data and gathering user input, the Business Services Tier contains the business rules and associated logic, and the Data Services Tier contains the components needed to manage persistent storage, usually using a DBMS.

Figure 1-3 depicts an example of a three-tier architecture.

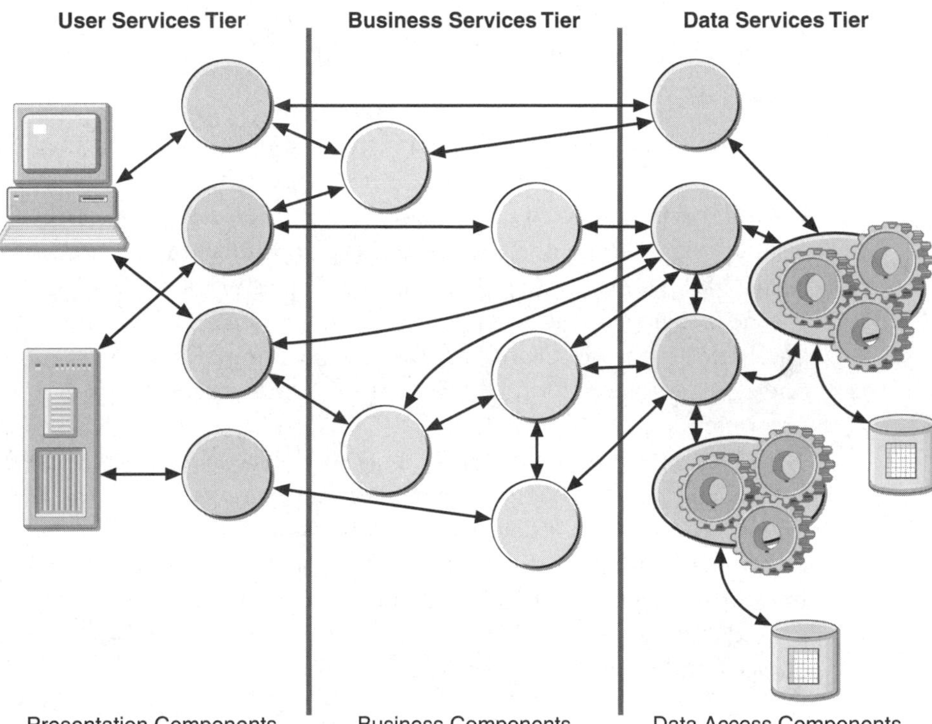

Figure 1-3 A three-tier architecture

This all sounds simple. But in practice, things can become very complicated very quickly, and there's a lot of room for developers to have deep and meaningful debates about the following issues:

- What code should actually go into each tier?
- How should components in one tier communicate with components in another tier?

To answer these questions, you should take a step back and consider the issues that led to the development of this architecture in the first place. For example

- What type, or types, of client will your system have to support: a GUI desktop application, an HTML browser, a batch application that requests and processes data but has no interactive user interface?

- Where is the data held, and in what format? Is there more than one data store?
- What are the data integrity requirements of the system? Where is the integrity of data checked? How do the business rules change over time?

You should also bear in mind that the tiers that result from partitioning a system in this manner are logical rather than physical. Naïve developers have been known to mistakenly assume that a three-tier architecture implies three separate computers: one for the desktop, another running the business components, and a third holding the database. This is not always so. Often, part of the business logic is located on the user's physical machine, some of the data storage logic might be located on the machine implementing the business rules, and the implementation of the business rules might be spread across several computers.

The choice of what components should go where is all part of the design. Many patterns have been proposed for automating some of the decisions developers have to make. (See *www.theserverside.com/patterns/index.jsp* for useful examples relating to distributed Java applications. They are based on Java 2 Enterprise Edition but can be adapted to .NET.) But by and large, you still have to understand the nature of the system being built in order to make the best choices and design a good structure.

The Northwind Traders Example

Consider an implementation of the Northwind Traders system—the sample database you're familiar with if you've spent any time using Microsoft SQL Server, Microsoft Access, Microsoft Visual Basic, or many other Microsoft applications. Northwind Traders is a fictitious organization that sells exotic edible goods. The Northwind database contains information about the goods that customers can order, information about the orders themselves, and the names and addresses of all the customers. Northwind Traders does not manufacture the goods; it orders them from suppliers as stock levels demand. Orders are sent to customers using a designated shipping company, depending on the location of the customer. Northwind Traders also maintains information about its employees and assigns each employee a target territory; the employee is responsible for maintaining and growing the customer accounts in the specified territory. Each territory belongs to a region. Figure 1-4 shows the schema for the Northwind database. The physical diagram of the database is shown in Figure 1-5.

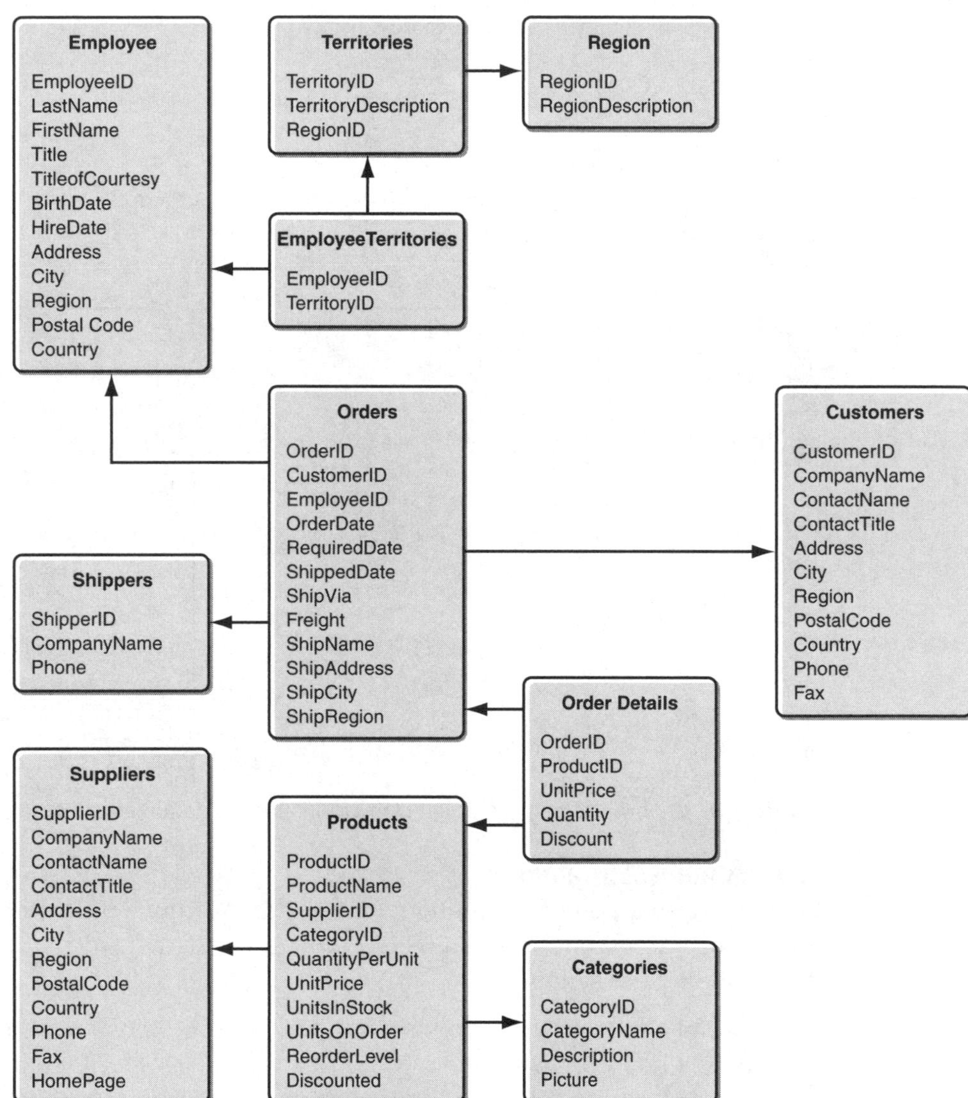

Figure 1-4 The Northwind Traders database schema

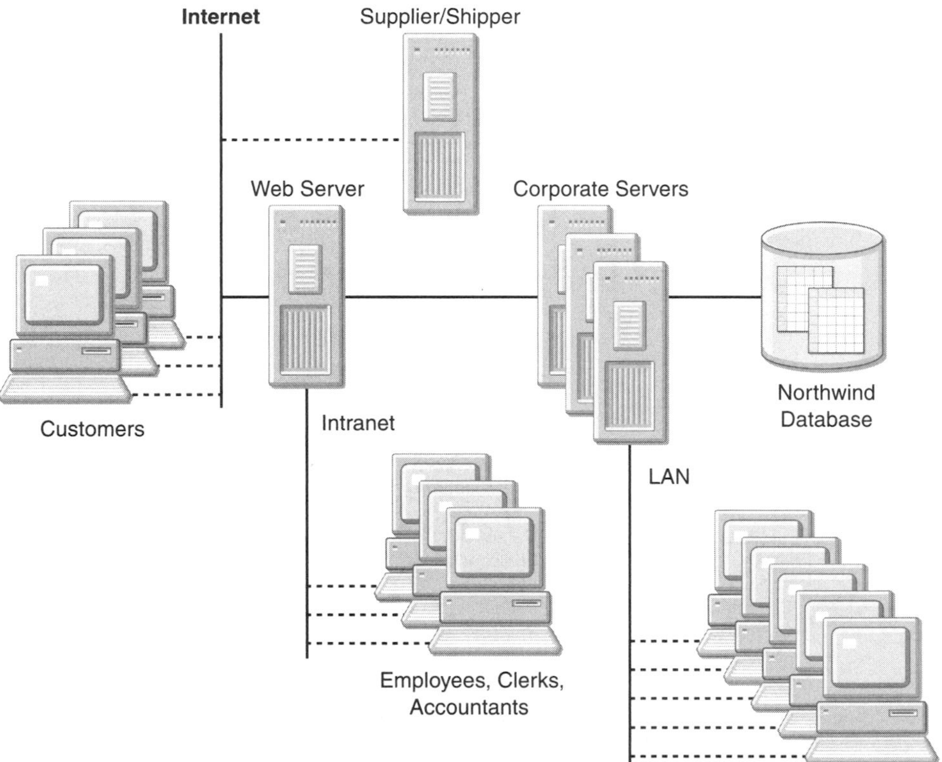

Figure 1-5 A physical diagram of the Northwind Traders database schema

Application Requirements

Here is a description of the requirements for the Northwind Traders system, as elicited by the user representative temporarily assigned to the development team building the system:

The Northwind Traders system must support several kinds of users, including customers who want to order goods and track their orders, employees who need access to customer and product information, clerks who dispatch orders and maintain inventory levels in the warehouse, and accountants who need to ascertain whether the company is making a profit. Customers will access the system using the Web and a browser. Employees, clerks, and accountants might use an internal desktop system or possibly an intranet. Part of the clerks' role in interacting with external agencies (suppliers and shippers) can be automated using a business-to-business (B2B) solution and the Internet. And further enhancements might be added in the future.

This list is complex but is by no means an atypical set of requirements. It would be easy to start throwing together pieces of code and components that support selected parts of the functionality, but unless you understand the bigger picture—how the system might need to collaborate with other systems—and can predict reasonably accurately any future needs, such an approach is unlikely to be successful.

Design Patterns

Fortunately, designers and developers tend to be pretty open about solutions they've discovered. There are few unique puzzles in the realm of distributed system design, and many common design patterns are publicly available, each designed to solve a particular problem in a defined context. The designer's job has become a matter of recognizing the problem and the context and then applying the appropriate pattern.

Perhaps the most famous design patterns are those published by the "Gang of Four"—Erich Gamma, Richard Helm, Ralph Johnson, and John Vlissides—in *Design Patterns: Elements of Reusable Object-Oriented Software* (Addison-Wesley, 1995). The 23 patterns in this book have passed into software folklore, and I won't repeat them all here. Other organizations have also proposed and published patterns, some of which are specializations of the original 23 (to target Web-based applications, for example). However, here are the keys to designing components in a flexible architecture that supports a dynamic distributed system:

- Use interfaces to decouple the functionality from the implementation.
- Hide as much detail as possible. The less you expose, the less you risk having to change "consuming code" if your component is modified in the future.
- Use generic interfaces that can be implemented by a range of components; don't define a business component that expects the GUI consumer to be a desktop application because you might end up having to rewrite the component (for example, if the consumer changes to a Web browser).

Any platform or toolset that you use to implement a distributed system using a patterns-based approach must provide support for these goals.

Connectivity and Data Formats

One major feature of distributed systems is that they are *distributed*—that is, components reside at different locations on different computers. These components and other pieces of software, such as a Web browser or a database server, need to communicate with each other across process boundaries. This communication is made possible by the middleware, formats, and protocols that components use. Another interesting challenge is that you might have to integrate a number of legacy components that still perform their tasks perfectly well—discarding and rewriting them in order to use new technologies might not be a cost-effective option.

Sockets

The great-granddaddy of connection mechanisms is the socket. Most modern connectivity solutions use sockets somewhere under the hood, but these days they're well hidden. Sockets themselves are an abstraction designed to hide the complexities of transmitting data over a network using TCP/IP, the protocol that underpins the Internet.

In a socket-based architecture, one process (often the server) creates a network endpoint on a machine, which is associated with a process, and waits for clients to connect to the endpoint. When the client connects to the server using the socket, the associated process receives data sent by the client, performs some piece of processing, and then possibly sends a response back to the client. A socket endpoint comprises the TCP/IP address of the computer and a port number (a positive integer). Any client that knows the TCP/IP address of the server machine and the port number can attempt to connect to the server process. The server process can examine the address of the client making the request (the TCP/IP address is passed as part of the protocol) and can accept or reject the request as it sees fit.

If you've written a program that uses sockets, you'll know that a lot of decisions are left up to the programmer's discretion. For example, what happens if a second request is sent to a server while the server is already handling a request? The answer is that the server should be implemented using multiple threads. One thread should sit and wait for a client request, and when a request arrives it should create and dispatch a new thread to handle the client while the original thread waits for the next request.

Another issue that the programmer is expected to handle is that the client must know the format of the data that the server requires. If the server expects an integer and the client sends it a string, the server will try to interpret the string as an integer and get it wrong. Even if the client knows that the server expects an integer, there is still plenty of room for confusion. How big (in bytes) is an integer? Are the client and server running on machines that use a big endian or little endian processor architecture?

Big Endian vs. Little Endian

The terms *big endian* and *little endian* refer to the byte ordering used by processors. A processor using big endian byte ordering stores the most significant byte of any multibyte value in the lowest memory address used by the data, the second most significant byte in the next location, and so on. A little endian processor stores the least significant byte in the lowest memory address used by the data, and so on.

For example, suppose a processor uses two-byte integers and the little endian byte-ordering scheme. The decimal integer 32000 will be represented in binary as 01111101 00000000. If the processor uses big endian byte ordering, the two bytes will be reversed: 00000000 01111101. If the value 32000 is transmitted from a little endian to a big endian computer, the big endian machine will wrongly interpret it as 125. Therefore, when you send data over a network, you should always be sure that it's transmitted using an agreed-upon byte-ordering scheme understood by both the sending and receiving computers.

Many UNIX machines are big endian, and big endian byte ordering is the convention used for transmitting data over the Internet. The Intel processors used by PCs running Microsoft Windows are little endian.

For those who are curious, the terms *big endian* and *little endian* can be traced back to Jonathan Swift's *Gulliver's Travels*. The Big-endians of Lilliput were so called because they cracked their boiled eggs at the big end; they were considered rebels by the Small-endians, who were commanded by the King of Lilliput to crack their eggs at the small end.

In general, binary data can be awkward to handle at the socket level because of the many ways it can be interpreted. Many designers and developers avoid using binary data and instead prefer to convert data into character streams, although streams present their own problems.

Another major concern with sockets is a lack of atomicity. When a client sends a large volume of data to a server over a socket, it might appear to the client as if it is sending a single piece of data. However, the vagaries of most modern operating system schedulers allow processes to be interrupted and suspended while they're performing input/output (I/O) operations. Behind the scenes, therefore, a single client operation that sends several kilobytes of data to a server might actually be broken down by the operating system into a series of smaller transmissions.

The client is not aware of this fact, but the server might be. The first chunk of data will be read, and the server might not realize that more is to follow; it will begin processing using the incomplete information it has received, once again making a mess of things! To counter this problem, designers end up defining data streams that contain additional information indicating how big a request is so the server can make sure it reads all of it. In short, when you use sockets, you can end up spending more time and effort worrying about the mechanics of data transmission than defining the actual business logic that needs to be performed.

Remote Procedure Calls

To free designers from the cumbersome task of handling sockets, a different mechanism was needed. One such mechanism is the Remote Procedure Call (RPC), which is a further abstraction of the network. (See Figure 1-6.) The purpose of the RPC is to make a request to a remote server look exactly the same as a call to a local procedure.

RPCs work by intercepting procedure calls using a proxy object (described by the Gang of Four, although proxies predate their design patterns book by a number of years) that packages up any parameters into a format suitable for transmission over the network and sends this data to a server (probably via a socket). A stub on the server receives the request, unpacks the data, and then invokes the corresponding procedure in the server process. Any return values are packed, sent from the server through the stub and the proxy back to the client, and then unpacked.

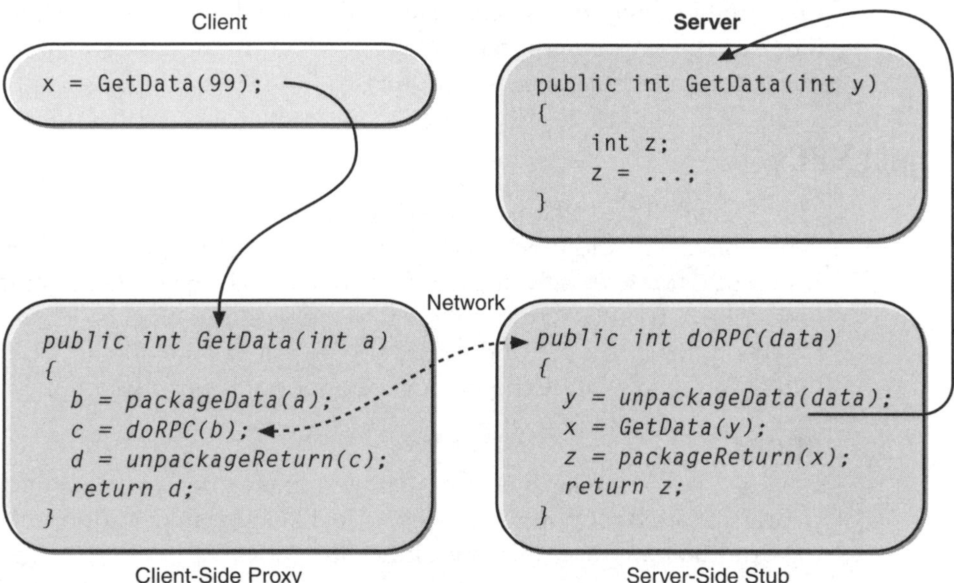

Figure 1-6 The RPC architecture (with proxy and stub pseudocode)

Most platforms that support RPCs provide tools that allow the proxy and stub code to be generated from a specification of the procedure that is to be remoted. For example, Microsoft supplies the MIDL compiler, which takes the definition of remote procedures in an Interface Definition Language (IDL) file and produces source code in C for the proxy and stub objects. Client code is compiled and linked with the proxy code, and the server is compiled and linked with the stub. The server itself must supply a real implementation of the remote procedure specified in the IDL file.

For transparency, RPCs often use a name service that allows the proxy to locate the RPC server by name rather than having to have hardcoded network addresses built in to the application. Using a name service permits the server to be relocated (for example, in the event of hardware failure) without needing to rebuild the client. Another advantage of a name service is that it can support advanced features such as load balancing by redirecting client requests to one of a number of servers that are implementing the same service.

The act of converting data into a portable format suitable for transmission over a network is called *marshaling*. The act of unpacking the data at the other end and converting it back into its original binary representation is called *unmarshaling*. IDL allows you to define how data structures should be marshaled if you don't want to use the default format. You should understand one important point at this juncture: Several vendors and consortia have implemented their own RPC mechanisms and marshaling schemes. They are all similar, but there are incompatibilities between them, so using RPCs does not guarantee portability across platforms.

Object RPCs

The original RPC mechanism was designed when procedural languages such as C predominated and object orientation was struggling to gain acceptance. As a result, RPCs were closely aligned with procedural semantics rather than objects. Object RPCs (ORPCs) extend RPCs into the world of objects—they allow entire objects, rather than just individual procedure calls, to be accessed remotely. ORPCs bring in a whole new range of opportunities and design issues.

CORBA

Having a set of similar but incompatible frameworks for performing RPCs was clearly not good for portability. The Object Management Group (OMG) decided to avoid making the same mistakes with ORPCs. It worked with its member organizations to come up with a common set of principles and techniques for allowing objects to be accessed remotely. The result was the Common Object Request Broker Architecture (CORBA), shown in Figure 1-7.

CORBA defines its own dialect of IDL. It extends the use of interfaces and adds support for objects in a language-independent manner. CORBA also dictates how objects should communicate, using an object request broker (ORB). An ORB is a piece of middleware that locates CORBA-compliant objects and is responsible for marshaling and unmarshaling data as the data is transmitted over the network.

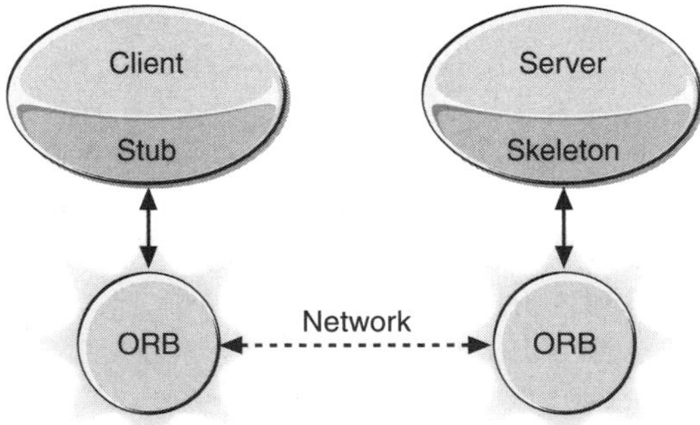

Figure 1-7 CORBA

With the advent of language bindings that map common (and some not-so-common) programming languages into IDL, cross-language interoperability was achieved. A server application can be written in one language, and the client can be written in another. The ORB handles the communication between the client and the server and the marshaling and unmarshaling of data, and the proxy (actually called a *client stub* by CORBA) and stub (called a *server skeleton*) code generated from the IDL definition of the server handles communication with the ORB. All you need to do when you generate the stub and skeleton is to specify which language (or languages) you want to generate code for.

The original CORBA specification defined how clients and servers should communicate with an ORB, but it was vague about how one ORB should communicate with another if it were ever necessary to do so. (ORBs originally used their own proprietary over-the-wire format). This rendered ORBs incompatible with one another. (Who says history never repeats itself?) The CORBA 2.0 specification plugged this gap by defining the Internet Inter-ORB Protocol (IIOP), which specifies the wire formats and messages that ORBs should use when communicating with other ORBs over TCP/IP (the network protocol used by the Internet and most intranets). Most modern ORBs implement IIOP.

An additional feature that CORBA provides is server activation. In the original world of RPCs, a server process that implemented an RPC had to be started manually in order for a client to find it, connect to it, and use it. CORBA defines activation policies that allow the ORB to start an object server on demand.

Distributed COM

Microsoft began its foray into the world of ORPCs with Distributed COM (DCOM). DCOM's functionality is similar to that of CORBA, except it is highly tuned and optimized for the Windows family of operating systems. (The German company Software AG created a version of DCOM for Linux platforms.) DCOM is essentially incompatible with CORBA, although COM-CORBA bridges are available if you need to combine the two systems. DCOM has provided the foundation for COM+, which is an important technology for building distributed applications under Windows and Microsoft .NET.

Remote Method Invocation

Java has its own native ORPC mechanism called Remote Method Invocation (RMI). RMI is optimized for Java and uses its own internal formats and mechanisms for marshaling data, and it is incompatible with most other RPC mechanisms (apart from CORBA using the RMI-IIOP protocol, which is an IIOP-conformant implementation of RMI). As a result, it can be difficult (but not impossible) to mix Java objects developed using the standard Java Developers Kit (JDK) with non-Java objects in a distributed system.

Serialization

The JDK includes its own name service—the RMI registry. (Version 1.2 of the JDK also includes *tnameserv*, which is a simple CORBA name server.) RMI uses serialization to marshal and unmarshal data. *Serialization* is just another term for the conversion of data into a portable binary representation. The binary version of the data can then be transmitted and reconstituted at the receiving end. Serialization is also used by Java for saving objects to a disk file or a database. Java is designed to work on multiple platforms, so even though RMI does not always interoperate well with other RPC services, it does guarantee cross-platform compatibility for applications developed using Java. A Java client running under Windows can communicate with an RMI server running under UNIX, and you don't need to worry about issues such as big endian versus little endian byte ordering.

Reference and Value Objects

Although Java objects can be complex, you can serialize most of them with little or no difficulty. Java has the *Serializable* interface, which a class must implement in order for its objects to allow serialization. The *Serializable* interface is actually just a marker interface that indicates that the class supports serialization; you do not need to write any additional code.

Objects instantiated from classes that implement the *Serializable* interface are copied by value when they're referenced as parameters or return types to RMI method calls. This means that if an RMI client obtains a serializable object as a return value from an RMI method call, the client actually receives a copy of the original data. Any changes that the client makes to this copy will not be reflected in the original object in the server. On the other hand, if a class is descended from the *java.rmi.server.RemoteObject* class, objects of that class are passed by reference between an RMI server and the client. Changes made by the client will be transmitted as RMI method calls to the original object residing in the address space of the server, thereby changing the state of the original object.

The decision about whether to pass remote objects by *value* or by *reference* is an important one that you should make on a case-by-case basis. It might make sense for objects whose data does not change (and that the client will want to browse) to be marshaled by value because this will result in a single transfer of data over the network. Objects whose state can be changed are better marshaled by reference, although this can result in numerous small network exchanges as individual pieces of state are modified. Design patterns are available if you need an object to be mutable but want to avoid the network overhead of repeated network calls. One example of such a pattern is using a value object with a batch update method that propagates the entire object back to the RMI server for updating after a number of changes have been made.

The Web

The explosion of the Internet and the increased access to network bandwidth has allowed more and more companies to consider using the Web to provide a transport for engaging in e-commerce. The same distributed design principles can be applied to local intranet solutions.

HTTP

Hypertext Transfer Protocol (HTTP) is the network protocol of the World Wide Web. HTTP is most commonly used by Web servers for receiving a request from a Web browser and responding with an HTML stream that contains information that the Web browser can render and display to the user. Much of the information that passes over HTTP is text-based, although this protocol can also be used to transmit binary data if the Web browser and the Web server use an agreed-upon format. (HTTP specifies a number of common formats that can be used.)

Although HTTP is suitable for transmitting text and surfing the Web, it has its limitations. An increasing number of companies that want to use the Internet as a conduit for sending business data require RPC calls over the Internet, which raw HTTP is not so good at.

Web Services

Web services are one way of addressing the need to make RPC calls over the Internet. You can think of a Web service as a component, or black box, that provides some useful facility to clients or consumers. Just as DCOM is often thought of as "COM with a longer wire," you can think of a Web service as a component with a truly global reach.

A Web service can be implemented in a variety of languages. Currently, the .NET Framework allows you to develop Web services using C++, Microsoft JScript, C#, J#, and Visual Basic .NET, and other languages will likely be available in the future. The Web server listens for incoming Web service requests and directs them to the appropriate Web service code. The Web server is also responsible for converting these requests (which arrive using HTTP) into a form that appears to the Web service code to be a local procedure call. In other words, the Web server acts like a server-side stub or CORBA skeleton.

As far as the consumer is concerned, the language used by the Web service, and even how the Web service performs its tasks, is not important. The consumer's view of a Web service is as an interface that exposes a number of well-defined methods. The consumer calls these methods using the standard Internet protocols, passing parameters in eXtensible Markup Language (XML) format and receiving responses in XML format.

XML has become a widely accepted standard for data transmission. It is well understood and extremely portable. The fact that XML is text-based makes it convenient to transmit over HTTP. There are the issues of marshaling and unmarshaling data to and from the required XML format, but the complexity of this process can be hidden using client-side proxies.

SOAP

SOAP is the protocol used by Web service consumers for sending requests to and receiving responses from Web services. SOAP is a lightweight protocol built on top of HTTP. It is possible to exchange SOAP messages over other protocols, but as of summer 2002 only the HTTP bindings for SOAP have been defined. SOAP defines an XML grammar for specifying the names of methods that a consumer wants to invoke on a Web service, for defining the parameters and return values, and for describing the types of parameters and return values.

When a client calls a Web service, it must specify the method and parameters using this XML grammar. Most tools for building applications that consume Web services create a client-side proxy that makes a call to a Web service appear to the client like a local procedure call. The proxy converts any parameters into the appropriate XML format and then calls the Web service using HTTP on behalf of the client. Any return values (which are passed back as XML) are unmarshaled into the native format expected by the client. Figure 1-8 shows a Web service consumer invoking a Web service using SOAP.

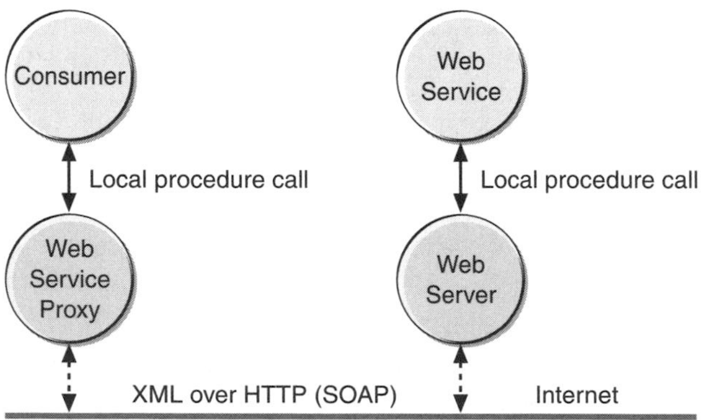

Figure 1-8 The Web service and the consumer

SOAP is becoming an industry standard. Its function is to improve cross-platform interoperability. The strength of SOAP lies in its simplicity, as well as the fact that it is based on two other industry-standard technologies, HTTP and XML.

Data Access

Business applications inevitably need to use data. Most systems use a database of some sort, often a relational database. Applications can use SQL for querying and maintaining relational data.

SQL has a long and checkered history, which I won't relate. Suffice it to say that SQL is useful for identifying data and specifying operations to be performed in a standard manner, but that there are two things SQL does not do:

- It does not specify how an SQL operation should be performed; it defines only what the results should be. This is not a problem for most developers (unless you're building your own DBMS). Database vendors fall over themselves trying to prove that their solution operates several orders of magnitude faster than the competition.
- It does not define how SQL statements should be transmitted to the DBMS or how the DBMS should send back the results. As a result, database vendors use their own formats for transmitting data over the network, which in turn means that database clients end up locked into a particular vendor's DBMS. This can be a problem for the developer.

Open Database Connectivity

Microsoft has addressed the data transmission issue with Open Database Connectivity (ODBC). The ODBC architecture defines an extended SQL grammar and an API aimed at C programmers for submitting SQL requests to a data source. The ODBC architecture requires an ODBC driver for the target DBMS. The role of the driver is to act as an adapter that converts ODBC procedure calls and data into the format used by the underlying DBMS. Data returned by the DBMS passes back through the ODBC driver and is converted into a vendor-neutral format. The result is a decoupling of the client from the DBMS, which leads to increased portability.

This decoupling can be a drawback. Many vendors supply extended facilities in their DBMS products (such as stored procedures, triggers, procedural extensions to SQL, or nonstandard functions), which are of course nonstandard and are therefore not directly accessible using ODBC. So ODBC has a pass-through mechanism that permits nonstandard SQL requests to be submitted by a client directly to the ODBC driver without being intercepted, checked, or modified in any way. Back to vendor lock-in!

Java Database Connectivity

Java Database Connectivity (JDBC) is a similar model to ODBC except that it is aimed at the Java programming language rather than at C or C++. The JDBC driver manager uses a JDBC driver to convert client requests into a format suitable for transmission to the target DBMS and to convert data from the DBMS back into JDBC format.

JDBC defines several categories of driver. Type 1 involves using the JDBC-ODBC bridge supplied with the JDK and an ODBC driver. The bridge converts JDBC requests into ODBC requests, and the ODBC driver is then used to access the DBMS. At the other end of the spectrum, Type 4 drivers are written in "pure Java" and use the vendor's proprietary formats and protocol for sending and receiving data. Types 2 and 3 are hybrids of Java and non-Java code. Most modern Java applications use Type 4 drivers to access a database.

ADO and ADO.NET

ODBC was fine at the time, but it had its limitations. By the mid-1990s, Microsoft realized that other nonrelational databases (or data sources, as Microsoft prefers to call them) did not fit into the ODBC model of processing. Microsoft decided to create a new API that encompassed relational and nonrelational databases, and the concept of Universal Data Access (UDA) was born.

Microsoft's architecture was called OLE DB (pronounced "olay dee bee") and comprised three parts. The upper part defined a *consumer* interface, and the lower part defined a *provider* interface. The bit in the middle was the OLE DB infrastructure supplied by Microsoft that connected the two halves. The idea was that data source vendors would provide access to their systems and implement the provider interface. Microsoft itself created an OLE DB provider that could convert OLE DB requests into ODBC calls, allowing continued (albeit a little slower) access to relational databases even if the corresponding vendor had not yet implemented an OLE DB provider. Developers writing programs that needed to access a database could use the consumer interface. The consumer interface was still a bit low-level for many programmers, so Microsoft built another, more abstract layer on top, called ActiveX Data Objects (ADO).

The neat thing about ADO was that you could easily use it from Visual Basic. (ODBC was more difficult to use because the API was designed for C programmers; the OLE DB consumer interface was designed for C++ programmers.) Abstractions in ADO included objects for handling connections to the data source, commands (which could be SQL statements or something else, depending on the data source), and *Recordset* objects (which you can think of as data in a tabular format). ADO also exposed events, allowing a program to submit a command to a data source and then do something else while the command was processed. When the command completed, the program would be notified using an event, and the program could determine whether the command was completed successfully. Events were used in other parts of ADO as well.

With the advent of .NET, Microsoft decided to update ADO and created ADO.NET. ADO.NET contains several enhancements over the original ADO architecture, providing improved interoperability and performance. If you're familiar with ADO, you'll notice that the ADO.NET object model is a little different. For one thing, it has no *Recordset* objects—Microsoft has created the *DataAdapter* and *DataSet* classes to support disconnected data access and operations. Using these classes allows for greater scalability because you no longer have to be connected to the database all the time. (To be fair, ADO also provided disconnected *Recordset* objects, but their use was the exception rather than the rule, especially among inexperienced programmers!) This means that your applications can consume fewer resources. The ADO.NET connection pooling mechanisms allow database connections to be reused by different applications, thereby reducing the need to continually connect to and disconnect from the database, which can be time-consuming.

Although you can use JDBC from J#, ADO.NET's close integration with Windows makes it the natural choice for accessing data in J# applications.

Nonfunctional Requirements

In most applications, security, scalability, and reliability are important issues. In a distributed system, these issues are far more pronounced—a lot more can go wrong, and once you start using the Internet as part of your infrastructure, you never know who or what will be monitoring the data emanating from your site.

Security

If you're building a system based on a local area network (LAN) or an intranet, you can use the security features of Windows domains. This ability is convenient because users will have a single point of sign-in and because identity information can be passed around the network by the operating system quickly and easily as components are accessed. Impersonation allows controlled access to sensitive resources, and the declarative role-based nature of most Windows .NET security components permits a high degree of flexibility.

Using the Internet is more problematic. For example, external customers browsing a company's Web site are unlikely to be members of any internal Windows domain that the application can use. Security must therefore be performed using other mechanisms. One of the common techniques that Microsoft Internet Information Services (IIS) can use in conjunction with .NET is forms-based security, whereby the user is presented with a form that asks for a valid username and password. The login form is responsible for authenticating the user and caching the user's credentials so they can be verified as the user attempts to access other resources at the site. You can combine this technique with Secure Sockets Layer (SSL) to encrypt the exchanges passing over the Internet between the browser and Web server.

An alternative is to use client certificates. Each client obtains a digital certificate that verifies the user's identity. In order for this approach to be totally effective, each client must be mapped to an internal Windows domain account, which IIS then uses to determine whether to authorize access. Client certificates are more useful on sites that require user membership and registration.

Microsoft Passport

Microsoft Passport is a Web service that provides a single sign-in across multiple Web sites. Microsoft maintains a secure database that holds usernames, passwords, and other personal information. A user can subscribe to the Passport service, create an ID, and store his or her details in the database. Web sites can use the Passport SDK to obtain a user's credentials when the user attempts to access the Web site, and thus verify that the user is valid. Companies who build these Web sites have to sign a license agreement with Microsoft. Passport currently has over 160 million subscribers worldwide.

Passport is a proprietary technology. In the future, you're likely to see standardized security mechanisms available over Web services as part of the Global XML Web Services Architecture (GXA).

Scalability and Availability

As more users access your system, they'll place an increasingly heavy load on it. In an ideal world, the system should never reach a point where it might suddenly stop because it is overloaded, although you have to be pragmatic about this. The best you can do is to design your systems so the point at which operations slow is pushed further and further back, making slowdown less and less likely. Achieving scalability and high availability involves careful design and ensuring that resources are not locked for longer than they need to be, that data is cached effectively, and that the network is not swamped. Also, if you're building a 24×7 system, you must guarantee that the system will function even if a hardware failure occurs. You can achieve high availability by using redundancy (duplicating hardware), clustering, and load balancing. You should also make sure that your basic infrastructure is up to the job.

The Windows .NET Server operating system can run on an ever-expanding range of high-end computers. It has built-in facilities for monitoring performance and raising alerts to identify potential problems and bottlenecks so you can prevent them before they occur. If you make use of COM+, you also have access to load balancing, object pooling and caching, asynchronous operations, remote events, and many other features designed to improve throughput.

Integrity and Transactions

Another major feature of COM+ is its ability to preserve integrity through transactions. Integration with Microsoft Distributed Transaction Coordinator makes it easy to ensure that state is consistent across multiple machines.

Transactions are often associated with databases, but transactions in COM+ can be used to maintain consistency across other resources as well. For example, a message queue can be transactional; the act of retrieving a message from a queue and processing it can constitute a transaction. If the processing fails for some reason, rolling back the transaction will return the message to the message queue, thus restoring the system to the state it was in when the transaction commenced.

Transactions determine how long shared resources are locked. It is important to keep transactions short when you design distributed applications, in order to reduce contention and retain locks only for as long as absolutely necessary.

.NET Enterprise Servers

You're unlikely to ever write your own custom DBMS or your own messaging service or any of the other items of software infrastructure required to build a robust distributed application. More likely, you'll buy a package off the shelf or use whatever facilities are supplied with the operating system. However, this strategy poses a challenge: How do you integrate all these disparate pieces of software into a coherent system? To help solve this problem, Microsoft developed .NET Enterprise Servers. Each server is designed to fulfill a particular role in an enterprise system.

The most commonly used .NET Enterprise Servers are

- **SQL Server** This is Microsoft's flagship DBMS. It is SQL-based but also has comprehensive support for manipulating XML, and it has the ability to perform queries across the Internet.
- **Exchange Server** Exchange Server provides an infrastructure that supports messaging and collaboration. Its main features are scheduling facilities, e-mail, and workflow.
- **BizTalk Server** BizTalk Server allows you to define and deploy integrated business processes that incorporate components built using a range of technologies. You can implement secure trading partner relationships and specify, validate, and transform documents that are passed to and from trading partners. BizTalk Server Orchestration allows you to automate and manage business processes within your organization as well as the flow of data to trading partners.
- **Application Center** This server aids in the deployment and maintenance of Web applications. Its features allow easy maintenance of applications across groups of computers for high availability.
- **Commerce Server** Commerce Server provides a framework for building and deploying e-commerce solutions.

Java and .NET

Java was developed as a language that could run anywhere, on anything. Java's portability has both solved and caused problems. The language itself is neat, but some of the "bolt-ons" that have emerged since the language first emerged have not been quite so effective.

The Java language was designed to let developers write generic software. Java runs using a Java Virtual Machine (JVM), which is usually a piece of software that executes Java bytecodes. Bytecodes are the low-level instructions that the Java compiler converts Java source code into—they are the "machine code" of the JVM. Java applications run on any compliant JVM, regardless of the underlying operating system, without ever needing to be recompiled.

The problem is that different operating systems provide different facilities, so the Java language and the JVM occasionally have to take responsibility for implementing what could be considered operating system–level features. Take events, for example. Some operating systems have built-in support for events, but others do not. A JVM has to emulate events on operating systems that provide no intrinsic support. This is OK. But when the operating system does supply events, Java applications must still go through the JVM to use them, and this adds an extra level of indirection, which is bound to impair performance. If you require direct access to the underlying operating system, or to non-Java code, you can use the Java Native Interface (JNI). But be prepared to spend time debugging your code—the JNI is not the most friendly of environments.

To build enterprise applications in Java, you need to use Java 2.0 Enterprise Edition (J2EE). J2EE is simply a specification of the infrastructure required to build enterprise applications. It includes elements such as Enterprise JavaBeans (EJB) for building shared business components, the Java Naming and Directory Interface (JNDI) for locating various Java services, the Java Transaction Service (JTS) for managing distributed transactions, JavaServer Pages (JSP) and Servlets for creating dynamic Web applications, and the Java Messaging Service (JMS) for using message queues. To build and deploy an enterprise application using J2EE, you must obtain a separate J2EE server that implements these features. The J2EE server effectively runs as an application on top of the operating system, and your Java code runs inside the environment created by the J2EE server.

Microsoft has recognized the strengths and weaknesses of Java and J2EE, and with J# and .NET it offers a solution ideally suited to the Windows platform. J# uses the syntax and semantics of the Java programming language while integrating with .NET to provide the enterprise infrastructure. You don't need to purchase a J2EE server because everything you need is built into Windows and .NET. Much existing Java code (not J2EE) will run unchanged under .NET. Where there are weaknesses in the JVM, Microsoft has replaced them with its own Windows-specific features. (For example, RMI has been supplanted by .NET Remoting.)

Summary

This chapter has presented many of the issues developers face when they design and implement a distributed system. The Microsoft .NET Server operating system together with the .NET servers provides a solid platform that you can use to meet these challenges. If you're a Java developer and want to continue developing using the Java programming language, you can do so using Visual J# .NET.

The remainder of this book will look in detail at each aspect of distributed application development with J#.

2

Microsoft .NET

Microsoft .NET—which at the time of writing consists of Visual Studio .NET, the .NET Framework SDK, .NET servers, and Windows .NET—is Microsoft's strategic platform and toolset for building and deploying the next generation of enterprise applications. If you're going to be involved in any way with designing and creating applications running under Microsoft Windows, you need to understand .NET.

Microsoft created .NET to provide a comprehensive platform for building and running distributed applications. The .NET Framework and Visual Studio .NET provide a core set of services that take much of the drudgery out of building such applications, while the .NET servers supply additional extended functionality for exploiting .NET and for deploying and managing distributed systems. In this chapter, we'll take a tour of Microsoft .NET and examine the main features. In particular, we'll look at the common language runtime and how it supports cross-language development, memory management, deployment of .NET applications and libraries, the .NET Framework Class Library, and security.

Compilers and Language Support

You can write .NET applications using any of the languages supported by .NET—C#, Visual Basic .NET, C++, and J#. As with most modern languages, the code you write must be compiled to machine code. In a departure for Microsoft, however, the compilers for languages supported by .NET do not generate machine instructions for a specific processor. Instead, they generate a pseudomachine code called Microsoft Intermediate Language (MSIL).

The Common Language Runtime

The common language runtime is the execution system that runs code written for .NET. When an application is executed, the runtime uses just-in-time (JIT) compilation to convert the MSIL code into real machine instructions and runs them. If you're familiar with the operation of the Java runtime environment, you already know about this kind of operation because like a Java Virtual Machine (JVM), the common language runtime aims to provide portability. The MSIL code can be transported onto any machine that has the runtime installed.

With .NET, Microsoft has extended the concept underlying the JVM. The deployment and dynamic linking mechanisms used by the common language runtime allow compiled code to be built on one machine and transported to another machine for execution. More on this later. Also, by enabling a number of languages to compile to the same MSIL code and, more important, by standardizing many of the data types used by these languages (for example, a *Long* in Visual Basic .NET is the same as a *long* in C#, which is the same as a *long* in J#, and so on), .NET not only allows applications to be portable across hardware, but it enables the data processed by them to be understood across all languages. All languages running under .NET use the same method-calling conventions, which makes it easy to perform interlanguage method calls. (We'll discuss this in detail later in the chapter.)

When an application is compiled into MSIL, the result is a module. A module can be linked with resources from other modules and DLLs into an executable (EXE) file or another DLL. Although the filename extensions used are still EXE and DLL, the content and format of these files are a little different from native EXEs and DLLs. The runtime uses an extended version of the Portable Executable (PE) file format used by regular Windows executables. The main difference is that runtime PE files contain sections with information about the types defined by your code (or classes, if you're writing J# code, or classes, structs, enums, and attributes if you're writing C# code). They also contain security information and any dependencies on types defined by other modules. This information is required when you link modules.

A Closer Look at MSIL

To understand the runtime, it helps to look closely at MSIL. Let's look at a variation on the familiar "Hello, World" program:

```
package Greeting;

public class Hello
{
public static void main(String[] args)
```

```
{
for (int i = 0; i < 10; i++)
System.out.println("Hello, World");
}
}
```

If you create a text file called Greeting.jsl using Wordpad, or download it from the book sample files, and then type in this code and compile it, the result will be an executable named Greeting.exe. (The convention is to use the .jsl extension for J# source code.) To compile the program, you can use the J# compiler from the command line:

```
vjc Greeting.jsl
```

Tip The J# compiler is called vjc. Don't fall into the trap of thinking that just because the C# compiler is called csc, the J# equivalent is jsc. Visual Studio .NET includes a jsc compiler that is used for compiling JavaScript code. If you use it over your J# code, you'll get what looks like meaningful errors as the compiler understands some Java language syntax, but not all of it. If you don't realize this difference, you can spend hours telling the compiler that your code is perfectly valid and hoping that it will compile your program if you shout loudly enough!

When you run Greeting.exe, you'll be rewarded with the message "Hello, World" displayed 10 times.

Tip To run vjc or any of the other command-line tools supplied with the .NET Framework SDK, you must set your environment variables appropriately. Microsoft supplies the batch file Corvars.bat, which you can run from the command line for this purpose. Corvars.bat is located at C:\Program Files\Microsoft Visual Studio.NET\FrameworkSDK\bin.

You can look at the MSIL generated for this executable using the Intermediate Language Disassembler tool, better known as ILDASM. Figure 2-1 shows ILDASM being used to disassemble Greeting.exe.

Figure 2-1 Using ILDASM to disassemble the sample code

The first item you'll notice is labeled Manifest. Every executable program has a manifest. A manifest contains information about the DLL or EXE as well as any dependencies on other DLLs needed to run this executable. Figure 2-2 shows the manifest for the Greeting executable. If you double-click the manifest entry, you'll see another window containing the details. There is much more to the manifest than we'll cover here; for now, we'll just concentrate on the pertinent information.

You can see that the Greeting application requires three other assemblies when it runs: vjscor, mscorlib, and vjslib. For the time being, you can think of an assembly as a DLL containing runtime support code needed to execute your application. The mscorlib assembly contains the core base class libraries needed by every .NET application and is always present. Vjslib and vjscor contain J# runtime and type information and are used only by J# applications.

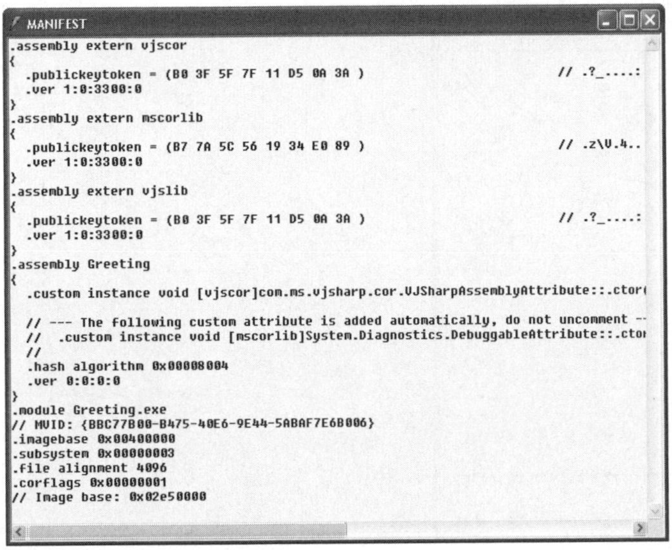

```
MANIFEST
.assembly extern vjscor
{
  .publickeytoken = (B0 3F 5F 7F 11 D5 0A 3A )                        // .?_....:
  .ver 1:0:3300:0
}
.assembly extern mscorlib
{
  .publickeytoken = (B7 7A 5C 56 19 34 E0 89 )                        // .z\V.4..
  .ver 1:0:3300:0
}
.assembly extern vjslib
{
  .publickeytoken = (B0 3F 5F 7F 11 D5 0A 3A )                        // .?_....:
  .ver 1:0:3300:0
}
.assembly Greeting
{
  .custom instance void [vjscor]com.ms.vjsharp.cor.VJSharpAssemblyAttribute::.ctor(

  // --- The following custom attribute is added automatically, do not uncomment --
  //  .custom instance void [mscorlib]System.Diagnostics.DebuggableAttribute::.cto
  //
  .hash algorithm 0x00008004
  .ver 0:0:0:0
}
.module Greeting.exe
// MVID: {BBC77B00-B475-40E6-9E44-5ABAF7E6B006}
.imagebase 0x00400000
.subsystem 0x00000003
.file alignment 4096
.corflags 0x00000001
// Image base: 0x02e50000
```

Figure 2-2 An application manifest

Underneath the reference to vjslib is information about the Greeting application itself. The first piece of information concerns an attribute (*DebuggableAttribute*). Attributes are additional items of data that can be examined and acted upon by the runtime to modify the way in which the program runs. They typically contain configuration or other declarative information; we'll cover them in more detail in Chapter 3.

Close the Manifest window, return to the main ILDASM window, and expand the Greeting node to see the *Hello* class. The Greeting node corresponds to the package created in the application. If you expand the *Hello* class, you'll see its contents as shown in Figure 2-3.

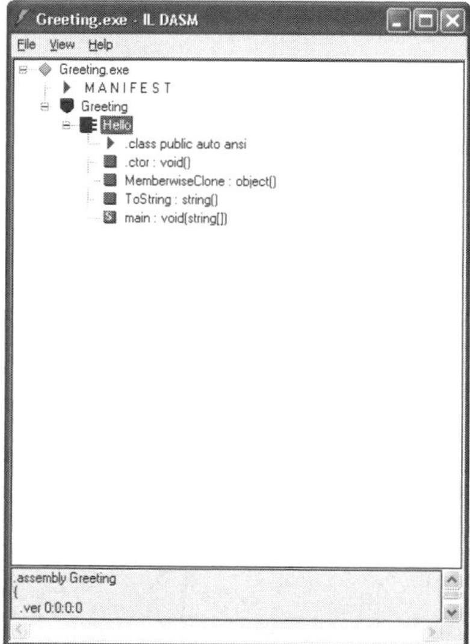

Figure 2-3 The ILDASM window showing the *Hello* class

Items with a red triangle symbol provide more information. In this case, the information is the pedigree of the *Hello* class. If you double-click the item marked .class public auto ansi, another window will appear, as shown in Figure 2-4.

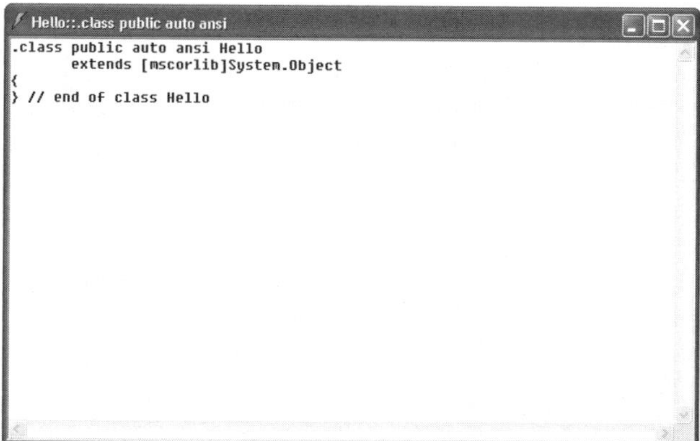

Figure 2-4 The definition of the *Hello* class

Again, there is more information in here than you might care to know, but you should be able to gather that the *Hello* class is descended from *System.Object* (as all .NET classes are by default) and that the implementation of *System.Object* is found in the mscorlib assembly.

If you close this window and return to ILDASM, you'll notice four methods in the *Hello* class, denoted by pink squares. A square containing an *S* indicates that the method is static. The method marked *.ctor* is the constructor for the *Hello* class. Although you didn't define a constructor yourself, in this situation the semantics of the Java language are such that the compiler will create a default constructor for you automatically. If you double-click the constructor, you'll see the MSIL code generated for you. We won't describe the entire MSIL instruction set here, but you can probably guess that the instruction at address IL_001 invokes the constructor inherited from *System.Object* (the parent class of *Hello*), as shown in Figure 2.5.

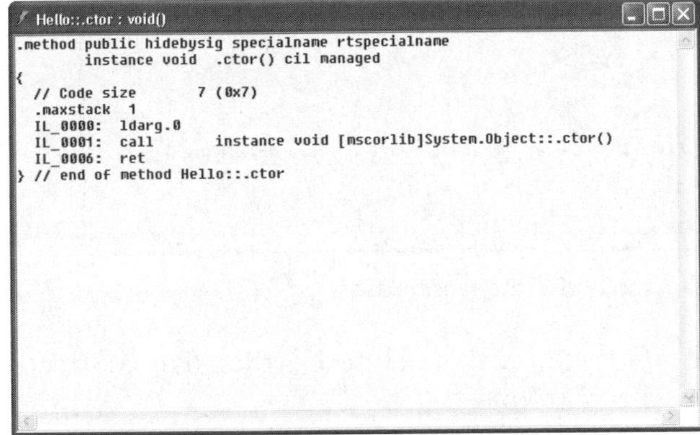

Figure 2-5 The default constructor for the *Hello* class

Close this window and return to the main ILDASM window. All .NET classes inherit a number of methods from *System.Object*. In some cases, the default implementation provided by *System.Object* is sufficient for the class, but in other cases you might want to override the default implementation and provide your own code. *MemberwiseClone* and *ToString* are two methods that are normally inherited from *System.Object*. The *MemberwiseClone* method is used for creating a copy of an object, and *ToString* generates a printable (string) representation of an object. However, the requirements of J# objects are subtly different from those of objects written in other languages (for reasons of interoperability with the Java programming language), and the J# compiler automatically generates specialized versions of *MemberwiseClone* and *ToString* for you. The other methods inherited from *System.Object* are not affected by the requirements of the Java language.

Double-click the *main* method to display its MSIL code, as shown in Figure 2-6. The *main* method is the entry point for the application. You'll see a few directives (the lines that start with a dot, as in *.entrypoint*) followed by some real MSIL code.

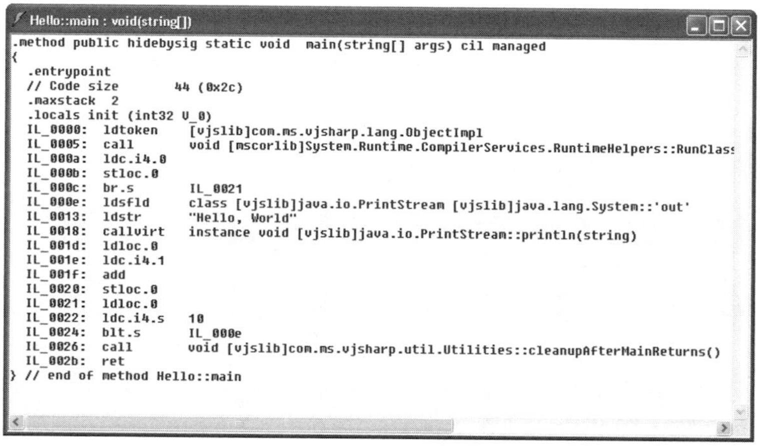

```
Hello::main : void(string[])
.method public hidebysig static void  main(string[] args) cil managed
{
  .entrypoint
  // Code size       44 (0x2c)
  .maxstack  2
  .locals init (int32 V_0)
  IL_0000:  ldtoken    [vjslib]com.ms.vjsharp.lang.ObjectImpl
  IL_0005:  call       void [mscorlib]System.Runtime.CompilerServices.RuntimeHelpers::RunClass
  IL_000a:  ldc.i4.0
  IL_000b:  stloc.0
  IL_000c:  br.s       IL_0021
  IL_000e:  ldsfld     class [vjslib]java.io.PrintStream [vjslib]java.lang.System::'out'
  IL_0013:  ldstr      "Hello, World"
  IL_0018:  callvirt   instance void [vjslib]java.io.PrintStream::println(string)
  IL_001d:  ldloc.0
  IL_001e:  ldc.i4.1
  IL_001f:  add
  IL_0020:  stloc.0
  IL_0021:  ldloc.0
  IL_0022:  ldc.i4.s   10
  IL_0024:  blt.s      IL_000e
  IL_0026:  call       void [vjslib]com.ms.vjsharp.util.Utilities::cleanupAfterMainReturns()
  IL_002b:  ret
} // end of method Hello::main
```

Figure 2-6 The *main* method of the *Hello* class

We wrote the J# code for this method earlier. The MSIL code resulting from the compilation is reproduced here:

main (MSIL)

```
.method public hidebysig static void main(string[] args) cil managed
{
  .entrypoint
  // Code size       44 (0x2c)
  .maxstack  2
  .locals init (int32 V_0)
  IL_0000:  ldtoken    [vjslib]com.ms.vjsharp.lang.ObjectImpl
  IL_0005:  call       void [mscorlib]System.Runtime.CompilerServices.
    RuntimeHelpers::RunClassConstructor(valuetype [mscorlib]
    System.RuntimeTypeHandle)
  IL_000a:  ldc.i4.0
  IL_000b:  stloc.0
  IL_000c:  br.s       IL_0021
  IL_000e:  ldsfld     class [vjslib]java.io.PrintStream
    [vjslib]java.lang.System::'out'
  IL_0013:  ldstr      "Hello, World"
  IL_0018:  callvirt   instance void
    [vjslib]java.io.PrintStream::println(string)
  IL_001d:  ldloc.0
  IL_001e:  ldc.i4.1
```

```
    IL_001f:  add
    IL_0020:  stloc.0
    IL_0021:  ldloc.0
    IL_0022:  ldc.i4.s   10
    IL_0024:  blt.s      IL_000e
    IL_0026:  call       void
      [vjslib]com.ms.vjsharp.util.Utilities::cleanupAfterMainReturns()
    IL_002b:  ret
} // end of method Hello::main
```

This code needs a little explanation. MSIL is a stack-based language. The *.maxstack* directive at the start of the method indicates the maximum number of values that will be pushed onto the stack (maximum depth of stack) while the method runs. If this value is exceeded, the program will terminate with an exception for security reasons. The MSIL verification process conducts this check by analyzing the MSIL code as it is JIT-compiled but before it is run.

Local variables are identified by number in MSIL. The *.locals* directive at the start of the *main* method indicates that that a 32-bit integer value (the variable *i* created in the *for* loop) is local variable *V_0*. If there were more variables, they would be called V_1, V_2, V_3, and so on, in the order in which they were defined in the original code.

The instructions at addresses IL_0000 and IL_0005 initialize the object calling the class constructor for the *ObjectImpl* class. *ObjectImpl* is an internal class defined in the vjslib assembly that implements most of the methods normally inherited by Java language objects from the *java.lang.Object* class. The way in which J# objects are implemented and mapped into the Java language object hierarchy is discussed in more detail in Chapter 3.

The MSIL instruction *ldc.i4.0* at address IL_000a pushes the 4-byte constant value 0 onto the top of the stack. The next instruction, *stloc.0*, pops the value from the top of the stack (containing 0) into local variable 0. The net effect of this action is to set the variable *i* to 0. The instruction *br.s* is an unconditional transfer that causes a jump to address IL_0021. At this address, the *ldloc.0* instruction copies the value in local variable 0 (variable *i*) back onto the stack.

The instruction *ldc.i4.s 10* at address IL_0022 pushes the 4-byte integer value 10 onto the stack, so the stack now contains two values: 0 (variable *i*) and 10. The instruction *blt.s* compares the top two items of the stack and transfers execution to address IL_000e if the penultimate value in the stack is less than the value at the top of the stack. Because *i* contains 0, this condition is true and execution continues at IL_000e.

The *ldsfld* instruction at address IL_000e pushes the value of *System.out*, which is the static variable of type *PrintStream* used for printing to the console, onto the top of the stack. The definitions of *PrintStream* and *System* are held in the vjslib assembly. The next instruction, *ldstr "Hello, World"*, pushes the constant string *"Hello, World"* onto the stack as well. Once again, the stack contains two items: the *System.out* static field and the *"Hello, World"* string.

The *callvirt* instruction calls an instance method using the information on the stack. In this case, the MSIL instruction invokes the *println* method and expects a single string parameter (which is currently at the top of the stack). The object below this on the stack, *System.out*, is the object whose *println* method is invoked. Both items are popped from the stack, and because the *println* method does not return a value, nothing is pushed back onto the stack. At this point, the text "Hello, World" appears on the console for the first time.

The instruction at IL_001d, *ldloc.0*, loads the value of local variable 0 (variable *i*) onto the stack; this value is still 0. The next instruction, *ldc.i4.1*, pushes the constant value 1 onto the stack, and the *add* instruction adds the top two items on the stack and replaces them with the result. The *stloc.0* instruction at IL_0020 pops the new value at the top of the stack and places it in variable 0. The local variable *i* has now been incremented to 1. We are now back at address IL_0021, where the *ldloc.0* instruction copies the new value of *i* back onto the stack, the *ldc.i4.s 10* instruction pushes the constant 10 onto the stack, and the *blt.s IL_000e* instruction jumps back to address IL_000e if *i* is still less than 10.

When variable *i* eventually reaches 10, the method *cleanupAfterMainReturns* defined in the *utilities* class in the vjslib assembly performs some housekeeping, and then the *ret* instruction at IL_002b exits the method.

Now you can see how the Java code in the original program is transformed into MSIL. If you want to know more about MSIL, see the document called Partition III CIL.doc that comes with Visual Studio .NET Enterprise Edition (in \Program Files\Microsoft Visual Studio .NET\FrameworkSDK\Tool Developers Guide\docs\Partition III CIL.doc).

MSIL Verification

If you're feeling brave, you're welcome to write MSIL code yourself. Microsoft supplies the MSIL assembler (ILASM.exe) for compiling raw MSIL code files into PE format. However, this option raises a difficult issue. MSIL code is not as easy to write as J#, C#, Visual Basic .NET, or even C++ code. It's fair to assume that if you write in one of these languages and use the appropriate compiler, the resulting MSIL code in the PE file will be valid. If you're handcrafting MSIL code, this assumption is not applicable. For example, you could easily forget to push the correct number of items onto the stack before executing an add instruction, which would result in a nasty problem.

The runtime guarantees that the code it executes will not crash in an uncontrolled manner. To achieve this guarantee, the runtime performs code verification on each assembly as it's compiled from PE format into native code immediately before it is executed. The runtime checks for many problems, including attempts to use uninitialized variables, illegal memory accesses, and assignment of incompatible values to types. These checks eliminate a whole range of common programming errors and ensure that your program is type-safe and not prone to security failures.

For example, an attempt to read a piece of memory that was not directly allocated to the program could allow a devious programmer to gain access to all sorts of private data. Not all errors can be trapped at this time, but the runtime performs numerous checks at run time as well, preventing problems such as "out by one" errors when reading an array (stepping off the end of an array) or invalid type-casts. If these occur, the runtime will throw an exception.

If you're writing your own MSIL code, you can use the PEVerify tool, PEVerify.exe (in \Program Files\Microsoft Visual Studio .NET\FrameworkSDK\Bin), to check that your PE file contains valid and verifiable code.

Java Bytecodes

You've seen the .NET code for the "Hello, World" program. Now compare it to the Java bytecodes for the same program generated by the standard Java compiler supplied with Sun Microsystems' Java Development Kit (JDK). This output was generated using the javap tool, which also comes with the JDK.

```
Compiled from Hello.java
public class Greeting.Hello extends java.lang.Object {
    public Greeting.Hello();
    public static void main(java.lang.String[]);
}

Method Greeting.Hello()
   0 aload_0
   1 invokespecial #1 <Method java.lang.Object()>
   4 return

Method void main(java.lang.String[])
   0 iconst_0
   1 istore_1
   2 goto 16
   5 getstatic #2 <Field java.io.PrintStream out>
   8 ldc #3 <String "Hello, World">
  10 invokevirtual #4 <Method void println(java.lang.String)>
  13 iinc 1 1
  16 iload_1
```

```
17 bipush 10
19 if_icmplt 5
22 return
```

We won't go into the Java bytecodes here, but if you look at the *main* method you should recognize the pattern. The algorithm used by the MSIL code is exactly the same. (The JVM is also stack-based.) If you're interested in learning more, Bill Venner's book *Inside the Java 2 Virtual Machine* (McGraw-Hill, 1999) is a good place to start.

Compiling MSIL to Native Code

To speed up the execution process, you can compile MSIL executables and DLLs using the Ngen.exe utility. Ngen stands for Native Image Generator. When you run Ngen over an MSIL EXE or DLL, the file is compiled into native code and placed in the native image cache on your computer. Currently, this cache is a folder called NativeImages_<*.NETVersion*> under \Windows\assembly, where <*.NETVersion*> is the version of the .NET Framework that you have installed. When you invoke a .NET EXE or DLL, the runtime will check in the native image cache for a compiled version and will use it if it finds one; otherwise, it will load and compile your MSIL using the JIT compiler.

You can remove an image from the native image cache using the */delete* parameter with Ngen.

Cross-Language Development

Earlier, we said that the runtime makes data portable across languages and that languages that execute using the runtime obey the same method-calling conventions. What does this mean for developers? For one thing, it eliminates the headaches you used to have in attempting to call a method in a DLL written using Visual C++ from your Visual Basic 6.0 application. Because the data types in C++ and Visual Basic are different—an *int* in C++ is a different length from an *Integer* in Visual Basic—you always had to remember to use a *Long* in Visual Basic instead. Then you had to make sure that the C++ methods used the standard calling convention; otherwise, you could end up with a corrupt stack. You also had to turn off name decoration in C++ so Visual Basic would actually find the names of the methods in the DLL. The final hurdle was using the *Declare Function* or *Declare Sub* statements in Visual Basic, making sure that you specified the correct path to the DLL to pretend that the methods you were calling were written in Visual Basic.

So many errors could creep in, and you wouldn't know about them until you tried to run your program. If you were lucky, you'd get a message box saying "Bad calling convention." Of course, more often than not, applications would crash, your computer would freeze, and you'd lose hours of work. (Developers never save anything until it all works!). Once you had the program functioning correctly, someone in the C++ development team would update the DLL—maybe by adding a parameter or two to an existing method or changing its return type—and ship a new version that broke your Visual Basic application again. Thankfully, Windows XP and the .NET Framework provide solutions to these problems.

Combining Visual Basic and J#

Calling C++ routines from Visual Basic was a complex process, often involving the use of additional software such as the ActiveX Bridge for JavaBeans. Then along came the common language runtime, and what was complicated became simple. Look at the following sample J# package, CakeUtils.jsl:

```
package CakeUtils;

public class CakeFilling
{
  public static final short Sponge = 0, Fruit = 1;
}

public class CakeShape
{
  public static final short Square = 0, Round = 1, Hexagonal = 2,
    Other = 3;
}

public class CakeInfo
{
  // Work out how many people a cake of a given size, shape,
  // and filling will feed
  public static short FeedsHowMany(short diameter, short shape,
    short filling)
  {
    double munchSizeFactor = (filling == CakeFilling.Fruit ? 2.5 : 1);
    double deadSpaceFactor;

    switch (shape)
    {
      case CakeShape.Square:    deadSpaceFactor = 0;
        break;
      case CakeShape.Hexagonal: deadSpaceFactor = 0.1;
        break;
      case CakeShape.Round:     deadSpaceFactor = 0.15;
        break;
      default:                  deadSpaceFactor = 0.2;
```

```
          break;
      }

      short numConsumers = (short)(diameter * munchSizeFactor *
        (1 - deadSpaceFactor));

      return numConsumers;
    }
}
```

For years, John's wife has been baking and decorating cakes for birthdays, weddings, and other occasions. Customers would often ask her, for example, how big a birthday cake they would need to feed 25 people. The answer depends on several factors: primarily the shape of the cake (a square cake has more volume than a round cake and will feed more people) and the type of filling (a fruit cake of a given size feeds more people than a sponge cake of the same size). She tended to base her answers on past experience, but we thought we'd try to add a bit of science to the process and write some code to make the calculation. The result is the *FeedsHowMany* method in the *CakeInfo* class shown previously.

The CakeUtils package also defines classes exposing constants for the shape and filling of the cake. If you want to follow along, save the code in a file called CakeUtils.jsl. (You could do all of this in Visual Studio .NET, but it's more instructive to perform the build tasks manually for this example.)

You can compile the package into a DLL from the command line:

```
vjc CakeUtils.jsl /target:library
```

The result is an assembly called CakeUtils.dll.

To test the package, use the following Visual Basic .NET class. Save it in a file called SizeCake.vb in the same folder as your J# source code and DLL.

```
Imports CakeUtils, System

Module SizeCake

  Sub Main()

    Dim numEaters As Short

    ' How many people will a 10" hexagonal sponge cake feed?
    numEaters = CakeInfo.FeedsHowMany(10, CakeShape.Hexagonal, _
        CakeFilling.Sponge)
    Console.WriteLine("This will feed " & numEaters & " people")

  End Sub
```

```
End Module
```

You should notice a number of things about this Visual Basic application. It uses the *CakeShape* and *CakeFilling* classes exposed by the J# package, it calls the *FeedsHowMany* method, and the result is a short integer. These steps might seem obvious, but what's not obvious from the Visual Basic code is the language that was used to create the *CakeInfo* class. The code contains no *Declare* statements. You don't have to worry about how Visual Basic data types map to J# (or vice-versa) or about using the wrong calling convention. In fact, the developer writing the Visual Basic application does not need to know what language was used for the *CakeInfo* class.

To compile the SizeCake program and link it to use CakeUtils.dll, use the vbc compiler from the following command line:

```
vbc SizeCake.vb /reference:CakeUtils.DLL
```

If you run the SizeCake.exe program, you'll be informed that a 10-inch hexagonal sponge cake will feed nine people. Besides working out how big a cake you need to order from John's wife, this little exercise proves how easy it is to combine code written in different languages when you use .NET.

The Common Language Specification

Even though the common language runtime looks wonderful, it can't do everything. Cross-language method calls work because of the way the source code for each language is compiled into MSIL. Microsoft has made the data types as compatible as possible across all the languages supported by .NET it has built compilers for, including J#. And because all the code is converted to MSIL, the calling convention and name decoration issues evaporate. (MSIL does not use name decoration as we would recognize it.)

However, different languages inevitably have different data types. Compiler writers can map many of them into common formats and sizes, but there will always be types in one language that have no corresponding type in another. For example, Visual Basic has no direct equivalent to a C++ pointer. Naming conventions used by different languages can also be problematic; a valid identifier in one language might not be valid in another. To help address this problem, Microsoft has developed a set of rules for building cross-language classes, called the Common Language Specification (CLS).

The CLS is a large subset of all the runtime types and other features available for writing components that can be used by any of the languages supported by .NET. If you abide by these rules, your classes will be universally accessible. If you break any of the rules, you'll restrict the audience for your code. Bear in mind that the CLS applies only to the exposed elements of your components (public methods, fields, and so on). You can use any language features you like internally.

Common CLS rules The first rule of the CLS is that global static fields and methods are banned. The *CakeFilling* class shown earlier is not actually CLS-compliant because it violates the first rule:

```
public class CakeFilling
{
  public static final short Sponge = 0, Fruit = 1;
}
```

Nevertheless, you can still use the class from Visual Basic. Nonconformance with the CLS doesn't mean that your class can't be used from other languages; it just means it might not be usable if the language doesn't know how to handle the noncompliant construct.

The CLS restricts the data types you can use. The available primitive types are *Byte*, *Int16*, *Int32*, *IntPtr*, *Int64*, *Single*, *Double*, *Boolean*, *Decimal*, *Char*, and *String*. These are the official language-independent names of the types, and they can map to different named types in each of the languages supported by .NET. For example, the *Int64* data type of the CLS corresponds to the *long* data type in J#, and a CLS *Single* is a J# *float*. For a method to be CLS-compliant, you must restrict its parameters and return types to CLS-supported types. You can use classes as parameter types and return values if the classes themselves conform to the CLS.

Another important rule concerns identifiers. In the CLS, for two identifiers to be considered distinct, they must vary by more than just their case. This rule is necessary because some languages, such as Java, are case sensitive but others, such as Visual Basic, are not. For example, if you define two methods in J# called *MyMethod* and *Mymethod*, Visual Basic will not be able to distinguish between them. Also, for strict CLS compliance, all names in the same scope must be distinct. You cannot have a class and a method that share the same name even if the language used to create the class allows it. Overloading is also an issue. The CLS allows methods to be overloaded based only on the number and types of their parameters; the return type cannot be used to distinguish between overloaded methods. Operator overloading is not supported, and neither are methods that take variable numbers of parameters.

A CLS-compliant class cannot inherit from a class that is not CLS-compliant. Arrays are allowed if the elements conform to the CLS, the array has a fixed number of dimensions, and each dimension has a zero lower bound.

We've covered a lot of information, but you've seen just the highlights. Most of the remaining CLS rules don't apply to the Java language, so we won't elaborate further. One final point: A language does not have to implement every feature of the CLS in order for you to use it to write CLS-compliant code. For example, the CLS includes enumerations, which are not part of the Java language, but that does not prevent you from writing components in the Java language that meet the requirements of the CLS.

Memory Management

If you have a C++ background, you're accustomed to watching how your objects use memory. C++ allows programmers to grab large chunks of memory and not release it, making memory management a constant issue. Applications use the *new* operator to allocate a piece of memory and create an object, but then they forget to delete the object and release the memory when they're done. The essential rule of C++ and similar languages that allow you direct access to memory is "That which you *new*, you shall also *delete*." Failure to adhere to this decree means that your application will consume more and more memory, causing the application to run slower and slower until it eventually halts.

A second rule regarding memory access in C++ and similar languages is "Use only that which you created." C++ allows you to create pointers to blocks of memory. A well-behaved application restricts itself to pointing at memory that actually belongs to the address space of the process running the application. More rebellious applications attempt to read and write random pieces of memory anywhere on the computer, sometimes because the programmer failed to point the pointer to a valid location and other times for more insidious reasons. (Some systems have been known to exhibit a security loophole, allowing a developer to read and write memory that is not part of the running process.) Many modern operating systems will trap such memory accesses and terminate the offending application before it can cause damage to the operating system or to other processes running at the same time.

If you're a Java programmer who has never used C++, the previous two paragraphs might not mean anything to you because the Java language doesn't have pointers. Neither does the common language runtime. Instead, both the Java language and the common language runtime have *reference types*. A reference type is an object whose lifetime and memory are managed by the common language runtime. The common language runtime grabs memory on behalf of applications when those applications create new objects. The common language runtime tracks the use of these objects and releases the memory they use automatically after the last references to them disappear. Neither J# nor the Java language have a *delete* operator as C++ does to indicate when an object can be disposed of. Instead, the runtime used by both languages performs automatic garbage collection. In the case of the common language runtime, the objects are said to be *managed*.

Reference Types and Value Types in the Common Language Runtime

Reference types in the runtime are heap-based. The *heap* is the large block of memory that is managed by the common language runtime. When you create a new object, the common language runtime allocates memory from the heap and assigns it to your object. The garbage collector (part of the common language runtime) returns this memory to the heap when it collects your object.

All classes are reference types. The common language runtime also has value types. These are items that are allocated memory on the stack when they're created, and they automatically disappear when they go out of scope—they're not subject to garbage collection. Most of the primitive types in the common language runtime (*int*, *long*, *float*, *short*, *bool*, and so on) are value types. For example, in the *DoSomething* method shown here, *int* is a value type and the class *MyClass* is a reference type:

```
public void DoSomething()
{
  int j = 99;
  MyClass myThing = new MyClass();
  ⋮
  // j disappears; the MyClass object will be garbage collected later
}
```

When the method runs, the integer *j* will be created on the stack and the *new* operator will create an instance of *MyClass* on the heap. At the end of the method, the variable *j* will disappear from the stack and its memory will be reused by the next variable that is created on the stack. The reference (*myThing*) to the *MyClass* object will disappear, rendering the object inaccessible when the method finishes. However, the object itself will remain in memory until the garbage collector decides to dispose of it.

The fact that the common language runtime grabs chunks of memory on your behalf means that neither the Java language nor the languages supported by .NET need pointers, so they don't have them. (There is one exception: You can use pointers in C++ and C# running under .NET, but this code runs in unmanaged space, which we'll describe later in the chapter). If you don't have pointers, you cannot point at specific blocks of memory outside the address space of the current process; therefore, no one can try to read them in an attempt to compromise the security of the computer.

To plug the gap totally, the verification process that MSIL code goes through as it is compiled ensures that all variables are initialized before use; using an uninitialized reference won't accidentally damage some random system memory. Also, the type-safety verification checks performed by the common language runtime prevent you from assigning invalid values to references. For example, you cannot assign the value 99 to a reference with the expectation that you can use it to access memory address 99.

Garbage Collection

Some programmers like automatic garbage collection, and others loathe it. On the positive side, garbage collection removes the need for your application to track the objects that it created and make sure they're deleted when no longer required. On the negative side, you can never be quite sure when your objects are reclaimed by the runtime because the garbage collection process is nondeterministic. Essentially, garbage collection happens when the common language runtime decides to do it. Garbage collection is a potentially expensive operation, so the common language runtime does it only when absolutely necessary.

Note The documentation supplied with the .NET Framework SDK provides details on the algorithms used by the garbage collector (\Program Files\Microsoft Visual Studio .NET\FrameworkSDK\Tool Developers Guide\docs\Partition I Architecture.doc). Be aware that they might change in future versions of the common language runtime.

If you come from a C++ background, the garbage collector will affect how you design your classes. The most important point is that when you use the common language runtime, you cannot necessarily count on destructors running when your objects disappear. Just because you've finished using an object doesn't mean that the garbage collector will dispose of it immediately.

Finalizers

If your objects obtain further resources (file handles or database connections, for example), you can arrange for these resources to be reclaimed when the object is garbage collected using a *finalizer*. A finalizer is a method, called *finalize*, that runs when the garbage collector wants to remove the object from memory but before the object actually disappears, as the following code shows:

```
public class MyClass
{
  ⋮
  protected void finalize()
  {
    // Put finalization code here
    ⋮
  }
  ⋮
}
```

Remember, you cannot guarantee when garbage will be collected, so you should not put critical code in a finalizer!

By default, the garbage collector runs as a separate thread inside the common language runtime. The runtime exposes the *GC* class, which contains static methods that you can use to influence and query the status of the garbage collection process. For example, the method *GC.Collect* forces garbage collection to start. Bear in mind, though, that all this does is signal to the thread running the garbage collector that it should do some work—it does not wait for that work to be completed. There is also a *KeepAlive* method you can use to prevent an object from being collected. Use these methods only when you have a really good reason to do so. The garbage collector works best when left to its own devices.

Deterministic Garbage Collection

So far, you haven't seen much difference between the way the JVM and the runtime manage memory. However, the runtime does provide a mechanism for deterministic garbage collection through the *IDisposable* interface.

The *IDisposable* interface specifies a single method called *Dispose*. You call this method to free up any resources used by the object, just like a finalizer would do. You should also create a finalizer that calls the *Dispose* method. The *Dispose* method should include a call to the method *GC.SuppressFinalize*, which prevents the garbage collector from calling the finalizer again. There's a good reason to do this: The resources have already been released, and trying to release them again can cause errors. Not calling the finalizer again also speeds up garbage collection because the collector can simply reclaim the object without doing any further finalization.

The following code fragment shows the general shape for a J# class that implements *IDisposable*:

Note The structure shown here is a précis of the Dispose pattern documented by Microsoft. For more details, consult the .NET Framework SDK documentation.

```
public class CollectedClass implements System.IDisposable
{

  public void Dispose()
  {
    // Release resources
    ⋮

    // Remove object from garbage collection queue
    System.GC.SuppressFinalize(this);
  }

  protected void finalize()
  {
    Dispose();
  }

  // Other methods
  ⋮}
```

A consumer program that creates instances of a disposable class can call the *Dispose* method explicitly when the application is done with the object, but the runtime also provides an automatic mechanism that allows the consumer to specify when those objects should be disposed of. This feature is not available for consumers written in J#. However, it's still good practice to implement *IDisposable* in your J# components because they might be used from other languages.

The following example shows some C# code that creates and disposes of an instance of the *CollectedClass* shown earlier. It employs the *using* construct of C#.

```
public static void Main()
{
```

```
    using (CollectedClass myThing = new CollectedClass())
    {
        // myThing is accessible in this block
        ⋮
    } // myThing is disposed of at this point

    ⋮
}
```

Integrating Unmanaged Code into .NET Applications

A lot of code was written before Microsoft created .NET. Some of it still runs and is still in use. Rather than forcing you to throw away perfectly good components and rewrite them for .NET, Microsoft allows you to integrate them into your .NET applications as-is. You have several techniques available to incorporate your old code into .NET. Your choice will depend on the type of component. All of these methods involve calling unmanaged code—that is, code that does not run under the common language runtime. Unmanaged code cannot be verified by the common language runtime and might corrupt the memory used by the process. Applications that execute unmanaged code have to be granted special access rights. Furthermore, method calls from managed to unmanaged code have to be marshaled into and out of the common language runtime, which will hurt performance if it occurs often.

To integrate .NET applications with unmanaged DLLs, you can use the Platform Invoke Service, also known as PInvoke. PInvoke locates a specified DLL and loads it into unmanaged space before invoking the required function in the DLL. The techniques used for specifying the DLL to be loaded and the method to be invoked are reminiscent of those required when you integrated DLLs into Visual Basic 6.0 applications. The major difference is that PInvoke is far more robust than the Visual Basic 6.0 runtime, and a bad method call is unlikely to crash your application, although it might generate exceptions that you can trap. If you're familiar with Visual J++ 6.0, you might have used a similar facility called J/Direct for making method calls into DLLs from Java. J/Direct is still available with J#.

COM is still an important technology, and you can use COM components from managed code by creating COM Callable Wrappers (CCWs). These are pieces of code that act as proxies, making COM components appear as if they are ordinary .NET components. The CCW is responsible for locating and loading the COM component into unmanaged space, marshaling and converting managed parameters into unmanaged data, and converting returned data back into managed types. You can also call a .NET component from COM. This involves creating a Runtime Callable Wrapper (RCW), which acts as a proxy for the .NET component, marshaling COM data into the managed space of the common language runtime.

We'll look at integrating J# with legacy code in more detail in Part IV of this book.

Assemblies and Deployment

One of the most frustrating aspects of Windows-based applications in the past has been the problem of "DLL hell." To promote reuse and allow for the upgrading of applications without completely reinstalling them, developers have made use of shared DLLs. Windows itself comprises a collection of DLLs containing many of the core operating system routines and functions. The idea was that developers could invoke a well-written piece of code packaged in a DLL in much the same way that they would invoke an ordinary procedure. At run time, the DLL would be located and loaded into the calling process's address space and the required procedure would be executed. The dynamic nature of a DLL allowed it to be shared by a number of processes simultaneously, reducing the overall memory requirements of those processes. A DLL could also be overwritten with a later release, perhaps fixing a bug or two, adding new procedures, or changing an existing procedure to use some new, faster algorithm. Applications using the DLL would automatically pick up and use this new version without being aware that anything had changed.

But then the fun would begin!

The Joy of DLLs: The Movie

The joy of DLLs is that they can be replaced dynamically. And the trouble with DLLs is that they can be replaced dynamically! Consider the following screenplay concerning the intrigue sparked by a typical application (definitely not coming to a movie screen near you):

Scene 1: A small dark room in Upper Gumtree. A developer named Honest John writes an application that makes use of one of the common redistributable DLLs found in Windows: CTL3D32.dll (the 3-D controls). He assumes that the DLL might not always be present on the user's machine, so he makes sure that the application installation package includes the DLL and installs it along with the application.

Scene 2: A plush development lab in Redmond. A developer at Microsoft uncovers a bug in the current release of CTL3D32.dll. The development team does the honorable thing and fixes the bug, making it available for download and redistribution. They also take the opportunity to add some extra functionality that the Windows community at large has been calling for—a few new procedures and a couple of enhancements to some of the controls. After a while, this becomes the "standard" version of the DLL; all new applications use this updated DLL, and many make use of the new features.

Do you follow the plot so far? Good.

Scene 3: An unsuspecting user's desktop computer. The user has just taken delivery of a brand-new desktop computer with all the latest software. Everything works well—Tetris in 32-bit color has never looked so good! Then the user installs Honest John's application (which uses CTL3D32.dll). As the installation progresses, the user suddenly see the message "Target file CTL3D32.dll exists and is newer than the source. Copy anyway?" She thinks hard, has a cup of coffee, and then clicks Yes. What could possibly go wrong? The application installation finishes, and she runs it to test it—it works fine.

Scene 4: The user's computer on deadline day. It is Friday and the weekend beckons. The user has to process the current week's sales and then go home. She fires up the sales processing application, which pops up an error message and won't let the sales processing application run. She tries again, with the same result. Three hours later, after several hundred more attempts to run the application, all with the same result, and a long call to the help desk of the company that supplied the computer in the first place (which yields no help), the user gives up and throws the computer out the window. The reason for the failure? The sales processing application was built using a later version of CTL3D32.dll than that installed with Honest John's application.

We admit that we might have taken some dramatic license here, but we're sure you can empathize with the unsuspecting user. The key problem is that a DLL was overwritten with an earlier, less functional version. Wouldn't it be nice if you could have multiple versions of the same DLL installed on the same computer at the same time, and have applications automatically use the correct version? This ability is one of the major features of .NET and is achieved using versioned assemblies.

.NET Assemblies

We used the word *assembly* when we discussed MSIL, and we said that an assembly was like a DLL. That was only partly true. An assembly is more like a logical DLL that can comprise several physical files, each of which is called a *module*. An assembly is the unit of deployment and code access security used by .NET.

You can compile individual source code files into .NET modules using the appropriate language compiler. For example, you can use the */target:module switch* with vjc. You can then combine them in an assembly using the Assembly

Linker tool (AL.exe, located in \Windows\Microsoft.NET\Framework\<*version*>). Alternatively, most compilers will let you compile and link multiple source files in an assembly without your needing to build separate modules and use the Assembly Linker—it depends on the compiler.

When any module is compiled, the PE file that is generated contains a description of the module's contents. This description is referred to as metadata. Tools such as the Assembly Linker use the metadata exposed by modules to determine how to link them together. The difference between a module and an assembly is that an assembly also contains a *manifest*. The manifest holds additional information (version, load address, internal flags, and so on) about the assembly and about any dependencies on other assemblies or other resources (such as bitmaps, cursors, and icons). You can use ILDASM to examine the manifest of an assembly, as you saw earlier.

When you compile an application that uses the classes and methods in one or more assemblies, you use the */references* option to indicate which assembly or assemblies are required. The compiler will locate each assembly and examine the metadata for the methods and types they contain, checking to make sure that they satisfy those needed by the application. If there are any unresolved references, the application will not compile.

For example, the following code (SizeCake.jsl) shows a J# client application that uses the CakeUtils package to determine how many people a 10-inch sponge cake will feed. (You saw the Visual Basic version of this class earlier.)

SizeCake.jsl

```
package SizeCake;

import CakeUtils.*;
import System.*;

public class SizeTest
{

  public static void main(String [] args)
  {

    short numEaters;

    // How many people will a 10" hexagonal sponge cake feed?
    numEaters = CakeInfo.FeedsHowMany((short)10, CakeShape.Hexagonal,
      CakeFilling.Sponge);
    Console.WriteLine("This will feed " + numEaters + " people");
  }
}
```

The CakeUtils package was previously compiled in an assembly called CakeUtils.dll. To compile the SizeCake application, you use the following command:

```
vjc SizeCake.jsl /reference:CakeUtils.dll
```

The result of this command is an executable, SizeCake.exe, which is also an assembly. If you use ILDASM to examine it and look at its manifest, you'll see the reference to the CakeUtils assembly, as in Figure 2-7:

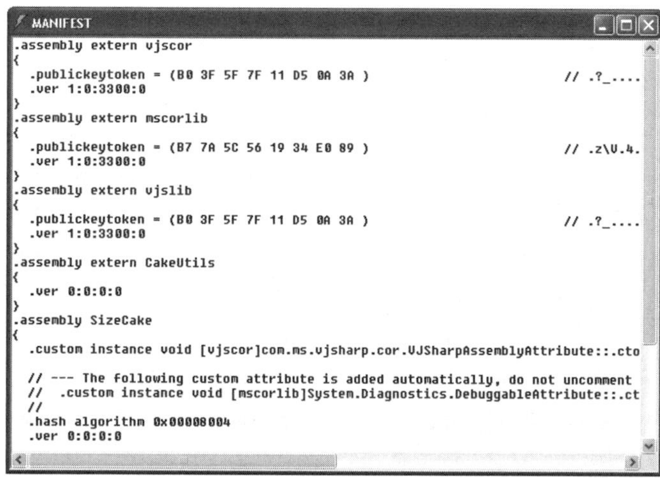

Figure 2-7 The SizeCake assembly manifest

Bear in mind that this is just a logical link. The SizeCake assembly simply contains a reference to the CakeUtils assembly. At run time, the common language runtime will locate and load the CakeUtils assembly dynamically as and when required.

Single-File Assemblies

The simplest applications that use no any additional assemblies other than the standard runtime (mscorlib.dll and, for J# applications, vjslib.dll and vjscor.dll) are compiled in an EXE file without use of the *references* option. These are referred to as *self-contained* or *single-file* assemblies. The Greetings program you saw at the start of this chapter was an example of such an application.

Private Assemblies

When you run an application, the common language runtime will locate and load any assemblies that are needed. This process is known as *binding*. The common language runtime uses a specific search algorithm to locate assemblies, which will be described shortly, in the section "Configuring an Application." The simplest way to make sure the runtime is successful is to use private assemblies. In this configuration, the assemblies used by your application are copied to the folder containing the application's EXE file when the application is installed. Alternatively, the runtime can also look in subfolders named after each assembly. You can additionally specify a private binpath using an application configuration file. (More on this later.)

For example, you could use the directory structure shown in Figure 2-8 for the SizeCake application. The SizeCake.exe program is located in the SizeCake folder, which also contains a subfolder named CakeUtils, which contains CakeUtils.dll.

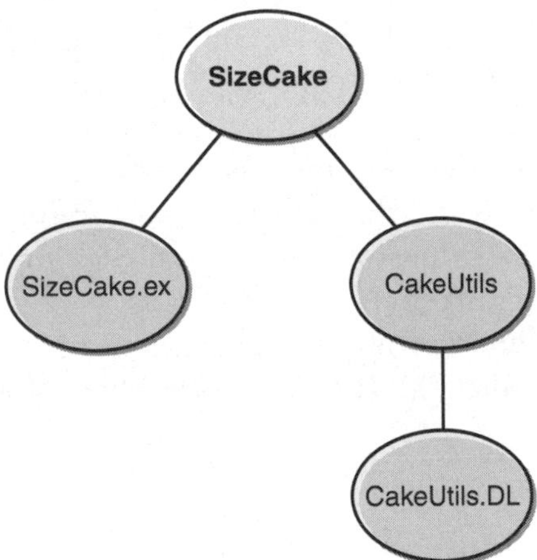

Figure 2-8 SizeCake application directories

The binding mechanism of the runtime requires only that it can locate the assemblies needed by the application. It does not rely on any settings in the Windows Registry. Application installation is therefore easy—you simply copy the EXE and the DLLs onto the computer. This is known as *XCOPY* deployment (you can use the *XCOPY* command to copy directory structures). Uninstallation is equally easy—you delete the folder and subfolders that contain the application and its assemblies. You won't leave any ghosts behind in the Registry that will come back to haunt you later!

Private assemblies are fine, and because they're private to your application they will not be accidentally overwritten if another application uses a later, incompatible release of the same assembly. Both applications will have their own private copies of the assembly and will not interfere with one another. However, if you have limited disk space, you might not want to have 1001 copies of the same assembly installed on your computer. You also have to consider maintenance issues. Suppose you actually want to replace an assembly with a later version because the developers have found and corrected a bug. Hunting down every copy of the assembly and replacing it with the fixed version would be time consuming. Handily, the runtime provides some different places to store assemblies.

The Global Assembly Cache

One place you can store assemblies is the Global Assembly Cache (GAC). The GAC is a set of system folders managed by the runtime, and it allows multiple applications to share assemblies. The current location of the GAC is \WINDOWS\assembly, although this site may change in future versions of .NET. The simplest way to examine the GAC is to use Windows Explorer.

The GAC is an intricate structure consisting of folders and subfolders that can hold many different versions of the same assembly. The GAC Viewer (shown in Figure 2-9), which is displayed when you navigate to the \WINNT\assembly folder, is a shell extension that is installed with .NET. It presents the contents of the GAC in a more friendly way. If you want to look at the raw GAC, you can open a command prompt window and examine it from the command line by moving around the \WINDOWS\Assembly subfolders. Don't change anything, though!

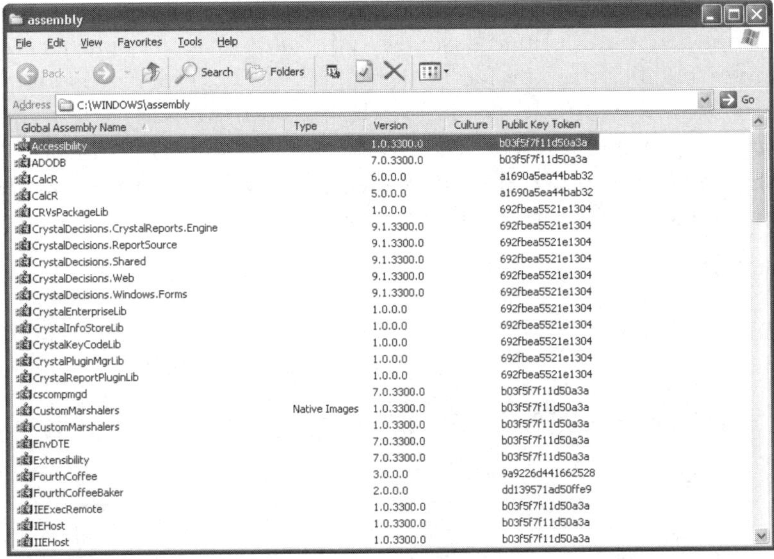

Figure 2-9 The GAC Viewer

Strong Names and Version Numbers

You can place your own assemblies in the GAC, but they must first meet a couple of requirements. The first condition is that an assembly must have a *strong name*. This is a name that uniquely distinguishes your assembly from any other. The earlier examples used the filename of an assembly to identify it. This is fine for private assemblies where there is little scope for ambiguity, but filename uniqueness is not guaranteed once you start using the GAC—two developers might use the same name for two different assemblies. A strong name combines the filename with version information, culture information (you can provide a different build of the assembly for different cultures—a Japanese version, for example), a public key, and a digital signature. Strong names not only ensure that your assemblies are unique, but they also add a degree of protection to your code through public/private key encryption. If you reference a strongly-named DLL, you can be sure where it originated and that it has not been tampered with. It could still be malicious, but at least you know who to sue!

The .NET Framework SDK provides the strong name utility, sn.exe, in the folder \Program Files\Microsoft Visual Studio .NET\FrameworkSDK\Bin, for generating public/private key pairs. The sn utility creates a file containing the keys if you use the *–k* option. The key file is conventionally given the SNK extension, for *Strong Name Keys*:

```
sn -k CakeUtilsKeys.snk
```

You can indicate that your assembly should be signed with the keys in this file using some predefined assembly attributes. The *AssemblyKeyFileAttribute* attribute specifies the key file (CakeUtilKeys.snk), and the *AssemblyVersionAttribute* attribute should be set to the version number for your assembly. Attributes in J# are added using Javadoc-style comments. The J# compiler will pick them out and process them. Notice that you must import the *System.Reflection* package in order to use these attributes:

```
package CakeUtils;

import System.Reflection.*;

/** @assembly AssemblyVersionAttribute("1.0.*") */
/** @assembly AssemblyKeyFileAttribute("CakeUtilsKeys.snk") */
⋮
```

Note If you use Visual Studio .NET to write your assembly, it will create a file called AssemblyInfo.jsl and add it to your project automatically. This file contains placeholders where you can insert values for the *AssemblyVersionAttribute* and *AssemblyKeyFileAttribute* attributes (among others).

The second condition for using the GAC is that your assembly must have a version number. The versioning scheme used by .NET has four parts:

```
<Major Version>.<Minor Version>.<Build Number>.<Revision>
```

You must specify a major and minor version number for your assembly, but the compiler can automatically generate a Build Number and Revision every time you rebuild the assembly. You simply specify * for the build number and revision. When an application is linked to a particular assembly using the */references* option, the strong name and version number of the assembly are noted and stored in the manifest of the application.

A sample manifest is shown in Figure 2-10. You can see the strong name and version number of the assembly using ILDASM. At run time, the runtime will make sure the correct version is loaded. To make sure the correct assembly is used (and not the correct version of the wrong assembly that has the same filename), the runtime also uses the *publickeytoken* value specified in the manifest of the consuming application. This is a hexadecimal version of the strong name of the required assembly.

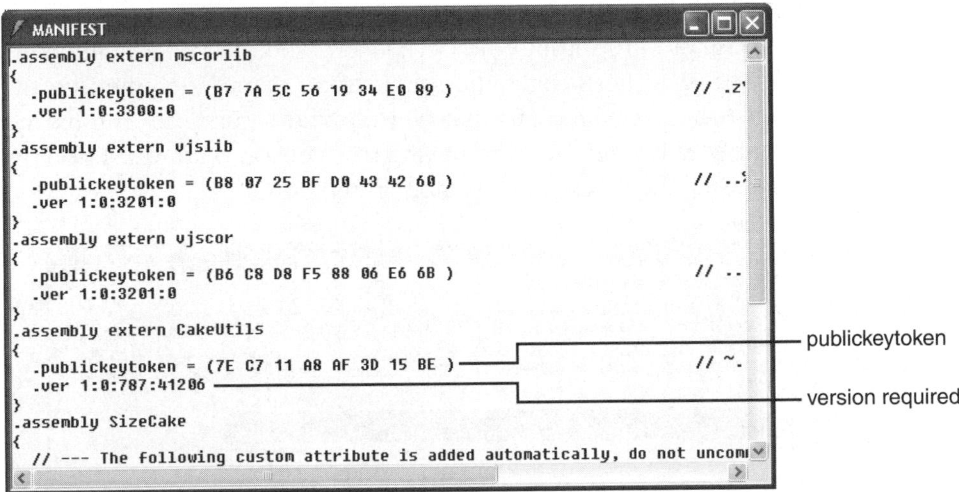

```
MANIFEST
.assembly extern mscorlib
{
  .publickeytoken = (B7 7A 5C 56 19 34 E0 89 )                    // .z'
  .ver 1:0:3300:0
}
.assembly extern vjslib
{
  .publickeytoken = (B8 07 25 BF D0 43 42 60 )                    // ..
  .ver 1:0:3201:0
}
.assembly extern vjscor
{
  .publickeytoken = (B6 C8 D8 F5 88 06 E6 6B )                    // ..
  .ver 1:0:3201:0
}
.assembly extern CakeUtils
{
  .publickeytoken = (7E C7 11 A8 AF 3D 15 BE )                    // ~.
  .ver 1:0:787:41206
}
.assembly SizeCake
{
  // --- The following custom attribute is added automatically, do not uncom
```


Figure 2-10 The manifest of SizeCake.exe

When the application runs, the runtime will search for required strongly named assemblies in the GAC. (Assemblies without strong names cannot be held in the GAC and will most likely be deployed as private assemblies.) If any assemblies are missing, the runtime will look for them elsewhere using application configuration files or will probe for them under the application's base directory using the same strategy it uses to search for a private assembly.

Deploying to the GAC

You can add an assembly to the GAC in at least two ways. The first and simplest way is to use Windows Explorer to drag and drop the DLL comprising your assembly into the \WINDOWS\assembly folder. The GAC Viewer will create the appropriate directory structure and put your assembly in the correct place. You'll see the assembly appear in the GAC, together with its version number and public key token. You can remove an assembly from the GAC by clicking it and pressing the Delete key.

Warning Never use the *copy* command from the command line to put assemblies into the GAC. Deploying an assembly to the GAC is more involved than just copying a file. For the same reason, never use the command line to delete files from the GAC.

If you update an assembly and rebuild it with a new version number, you can drag and drop it into the GAC again. The old version and the new version will coexist. (They'll have the same strong name, identified by the public key token.) Also, applications that were linked to use the original version of the assembly will continue to run using that version. Figure 2-11 below shows two versions of the CakeUtils assembly in the GAC.

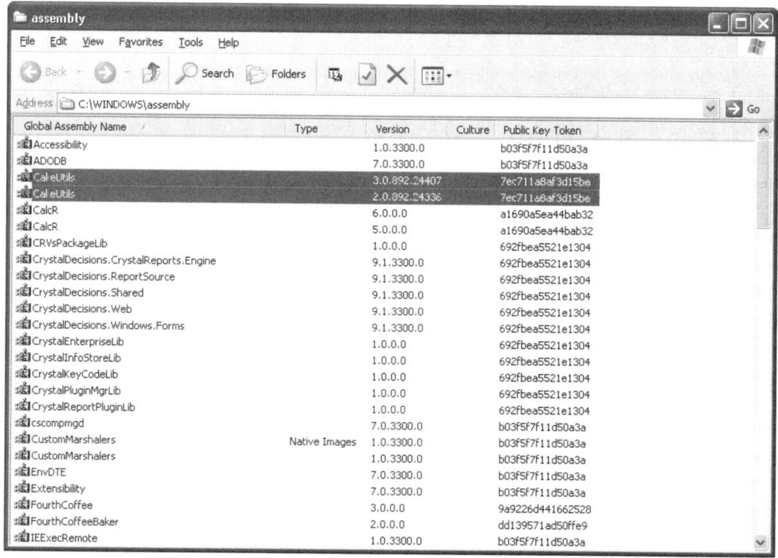

Figure 2-11 Two versions of CakeUtils in the GAC

Microsoft also supplies a command-line tool called Gacutil that you can use to query and maintain the GAC. To install an assembly to the GAC, you use *Gacutil /i*. To uninstall an assembly, you use *Gacutil /u*. To list the contents of the GAC, use *Gacutil /l*.

Configuring an Application

You can configure an application using an optional application configuration file. An application configuration file can contain information about the locations and versions of assemblies that the application references. The application configuration file has the same name as the application, with *.config* tacked onto the end. Assembly DLLs can also have configuration files, which can be useful if they reference other assemblies. The configuration file resides in the same folder as the application executable. Application configuration information is specified using an XML schema. The following example below shows

SizeCake.exe.config, a configuration file for the SizeCake application, specifying that the SizeCake application requires the CakeUtils assembly to run:

```
<?xml version="1.0"?>
<configuration>
  <runtime>
    <assemblyBinding xmlns="urn:schemas-microsoft-com:asm.v1">
      <dependentAssembly>
        <assemblyIdentity name="CakeUtils"
        publicKeyToken="7ec711a8af3d15be" />
      </dependentAssembly>
    </assemblyBinding>
  </runtime>
</configuration>
```

The *<assemblyBinding>* tag specifies the assemblies that the application uses.

Binding Policies

If a new version of an assembly is released, you can arrange for the application to use it without relinking it, using a *bindingRedirect* tag:

```
<?xml version="1.0"?>
<configuration>
  <runtime>
    <assemblyBinding xmlns="urn:schemas-microsoft-com:asm.v1">
      <dependentAssembly>
        <assemblyIdentity name="CakeUtils"
        publicKeyToken="6bf6f09321e683a7" />
        <bindingRedirect oldVersion="2.0.0.0-2.0.65535.65535"
        newVersion="3.0.892.24407" />
      </dependentAssembly>
    </assemblyBinding>
  </runtime>
</configuration>
```

The example configuration causes all requests for any version of the CakeUtils assembly between versions 2.0.0.0 and 2.0.65535.65535 to be redirected to use version 3.0.892.24407 instead. (The newer version was shown earlier in Figure 2-11.)

Note Binding policies apply only to assemblies that have strong names.

If the creator of an assembly wants to ensure that all applications that use the assembly are directed to a specific version of that assembly, she can create a publisher policy file and deploy it in the GAC with the assembly. The publisher policy file also uses an XML schema and contains a *bindingRedirect* tag similar to that used by the application configuration file. Publisher policy files are sometimes referred to as Quick Fix Engineering (QFE) files because they're designed to be deployed as a "quick fix" to redirect requests from a faulty assembly to a "fixed" one!

By default, the publisher policy file overrides any binding redirects performed by an application configuration file, but you can have an application ignore the publisher policy file settings by using the safe mode and specifying the *<publisherPolicy apply="no" />* tag, as shown here:

```
<?xml version="1.0"?>
<configuration>
  <runtime>
    <assemblyBinding xmlns="urn:schemas-microsoft-com:asm.v1">
      <dependentAssembly>
        <assemblyIdentity name="CakeUtils"
        publicKeyToken="6bf6f09321e683a7" />
        <bindingRedirect oldVersion="2.0.0.0-2.0.65535.65535"
        newVersion="3.0.892.24407" />
        <publisherPolicy apply="no" />
      </dependentAssembly>
    </assemblyBinding>
  </runtime>
</configuration>
```

Downloading Assemblies

An application configuration file (and the publisher policy file) can contain a *<codeBase>* element as part of the *<dependentAssembly>* entry. Using a code base lets you specify a location other than the GAC from where the assembly should be retrieved. It can be a folder on your computer or a URL on some Web server. Different versions of the same assembly are accessed from different code bases. If the code base specifies a URL, the assembly will be retrieved over the Internet (or your local intranet) and held in the download cache. If a subsequent request is made to the same assembly, the runtime will check the download cache first. If the required version of the assembly has already been retrieved from the same code base, it will be used rather than being fetched again.

Downloading assemblies from the Internet and running them poses some interesting security issues, which we'll address later in the chapter. The following example downloads the CakeUtils assembly from a URL on my local intranet:

```
<?xml version="1.0"?>
<configuration>
  <runtime>
    <assemblyBinding xmlns="urn:schemas-microsoft-com:asm.v1">
      <dependentAssembly>
        <assemblyIdentity name="CakeUtils"
        publicKeyToken="6bf6f09321e683a7" />
        <publisherPolicy apply="no" />
        <bindingRedirect oldVersion="2.0.0.0-2.0.65535.65535"
        newVersion="3.0.892.24407" />
        <codeBase version="3.0.892.24407"
        href="http://cheshirecat/CakeAssemblies/CakeUtils.dll" />
      </dependentAssembly>
    </assemblyBinding>
  </runtime>
</configuration>
```

Search Paths

If the configuration file for an application does not specify a code base and the assembly cannot be found in the GAC, the runtime will assume that the assembly is private and will look for it in the folder containing the application, and then in any subfolder named after the assembly (and in sub-subfolders as well—for example, you could place the CakeUtils.dll assembly in a folder named CakeUtils\CakeUtils under the application folder). If the assembly uses culture information, the search path will also include subfolders named after the required culture. Finally, you can specify a manual search path, called a *binpath*, that will also be searched for folders, subfolders, and culture folders that might contain the assembly. This whole process is known as *probing*.

The following file contains a binpath (the *<probing privatePath>* element) comprising \bin\retail and \assemblies. Notice the use of a semicolon to specify multiple paths. You should also be aware that these paths are relative to the application folder, not absolute path names.

```
<?xml version="1.0"?>
<configuration>
  <runtime>
    <assemblyBinding xmlns="urn:schemas-microsoft-com:asm.v1">
      <dependentAssembly>
        <assemblyIdentity name="CakeUtils"
        publicKeyToken="6bf6f09321e683a7" />
        <publisherPolicy apply="no" />
        <bindingRedirect oldVersion="2.0.0.0-2.0.65535.65535"
        newVersion="3.0.892.24407" />
```

```
      </dependentAssembly>
      <publisherPolicy apply="no" />
      <probing privatePath="\bin\retail;\assemblies" />
    </assemblyBinding>
  </runtime>
</configuration>
```

If the probe fails, the runtime will ask the Windows Installer to provide the assembly. The Windows Installer allows assemblies to be packaged as install-on-demand Windows Installer (MSI) files. If the Windows Installer cannot install the assembly (most likely because there is no such install package), the common language runtime will give up and generate an *exception*.

To summarize, here is the search algorithm the common language runtime uses to locate an assembly:

1. Determine the version of the assembly using the metadata in the application's EXE file.
2. Examine the application configuration file (if it exists) for a binding policy to determine whether a different version of the assembly should be used.
3. Look in the GAC for the assembly. If a publisher policy file is present, use it to redirect to an appropriate version of the assembly (unless the application configuration file specifies that the application is using safe mode).
4. If the assembly is not found in the GAC, check to see whether the application configuration file specifies a code base for the assembly.
5. If no code base is specified, probe for the assembly in the application's folder based on the name of the assembly and using any *bin-path* specified.
6. If the assembly is still not found, ask Windows Installer to install it. If this fails, raise an *exception*.

.NET Configuration Tool

You can edit application configuration files and publisher policy files manually, but the .NET Framework SDK has a Microsoft Management Console snap-in called .NET Framework Configuration (shown in Figure 2-12) that makes life a little easier. Under Windows XP, you can find this in Control Panel, under Performance and Maintenance and then under Administrative Tools. (Alternatively, you can find the snap-in, called Mscorcfg.msc, under \WINDOWS\Microsoft.NET\Framework\<*version*>).

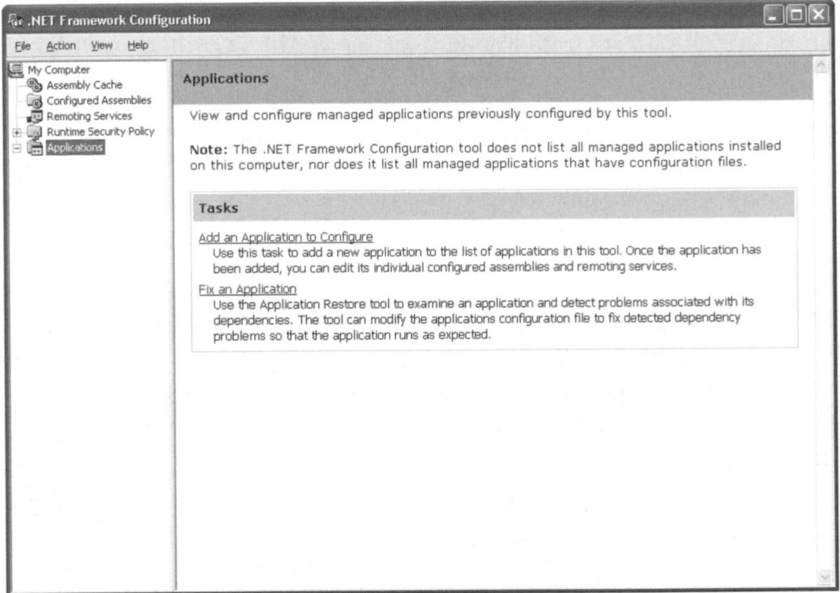

Figure 2-12 The .NET Framework Configuration tool

The Applications folder lets you configure an application. Simply click Add an Application to Configure, and a wizard will appear, allowing to you to browse to the application. The wizard will list the dependent assemblies and let you specify any binding policy and code base entries you require. The result will be a configuration file, created in the same folder as the application. You can also use the Applications folder to maintain existing application configuration files.

The Configured Assemblies folder allows you to create and maintain publisher policy files. Again, you can specify binding policy and code base entries for an assembly.

The .NET Framework Class Library

The .NET Framework incorporates a comprehensive library of classes and other types that are essential for building applications. This library provides access to the underlying operating system and adds a level of abstraction that allows you to write portable code that can run on any machine that has the common language runtime installed.

In developing the .NET Framework Class Library, Microsoft paid particular attention to the fact that the routines and objects contained in it had to be usable by a wide (and indeterminate) range of programming languages. Therefore, as much functionality as possible had to be made available using only CLS-compliant types and methods. Microsoft also met the following goals:

- The library has functionality at least equivalent to that of the ISO C standard library. This is the library that many C and C++ programmers are familiar with, and it is widely acknowledged as the benchmark for portable libraries designed to remove dependencies on the operating system.
- The structure of the library is consistent, allowing it to be factored into smaller, self-contained units with as few interdependencies as possible. The rationale behind this is twofold: First, the library can be split into mandatory and optional components for porting to mobile environments in which resources are at a premium. Second, the library can be implemented as a series of relatively independent assemblies. This reduces the runtime overhead of applications using it, because applications load only the assemblies containing the needed routines rather than the entire library.
- The library supports modern programming paradigms that go beyond those of the ISO C standard. Examples include support for a consistent model for events, delegates (callbacks), and consistent properties across all languages.
- The library provides consistent APIs for networking, processing XML, handling runtime type information, dynamic object creation, and dynamic method dispatching. These last three items give applications a high level of flexibility, postponing many decisions about object creation and method invocation until run time, which is useful when interoperating with COM.

The .NET Framework Class Library also includes additional utility objects and methods, including implementations of useful collection classes, classes for building Windows GUI applications (called Windows Forms), classes for interacting with the graphics subsystems, and many others. These features are optional and might be partially present or not present at all in any given implementation of the .NET Framework. The .NET Compact Framework, which is aimed at mobile and other devices, contains a stripped-down version of the library, for example.

Namespaces

The .NET Framework Class Library is split into namespaces. A *namespace* is a logical partitioning of the library. The namespace scheme used in the library is hierarchical and can be further subdivided into child namespaces. Each namespace contains a set of related types, resulting in the division into namespaces that is functional, and which makes a large library easier to understand.

Microsoft uses the following convention for namespace names. You should adopt the same approach when defining your own namespaces, especially if you're going to publish them:

```
<Company>.<Technology>[.<Feature>][.Design]
```

Features can be split into subfeatures. You use the *Design* suffix only for namespaces that implement design-time functionality. Some examples of namespaces in the .NET Framework Class Library are *Microsoft.Win32*, *System.Web.Services*, *System.Security.Cryptography.Xml*, and *System.Windows.Forms.Design*. Notice that Microsoft makes extensive use of the pseudocompany *System*. You should not use *System* for your own namespaces.

From a J# perspective, a namespace is treated syntactically like a Java package: You can use the *import* statement to bring the contents of a namespace into scope. However, unlike regular Java packages, a namespace is purely a logical organization of types and does not imply any physical directory structure.

The relationship between assemblies and namespaces can be confusing. A single assembly can implement more than one namespace. For example, the primary runtime assembly, mscorlib.dll, contains code for the *System* namespace as well as *System.Collections*, *System.Reflection*, *System.Security*, *System.Threading*, and several others.

Frequently Used Namespaces

The most important namespace is *System*. This namespace contains the fundamental base classes, types, and other services exposed by .NET.

The *System* Namespace and the *System* Object

Although the .NET Framework is designed to provide cross-language support, its use of namespaces and how they are mapped to Java packages can lead to confusion for the unwary developer. An example of this is the *System* namespace.

In the .NET Framework Class Library, the *System* namespace contains the fundamental types and objects, plus some utility classes. However, the Java language also defines its own core set of class libraries; to maintain interoperability with programs written in Java, Microsoft has tried to support many of these in J#. In the java.lang package of the Java class libraries, you'll find an object that is also called *System*. It contains a field named *out*. The *out* field exposes a method called *println* that you can use to display data on the console screen, using the following statement:

```
System.out.println("Hello, World");
```

The J# compiler has to use its knowledge of the *System* namespace and the *System* object in the java.lang package to determine which particular "System" it should be using in any given context. For example, the following statement refers to the *System* namespace rather than the *java.lang.System* object:

```
System.Console.WriteLine("Hello, World");
```

This can all be very confusing. I'm afraid you just have to live with it and make sure you know which *System* is which! This ambiguity occurs elsewhere as well. The Java language and .NET both have their own *Object* and *String* types, for example. Chapter 3 describes in more detail how the Java language class libraries and types are reconciled with those of .NET.

The *System.Collections* and *System.Collections.Specialized* namespaces define useful utility classes for maintaining collections of data. Examples include lists, queues, dictionaries, dynamic arrays, and hash tables.

System.Reflection provides classes that allow you to examine the metadata of objects found in assemblies. You can use this information to dynamically create objects, invoke methods, and process attributes.

The *System.Security* namespace and its child namespaces *System.Security.Cryptography*, *System.Security.Permissions*, *System.Security.Policy*, and *System.Security.Principal* give you access to the security system underlying the runtime.

The *System.Threading* namespace implements the .NET multithreading primitives and synchronization objects.

System.Data and its child namespaces contain the classes needed to manipulate databases using ADO.NET and SQL.

System.Net and *System.Net.Sockets* provide low-level programmatic access to the Internet and the Web.

System.Runtime.Remoting and its child namespaces contain classes and methods useful for building distributed applications.

System.Web and its subnamespaces implement classes that support Web server and Web browser interaction and well as Web services. This namespace contains child namespaces that you can use for defining specialized Web controls and for building GUI applications running using a Web browser.

The *System.Windows.Forms* and *System.Windows.Forms.Design* namespaces provide classes for building GUI applications and controls that are designed to run using the Windows operating system.

System.Xml and its child namespaces contain classes for handling XML, XML Schemas, XSL/T Transformations, XPath expressions, XML namespaces, and SOAP.

.NET Remoting and the Web

Programming with .NET is all about building distributed applications. You can use the .NET Remoting framework to build applications that communicate with remote objects—over a network, for example. ASP.NET is another programming framework designed for building scalable applications that present Web pages as the user interface.

The .NET Remoting Architecture

Remoting in .NET is based on object references and proxies. Figure 2-13 shows the .NET Remoting architecture. When a client application wants to use a remote object, it can obtain a remote object reference, called an *ObjRef*, from an Activator (which is part of the Remoting runtime). The Activator can use information specified in the application configuration file to create the object reference, or the client application can specify in code the type of object reference it requires. The object reference contains information about the remote class, its address, and the transport mechanisms that can be used to contact it.

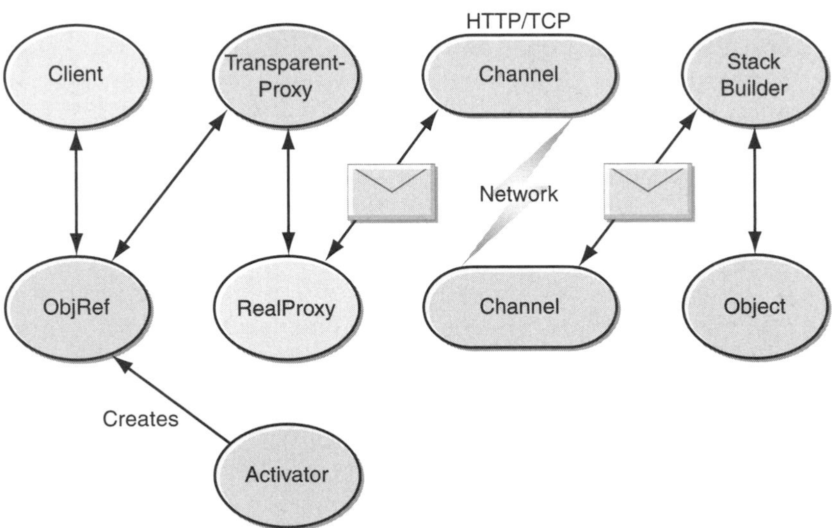

Figure 2-13 The .NET Remoting architecture

A client can activate a remote reference using the *new* operator or one of the *Activator* methods, such as *CreateInstance* or *GetObject*. When the reference is activated, a *TransparentProxy* object is instantiated. This object is responsible for intercepting method calls and bundling parameters into a format suitable for transmission over the network. It passes the bundled data to a *RealProxy* object, which does the actual sending and receiving of data. If you want to customize the manner in which data is transmitted (to use load balancing and direct requests to different servers, for example), you can create your own *RealProxy* classes using inheritance. (The *TransparentProxy* class cannot be extended, however.)

The *RealProxy* object transmits the bundled data as a message using a channel. A channel is an object that is responsible for sending and/or receiving physical data using a given format and protocol. A message is a serialized request, formatted according to the type of transport implemented by the channel. The .NET Framework supports two types of channels: HTTP, which uses SOAP encoding, and TCP, which uses a binary encoding.

When a request has been transmitted to a server, a channel on the server side of the network unmarshals the data and passes it to the *stack builder*. The stack builder creates a stack frame comprising the details passed from the client, and then it invokes the appropriate method in the target object. The target object itself sees the request as an ordinary method call. Any return values are passed back from the object and are intercepted by the Remoting runtime services on the server. They are marshaled and sent back through the channel to the *RealProxy* object on the client machine, where they are unmarshaled and eventually returned to the client process.

The whole architecture is highly customizable—you can implement custom marshaling, encryption, auditing, or any other type of processing—but you can use the standard predefined components if you have no special requirements.

Remote Object Activation

A remote object can be managed and activated by a client or by a server. Server activation is useful if an object does not maintain private state between method calls, or if multiple clients need to access the same remote object. In this model, a host application, running on the server machine, is responsible for creating a channel that clients can contact and then registering a class that implements the remote object. A client that sends a request to the channel is then connected to an instance of the registered object. When an object is registered by a host application in this way, it can specify one of two modes, *Singleton* or *SingleCall.*

The *Singleton* mode specifies that all client requests be directed to the same long-running instance of the object. The object is created once, when the first client requests a connection, and the next client will access the same object. This arrangement allows multiple clients to share the object's data. You should make sure that such an object is capable of handling and synchronizing multiple simultaneous client requests.

The *SingleCall* mode creates a new instance of the remote object on each method call. The target object is destroyed at the end of the method call.

Client activation allows the client application to control the lifetime of an object and does not require a server host application. The *Activator* object that the client uses to obtain the *ObjRef* causes the .NET Remoting runtime to instantiate an object on the server machine. A client-activated object is private to the client—two clients cannot share the same object. The client controls the lifetime of the remote object in the same way it would a local object.

Chapter 11 covers remoting and activation in more detail.

ASP.NET

Originally, Web pages contained just HTML. HTML allowed you to create static Web pages. Then Microsoft invented Active Server Pages (ASP), which allowed you to build Web pages whose content was determined dynamically. The contents of a Web page could be generated using embedded code mixed in with static HTML markup. While this was good in its time, it did have its problems.

The first issue was speed. ASP pages are interpreted, and the code embedded on an ASP page has to be examined, parsed, and compiled to machine code every time the page is accessed. While this delayed compilation makes ASP pages easy to deploy and update (you just copy the ASP file that comprises your page to the correct folder on the Web server), speed and scalability are affected.

With .NET, Microsoft updated the ASP model and created ASP.NET. ASP.NET compiles pages the first time they are accessed and caches them on the Web server. A subsequent request for the same page causes the previously compiled version to be retrieved from the cache and used. If the page is updated, the ASP.NET runtime detects the change, throws away any cached version of the page, and recompiles the new version the next time the page is accessed.

Another issue with ASP is that script code implementing business logic and HTML presentation logic are mixed together. This can make pages difficult to maintain. ASP.NET allows you to separate the business logic from the presentation logic. An ASP.NET file can contain just HTML, but with a directive that refers to a file containing the business logic code. This is known as *code behind forms*. The code itself can be written in a number of languages, including C#, J#, Visual Basic .NET, and JScript.

A major feature of ASP.NET is the ability to use Web Forms and Web Controls. Web Forms provide the user interface. You can create them using the Visual Studio .NET IDE. You can drop Web Controls onto forms, resize them, and set properties—it's as simple as programming in Visual Basic! Web Forms and Web Controls also define events—a command button has a *clicked* event, for example. You write handlers that respond to these events in your chosen language. All these features allow you to create Web Forms very quickly. The event handlers themselves run on the Web server. The code generated by ASP.NET can automatically remember the state of the controls on a form. After an event has been processed, the same form can be redisplayed with its contents intact or updated.

You'll learn a lot more about ASP.NET in Chapter 16.

Web Services

ASP.NET also provides support for Web services. When Microsoft Internet Information Services (IIS) is configured to use ASP.NET, it listens for incoming SOAP requests as well as requests for regular ASP.NET Web pages. The listener component inside ASP.NET decodes each SOAP request and loads the component that actually implements the service (which is referred to as a *Web method*). The listener then unmarshals any parameters in the SOAP request and invokes the

Web method in the component, passing the parameters to it. As far as the Web service component is concerned, it is dealing with an ordinary method call, and it knows nothing about SOAP. When the method call is completed, the Web service component passes any return values and output parameters back to the listener, which marshals them into a SOAP response and sends them back to the client. This scenario is illustrated in Figure 2-14.

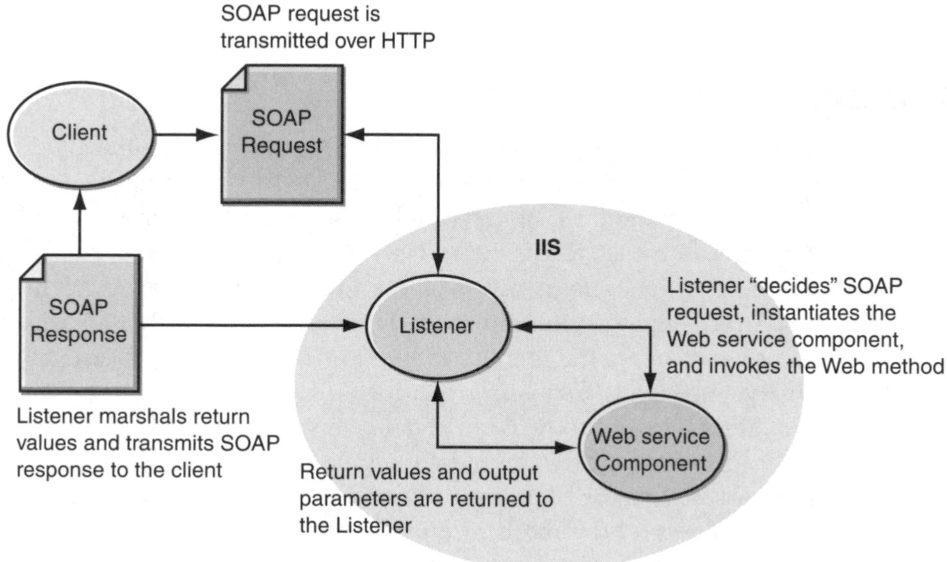

Figure 2-14 IIS handling a Web service request

Chapter 17 and Chapter 18 cover Web services in detail.

.NET Security

.NET security applies at a number of levels. The first level is the user's ability to run a piece of code that might perform a privileged operation or access sensitive data. A .NET component or ASP.NET Web application can be configured to use role-based security, which can check the identity of the user who is running a method or instantiating a class, and then grant or deny access based on that identity.

The second aspect of security concerns the code itself. The dynamic nature of the common language runtime and assemblies allows an application to download code from a remote site, load it, and run it. Using strong names and certificates to sign an assembly provides confidence in the authenticity of the code and ensures that it is not some spoof put in place by a malicious individual. We described this earlier.

The third and final aspect concerns what the code can do and what it has access to. For example, you might want to restrict the ability of assemblies downloaded from the Internet to write to your hard disk or access some other valuable resource. An administrator can set the security policy that governs what an assembly can and cannot do.

Application Domains

In a conventional operating system, each application is executed in a separate process. The purpose of this separation is to isolate applications from each other. The operating system typically ensures that one process cannot, inadvertently or otherwise, access the address space of another process, corrupt another process, or generally cause mayhem to other processes by going awry. Most modern operating systems also apply security at the process level—the application often inherits the identity of the user running the process, and the operating system can use this information to determine whether the application should be allowed to perform certain sensitive operations.

This scheme provides a high degree of protection between processes, but at a cost. A process consumes resources (mainly memory), and the more processes there are, the more resources you need to have available to run them. Also, an application that requests the services of another application (as is the case in a distributed system) will have to make cross-process calls. This involves marshaling and unmarshaling of data between process boundaries, which can be expensive. You cannot avoid this for processes running on different computers, but if both processes are executing on the same machine, this overhead can become a burden.

.NET uses a different model: It uses *application domains*—environments created by a host process for running a .NET application. A single process can host several application domains. The managed nature of .NET applications and the common language runtime guarantees that different applications running in different application domains in the same process cannot interfere maliciously with each other because assemblies are verified when they are loaded (as we explained earlier in this chapter).

An application domain is actually an instance of the *System.AppDomain* class. It implements methods that allow the runtime to load and execute assemblies, enumerate the assemblies and threads being used by the application domain, and even terminate the domain. If several application domains being hosted by the same process load the same assembly, the host process can share a single instance of the assembly (but not the data) between application domains.

A major benefit of application domains is realized with server-side applications (Web server applications and .NET Remoting servers). A single server process can create, destroy, or even recycle application domains as client requests arrive. This makes it possible for a single process to handle many simultaneous requests in a safe and secure manner, and it greatly improves scalability. For example, a Web application being accessed by dozens of clients can run in a single process and share the same assemblies in memory across all clients. If code in one application domain needs to communicate with code in another application domain in the same process, there is no need for costly cross-process marshaling—the application host effectively performs local procedure calls!

Application hosts are transparent as far as the user running .NET applications is concerned. This is because much of the work in creating application domains is carried out silently behind the scenes. Internet Explorer 6.0 and later acts as a host, loading the runtime and creating application domains when it is called on to execute managed browser-based controls. (One application domain is created for each Web site by default.) Similarly, when you launch a .NET executable from the shell or the command line, a host application is created automatically and the .NET executable runs in a domain created by that host.

You can create custom runtime hosts using the methods documented in the runtime Hosting Interfaces specification. A host contains an unmanaged stub, which is responsible for performing initialization and loading the runtime. The common language runtime creates an initial default application domain for running managed code. The purpose of this domain is to run the managed part of the host process rather than user code. The host application obtains a reference to the new application domain from the common language runtime and loads the managed portion of its code into this domain. The managed portion of the host process is responsible for creating additional application domains and loading assemblies as needed by the runtime. At this point, the unmanaged stub of the host application is no longer required and can be discarded.

The host application itself determines the policy for creating application domains based on application configurations, security, and the need to manage resources (unloading code that is no longer required). Individual assemblies cannot be unloaded; instead, the entire application domain must be terminated. You can see that the policies adopted for creating application domains can have a major impact on the footprint of a host process. Creating custom host applications is a specialized art!

You should note one interesting fact about threads and application domains. Threads belong to a host process rather than a single application domain, so there is not a 1:1 correspondence between threads and application domains. Several threads can execute in the same application domain at the same time, and a single thread can cross from one application domain to another (when making calls from one application domain to another, for example). The common language runtime keeps track of which threads are executing in which application domain.

Figure 2-15 shows how the unmanaged stub loads the common language runtime, which in turn creates the default application domain. Further application domains can be created (and destroyed) by code running in the default application domain. These application domains load and use assemblies, which are then executed by the common language runtime.

Figure 2-15 Host processes, application domains, and assemblies

Host applications have intimate knowledge about the assemblies being run by the various application domains they have created, so they play an important part in the code access security model implemented by .NET.

Role-Based Security

Role-based security is used to specify who can execute your code. A .NET component can tag classes and methods declaratively, stating the identity and/or roles that can execute the code. If the user running the code does not meet these requirements, the result is a *SecurityException*. You should be prepared to trap and handle this exception in your code and report a meaningful error to the user—and possibly record the security exception in the Windows Event log as well.

If you prefer, you can use the features of the .NET Framework *System.Security.Permissions* and *System.Security.Principal* namespaces to perform imperative security checking in your own code.

Principals

Role-based security uses *principals* to represent the identity and role of a user attempting to run a piece of code. If you're operating within a Windows domain, you can use Windows users and groups to implement an integrated security scheme that encompasses both Windows and .NET. Windows users can be mapped to .NET users, and Windows groups can be mapped to .NET roles. Using this approach means you can use the built-in Windows tools to administer users and roles, which are known as Windows Principals. Windows Principals also support impersonation—the ability of a component configured to run using one identity to switch to the identity used by a calling component and perform operations as this new identity.

If this is not convenient—for example, if you cannot guarantee that your users will be members of a particular domain—the .NET security scheme also allows you to use Generic Principals, which are independent of Windows users and groups.

Finally, you can define your own custom classes that implement the *IPrincipal* interface found in the *System.Security.Principal* namespace. This interface defines an *Identity* property and a method called *IsInRole*. The *Identity* property identifies the principal (user) in some application-defined manner. The *IsInRole* method is used to determine whether the principal belongs to a specified role. You write your own code to implement this property and method.

Note The common language runtime security mechanisms are independent of any operating system security. Using Windows Principals allows you to map Windows security information to the runtime, but it is a manual rather than automatic operation—you must explicitly configure the application domain to use Windows security. If you're running on an operating system that has little or no inherent security (Windows 98 or Windows ME, for example), the common language runtime security mechanisms will still apply.

Declarative Security

You can use *System.Security.Permissions.PrincipalPermissionAttribute* to indicate the identities and roles of users that can run your code. The following example shows the *CakeInfo* class with the *FeedsHowMany* method restricted to members of the *Bakers* group in the *Wonderland* domain and the user *JSharp*. If you apply *PrincipalPermissionAttribute* several times (as shown in the example), identities that match any of the attributes shown will be allowed to execute the method. If you specify a *Name* and a *Role* in the same attribute, you will restrict access to identities that satisfy both criteria—that is, the identity must match the specified name *and* the role.

```
package CakeUtils;

import System.Reflection.*;
import System.Security.Permissions.*;
⋮
public class CakeInfo
{

  /** @attribute PrincipalPermissionAttribute(SecurityAction.Demand,
  Role="WONDERLAND\\Bakers") */
   /** @attribute PrincipalPermissionAttribute(SecurityAction.Demand,
  Name="WONDERLAND\\JSharp") */

  // Work out how many people a cake of a given size, shape,
  // and filling will feed
  public static short FeedsHowMany(short diameter, short shape,
  short filling)
  {
      ⋮
   }
 }
```

You can tag a class with *PrincipalPermissionAttribute*—the restrictions will be applied to every method in the class. However, if you also tag a method, the restrictions of the method will override those of the class (even if they're less restrictive).

A client application that calls this method must make sure that the application domain is using the appropriate authentication provider. Authentication will fail otherwise. The following example executes the *SetPrincipalPolicy* method of the current application domain (which is retrieved using the *AppDomain.get_CurrentDomain* method). The authentication provider is set to *PrincipalPolicy.WindowsPrincipal*, which indicates that Windows Principals should be used. This authentication provider then validates the user when the *FeedsHowMany* method is called.

```
package SizeCake;

import CakeUtils.*;
import System.*;
import System.Security.Principal.*;

public class SizeTest
{

  public static void main(String [] args)
  {

    short numEaters;

    // Configure the application domain to use the Windows Principal
    // authentication provider
    AppDomain.get_CurrentDomain().SetPrincipalPolicy(
         PrincipalPolicy.WindowsPrincipal);

    // How many people will a 10" hexagonal sponge cake feed?
    numEaters = CakeInfo.FeedsHowMany((short)10, CakeShape.Hexagonal,
        CakeFilling.Sponge);
    Console.WriteLine("This will feed " + numEaters + " people");
  }
}
```

Security Demands

The value *SecurityAction.Demand*, which is invoked by *PrincipalPermissionAttribute*, forces a security check not only on the direct calling method (in the client, in this case) but also on the method that called the calling method, and so on all the way up the call stack. In this case, the call to *FeedsHowMany* will fail the security check if the identity of the caller was changed at any point in the call stack. This type of thorough security checking is vital if you cannot guarantee the trustworthiness of the calling code!

A less powerful option is *SecurityAction.LinkDemand*. This value causes the identity of the immediate caller to be checked but does not proceed any further up the call stack. Use this option only for trusted code.

Imperative Security

Instead of using attributes, you can implement what's known as imperative security by writing your own code to check the identity of a user executing your methods. Imperative security is a little more involved than declarative security, but it gives you a lot more flexibility if you need it. Declarative security is fixed when your assembly is compiled, but imperative code allows you to adapt to changing circumstances dynamically.

The following code shows the *FeedsHowMany* method again, but this time using imperative rather than declarative security:

```
package CakeUtils;

import System.Reflection.*;
import System.Security.Permissions.*;
⋮
public class CakeInfo
{

  // Work out how many people a cake of a given size, shape, and filling
  // will feed
public static short FeedsHowMany(short diameter, short shape,
   short filling)
  {
    // Imperative security check - make sure caller is in
    // WONDERLAND\Bakers role
    // or has the WONDERLAND\JSharp identity
    PrincipalPermission rolePermission =
       new PrincipalPermission(null, "WONDERLAND\\Bakers");
    PrincipalPermission namePermission =
      new PrincipalPermission("WONDERLAND\\JSharp", null);
    rolePermission.Union(namePermission).Demand();

    ⋮
  }
}
```

The method creates two *PrincipalPermission* objects: *rolePermission* and *namePermission*. The *rolePermission* object comprises the *WONDERLAND\Bakers* role. The first parameter of the constructor is the identity to use. If you want to include all the members of a certain role, you can set the first parameter to *null*. Similarly, if you set the identity parameter to a name, you can set the role parameter to *null* if you do not want to restrict the identity to any particular role, as the *namePermission* object does. The *Union* method combines permissions, and the *Demand* method performs the security check. If the check fails, an exception will be raised; otherwise, execution will continue with the remainder of the method.

Code Access Security

Role-based security determines who can access your code, and code access security determines what your code is allowed to do when it runs. Code access security examines characteristics of an assembly, such as its source, which it refers to as evidence. The .NET security system uses configuration files that map evidence to permission sets, which specify what the code is and isn't allowed to do. The mapping between evidence and permission sets is called a security policy.

Code access security policies can be defined at three levels: enterprise, machine, and user. Policy information is held in XML format in files located in *\Windows\Microsoft.NET\Framework\<version>\config*. These files should be protected appropriately to prevent unauthorized editing. An administrator can make use of the .NET Framework Configuration tool to maintain this information. A command-line tool, Caspol.exe, is also available, but it is not very friendly.

Evidence

Evidence is information passed to the runtime from the host application loading an assembly about the origin of that assembly. As you'll recall, assemblies can be loaded from almost anywhere, such as a URL over the Internet, a network file share, or a local disk. What's more, the location of an assembly can change during the lifetime of an application as new versions are released and configuration files are updated with different code bases.

Evidence takes many forms, but the most common ones are

- The installation directory (local machine, network share, and so on)
- The assembly publisher's signature (created using Authenticode)
- The strong name of the assembly
- The URL the assembly was loaded from
- The zone of origin

Runtime security uses zones in a similar way to Internet Explorer. Assemblies originating from different zones (the Internet, a local intranet, My Computer, and so on) can be granted different levels of trust. The .NET Framework Configuration tool lets you modify the degree of trust for each zone, but unless you have good reason to do so, you should probably leave them at their default settings. Zone information can be modified for a single user or for the computer.

Figure 2-16 shows the Security Adjustment Wizard, which is part of the .NET Framework Configuration tool.

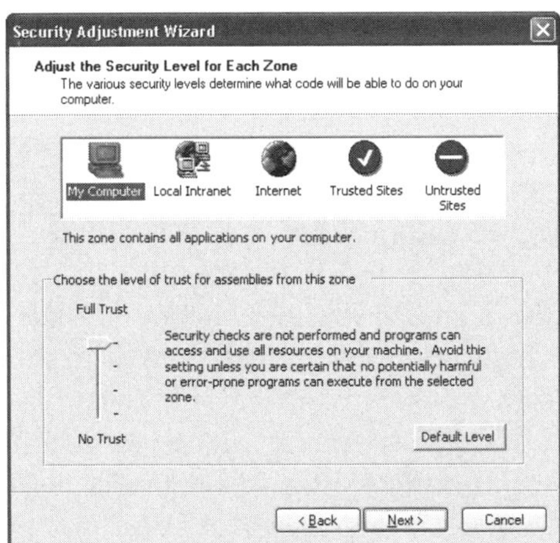

Figure 2-16 The Security Adjustment Wizard

Permissions and Permission Sets

Runtime security has a set of built-in code access permissions that can be granted to assemblies, depending on their origin (as determined by the available evidence). Table 2-1 summarizes these permissions. If these are insufficient for your requirements, you can create your own custom permissions. See "Creating Your Own Code Access Permissions" in the *.NET Framework Developer's Guide* for details.

Table 2-1 Code Access Permissions

Permission Name	Description
DirectoryServicesPermission	Allows the assembly to programmatically access Directory Services.
DnsPermission	Grants access to the Domain Name System.
EnvironmentPermission	Allows the assembly to read and write environment variables.
EventLogPermission	Allows the assembly to use the Windows Event Logs.
FileDialogPermission	Permits access to files selected by the user in the Open File common dialog box.

Table 2-1 Code Access Permissions

Permission Name	Description
FileIOPermission	Grants the ability to read, write, and append to files and directories.
IsolatedStorageFilePermission	Allows access to private virtual file systems.
IsolatedStoragePermission	Grants access to user-specific isolated storage.
MessageQueuePermission	Allows the assembly to manipulate MSMQ message queues.
OleDbPermission	Grants access to databases using OLE DB.
PerformanceCounterPermission	Allows the assembly to access Windows performance counters.
PrintingPermission	Provides access to printers.
ReflectionPermission	Allows the assembly to use reflection to discover run-time information about types.
RegistryPermission	Grants access to the Windows Registry.
SecurityPermission	Allows code to query and manipulate runtime security information. Also permits calls to unmanaged code and allows assemblies to skip code verification.
ServiceControllerPermission	Allows an assembly to start, stop, and query Windows Services.
SocketPermission	Allows an assembly to make and accept connections using a socket.
SqlClientPermission	Grants access to the SQL Server data provider.
UIPermission	Allows the assembly to use user interface functionality.
WebPermission	Allows the assembly to make and accept connections on a Web address.

To simplify the task of assigning permissions, you can group permissions into permission sets. Figure 2-17 shows the built-in .NET permission sets. You can also define your own permission sets in code or by using the .NET Framework Configuration tool.

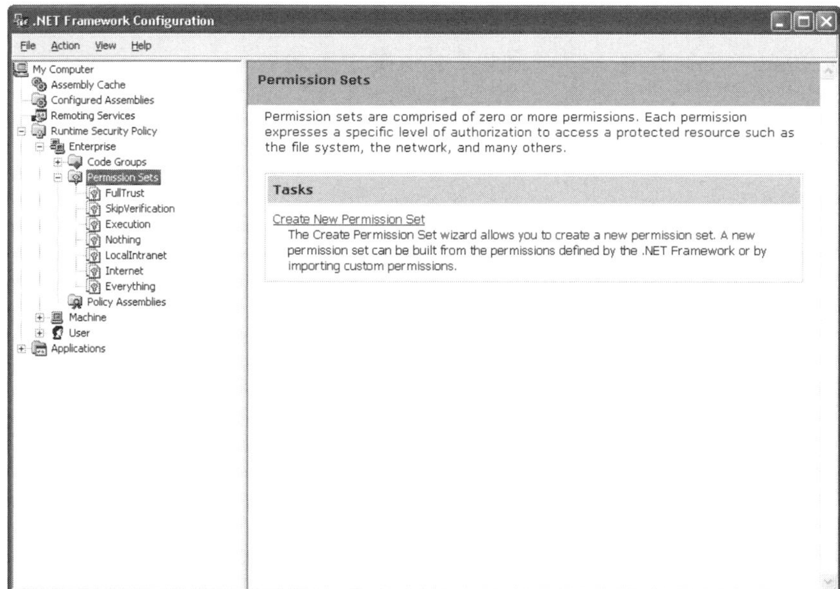

Figure 2-17 Permission sets in the .NET Framework Configuration tool

Table 2-2 below describes the default permissions assigned to the various permission sets.

Table 2-2 Built-In Permission Sets

Permission Set	Permission(s)
Nothing	No permissions
Execution	*SecurityPermission*
FullTrust	N/A
Internet	*FileDialogPermission, IsolatedStorageFilePermission, SecurityPermission, UIPermission, PrintingPermission*
LocalIntranet	*EnvironmentPermission, FileDialogPermission, IsolatedStorageFilePermission, ReflectionPermission, SecurityPermission, UIPermission, DnsPermission, PrintingPermission, EventLogPermission*
SkipVerification	*SecurityPermission*
Everything	All permissions

With the exception of *Everything*, you cannot modify these permission sets. The *FullTrust* permission set causes security checking to be bypassed, so it does not need to contain any permissions. Naturally, you should be very careful when using this permission set!

You can define permission sets at the user, machine, and enterprise levels.

Security Policy and Code Groups

As we mentioned earlier, the sets of permissions that are ascribed to assemblies based on evidence is referred to as a security policy. The .NET Framework Configuration tool lets you configure security policies by using code groups. .NET defines a number of built-in code groups, but you can edit them and change their associated permission sets. The Create Code Group Wizard in the .NET Framework Configuration tool also allows you to create your own custom code groups. You specify the evidence to use, plus a permission set. Code groups can be defined at the enterprise, machine, and individual user levels.

All assemblies are evaluated against all code groups when they are loaded, and they are granted the permissions associated with any corresponding evidence. A single assembly might match the evidence in more than one code group, in which case the assembly will be granted the union of all the permissions of the matching code groups. If the assembly subsequently attempts to perform an operation that is incompatible with the permissions granted, the runtime will raise a *SecurityException*.

Requesting and Refusing Permissions

An assembly can specify a minimum set of permissions needed in order to use it successfully, or it can filter certain permissions that it doesn't need to prevent malicious use. The assembly developer can specify this information declaratively (using attributes) or with code. For example, the *SecureLibrary* assembly shown below specifies that the *System.Diagnostics.EventLogPermission* is required to use any of the classes in the assembly, but any operations calling methods that require *System.Security.Permissions.FileIOPermission* will be refused, even if the calling assemblies have been granted this permission.

```
package SecureLibrary;
import System.Diagnostics.*;
import System.Security.Permissions.*;


/** @assembly EventLogPermissionAttribute(SecurityAction.RequestMinimum) */
/** @assembly FileIOPermissionAttribute(SecurityAction.RequestRefuse) */
public class Auditor
{
```

```
  ⋮
}
```

You can also tag individual methods and classes. The *TransmitData* method shown below specifies that it must have *System.Net.SocketPermission*. It also revokes *System.Security.Permissions.UIPermission* to prevent potentially malicious use:

```
import System.Net.*;
import System.Security.Permissions.*;
⋮
public class Auditor
{
  /** @attribute SocketPermissionAttribute(SecurityAction.Demand) */
  /** @attribute UIPermissionAttribute(SecurityAction.Deny) */
  public void TransmitData(String data)
  {
      ⋮
  }
}
```

Microsoft provides the PERMVIEW.exe tool (in the folder \Program Files\Microsoft Visual Studio .NET\FrameworkSDK\Bin), which you can use to display the permissions requested, refused, demanded, and denied by the code in an assembly.

Java Security Policy

If you're familiar with security features of the Java language implementation, you're aware that, by default, applications written in the Java language that are installed and executed on the same local machine have no security manager. Essentially, local applications written in the Java language are considered fully trusted.

With .NET, the situation is subtly different. Assemblies that are loaded from the hard disk of the user's machine are members of the My Computer zone, which by default also has full trust status. However, if you change the degree of trust that the My Computer zone enjoys, you'll find that your local assemblies are subject to the corresponding security constraints and might no longer work as a result.

In other words, plan your security policies carefully.

Summary

This chapter has taken a detailed look at the execution environment implemented by .NET and the runtime. You've seen how programs are compiled into MSIL and then linked into assemblies. When an assembly is loaded and run, its contents are verified and the JIT compiler converts the assembly into machine code. Assemblies can be installed privately with an application's executable code, they can be shared in the GAC, or they can be downloaded from a remote URL. Application configuration files and publisher policy files allow the version and location of assemblies used by an application to vary as new releases occur. Assemblies are executed in the context of an application domain.

The .NET Framework also supplies a comprehensive class library containing the objects and methods needed to create applications. The .NET Remoting architecture and ASP.NET allow you to implement a range of distributed solutions spanning the LAN, intranet, or Internet.

The .NET security features are highly configurable using the .NET Framework Configuration tool. Role-based security allows you to restrict access to your assemblies to specified users and roles. Code access security enables you to determine the degree to which you trust assemblies that have been loaded from a variety of sources.

3

Java and the Common Language Runtime

The Java programming language was designed with a number of aims in mind. James Gosling and Henry McGilton, two of the creators of the Java language, wrote a famous white paper called "The Java Language Environment" in which they discussed the goals of the language. (You can read the white paper at *http://java.sun.com/docs/white/langenv*.) The goals were that Java should be

- Simple, object-oriented, and familiar
- Robust and secure
- Architecture-neutral and portable
- High-performance
- Interpreted, threaded, and dynamic

Microsoft .NET fulfills these same goals. The only difference is the underlying platform—Java-language programs built using the Java Development Kit (JDK) execute using the Java Virtual Machine (JVM), while .NET programs execute using the common language runtime. Object technologies have advanced since the Java language was first introduced, and the common language runtime actually provides much more functionality than the JVM does. The JDK has attempted to keep up with the rest of the world while remaining true to its roots by having additional optional packages and specifications appended to it—for example, the JavaBeans framework that provides a model for building and consuming components. Further extensions include Java 2 Enterprise Edition

(J2EE), the specification of a framework for building and deploying enterprise applications.

With .NET, Microsoft has its own infrastructure that uses the features of the underlying Windows platform. Microsoft made the strategic decision that even though Visual J# would implement the syntax of the Java language, it would not support many of the additional specifications. Instead, you can use the enterprise features of .NET directly from J#. This chapter describes how Microsoft has retained the integrity of most of the semantics of the Java language while allowing you to access the features of .NET, and how the functionality of J2EE is matched, or in some cases exceeded, by that of .NET.

Visual J#, Visual J++, and the JDK

When Microsoft released Visual J++ 6.0, the current version of the JDK was 1.1.4. Microsoft implemented all the standard JDK 1.1.4 class libraries except Remote Method Invocation (RMI), and it offered some additional extensions for integrating with the Component Object Model (COM), Microsoft Windows, DLLs, and Microsoft Windows Foundation Classes for Java (WFC)—Microsoft's own Windowing library.

Although the Java language has been stable for the last few years, some additions have been made to the standard class libraries, notably Swing, which is an updated GUI framework that replaced the Abstract Window Toolkit (AWT) of earlier releases, and Java Interface Definition Language (IDL), a tool that allows you to define Java objects that communicate with CORBA using Internet Inter-ORB Protocol (IIOP). Many of the existing libraries, such as those that handled security and serialization, were also modified and extended. Microsoft had already addressed these areas with its own extension libraries, so it decided that there was no need to support the additional libraries and updates. Visual J++ 6.0 thus retained the JDK 1.1.4 libraries throughout its lifetime.

In Visual J#, Microsoft provides independently developed class libraries that support many of the features of JDK1.1.4. For compatibility with Visual J++ 6.0, Microsoft has also kept many of the existing extension classes. The primary packages that are no longer supported are *sun.io.**, *sun.net.**, and *netscape.**. There is some overlap between the extension class libraries of Visual J++ and the .NET Framework Class Library. If you have a choice, you should use the

.NET Framework Class Library when you build new applications with Visual J#. For example, you should now use Windows Forms rather than WFC.

Components and Java

First, there was structured design and programming, which promoted the ideas of abstraction and encapsulation but was unable to enforce them effectively. Then came object-oriented development, which was able to implement these concepts but sometimes did so clumsily. Finally, there came component-oriented development, whereby developers no longer built ordinary classes but instead created "components." But what distinguishes a component from a class, and which camp do Java, J#, and .NET fall into?

The problem with classes is that, well, they're not components. To understand this point, ask yourself a couple of questions: What goes in a class? What is the purpose of a class? Typically, a class contains some private data and some public methods that a consumer can call to query or manipulate the private data. A class might contain some private methods as well, or even some public data (ugh!), but we'll ignore those for now. The purpose of a class is to model some object in the real world.

At issue is the way in which you interact with objects in the real world. You can ask an object to perform an action, and it will do it if it understands the request. How it performs the action shouldn't matter to you as long as it does it. Methods are good for implementing this sort of behavior in computer programs that model objects. However, most objects also have properties—values that you can inquire about or change. A bank account object might have a current balance property, for example. Given that public data is often considered a bad thing, you should use methods to implement properties because they can be used to provide access to data values while vetoing any changes that violate business rules. However, the drawback of using methods in this case is that you generally need two of them for each property—one to ask about the current value and one to change it. These are referred to as accessor methods, or getters and setters.

Another aspect of object modeling that's often ignored by the classic object-oriented view of the universe is that sometimes objects need to tell the outside world that something significant has happened. For example, the nuclear power station core object might find it necessary to inform the safety-valve object that it is overheating! In other words, objects need to be able to raise events. Objects must also be able to receive events—it's no good shouting if no one is listening.

Component-oriented development addresses these issues. A component is a self-contained object that can interact with the world in a well-defined manner by exposing methods, properties, and events.

JavaBeans

The JDK includes the JavaBeans framework for creating and consuming components. A JavaBean is essentially just a Java class that exposes properties and events as well as methods. However, when the JavaBeans framework was proposed, one requirement was to not change or extend the JVM. As a result, the JavaBeans framework relies on specific naming conventions to indicate to JavaBeans-aware tools (such as the BeanBox supplied with the Bean Development Kit [BDK]) that a particular item is a property or an event.

For example, properties are indicated by implementing a pair of methods called *getXXX* and *setXXX*, where *XXX* is the name of the property and read-only properties are defined by creating a *getXXX* method but no *setXXX* method. Similarly, a JavaBean that publishes events implements *addYYYListener* and *removeYYYListener* methods, where *YYY* is the name of the event. These methods allow other classes to subscribe to and unsubscribe from the *YYY* event. Subscribing classes must also implement the *java.util.EventListener* interface (which is just a tag interface). When a JavaBean raises an event, it creates an event state object to hold any information needed by the event subscribers—this is a class that inherits from *java.util.EventObject*. The event state object is then passed to each subscribing object for processing.

Development tools that understand JavaBeans can use reflection to examine the structure of a bean and discover its properties and events. (*Reflection* is a technique that allows an object to examine the internal structure of classes.) Many JavaBeans are graphical components, and tools such as the BeanBox (shown in Figure 3-1) allow a developer to drag and drop them onto a form, set their properties, and wire them together automatically using events. Most graphical JavaBeans also provide editors, which allow a developer to set complex properties at design time.

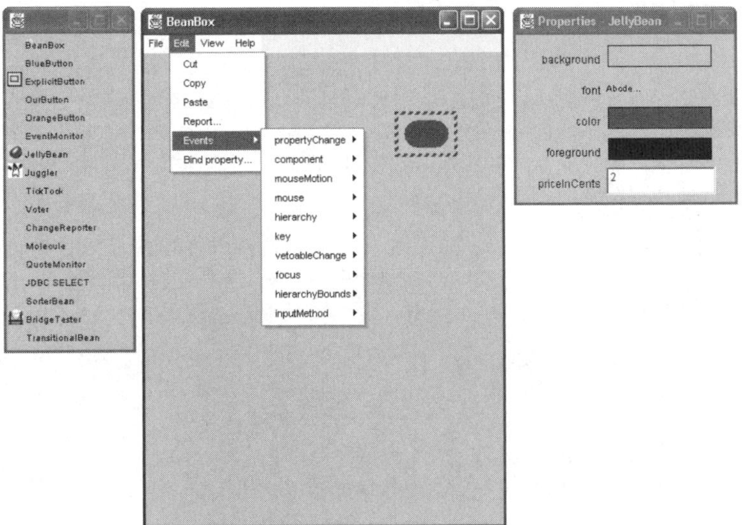

Figure 3-1 The BDK BeanBox

Ordinary Java classes can also use JavaBeans, but the process is more akin to consuming an ordinary class—you should use the *setXXX* and *getXXX* methods explicitly to access properties, for example.

Business-Oriented JavaBeans

You can build JavaBeans that act as business components. The *OvenBean* class shown below (which is available in the JDK OvenBean folder) is a JavaBean that models a simple kitchen oven. It exposes a property called *Temperature*, which is accessible through the *setTemperature* and *getTemperature* methods, and an event called *TemperatureEvent* that is raised whenever the oven gets too hot or cold. The *TemperatureEvent* state object contains information about the current temperature of the oven and is passed to each subscriber when the event is raised. A class subscribes to the *TemperatureEvent* using the *addTemperatureEventListener* method and can unsubscribe using the *removeTemperatureEventListener* method. The signatures and naming conventions used by the property and event are those mandated by the JavaBeans framework. The method *fireTemperatureEvent* actually raises the *TemperatureEvent* and is called by the *setTemperature* method if the requested temperature is outside the operational bounds of the oven. Each subscriber must implement the *TemperatureEventListener* interface (shown later), which specifies a method called *handleOvenEvent*. The *fireTemperatureEvent* method invokes the *handleOventEvent* method in each subscriber in turn.

OvenBean.java

```
import java.util.*;

// JavaBean that models a simple oven for baking cakes.
// OvenBean exposes a property to get/set the oven temperature
// OvenBean raises a TemperatureEvent if the oven overheats or underheats
public class OvenBean
{
   // Constants that define the working temperature range of the oven
   public static final int LOW_OVEN_TEMP = 100;
   public static final int HIGH_OVEN_TEMP = 500;

   // Current temperature of the oven
   private int temperature = LOW_OVEN_TEMP;

   // Event subscribers
   private Vector listeners = new Vector();

   // Subscribe to the TemperatureEvent
   public void addTemperatureEventListener(TemperatureEventListener l)
   {
      listeners.addElement(l);
   }

   // Unsubscribe from the TemperatureEvent
   public void removeTemperatureEventListener(TemperatureEventListener l)
   {
      listeners.removeElement(l);
   }

   public void fireTemperatureEvent()
   {
      Vector listenerCopy;

      // No listeners - do nothing
      if (listeners.isEmpty())
         return;

      // Otherwise build a state object holding the current temperature
      TemperatureEvent te = new TemperatureEvent(this, temperature);

      // create a copy of the listeners' vector (to prevent race conditions)
      synchronized(this)
      {
         listenerCopy = (Vector)listeners.clone();
      }

      // iterate through the copy, invoking each listener's "action" method
```

```
        for (Enumeration l = listenerCopy.elements(); l.hasMoreElements();)
        {
            ((TemperatureEventListener)(l.nextElement())).handleOvenEvent(te);
        }
    }

    // Methods for getting and setting the oven temperature
    public int getTemperature()
    {
        return temperature;
    }

    public void setTemperature(int newTemperature)
    {
        temperature = newTemperature;

        // If the new temperature is outside the working range of the oven,
        // raise a TemperatureEvent
        if (newTemperature < LOW_OVEN_TEMP || newTemperature >
            HIGH_OVEN_TEMP)
            fireTemperatureEvent();
    }
}
```

The *TemperatureEvent* state object, shown in the TemperatureEvent.java code that follows, obeys the requirement that all event state objects must inherit from *java.util.EventObject*. The *EventObject* constructor (which you should call from any constructor in the state object) requires a reference to the object raising the event. The only other data held in the state object is the current temperature of the oven.

TemperatureEvent.java

```
import java.util.*;

// The event state object for the TemperatureEvent
public class TemperatureEvent extends EventObject
{
    private int temperature;

    public TemperatureEvent(Object source, int temperature)
    {
        super(source);
        this.temperature = temperature;
    }

    public int getTemperature()
    {
```

```
        return temperature;
    }
}
```

A subscribing class must implement the *TemperatureEventListener* interface shown in TemperatureEventListener.java below. The *TemperatureEventListener* extends the *java.util.EventListener* tag interface required of all event listener objects. The *TemperatureEventListener* interface defines the *handleOvenEvent* method, which is executed when the *TemperatureEvent* is raised by the *OvenBean* class.

TemperatureEventListener.java

```
import java.util.*;

public interface TemperatureEventListener extends EventListener
{
    // Define the signature of the method that handles the TemperatureEvent
    public void handleOvenEvent(TemperatureEvent te);
}
```

The *TemperatureWarning* class shown next implements the *TemperatureEventListener* interface. This class can subscribe to the *TemperatureEvent* published by the *OvenBean* class.

TemperatureWarning.java

```
import java.util.*;

// Subscriber for the TemperatureEvent
public class TemperatureWarning implements TemperatureEventListener
{
    // Implement the method that handles the TemperatureEvent
    public void handleOvenEvent(TemperatureEvent te)
    {
        System.out.println("TemperatureEvent raised. Temperature is " +
            te.getTemperature());
    }
}
```

JavaBeans and J#

The OvenBean example was originally developed using the JDK 1.1.4, and you can compile it to Java class files using the javac compiler. However, you can also compile the classes, unchanged, into an assembly using the J# compiler. The following command will create OvenBean.dll:

```
vjc /target:library /out:OvenBean.dll OvenBean.java TemperatureEvent.java
TemperatureEventListener.
java TemperatureWarning.java
```

Using ILDASM will confirm that it contains the *OvenBean*, *TemperatureEvent*, *TemperatureWarning* and *TemperatureEventListener* classes, as shown in Figure 3-2.

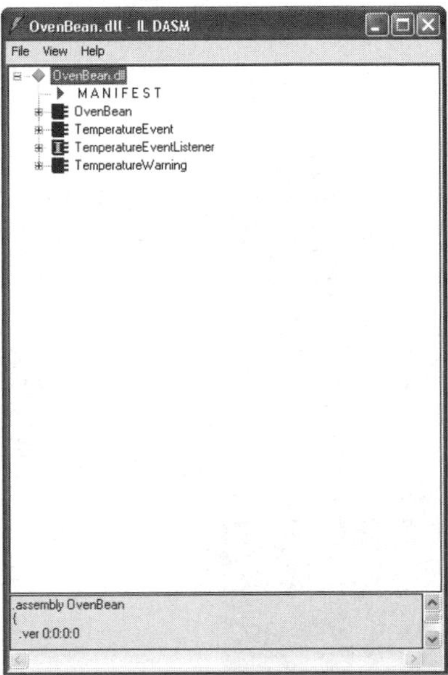

Figure 3-2 ILDASM displaying the contents of OvenBean.dll

The *BeanClient* class is a simple test harness for *OvenBean*. It creates an *OvenBean* and a *TemperatureWarning* object. The listener object subscribes to the *TemperatureEvent*. The program makes several calls to *setTemperature*. The first call (150) will not raise an event, but the two calls that follow (99 and 501) will change the oven temperature to values outside the valid range. Both of these calls will result in the *TemperatureEvent* being raised, and the listener object will respond by running its *handleOvenEvent* method.

BeanClient.java

```
public class BeanClient
{
    public static void main(String [] args)
    {
        // Create an OvenBean
        OvenBean ob = new OvenBean();

        // Create an event listener - for testing
        TemperatureEventListener tel =
           new TemperatureWarning();
```

```
            // Subscribe to the TemperatureEvent
            ob.addTemperatureEventListener(tel);

            // Test the oven by setting its temperature to different values
            ob.setTemperature(150);  // Should not raise an event
            ob.setTemperature(99);   // Should raise an event
            ob.setTemperature(501);  // Should raise an event
        }
    }
```

Again, this program will compile using the javac compiler. You can also compile the program using the J# compiler and link it with the OvenBean DLL using the following command:

```
vjc BeanClient.java /reference:OvenBean.dll
```

If you run the program BeanClient.exe, you'll see the output shown in Figure 3-3.

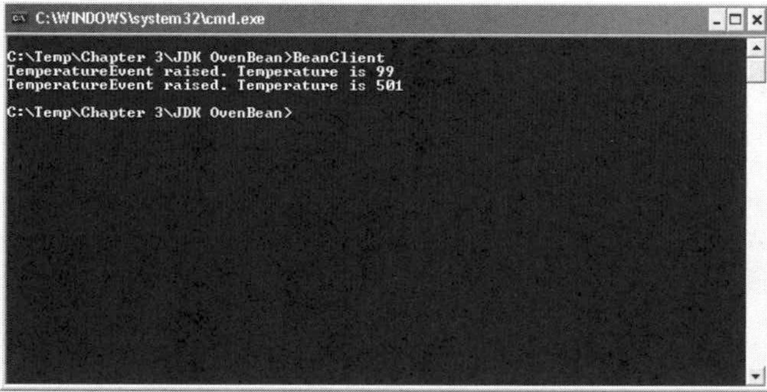

Figure 3-3 The output of the BeanClient program

Components in .NET

You can see that the JavaBeans framework allows you to create graphical and business components using the Java language and the JDK, and you can also use this framework from J#. But the .NET Framework has an arguably more elegant architecture for publishing events and properties.

Defining Properties

Properties are a built-in feature of the common language runtime. Properties are implemented in a similar manner to properties in JavaBeans. You can access a property by using a pair of accessor methods. The naming rules are slightly different, though; the *get* accessor must be called *get_XXX* (where *XXX* is the name of the property—note the underscore in the name), and the *set* accessor must be called *set_XXX*. Furthermore, both accessors must be tagged with the */ ** @property */* directive, as shown in the following example, which is from the J# implementation of the OvenBean component in the NET OvenBean folder:

```
public class OvenBean
{
    // Constants that define the working temperature range of the oven
    public static final int LOW_OVEN_TEMP = 100;
    public static final int HIGH_OVEN_TEMP = 500;

    // Current temperature of the oven
    private int temperature = LOW_OVEN_TEMP;
    ⋮
    // The Temperature property
    /** @property */
    public int get_Temperature()
    {
        return temperature;
    }

    /** @property */
    public void set_Temperature(int value)
    {
        temperature = value;
        ⋮
    }
}
```

To access a property from a J# client, you use the regular method call syntax. The following code is from the *ComponentClient* class, which is also in the .NET OvenBean folder:

```
public class ComponentClient
{
   ⋮

   public ComponentClient()
   {
      // Create an OvenBean
      OvenBean ob = new OvenBean();

      ⋮
      // Test the oven by setting its temperature to different values
      ob.set_Temperature(150);  // Should not raise an event
      ob.set_Temperature(99);   // should raise an event
      ob.set_Temperature(501);  // should raise an event
   }
}
```

The syntax for accessing a property from other languages such as C#, however, uses direct assignment (the same syntax you use when you access a variable), as shown below. Assigning to a property causes the *set* accessor to be invoked, and reading a property executes the *get* accessor. When the J# *OvenBean* class is compiled, the */** @property */* directive causes metadata to be generated for the property methods, allowing them to be called in this fashion from other languages.

```
// C#
OvenBean ob = new OvenBean();
⋮
ob.Temperature = 150;     // calls ob.set_Temperature(150)
int tp = ob.Temperature; // calls ob.get_Temperature()
```

Note This syntactic feature is also true of properties belonging to classes defined in the .NET Framework Class Library—you'll always have to use *set_XXX* and *get_XXX* methods when you access properties from J# code. Fortunately, the IntelliSense feature of Visual Studio .NET generates the correct syntax for you automatically.

Defining Events and Delegates

The .NET model of events is based on delegates. A delegate holds a reference to a method—a little like a function pointer or a callback if you're familiar with C++. However, unlike function pointers, delegates are type-safe; a delegate specifies a method signature, and it can be used only to refer to a method that has a matching signature. For example, the *TemperatureEventHandler* delegate shown in the following code (taken from the J# *OvenBean* class) specifies that any referenced method should not have a return value and must take two parameters—an *Object* and a *TemperatureEventArgs* (which we'll describe shortly). Delegates must be tagged with the */** @delegate */* directive for the J# compiler to recognize them and generate the metadata needed by the common language runtime. If you omit this directive, the code will not compile.

```
public delegate void TemperatureEventHandler(System.Object sender,
   TemperatureEventArgs args);
```

Declaring a delegate in this way creates a new type of object. You can then create a delegate variable using this type:

```
private TemperatureEventHandler onTemperatureEvent = null;
```

Once a delegate variable has been defined, it can be used to hold references to zero or more methods. When the *Invoke* method of the delegate variable is executed, all of the referenced methods will be called—this is how you raise an event. You should contrast this operation with the manual event-firing mechanism used by the JavaBeans example you saw earlier. For example, the *OnTemperatureEvent* method shown in the following code raises the *TemperatureEvent* by invoking the *onTemperatureEvent* delegate variable. The parameters passed to the *Invoke* method will be forwarded on to each method pointed to by the delegate variable. (It is conventional for the first parameter to be a reference to the object raising the event and for the second parameter to contain any additional data required to handle the event, as described in the next section.)

```
protected void OnTemperatureEvent(TemperatureEventArgs args)
{
    if (onTemperatureEvent != null);
        onTemperatureEvent.Invoke(this, args);
}
```

You must provide a mechanism to allow clients to subscribe to or unsubscribe from an event. You achieve this by providing a pair of methods that can add a subscribing method to the delegate or remove a method from the delegate. In J#, these methods must be called *add_XXX* and *remove_XXX*, where *XXX* is the name of the event. These methods must take a delegate variable as a single parameter that refers to the method to be added or removed. (The client will create and populate this variable.) Furthermore, both methods must be marked with the */** @event */* directive so the compiler can generate the appropriate metadata to allow clients written in other languages to subscribe to the event. In the following code, note the use of the static methods *Delegate.Combine* and *Delegate.Remove* to add or remove a delegate from a delegate variable. The result of these operations is a delegate variable with the new delegate added or removed, which is then assigned to the private *onTemperatureEvent* variable. A cast is necessary because the *Combine* and *Remove* methods return a generic *Delegate* object.

```
// Subscribe to the TemperatureEvent
/** @event */
public void add_TemperatureEvent(TemperatureEventHandler handler)
{
  onTemperatureEvent =
    (TemperatureEventHandler)Delegate.Combine(onTemperatureEvent, handler);
}

// Unsubscribe from the TemperatureEvent
```

```
/** @event */
public void remove_TemperatureEvent(TemperatureEventHandler handler)
{
  onTemperatureEvent =
    (TemperatureEventHandler)Delegate.Remove(onTemperatureEvent, handler);
}
```

Event Arguments

We mentioned earlier that when you raise an event, it is conventional for the delegated method to take two parameters. The first parameter is a reference to the object raising the event (passed as an *Object*), and the second contains any additional information needed by the subscriber to handle the event—the equivalent of the event state object in the JavaBeans model. A further convention is that the second parameter should subclass the *System.EventArgs* class. (Your code will still work if you don't do this, but it is considered poor practice if you don't.) The *TemperatureEvent* raised by the J# *OvenBean* class passes the temperature of the oven to subscribers. The *TemperatureEventArgs* class shown below wraps the temperature in an *EventArgs* object:

```
public class TemperatureEventArgs extends EventArgs
{
    private int temperature;

    public TemperatureEventArgs(int temp)
    {
        temperature = temp;
    }

 /** @property */
    public int get_Temperature()
    {
        return temperature;
    }
}
```

The *TemperatureEvent* is raised by the *set_Temperature* accessor method when the oven becomes too hot or too cold. The method creates a new *TemperatureEventArgs* object containing the requested temperature and then calls the *OnTemperatureEvent* method to invoke the subscribing delegates. The *set_Temperature* method is shown here—you saw an abbreviated version of this method earlier.

```
    /** @property */
    public void set_Temperature(int value)
    {
        temperature = value;
```

```
        if (temperature < LOW_OVEN_TEMP || temperature > HIGH_OVEN_TEMP)
            OnTemperatureEvent(new TemperatureEventArgs(temperature));
    }
```

A complete listing of the *OvenBean* class is shown below. You might find it useful to compare it to the JDK implementation covered earlier.

OvenBean.jsl

```
package OvenBean;
import System.*;

public class OvenBean
{
    // Constants that define the working temperature range of the oven
    public static final int LOW_OVEN_TEMP = 100;
    public static final int HIGH_OVEN_TEMP = 500;

    // Current temperature of the oven
    private int temperature = LOW_OVEN_TEMP;

    // Delegate defining the signature of the event callback
    /** @delegate */
    public delegate void TemperatureEventHandler(Object sender,
      TemperatureEventArgs args);

    // The event itself, declared as a delegate
    private TemperatureEventHandler onTemperatureEvent = null;

    // Subscribe to the TemperatureEvent
    /** @event */
    public void add_TemperatureEvent(TemperatureEventHandler handler)
    {
        onTemperatureEvent = (TemperatureEventHandler)Delegate.Combine(
          onTemperatureEvent, handler);
    }

    // Unsubscribe from the TemperatureEvent
    /** @event */
    public void remove_TemperatureEvent(TemperatureEventHandler handler)
    {
        onTemperatureEvent = (TemperatureEventHandler)Delegate.Remove(
           onTemperatureEvent, handler);
    }

    // Raise TemperatureEvent
    protected void OnTemperatureEvent(TemperatureEventArgs args)
    {
        if (onTemperatureEvent != null);
```

```
            onTemperatureEvent.Invoke(this, args);
        }

        // The Temperature property
        /** @property */
        public int get_Temperature()
        {
            return temperature;
        }

        /** @property */
        public void set_Temperature(int value)
        {
            temperature = value;
            if (temperature < LOW_OVEN_TEMP || temperature > HIGH_OVEN_TEMP)
                OnTemperatureEvent(new TemperatureEventArgs(temperature));
        }
    }
```

You can compile the OvenBeans.jsl and TemperatureEventArgs.jsl files into a DLL (OvenBean.dll) and reference the component from other applications:

```
vjc /target:library /out:OvenBean.dll OvenBean.jsl TemperatureEventArgs.jsl
```

Consuming a .NET Component

When you use a .NET component, the J# compiler maps properties and events into Java-language constructs. The *ComponentClient* class is a test program that exercises the J# OvenBean component.

The *handleOvenEvent* method matches the signature of the *TemperatureEventHandler* delegate and is used for handling the *TemperatureEvent* when it is raised. All the method actually does is print out the temperature of the oven, which is passed in through the *TemperatureEventArgs* parameter:

```
System.out.println("TemperatureEvent raised. Temperature is " +
   args.get_Temperature());
```

The bulk of the work is performed in the *ComponentClient* constructor. It instantiates an *OvenBean* object using regular Java syntax. The constructor then creates a *TemperatureEventHandler* delegate based on the *handleOvenEvent* method:

```
OvenBean.TemperatureEventHandler handler =
   new OvenBean.TemperatureEventHandler(handleOvenEvent);
```

This delegate is used to subscribe to the *TemperatureEvent* of the *OvenBean* object:

```
ob.AddOnTemperatureEvent(handler);
```

Finally, the temperature of the *OvenBean* is set to different values. Again, notice how the *Temperature* property is assigned, using *set_Temperature* method calls:

```
ob.set_Temperature(150);  // Should not raise an event
ob.set_Temperature(99);   // Should raise an event
ob.set_Temperature(501);  // Should raise an event
```

The code can be compiled and linked with the OvenBean component from the command line:

```
vjc ComponentClient.jsl /reference:OvenBean.dll
```

If you execute this program, you'll find that the C# component behaves in much the same way as the original JavaBean, and you'll get output that looks like that shown in Figure 3-4.

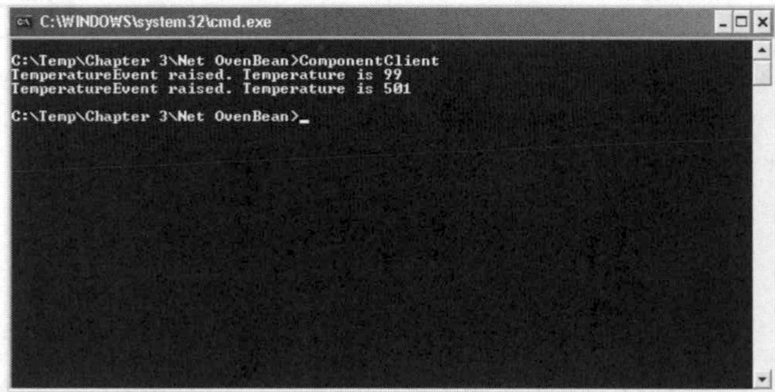

Figure 3-4 The output of the ComponentClient program

ComponentClient.jsl

```
package ComponentConsumer;
import OvenBean.*;

public class ComponentClient
{
   public static void main(String[] args)
   {
      ComponentClient cc = new ComponentClient();
   }

   public ComponentClient()
   {
      // Create an OvenBean
      OvenBean ob = new OvenBean();

      // Create a delegate that refers to the handleOvenEvent method
```

```
        OvenBean.TemperatureEventHandler handler =
           new OvenBean.TemperatureEventHandler(handleOvenEvent);

        // Subscribe to the TemperatureEvent
        ob.AddOnTemperatureEvent(handler);

        // Test the oven by setting its temperature to different values
        ob.set_Temperature(150);  // Should not raise an event
        ob.set_Temperature(99);   // should raise an event
        ob.set_Temperature(501);  // should raise an event
    }

    private void handleOvenEvent(System.Object sender,
        TemperatureEventArgs args)
    {
        System.out.println("TemperatureEvent raised. Temperature is " +
           args.get_Temperature());
    }
}
```

Which component model should you use for your J# applications, JavaBeans or .NET? We recommend using the .NET functionality when you have a choice.

Java, J#, and the .NET Framework

J# includes independently developed libraries that provide the same functionality as that of the JDK 1.1.4 libraries, which makes it easier to take existing Java code and port it to .NET. If your Java application uses the Abstract Window Toolkit (AWT), JDBC or other features of the JDK 1.1.4 class libraries, you can compile your source code using the J# compiler and generate a .NET executable. However, there are a few features that Microsoft does not support, and there are some areas of overlap between the JDK 1.1.4 class libraries and the .NET Framework Class Library that might cause confusion. We'll discus these in the next few sections.

Packaging and Locating Classes

Java uses *packages* as containers for classes. In many implementations, a package is a directory structure held on disk or in a compressed ZIP folder. For example, in the JDK 1.1.4 under Windows, the compressed folder classes.zip contains the JDK library. Classes.zip is located in the \JDK1.1.4\lib folder by default. If you're using Windows XP, you can examine the contents of classes.zip. You'll see that the folder contains compressed folders called java, sun, and sunw. (The latter two folders contain extension classes provided by Sun Microsystems and are not strictly part of the standard JDK library.) If you open the java folder, you'll see a range of further folders corresponding to the various packages in the JDK library, as shown in Figure 3-5.

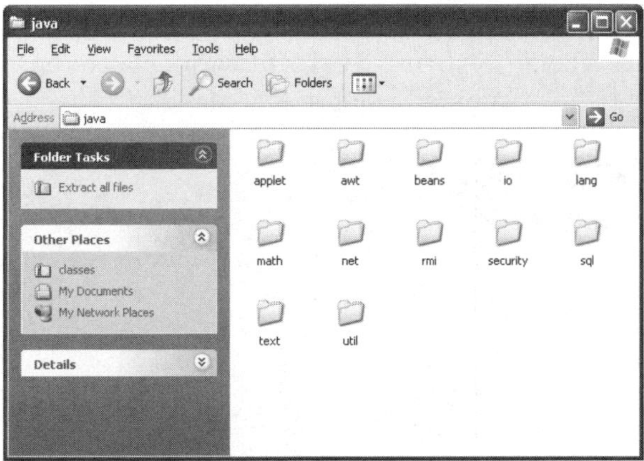

Figure 3-5 The JDK 1.1.4 class library

If you open one of these folders—lang, for example—you'll find all the classes in the java.lang package as well as a further folder called reflection, which contains the classes in the java.lang.reflection package.

In version 1.2 of the JDK, packages can also be held in a Java Archive (JAR) file, which is similar to a ZIP file except it contains a manifest describing the contents of the archive, which makes it quicker to search.

At run time, the class loader in the JVM uses the *CLASSPATH* environment variable to provide a list of locations used for resolving class references. These locations can be folders, references to ZIP files, or both. If the *CLASSPATH* variable does not exist, the JVM uses a default path that includes the classes.zip file in the lib subfolder, under the folder created for the JDK when it was installed. Each location in the *CLASSPATH* is examined in turn until the required package and class is located or the *CLASSPATH* is exhausted. If the class is found, the JVM will load it and use it. If not, it will generate a *NoClassDefFoundError*.

As you might recall, the mechanism used by the common language runtime for locating and loading classes is quite different. For one thing, the common language runtime uses assemblies and namespaces rather than ZIP files and packages. Like Java, J# also uses the *import* statement, but you perform namespace resolution at compile time by specifying the assemblies being used with the */reference* flag to the vjc compiler. At run time, the J# class loader uses the common language runtime mechanisms described in Chapter 2 to locate and load the correct assembly and class. J# does not use the *CLASSPATH* variable. The *Class.forName* methods, which you can use to load a class dynamically, also use the assembly search mechanisms of .NET rather than the *CLASSPATH* variable.

Incidentally, you'll find the Microsoft libraries that support the functionality of the JDK 1.1.4 libraries used by J# in the assembly Vjslib.dll located under \Windows\Microsoft Visual JSharp. NET\Framework\<version>. Figure 3-6 shows this assembly being examined using ILDASM.

Figure 3-6 The contents of the Vjslib.dll assembly

The Java Class Hierarchy

If you're familiar with the JDK, you know that it implements an object-oriented hierarchy of types. The same is true of the .NET Framework. There are similarities and differences between these two hierarchies, and one task that J# has to perform is provide access to both in as seamless a manner as possible. This task is complicated by name clashes. For instance, at the top of the JDK hierarchy is the generic *Object* type in the java.lang package. Likewise, there is an *Object* class at the top of the .NET Framework hierarchy in the *System* namespace. Also, both the JDK and .NET contain a *String* type, arrays, exceptions, and their own primitive types. The J# compiler must handle all of these potential conflicts.

J# Objects

In the Java language, the unqualified type *Object* is resolved as *java.lang.Object*. In the common language runtime, the unqualified type *Object* is resolved as *System.Object*. J# addresses this ambiguity by effectively making *java.lang.Object* an alias for *System.Object*, so they are both the same thing. When a J# object is compiled, any *java.lang.Object* methods called using it (such as *toString*, *wait*, *getClass*, and so on) that are not part of the *System.Object* class are silently redirected to the *com.ms.vjsharp.lang.ObjectImpl* class implemented in the vjslib.dll assembly. We won't get into the details of how this is done because they might change in the future, but suffice it to say that in J# *java.lang.Object* and *System.Object* are interchangeable. (You can even execute *java.lang.Object* methods against a variable explicitly declared as *System.Object*, and vice-versa.)

All the classes you create in J# are descended directly from *System.Object*, and you can assign any J# class object (as opposed to a primitive J# type) to a *System.Object* with impunity. Effectively, the types in Microsoft's version of the JDK are treated just like the types in any other assembly, and you can even access them from other languages. You add a reference to the Vsjlib.dll assembly, and then you can use the types in the *java* namespace (and any other namespaces defined in Vjslib.dll). Here's a fragment of C# that creates a Java *Long* variable:

```
using System;
using java;
⋮

class MyClass
{
  public static void Main(string[] args)
  {
    ⋮
    java.lang.Long test = new java.lang.Long(99);
    ⋮
  }
}
```

Primitive Types

The Java language distinguishes between object types (classes) and primitive types. In the JDK, all object types are instantiated using the *new* operator, created on the heap, and thereafter subject to the memory management implemented by the JVM. Primitive types (the numeric types, *char*, and *boolean*) are created on the stack and come into existence automatically when execution reaches the point at which they are declared. Primitive types are removed as soon as they go out of scope and are not garbage collected in the same way that object types are.

The same is true in the common language runtime—so far. However, in Java the primitive types are built into the JVM. In contrast, the .NET Framework Class Library defines the primitive types as structures in the *System* namespace. A structure is a bit like a class. It can have methods as well as data, but it is created on the stack. For example, the native integer type in the common language runtime is actually the structure *System.Int32*. When you create a variable of type *Integer* in Visual Basic .NET, or *int* in C#, these are actually aliases for *System.Int32*. In many ways, the primitive types of the common language runtime are more like the wrapper classes (such as *java.lang.Integer*) of the JDK. In languages other than J#, the common language runtime further blurs the distinction between the primitive and object types by allowing you to directly assign a primitive to an object. For example, in C# you can use statements such as this:

```
// C#
int anInt = 99;
Object thing = anInt;
```

If you think about this from a Java perspective, it looks quite odd because in Java the primitive types and the object types do not mix. To do the equivalent in Java or J#, you would have to write this:

```
// Java and J#
int anInt = 99;
Object thing = new Integer(anInt);
```

What the preceding code does is use the *Integer* wrapper class to create an object that contains a copy of the integer value inside it. You can then assign the *Integer* to an *Object* instance. In essence, what you're doing is creating a "box" on the heap, sticking an integer value in that box, and then referencing it with the *Object*, as shown in Figure 3-7.

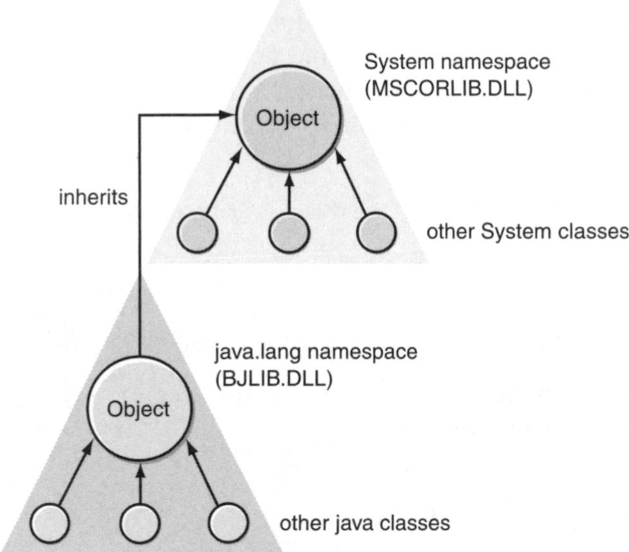

Figure 3-7 Using a wrapper

The common language runtime actually performs the same trick, but it does so silently, without you having to write any code to do it. This is called *boxing*. The common language runtime also performs *unboxing*, which allows you to assign an object to a primitive type:

```
// C#
int anInt = 99;
Object thing = anInt;  // boxing
⋮
anInt = (int)thing;    // unboxing
```

Unboxing must use a cast, and if the object does not refer to a boxed value of the appropriate type, the common language runtime will raise an *InvalidCastException*.

The JVM does not perform boxing, so it should come as no surprise that it does not perform unboxing either. Instead, many of the wrapper classes that you use for boxing provide methods that allow you to gain access to the primitive data inside. For example, the *Integer* class has the *intValue* method:

```
// Java and J#
int anInt = 99;
Object thing = new Integer(anInt);
⋮
anInt = ((Integer) thing).intValue();
```

What this all means is you cannot treat the Java primitive types in the same way as the .NET primitive types when you write J# code. Nevertheless, in the .NET world, the common language runtime performs the role of the JVM, and the J# compiler uses the same underlying Microsoft Intermediate Language (MSIL) data types used by the .NET primitive types. To see what we mean, look at this method implemented in J#:

```
public static double CalculatePay(int numHours, double ratePerHour)
{
  return numHours * ratePerHour;
}
```

The MSIL code for the *CalculatePay* method looks like this:

```
.method public hidebysig static float64  CalculatePay(int32 numHours,
   float64 ratePerHour) cil managed
{
  ⋮
} // end of method JavaCalcPay::CalculatePay
```

Notice how the Java *double* type is compiled into an MSIL *float64*, and a Java *int* becomes an *int32*. Suppose you write the equivalent method in another language that uses the .NET types (Visual Basic .NET, for example):

```
Public Function CalculatePay(numHours as Integer, _
   ratePerHour as Double) as Double

    Return numHours * ratePerHour

  End Function
```

Here is the MSIL code for this version:

```
.method public static float64  CalculatePay(int32 numHours,
   float64 ratePerHour) cil managed
{
  ⋮
} // end of method VBCalcPay::CalculatePay
```

You can see that the Visual Basic *Integer* (which is actually a *System.Int32*) is also compiled into an *int32*, and the Visual Basic *Double* (*System.Double*) becomes a *float64*. So although the .NET and Java primitive types are different when you're writing code (J# retains the semantics of Java primitive types), by the time your code has been compiled, they are interchangeable. You can call a method written in J# from Visual Basic and pass parameters whose underlying types are the same in both languages.

Value Types

The primitive types in .NET are examples of *value types*. In .NET, a value type is a type that is created on the stack rather than the heap. The most common value types used by .NET are structures and enumerations. The .NET Framework Class Library contains numerous value types, and if you're writing programs in C#, Visual Basic .NET, or C++, you can also define your own. Java and J# do not have value types, and you cannot create them using J#. However, you can employ existing value types from J#. With the exception of the primitive types, the J# compiler performs automatic boxing and unboxing conversions when you access them. You just use them as if they were ordinary Java types.

One common example of a value type in .NET is the enumeration. An enumeration is a set of named constants, usually applied to a specific domain. For example, the *DayOfWeek* enumeration in the *System* namespace defines constants representing each day of the week. You can create a variable whose type is *DayOfWeek*, assign it one of the defined constant values, and read it back. You can also compare a *DayOfWeek* variable against the constant *DayOfWeek* values. The following code creates a variable called *day*, assigns it the value *Monday*, and then prints it out. This is all valid J# code.

```
System.DayOfWeek day = new System.DayOfWeek();
day = System.DayOfWeek.Monday;
System.out.println("The day is " + day.ToString());
```

Internally, enumeration constants are actually integer values, and you can cast an enumeration constant to and from a Java *int*. You can even perform arithmetic on them, but be careful not to go out of range—if you subtract 1 from a variable holding *DayOfWeek.Sunday* (which has the value 0), you'll end up with *–1*, which doesn't stand for any day of the week.

Note Although you can create local variables using the value types defined in the .NET Framework Class Library, J# does not currently allow you to use value types such as *System.Int32* or *System.Int64* in any definitions that generate metadata (method signatures, fields, and properties). Instead, you should use the corresponding equivalent primitive types (*int*, *long*, and so on).

Strings

The .NET Framework defines a *String* type in the *System* namespace. There is also a *String* type in the java.lang package in the JDK. The situation is similar to that of the *Object* types, and the solution to any ambiguity is equally similar. When you use J#, *System.String* and *java.lang.String* are interchangeable. You can assign a *System.String* to a *java.lang.String*, and you can execute *System.String* and *java.lang.String* methods against objects of either type.

Arrays

Arrays in Java are first-class objects that descend from *java.lang.Object*. As such, each array has a type, fields, and methods. The class for a given Java array is actually generated by the Java compiler. Programmers tend not to concern themselves with such details, but if you're curious, you can see the name of the class by printing this array:

```
int [] data = new int[5];  // Could be any size for this demo
System.out.println(data);
```

The results will vary. Using the J# compiler, the *data* array was called *[I@1f*. Using the JDK 1.1.4 compiler from Sun, the data array was called *[I@273d3c*. These names will vary.

Array Class Names in Java

The class name that Java generates for an array comprises a *[* for each dimension, followed by a letter or a string indicating the type of the array elements, followed by an @ sign, and then a unique hexadecimal integer. The name *[I@5b* indicates that the array has one dimension and contains integers. An array of *floats* would start with the prefix *[F@*, and a two-dimensional array of *long*s would start with the prefix *[[J@*. Why *J*? Well, *L* is used if the array contains nonprimitive types, and *J* is the next available letter. For example, a one-dimensional array of *Object*s has the prefix *[Ljava.lang.Object;@*.

The .NET Framework also contains arrays. .NET has the *Array* class defined in the *System* namespace, and every non-J# .NET array inherits from *System.Array*. The .NET arrays have their own properties and methods, which are different from but sometimes similar to those of Java arrays. For example, Java arrays have a *length* field that you can examine to determine the length of the array, and .NET arrays have a *Length* property. (Note the uppercase L). What this means is that J# arrays and arrays used by the other .NET languages are not the same. Happily, this is only of minor concern. First, you cannot create *System.Array* objects directly in J#, so there is little scope for ambiguity. Second, the J# compiler will freely convert from Java arrays to .NET arrays and back again. You can pass arrays from your C# code as parameters to methods written in J#, and vice-versa.

Java allows you to create multidimensional arrays. In the following example, variable *i* is a two-dimensional array of *int* elements:

```
int [][] i;
```

Strictly speaking, variable *i* is an array of arrays of *int* elements. The Java language permits such arrays to be ragged—the second dimension can vary in length. For example, in the *data* array shown below, the second dimension comprises five elements in the first row of the array and three elements in the second row:

```
int [][] someData = {{1, 2, 3, 4, 5}, {6, 7, 8}};
```

The .NET Framework supports *jagged* arrays (notice the different nomenclature—*jagged* rather than *ragged*), which are essentially the same, and the J# compiler will convert Java ragged arrays into .NET jagged arrays and back again. However—and this is a big however—jagged arrays are not part of the Common Language Specification (CLS), and some languages, including Visual Basic .NET, do not have them! Instead, the CLS mandates *rectangular* arrays, where each dimension length is fixed and therefore cannot vary once it has been defined. In C#, a 5-by-3 two-dimensional rectangular array is declared using the following syntax:

```
int [ , ] moreData = new int[5, 3];
```

Rectangular arrays are different beasts from jagged arrays, and you cannot assign a two-dimensional jagged array to a two-dimensional rectangular array (not even in C#). This posed a slight problem for J#. The Java language has only ragged arrays, which meant that J# would not be able to use any of the methods in the .NET Framework Class Library that passed or returned multidimensional arrays (because they're all rectangular, for CLS compliance). So Microsoft bit the bullet and added rectangular arrays to J#.

Exceptions

Both Java and .NET allow you to define, throw, and catch exceptions. Java exceptions descend from the generic *Exception* class in the java.lang package, but .NET exceptions descend from *System.Exception*. Java exceptions and .NET exceptions are different types that expose a similar functionality. To make interoperability with Java possible, an unqualified *Exception* refers to the *java.lang.Exception* class:

```
try
{
  ⋮
}
catch (Exception e) // defaults to java.lang.Exception
{
  ⋮
}
```

If you want to catch the .NET *Exception* class instead, you must qualify the *Exception* object:

```
try
{
  ⋮
}
catch (System.Exception e)
{
  ⋮
}
```

One result of the way in which the *Exception* classes are defined with J# is that *System.Exception* will mask and catch *java.lang.Exception* (and consequently any other Java exceptions). However, the converse is not true—*java.lang.Exception* will not catch *System.Exception* or any other .NET exceptions. So if your application throws a *System.Exception* or any of the other .NET exceptions, using a *catch(Exception e)* statement will not actually catch them. (You'll most likely get an error when you compile your code, informing you that possible exceptions have not been caught.) This has significant implications if you're using the .NET Framework Class Library with J# because many of the methods raise .NET exceptions. You should be prepared to handle them.

Interfaces

Java has interfaces, and .NET has interfaces. A J# class can implement a .NET interface, and a class written using one of the other .NET languages can implement a J# interface. An example C# interface is shown here:

```
// C#
public interface CBase
{
  void doProcessing();
}
```

The J# *JChild* class that follows can implement this interface and even add a *throws* clause if the method can raise an exception:

```
// J#
public class JChild implements CBase
{
  public void doProcessing() throws Exception
  {
    ⋮
    throw new Exception("Processing failed");
  }
}
```

The important point to remember when you use interfaces is that the specified methods must use types that are available in the implementing languages. (Trying to implement a C++ interface that uses pointer types in J# could be tricky, for example.) If you stick to the types in the CLS, you should not have any problems.

You might need to perform a bit of translation when you implement interfaces that define properties. For example, the following interface is valid in C#:

```
// C#
interface CSharpInterface
{
   int data
   {
      get;
      set;
   }
}
```

An implementation in J# would look like this:

```
public class JSharpProperties implements CSharpInterface
{
   /** @property */
   int get_data()
   {
       ⋮
    }

    /** @property */
    void set_data(int value)
    {
       ⋮
    }
}
```

Other Issues

You should be aware of some other issues that will affect the way that your J# programs interact with the .NET Framework, as described in the following sections.

Methods with Variable Numbers of Arguments

The CLS allows you to create methods that take variable numbers of arguments (as opposed to creating overloaded methods). The following C# method allows the caller to pass in a variable number of *int* parameters. The *params* keyword indicates that the array parameter that follows can be interpreted as a list of *int* elements by the compiler. If you are a C or C++ developer, you might be familiar with *varargs*, which performs a similar function:

```
// C#
public void UseParams(params int[] list)
{
    for (int i = 0; i < list.Length; i++)
    {
        // process element i
        ⋮
    }
}
```

If you want to pass a selection of different types, you can create a *params* array comprising *Object* elements. You can invoke this method from C# using statements such as this one:

```
// C#
UseParams(99, 100, 120);
UseParams(5);
```

At run time, the actual parameters will be packaged into an *int* array and passed to the *UseParams* method as the formal parameter list. However, if you try calling the method from J# using the same syntax, you'll receive a compile-time error because the Java language does not permit methods that take variable parameter lists. Instead, you must manually package the parameters into an array yourself, as shown here:

```
// J#
int [] i = {99, 100, 120};
UseParams(i);
```

Console I/O

The JDK provides the *System.out PrintStream* object, which has the method *println* for displaying information on the console. The *println* method is overloaded, which allows you to output a single value of any type—most often a *java.lang.String*. The .NET Framework contains the *Console* object in the *System* namespace, which fulfills a similar role. It has a method called *WriteLine*, which you can use to display information to the screen. You can print Java strings, objects, and primitive types, as shown here. (Objects will be rendered using the *ToString* method inherited from *System.Object*.)

```
import System.*;  // Console is in the System namespace
⋮
String message = "Hello, World";
Console.WriteLine(message);
```

You might find it more convenient to use *Console.WriteLine* rather than *System.out.println* when you develop J# programs.

Getting keyboard input is notoriously troublesome in Java. The *System.in InputStream* object supplies a *read* method that you can use to read individual bytes from the keyboard, but it is all very low-level and error-prone. In contrast, the *System.Console* class in the .NET Framework Class Library contains the *ReadLine* method, which reads a *System.String* from the keyboard, up to the next carriage return. This method is easier to use, as this code shows:

```
import System.*;
⋮
System.String input = Console.ReadLine();
```

The *ubyte* Type

Microsoft has tried hard to not make too many additions to the Java language in J#. You've already seen that rectangular arrays were added to maintain compliance with the CLS. One data type in the CLS that is used by a number of methods in the .NET Framework Class Library is *Byte*, which can hold 8-bit unsigned values. Java also has a *byte* data type, but it is signed. (.NET has the *SByte* data type for signed 8-bit values.) Microsoft therefore created the data type *ubyte* for J#, for 8-bit unsigned data. Try not to get too confused—a .NET *SByte* corresponds to a J# *byte*, and a .NET *Byte* corresponds to a J# *ubyte*!

Threads

The JDK defines the *Thread* class in the java.lang package. Classes that extend *Thread* and override the *run* method can be executed asynchronously. If an object instantiates a *Thread* object and calls the *start* method, the JVM will invoke the *Thread* object's *run* method and return to the calling object without waiting for *run* to finish. Both the calling object and the *Thread* object can then execute concurrently. The *Thread* class also provides the *stop* method, which can halt a *Thread* object in its tracks, and the *join* method, which causes the creating object to wait for the *Thread* object to complete. Classes can define methods as *synchronized*, which prevents two concurrent threads from executing the same code in the same object at the same time—the second thread will have to wait for the first to exit the method.

The following classes illustrate a simple *Thread* class called *WorkerThread*. The *run* method prints the values 0 through 499. The *ThreadRunner* class creates a new *WorkerThread* and invokes its *run* method asynchronously by executing the *start* method. The *ThreadRunner* then prints a farewell message and finishes.

JDK Threads

```
class WorkerThread extends Thread
{
   public void run()
   {
      for (int i=0; i < 500; i++)
         System.out.print(i + " ");
   }
}

class ThreadRunner
{
   public static void main(String [] args)
   {
      WorkerThread wt = new WorkerThread();
      wt.start();
      System.out.println("ThreadRunner finished");
   }
}
```

You can compile and run this program using the JDK or J#—it will work with either. On our uniprocessor machine, both the JDK and the J# implementations cause the "ThreadRunner finished" message to be displayed before the numbers 0 to 499 are printed. The results you get when you run the program might not be the same, especially if you have a multiprocessor machine.

Bear in mind that when you use JDK threads, the JVM implements the threading model itself. Many operating systems, including Windows, have native support for threads, and the JVM might use this facility behind the scenes, but it will use its own data structures internally for managing them. The reason for this, once again, is portability. Any Java application can use threads whether the underlying platform supports them or not, and all implementations of the JDK must provide a consistent implementation of the *Thread* class.

Windows has its own multithreading capability, and the common language runtime permits managed access to it through the *System.Threading* namespace. This namespace is feature-rich compared to the JDK, and it exposes the *System.Threading.Thread* class, which you can use from J#. To some extent, common language runtime threads and JDK threads will interoperate—they can be coordinated with each other using either *synchronized* methods or common language runtime *Monitor* objects. However, the *System.Threading.Thread* class is different from *java.lang.Thread* and they are not interchangeable. A common language runtime thread cannot be a member of a JDK *ThreadGroup*, for example. The main reason that the *java.lang.Thread* class exists is to support existing JDK code that you don't want to rewrite. If you're undertaking new development that involves threads, you should use the *System.Threading* namespace in preference to the *java.lang.Thread*.

You have probably gathered that threads are another area in which there's a namespace clash. By default, the J# compiler assumes that an unqualified *Thread* reference refers to a *java.lang.Thread*. If you want to use a common language runtime thread, you must qualify it as a *System.Threading.Thread*. Threads under the common language runtime will be explained in detail in Chapter 8.

Omissions from the JDK

Microsoft has implemented much of the JDK 1.1.4 functionality. The omissions include RMI, which we already mentioned, and there is also no support for the Java Native Interface (JNI) or for applets. However, .NET, together with Windows, does supply eminently suitable alternatives. Instead of RMI, you can use .NET Remoting or COM. JNI has been replaced by J/Direct (originally introduced with Visual J++) and the Platform Invoke service, and applets have been superseded by ASP.NET Web Forms.

Migrating to J#

Microsoft supplies some useful tools with the Visual Studio.NET IDE to help you migrate existing JDK and Visual J++ 6.0 applications to J#. You can migrate the source code, or you can convert class files. We'll look at these possibilities next.

Migrating Source Code

By now, you should appreciate that you can compile ordinary *.java* source code using the jc compiler to produce DLLs and EXEs. The compiler can take source code that conforms to the Java Language Specification version 2.0. If you have existing J++ 6.0 solutions, you can open them in Visual Studio .NET if you have Visual J# installed. Solution and project files will be upgraded automatically (the Visual J# Upgrade Wizard takes you through the process), but you should be aware of a few issues:

- The *CLASSPATH* variable is no longer used. Instead, you must add references to each assembly that implements the packages your application uses. This means you must first have upgraded those packages and converted them into assemblies.
- References to COM components are not preserved automatically. You must add them manually to the Visual J# project either during the upgrade process (the wizard will prompt you) or using the Add Reference command on the Project menu.
- The project upgrade process ignores Microsoft Visual SourceSafe (VSS) settings. You must check out all source files from VSS before upgrading.
- Not all deployment options are preserved, and neither are any prebuild or postbuild steps.

The compiler understands many of the directives Microsoft introduced with J++, such as *@dll*, *@com*, *@conditional*, and *#if*. This means you can quickly migrate much of your code that uses J/Direct for accessing native APIs and that implements COM components using JActiveX wrappers. (For more information about using J/Direct and migrating COM components, see Part IV of this book.) Also, alongside the JDK libraries, Microsoft has also implemented some of the extension packages that ship with J++, most notably com.ms.com, com.ms.dll, and com.ms.win32. The class libraries include an implementation of the JDBC-ODBC bridge driver in com.ms.jdbc.odbc. This driver requires an ODBC 3.0 or later driver. These packages are all held in the Vjslib.dll assembly. You'll also find an implementation of the WFC libraries in the Vjswfc.dll assembly.

The Profiler, Heap Monitoring, and Debug APIs that were provided with J++ have been omitted from J#. You should use the corresponding .NET Framework Class Library APIs instead.

Converting Class Files

If you do not have the source code for a given set of Java classes available, you can still migrate an application to .NET. Microsoft's Java Binary Converter tool, jbimp, converts *.class* files into MSIL assemblies—DLLs and EXEs. The simplest way to use jbimp is to run it from the command line. You'll find jbimp.exe in the folder \Program Files\Microsoft Visual J# .NET\Framework\Bin. If you're migrating several class files, you can combine them into a single DLL using the

/target:library switch, which is similar to that used by the vjc compiler. The name of the DLL is taken from the first class file supplied on the command line, or you can specify a name using the */out* parameter.

Let's take the *OvenBean, TemperatureEvent, TemperatureEventListener,* and *TemperatureWarning* classes used by the components example earlier in this chapter. (These files are in the JDK OvenBean folder.) Pretend that you've lost the source code and have only the *.class* files created as a result of compiling using the JDK. You can convert them into a .NET DLL using the following command:

```
jbimp /target:library /out:OvenBean.dll OvenBean.class
TemperatureEvent.class TemperatureEventListener.class TemperatureWarning.class
```

You can build an EXE using the */target:exe* parameter (the default), as long as one of the classes has a *main* method. You can also use the */reference* parameter to link to another .NET assembly. Continuing with the OvenBean example, you can convert the test client (*BeanClient.class*) and link it to the OvenBean.dll assembly by using the following command:

```
jbimp /reference:OvenBean.dll BeanClient.class
```

Running this command will result in a .NET executable called BeanClient.exe. (You can use the */out* parameter to generate an executable with a different name.)

The jbimp tool has a number of other options available, including */recurse*, which will recursively process *.class* files in subdirectories. This option is useful if you have an entire package that you need to convert.

Metadata and Attributes

In Chapter 2, you saw how classes are compiled into assemblies. Alongside the compiled (MSIL) version of the application code, assemblies contain additional information about each type they contain—the name, together with methods, properties, events, and other items. This is *metadata*.

Note Do not confuse metadata with manifests. A manifest contains information about the contents of the assembly and about other assemblies that the contents reference. An assembly contains a single manifest. Metadata holds information about a single type in an assembly, and each type has its own set of metadata.

The ILDASM utility uses the metadata of each type in an assembly to present the contents of that assembly in a tree structure. The .NET Framework supplies the *System.Reflection* namespace, which allows you to write your own code to examine the metadata of a type. If you're familiar with Java, you know that it provides the package java.lang.reflect, which also contains classes and methods for examining metadata. Much of this package has been implemented with J#, and you can also use it for examining types implemented in languages other than J#. However, as with many features in J#, this package was created to allow you to port existing Java code to J# with the minimum of fuss, and you should use the *System.Reflection* namespace when you build new applications.

Reflection in .NET

Reflection is used throughout .NET. In addition to allowing you to write programs that analyze other types and classes, it has many uses. It is required by languages that use late binding (most of the interpreted scripting languages), for generating wrappers when interoperating with COM, for processing attributes, and for serializing objects when using .NET Remoting.

The *System.Type* Object and the *System.Reflection* Namespace

The *System.Reflection* namespace has a very regular structure, making it easy to understand. (The JDK has a similar set of methods in *java.lang.reflect.*) Essentially, you extract information about a type using the *GetType* method. This method returns a *System.Type* object. The *Type* class exposes a multitude of properties that allow you to determine information such as whether the type is public (*get_IsPublic*) or private (*get_IsPrivate*), is a class (*get_IsClass*), or is an interface (*get_IsInterface*), as well as retrieve useful information such as the name of the type (*get_Name*) and the type that the current class inherits from (*get_BaseType*). The *Type* class also exposes methods that allow you to obtain arrays of methods (*GetMethods*), constructors (*GetConstructors*), and fields (*GetFields*), as well as non-Java items such as events (*GetEvents*) and properties (*GetProperties*) if the type was created in a language other than J#. You can search for specific methods, constructors, and fields using the *GetMethod* (singular), *GetConstructor*, and *GetField* methods, respectively. For more information, look up the *Type* class in the *System* namespace in the .NET Framework Class Library documentation that ships with Visual Studio .NET.

The various *GetXXXs* methods return arrays of *XXXInfo* objects. For example, *GetMethods* returns an array of *MethodInfo* objects. Like the *Type* class, the *XXXInfo* classes have properties that you can query to determine information such as the accessibility of a class member (private, public, protected, and so on), whether the member is static, virtual, abstract, final, and so on. In addition to these common properties that all members have (these methods are defined in the *MethodBase* class that the various *XXXInfo* classes inherit from), each *XXXInfo* class exposes additional methods and properties peculiar to the member type. For example, *MethodInfo* has a *get_ReturnType* property that indicates the type returned by the method, as well as an *Invoke* method that allows you to call the corresponding method dynamically. (This is very useful when you perform late binding). All the *XXXInfo* classes are defined in the *System.Reflection* namespace.

Using Reflection

Perhaps the best way to understand the *Type* class and the *System.Reflection* namespace is to see an example in action. The ReflectionDemo program contains a class (also called *ReflectionDemo*) that prompts the user for the name of an assembly—either a DLL or an EXE—and then uses reflection to display the metadata for every type in that assembly. The program dynamically loads the assembly using the static method *Assembly.LoadFrom*, as shown here:

```
Assembly assembly = Assembly.LoadFrom(assemblyName);
```

The *Assembly* class provides a useful mechanism for querying, loading, and manipulating assemblies; you'll find it in the *System.Reflection* namespace. The program then calls the *GetTypes* method of the newly loaded assembly, which returns an array of all the types defined in the assembly:

```
Type[] typeList = assembly.GetTypes();
```

The program iterates through each type in the array, determining the class that the type inherits from by invoking *get_BaseType*. This approach works because all Java and J# classes inherit from something, even if it is just the generic *Object* class. The program also obtains a list of interfaces (if any) that are being implemented by the type by calling the *GetInterfaces* method. The name of each interface is printed. Here's the code:

```
Type t = typeList[i];
```

```
// Determine the direct ancestor
Type superT = t.get_BaseType();
Console.Write("class " + t.get_Name());
if ((superT != null) && (superT.get_IsClass()))
   Console.Write(" extends " + superT.get_FullName());

// Does this class implement any interfaces?
Type[] interfaceList = t.GetInterfaces();
for (int j = 0; j < interfaceList.length; j++)
{
   if (j == 0)
      Console.Write(" implements ");
   else
      Console.Write(", ");
   Console.Write(interfaceList[j].get_Name());
}
```

The program continues by displaying the details of all constructors (using the *printConstructors* method), methods (*printMethods*), and fields (*printFields*) for each type in the assembly. The *printConstructors* method calls *GetConstructors* to retrieve a list of the constructors for the current type being examined:

```
ConstructorInfo[] constructors = t.GetConstructors(flags);
```

The *flags* parameter specifies which constructors will be found. By default, only public constructors are returned. If you look at the private fields at the start of the class, you'll see that the *flags* variable is a bitwise combination that specifies public and nonpublic (private and protected) static and instance members. The *flags* variable itself is actually a *BindingFlags* enumeration:

```
private static BindingFlags flags = (BindingFlags)
   (BindingFlags.Public | BindingFlags.NonPublic |
   BindingFlags.Instance | BindingFlags.Static);
```

GetConstructors returns an array of *ConstructorInfo* objects. The *printConstructors* method investigates each constructor in turn; accessibility is determined and displayed by examining the *get_IsPublic*, *get_IsPrivate*, and *get_IsFamily* properties:

```
// Display modifier information and the name of the constructor
ConstructorInfo c = constructors[i];
System.String name = c.get_Name();
if (c.get_IsPublic())
   Console.Write("public");
if (c.get_IsPrivate())
   Console.Write("private");
if (c.get_IsFamily())
```

```
   Console.Write("protected");
Console.Write(" " + name + "(");
```

The *GetParameters* method is used to extract the parameters as a *ParameterInfo* array. The type and name of each parameter is also displayed. The code looks like this:

```
// Display information about each parameter
ParameterInfo[] params = c.GetParameters();
for (int j = 0; j < params.length; j++)
{
   if (j > 0)
      Console.Write(", ");
   Console.Write(params[j].get_ParameterType().get_Name() + " " +
      params[j].get_Name());
}
```

The *printMethods* method is similar. The major difference is that it calls *GetMethods* to find all the methods for the specified type:

```
MethodInfo[] methods = t.GetMethods(flags);
```

The list of methods is returned as a *MethodInfo* array. As each method is processed, the *printMethods* determines its accessibility and return type and displays them. Another small difference is that *printMethods* also looks at the *get_IsStatic* property to determine whether the method is a static method or an instance method. (This does not apply to constructors because they cannot be static.)

```
if (m.get_IsStatic())
Console.Write(" static");
```

The *printMethods* method then outputs the names and types of each parameter using the same technique as *printConstructors*.

Finally, the *printFields* method calls *GetFields* to return an array of *FieldInfo* objects. The type of the field is extracted using the *get_FieldType* method of the field:

```
Type type = f.get_FieldType();
```

The modifiers, type, and name of each field are obtained and displayed.

ReflectionDemo.jsl

```
import System.*;
import System.Reflection.*;

public class ReflectionDemo
{
   private static BindingFlags flags =
```

```
      (BindingFlags)(BindingFlags.Public | BindingFlags.NonPublic |
      BindingFlags.Instance | BindingFlags.Static);

   public static void main(String[] args)
    {

      String assemblyName;
      Console.Write("Please enter an assembly name: ");
      assemblyName = Console.ReadLine();

      try
      {
         // Load the assembly
         Assembly assembly = Assembly.LoadFrom(assemblyName);

         // Find all the types in the assembly
         Type[] typeList = assembly.GetTypes();

         // Iterate through each type and print its details using
         // the metadata in the assembly
         for (int i = 0; i < typeList.length; i++)
         {
            Type t = typeList[i];

            // Determine the direct ancestor
            Type superT = t.get_BaseType();
            Console.Write("class " + t.get_Name());
            if ((superT != null) && (superT.get_IsClass()))
               Console.Write(" extends " + superT.get_FullName());

            // Does this class implement any interfaces?
            Type[] interfaceList = t.GetInterfaces();
            for (int j = 0; j < interfaceList.length; j++)
            {
               if (j == 0)
                  Console.Write(" implements ");
               else
                  Console.Write(", ");
               Console.Write(interfaceList[j].get_Name());
            }

            // Print the details for the type
            Console.WriteLine("\n{");
            printConstructors(t);
            Console.WriteLine();
            printMethods(t);
            Console.WriteLine();
            printFields(t);
```

```
            Console.WriteLine("}\n");
        }
    }
    catch(System.Exception e)
    {
        Console.WriteLine("Exception: " + e);
    }
}

// Display information about constructors
public static void printConstructors(Type t)
{
    // Find all constructors for the type
    ConstructorInfo[] constructors = t.GetConstructors(flags);

    for (int i = 0; i < constructors.length; i++)
    {
        // Display modifier information and the name of the constructor
        ConstructorInfo c = constructors[i];
        String name = c.get_Name();
        if (c.get_IsPublic())
            Console.Write("public");
        if (c.get_IsPrivate())
            Console.Write("private");
        if (c.get_IsFamily())
            Console.Write("protected");
        Console.Write(" " + name + "(");

        // Display information about each parameter
        ParameterInfo[] params = c.GetParameters();
        for (int j = 0; j < params.length; j++)
        {
            if (j > 0)
                Console.Write(", ");
            Console.Write(params[j].get_ParameterType().get_Name() +
                " " + params[j].get_Name());
        }
        Console.WriteLine(");");
    }
}

// Display information about methods
public static void printMethods(Type t)
{
    // Find all methods for the type
    MethodInfo[] methods = t.GetMethods(flags);

    for (int i = 0; i < methods.length; i++)
```

```
        {
            // Display the modifiers, return type, and name of the method
            MethodInfo m = methods[i];
            String name = m.get_Name();
            if (m.get_IsPublic())
                Console.Write("public");
            if (m.get_IsPrivate())
                Console.Write("private");
            if (m.get_IsFamily())
                Console.Write("protected");
            if (m.get_IsStatic())
                Console.Write(" static");

            Type retType = m.get_ReturnType();
            Console.Write(" " + retType.get_Name() + " " + name + "(");

            // Display the type and name of each parameter
            ParameterInfo[] params = m.GetParameters();
            for (int j = 0; j < params.length; j++)
            {
                if (j > 0)
                    Console.Write(", ");
                Console.Write(params[j].get_ParameterType().get_Name() +
                    " " + params[j].get_Name());
            }
            Console.WriteLine(");");
        }
    }

    // Display information about fields
    public static void printFields(Type t)
    {
        // Find all fields for the type
        FieldInfo[] fields = t.GetFields(flags);

        for (int i = 0; i < fields.length; i++)
        {
            // Display the modifier, type, and name of each field
            FieldInfo f = fields[i];
            Type type = f.get_FieldType();
            String name = f.get_Name();
            if (f.get_IsPublic())
                Console.Write("public");
            if (f.get_IsPrivate())
                Console.Write("private");
            if (f.get_IsFamily())
                Console.Write("protected");
            if (f.get_IsStatic())
```

```
                Console.Write(" static");

            Console.WriteLine(" " + type.get_Name() + " " + name + ";");
        }
    }
}
```

You can run this program over any of the .NET-supplied assemblies or those you've written yourself. It is actually quite instructive to use it to examine the ReflectionDemo.exe assembly, as you can see in Figure 3-8.

```
C:\WINDOWS\system32\cmd.exe

C:\Temp\Chapter 3\Reflection>ReflectionDemo
Please enter an assembly name: ReflectionDemo.exe
class ReflectionDemo extends System.Object
{
public .ctor();
private .cctor();

public Object MemberwiseClone();
protected Void Finalize();
public Int32 GetHashCode();
public Boolean Equals(Object obj);
public String ToString();
public static Void main(String[] args);
public static Void printConstructors(Type t);
public static Void printMethods(Type t);
public static Void printFields(Type t);
public Type GetType();
protected Object MemberwiseClone();

private static BindingFlags flags;
}

C:\Temp\Chapter 3\Reflection>
```

Figure 3-8 ReflectionDemo running over the ReflectionDemo.exe assembly

You'll notice that a certain amount of mapping from Java to .NET types occurs. In addition, there are two constructors, *.ctor* and *.cctor*. The *.ctor* constructor is the default instance constructor. In Java, if you don't define any constructors, a default constructor is created for you automatically. The *.cctor* constructor is the *type constructor*. Its purpose is to initialize the static fields in the class, and it will also be created automatically if a class contains static data.

Attributes

We talked about attributes in Chapter 2. An *attribute* is a piece of declarative information that is stored with the metadata of a type. At run time, this metadata can be examined and used to modify the way in which the type operates. The .NET Framework defines a large number of attributes. Most cause annotations to be inserted into the compiled code and are interpreted by the common language runtime. The examples in Chapter 2 included *PrincipalPermissionAttribute*, which the common language runtime uses to determine whether a user can execute a particular method. The use of this attribute is shown in the following code:

```
public class CakeInfo
{
   /** @attribute PrincipalPermissionAttribute(SecurityAction.Demand,
       Role="WONDERLAND\\Bakers")
    */
   /** @attribute PrincipalPermissionAttribute(SecurityAction.Demand,
       Name="WONDERLAND\\JSharp")
    */

   public static short FeedsHowMany(short diameter, short shape,
      short filling)
{
      ⋮
}
}
```

If you use ILDASM to examine the *FeedsHowMany* method of the *CakeInfo* class in the *CakeUtils* assembly, you'll see the effects of these attributes on the code—a *.permissionset* block is added to the start of the method, and the common language runtime will examine this information to determine whether to allow the current user to execute the code, as shown in Figure 3-9.

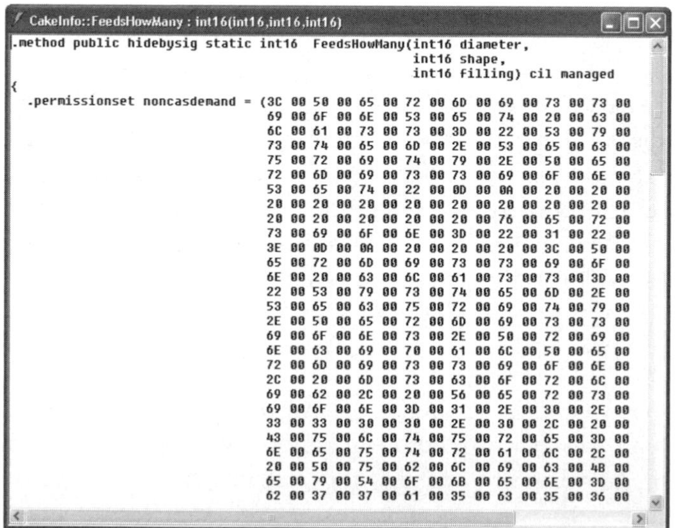

```
CakeInfo::FeedsHowMany : int16(int16,int16,int16)
.method public hidebysig static int16  FeedsHowMany(int16 diameter,
                                                    int16 shape,
                                                    int16 filling) cil managed
{
  .permissionset noncasdemand = (3C 00 50 00 65 00 72 00 6D 00 69 00 73 00 73 00
                                 69 00 6F 00 6E 00 53 00 65 00 74 00 20 00 63 00
                                 6C 00 61 00 73 00 73 00 3D 00 22 00 53 00 79 00
                                 73 00 74 00 65 00 6D 00 2E 00 53 00 65 00 63 00
                                 75 00 72 00 69 00 74 00 79 00 2E 00 50 00 65 00
                                 72 00 6D 00 69 00 73 00 73 00 69 00 6F 00 6E 00
                                 53 00 65 00 74 00 22 00 0D 00 0A 00 20 00 20 00
                                 20 00 20 00 20 00 20 00 20 00 20 00 20 00 20 00
                                 20 00 20 00 20 00 20 00 20 00 76 00 65 00 72 00
                                 73 00 69 00 6F 00 6E 00 3D 00 22 00 31 00 22 00
                                 3E 00 0D 00 0A 00 20 00 20 00 20 00 3C 00 50 00
                                 65 00 72 00 6D 00 69 00 73 00 73 00 69 00 6F 00
                                 6E 00 20 00 63 00 6C 00 61 00 73 00 73 00 3D 00
                                 22 00 53 00 79 00 73 00 74 00 65 00 6D 00 2E 00
                                 53 00 65 00 63 00 75 00 72 00 69 00 74 00 79 00
                                 2E 00 50 00 65 00 72 00 6D 00 69 00 73 00 73 00
                                 69 00 6F 00 6E 00 73 00 2E 00 50 00 72 00 69 00
                                 6E 00 63 00 69 00 70 00 61 00 6C 00 50 00 65 00
                                 72 00 6D 00 69 00 73 00 73 00 69 00 6F 00 6E 00
                                 2C 00 20 00 6D 00 73 00 63 00 6F 00 72 00 6C 00
                                 69 00 62 00 2C 00 20 00 56 00 65 00 72 00 73 00
                                 69 00 6F 00 6E 00 3D 00 31 00 2E 00 30 00 2E 00
                                 33 00 33 00 30 00 30 00 2E 00 30 00 2C 00 20 00
                                 43 00 75 00 6C 00 74 00 75 00 72 00 65 00 3D 00
                                 6E 00 65 00 75 00 74 00 72 00 61 00 6C 00 2C 00
                                 20 00 50 00 75 00 62 00 6C 00 69 00 63 00 4B 00
                                 65 00 79 00 54 00 6F 00 6B 00 65 00 6E 00 3D 00
                                 62 00 37 00 37 00 61 00 35 00 63 00 35 00 36 00
```

Figure 3-9 ILDASM showing the effects of *PrincipalPermissionAttribute*

Other attributes are handled in different ways by the compilers and the common language runtime. Depending on the attributes being used, they can be applied to an entire assembly (the *AssemblyVersionAttribute*, for example), a class, individual methods, constructors, fields, interfaces, and even parameters and return values. You'll see many more examples of attributes later in this book.

Enterprise Java

The J2EE specification defines a framework for building and deploying distributed applications using Java. Many vendors implement J2EE in their server products—BEA WebLogic Server, IBM WebSphere, Sun Microsystems iPlanet Application Server, and Oracle Application Server are four popular examples. Java components that execute in a J2EE environment communicate using Java's own RMI protocol. J2EE specifies a core set of services, and it should be possible to build applications that are independent of any particular vendor's implementation. Many vendors have adopted the tried and true strategy of "adding value" to the J2EE specification by implementing proprietary extensions with their products, leading to inconsistencies between implementations. However, it is worth reviewing the individual elements that comprise J2EE so you can see where the equivalent functionality lies in .NET.

The upcoming material is not intended to be a detailed treatise on J2EE. If you want more information about the elements that comprise J2EE, you should study one of the many other books available, such as *Teach Yourself J2EE in 21 Days* by Dan Haywood, Martin Bond, and Peter Roxburgh (Sams Publishing, 2002).

The Elements of J2EE

J2EE is used for building *n*-tier applications. The elements that comprise the J2EE specification are generally aimed at individual tiers. Figure 3-10 depicts the general structure of J2EE and its components, broken down by tier. The following sections discuss each of these areas in turn.

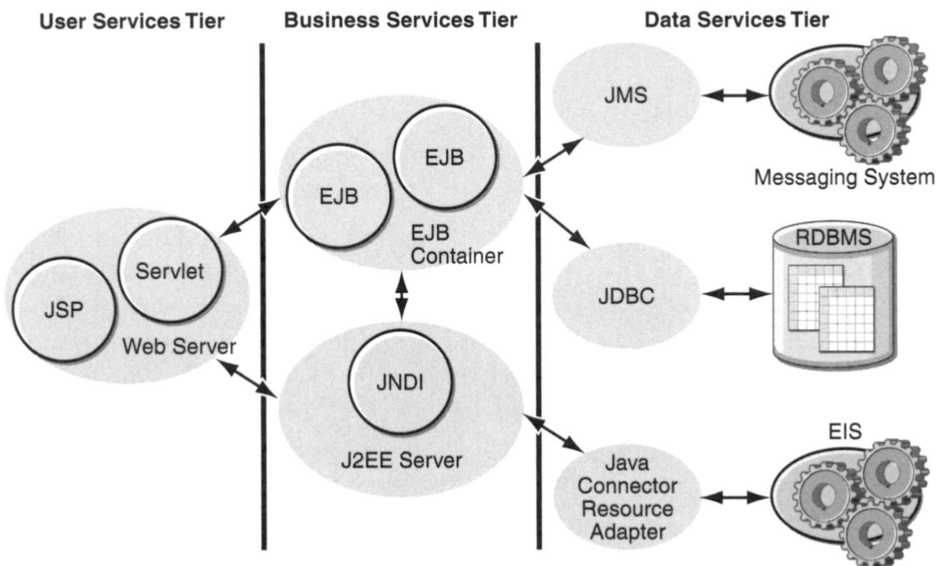

Figure 3-10 The structure of J2EE

Data Services in J2EE

J2EE provides Java Database Connectivity (JDBC) and the Java Connector Architecture for manipulating data retrieved from a data store and saving it again. We'll cover the Java Messaging Service (JMS) shortly.

JDBC actually predates J2EE but has become an integral part of it. JDBC is used to interface with relational databases, and it allows a developer to submit SQL requests and retrieve tabular data. Batch optimizations allow a developer to submit blocks of requests to a database to try to reduce the network bandwidth used by an application. One enhancement of JDBC that appeared as part of the J2EE specification is the *RowSet* interface. A *RowSet* is basically a JavaBean that allows a developer to package a set of rows into an abstract object that hides the details of the underlying database and tables. JDBC also allows connection pooling (depending on the functionality implemented by the JDBC driver), permitting database connections to be shared among multiple components.

The Java Connector Architecture defines a mechanism that allows a developer to integrate Enterprise Information Systems (EIS) into the J2EE framework. The Java Connector Architecture is based on adapters (another one of Gamma's patterns) that convert J2EE server requests into those understood by the EIS. The adapter also has to implement a number of *system contracts* for handling connection, transaction, and security management in a standard way, as directed by the J2EE server. This allows a degree of pluggability between EISs and J2EE servers—in theory, an EIS that implements a particular service can be replaced by an alternative, and the same applies to the J2EE server! A J2EE application can call upon an EIS as if it were part of the J2EE server and treat it as an integral piece of the system.

You should notice that neither XML nor Web services feature in J2EE. This is intentional. Although they can both play an active part in building solutions that integrate third-party services into J2EE, both have much broader appeal than just Java applications. To tie them to J2EE at this stage in their development would be severely limiting—remember that J2EE is a specification, and if Java-based support for XML and/or Web services were to form part of the same specification, they would be updatable only when a new version of J2EE was released.

Instead, you'll find a host of separate Java APIs for handling different aspects of XML and implementing Web services. They currently include

- JAXP (Java API for XML Processing) for manipulating XML documents using DOM, SAX, and XSLT
- JAXB (Java Architecture for XML Binding) for serializing Java objects to XML files and vice versa
- JAXM (Java API for XML Messaging), which implements SOAP-based messaging and provides support for more sophisticated messaging such as that found in ebXML (the UN/CEFACT initiative for designing business-to-business interaction)
- JAX-RPC (Java API for XML-based RPC) for implementing portable remote procedure calling mechanisms based on SOAP and WSDL
- JAXR (Java API for XML Registries) for providing uniform access to different types of XML Registries (such as UDDI and ebXML)

Web service toolkits for building Web services in Java are available from several sources. These toolkits generally track the various XML APIs listed above.

Business Services in J2EE

Perhaps the best-known part of the J2EE specification concerns Enterprise JavaBeans (EJBs). These are components designed to run on the server side to implement business logic, potentially for multiple clients. EJBs come in two flavors, Session and Entity. A Session EJB implements a service, such as submitting an order in a sales application, and can be either stateful (maintaining state between method calls) or stateless (no state is maintained). Entity EJBs are used to model persistent objects—often rows from a database. Entity EJBs are highly stateful!

Both kinds of EJBs are managed by *containers*, which are provided by the J2EE server. When the J2EE server starts, it creates containers for the various EJBs it supports, and each container can create a pool of EJB instances that are ready for use. When a J2EE application requests the use of an EJB, the J2EE server will respond by passing back a reference to an appropriate EJB. When the application has finished with the EJB, the J2EE server can return it to the pool for recycling. All of this is often hidden from the client application, which only sees EJBs being "manufactured" (or so it thinks) on demand.

The container manages the lifetime of an EJB. An EJB developer defines an EJB using a pair of interfaces: the Remote interface, which contains the business methods exposed by the EJB that the J2EE application can use, and the Home interface, which defines the methods used by the J2EE client to create, find, or delete EJBs. Session EJBs tend to be short-lived, often executing a single method on behalf of a client application before being returned to the pool.

Entity EJBs model business or data entities. Entities are expected to outlive the J2EE application processes that use them. The Entity EJB model defines a mechanism for saving the contents of an EJB back to a database and for re-creating the EJB from data held in a database. To actually load and unload data to or from persistent storage, Entity EJBs can use Bean-Managed Persistence (BMP) or Container-Managed Persistence (CMP). In BMP, the Entity EJB contains the code necessary to populate or save the entity's data using life-cycle methods defined as part of the contract between the EJB and the container. With CMP, the container itself populates the EJB using configuration information supplied when the EJB is deployed.

User Services in J2EE

J2EE is largely intended for building Web-oriented applications, so the infrastructure it specifies for presenting user interfaces comprises technologies for generating XML and HTML. These technologies are *servlets* and *JavaServer Pages* (JSP).

A *servlet* is a Java class that executes in a JVM running in a supporting Web server. (Many common Web servers that support servlets are descended from Tomcat, which is the servlet container that forms part of the Apache Web server.) Most servlets are designed to handle and process HTTP requests originating from a Web browser, although servlets can handle other protocols as well. When a Web server receives a request for a particular HTML page (or set of pages), it can redirect that request to an HTTP servlet, passing it any HTTP parameters that were submitted by the client. The servlet can examine these parameters and generate an HTML (or XML) response, which is sent back, via the Web server, to the client. The same JVM can run multiple servlets, and it is possible to share data between servlets servicing different clients.

The Servlet API contains the abstract class *HttpServlet*, which you can extend and add your own functionality to. Most implementations override the *init* method (which executes when the servlet is first loaded) and the *doGet* and *doPost* methods (which run when the servlet receives an HTTP *Get* or HTTP *Post* request, respectively). The servlet sends its HTML reply to an output stream—the Web server captures this stream and converts it into an HTTP response.

The model used by servlets is similar to the compile-and-cache technique implemented by ASP.NET. When the Web server runs a servlet, it looks to see whether a compiled class file already exists for that servlet. If the file exists, the Web server loads it; if not, the Web server compiles the source code to produce the class file. Multiple clients can run the same servlet concurrently. Having said that, we must concede that you can simply deploy precompiled .class files with the Web server, packaged up as Web Archive (WAR) files. This is the approach most commonly adopted by J2EE servers that are integrated with Web servers these days.

Much of the code in a servlet is concerned with parsing input parameters and formatting an HTML or XML response. JSPs simplify this task by abstracting the mechanics of these tasks out to automatically generated code, allowing the developer to concentrate on the layout and any associated user interface logic. A JSP contains ordinary HTML markup along with Java statements embedded between special tags that perform any additional processing required. Conceptually, the model is similar to that used by Microsoft for ASP, although Microsoft adapted it for languages other than Java. Behind the scenes, a JSP is converted into a servlet by the JSP engine in the Web server. The servlet is then compiled into a Java .class file that can be loaded and run as described earlier. Hence, as with servlets, multiple clients can execute the same JSP simultaneously and share data.

JSP is tightly integrated with Java, so it has a close association with JavaBeans. JSP defines shorthand syntax for instantiating a JavaBean and accessing its properties. A common approach is to limit a JSP to performing tasks associated with the layout of an HTML page and to use a JavaBean to encapsulate any business logic or other processing. JSP also lets a developer define custom tags (by creating tag libraries) and embed them in pages.

The J2EE Infrastructure

J2EE makes heavy use of the Java Naming and Directory Interface (JNDI) for providing access to directory services. JNDI provides a uniform API to the different directory services that are available. For example, J2EE servers implement a directory service that makes EJBs available through JNDI names. Other resources, such as databases, connection pools, and even the file system, can be accessed through JNDI using a suitable JNDI service provider. (A JNDI service provider is an adapter that converts JNDI requests into a format understood by the underlying technology.) The list of JNDI providers is continually growing and includes providers for DNS, LDAP, and CORBA.

The Java Messaging Service (JMS) is the J2EE API for integrating message-oriented middleware into a Java application. As is so often the case in J2EE, JMS essentially defines a series of interfaces and adapters that messaging systems vendors should implement to make their products available to J2EE. JMS implementations are available for many of the widely used messaging systems, including IBM MQ Series and MSMQ. The current release of the J2EE specification allows EJBs to be combined with JMS to provide asynchronous activation of middle-tier services through messaging. An EJB client can post a message to a queue and have that message processed asynchronously by an EJB. This is useful for *mostly-disconnected* clients; requests can be sent to a local message queue on the client machine and posted by the message queuing software as a batch the next time the client connects to the network.

Transaction Management

Transactions have always been important but difficult to implement correctly, especially in a distributed environment. The problem is that the participants might be spread over the network (possibly the Internet), where speed and reliability become challenging issues. Transactions also determine when a J2EE server can discard, save, or recycle an EJB. Managing distributed transactions is best left to specialist transaction servers. J2EE defines the Java Transaction API (JTA) to help in this situation.

The JTA is an interface used for initiating, committing, and rolling back transactions. The JTA can be used directly by J2EE component developers, but it is more commonly employed by EJB containers. EJB containers allow developers to specify declarative transactions as EJB method attributes, and the container will start and control any transactions required using the JTA. The JTA relies on a transaction service provider that implements the JTA to actually create and manage transactions as directed by the application or the J2EE container. Many application servers that implement J2EE also double as transaction servers.

Comparing .NET to J2EE

It's always risky to compare one technology to another. Inevitably, interest groups on one side or the other will claim that the comparison was unfair or that it omitted details to show one product in a favorable light over another or was otherwise prejudicial. This is especially true in the "J2EE vs. .NET" debate, which can degenerate into "Sun vs. Microsoft" if one is not careful. So, before we continue, let us state something that might disappoint or surprise you: We like J2EE. We've used it to build applications and will probably continue to use it in the future.

If you're building or designing a solution that's based on Windows, you should probably use .NET. If, however, the system is heavily based on UNIX, for example, you'd be crazy not to go for J2EE. The challenge is to know what to use in hybrid UNIX/Windows systems, but the integration features of .NET make it ideal for building components that run on Windows but need to interface with J2EE, particularly with the advent of Web services.

Another point is worth making: Comparing .NET to J2EE is a little like comparing apples to oranges. The most important difference is that J2EE is a specification, whereas .NET is an actual product suite. There are many implementations of J2EE; some are great, some are not, so we'll refrain from even attempting to compare the performance of J2EE and .NET and will instead stick to the functionality exposed by each.

Data Services in .NET

In the Data Services Tier, .NET provides ADO.NET as an alternative to JDBC. You can still use JDBC from J# if you want. JDBC is used primarily to access relational databases, whereas ADO.NET uses a more generalized model and can access many different types of data stores. That being said, the most common use for ADO.NET is as an interface to SQL Server, and Microsoft supplies an optimized implementation (packaged in the *System.Data.SqlClient* namespace) just for SQL Server. The *System.Data.OleDb* namespace contains the generic OLE DB data provider that you can use to query other data sources. It is anticipated that third-party database vendors will supply their own ADO.NET libraries for accessing their products. We'll cover ADO.NET in detail in Chapter 7.

As far as integration with EISs is concerned, .NET provides a wealth of features and tools that you can use, depending on the circumstances, ranging from low-level solutions involving COM and J/Direct to highly functional schemes such as building Web service facades. Chapter 13 describes how to integrate with legacy systems.

.NET has good support for common XML features such as schemas, namespaces, XPath, and XSL/T. The *System.Xml* namespace and its child namespaces in the .NET Framework class contain classes and methods for creating and manipulating XML documents. However, XML is not just an add-in appended to .NET for the convenience of developers. It is a fundamental part of .NET. Much of the .NET Framework relies on XML for its own use. For example, configuration information is held in XML files, the Remoting architecture can use XML as a format for serializing data, ADO.NET uses XML internally to represent data in a portable manner, and SOAP relies on XML as the format for sending and receiving requests. The implementation of SOAP underpins Web services, which are also an integral feature of .NET. Chapter 5 and Chapter 6 cover XML in detail. Chapter 17 and Chapter 18 describe Web services under .NET.

Business Services in .NET

Microsoft has had a middle-tier technology available for some time. It was originally called Microsoft Transaction Server, but it has matured over the last few years into COM+. Strictly speaking, COM+ is part of the Windows operating system rather than .NET, but you should expect to see Windows and .NET become increasingly intertwined, in much the same way that COM+ and Windows have.

COM+ components are the closest that .NET gets to Java EJBs (although it does not currently supply an equivalent to CMP). You cannot create EJBs with J#, but you can create COM+ components. COM+ components can be stateful or stateless, and the integration with other operating-system-level features such as events and messaging allows you to build asynchronous components. In .NET, COM+ components are called *serviced components*. A nice touch is the just-in-time deployment feature—you don't have to manually deploy a serviced component because it will be automatically installed into the Component Services framework when it is first used. Serviced components are described in detail in Chapter 14.

User Services in .NET

J2EE has JSP, and .NET has ASP.NET. Actually, there is considerably more in ASP.NET than the functionality of JSP. For one thing, ASP.NET supplies intelligent server controls. A server control is an ASP.NET component, embedded in a Web Form, that can programmatically respond to events generated by the user interacting with the form—clicking a button, for example. The code that responds to the event will execute on the Web server and can generate a new page or update the contents of the current one. (It does this using sleight of hand—it actually creates a new page that looks like the old one, but with any values typed in by the user preserved, and possibly new data added as a result of the processing performed by the event handler. All of this is performed automatically by the ASP.NET runtime so you don't have to write any intricate code!)

Because the event-handling code that you add to a Web Form is ordinary J# code (or C# code, or Microsoft Visual Basic .NET code, or code in any other language supported by the runtime), you can do anything that you can from an ordinary application, security permitting, including invoking a serviced component, calling a remote object, or querying a database.

You'll see a lot more of ASP.NET in Chapter 16.

The .NET Infrastructure

J2EE uses JNDI as a naming service that allows an application to locate and activate components and resources. This practice gives the application a high level of configurability that allows individual components to be replaced without a programmer having to rebuild and redeploy an entire application. .NET also has this capability. But instead of using a naming service, the common language runtime uses the mechanisms described in Chapter 2 for locating and loading assemblies. This mechanism depends on individual application configuration files and publisher policy files, or a specific search sequence if no configuration files are present. Some configuration information can also be held centrally in the machine and enterprise configuration files.

The .NET Framework class library provides the *System.DirectoryServices* namespace. The classes in this namespace can be used to access any of the Active Directory service providers. In this respect, it fulfills a role similar to that of JNDI. Microsoft currently supplies providers for Microsoft Internet Information Services (IIS), Novell Netware Directory Service (NDS), Lightweight Directory Access Protocol (LDAP), and WinNT. Windows uses Active Directory as a repository for system information, and it is possible to store details about almost any type of resource using it.

MSMQ is another example of a technology that started out as an add-on (the original version was part of the Windows NT Option Pack) but is now a critical part of the operating system. The COM+ runtime relies on MSMQ to support its asynchronous operations. You can create applications based on MSMQ using the classes in the *System.Messaging* namespace. Message queuing is covered in Chapter 12.

Transaction Management

.NET makes use of the transaction services exposed by the COM+ runtime and the Distributed Transaction Coordinator. What this means in practical terms is that you don't have to learn any new tricks to use transactions with .NET—you just have to learn how to apply all the old ones!

Classes and methods can be tagged with *TransactionAttribute* (found in *System.EnterpriseServices*) to indicate any transactional requirements, and the common language runtime in conjunction with COM+ does the rest:

```
import System.EnterpriseServices.*;
:
/** @attribute TransactionAttribute(TransactionOption.Required) */
public class CakeOrderComponent extends ServicedComponent
{
    :
}
```

Individual methods can also be tagged with *AutoCompleteAttribute* (also in *System.EnterpriseServices*), indicating that the runtime should determine whether to commit or roll back the current transaction automatically at the end of the method, depending on whether the method was successful (whether it raised an exception).

```
/** @attribute AutoCompleteAttribute() */
public void CancelOrder(int orderId)
{
    :
}
```

COM+ applications can also take charge of their own transactions in a similar manner to the JTA, if they really need to. Transactions are also covered in Chapter 14.

The Java Pet Store

Having a comprehensive set of tools for building applications is one thing, and actually using them to successfully implement a complex distributed system is another. More often than not, it helps to have an example system that you can take apart so you can see how things should be done. For this purpose, we'll take a look at the Java Pet Store example.

The Java Pet Store is an e-commerce application that allows customers to browse the animals stocked by a pet shop, place orders, pay for goods, and so on—all the usual e-commerce type of stuff. The original application was designed and documented by consultants working at Sun Microsystems, and it shows best practices (referred to as the J2EE Blueprints) for building Web-based applications using J2EE. You can download the Java Pet Store source code and documentation from *http://java.sun.com/blueprints/code/index.html#java_pet_store_demo*.

For comparison purposes, an implementation of a similar application called the Microsoft .NET Pet Shop (shown in Figure 3-11 on page 144) is available from the .NET Framework Community Web site at *http://gotdotnet.com/team/compare/petshop.aspx*. This version uses .NET and is written in C# because J# was not available when the .NET Pet Shop was developed. Ignoring any relative performance benchmarks (which are always subjective), one interesting statistic concerning the two applications is the amount of code that was written: The Java Pet Store contains over 14,000 lines of Java, but the equivalent parts of the .NET Pet Shop comprise under 3500 lines of C#. There are some differences between C# and J#, but we would expect a J# version to be a similar size.

As with any implementation based on a set of requirements, each of these applications makes use of the strengths of the particular technologies on which it is based. It also makes its own trade-offs when mapping the required functionality into components. As developers who are fluent in both Java/J2EE and J#/.NET, we would encourage you to examine the two implementations and form your own opinion about which is the best tool for your purposes. When you examine the .NET Pet Shop (or any equivalent Microsoft examples, such as Duwamish Books), bear in mind that even though the examples are meant to show the best way of applying particular technologies, there's also the tendency to show off as many technologies as possible, which is not always the best way to design an application!

Note The Java Pet Store and the .NET Pet Shop do have some functional differences. For example, the Java Pet Store defines mailing and administrative operations, and the .NET Pet Shop does not. Similarly, the .NET Pet Shop contains features that handle mobile devices and a Web service not found in the Java version. Our comparison of the lines of code includes only the areas that are common to both applications, so it is a fair comparison.

Figure 3-11 The .NET Pet Shop

Summary

In this chapter, you saw how Microsoft's implementation of J# includes Java language and JDK 1.1.4 functionality while being flexible enough to take advantage of the features of .NET. In particular, you saw how the J# compiler allows you to write Java-language code that can consume .NET components and how the JDK 1.1.4 object hierarchy has been integrated into the .NET Framework Class Library.

This chapter also presented a brief comparison between J2EE (the framework often used for building enterprise applications in Java) and .NET. It showed how .NET addresses the requirements of enterprise applications. In later chapters, you'll learn about how to implement the individual elements of an enterprise application using J# with .NET.

4

Graphical User Interfaces

Java has had libraries for building graphical user interfaces (GUIs) since the earliest days of the JDK. The original library was called the Alternative Window Toolkit, and it later became the Abstract Window Toolkit (AWT) in version 1.1 of the JDK. The goal of the AWT was to provide a set of tools for defining the essential structure of a GUI application that would be independent of the operating system. This circumstance would allow a developer to build applications that could function on a wide range of desktops, ranging from X-Windows under UNIX, to Apple Macintosh, to Microsoft Windows.

A GUI application typically comprises forms, controls that can be placed on those forms, and code that's executed in response to events raised by those controls. With Visual J++ 6.0, Microsoft extended the AWT and added some features specific to Windows, which resulted in the Windows Foundation Class (WFC) library. Meanwhile, the AWT followed its own development track and was later replaced by Swing in version 1.2 of the JDK. As we've mentioned in earlier chapters, Microsoft made the strategic decision to use the JDK 1.1.4 as the foundation for Visual J# .NET but to also support much of the added functionality in Visual J++ 6.0. This means that Visual J# .NET allows you to use the AWT and WFC to support existing applications that are ported to J#. But what about Swing? Well, the Microsoft .NET Framework includes the Windows Forms library, which is comparable to Swing and is available to any program that executes using the common language runtime. It can also be used by programs written in languages other than J#, such as C# and Microsoft Visual Basic .NET.

In this chapter, you'll learn more about the implementation of the AWT in J#, and you'll learn how to use the Windows Forms library for building GUIs from scratch with Visual Studio .NET. However, this chapter is intended only to be an overview of the Windows Forms library, so it does not cover building GUI applications with .NET in detail.

Desktop GUIs

Despite all the excitement about Microsoft ASP.NET and Web services, writing desktop GUI applications is what many of us are really interested in. If you've developed applications specifically for Windows in the past, prepare yourself for a pleasant surprise—things have changed and gotten easier. If you're taking your first steps into pure Windows-based GUI development, you'll find yourself in familiar surroundings because building Windows applications under .NET is similar to traditional Java GUI development.

But before we start looking at GUI development using the.NET Framework, let's take a step back and ask why you'd want to develop applications specifically for Windows. We can answer that question by first looking at how GUIs can be created using Java.

Revisiting Java GUI Development

In a nutshell, Java offers two GUI libraries: the AWT and Swing. The AWT was the first of the libraries to appear. It operates on the premise that a developer can write code that in effect defines an abstraction of a GUI. Specifically, you use generic components to create a GUI, and position these components using a layout manager rather than absolute coordinates. The layout manager is responsible for managing the exact position of controls placed inside it. The AWT defines a number of layout managers that lay out controls in different ways. (The *GridLayout* class, for example, displays its contents in a rectangular grid format.) The layout manager removes the need for you to understand how the underlying platform manages, sizes, and positions controls. You can write code once and deploy it across many platforms, ensuring that it appears as if it is a native program running on each platform. You don't have to change a single line of code.

At run time, the AWT libraries map AWT forms and widgets onto the structures used by the underlying platform. However, working with an abstract model poses some disadvantages. The most significant of these are

- The developer has little control over the appearance of the GUI when it executes in an environment other than that in which it was originally written.
- Applications have a look and feel based on the operating system they are executing against. There might be inconsistencies when you run the same application on different platforms.

- The AWT model is a highly layered system, with the native platform at the lowest level. As a result, performance can be hindered as the code passes through several levels of indirection at run time.

Figure 4-1 shows a simple text editor application that was developed using AWT running under Windows XP. The AWT implementation under Windows makes the application appear as similar to a native Windows application as possible.

Figure 4-1 An AWT editor application running under Windows XP

The AWT will present the same application running on a different operating system using that operating system's look and feel. For example, Figure 4-2 shows the editor application running using the Enlightenment Window Manager under Linux. (The Java class file was copied to the Linux machine and run unchanged.)

Figure 4-2 The AWT editor application running under Linux

Lack of control over the presentation style was a major factor that led to the creation of the Swing libraries. Unlike the AWT, Swing applications can be configured to always have the same look and feel regardless of the underlying operating system. This is achieved using the Pluggable Look and Feel (PLAF) feature of the Swing user interface manager. PLAF schemes are available for a variety of operating systems, including Windows and Motif (X-Windows), as well as a generic cross-platform scheme called Metal (which is actually the default). Figure 4-3 shows a Swing implementation of the editor application running under Windows XP, using the Metal PLAF scheme. (The differences between this figure and Figure 4-1 are subtle but significant—look at how the menu items are rendered, for example.)

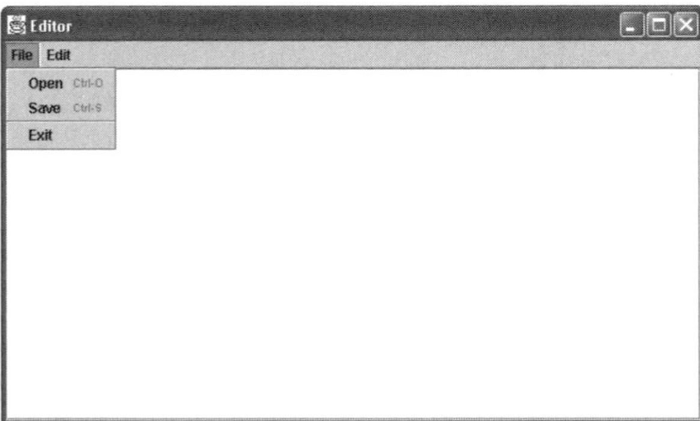

Figure 4-3 The Swing editor application running under Windows XP, using the Metal PLAF scheme

The Swing libraries also simplify many of the day-to-day tasks that a GUI developer might need to perform, such as writing to and from the system clipboard.

Today, some Java developers use Swing, and others use the AWT. The actual choice of library is generally based on which platforms the application will be deployed on and how that application should look on those platforms. Just remember that you can write Swing applications and run them on Windows, but you cannot use Visual J# .NET to do it! However, you can use Visual J# .NET to build AWT applications. You'll find an implementation of the java.awt package, along with java.awt.datatransfer, java.awt.event, and java.awt.image, in the assembly vjslib.dll. However, the main reason for the existence of these packages in .NET is to allow you to migrate existing AWT code rather than develop new applications with it.

One issue not directly addressed by Swing is speed. A benefit of using the .NET implementation of the AWT is that it targets only the Windows platform and is less concerned about dynamically adjusting itself to the look and feel of different environments. (The Windows operating system itself handles any adjustments required by different desktop themes.) As a result, the code usually executes faster than the same AWT application running using the Java Virtual Machine (JVM).

Note If you're porting a J++ application to .NET, the assembly vjswfc.dll supplied with J# contains a .NET implementation of the WFC classes.

If you're developing an application specifically to run under Windows from scratch using Visual J# .NET, you should consider using the Windows Forms library. This library was written and optimized for Windows. The model used is different from that of the AWT or WFC but is arguably more intuitive. And because it is a native .NET library, it is faster still than the Microsoft implementation of the AWT and WFC.

The Windows Forms Library

The Windows Forms library comprises a set of classes and other types located in the *System.Windows.Forms* namespace. The *Form* class represents a window or dialog box, and many of the other classes implement the various controls (such as *ListBox*, *DataGrid*, and *Label*) that you can place on a form.

Unlike some earlier Windows GUI development tools such as Visual Basic 6.0, forms and controls are themselves first-class types that support inheritance. This should not be a surprise to seasoned Java developers because the same is true in the models used by Swing and the AWT, but it is in fact a big change in the Windows GUI development paradigm. This change in Windows GUI development brings Windows much closer to the concepts used by Java, making the transition from Java development to .NET development as painless as possible. Later in this chapter, we'll take a closer look at Windows Forms and compare them to selected aspects of the Swing library.

Porting Existing Java Applications

If you've spent time writing an application in Java, the last thing you want to do is to rewrite it using the .NET classes. In this section, we'll look at how you can compile and run an AWT application under .NET. The code we'll use is for a simple text editor. In this section, the code will use the AWT libraries.

The code for the application follows, in the class *EditorFrame*. We won't walk you through how the AWT works (this is a book about .NET, after all), but to summarize, the *EditorFrame* constructor calls the initComponents method, which creates new instances of all the components used within the application. The bulk of this method builds the menu structure for the application. For each menu item instance, the code sets shortcut and name properties and adds an ActionListener, which wires the event that each menu item fires to a corresponding event handler method. Most of the event handlers perform fairly straightforward operations, but it is important to note that the *cut*, *copy*, and *paste* methods in this application use the system clipboard, so the *EditorFrame* class also implements the ClipboardOwner interface:

EditorFrame.java

```
import java.io.*;
import java.awt.*;
import java.awt.event.*;
import java.awt.datatransfer.*;

public class EditorFrame extends Frame implements ClipboardOwner {

    // This method is called from within the constructor to
    // initialize the form.
    private void initComponents() {

        // Initialize the components and menus
        mainMenuBar = new java.awt.MenuBar();
```

```
fileMenu = new java.awt.Menu();
openMenuItem = new java.awt.MenuItem();
saveMenuItem = new java.awt.MenuItem();
exitMenuItem = new java.awt.MenuItem();
editMenu = new java.awt.Menu();
cutMenuItem = new java.awt.MenuItem();
copyMenuItem = new java.awt.MenuItem();
pasteMenuItem = new java.awt.MenuItem();
textEditor = new java.awt.TextArea();

// Initialize the File menu and its menu items
fileMenu.setLabel("File");

// The Open file menu item
openMenuItem.setShortcut(new MenuShortcut(79));
openMenuItem.setLabel("Open");
openMenuItem.addActionListener(new ActionListener() {
   public void actionPerformed(ActionEvent evt) {
       openMenuItemActionPerformed(evt);
   }
   }
);
fileMenu.add(openMenuItem);

 // The Save file menu item
saveMenuItem.setShortcut(new MenuShortcut(65));
saveMenuItem.setLabel("Save");
saveMenuItem.addActionListener(new ActionListener() {
    public void actionPerformed(ActionEvent evt) {
        saveMenuItemActionPerformed(evt);
    }
    }
);
fileMenu.add(saveMenuItem);

fileMenu.addSeparator();

// The Exit file menu item
exitMenuItem.setLabel("Exit");
exitMenuItem.addActionListener(new ActionListener() {
    public void actionPerformed(ActionEvent evt) {
        exitMenuItemActionPerformed(evt);
    }
    }
);
fileMenu.add(exitMenuItem);

// Add the File menu to the main menu bar
```

```
mainMenuBar.add(fileMenu);

// Initialize the Edit menu and its menu items
editMenu.setLabel("Edit");

// The Cut edit menu item
cutMenuItem.setShortcut(new MenuShortcut(88));
cutMenuItem.setLabel("Cut");
cutMenuItem.addActionListener(new ActionListener() {
    public void actionPerformed(ActionEvent evt) {
        cutMenuItemActionPerformed(evt);
    }
    }
);
editMenu.add(cutMenuItem);

// The Copy edit menu item
copyMenuItem.setShortcut(new MenuShortcut(67));
copyMenuItem.setLabel("Copy");
copyMenuItem.addActionListener(new ActionListener() {
    public void actionPerformed(ActionEvent evt) {
        copyMenuItemActionPerformed(evt);
    }
    }
);
editMenu.add(copyMenuItem);

// The paste edit menu item
pasteMenuItem.setShortcut(new MenuShortcut(86));
pasteMenuItem.setLabel("Paste");
pasteMenuItem.addActionListener(new ActionListener() {
    public void actionPerformed(ActionEvent evt) {
          pasteMenuItemActionPerformed(evt);
    }
    }
);
editMenu.add(pasteMenuItem);

// Add the Edit menu to the main menu bar
mainMenuBar.add(editMenu);

// Set the title of the frame to something meaningful
setTitle("Editor");

// Allow the window to close cleanly
addWindowListener(new WindowAdapter() {
    public void windowClosing(WindowEvent evt) {
        exitForm(evt);
```

```
            }
            }
        );

        // Define the properties of the text box that is used as
        // the main edit areas
        textEditor.setBackground(java.awt.Color.white);
        textEditor.setFont(new java.awt.Font ("Dialog", 0, 11));
        textEditor.setColumns(120);
        textEditor.setForeground(java.awt.Color.black);
        textEditor.setRows(30);

        // Add the text editor text box to the window
        add(textEditor, java.awt.BorderLayout.CENTER);

        // Add the main menu bar to the window
        setMenuBar(mainMenuBar);
    }


    // Event handling methods for the various menu items


    // Open a file and display its contents in the textEditor text area
    private void openMenuItemActionPerformed(ActionEvent evt)
    {
        BufferedReader br=null;
        String text="";
        String line;
        String theFile = null;

        // Display a file dialog to allow the user to select the file
        FileDialog fd = new FileDialog(this, "Pick a file",
           FileDialog.LOAD);
        fd.show();
        theFile = fd.getDirectory() + fd.getFile();
        if (theFile == null)
        {
            System.err.println("the file is null");
        }

        // read the contents of the text file
        try
        {
            br = new BufferedReader(new FileReader(theFile));
            while ((line = br.readLine())!= null)
            {
                text += line + System.getProperty("line.separator");
```

```
            }
        }
        catch (IOException ioe)
        {
            System.err.println("Exception: " + ioe.getMessage());
        }

        // Update the display
        textEditor.setText(text);
    }

    // Save the contents of the textEditor text area to a file
    private void saveMenuItemActionPerformed(ActionEvent evt) {
        String theFile;
        BufferedWriter bw = null;

        //First find out what they want to save it as
        FileDialog fd = new FileDialog(this, "Save as", FileDialog.SAVE);
        fd.show();
        theFile = fd.getDirectory() + fd.getFile();

        // Now write the contents to the file
        try {
            bw = new BufferedWriter(new FileWriter(theFile));
            bw.write(textEditor.getText());
        }
        catch (IOException ioe) {
            System.err.println("Exception: " + ioe.getMessage());
        }
        finally {
            try {
                bw.flush();
                bw.close();
            }
            catch (IOException ioe) {
                System.err.println("Exception: " + ioe.getMessage());
            }
        }
    }

    // Exit the application (called by the exit menu item)
    private void exitMenuItemActionPerformed(ActionEvent evt) {
        System.exit(0);
    }

    // Exit the Application (called by the window itself)
    private void exitForm(WindowEvent evt) {
        System.exit (0);
```

```
}

// Cut the selected text from the textEditor text area to the clipboard
private void cutMenuItemActionPerformed(ActionEvent evt) {

    // Copy the selected text to the clipboard, reusing
    // the Copy event handler defined below
    copyMenuItemActionPerformed(evt);

    // Delete the selected text from the text area
    // by overwriting it with an empty string
    int startPos = textEditor.getSelectionStart();
    int endPos = textEditor.getSelectionEnd();
    textEditor.replaceRange("", startPos, endPos);
}

// This method places stuff on the clipboard when a user copies
// in this example using the system clipboard through the Toolkit
// however, this is not platform portable. If we wish platform
// independence we should use the Clipboard in the
// java.awt.datatransfer package
private void copyMenuItemActionPerformed(ActionEvent evt)
{
    // Get the selected text
    String s = textEditor.getSelectedText();

    // The clipboard holds only Transferable types, so we use
    // one of its implementations
    StringSelection ss = new StringSelection(s);

    // Copy the string into the system clipboard
    this.getToolkit().getSystemClipboard().setContents(ss,this);
}

// Paste the contents of the clipboard to the textEditor text area
private void pasteMenuItemActionPerformed(ActionEvent evt)
{
    // Get the clipboard
    Clipboard c = this.getToolkit().getSystemClipboard();

    // Get the contents of the clipboard
    Transferable t = c.getContents(this);
    try
    {
        if (t.isDataFlavorSupported(DataFlavor.stringFlavor))
        {
            String s= (String)
```

```
                    t.getTransferData(DataFlavor.stringFlavor);

                // Obtain the caret posistion
                int p = textEditor.getCaretPosition();

                // Insert the text at this point
                textEditor.insert(s,p);
            }
        }
        catch (Exception e) {
            System.err.println("Exception: " + e.getMessage());
        }
    }

    // Miscellaneous methods and constructors


    // Required method because we are implementing ClipboardOwner
    public void lostOwnership(Clipboard c, Transferable t) {

    }

    // Creates new form EditorFrame
    public EditorFrame()
    {
        initComponents ();
        pack ();
    }

    // The entry point to the program
    public static void main (String args[]) {
        new EditorFrame().show ();
    }

    // Variable declarations
    private java.awt.MenuBar mainMenuBar;
    private java.awt.Menu fileMenu;
    private java.awt.MenuItem openMenuItem;
    private java.awt.MenuItem saveMenuItem;
    private java.awt.MenuItem exitMenuItem;
    private java.awt.Menu editMenu;
    private java.awt.MenuItem cutMenuItem;
    private java.awt.MenuItem copyMenuItem;
    private java.awt.MenuItem pasteMenuItem;
    private java.awt.TextArea textEditor;
}
```

You can compile and run this application using the JDK version 1.1.4 or later. However, the main purpose of showing this code is to demonstrate that it will also work unchanged with J#. You can compile the EditorFrame.java file using vjc to produce EditorFrame.exe, which will run like any other .NET executable program.

The Visual Studio .NET IDE

Some of us love to lock ourselves away, open up a text editor, and start hacking away at code. But when it comes to real-life GUI development, you have to put aside your text editor and get serious with an IDE.

A good IDE takes the pain out of GUI development. The IDE for Windows .NET development is Visual Studio .NET. It has many great features, such as

- **Dynamic help** The IDE provides context-sensitive help based on what you've just written or are writing
- **IntelliSense** Fast tool-tip prompts display method overloads and valid parameter types
- **Drag-and-drop** Visual Studio .NET is also simple to use: You just drag-and-drop components from the Toolbox onto your Windows Form in the Visual Studio .NET Design View and then double-click to access the code behind the GUI.

Visual Studio .NET provides a number of project templates that can give you a head start on building different types of applications. For building GUI applications, you'll probably find the Windows Application template most useful, as described later.

Porting AWT Applications to .NET

You've seen that you can compile ordinary Java (.java) source files from the command line using the vjc compiler to build a .NET executable. You can also use the Visual Studio .NET IDE.

The simplest way to edit and compile existing .java files with Visual Studio .NET is to create a new empty project and then import the Java source code:

From the Visual Studio IDE, choose New and then Project from the File menu. The New Project dialog box will appear, as shown in Figure 4-4.

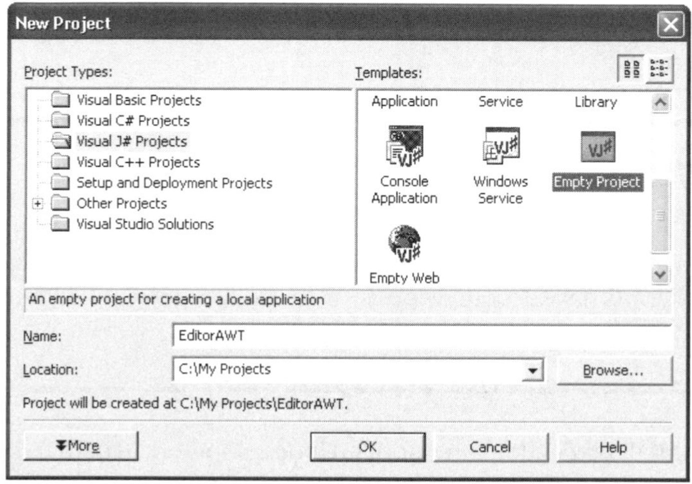

Figure 4-4 The New Project dialog box in Visual Studio .NET

In the Project Types pane, select Visual J# Projects, and in the Templates pane, select Empty Project. To create the project, give the project a name—for example, *EditorAWT*—and then click OK. Your first impression might be that nothing has happened. But if you look at the right side of the IDE, you'll see Solution Explorer displaying the project you just created. The project is currently empty, so to add the existing source file choose Add Existing Item from the Project menu. The Add Existing Item dialog box will appear, as shown in Figure 4-5. Browse to the folder containing your .java files, select the file you want to add to the project, and then click Open. Visual Studio .NET will add the file to the current project.

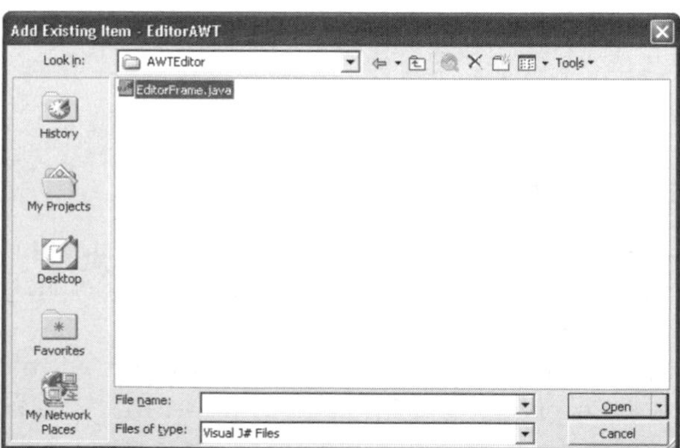

Figure 4-5 The Add Existing Item dialog box in Visual Studio .NET

You should see the code appear in the main window of the IDE. Although we won't be changing this code, go ahead and browse through it to appreciate the colorized highlighting that identifies key words and comments. (How many times have you opened a multiline comment and forgotten to close it again? This sort of error is easier to spot in a colorized environment!)

The Visual Studio Folding Editor

Visual Studio uses a folding editor that allows you to contract or expand blocks of code, such as methods and classes. On the left side of the Code View window, you can see grayed-out plus and minus signs adjacent to the start of each method or class. If you click a minus sign, it will turn into a plus sign and the corresponding code block will contract, leaving just the method or class definition.

This feature allows you to focus on the areas of the program you're currently developing, without needing to scroll through large quantities of code to find various methods.

To build and run the project, choose Start from the Debug menu. If there are any errors in your source, these will be displayed in the Output window of the IDE. Otherwise, the application will open a command window and execute.

Writing a GUI Application Using the .NET Classes

If you have an existing AWT Java application you want to deploy under .NET, porting it is a sensible approach. But if you have an application built using Swing, you'll most likely want to redevelop the GUI using .NET classes, for three main reasons:

- J# does not provide support for Swing.
- You can take advantage of the wide variety of GUI components that .NET offers.
- Applications built using .NET classes can run much faster than their Java peers.

In this section, we'll continue with the theme of the text editor. Specifically, rather than using JDK constructs, we'll build an equivalent application using the .NET Framework. As you walk through the code, pay particular attention to areas where .NET development differs from traditional Java development. In particular, notice the object model implemented by Windows Forms and the way in which events are raised and handled.

Creating the Windows Form

To create the Windows Form, you must first create a new solution in Visual Studio .NET: open the IDE, and click New Project. The New Project dialog box will appear. In the Project Types pane, select Visual J# Projects, and in the Templates pane, select Windows Application. Give the project a name (use Editor for this example), and then click OK.

When the application is created, Visual Studio .NET will also create a default form called Form.jsl and a file containing assembly and attribute information called AssemblyInfo.jsl (which you can ignore for now). The Design View window, will display a GUI representation of Form1. To the left of the Design View window is the Toolbox (Figure 4-6), which contains controls that you can drag-and-drop onto the form.

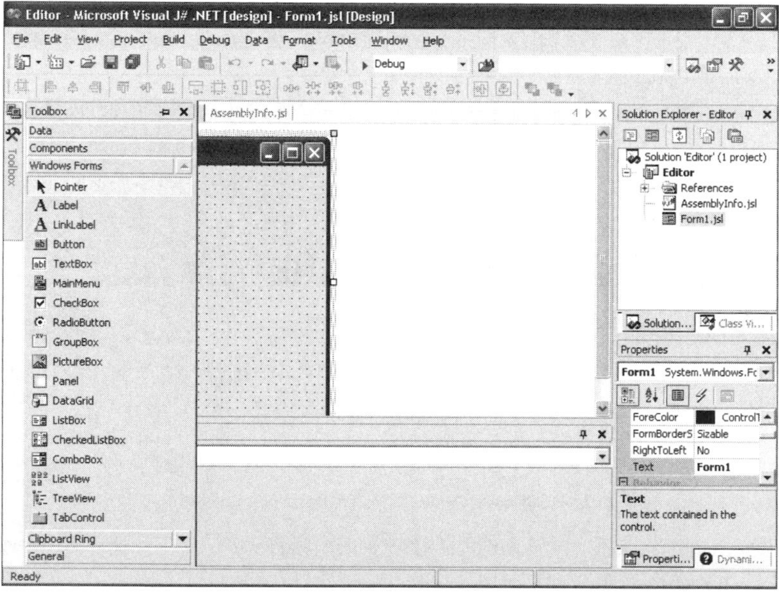

Figure 4-6 The Toolbox and Design View in Visual Studio .NET

Before you start adding controls to the form, look at the code behind Form1. To view the code, choose Code from the View menu. The code should look like that shown on the facing page. (You might need to expand some of the contracted code to see everything.)

Form1.jsl

```
package Editor;

import System.Drawing.*;
import System.Collections.*;
import System.ComponentModel.*;
import System.Windows.Forms.*;
import System.Data.*;

/**
 * Summary description for Form1.
 */
public class Form1 extends System.Windows.Forms.Form
{
/**
 * Required designer variable.
 */
private System.ComponentModel.Container components = null;

public Form1()
{
//
// Required for Windows Form Designer support
//
InitializeComponent();

//
// TODO: Add any constructor code after InitializeComponent call
//
}

/**
 * Clean up any resources being used.
 */
protected void Dispose(boolean disposing)
{
if (disposing)
{
if (components != null)
{
components.Dispose();
}
}
super.Dispose(disposing);
}

#region Windows Form Designer generated code
/**
```

```
 * Required method for Designer support - do not modify
 * the contents of this method with the code editor.
 */
private void InitializeComponent()
{
this.components = new System.ComponentModel.Container();
this.set_Size(new System.Drawing.Size(300,300));
this.set_Text("Form1");
}
#endregion

/**
 * The main entry point for the application.
 */
/** @attribute System.STAThread() */
public static void main(String[] args)
{
Application.Run(new Form1());
}
}
```

This is actually a complete working application. You can build and run it, and it will display an empty form! Your task as a developer is to add functionality to make it useful.

Before we examine this code in detail, we need to change the filename and form name to something more meaningful.

Note In a difference from the JDK, the name of a class or form in J# does not have to be the same as the filename in which the form or class is defined. Furthermore, a single J# (JSL) file can contain the definitions of multiple public classes. However, this means that if you change the name of a file to something meaningful, you should also change the names of all forms or classes in that file to something equally meaningful because it will not happen automatically!

To change the filename, right-click on Form1.jsl in Solution Explorer (normally found on the right side of the Design View window). Choose Solution Explorer from the View menu if it is not displayed. Select Rename, and change the filename to Editor.jsl. To change the form name, switch back to the Design View window (choose Designer from the View menu), click anywhere on the form, and then change the value of the *(Name)* property to *Editor* in the Properties window. (The Properties window is normally displayed below Solution Explorer; you can display it if it is not visible by choosing Properties from the View menu.) You can change the caption of the form by setting the *Text* property to *Editor* as well.

Returning to Code View, the program commences by declaring the package name to which this form belongs, and then it imports a number of namespaces that the application uses. Although Visual Studio imports all these namespaces, you might not necessarily use classes from all of the namespaces. For example, in this application you won't use any of the classes or interfaces that the *System.Data* namespace contains. Table 4-1 lists the imported namespaces and describes their contents.

Table 4-1 Visual Studio .NET Default Imports for a Windows Form

Namespace	Description
System.Drawing	Provides basic graphics functionality through GDI+. It is similar in functionality to the graphics classes located in the java.awt package in the JDK.
System.Collections	Provides collection classes and interfaces, such as arrays, queues, and hash tables. The nearest equivalent in the JDK is the java.util package.
System.ComponentModel	Provides classes and interfaces that define the runtime and design-time behavior of controls and components.
System.Windows.Forms	Provides the essential classes for creating Windows-based applications.
System.Data	Provides the classes that constitute the ADO.NET architecture. (You'll learn about ADO.NET in Chapter 7).

After the *import* statements, the code defines the *Editor* class. This class represents a form—that is, a window displayed in an application. A standalone form, the parent form of an application, and a dialog box (such as a file dialog box) are all examples of forms as defined by the .NET Framework. This class, like all other Windows Forms, extends the *System.Windows.Forms.Form* class in much the same way that an AWT frame extends *java.awt.Frame* or a Swing frame extends *javax.swing.JFrame*.

The default constructor for this class simply calls the *InitializeComponent* method, which on the surface performs a similar role to the *initComponents* method in the AWT application shown earlier. One thing that might strike you about this method is that there is no reference to a layout manager. This is because both forms and individual controls are positioned and sized using coordinates, or absolute sizes. This means you can catch up on all that sleep you lost when you were working out how to fit all those Java components into a *GridBag* layout! We'll take another look at this method when you start adding controls to the form.

The *Dispose* method frees any resources associated with the particular form. You do not need to call this method explicitly because it is called when you invoke the form's *Close* method.

Finally, the *main* method executes the static *Run* method of the *Application* class to start the application. The *Application* class exposes methods and properties that you can use to control the current application. For a complete list of the *Application* class's members, see the .NET Framework Class Library documentation. The *Run* method has three overloads, all of which run an application in the current thread:

- **Application.Run()** This method starts the application but does not display a form.
- **Application.Run(Form mainForm)** This method starts the application and makes the specified form visible.
- **Application.Run(ApplicationContext context)** This method starts the application within the specified context. You can use an *ApplicationContext* to change the circumstances that cause the program to exit. By default, it waits for the *Closed* event on the main form (Form1 in this case) of the application. For more information, see the .NET Framework Class Library documentation.

Caution Much of the time, if you use the Properties window or Solution Explorer to change the properties of forms and controls, Visual Studio .NET will update the corresponding statements in the code behind the form and keep everything synchronized. (This applies only to code that the Visual Studio .NET generates, not to code that you write yourself.) There is one major exception to this rule. If you change the name of a form, the *Application.Run* statement will not change—it will still attempt to execute Form1. For this reason, if you change the name of a form, you should change the *Application.Run* statement as well (as shown below); otherwise, your application will not compile.

```
Application.Run(new Editor());
```

Adding Controls to the Form

Once you've defined a form, you can add controls to it. In the Design View window, you can drag controls from the Toolbox onto the form. You'll notice that most of the controls in the Toolbox offer similar functionality to many of the Java Swing components and have similar names. To start building the Editor application, drag a *MainMenu* component and drop it anywhere on the form. A *MainMenu* control called *mainMenu1* will appear in the area below the form, and a menu bar will be added to the form. You can rename this component, and any other controls, by selecting it and changing the *(Name)* property in the Properties window. In this case, change the name of the *mainMenu1* control to *editorMenu*.

Creating menus, even complex ones, is a relatively simple procedure in Visual Studio .NET. Click where it says "Type Here" in the menu bar near the top of the form displayed in the Design View window, and type the text (the *menu label*, in AWT and Swing parlance) for the first menu item (File, in this case). The display will change to allow you to add this menu and additional menus, as shown in Figure 4-7.

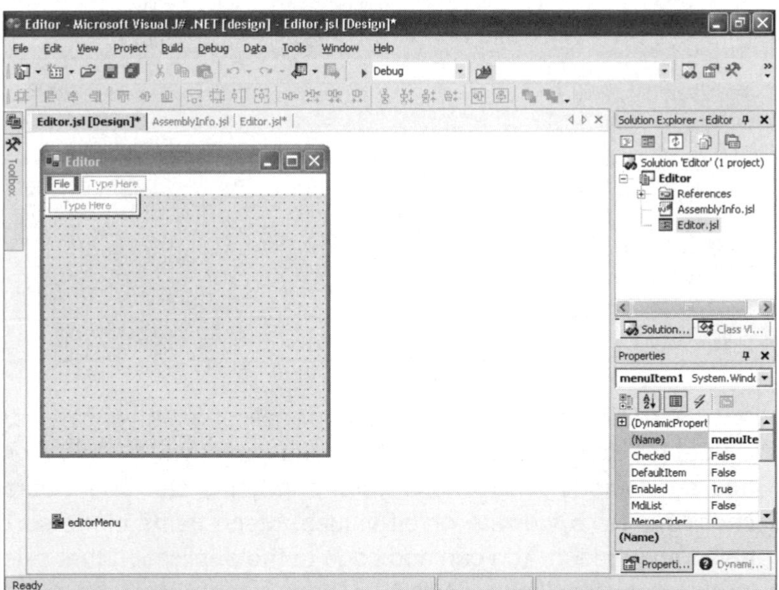

Figure 4-7 Creating a menu in Visual Studio .NET

As you type the name of the menu item, the item will be created and added to the main menu automatically (as you'll see shortly, when we examine the code that is generated). You can use the same technique to add the remaining menu items to create the menus for the application. Table 4-2 lists the menu items you should create for this application. You should notice that unlike the AWT or Swing, the *Windows.Forms* library does not differentiate between menus and menu items; a menu (such as File—or Edit, in this example) is a menu item that happens to contain child menu items (such as Open, Save, Exit, and so on). Note that to insert a separator, you can either right-click at the place where you want to place the separator and then choose Insert Separator from the shortcut menu, or you can type a "-" sign. As you add the menus items, also change the *Name* property of each item as shown in Table 4-2. (You must click away from the new menu item and select it again for the properties to be displayed in the Properties window.)

Table 4-2 Menus and Menu Items for the Editor Application

Top-Level Menu Item	Child Menu Item	Name Property Value
File		*fileMenu*
	Open	*openMenuItem*
	Save	*saveMenuItem*
	Separator	*separator1*
	Exit	*exitMenuItem*
Edit		*editMenu*
	Cut	*cutMenuItem*
	Copy	*copyMenuItem*
	Paste	*pasteMenuItem*

Note The menu built for the Editor application is very basic. If you look at the properties available for menu items, you'll see that you can add shortcuts for each menu item, and items can be rendered with check boxes to indicate on/off values. Menu items can also be disabled and hidden. You can add code to the application that selectively enables or disables, or shows or hides, menu items by dynamically modifying these properties.

If you look at the variables added to the *Editor* class and *InializeComponent* method for the form in the Code View window, you'll see the code that initializes the menu items you've just added to the form:

```
public class Editor extends System.Windows.Forms.Form
{
   private System.Windows.Forms.MainMenu editorMenu;
   private System.Windows.Forms.MenuItem fileMenu;
   private System.Windows.Forms.MenuItem openMenuItem;
   private System.Windows.Forms.MenuItem saveMenuItem;
   private System.Windows.Forms.MenuItem seperator1;
   private System.Windows.Forms.MenuItem exitMenuItem;
   private System.Windows.Forms.MenuItem editMenu;
   private System.Windows.Forms.MenuItem cutMenuItem;
   private System.Windows.Forms.MenuItem copyMenuItem;
   private System.Windows.Forms.MenuItem pasteMenuItem;
   ...
private void InitializeComponent()
   {
      this.editorMenu = new System.Windows.Forms.MainMenu();
      this.fileMenu = new System.Windows.Forms.MenuItem();
      this.openMenuItem = new System.Windows.Forms.MenuItem();
      this.saveMenuItem = new System.Windows.Forms.MenuItem();
      this.seperator1 = new System.Windows.Forms.MenuItem();
      this.exitMenuItem = new System.Windows.Forms.MenuItem();
      this.editMenu = new System.Windows.Forms.MenuItem();
      this.cutMenuItem = new System.Windows.Forms.MenuItem();
      this.copyMenuItem = new System.Windows.Forms.MenuItem();
      this.pasteMenuItem = new System.Windows.Forms.MenuItem();
      ...
   }
}
```

The *InitializeComponent* method also sets the properties of each menu item using the values that you specified in the Properties window. You'll notice that the way in which menus are constructed at run time is not dissimilar to the procedure followed by the AWT or Swing. The main difference between a .NET menu and its Java equivalents is that in .NET menu items are added to menus, and menus are added to the menu bar, in the same way—by calling the *AddRange* method. This method accepts an array of *MenuItem* objects, which are then associated with that particular menu or menu bar. For example, the following code fragment generated by Visual Studio .NET adds the File and Edit menus to the main menu bar:

```
this.editMenu.get_MenuItems().AddRange
   (new System.Windows.Forms.MenuItem[]  {this.fileMenu, this.editMenu});
```

The next task for you to perform is to add a control that the user can type text into. The AWT application used a *TextArea*. The Toolbox has two controls that at first glance look like they might provide the functionality the application requires, namely *TextBox* and *RichTextBox*. *TextBox* is typically used for single-line text entry, much like a Swing *JTextField* or an AWT *TextField*. However, setting its *Multiline* property to *true* and its *Scrollbars* property to *Vertical* allows it to display multiple lines of text in a way that is almost the same as a Swing *JTextArea*. The *RichTextBox* control provides richer functionality than the *TextBox*. For example, you can assign character and paragraph formatting. The *RichTextBox* control is probably overkill for this application.

In the Design View window, drag a *TextBox* control anywhere onto the form and then display its properties by choosing Properties from the View menu. Many of the *TextBox* properties are common to all controls because its parent class (*TextBoxBase*) inherits from *System.Windows.Forms.Control*, which is the base class for all controls that display information to a user, as Figure 4-8 shows.

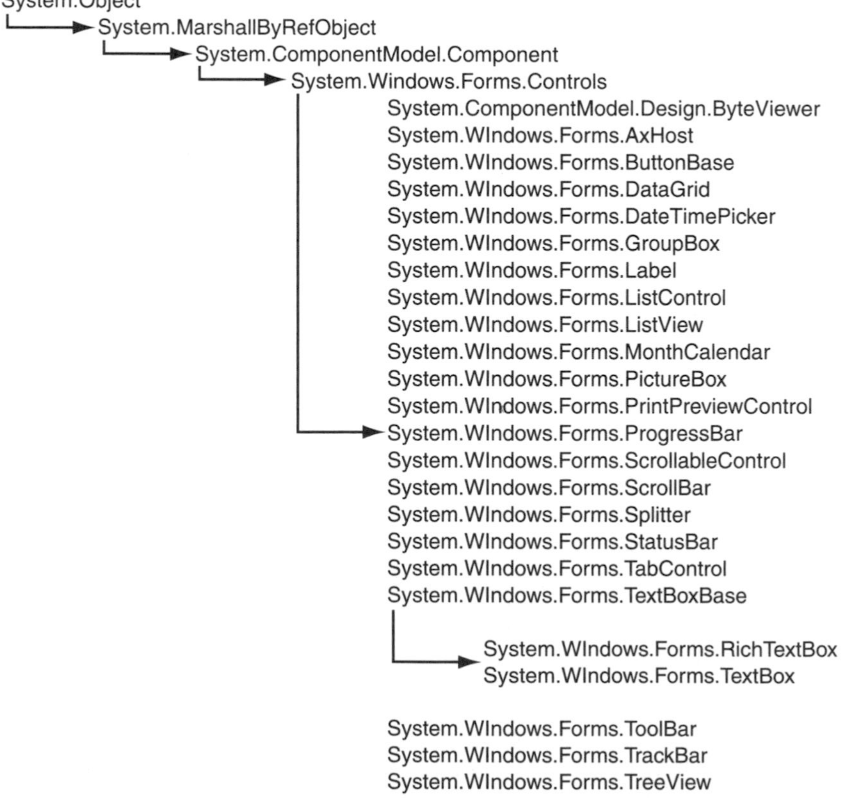

Figure 4-8 The *TextBoxBase Control* class hierarchy

As you scroll through the list of properties, you'll see some that are familiar from an AWT and Swing perspective, but many others might be less so. You should consult the Visual Studio .NET documentation for a definitive list of all the *TextBox* properties. Table 4-3 shows a selection of *TextBox* properties that might be unfamiliar to Java developers and indicates the class from which each property originates in the *Control* hierarchy:

Table 4-3 TextBox Control Properties

Property	Inherited From	Description
AcceptsTab	*TextBoxBase*	A Boolean property that indicates whether pressing the Tab key will type a Tab character or move the focus to the next control in the tab order. Default value is false.
AccessibleDescription	*Control*	A string that provides a textual description of a control appearance. Typically used as an accessibility feature, for example, for users with poor vision. The default value is null.
AccessibleName	*Control*	A string that provides a short name for a control. Typically used as an accessibility feature. The default value is null.
AccessibleRole	*Control*	An AccessibleRole enum member that indicates the type of user interface element the control represents. For example, AccessibleRole members include Alert, Border, Caret, and DropList. The default value is Default.
AllowDrop	*Control*	A Boolean that indicates whether drag-and-drop is allowed. The default value is false.
Anchor	*Control*	A bitwise combination of AnchorStyles enum members that indicates which edges of a container the control is anchored to. The AnchorStyles enumeration has five members: Bottom, Left, None, Top, and Right. The default value is Top and Left.
AutoSize	*TextBoxBase*	A Boolean that indicates whether the size of the control will automatically adjust when the font changes. The default value is true.
CausesValidation	*Control*	A Boolean that indicates whether the control, on receiving focus, will cause the validation of other controls. The default value is true.

Table 4-3 TextBox Control Properties

Property	Inherited From	Description
CharacterCasing		A CharacterCasing enum member that indicates whether the control will change the case of text as the user types it. The CharacterCasing enumeration contains three values: Lower, Normal, and Upper. The default value is Normal.
ContextMenu	*Control*	A ContextMenu item that indicates whether a shortcut menu will be associated with the control. See the product documentation for usage guidelines.
Dock	*Control*	A DockStyle enum member that indicates whether the control will be docked to its parent container, and if it is, which edges it will dock to. The DockStyle enum values are: Bottom, Fill, Left, None, Right, and Top. The default value is None.
ImeMode	*Control*	An ImeMode enum member that indicates the Input Method Editor (IME) mode of the control. An IME is typically a program that allows a user to enter characters that are not found on a standard keyboard. The values for the ImeMode enum are Alpha, AlphaFull, Disable, Hangul, HangulFull, Hirgana, Inherit, Katakana, KatakanaFull, NoControl, Off, and On. The default is Inherit. In this instance, the control will normally inherit from Form, which has a default value of NoControl.
Location	*Control*	A Point (a Point structure represents an integer x-y coordinate pair) that indicates the position of the top-left corner of the control relative to the top-left corner of its containing control.

For the Editor application, you should change the values of the *TextBox* properties shown in Table 4-4. Leave the remaining properties at their default values.

Tip You might find it easier to locate each property if you select the Alphabetic toggle button in the toolbar directly above the Properties window. (It has an image showing an *A* above a *Z* alongside an arrow.) The properties will then be displayed in alphabetical order.

Table 4-4 *TextBox* Properties in the Editor Application

Property	Value
(Name)	textEditor
AcceptsTab	*True*
Dock	*Fill* (You can either type the word *Fill* or select the square in the middle of the diagram that appears when you click the drop-down arrow.)
MultiLine	*True*
ScrollBars	*Both*
Text	Leave blank

If you return to the Code window and examine the *InitializeComponent* method again, you can observe the changes that resulted from your adding the *TextBox* and setting its properties. As the following code shows, the two points where the .NET-generated code radically departs from the Java GUI development model are the *set_Size* and *set_Dock* accessor methods. These two methods, which were described in Table 4-3, further illustrate that the Windows GUI development model revolves around coordinate sizes (and positioning) and relative positioning.

```
this.textEditor.set_AcceptsTab(true);
this.textEditor.set_Dock(System.Windows.Forms.DockStyle.Fill);
this.textEditor.set_Multiline(true);
this.textEditor.set_Name("textEditor");
this.textEditor.set_ScrollBars(System.Windows.Forms.ScrollBars.Both);
this.textEditor.set_Size(new System.Drawing.Size(292, 266));
this.textEditor.set_TabIndex(0);
this.textEditor.set_Text("");
```

Handling Events

The next step is to write code to handle the events that are triggered when the user chooses the various menu items.

To understand the event model used by Windows Forms, we'll examine the simplest of the events in the application—the event associated with the *Click* event of the Exit menu item. To create the event handler method, use the Design View windows and choose the File menu item belonging to the Editor form. Click the Exit menu item when it appears. With the Exit menu item highlighted, switch to the Properties window (which should now be displaying the properties for the *exitMenuItem* control) and click the "lightning bolt" button (the Events button) on the toolbar. This action will display the events available for the menu item. Type the method name *exitMenuItemClick* in the slot adjacent to the *Click* event and press the Enter key. The display will automatically change to the Code View window, and a new method called *exitMenuItemClick* will be created to handle the Click event.

Following the conventions discussed in Chapter 3, the *exitMenuItemClick* method accepts two parameters rather than the single parameter you normally expect with Swing and AWT events:

```
private void exitMenuItemClick (System.Object sender, System.EventArgs e)
```

The first parameter, *sender*, is a reference to the object that raised the event. The second parameter contains additional information specific to the event. For example, for some events it might contain information about which key the user pressed or the position of the cursor when the event fired. All events for Windows Forms components are passed this parameter, even if there's no useful additional information.

The click event is just one of the events supported by the menu item. All controls, and the form itself, expose other events. For a complete guide to the use of each of these events, see the Visual Studio .NET documentation.

When you work with an IDE, the actual mechanics of how events are connected to event handlers is often hidden from you. But sometimes you might need to explicitly wire events to their corresponding handlers. In a .NET Windows Forms application, you can think of an event as an action that you can code against. A user might trigger this action by moving a mouse, or code within your application or the system itself might invoke the action. The code that handles the event is the *event handler*.

As discussed in Chapter 3, a *delegate* performs the binding between an event and an event handler. Event handler methods are *added* to the delegate. When an event fires, the runtime will execute the delegate and cause all the associated event handlers to run. If you're using an IDE such as Visual Studio .NET, the binding of an event method to a delegate will occur automatically, but you can also write code to do it manually. This technique is useful if you want to exploit the event model in your own applications, but without using GUI components. The following code fragment, which is part of the *InitializeComponent* method in the Editor application, shows how Visual Studio .NET uses a delegate to bind the *Click* event of the *exitMenuItem* control to the *exitMenuItem_Click* method. The type of delegate used is *System.EventHandler*:

```
this.exitMenuItem.add_Click
(new System.EventHandler(this.exitMenuItemClick));
```

The menu item control inherits the method *add_Click* from its ancestor class, *Control.* For each type of event that a control or .NET class exposes, there is a corresponding *add_XXX* subscriber method and a corresponding *remove_XXX* unsubscriber method. The *add_Click* method accepts a single parameter, which is an instance of *System.EventHandler* that refers to the method to be executed when the delegate is invoked. (See Chapter 3 for more details about how events are raised.)

Note In .NET, delegates support *multicasting*, in which multiple event handlers can be associated with a single delegate. For example, the following code fragment shows how to bind three event handlers to a button that fires when the button is resized:

```
this.button1.add_Resize(new
    System.EventHandler(this.firstB1_Resize());
this.button1.add_Resize(new
    System.EventHandler(this.secondB1_Resize());
this.button1.add_Resize(new
    System.EventHandler(this.thirdB1_Resize());
```

In the Editor application, the purpose of the *exitMenuItemClick* event handler method is to quit the application. You can implement this in three main ways. The first approach is to use the *Application.Exit* method, but this is rather draconian—it terminates the form without giving it a chance to perform any tidying up or without saving any unsaved data. (*System.exit* is the equivalent method in the JDK, and it has much the same effect.) A better solution is to use the *Close* method of the *Form* class. This method raises the *Form.Closing* and *Form.Closed* events, which can be intercepted by event handlers attached to the form and can be used to save any data or even give the user the option of vetoing the close operation. (The *Form.Closing* method can set a flag that prevents the form from terminating.)

The *Exit* event handler method should appear as follows:

```
private void exitMenuItem_Click (System.Object sender, System.EventArgs e)
{
    this.Close();
}
```

Tip If you want to simply hide a form rather than dispose of it, you can call the form's *Hide* method (which is inherited from *Control*). This method makes the form invisible but allows you to redisplay it later by calling its *Show* method. Note also that the *Hide* method, unlike the *Close* method, does not release the resources associated with the form.

Using File Dialog Boxes

The next task in creating the Editor application is to provide the code that allows a user to open and save files. Unlike Swing and the AWT, .NET provides dedicated file dialog boxes for both Save and Open operations. Figure 4-9 shows an example of the Open File dialog box. The user can navigate to a folder, select a file (or type in a name), and click OK. Clicking Cancel aborts the operation:

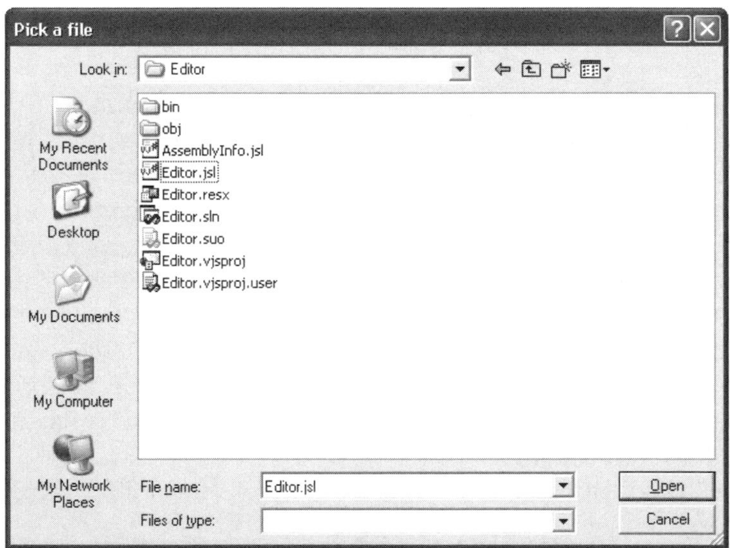

Figure 4-9 The Open File dialog box

Inheriting File Dialog Box Functionality

Both of the classes that represent the dialog boxes for Open and Save operations inherit from the *System.Windows.Forms.FileDialog* class. This is an abstract class that defines the common functionality of the Open and Save file dialog boxes. It defines just these two classes' functionality. You cannot directly inherit from the *FileDialog* class. If you want to create your own custom file dialog box, you must either inherit from the *FileDialog* class's parent class, *CommonDialog*, or from *SaveFileDialog* or *OpenFileDialog*. Figure 4-10 shows the class hierarchy of the most commonly used .NET Framework dialog boxes.

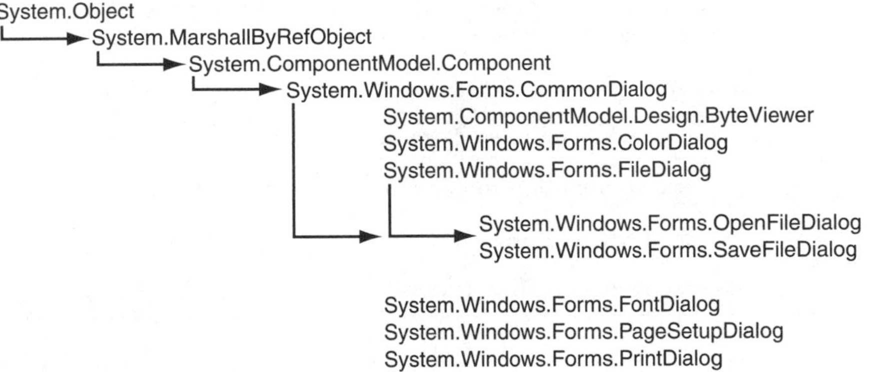

Figure 4-10 The *FileDialog* class hierarchy

To display a file dialog box, you call its *ShowDialog* method. There are two overloaded versions of this method. The first accepts no parameters, and the second accepts a single parameter that indicates the dialog box's parent form. If you pass the *ShowDialog* method a reference to a form, the dialog box will be modal; if you do not, it will be modeless.

Note A modal dialog box is one that blocks the application until the user closes it. A modeless dialog box allows other forms in the same application to receive the focus.

You'll also notice that the *ShowDialog* method returns a member of the *DialogResult* enumeration, which indicates which button the user clicked to close the dialog box. In our sample application, the code tests to determine whether the value returned is equal to *OK*. The *ShowDialog* method returns the *OK* value when the user makes a positive choice—for example, by clicking the OK button or double-clicking on a file. The values from this enumeration are used as the return values not just from the file dialog boxes but by other dialog boxes throughout the .NET Framework Class Library.

Table 4-5 describes the members of the enumeration.

Table 4-5 The *DialogResult* Enumeration Members

Value	Description
OK	Returned when the user clicks OK or double-clicks a file
Abort	Returned when the user clicks Abort
Cancel	Returned when the user clicks Cancel or when the user closes a dialog box without making a choice
Ignore	Returned when the user clicks Ignore
No	Returned when the user clicks No
None	The dialog box is still running (modeless), so nothing is returned
Retry	Returned when the user clicks Retry
Yes	Returned when the user clicks Yes

The following code shows the Open menu item event handler. You should add this method to the Editor form and connect it to the *Click* event of the Open menu item; in the Design View window, select the File menu item, click the Open menu item, and then use the Properties window to set the *Click* event of the Open menu item to the *openMenuItemClick* method. The code for the *openMenuItemClick* is shown here—type it in:

```
private void openMenuItemClick (System.Object sender, System.EventArgs e)
{
    String theText = "";

    // Opens a file that a user selects
    OpenFileDialog ofd = new OpenFileDialog();
    ofd.set_Title("Pick a file");

    // Pass owner to ensure that it is modal
    DialogResult dr = ofd.ShowDialog(this);
    if (dr == dr.OK)
```

```
    {
        String theFile=ofd.get_FileName();
        try
        {
            StreamReader sr = new StreamReader(theFile);
            theText = sr.ReadToEnd();
            textEditor.set_Text(theText);
        }
        catch (System.Exception ioe)
        {
            MessageBox.Show(this,ioe.get_Message());
        }
    }
}
```

In the .NET Framework Class Library, as in Swing, the file dialog classes provide the functionality that allows the user to select a file, but they do not actually read or write to the file that has been selected. You must write the code to do this. You could use the objects in the java.io package of the JDK to read or write a file, but because the purpose of this chapter is to show you how to develop Windows Forms applications, the preceding *openMenuItemClick* method uses classes from .NET Framework Class Library to perform the I/O. As you can see, the I/O elements of the method use a *StreamReader* in much the same way that you'd use a Java *FileReader*. To use the *StreamReader* class (and all of the other .NET-related I/O classes), you must import the System.*IO* package at the start of the file:

```
import System.IO.*;
```

You can read data from a text input stream a line at a time using the *Read* method of the *StreamReader* class, but an alternative is to use the *ReadToEnd* method, which reads the entire contents of the file, including any carriage return characters. This is the approach taken by the *openMenuItemClick* method.

Like the event handler for the Open menu item, the event handler for the Save menu item uses .NET classes for both the dialog box and I/O. The following code shows the completed method; it also illustrates that the *SaveFileDialog* object is instantiated and used in the same way as the *OpenFileDialog* object. You should add this method to the Editor form and attach it to the *Click* event of the Save menu item. (You can select an existing method when you define an event handler as well as create a new one—in this way, it is possible for two handlers to refer to the same method and execute the same code.)

```
private void saveMenuItemClick (System.Object sender, System.EventArgs e)
{
    // the save file method
    String theFile = null;
    StreamWriter sw = null;
```

```
        // get the file name to save as
        SaveFileDialog sfd = new SaveFileDialog();
        DialogResult dr = sfd.ShowDialog(this);
        if (dr==dr.OK)
        {
            theFile=sfd.get_FileName();
            try
            {
                sw = new StreamWriter(theFile);
                sw.Write(textEditor.get_Text());
            }
            catch (System.Exception ioe)
            {
                MessageBox.Show(this, ioe.get_Message());
            }
            finally
            {
                try
                {
                    sw.Flush();
                    sw.Close();
                }
                catch (System.Exception ex)
                {
                    MessageBox.Show(ex.get_Message());
                }
            }
        }
    }
```

You might notice in both of the event handlers described in this section that a *MessageBox* is displayed when an exception is caught. We've included this because it is a really useful class that has similar functionality to the Swing *JOptionPane* class—that is, it displays simple dialog-type boxes. The code in these examples calls the static *Show* method to display a message box. In both fragments, the code passes two parameters: a form to ensure that the box is modal, and a message. However, the *Show* method has 12 overloads, allowing you to specify parameters that indicate objects such as captions, buttons, icons, and default buttons. For a full guide to these overloads, see the Visual Studio .NET documentation.

Working with the System Clipboard

Working with the system clipboard is straightforward, and the code is almost identical to using the system clipboard with the *JTextArea* class in Swing. The

.NET *TextBox* class inherits three system clipboard manipulation methods from its parent class, *TextBoxBase*: these are *cut*, *copy*, and *paste*. Implementing the event handler methods for the Cut, Copy, and Paste menu items is straightforward, as shown in the following code. These methods should be added to the Editor form and the methods attached to the *Click* event handlers of the appropriate menu items:

```
private void copyMenuItemClick (System.Object sender, System.EventArgs e)
{
    textEditor.Copy();
}

private void pasteMenuItemClick (System.Object sender, System.EventArgs e)
{
    textEditor.Paste();
}

private void cutMenuItemClick (System.Object sender, System.EventArgs e)
{
    textEditor.Cut();
}
```

This is all the code that most applications will need to interact with the clipboard. However, you can also access the clipboard through the *System.Windows.Forms.Clipboard* class, which gives you much greater control. The *Clipboard* class has only two members, both of which are static methods: *GetDataObject* to retrieve from the clipboard, and *SetDataObject* to place items on the clipboard. The *SetDataObject* method has two overloads: You can either pass it an object or you can pass it an object and a Boolean flag to indicate whether the data should remain on the clipboard after the application exits. (Pass the value *true* to indicate this.) As the generic names of the methods suggest, you can copy and retrieve objects of different types to the clipboard.

In much the same that as you work with data flavors in the AWT, you can test the data types held on the clipboard within .NET. The following code fragment shows a modified Paste menu item event handler that tests whether the data on the clipboard is of the type *Text*:

```
private void pasteMenuItemClick (System.Object sender, System.EventArgs e)
{
    String theText="";
    DataObject dobj = (DataObject)Clipboard.GetDataObject();
    if (dobj.GetDataPresent(DataFormats.Text))
    {
        theText = (System.String)dobj.GetData(DataFormats.Text);
        textEditor.set_SelectedText(theText);
```

```
    }
}
```

This event handler obtains the data from the clipboard by calling the *GetDataObject* method. The returned type is an object that implements the *IDataObject* interface. The object is cast to the *DataObject* type, which is the generic class used for storing data on the clipboard (all objects stored on the clipboard must descend from the *DataObject* class), and implements the *IDataObject* interface. The interface defines four methods, as listed in Table 4-6.

Table 4-6 Methods of the *IDataObject* Interface

Method	Description
GetDataPresent	Checks whether data held on the clipboard is of a given data format or can be converted to a given format. You should specify one of the formats from the *DataFormat* enumeration.
GetData	Retrieves data of a given data format. You should cast the return value appropriately.
GetFormats	Returns a list of all the data formats associated with the stored data. The stored data can be safely converted to any of the formats returned.
SetData	Stores data of a specified data format in the current instance.

In the preceding code fragment, if the data is of the type specified (*Text*), it is assigned to the local variable *theText*, and the data is then inserted into the text of the *TextBox* using the *Textbox* class's *set_SelectedText* method. Note that the code casts *Text* format data to a *System.String* because an unqualified *String* would be a *java.lang.String*, which would trip an invalid cast exception. In our example, the code specifically tests for a data type of *Text*; however, the *DataFormats* class defines a large number of other data types, including *Bitmap*, *HTML*, *RTF*, *Serializable*, and *WaveAudio*. For a complete list of supported formats, see the Visual Studio .NET documentation.

Building and Running the Application

To compile the application, choose Build Solution from the Build menu. Any syntax errors will be displayed in the Output window. Once you have successfully compiled the application, you can run it from within Visual Studio .NET by choosing Start or Start Without Debugging from the Debug menu. Alternatively, you can run the program from the command line by navigating to the bin\Debug folder under the project folder and executing Editor.exe. Figure 4-11 shows the application running. (The form has been expanded slightly.)

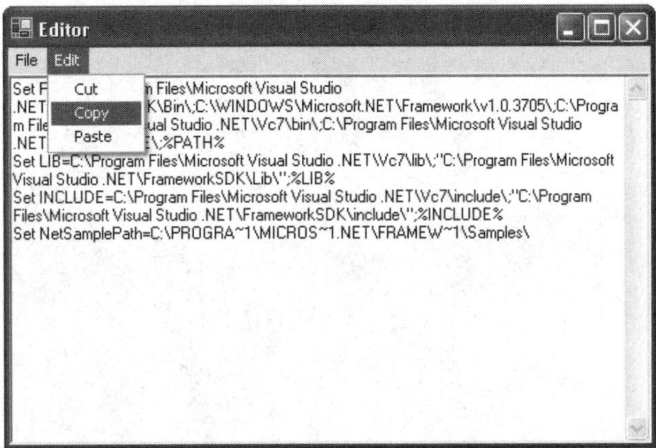

Figure 4-11 The .NET Editor application running

A completed version of the Editor application is available in the Editor folder among the book's sample files.

Summary

This chapter provided a brief overview of Java GUI development. It explained why you might want to port an existing AWT application to .NET and how to do it using Visual Studio .NET. Finally, this chapter introduced Windows Forms, a library that allows you to build GUI applications for deployment on .NET platforms.

Part II

Managing and Manipulating Data

5

Processing XML

XML is one of the key technologies underpinning the Microsoft .NET Framework. In fact, XML is a significant feature in almost all recent environments and frameworks, including later versions of Java 2 Enterprise Edition (J2EE). Due to its flexibility, XML is applied in many ways and at many levels. At higher levels, business data can be represented in an XML format, as can business concepts such as workflows between organizations. At lower levels, XML can be used as a convenient format for application configuration information and component metadata. Also, XML provides the packaging and structure that make Web services possible. It's no surprise, then, that the processing and manipulation of XML is well supported within the .NET Framework.

As an application developer, you'll encounter XML in many places. Components used by your application might generate XML documents that your application will then need to process and from which you will need to extract information. Conversely, your applications and components might themselves generate data in XML format to exchange it with other systems or store it.

The type of processing required and the source (or destination) of the XML to be processed will vary based on the context of your application. To help you address these scenarios, you need a set of tools and libraries that provide different ways to manipulate XML. The .NET Framework and Microsoft Visual Studio .NET provide such tools and libraries. These include GUI tools for designing and manipulating XML, XML parsers and processors, and APIs that let you create, access, and manipulate data in XML format. You can choose from a range of facilities, ranging from low-level manipulation of XML documents to transformation of XML data using a stylesheet to sophisticated binding between XML and ADO.NET *DataSet* objects. These tools allow you to apply the right level of functionality to address your requirements.

This chapter will examine the XML support available to J# developers through Visual Studio .NET and the .NET Framework. It will look at how you can use XML as a convenient format for platform-independent and cross-language documents and how applications can produce and consume valid XML. It will also examine the relationship between XML and relational data as typically stored in databases.

Note The transformation of XML documents using XML Stylesheet Language for Transformations (XSLT) and the navigation of XML documents using XPath syntax is described in Chapter 6.

Using XML in a .NET Application

If you're working in an environment that consists entirely of platforms that support the .NET Framework, you might wonder why you need XML. You can use the facilities of ADO.NET to manipulate and transport your data, so why bother converting to and from a text format? The answer lies largely in the ubiquity of XML; XML has become the universal data representation of modern distributed applications. This representation allows data to be passed relatively easily between different platforms, different vendors, new and old applications, and so forth. The generic integration provided by Web services relies on XML to deliver interoperability. Almost all applications now have some ability to import and export XML, regardless of their background. Because of its ubiquity, XML forms an important part of the world that your applications will occupy.

XML as a Data Format

XML documents consist of data and tags that provide meaning and context for that data. XML is a text format rather than a binary one. If you need to, you can read and write XML using an ordinary text editor, such as Notepad. An XML document consists of tags, which are delimited by less-than (<) and greater-than (>) characters, and text content.

The following is a simple XML document that describes a catalog of cakes:

```
<?xml version="1.0" encoding="utf-8" ?>
<CakeCatalog xmlns="http://www.fourthcoffee.com/CakeCatalog.xsd">
   <CakeType style="Celebration" filling="sponge" shape="square">
      <Message>Congratulations</Message>
      <Description>General achievement</Description>
```

```
      <Sizes>
        <Option sizeInInches="10" />
        <Option sizeInInches="12" />
      </Sizes>
    </CakeType>
    <CakeType style="Celebration" filling="fruit" shape="round">
      <Message>Hi!</Message>
      <Description>Quite casual</Description>
      <Sizes>
        <Option sizeInInches="12" />
        <Option sizeInInches="18" />
      </Sizes>
    </CakeType>
    <CakeType style="Christmas" filling="fruit" shape="square">
      <Message>Season's Greetings</Message>
      <Description>Traditional, spiced Christmas cake</Description>
      <Sizes>
        <Option sizeInInches="15" />
        <Option sizeInInches="18" />
        <Option sizeInInches="20" />
      </Sizes>
    </CakeType>
    <CakeType style="Celebration" filling="sponge" shape="hexagonal">
      <Message>Happy Birthday</Message>
      <Description>An excellent cake.</Description>
      <Sizes>
        <Option sizeInInches="15" />
      </Sizes>
    </CakeType>
</CakeCatalog>
```

Within this document, you can see some common aspects of XML:

- An XML document is made up of a series of XML elements. An element consists of a start tag (*<CakeType>*, for example), an end tag (*</CakeType>*, for example), and possibly some content. This content can be a combination of text and other elements.
- Each *CakeType* element has three attributes. Attributes are name/value pairs that provide metadata relating to the text content of an element. An example of an attribute is *filling="fruit"*. In some cases, there might be no text content at all—simply the attribute values that are used to contain all of the relevant data. Be careful not to confuse XML attributes with the .NET attributes you've already encountered—they are completely unrelated.

- An XML document has a defined structure. It starts with an XML declaration, *<?xml ... ?>*, that states the version and encoding of the document. Most XML documents are encoded in some form of Unicode, such as UTF-8. The document then has a single *root* element. The root element contains all the other elements and content, except for the XML declaration and a few other document-level tags. The structure of a document is governed by simple rules, such as the requirement that elements be correctly nested and not overlap. There are also some encoding rules that govern the validity of names that can be used in an XML document. If an XML document conforms to these basic rules as defined in the XML standard, it is said to be *well formed.*

- Parts of a document can be associated with different XML namespaces. A namespace provides a way of differentiating tags defined by different organizations or for different purposes (similar to packages or namespaces in Java and the .NET Framework). A namespace can be applied to all elements in a document or associated with a particular prefix. The namespace attribute (*xmlns= "http://www.fourthcoffee.com/CakeCatalog.xsd")* defined on the *CakeCatalog* element shown in the example document indicates that the default namespace for the document is *http://www.fourthcoffee.com/CakeCatalog.xsd*. This default namespace is associated with all elements and attributes in the document. You can alter this definition to indicate that only elements and attributes annotated with a particular prefix are associated with that namespace. To use a prefix, you can alter the namespace attribute to *xmlns:cakes="http://www.fourthcoffee.com/CakeCatalog.xsd"* so this namespace is associated only with the *cakes* prefix. You can then annotate particular elements and attributes with that prefix so that, for example, the *CakeType* element is changed to *cakes:CakeType*. You can define and use multiple namespace prefixes in a document. The document author can also combine elements and attributes that use namespace prefixes with a default namespace. In this case, any elements and attributes that do not have a prefix are associated with the default namespace.

You can define the expected structure of an XML document using one of two mechanisms. The XML specification itself defines a structure definition syntax known as Document Type Definition (DTD). As you'll see later, DTDs have some drawbacks, so they have been superseded by a newer standard for document structure definition called XML Schema. An XML document can be checked against an associated DTD or XML schema—this check is called *validation*. If the document conforms to the DTD or XML schema, it is said to be valid.

One thing that is not shown in our sample XML document is an *entity*. Entities are among the more obscure parts of the XML standard. An entity shows up in an XML document as a placeholder, and at some point during the processing of the XML document, a value is typically inserted into the placeholder. Entities can be either internal or external. The value for an internal entity is defined as part of the DTD or schema. The value for an external entity is obtained from an external source, such as a URL. The act of retrieving the value of an external entity is called *resolving* the entity. We will not cover entities in great detail in this chapter, but you'll learn more about them at certain points, when they're relevant.

Because XML is a text-based format, it has certain disadvantages over native data formats, such as

- It is comparatively bulky.
- Data generally needs to be converted back and forth between XML and an internal or native format, which adds processing overhead.

However, XML also has advantages:

- XML is independent of any platform or vendor.
- A text format is comparatively easy to process in almost all programming languages.
- The flexibility of XML means that almost any type of data can be described.
- Because XML it is text-based, there is little danger that XML documents will become obsolete and unreadable in the way that some proprietary binary formats have over the years.

Roles for XML

XML can perform various roles within an enterprise application:

- XML can be used to encode data and documents that need to be exchanged between business partners. Earlier initiatives in this area, such as Electronic Data Interchange (EDI), used a fairly specialized, binary format that was comparatively difficult to process and usually required specific software. However, many XML processors are available, some of them free.

- All but the simplest applications need to access and store configuration information. This has traditionally taken the form of INI files and various proprietary formats, either text or binary. XML provides a flexible way of storing such information that is easy to read and maintain.
- XML can be used for the long-term persistence of data—within an XML-aware database or as standalone files.
- Because XML is machine-readable while still being very flexible, it can be used to encode information at different levels in the application architecture, including middleware and support services. The best example of this is the use of XML in SOAP and other Web service technologies to describe the data being transported and the services being offered.

What Applications Need from XML Support

As you've seen, XML is a flexible, text-based format. However, you still need facilities that make it easy to manipulate and apply XML:

- You need high-level abstractions—this means no low-level string parsing and a reduction in the amount of work involved in marshaling XML into and out of memory.
- You need simple ways to validate the format of the XML documents. Data might arrive from a variety of sources, so one of the first requirements is to ensure that it has the correct structure—that is, you need to know whether the document is both well formed and valid.
- It must be easy to read XML from many sources, such as files, URLs, streams, and so forth.
- XML might need to be processed in different ways. When you handle large documents, it is far more convenient to be able to process the data as a stream than having to load the whole document into memory. In contrast, some applications move back and forth (or up and down) through the data, adding, changing, and removing as they go. This implies that the document must be held in memory. Both of these processing styles must be accommodated.

Regarding the last point, you'll see throughout this chapter that two distinct techniques are used for manipulating XML data. Stream-based processing reads the data through once, presenting the data as soon as it arrives and discarding it once it has been read. This type of processing is ideal when you're dealing with large amounts of data or data with little context, and it's ideal for filtering or when no manipulation of the data is needed. The use of a stream results in comparatively fast processing and a comparatively small memory footprint. However, one problem with stream-based processing relates to context sensitivity. If the meaning of tags and text in your document is dependent on the context in which you find them, you might have to keep a track of the current context when you use stream-based processing. This can mean using many Boolean flags or building complex state models.

The alternative mechanism, in-memory processing of XML documents, tends to be slower and more memory intensive, but you have completely random access to the document and you can add, remove, or change parts of it as you see fit. In-memory processing does not have the same context issues that are inherent in the stream-based processing model. Because you can revisit any piece of the document, you can work out the context of any part when you need it rather than having to cache the current context.

Processing XML Data

Given data in an XML format, what might you do with it? There are certain tasks you will often perform when manipulating XML. These include

- Accessing the data and metadata in an XML document using low-level APIs. You might also need to generate your own XML documents programmatically at the same low level. APIs such as the Document Object Model (DOM) and the Simple API for XML (SAX) provide this level of processing. (The use of APIs is covered later in this chapter.)
- Importing or exporting XML data to or from relational databases. In this case, you might need to interact with ADO.NET *DataSet* objects to exchange such data with a relational database. (More about this later in the chapter.)
- Using XML as a convenient, in-memory data format, especially in a Web browser. As such, you'll often find that XML is bound to visual user interface components to provide information for the user. (See Chapter 16.)
- Converting XML from one format to another—for example, when data is exchanged with a business partner. You can achieve this by applying XSLT (which is covered in Chapter 6).

Support for XML in Visual J# and the .NET Framework

Visual J# and the .NET Framework provide a great deal of support for the generation, consumption, and manipulation of XML when you develop applications.

Standards and Mechanisms Supported by the .NET Framework

As mentioned previously, there are two primary approaches to processing XML programmatically. The first is to perform forward-only, noncached parsing. This approach is well supported by classes in the .NET Framework. Although there is no official standard for this style of processing, it is commonly used when processing XML. (SAX provides a similar mechanism, but with a different philosophy, and it is in itself not a standard.) The second approach is to use in-memory manipulation through the DOM model. DOM is a standard defined by the World Wide Web Consortium (W3C) and is fully supported by classes in the .NET Framework.

The .NET Framework supports XML standards for document structure, namespaces, XSLT, and XPath. Other applicable XML-related standards might be supported in the future as they are formalized under the W3C.

Classes in the .NET Framework

The .NET classes for XML manipulation are split across several namespaces in the .NET Framework Class Library. These namespaces are

- *System.Xml*, which contains the core classes for XML document manipulation and validation. This namespace also provides classes that support integration with ADO.NET *DataSet* objects.
- *System.Xml.Schema*, which holds classes for the manipulation of XML schemas and support classes for performing validation.
- *System.Xml.Serialization*, which defines classes for converting objects into an XML representation for storage or streaming.
- *System.Xml.XPath*, which contains classes that support the navigation of XML documents in a flexible way based on XPath expressions.
- *System.Xml.Xsl*, which comprises classes that support the transformation of XML documents using XSLT stylesheets.

In this chapter, we'll focus primarily on the document manipulation and validation capabilities provided by the classes in the *System.Xml* and *System.Xml.Schema* namespaces. Chapter 6 covers the transformational and navigational capabilities supported by the classes in *System.Xml.Xsl* and

System.Xml.XPath. The serialization capabilities provided by the classes under *System.Xml.Serialization* are discussed in Chapter 10.

Manipulating XML Files in Visual J#

If your application uses XML, you might need to edit XML documents, define XML schemas, and so on. Naturally, you are free to do this manually (in Notepad) or in a specific XML-oriented tool. However, you can perform most XML-related tasks without leaving the Visual Studio .NET environment. You can add any relevant XML files or schemas to your Visual Studio .NET project by importing existing files or by creating new ones, as shown in Figure 5-1.

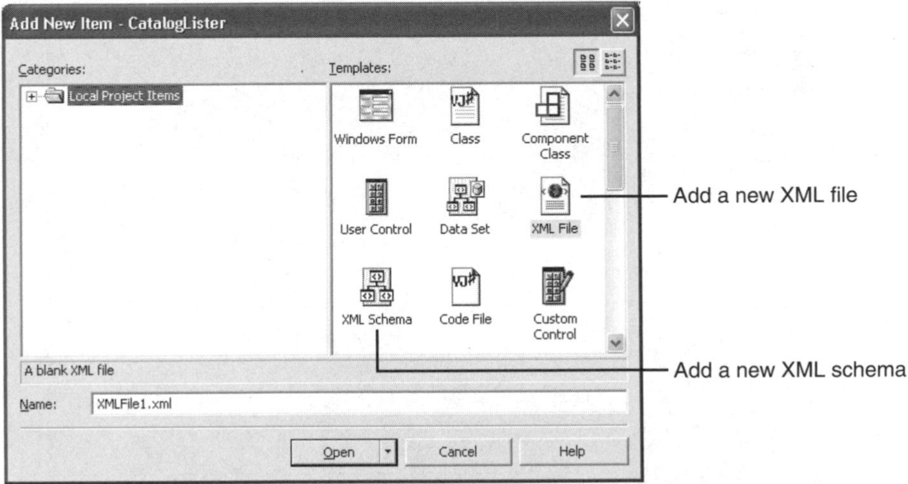

Figure 5-1 XML File and XML Schema options in the Add New Item dialog box

You can edit an XML document or schema in Visual Studio .NET using the XML Designer. The XML Designer allows you to view and edit an XML file in two ways. You can manipulate the raw XML as shown in Figure 5-2, or you can work with a structured data grid form of the data, as shown in Figure 5-3. You can easily switch between the views by choosing the appropriate command from the View menu. The XML Designer ensures that the two views are kept synchronized—any changes, additions, or deletions made in one view will be reflected in the other.

Note Data view in the XML Designer can show only regular, structured data, such as the results of a database query or a business document such as a purchase order. Other XML documents that use irregular tagging, such as marked-up text produced by an XML-based word processor, will not display correctly in Data view.

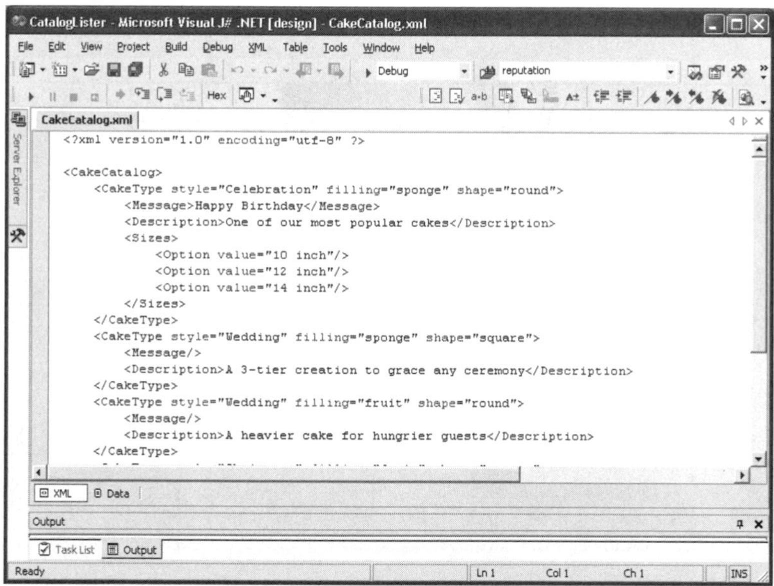

Figure 5-2 Working with raw XML in Visual Studio .NET

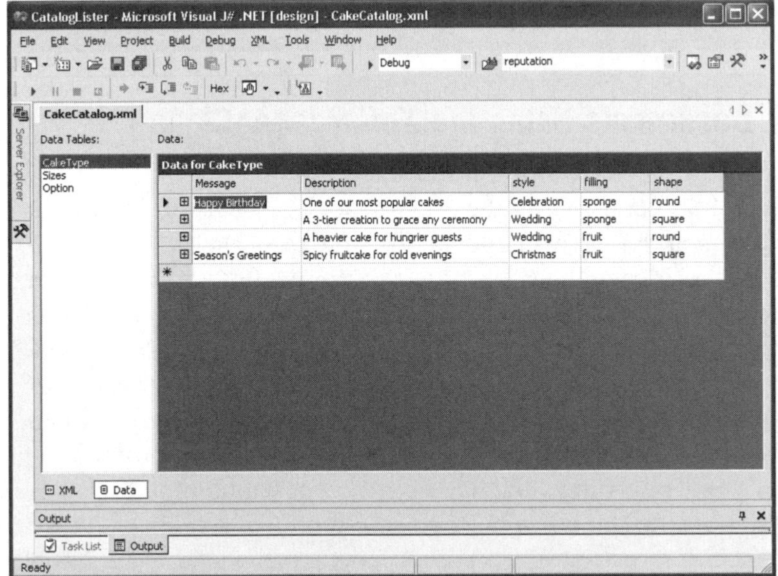

Figure 5-3 Working with XML in a data grid in Visual Studio .NET

The XML Designer also lets you create and manipulate XML schema documents (XSD files). Because XML schemas are themselves XML documents, the XML Designer again provides two views of the document. You can view the XML schema as raw XML or in a graphical view that shows the relationships between the different types of data in the document. (If you're familiar with databases, this will look very similar to the representation of a database schema.) You can create a schema from an existing XML document, import a preexisting schema, or create your own schema from scratch. You can then associate the XML file with a schema within the project through the XML document's properties. Once the file has a schema associated with it, it can be validated within Visual Studio .NET.

For more information about the XML Designer, see the Visual Studio .NET documentation.

Single-Pass Processing of XML Documents

As mentioned previously, it is often convenient to process an XML document in a single pass without retaining the document in memory. This is true both when you're reading a document from an external source and when you're creating a document to be transmitted to an external destination. The .NET Framework provides XML readers and XML writers for reading and creating XML documents in a serial fashion.

Parsing XML Documents Using the *XMLReader* Class

Historically, forward-only, noncached parsing of XML has been performed using the SAX API. Under the SAX model, you register a callback interface that acts as a sink for events generated by the SAX parser. The parser will generate an event as it encounters each part of the document, such as a start tag, some text content, or an end tag. In effect, the parser pushes the information from the document at your callback handler, so SAX is termed a *push* model. The parser will inform you of every part of the document it discovers—elements, text, white space, and so forth—even if you're not interested in them. You cannot unregister a particular type of information event; you must simply ignore those calls by not providing any code in the event handler method. This has obvious implications for the efficiency and speed of processing.

The forward-only, noncached parsing provided by the .NET Framework is similar in concept to SAX processing, with one important difference. In the equivalent .NET model, data is *pulled* from the parser on request. This means that the application never sees data in which it has no interest. As you'll see, it is possible to skip unwanted data and to process only elements with specific names.

The central class for forward-only, noncached processing in the .NET Framework is *System.Xml.XmlReader*. *XmlReader* is an abstract class that defines the properties and methods required to process an XML document under the pull model. As such, you can use it polymorphically to process XML documents from different sources. Because *XMLReader* is an abstract class, you must pick a concrete subclass to use the features defined. Three concrete subclasses of *XmlReader* are provided in the *System.Xml* namespace:

- *XmlTextReader*, which is the fastest form of *XmlReader*. *XmlTextReader* ensures that the document is well-formed, but it does not validate the document being processed, nor does it resolve entities (either internal or external) except to ensure their well-formedness. If no validation or entity resolution is required, this is usually the best choice.

- *XmlValidatingReader*, which adds a validation layer on top of an *XmlTextReader*. It can validate the document against a DTD or a schema, depending on the properties set.
- *XmlNodeReader*, which provides forward-only processing over an *XmlNode* that forms part of a DOM tree. The *XmlNodeReader* does not implement any validation of the document being processed. (The *XmlNode* class is discussed later in the chapter.)

All of these subclasses ensure the well-formedness of the document being processed. Each one will be described later in the chapter.

Processing XML Using an *XMLTextReader* Instance

The *XmlTextReader* provides fast and simple access to an XML document. The constructor specifies the source of the XML document to be processed. Many alternatives are available because the constructor is highly overloaded, but you can obtain the XML document from one of three sources:

- A file or other form of URL (such as the URL of an ASP.NET application that generates XML). If a single *String* is passed to the constructor, it is presumed to contain a URL.
- A *System.IO.Stream* that is passed in as one of the constructor parameters
- A *System.IO.TextReader* that is passed in as one of the constructor parameters

The XML Document

To start looking at how you can use an *XmlTextReader* to process an XML file, consider the sample file CakeCatalog.xml. (Yes, we're heading toward an online cake store.)

CakeCatalog.xml

```
<CakeCatalog>
  <CakeType style="Celebration" filling="sponge" shape="round">
    <Message>Happy Birthday</Message>
    <Description>One of our most popular cakes</Description>
    <Sizes>
      <Option value="10 inch"/>
      <Option value="12 inch"/>
      <Option value="14 inch"/>
    </Sizes>
```

```
    </CakeType>
    <CakeType style="Wedding" filling="sponge" shape="square">
        <Message/>
        <Description>A 3-tier creation to grace any ceremony</Description>
    </CakeType>
    <CakeType style="Wedding" filling="fruit" shape="round">
        <Message/>
        <Description>A heavier cake for hungrier guests</Description>
    </CakeType>
    <CakeType style="Christmas" filling="fruit" shape="square">
        <Message>Season's Greetings</Message>
        <Description>Spicy fruitcake for cold evenings</Description>
        <Sizes>
            <Option value="12 inch"/>
            <Option value="14 inch"/>
        </Sizes>
    </CakeType>
</CakeCatalog>
```

As you can see, there are different *CakeType* elements, each defined with attributes representing the style, filling, and shape of the cake. Within each *CakeType* element is more information about the message displayed on the cake, a description of the cake, and any size options. As a first pass, let's examine how to get hold of the *CakeType* elements and list out their attributes.

Finding and Processing Elements and Attributes

Before you can process the document, you must create an *XmlReader* based on it:

```
XmlReader reader = new XmlTextReader(args[0]);
```

Warning You might expect this line to generate an exception if the specified file does not exist or does not contain well-formed XML. However, the source file (or stream) and its contents are checked only on the first call to read content from the XML document.

Using an *XmlReader*, you can read nodes in sequence from the XML document. The *XmlReader* class exposes properties containing information about the current node, such as its name and value. If the current node is an element that has attributes or contains other XML or text, you can make calls to retrieve its attributes or contents. You can move the *XmlReader* on to the next node in the document by calling the *Read* method:

```
reader.Read()
```

The *Read* method returns a Boolean value indicating whether the operation was successful (*true*) or not (*false*). Initially, the *XmlReader* does not point to any node in the document. After the first call to *Read*, the *XmlReader* will refer to the first node in the document, which is typically the XML declaration. After each subsequent call to *Read*, the *XmlReader* will point to the next node in the document. When the current node changes, the exposed properties of the *XmlReader* will also change to reflect those of the current node. Remember, you cannot go back so you must ensure that you've obtained all the information you need from a node before proceeding further.

When the *XmlReader* encounters the end of the document, a call to *Read* will return *false*. The following code fragment shows how you can list out the nodes in a document and display certain information about them such as their type, local name, namespace, and their attribute and content information:

```
while (reader.Read())
{
   Console.WriteLine("---START NODE---");
   Console.WriteLine("Node type: " + reader.get_NodeType());
   Console.WriteLine("Name: " + reader.get_LocalName());
   Console.WriteLine("Namespace: " + reader.get_NamespaceURI());
   if (reader.get_HasAttributes())
   {
      Console.WriteLine("Has attributes: yes");
      Console.WriteLine("Num attributes: " +
         reader.get_AttributeCount());
   }
   else
   {
      Console.WriteLine("Has attributes: no");
   }
   if (reader.get_HasValue())
   {
      Console.WriteLine("Has value: yes");
      // Surround value with asterisks to delimit whitespace
      Console.WriteLine("Value: ***" + reader.get_Value() + "***");
   }
   else
   {
      Console.WriteLine("Has value: no");
   }
   Console.WriteLine("----END NODE----");
}
```

The output produced by processing the CakeCatalog.xml document using the code shown above looks like this:

```
---START NODE---
Node type: XmlDeclaration
Name: xml
Namespace:
Has attributes: yes
Num attributes: 2
Has value: yes
Value: ***version="1.0" encoding="utf-8"***
----END NODE----
---START NODE ---
Node type: Whitespace
Name:
Namespace:
Has attributes: no
Has value: yes
Value: ***

***
----END NODE ----
---START NODE ---
Node type: Element
Name: CakeCatalog
Namespace:
Has attributes: no
Has value: no
----END NODE ----
---START NODE ---
Node type: Whitespace
Name:
Namespace:
Has attributes: no
Has value: yes
Value: ***
   ***
----END NODE ----
---START NODE ---
Node type: Element
Name: CakeType
Namespace:
Has attributes: yes
Num attributes: 3
Has value: no
----END NODE ----
⋮
```

Note When performing read operations, the *XmlReader* does not consider the attributes of an element to be nodes in their own right. If you were to process the CakeCatalog.xml document using the code shown above, it would list out nodes of type *Element*, *EndElement*, *XmlDeclaration*, *Whitespace*, and *Text*. Attributes would not be listed. If you need to treat an attribute as a node, use the *MoveToAttribute* method to point the *XmlReader* at the given attribute.

You'll find the code to perform this simple listing of the CakeCatalog.xml file in the SimpleXmlReaderCatalogLister.jsl file in the SimpleXmlReaderCatalogLister sample project. This program takes the name of the XML document as a command-line parameter, creates an *XmlTextReader* for it, and performs the *while* loop shown previously to print out all of the nodes in the document.

If you were processing CakeCatalog.xml in an application, you would want to extract the *CakeType* elements and examine their attributes and contents. You'll find the code for extracting the different *CakeType* elements from CakeCatalog.xml in the XmlReaderCatalogLister.jsl sample file. This program takes the name of the XML document as a command-line parameter, creates an *XmlTextReader* for it, and calls the *listCakes* method. This method tests the type of each node encountered, ignoring any nonelements such as text or white space. To determine whether the current node is an element, the method retrieves the value of the *XmlReader* constructor's *NodeType* property and compares it to *XmlNodeType.Element*. Note that *XmlNodeType* is a .NET enumeration that contains values for each different type of node, so it has to be cast to a Java *int* to be used in a *switch-case* statement:

```
switch ((int)reader.get_NodeType())
{
   ⋮
}
```

The name of the current element can then be checked to see whether it is *CakeType*. If so, the attributes can be retrieved and output:

```
if (reader.get_Name().CompareTo("CakeType") == 0)
{
   ⋮
}
```

The name returned by *get_Name* is the qualified name of the element. As you saw earlier, you can retrieve the local name and namespace separately using *get_LocalName* and *get_NamespaceURI*.

The attribute information is extracted using the *GetAttribute* method. This is an overloaded method that allows you to access attributes by name or by index. Accessing attribute values does not change the current node.

The results of processing CakeCatalog.xml are shown here:

```
A round, sponge-filled Celebration cake
A square, sponge-filled Wedding cake
A round, fruit-filled Wedding cake
A square, fruit-filled Christmas cake
```

The two programs shown so far are fairly simple, but they introduce the basic processing model of the forward-only, noncached style:

- Use a method call to change the current node. You can skip nodes or ask for nodes by name.
- Retrieve the properties of the current node to access data and metadata.

As you progress through this chapter, you'll learn various techniques that improve on this style of processing.

Traversing Hierarchies and Reading Content

The document CakeCatalog.xml contains a lot more than just the *CakeType* elements. Each *CakeType* element contains a *Message*, a *Description*, and possibly a list of *Sizes*. To process these child elements, you have three choices:

- Add some extra *else if* statements to the element handling case. The extra *if* statements will check for the child element names and write out a message based on their content or attributes. This would work reasonably well for our simple document but not for any form of processing that needs to know the context of the child node (what type of cake is currently being processed, for example). Indeed, if a *Message* element were added to the document outside of a *CakeType* element, this simple processing would merrily print out a message for it even though it is not an appropriate place to find this element.
- Perform the same processing as described above but set flags as each element is encountered. You could, for example, set a Boolean flag called *inCakeTypeElement* to *true* when you encounter a *CakeType* element. All of the child element handling code would then verify that this flag is set to *true* before processing the child element. This is better, but it would mean that you'd be building a fairly complex state machine to process your document. In this case, the pull model has few advantages over the SAX push model.

- Extend the code that handles the *CakeType* element so that it walks through subsequent nodes, discovering and processing the child elements as it goes. This approach does not rely on any saved context or a complex state machine.

The code in the ChildElementXmlReaderCatalogLister.jsl sample file illustrates how the children of a *CakeType* element can be processed using the last approach described. After the attributes of the *CakeType* element are displayed, the *ReadStartElement* method checks that the current node is still the *CakeType* element and then moves to the next node. *ReadStartElement* is a useful way of ensuring that you know where you are before proceeding further:

```
reader.ReadStartElement("CakeType");
```

Depending on the amount of white space in the document, the next node might be the *Message* element or some white space. In many applications, the white space in the XML document will be irrelevant, so you'd want to skip over the white space and go right to the content. One way to do this is to use the *MoveToContent* method, which ignores any white space or comments and returns only when it finds the next node with meaningful content. *MoveToContent* returns the type of the node found (such as *Element*, *EndElement*, or some text). In the handling code for *CakeType*, you can check that the node found is an element and that its name is *Message*:

```
XmlNodeType content = reader.MoveToContent();

if (content == XmlNodeType.Element &&
   reader.get_Name().CompareTo("Message") == 0)
{
   ...
}
```

White space in an XML document is classified as significant or insignificant. Significant white space occurs in text content or where content is a mixture of text and elements. When you manipulate an XML document, you should usually preserve significant white space between the original document and the final document. Insignificant white space occurs, for example, between elements where tab and newline characters have been added for readability. This latter form of white space can be stripped out or ignored without affecting the contents of the document.

An alternative approach to avoiding insignificant white space is to set the *WhitespaceHandling* property on the *XmlReader* to *WhitespaceHandling.Significant* so that the insignificant white space between the tags is ignored:

```
XmlTextReader reader = new XmlTextReader(args[0]);
reader.set_WhitespaceHandling(WhitespaceHandling.Significant);
```

Note In this case, the *reader* variable is of type *XmlTextReader*, and not the superclass *XmlReader*. The *WhitespaceHandling* property is not part of the superclass, so you cannot set it using a reference to *XmlReader*.

Limiting white space notification to only significant white space can safely be combined with the use of the *MoveToContent* method.

Returning to the sample code (once you've found the *Message* element), you can use the *IsEmptyElement* property to determine whether the *Message* element has content to be processed. A simple way to retrieve the text content of the *Message* element is to move on to the text node and retrieve its value:

```
if (!reader.get_IsEmptyElement())
{
   reader.ReadStartElement("Message");
   // Process the text
   Console.WriteLine("    Message: " + reader.get_Value());
   reader.Read(); // Move to the EndElement
}
```

Once the text content has been retrieved, the *XmlReader* will still point at the text content node. If you issue a *MoveToContent* method call at this point, it will not move the position of the *XmlReader* because you're already on a content node (the text node). You must therefore move away from the text node to progress. Hence the call to *Read* after the content is retrieved; it moves the *XmlReader* on to the *EndElement* node.

If the node is a *Text* node or any other form of character data, an alternative to *get_Value* is the *ReadString* method. This method performs an explicit read operation, just like the simple *Read* method, so the call to this method moves the *XmlReader* on to the *EndElement* node. Therefore, there is no need for the additional *Read* method call as there is with *get_Value*. Making this change would improve the efficiency of the code, but this option is viable only for text-based nodes.

The next step is to issue another *Read* before the *MoveToContent* call. If text content is present in the *Message* element, doing this will move beyond the *EndElement* node. This move is necessary because an *EndElement* counts as content as far as *MoveToContent* is concerned. If there is no content in the element, this *Read* call will move beyond the *Message* element (on to white space or the *Description* element):

```
// Move to what should be the Description element
reader.Read();
content = reader.MoveToContent();
```

You can then perform the same testing and processing of the *Description* element as you did on the *Message* element.

If the *CakeType* element has a *Sizes* child element, the *Sizes* child element will contain a set of *Option* elements. You should traverse each of these *Option* elements, retrieving and displaying the value (the size of the cake). Again, you must issue a *Read* call to move away from the *Sizes* element, and you can then loop through the *Option* elements, calling *GetAttribute* on each of them to retrieve the value.

Other Options for Reading and Navigation

You've seen how to navigate and retrieve content in a straightforward way using *Read*, *MoveToContent*, and *get_Value*. Other methods are available that can help to simplify code that handles particular types of nodes.

When you read the content of a simple element that contains only a text string, you can execute the *ReadElementString* method. This method returns the text content of the element and moves the *XmlReader* onto the next node after the *EndElement*. This approach simplifies the message and description-reading code of the previous example:

```
if (content == XmlNodeType.Element &&
    reader.get_Name().CompareTo("Message") == 0)
{
   if (!reader.get_IsEmptyElement())
   {
      Console.WriteLine("    Message: " + reader.ReadElementString());
   }
   else
   {
      Console.WriteLine("    Empty message");
      reader.Skip();
   }
}

// Move to what should be the "Description" element
content = reader.MoveToContent();
if (content == XmlNodeType.Element &&
    reader.get_Name().CompareTo("Description") == 0)
{
```

```
        if (!reader.get_IsEmptyElement())
        {
            Console.WriteLine("    Description: " +
                reader.ReadElementString());
        }
        else
        {
            Console.WriteLine("    Empty description");
            reader.Skip();
        }
    }
```

As you can see, the use of *ReadElementString* removes the need to *Read* to the *EndElement*. Also, no extra read is required before the *MoveToContent* that takes the *XmlReader* on to the *Description* element. What is required, however, is an extra line of code in the *else* condition, where the element is empty. In this case, the *Skip* method is used to move the *XmlReader* beyond the empty element. This leaves the *XmlReader* in the right position for the next call to *MoveToContent*. You can use *Skip* anywhere that you would use the *Read* method, but *Skip* moves on to the next node without reading it. The code for this form of the application can be found in the ReadElementStringXmlReaderCatalogLister.jsl sample file.

Another option is to use the *ReadInnerXml* method to retrieve the contents of the element, as in this example:

```
Console.WriteLine("    Description: " + reader.ReadInnerXml());
```

In the case of a simple text-containing element, the call to *ReadInnerXML* has the same effect as *ReadElementString*. If the XML contained in the current element is more complex, the XML content is returned as a single string. You can use *ReadInnerXml* on elements or attributes. In the case of an element, the returned string represents all of the children of the current element, including any markup.

There is also the method *ReadOuterXml,* which returns a string representing the current node (and all of its children if the node is an element), including any markup. For example, if the *XmlReader* object points at the first *Message* element in the document, *ReadInnerXml* will return "Happy Birthday" and *ReadOuterXml* will return "<Message>Happy Birthday</Message>".

The *XmlReader* object allows you to navigate through attributes in a similar way to navigating through elements. Rather than just call *GetAttribute,* you can use *MoveToFirstAttribute*, *MoveToNextAttribute*, and *MoveToAttribute* to position the *XmlReader* on one of the attribute nodes of the current start element tag. When you point at an attribute, you can use all of the applicable methods and properties of the *XmlReader* object. The *MoveToElement* method repositions the *XmlReader* to point at the element to which the current attribute belongs.

Types and Namespaces

So far, you've encountered text strings as attribute and element values. In addition to strings, XML documents will regularly contain nontext values such as integer or floating point values, although these must be encoded as strings within the document. The *XmlConvert* class provides a convenient way of converting common XML types into .NET Framework types.

Consider a scenario in which the cake size information is held as a number:

```
<Option sizeInInches="12"/>
```

You can use *XmlConvert* to convert this into a runtime type:

```
String sizeStr = reader.GetAttribute("sizeInInches");
Console.WriteLine("    Size option: " + sizeStr + " inch");

int feedsApprox = XmlConvert.ToInt32(sizeStr) * 2;
Console.WriteLine("    This will feed " + feedsApprox + " people (approx)");
```

You can also use the *XmlConvert* class to create and interpret XML-compliant names. The XML standard sets out characters that are forbidden in names in an XML document. The methods *EncodeName* and *EncodeLocalName* convert a J# string into an XML-compliant name; *DecodeName* performs the reverse conversion.

The difference between *EncodeName* and *EncodeLocalName* is in the way they handle colons. This is important because the colon delimits namespace information in an XML-compliant name. All of the names we've looked at so far are simple names that do not include a namespace, so the local name and the qualified name have been the same. If you use namespaces, the code must change to handle this extra information.

Consider a version of the cake catalog that uses namespaces. This cake catalog is issued by the fictional Fourth Coffee company (whose URL is *http://www.fourthcoffee.com*). The URI for the namespace is based on Fourth Coffee's URL and specifies a prefix of *cakes*:

```
<cakes:CakeCatalog xmlns:cakes="http://www.fourthcoffee.com/xmlcakes">
   <cakes:CakeType cakes:style="Celebration" cakes:filling="sponge"
   cakes:shape="round">
        <cakes:Message>Happy Birthday</cakes:Message>
     ⋮
```

The prefix might change from document to document, so you should use the namespace-aware forms of methods to navigate through the document. To see what impact the use of namespaces will have, consider how it would change the first few lines of the *CakeType* handling:

```
String cakeNamespace = "http://www.fourthcoffee.com/xmlcakes";

if (reader.get_LocalName().CompareTo("CakeType") == 0 &&
    reader.get_NamespaceURI().CompareTo(cakeNamespace) == 0)
{
   Console.WriteLine("A " +
      reader.GetAttribute("shape", cakeNamespace) +
      ", " + reader.GetAttribute("filling", cakeNamespace) +
      "-filled " + reader.GetAttribute("style", cakeNamespace) +
      " cake");

   // Move to what should be the "Message" element
   reader.ReadStartElement("CakeType", cakeNamespace);
   XmlNodeType content = reader.MoveToContent();
```

The initial *if* test now makes sure that the *LocalName* of the element (*CakeTypes*) and the associated namespace (*http://www.fourthcoffee.com/xmlcakes*) are correct before proceeding. Using the *get_Name* method at this point would return *cakes:CakeTypes*. It is still possible for you to use the *get_Name* method and to look for names with a given prefix, in this case *cakes:*. However, you would have to have already ensured that the correct namespace was associated with *cakes* for this code to work correctly. Generally, you're better off sticking with the forms of methods that provide explicit namespace information.

The namespace-aware form of the *GetAttributes* method is used to retrieve the attribute values because these, too, are namespace-qualified in the XML document. You should also use the namespace-aware versions of any method to which you pass an element or attribute name, such as the *ReadStartElement* method. The code for processing a version of the cake catalog that uses namespaces (CakeCatalogNS.xml) can be found in the NamespaceXmlReaderCatalogLister.jsl sample file.

Exception Handling

While processing an XML document, you might encounter errors. Some of these might relate to the underlying source of the XML, such as an error when reading data from a file or stream. They will generate exceptions unrelated to XML, such as *FileNotFoundException*, and should be handled appropriately.

If there is a problem with the XML document itself, an *XmlException* will be raised. For example, an exception will be raised if the document is not well formed or if you request a node with a particular name, using a method such as *ReadStartElement*, and the current node is not an element with that name.

Note As with any other .NET exception, *XmlException* is not a Java language–checked exception, so you must remember to add an appropriate *try/catch* block.

Writing XML Documents Using the *XmlWriter* Class

The SAX API was developed because the preexisting DOM model of processing was too cumbersome for some applications that simply needed to parse XML documents. However, SAX is a read-only mechanism, so to output an XML document in the SAX world you could employ DOM to create an in-memory DOM tree and then write it out, or you could use a lot of *println* statements. The former can be too memory-intensive and unwieldy, and the latter is messy and prone to errors. What you need is a lightweight equivalent of the *XMLReader* that makes it easier for applications to write out XML documents.

The *XMLWriter* class in the *System.Xml* namespace provides what you might think of as a reverse-SAX mechanism. *XmlWriter* is an abstract class that contains a set of methods that allow you to write out individual pieces of an XML document, such as elements and attributes. The only subclass of *XmlWriter* is *XmlTextWriter*. *XmlTextWriter* contains additional properties, such as those that allow you to configure the output formatting of the document.

To see how a writer works, consider the operations required to write out a cake catalog with a single cake type. The cake type will have a message, description, and size options. All output should have the appropriate namespace information associated with it. For example, the output can look like this:

```
<?xml version="1.0" encoding="utf-8"?>
<cakes:CakeCatalog xmlns: cakes="http://www.fourthcoffee.com/xmlcakes">
  <cakes:CakeType cakes:style="Celebration" cakes:filling="sponge"
    cakes:shape="square">
    <cakes:Message>Congratulations!</ cakes:Message>
    <cakes:Description>General achievement</cakes:Description>
    <cakes:Sizes>
      <cakes:Option cakes:sizeInInches="10" />
      <cakes:Option cakes:sizeInInches="12" />
    </cakes:Sizes>
  </cakes:CakeType>
</cakes:CakeCatalog>
```

The first step is to create an *XMLWriter* object. As with the sources for an *XMLReader*, you can specify multiple types of destination for an *XMLWriter*:

- A filename passed as a string
- A *System.IO.Stream*
- A *System.IO.TextReader*

In the first two cases, you must also specify an encoding that will be used when writing the output document. The XML declaration that is output will contain this encoding as an attribute. The *System.Text.Encoding* abstract class has a set of encoding-specific subclasses, one of which is *UTF8Encoding*. It provides a standard Unicode-compliant, 8-bit encoding for the output document. You can use this to create a new *XmlTextWriter*:

```
XmlTextWriter writer = new XmlTextWriter("catalog.xml",
   new UTF8Encoding());
```

At this stage, nothing has been written to the document. Before you start to output the individual parts of the document, you should consider the formatting required. If you do not specify any formatting, the *XmlWriter* will output the XML document without any white space (that is, new lines or indentation). This is fine if the document is to be processed by another application, but it will be awkward for humans to read. To make the document friendlier, set the formatting to *System.Xml.Formatting.Indented*:

```
writer.set_Formatting(Formatting.Indented);
```

The *XmlWriter* also has properties you can set to define the character to be used for indenting (by default, a space) and the number of indenting characters for each level of nesting (by default, 2).

Because you are creating a well-formed XML document, you must write out the XML declaration, followed by the root element:

```
writer.WriteStartDocument();

String cakeNamespace = "http://www.fourthcoffee.com/xmlcakes";
writer.WriteStartElement("cakes", "CakeCatalog", cakeNamespace);
...
writer.WriteEndElement(); // CakeCatalog
```

The *WriteStartElement* method generates a start element tag with the given local name, namespace, and namespace prefix (if specified). This method has various overloaded forms. In this case, the call will create a *CakeCatalog* element with a declaration of the Fourth Coffee namespace associated with the *cakes* prefix. If you need to add additional namespace attributes, you can add them in the same way as any other attribute (as you'll see in a moment).

Because this information is being written as a sequential stream, at this stage only the start tag (and its attributes) will be in the output buffer. At some point before the end of the document, you should write out the associated end element using the *WriteEndElement* method.

Note In some cases, you can get away with not explicitly writing end elements. The code that handles start elements and other "major" changes, such as the end of the document, will automatically close any open elements for you. However, you must be careful to ensure that each element is at the correct level of nesting to take advantage of this feature. It is safest to write the end elements explicitly.

The next task is to write out the *CakeType* element and its attributes. The *WriteStartElement* method is used again, but this time no namespace prefix is required. Given the local name and the namespace, the *XmlWriter* can work out which namespace prefix should be used from the namespaces in scope. If you need to discover the namespace prefix associated with a namespace, use the *LookupPrefix* method. The *CakeType* element requires that the attributes *style*, *filling*, and *shape* be added to it and that their values to be defined. You can use the *WriteAttributeString* method to add an attribute to an element and to define its value. Again, the namespace is provided and the writer will work out the appropriate prefix:

```
writer.WriteStartElement("CakeType", cakeNamespace);
writer.WriteAttributeString("style", cakeNamespace, "Celebration");
writer.WriteAttributeString("filling", cakeNamespace, "sponge");
writer.WriteAttributeString("shape", cakeNamespace, "square");
```

All of the attributes are attached to the current start element tag. If the attribute value being generated is complex, you can use the sequence of method calls *WriteStartAttribute*, *WriteString*, and *WriteEndAttribute* to take more control of attribute writing.

The *Message* and *Description* elements are simple elements with text content and no attributes. To write these, you use the *WriteElementString* method, as in these two examples:

```
writer.WriteElementString("Message", cakeNamespace, "Congratulations!");
writer.WriteElementString("Description", cakeNamespace,
   "General achievement");
```

As with attributes, if the text content of an element is complex, you can use the sequence of method calls *WriteStartElement*, *WriteString*, and *WriteEndElement* to generate it.

The *Sizes* and *Options* elements can be written using methods you've already seen. Once you have output an end element for each of your start elements, you should end the document and close it:

```
writer.WriteEndDocument();
writer.Close();
```

The document will not be written to the underlying file until *Close* is called—the *XmlTextWriter* class uses buffered output for optimization. At any point, you can write the part of the document created so far using the *Flush* method. If you're creating a large document, you should flush the output buffer regularly to avoid taking up too much memory. (The size of a document for which you need to do this will vary depending on how much memory your system has, but certainly most applications would want to flush partial documents exceeding 500 KB.) You'll find the full code for writing the desired XML document in the book's XmlWriterCatalogWriter.jsl sample file.

Escaping and Copying When Writing

Certain characters are not allowed in XML documents. Characters that correspond to standard escaped entities, such as the ampersand (&), will automatically be converted into their entity equivalent (in this case, *&*), whether they occur in text content or as part of an element or attribute name. However, other characters that might occur as part of a name, such as the colon (:), will not be escaped. In this case, you should use the *XmlConvert* class to encode the name of the element or attribute before writing it out.

If your application is acting as a filter—that is, it is taking XML input and performing targeted transformations—you have several useful copying methods available in the *XmlWriter* class. For example, the *WriteAttributes* method will copy all of the attribute values from the node pointed to by an *XmlReader* into the current element being written by the *XmlWriter*:

```
writer.WriteStartElement("cakes", "CakeCatalog", cakeNamespace);
writer.WriteAttributes(reader, false);
```

The *boolean* flag parameter to *WriteAttributes* determines whether default attribute values are copied.

Validation and Entity Resolution

Once you use XML documents to exchange business information, you'll need additional functionality to help manage these documents. Data can flow smoothly between applications only if the applications agree on how the data will be formatted and what the structure of the data will be. XML provides the formatting and encoding for business data, but the required structure will depend on the applications involved.

Validating XML Documents

If XML documents are to be shared between applications, the receiving application must understand the contents of the document. Writing code to check that the document format is correct can be time consuming and prone to errors. To avoid coding, you can define the expected format of a document using a DTD or a schema.

The DTD syntax is inherited from the Standard Generalized Markup Language (SGML), which preceded XML, and it looks somewhat arcane. DTDs are limited in that they do not have a particularly strong type system—you cannot differentiate between strings and numbers, for example. There is also a limit of one DTD per document, which can cause problems if documents are being merged or parts are sourced from different places. The following sample file, CakeCatalog.dtd, shows the DTD for documents that contain a root element of *CakeCatalog*. I will not go into the precise syntax, but suffice it to say that this is not XML!

CakeCatalog.dtd

```
<!ELEMENT CakeCatalog   (CakeType)*>
<!ELEMENT CakeType      (Message, Description, Sizes?)>
<!ATTLIST CakeType  style CDATA #REQUIRED
                    filling CDATA #REQUIRED
                    shape CDATA #REQUIRED>
<!ELEMENT Message      (#PCDATA)>
<!ELEMENT Description  (#PCDATA)>
<!ELEMENT Sizes        (Option)*>
<!ELEMENT Option       EMPTY>
<!ATTLIST Option   sizeInInches CDATA #REQUIRED>
```

The XML Schema standard from the W3C defines document structure using an XML-based syntax. This standard has evolved from several early efforts to improve DTDs by using XML as the schema syntax and introducing a stronger type system. One of these early efforts was the XML Data submission to the W3C by Microsoft, DataChannel, and others. This standard was subsequently scaled down to a form known as XML Data Reduced (XDR). XDR was used for the first schema-based tools launched by Microsoft, so you might find many schemas still defined in this dialect. The latest XML Schema standard has many similarities to XDR, but the two are not interoperable. If you need to convert an XDR schema to an XML schema, you can use a tool such as the XML Schema Definition tool (XSD.exe), which comes with the .NET Framework SDK. A graphical schema editor is available with Visual Studio .NET.

The XML schema corresponding to the *CakeCatalog* is shown in the following sample file, SchemaCakeCatalog.xsd.

SchemaCakeCatalog.xsd

```
<?xml version="1.0" ?>
<xs:schema id="CakeCatalog" targetNamespace="http://www.fourthcoffee.com/Sche-
maCakeCatalog.xsd" xmlns:mstns="http://www.fourthcoffee.com/SchemaCakeCata-
log.xsd" xmlns="http://www.fourthcoffee.com/SchemaCakeCatalog.xsd"
xmlns:xs="http://www.w3.org/2001/XMLSchema"
xmlns:msdata="urn:schemas-microsoft-com:xml-msdata" attributeFormDefault="qual-
ified" elementFormDefault="qualified">
  <xs:element name="CakeCatalog" msdata:IsDataSet="true"
  msdata:Locale="en-GB" msdata:EnforceConstraints="False">
    <xs:complexType>
      <xs:choice maxOccurs="unbounded">
        <xs:element name="CakeType">
          <xs:complexType>
            <xs:sequence>
              <xs:element name="Message" type="xs:string" minOccurs="0"
                msdata:Ordinal="0" />
              <xs:element name="Description" type="xs:string" minOccurs="0"
                msdata:Ordinal="1" />
              <xs:element name="Sizes" minOccurs="0" maxOccurs="unbounded">
                <xs:complexType>
                  <xs:sequence>
                    <xs:element name="Option" minOccurs="0"
                      maxOccurs="unbounded">
                      <xs:complexType>
                        <xs:attribute name="sizeInInches"
                          form="unqualified" type="xs:string" />
                      </xs:complexType>
                    </xs:element>
                  </xs:sequence>
                </xs:complexType>
              </xs:element>
            </xs:sequence>
            <xs:attribute name="style" form="unqualified"
              type="xs:string" />
            <xs:attribute name="filling" form="unqualified"
```

```
              type="xs:string" />
            <xs:attribute name="shape" form="unqualified"
              type="xs:string" />
          </xs:complexType>
        </xs:element>
      </xs:choice>
    </xs:complexType>
  </xs:element>
</xs:schema>
```

Attaching a Schema or a DTD to an XML Document

A DTD can be associated with an XML document in one of two ways. First, a DTD can be defined within the XML document itself, as shown in the following sample file, DTDCakeCatalog.xml. The *DOCTYPE* statement indicates the name of the root element to which the DTD pertains.

DTDCakeCatalog.xml

```
<?xml version="1.0" encoding="utf-8"?>

<!DOCTYPE CakeCatalog [
   <!ELEMENT CakeCatalog   (CakeType)*>
   <!ELEMENT CakeType      (Message, Description, Sizes?)>
   <!ATTLIST CakeType  style CDATA #REQUIRED
                filling CDATA #REQUIRED
                shape CDATA #REQUIRED>
   <!ELEMENT Message      (#PCDATA)>
   <!ELEMENT Description   (#PCDATA)>
   <!ELEMENT Sizes         (Option)*>
   <!ELEMENT Option       EMPTY>
   <!ATTLIST Option       sizeInInches CDATA #REQUIRED>
]>

<CakeCatalog>
  <CakeType style="Celebration" filling="sponge" shape="square">
    <Message>Congratulations</Message>
    <Description>General achievement</Description>
    <Sizes>
      <Option sizeInInches="10" />
      <Option sizeInInches="12" />
    </Sizes>
  </CakeType>
</CakeCatalog>
```

Alternatively, you can provide the name of an external file that contains the DTD. The following *DOCTYPE* declaration could replace the *DOCTYPE* declaration in DTDCakeCatalog.xml. This declaration refers to the file CakeCatalog.dtd sample shown earlier:

```
<!DOCTYPE CakeCatalog SYSTEM "CakeCatalog.dtd">
```

In either case (internal or external DTD definition), a validating parser can discover, resolve, and apply the structure information given within the document.

Most structure definitions created recently use an XML schema rather than a DTD. To attach the schema defined in SchemaCakeCatalog.xsd to an XML document, you can use a namespace declaration. The following sample file, SchemaCakeCatalog.xml, shows how this can be done so that the schema becomes the default schema for that document. You can define multiple schemas on a single start element tag using different namespace prefixes. (There can be only one default.)

SchemaCakeCatalog.xml

```
<?xml version="1.0" encoding="utf-8"?>
<CakeCatalog xmlns="http://www.fourthcoffee.com/SchemaCakeCatalog.xsd">
    <CakeType style="Celebration" filling="sponge" shape="square">
        <Message>Congratulations</Message>
        <Description>General achievement</Description>
        <Sizes>
            <Option sizeInInches="10" />
            <Option sizeInInches="12" />
        </Sizes>
    </CakeType>
</CakeCatalog>
```

Again, any schema-aware, validating parser that encounters the document SchemaCakaCatalog.xml can resolve the location of the schema and use it to validate the XML document.

Handling Validation Errors

You now have a schema or DTD associated with your document. How do you ensure that the document is valid? The ability to validate documents programmatically is what adds value—you do not have to write low-level checking code yourself. The first thing to do is to obtain a validating parser. The *XmlValidatingReader* class provides such functionality. This class can obtain the XML to be validated from the following sources:

- An existing *XmlReader*—either an *XmlTextReader* or an *XmlNodeReader*
- A stream or a string. In this case, you must provide more information, including the type of XML fragment being parsed and the encoding used

The simplest approach is to wrap an *XmlValidatingReader* around an *XmlTextReader*:

```
XmlTextReader reader = new XmlTextReader(args[0]);
reader.set_WhitespaceHandling(WhitespaceHandling.Significant);
XmlValidatingReader vreader = new XmlValidatingReader(reader);
```

Calls to the *Read* method (or similar methods) of the *XmlValidatingReader* class will cause the document to be validated as the reading progresses. If an inconsistency is encountered, a *System.Xml.Schema.XmlSchemaException* will be thrown. This exception can then be caught and examined. However, there is a cleaner way of monitoring the progress of validation.

When a validation error occurs, the parser will raise an event to this effect; an exception will be thrown only if there is no event handler defined. Therefore, the preferred way of handling validation errors is to set an event handler. In J#, the event handler takes the form of a delegate with the signature containing the sender and validation event arguments, as shown here:

```
public delegate void ValidationEventHandler(object sender,
   ValidationEventArgs e);
```

You can define an event handler by creating a delegate and calling the *add_ValidationEventHandler* method to add this to the list of event handlers for the *XmlValidatingReader*:

```
ValidationEventHandler handler = new
   ValidationEventHandler(validationHandler);
vreader.add_ValidationEventHandler(handler);
```

If a validation problem is encountered, the handler will be invoked. The problem could be an error or a warning as defined by the *Severity* property of the *ValidationEventArgs* object passed into the event handler. The event handler can then decide on a suitable course of action. The DTDValidateCatalog.jsl sample file shows how to handle such validation errors. This sample is provided with three XML files. DTDCakeCatalog.xml is a valid XML file that uses an internal DTD, ExtDTDCakeCatalog.xml is a valid XML file that uses an external DTD, and InvalidDTDCakeCatalog.xml is an invalid XML file that uses an internal DTD.

Defining the Schema to Use

A document can be validated using an attached schema or a DTD. However, a particular document might have multiple schema types attached to it. In this case, you can set the *XmlValidatingReader class's ValidationType* property to indicate whether the document should be validated against a DTD, an XDR schema, or an XML schema.

Another issue is whether you're using the correct schema. In general terms, you might need to examine and possibly change the namespace attributes associated with a document to ensure that it is validated against the schema expected by your application.

The use of schemas can be made more efficient by caching the most frequently used schemas. You can create an *XmlSchemaCollection* and add common schemas to it. This collection can then be added to the schema collection held for each *XmlValidatingReader* used:

```
XmlSchemaCollection schemas = new XmlSchemaCollection();
schemas.Add("http://www.fourthcoffee.com/SchemaCakeCatalog.xsd",
   "SchemaCakeCatalog.xsd");
...
XmlSchemaCollection xsc = vreader.get_Schemas();
xsc.Add(schemas);
// Validate as before...
```

The code to perform the validation of an XML document using an XML schema and a schema cache can be found in the sample file SchemaValidate-Catalog.jsl, which uses the files SchemaCakeCatalog.xml and SchemaCakeCatalog.xsd.

Resolving Entities

An XML document might contain fixed markup or other content. For example, you might need to use the same supplier address in every XML-based invoice you issue. One way of inserting the address is to define the appropriate markup for the address in another file and include this file as the document is being processed. When used in this way, the external markup is referred to as an external entity. Such entities are defined as part of the DTD or schema for a document.

The .NET Framework Class Library contains a class designed for entity resolution, *XmlUrlResolver*. If you need to resolve entities in any other way, you can create a custom resolver class, which you can set on the *XmlReader* using the *XmlResolver* property. This resolver is then used for all external resolution, such as the location of external DTDs and schemas. A full examination of entity resolution, schema includes and imports, and the use of nondefault resolvers is beyond the scope of this book. For more information, see the .NET Framework documentation.

Processing XML Documents in Memory

As mentioned earlier, it is not always convenient to process information in one pass. For some types of applications, it will be more convenient to keep an in-memory copy of the data being processed. To process an XML document in this way, you could use single-pass processing, converting the document's contents into internal, application-specific objects. You could manipulate these objects and then serialize them out as XML again once they've been processed. However, you might find it easier just to keep the data in an XML format in memory so you can manipulate it *in situ* and write it out again quite easily.

In-Memory Processing

The DOM defined by the W3C provides a model of an XML document from a programmer's point of view. Interfaces are provided for searching, navigating, retrieving content, and creating content. DOM implementations provide this functionality by creating an in-memory replica of the document on which these operations can be performed. The advantages of using an in-memory replica include the ability to access any part of the document at any time and the ability to easily add and remove parts of a document. The main disadvantage of in-memory processing is that it can consume large amounts of memory when processing large documents.

DOM represents the document as a tree, with text content and attributes forming the *leaf nodes* and the hierarchy of elements providing the branches, as shown in Figure 5-4.

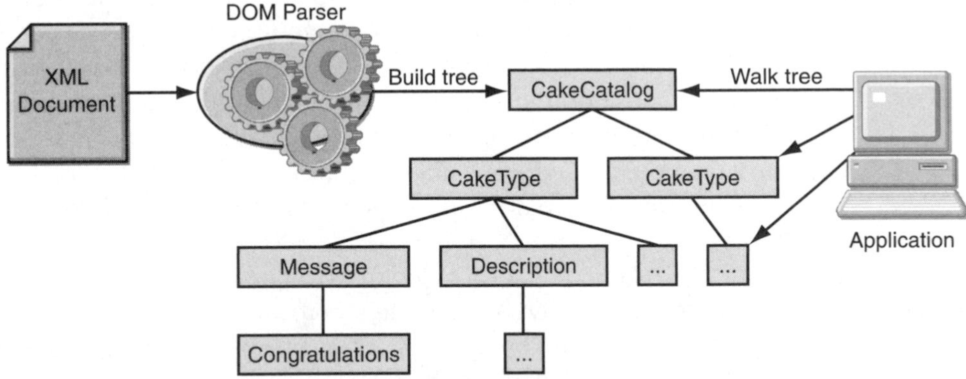

Figure 5-4 DOM representation of an XML document

To process a DOM tree, you start at a particular point in the tree and navigate or search relative to that point. From this position, you can retrieve individual objects representing elements, attributes, and content or collections of such objects. The DOM model specifies particular interfaces for different parts of an XML document, such as elements and text content, some of which are shown in Figure 5-5. You can use the DOM interfaces to process objects you have retrieved from the DOM tree.

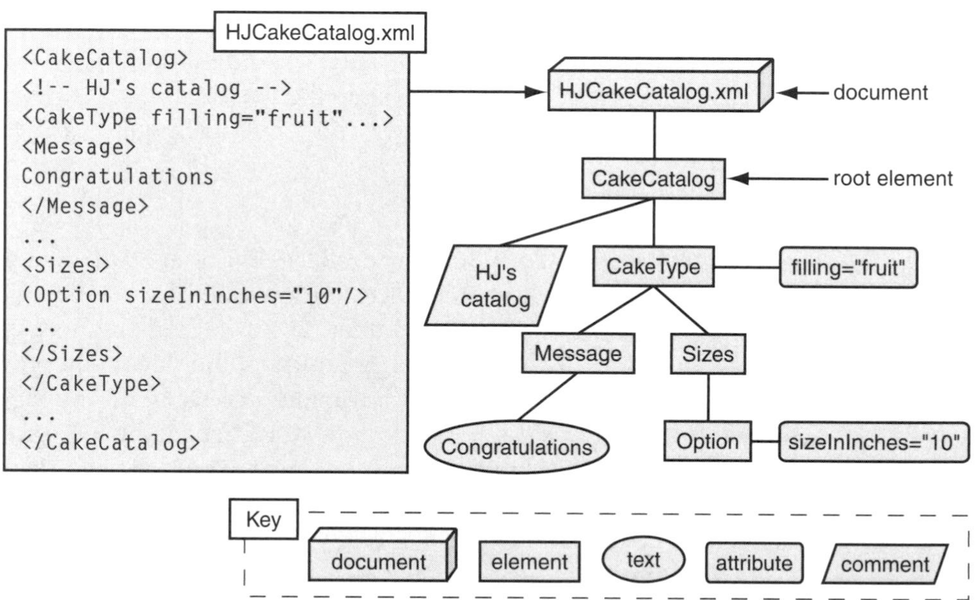

Figure 5-5 Mapping different parts of an XML document to different DOM interface types

The general principle of DOM is that everything is a node. The DOM Node interface exposes methods to navigate up (to the parent), down (to children), and sideways (to siblings) through the DOM tree. Because all nodes in the DOM tree support the *Node* interface, this provides a common navigational model. Individual nodes can be of particular types, such as elements or attributes. Additional type-specific interfaces are provided to make it easier to retrieve information from the node, such as the name and content of an element.

The .NET Framework Class Library contains a set of classes that represent the different parts of a DOM tree. The Microsoft DOM implementation extends the functionality offered by the W3C interfaces by supplying convenient helper functionality and extended capabilities.

Loading XML into the *XmlDocument* Class

The class *System.Xml.XmlDocument* provides access to an XML document through DOM interfaces. You can load an XML document into an instance of *XmlDocument* and then process it. The code to instantiate and load a document is straightforward:

```
XmlDocument doc = new XmlDocument();
doc.Load("CakeCatalog.xml");
```

The *Load* method has various overloaded forms that can accept XML from the following sources:

- A URL or filename passed as a string
- An instance of *System.IO.Stream* from which the XML document can be read
- A *TextReader* representing the XML document
- Any subclass of *XmlReader*

Alternatively, if the XML document is sent to an application as a *String*, you can use the *LoadXml* method to parse it. The *Load* and *LoadXml* methods will throw exceptions if the document being loaded is not well-formed.

If the XML document must be validated as it is read in, you must load it through an *XmlValidatingReader*—the *XmlDocument* class itself does not have any validation capabilities. You should instantiate an *XmlValidatingReader*, passing it the document to process, setting its schema cache, and supplying a validation event handler as described earlier. You should then pass this *XmlValidatingReader* to the *Load* method of the *XmlDocument*. Validation failures will be flagged to the event handler you defined.

As with validation, the *XmlDocument* class does not provide control over the handling of entities. Entities will be resolved when you load a document, but they will not necessarily be expanded. Control over entity expansion is governed by the input to the *Load* method. By default, entities will be represented in the DOM tree as instances of *XmlEntityReference*. If you use an *XmlValidatingReader* to load the XML document into the DOM, you can set the *EntityHandling* flag to *ExpandEntities*. This setting will replace all entities in the document with their values as the tree is created.

Obtaining Information from a DOM Document

After the document is loaded, you can extract information from it by locating particular elements within the document and retrieving their text content or attributes. You can locate elements in two principal ways:

- If you know the structure of the document, you can navigate through the DOM tree by moving up, down, or sideways.
- You can search the document for particular elements. Several search mechanisms are available. The standard DOM mechanisms are covered in this chapter along with a more powerful search method based on the *XPathNavigator* class. *XPathNavigator* uses *XPath* syntax, which is described in Chapter 6.

Naturally, there's nothing to stop you from combining these two models by searching for a particular part of the tree and then navigating manually within that tree fragment.

Retrieving Information from a DOM Element

To navigate the DOM tree, you must start from somewhere, and the logical place is the root element of the document. Remember that the root element is the outermost element of your document. You can obtain the root element (also known as the *document element*) directly from the *XmlDocument*:

```
XmlDocument doc = new XmlDocument();
doc.Load("CakeCatalog.xml");

XmlElement root = doc.get_DocumentElement();
```

All elements are represented by instances of the *XmlElement* class. You can retrieve name, namespace, attribute and content information from the element. The *XmlElement* class has properties for the name, local name, and namespace URI:

```
private void listElement(XmlElement element)
{
   Console.WriteLine("Element name: " + element.get_LocalName());
   Console.WriteLine("Element namespace: " +
      element.get_NamespaceURI());
  ⋮
}
```

You can test to see whether the element has attributes and, if so, you can retrieve them as an *XmlAttributeCollection* using the *Attributes* property. The *Count* property of the collection gives you the number of attributes contained in the collection. You can then retrieve individual attributes using the indexed *ItemOf* property, which can be accessed using the *get_ItemOf* method and which takes an *int* index value. Each attribute retrieved is of type *XmlAttribute*, which has properties reflecting the name, local name, namespace URI, and value of the attribute. Here is an example:

```
if (element.get_HasAttributes())
{
   XmlAttributeCollection attributes = element.get_Attributes();
   Console.WriteLine("Element has: " + attributes.get_Count() + "
       attributes");
   for (int i = 0; i < attributes.get_Count(); i++)
   {
      XmlAttribute attribute = attributes.get_ItemOf(i);
      Console.WriteLine("\tAttribute name: " +
         attribute.get_LocalName());
      Console.WriteLine("\tAttribute namespace: " +
         attribute.get_NamespaceURI());
      Console.WriteLine("\tAttribute value: " +
         attribute.get_Value());
   }
}
```

Alternatively, if you know the name of the attribute whose value you want to retrieve, you can use the *XmlElement* class's *GetAttribute* method, passing in the name and namespace information for the attribute. This method returns the value as a string. You can query the *XmlElement* class's *HasAttribute* method to determine whether the element has an attribute of a particular name.

You can retrieve the element's content in several ways. But you should first use the *IsEmpty* property to test that it actually has content. The simplest way of retrieving the content is then to examine the *InnerXml* property, as shown here:

```
if (!element.get_IsEmpty())
{
   Console.WriteLine("Element has content:\n***********************");
   Console.Write(element.get_InnerXml());
   Console.WriteLine("\n***********************");
}
```

Figure 5-6 shows a listing of the information about the root element of SchemaCakeCatalog.xml. One interesting point to note is that the inner XML has had the appropriate namespace attribute set on it. (It inherits this from the root element.)

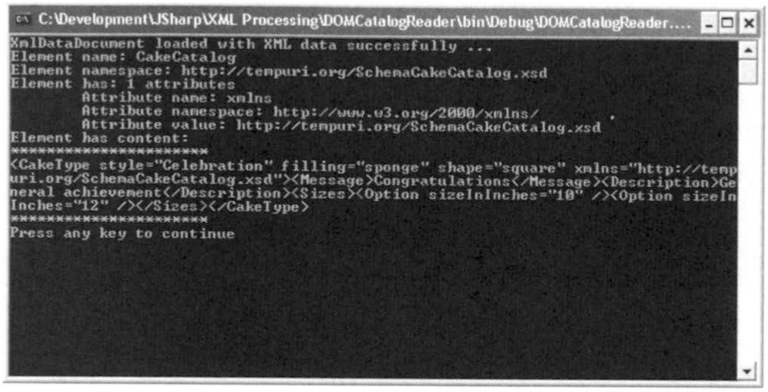

```
C:\Development\JSharp\XML Processing\DOMCatalogReader\bin\Debug\DOMCatalogReader....
XmlDataDocument loaded with XML data successfully ...
Element name: CakeCatalog
Element namespace: http://tempuri.org/SchemaCakeCatalog.xsd
Element has: 1 attributes
        Attribute name: xmlns
        Attribute namespace: http://www.w3.org/2000/xmlns/
        Attribute value: http://tempuri.org/SchemaCakeCatalog.xsd
Element has content:
**********************
<CakeType style="Celebration" filling="sponge" shape="square" xmlns="http://temp
uri.org/SchemaCakeCatalog.xsd"><Message>Congratulations</Message><Description>Ge
neral achievement</Description><Sizes><Option sizeInInches="10" /><Option sizeIn
Inches="12" /></Sizes></CakeType>
**********************
Press any key to continue
```

Figure 5-6 Listing the root element of the SchemaCakeCatalog.xml file

If you're handling an element containing text, you can use the *get_InnerText* method to retrieve just the text content. Alternatively, given that any text content of an element is held as a child node of that element, you can navigate downward and extract the content directly from the child node. To retrieve information from an *XmlText* node, you can use its *Value* property or *Data* property (which return the same value for an *XmlText* node).

Navigating the DOM Tree

You can use methods inherited from the *XmlNode* class to navigate the DOM tree relative to any given node. Unlike the *XmlReader*, the DOM does not retain the concept of a current node; you can hold references to as many nodes as you like and navigate relative to any node to which you have a reference. For example, consider the following method that searches for elements in a document:

```
private void lookForElements(XmlElement element)
{
   listElement(element);

   if (element.get_HasChildNodes())
   {
      for (XmlNode child = element.get_FirstChild();
         child != null;
         child = child.get_NextSibling())
      {
         if (child.get_NodeType() == XmlNodeType.Element)
         {
            lookForElements((XmlElement)child);
         }
      }
   }
}
```

The *listElement* method shown earlier displays the contents of an element to the console. Once the contents of the element passed in have been displayed, we use the *HasChildNodes* property to check whether the element has children. If so, the *FirstChild* of the element will be retrieved and its *NodeType* will be tested to see whether it is an *XmlNodeType.Element*. If the child is an element, a recursive call will be made to this method, and all the elements below this child will be listed. Once the first child has been processed, you can obtain the *NextSibling* and process it the same way. You can keep processing siblings until the *NextSibling* property is *null*. All of the DOM processing described so far is illustrated in the DOMCatalogReader.jsl file in the DOMCatalogReader sample project.

You have seen that you can navigate downward to children and sideways to the next sibling. You can also navigate to the previous sibling using the *PreviousSibling* property. To iterate through a list of the current node's children, you can invoke the Microsoft DOM extension method *GetEnumerator*. This method returns a *System.Collections.IEnumerator* interface reference that will iterate through that *XmlNode* class's children. An alternative implementation of the *lookForElements* method that uses an enumerator can be found in the sample file IteratorDOMCatalogReader.jsl.

To move upward to a node's parent, you can query the *ParentNode* property. If you want to go all the way to the top of the document, you can use the *OwnerDocument* property, which contains the *XmlDocument* containing this node.

Searching the DOM Tree

An alternative to walking through the whole document is to search the DOM tree. The simplest way to perform this search is to use the *GetElementsByTagName* method provided by the *XmlElement* and *XmlDocument* classes. This method expects the name and namespace information for the required element type, and it returns an *XmlNodeList* that contains matching elements. Here's a form of the *lookForElements* method (renamed *searchForElements*) that uses the *GetElementsByTagName* method:

```
private void searchForElements(XmlElement start, String name,
   String namespace)
{
   XmlNodeList nodes = start.GetElementsByTagName(name, namespace);

   System.Collections.IEnumerator enumerator = nodes.GetEnumerator();

   while (enumerator.MoveNext())
   {
      XmlElement element = (XmlElement)enumerator.get_Current();
```

```
        listElement(element);
    }
}
```

The *searchForElements* method is implemented in the sample file GetElementsByTagNameDOMCatalogReader.jsl.

The XML family of standards defines a powerful language for locating one or more nodes within an XML document. This standard is called *XPath*, and it is heavily used by XSLT for the identification of the parts of an XML document to be transformed. One of the Microsoft extensions to the DOM, the *XmlNode* interface, allows you to specify an XPath pattern and use it to locate nodes within a part of an XML document. Two methods are available in the *XmlNode* interface: *SelectNodes* and *SelectSingleNode*. The first of these returns an *XmlNodeList* containing all the nodes that match a given pattern. The *SelectSingleNode* method returns only the first node found that matches the pattern. These methods come in two forms, one of which uses an *XmlNamespaceManager* to associate prefixes with namespaces. This allows the prefixes to be used safely as part of the XPath string.

The following example, taken from the sample file SelectNodesDOMCatalogReader.jsl, shows how all of the *Option* elements can be retrieved from SchemaCakeCatalog.xml:

```
XmlDocument doc = ...
XmlNamespaceManager nsmgr = new XmlNamespaceManager(doc.get_NameTable());
nsmgr.AddNamespace("cakes",
   "http://www.fourthcoffee.com/SchemaCakeCatalog.xsd");

XmlElement root = doc.get_DocumentElement();
XmlNodeList nodeList = root.SelectNodes("//cakes:Option", nsmgr);

for (int i = 0; i < nodeList.get_Count(); i++)
{
   XmlElement element = (XmlElement)nodeList.get_ItemOf(i);
   listElement(element);
}
```

A more powerful (but more complex) strategy is to use an *XPathNavigator* object to search for nodes within a document. The *XmlDocument* class, and any other subclass of *XmlNode*, contains a *CreateNavigator* method. This method returns an instance of an *XPathNavigator* that is a read-only representation of the XML tree below the given node. You can then specify an XPath expression that will be used to search the tree by one of the *XPathNavigator* class's *Select* methods. These methods return an *XPathNodeIterator* that can be used to walk through the matching nodes. The detailed use of *XPathNavigator* is beyond the scope of this book, but Chapter 6 contains more on XPath expressions.

Treating a DOM Fragment as a Stream

When we examined the *XmlReader* class earlier in the chapter, you saw that one of its subclasses was *XmlNodeReader*. This class allows you to treat part or all of a DOM tree as a stream. You can pass an *XmlNode* to the constructor of an *XmlNodeReader* and use it as an *XmlReader* from then on.

Writing and Manipulating In-Memory XML Documents

One of the powerful features of the DOM is the ability to manipulate the XML document in memory. Let's now look at how to add, remove, and alter information in the DOM tree and how to write out the contents of the DOM once they've been changed.

Altering Content in a DOM Tree

The simplest thing you can do to alter the contents of a DOM tree is to delete part of it. The *RemoveChild* method of the *XmlNode* class allows you to remove a child of a given node. This operation will also delete any nodes below the given child. For example, the following code removes the first *Sizes* element in a *CakeCatalog* node together with the *Option* elements below it:

```
XmlElement root = doc.get_DocumentElement();
XmlNodeList nodes = root.GetElementsByTagName("Sizes",
   "http://www.fourthcoffee.com/SchemaCakeCatalog.xsd");
XmlElement sizesElement = (XmlElement)nodes.get_ItemOf(0);
sizesElement.get_ParentNode().RemoveChild(sizesElement);
```

Attributes can be removed collectively or individually by using one of the methods of the *XmlElement* class. *Remove*Attribute allows you to remove an attribute by name, RemoveAttributeAt removes an attribute by index, *RemoveAttributeNode* removes an attribute by reference, and *RemoveAllAttributes* clears all attributes of the element.

You can create new nodes to be added to a DOM tree using methods of the *XmlDocument* class. When you call type-specific creation methods, such as *CreateElement* and *CreateTextNode*, you supply the information to initialize the node. This information can include a name, namespace information, text content, and so on.

The following code shows a new element called *Gateaux* being created in the XML document, and some text content being added to that new element:

```
String namespace = "http://www.fourthcoffee.com/SchemaCakeCatalog.xsd";
XmlElement newElement = doc.CreateElement("Gateaux", namespace);
```

```
newElement.AppendChild(doc.CreateTextNode("A new product line!"));
root.AppendChild(newElement);
```

As you can see, when a new node is created, it is not attached to the document. You must use an appropriate method, such as *AppendChild*, to insert the node in the required place. *XmlNode* defines *PrependChild* and *AppendChild* to add a new child node at the start or end of the list of children, respectively. You can insert the new node relative to one of its siblings by passing that sibling to one of the *InsertAfter* or *InsertBefore* methods together with the new node. Another useful method is *ReplaceChild*, which allows you to replace a given child with a new one.

In addition to the type-specific creation methods, there is the generic *CreateNode* method. When you call *CreateNode*, you specify the type of node you want to create. (You cannot create a generic node!)

Note Nodes are associated with a particular document regardless of whether they are currently attached to that document. You cannot create a node on one document and add it to another document.

When you create a new element, you can add a new attribute to it using the *SetAttribute* method as defined on the *XmlElement* class:

```
String namespace = "http://www.fourthcoffee.com/SchemaCakeCatalog.xsd";
XmlElement newElement = doc.CreateElement("Gateaux", namespace);
newElement.SetAttribute("flavor", "chocolate");
```

You can also use *SetAttribute* to change the value of an existing attribute.

As with the node creation methods, *SetAttribute* is overloaded and has several variations to support different namespace options. In all cases, if a new namespace is specified and no prefix is provided for it, a new prefix will be generated.

Making Substantial Changes to XML Documents

You can add or change large amounts of content in an XML document using the *InnerXml* property. The following code adds a *Sizes* element containing two *Option* elements within the newly created *Gateaux* element:

```
XmlElement gateaux = doc.CreateElement("Gateaux");
...
XmlElement sizes = doc.CreateElement("Sizes", namespace);
sizes.set_InnerXml("<Option sizeInInches='10' />
```

```
    <Option sizeInInches='12' />");
gateaux.AppendChild(sizes);
```

All that has been explicitly created within the *Gateaux* element is a *Sizes* element. Setting the *InnerXml* of the *Sizes* element to a string containing the *Option* information then creates the *Option* elements. The DOM parses the given string and creates the required nodes. This approach requires a lot less programming than explicitly creating each required node in turn and adding them to the tree one by one. The best choice for your program will probably depend on whether you have the XML in a string format to begin with. (There's no point in creating a string yourself and then getting the DOM to parse it—you might as well make the individual method calls.)

Similarly, if you want to add text to an element, you can set its *InnerText* property:

```
XmlElement message = doc.CreateElement("Message", namespace);
gateaux.AppendChild(message);
message.set_InnerText("Sorry, writing messages on gateaux is too tricky!");
```

Warning Even though using the *InnerXml* property to set a large amount of content in one operation can be convenient, you must take great care about namespaces. If you add some XML without namespace information to a document with namespaces set, you might not get what you expect. For example, if your DOM document has a default namespace and you add an element without specifying a namespace, it will not inherit the default namespace. Instead, the new element will explicitly have its namespace set to the empty namespace "". An in-depth discussion of this issue is outside the scope of this book, so for more information on how namespaces are treated in this case, see the .NET Framework class library documentation for the *InnerXml* property of the *XmlDocument* class.

All of the code shown so far is contained in the sample file Manipulate-DOMDocument.jsl.

You can also create a completely new XML document using DOM. To do this, you just instantiate an *XmlDocument* and populate it using the methods you have seen in this section. Adding a child node to the *XmlDocument* creates the root node:

```
XmlDocument doc = new XmlDocument();
XmlElement root =
    (XmlElement)doc.AppendChild(doc.CreateElement("CakeCatalog"));
```

```
root.set_InnerXml("<CakeType style='celebration' filling='fruit'
shape='round'><Message>Hi!</Message></CakeType>");
```

A complete application to create a new DOM document is contained in the sample file CreateDOMDocument.jsl. This sample file also shows you how to persist a DOM document, as discussed in the next section.

Writing Out the DOM Tree

Once you have edited the contents of your DOM tree (or created a new one), you'll probably want to persist these changes. To do this, you must save the DOM to a file or a stream. The *XmlDocument* class has a *Save* method that can write its XML representation to

- A *System.IO.Stream*
- A file name, as specified by a string
- A *TextWriter* that wraps an appropriate destination
- An *XmlWriter* that wraps an appropriate destination

If you create a new DOM document as shown previously, you can save it to a file by adding this line:

```
doc.Save("BrandNewCatalog.xml");
```

You can omit part of a DOM tree using the *WriteTo* and *WriteContentTo* methods of the *XmlNode* class. Both of these methods take an *XmlWriter* that wraps up an appropriate destination. Again, referring to the newly created document, you can save just the *Message* element and its contents:

```
XmlTextWriter writer = new XmlTextWriter("JustTheMessage.xml",
   Encoding.get_UTF8());
root.get_FirstChild().get_FirstChild().WriteTo(writer);
writer.Close();
```

XML and Data

XML has become a popular choice for the representation of data in applications. Before XML, almost all "serious" data in applications was held in a database of some form, usually a relational database. Developers became accustomed to dealing with data from relational databases in terms of the structure and relationships between tables (embodied in the schema of the database) and the SQL statements used to retrieve data from those tables.

If you consider that XML data also has a schema and a query mechanism (XPath), you can see that the two models have many similarities. In some cases, it is easier to manipulate and transport application data in terms of database artifacts, such as set of database records as embodied in an ADO.NET *DataSet*. In other cases, it is preferable to manipulate and transport data in the form of an XML document. This convergence of XML and traditional data sources can be seen in the advent of XML generation and consumption facilities provided by database products, such as the SQLXML capabilities added to SQL Server.

Given the need for flexibility in data representation, and the similarities between the two models, the .NET Framework allows you to easily work with data that can be accessed using XML or traditional database techniques.

Links Between XML and ADO.NET Data

An ADO.NET *DataSet* is a powerful representation of underlying application data. ADO.NET is discussed in detail in Chapter 7, but for our purposes here, you need to know the following:

- An ADO.NET *DataSet* contains representations of one or more tables, views on those tables, and the definitions of relationships between them.
- A *DataSet* can contain data from one or more data sources.
- The tables in a *DataSet* appear as an indexed property of type *DataTable*.
- Each table has a *Rows* property, which represents the rows of data it contains. The type that represents a row is the *DataRow* class.
- You can obtain metadata from the tables, such as the number of columns, the names of the columns, and their data types.
- You can perform SQL queries based on the contents of the *DataSet* and retrieve an array of *DataRows*.

All of the classes you will see relating to the use of ADO.NET *DataSet* objects are defined in the *System.Data* namespace.

You can use the mechanisms you've seen so far, such as DOM, to read in the data from an XML document and use this data to programmatically populate an ADO.NET *DataSet*. You can also read the contents of an ADO.NET *DataSet* and generate an XML document from them using an *XmlWriter*. However, life is generally too short to indulge in this form of marshaling. As you'll see, you can create an ongoing relationship between an XML document, in the shape of an *XmlDataDocument*, and a *DataSet* such that you can use either view of the data when it suits you. The *XmlDataDocument* is a subclass of *XmlDocument*, and it provides DOM-style access to the data it contains. The really cool thing about the link between an *XmlDataDocument* and a *DataSet* is that any changes made while you work in one format are automatically reflected in the other format.

Viewing XML as Relational Data

If you're starting with XML data, you can load your data in one of two ways. One way is to create and populate an *XmlDataDocument*. You can use the *Load* and *LoadXml* methods you saw previously to load in the XML document. If you have an XML schema for your document, you can also load this into the *DataSet*. This helps the *XmlDataDocument* map your XML data into a table-based format. However, if you do not have a schema for your XML, don't panic—the *XmlDataDocument* can usually infer the required schema information from any well-structured XML.

The following code fragment, taken from the sample file XmlAsDataSet.jsl, shows how you can initialize an *XmlDataDocument*:

```
XmlDataDocument doc = new XmlDataDocument();
doc.get_DataSet().ReadXmlSchema("SchemaCakeCatalog.xsd");
doc.Load("SchemaCakeCatalog.xml");
DataTable cakeTypes = doc.get_DataSet().get_Tables().get_Item("CakeType");
```

The *XmlDataDocument* has a *DataSet* property through which you can obtain the related *DataSet*. In this instance, the *DataSet* is retrieved and its *ReadXmlSchema* method is used to read in the schema. The XML document is then loaded into the *XmlDataDocument* using the *Load* method. Once the data is in place, you can access it through the *DataSet* class, just as if it had been retrieved through a SQL query to a relational database. This process means that you can get hold of the *Tables* property of the associated *DataSet* that holds the collection of tables. You can then access the *Item* property to retrieve a table by name. The names of the tables will relate to the names of the elements in the XML document. In this case, the document consists of a set of *CakeType* elements, so this is reflected in the *DataSet* as a table called *CakeType*. You can use this name to retrieve the associated *DataTable*.

An alternative to starting with the *XmlDataDocument* is to commence with the *DataSet*. You can load XML directly into a *DataSet*, again optionally providing an XML schema before you do:

```
DataSet ds = new DataSet();
ds.ReadXml("SchemaCakeCatalog.xml");
DataTable cakeTypes = ds.get_Tables().get_Item("CakeType");
```

The *ReadXml* method is an overloaded method that takes a variety of sources of XML documents. The method also allows you to specify where to get a schema from if one has not been provided. If you do not provide an XML schema to the *DataSet* before loading the XML file, the *DataSet* will infer the schema from the XML document itself. You can see an example of loading an XML document into a *DataSet* in this way in the sample file InferDataSetSchemaFromXml.jsl.

Manipulating XML as Relational Data

Once you've obtained a *DataTable* to represent part of your XML document, you can access the content as if it were relational data. For example, you can read individual column values in particular rows, as shown here:

```
Console.WriteLine("First cake message is " +
   cakeTypes.get_Rows().get_Item(0).get_Item("Message"));
```

The *DataTable* has an indexed *Rows* property that allows you to retrieve a *DataRow* by offset. The code shown gets the first *DataRow* in the *DataTable* and then uses the *Item* property of the *DataRow* to access the contents of a particular column by name.

Even though it is useful to have access to all of the data in the table, you'll often want a subset of the data. When you connect to a relational database, you'll do so by issuing SQL queries that return rows that meet specified criteria. In the case of the *CakeCatalog*, this might be all of the cake types that have a fruit filling. The SQL statement for this would look something like this:

```
SELECT * FROM CakeType WHERE filling = 'fruit'
```

The code that you've seen already retrieved the equivalent of the CakeType table, so you can then query within those results using the *Select* method on the *DataTable*:

```
DataRow[] rows = cakeTypes.Select("filling = 'fruit'");
```

You can then loop through this array and print out the contents of each row. The *DataRow* has an *Item* collection property that you can use to access the individual column values. To use this property, you must obtain the number of columns from the *DataTable* as follows:

```
DataColumnCollection columns = cakeTypes.get_Columns();
int numColumns = columns.get_Count();

for (int i = 0; i < rows.length; i++)
{
      for (int j = 0; j < numColumns; j++)
      {
            Console.Write(rows[i].get_Item(j) + ", ");
      }
```

```
        Console.WriteLine();
}
```

The final task for now is to obtain the column names so that you know which data items relate to which parts of the XML document. You can do this by looping through the *DataTable* object's collection of columns and retrieving the name of each one in turn:

```
for (int i = 0; i < numColumns; i++)
{
        Console.Write(columns.get_Item(i).get_ColumnName() + ", ");
}
Console.WriteLine();
```

The code in the XmlAsDataSet.jsl and InferDataSetSchemaFromXml.jsl sample files show the whole sequence of events, starting from an *XMLDataDocument* and from a *DataSet*.

Viewing Relational Data as XML

Now that you know how an XML document is mapped into a *DataSet*, it should be fairly straightforward to see how data from a *DataSet* can be represented as an XML document:

- The contents of the *DataSet* class can be obtained in XML format using the *GetXml* method, which returns the XML as a *String*, or the *WriteXml* method, which sends the XML document to a file, a *Stream*, a *TextWriter*, or an *XmlWriter*.
- You can retrieve an XML schema that describes the data in the *DataSet* using the *GetXmlSchema* method, which returns the XML schema as a *String*, or the *WriteXmlSchema* method, which sends the XML schema to a file, a *Stream*, a *TextWriter*, or an *XmlWriter*.
- Given a *DataSet*, you can instantiate an *XmlDataDocument* by passing the *DataSet* into the constructor. This delivers an XML document representation that is synchronized with the contents of the *DataSet*.

Summary

The .NET Framework provides a wide range of features that allow you to process XML as part of your application. This chapter examined many of those features. You should now be able to process XML in a forward-only, noncached way using an *XMLReader* and to create XML in the same fashion using an *XMLWriter*. You can validate XML against a DTD or a schema by applying an *XmlValidatingReader*.

Alternatively, you can process XML documents in memory using the DOM model provided by an *XmlDocument*. This model allows you random access to information. DOM also allows you to add, remove, and alter parts of the document before writing it out. You can also now access XML data as if it were data from a relational database by using an *XmlDataDocument*, which synchronizes with an ADO.NET *DataSet*.

6

Transforming XML

Creating HTML pages for display in browsers used to be frustrating because of the lack of control over how page content was displayed. The arrival of cascading style sheets allowed Web developers to assign new styles to HTML tags and thus provided more control over how the HTML page was rendered. As the XML standard was being formalized, work began on the XML Stylesheet Language (XSL) to provide a facility for controlling the rendering of XML documents in browsers. The developers of XSL quickly worked out that they had two distinct problems to solve: the conversion of XML into a format that would display well in a Web browser and the general conversion of an XML document into another XML dialect (or any other text-based format, such as HTML).

The conversion of a document in one XML dialect to an XML document in another dialect is called *transformation*. Transformation is usually required in at least one place in an XML-based application because it makes it easier for your application to consume XML documents from external sources. One great advantage of XML is that it is extremely flexible and you can define your own data structures in it. However, one major drawback of XML is that it is extremely flexible and you can define your own data structures in it! In the absence of clearly defined and agreed-upon standards for the representation of a particular type data in XML, this flexibility can lead to XML spawning many different data formats to encode the same information.

This chapter will show how to transform XML data from one format to another and will explain the general support for the Extensible Stylesheet Language Transformations (XSLT) built into Microsoft .NET.

Transforming XML in .NET Applications

You might have many reasons for needing to transform XML in one dialect to XML in another dialect in your application. For example, you might be part of a supply chain in which orders are passed in XML format from customers to suppliers. Or you might have dozens of files containing medical records that must be converted to a common format. In such situations, you must know what conversion is required, obtain an XSLT stylesheet to perform this transformation, and then apply that transformation programmatically using the capabilities provided by the .NET Framework.

The Need for Transformation

In Chapter 5, you saw how the catalog information for the cakes sold by the Fourth Coffee company could be encoded in XML. One form of this catalog is shown in the CakeCatalog.xml sample file, shown here:

CakeCatalog.xml

```
<?xml version="1.0" encoding="utf-8" ?>
<CakeCatalog>
<CakeType style="Celebration" filling="sponge" shape="round">
  <Message>Happy Birthday</Message>
  <Description>One of our most popular cakes</Description>
</CakeType>
<CakeType style="Wedding" filling="sponge" shape="square">
  <Message />
  <Description>A 3-tier creation to grace any ceremony</Description>
</CakeType>
<CakeType style="Wedding" filling="fruit" shape="round">
  <Message />
  <Description>A heavier cake for hungrier guests</Description>
</CakeType>
<CakeType style="Christmas" filling="fruit" shape="square">
  <Message>Season's Greetings</Message>
  <Description>Spicy fruitcake for cold evenings</Description>
</CakeType>
</CakeCatalog>
```

Imagine that this catalog information will form part of a larger catalog—perhaps because another firm wants to offer these cakes as part of its own catalog. For this integration to be seamless, the cake catalog must be converted into a more generic form such as that shown in the TxCatalog.xml sample file here:

TxCatalog.xml

```
<?xml version="1.0" encoding="utf-8" ?>
<Catalog type="Cake" vendor="Fourth Coffee">
<Entry>
<EntryElement type="CakeStyle" value="Celebration" />
<EntryElement type="Filling" value="sponge" />
<EntryElement type="Shape" value="round" />
<EntryElement type="Message" value="TEXT_CONTENT">Happy
   Birthday</EntryElement>
<EntryElement type="Description" value="TEXT_CONTENT">One of our
   most popular cakes</EntryElement>
</Entry>
<Entry>
<EntryElement type="CakeStyle" value="Wedding" />
<EntryElement type="Filling" value="sponge" />
<EntryElement type="Shape" value="square" />
<EntryElement type="Message" value="TEXT_CONTENT" />
<EntryElement type="Description" value="TEXT_CONTENT">A 3-tier
   creation to grace any ceremony</EntryElement>
</Entry>
<Entry>
<EntryElement type="CakeStyle" value="Wedding" />
<EntryElement type="Filling" value="fruit" />
<EntryElement type="Shape" value="round" />
<EntryElement type="Message" value="TEXT_CONTENT" />
<EntryElement type="Description" value="TEXT_CONTENT">A heavier
   cake for hungrier guests</EntryElement>
</Entry>
<Entry>
<EntryElement type="CakeStyle" value="Christmas" />
<EntryElement type="Filling" value="fruit" />
<EntryElement type="Shape" value="square" />
<EntryElement type="Message" value="TEXT_CONTENT">Season's
   Greetings</EntryElement>
<EntryElement type="Description" value="TEXT_CONTENT">Spicy fruitcake
   for cold evenings</EntryElement>
</Entry>
</Catalog>
```

As you can see, the format of TxCatalog.xml is far more general than that of CakeCatalog.xml. Both documents contain the same information, but the structure is different. You saw in the previous chapter how you can access parts of an XML document and obtain information from it. You also saw how you can create a new XML document using the same APIs. Hence, you can perform such a conversion between these two document structures programmatically using a combination of *XmlReader* and *XmlWriter* or using the DOM features of an *XmlDocument*. However, such a conversion would require document-specific and potentially complex code.

The XSLT language and processing model is designed to aid transformation between XML dialects, so you should use it where transformation is required unless there is a compelling reason not to do so—for example, when the type of transformation you require is difficult to code in XSLT.

The XSLT Processing Model

XSLT stylesheets are themselves XML documents, so the basic XSLT processing model involves three documents:

- The source XML document that contains the XML to be transformed
- The XSLT document that specifies the transformation required
- The target XML document that will contain the results of the transformation

The source XML document and XSLT document are read and parsed by the XMLT processor, as shown in Figure 6-1. The XSLT transformation is applied to the source document to generate the target XML document.

Note The target document does not have to be in XML format—it can be plain text. However, for the purposes of this chapter we will concentrate on the generation of XML documents.

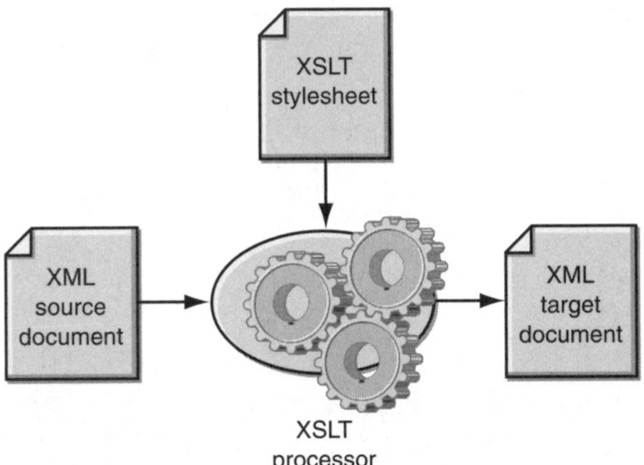

Figure 6-1 An XSLT processor transforms a source XML document based on an XSLT stylesheet.

XSLT is a declarative rather than a procedural language, so it can seem strange at first. An XSLT stylesheet consists of a set of rules that tell the processor what to output when it finds particular types of nodes or combinations of nodes in the source document. These rules are defined using XSLT templates. Each template consists of the following:

- An XPath expression that identifies a particular part of the source document to transform. XPath allows you to select attributes, elements, or other content by providing a pattern that describes a path into the structure of the source document based on such information as its location in the document or the name of a particular element or attribute.
- A rule dictating what should be output when that particular pattern is found in the source document.

We cannot go into all aspects of XSLT syntax at this point. If you need to investigate XSLT and XPath syntax in more detail, see Michael Kay's *XSLT Programmer's Reference 2nd Edition* (Wrox Press, 2001). However, to get an idea of what you can do, you can examine the sample file CatalogTransform.xsl, which defines an XSLT stylesheet that will transform CakeCatalog.xml into TxCatalog.xml:

CatalogTransform.xsl

```
<xsl:stylesheet xmlns:xsl="http://www.w3.org/1999/XSL/Transform"
version="1.0">
<xsl:output method="xml" />
   <xsl:template match="/">
      <xsl:apply-templates />
   </xsl:template>
   <xsl:template match="CakeCatalog">
      <Catalog type="Cake" vendor="Fourth Coffee">
         <xsl:apply-templates />
      </Catalog>
   </xsl:template>
   <xsl:template match="CakeType">
      <Entry>
         <EntryElement type="CakeStyle" value="{@style}" />
         <EntryElement type="Filling" value="{@filling}" />
         <EntryElement type="Shape" value="{@shape}" />
         <xsl:apply-templates />
      </Entry>
   </xsl:template>
   <xsl:template match="Message">
      <EntryElement type="Message" value="TEXT_CONTENT">
         <xsl:apply-templates />
      </EntryElement>
   </xsl:template>
   <xsl:template match="Description">
      <EntryElement type="Description" value="TEXT_CONTENT">
         <xsl:apply-templates />
      </EntryElement>
   </xsl:template>
</xsl:stylesheet>
```

Within this sample document, you can see some of the aspects common to all XSLT documents:

1. A namespace declaration indicates that the prefix *xsl* is used for XSLT-specific tags.
2. The root element indicates that it is an XSLT stylesheet (*xsl:stylesheet*).
3. The body of the document consists of a set of *xsl:template* tags. Each of these defines a rule to be applied.
4. The pattern in the source document to be matched by each template is defined by the *match* attribute. The first template matches the root node (indicated by "/").

Caution It is important to understand that in XSLT terms, the root node is not the same as the DOM root element. The XSLT root node is equivalent to the DOM *XmlDocument*.

---

5. The *xsl:output* element tells the XSLT processor that the output from the transformation will be an XML document and should include an XML declaration and all XML tags generated by the transformation.

6. When the root element is matched, the contents of the template are applied. In this case, the template simply contains an *xsl:apply-templates* element that tells the XSLT processor to carry on and examine the children of the root node to see if any of the other template rules apply to them.

7. The next node to be matched is the root element (or document element) of the document—the *CakeCatalog* element in our example. The template rule for this contains a mixture of literal output (for example, the *Catalog* tag and its attributes) and another *xsl:apply-templates* element.

8. The *xsl:apply-templates* instruction in the root element processing tells the XSLT processor to continue down the tree and process the child nodes of the root element. In the example document, this means that the children of the *CakeCatalog* (the *CakeType* elements) are then processed. Again, the template body contains a mixture of literal content and XSLT instructions. Some of these instructions relate to obtaining attribute values from the current element in the source document (*CakeType*) and substituting them into the output document. For example, the string *{@shape}* is replaced with the value of the *shape* attribute on the current *CakeType* element being processed from the input document.

9. The template body for *CakeType* element processing contains an *xsl:apply-templates* instruction. Once again, this tells the XSLT processor to process the children of such elements. In the example document, the *xsl:apply-templates* instruction causes the processing to cascade down to the *Message* and *Description* child elements. The rules for these elements are again a mixture of literal content and *xsl:apply-templates* instructions. Because there are no other elements

below *Message* and *Description*, this instruction simply causes their text content to be evaluated and transferred to the output document.

As you can see, with relatively few instructions, the contents of the document can be easily converted. The processing model for each type of element follows a similar pattern. Obviously, some transformations are easier to achieve than others, and sometimes it might be easier to perform a particular conversion using DOM or *XmlReader/XmlWriter*. However, stylesheets usually allow you to apply the Pareto principle of obtaining 80 percent of the result for 20 percent of the effort. As you'll see later, you can combine XSLT stylesheets with more traditional programmatic manipulation.

XSLT has certain advantages over programmatic mechanisms when it comes to performing transformations:

- All XSLT stylesheets are defined in standard XSLT syntax and therefore do not limit you to any particular procedural programming language, toolset, or platform.
- If a transformation is to be changed, it is generally easier to redeploy a stylesheet file than to redeploy application code.
- Many XSLT processors are available in a variety of programming languages. You can use the Microsoft XSLT processor (which is part of the MSXML component) from Visual Basic, C#, J#, and C++. Other XSLT processors are accessible from Java and C++, such as Apache Xalan and James Clarke's XT.

XSLT also has some drawbacks:

- You have to learn the XSLT stylesheet language and become familiar with XPath expressions.
- The use of stylesheets can be slower than programmatic transformation in some cases.

For most transformations, the advantages of using XSLT stylesheets will outweigh the disadvantages.

Applying Transformations

Transformations are required when an application or component needs data in a format different from the one that the data is currently in. When you're using XSLT, both of these formats will typically be XML, although the output can be almost any form of text. Transformations typically occur in the following situations:

- When the application is delivering information to the user—for example, to convert XML into HTML or WML for display in a Web browser or on a mobile phone.
- In a B2B scenario—for example, when you need to convert between your own data format and that of a customer or supplier. There might be a series of different transformations that convert multiple supplier formats into a common document structure for internal use. This form of conversion might also apply when you're dealing with legacy data.
- When you're dealing with multiple inputs to aggregate data from different sources.
- When filtering is required to reduce the amount of data being processed. Filtering creates a required subset of the data from a more data-rich document.

You can apply transformations as part of your application when it receives XML documents from external sources, when it generates documents as part of your application's output, or both. The appropriate type of transformation and the correct place to apply it will depend on your application. Figure 6-2 shows an application that accepts XML-based data from various sources and uses XSLT to convert it into a common format before it is processed and used to deliver information to various clients.

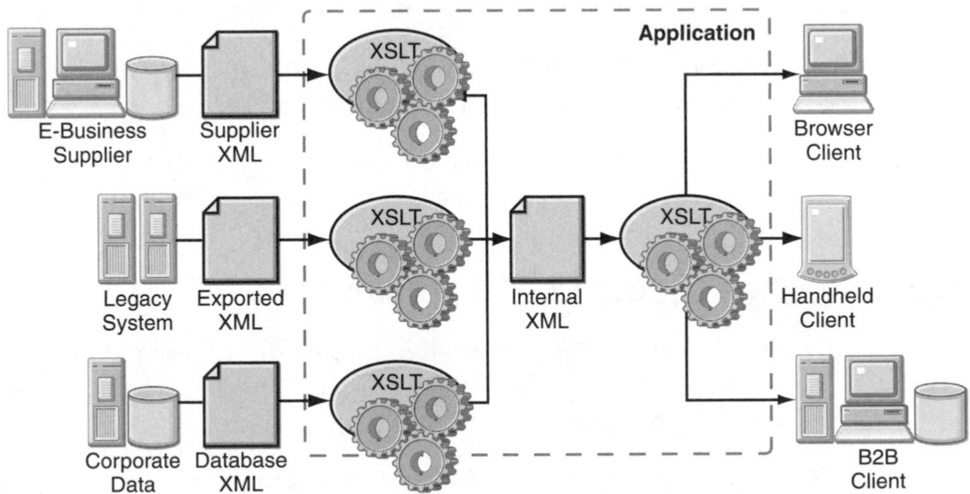

Figure 6-2 An application can apply XSLT in many ways for importing and exporting data.

.NET Support for XML Transformations

Visual J# and the .NET Framework provide support for the programmatic transformation of XML documents using XSLT. This support is based on widely accepted standards for the processing and transformation of XML.

Standards and Mechanisms Supported by the .NET Framework

To transform an XML document, you must identify parts of the input document to be converted and then specify the conversion to be performed. The W3C defines two standards to help define the transformation, both of which the .NET Framework supports. XPath defines a string-based syntax that allows you to traverse and search an XML document, which then allows you to specify the nodes in the input document that you want to transform. The XSLT standard builds on XPath and provides a set of element definitions with which you can define templates that specify the required structure of the output XML document.

Classes in the .NET Framework

As you saw in the previous chapter, the basic XML support required for document manipulation is provided in the *System.Xml* namespace. There are also two subnamespaces that provide functionality specific to XSLT and transformations:

- *System.Xml.XPath*, which contains classes that support the navigation of XML documents in a flexible way based on XPath expressions.
- *System.Xml.Xsl*, which comprises classes that support the transformation of XML documents using XSLT stylesheets.

This chapter will cover the use of the classes in these two namespaces and will use classes from the *System.Xml* namespace as required.

Applying Stylesheets to XML Documents

By now you should be convinced of the benefits of using XSLT stylesheets. The next step is to apply them in your J# applications. To do this, you have to answer certain questions:

- Where will you get the XML document from?
- Which transformation do you want to apply to it?
- What do you want done with the output XML document?

These three questions match up with the three documents involved in an XSLT-based transformation (source XML, XSLT stylesheet, output XML). In this section, we'll examine how the .NET Framework answers these questions. In one example, you'll also see how to apply transformations to data held in ADO.NET *DataSet* objects.

As test data for this section, we'll use the sample CakeCatalog.xml file and the CatalogTransform.xsl stylesheet shown earlier.

Simple Transformations Using *XslTransform*

The *XslTransform* class lies at the heart of the .NET Framework support for the transformation of XML. Using *XslTransform* is fairly straightforward—you simply provide it with the XML documents required and direct its output appropriately.

To perform any transformation, the first thing you do is instantiate an *XslTransform*. You can then prime it with the particular transformation you want to apply to your source document using the *Load* method:

```
XslTransform transformer = new XslTransform();
transformer.Load("CatalogTransform.xsl");
```

You can now use the *Transform* method of the *XslTransform* instance to apply this particular transformation to any XML document to which you have access:

```
transformer.Transform(sourceFile, targetFile);
```

The sample J# application Transformer.jsl in the Transformer sample project shows how you can apply this simplest form of transformation. The program takes the names of three files—one containing the source XML document, one containing the XSLT stylesheet, and another indicating the name of the target file in which to place the resulting XML document.

Transformer.jsl

```
package Transformer;

import System.*;
import System.Xml.*;
import System.Xml.Xsl.*;

public class Transformer
{
   public static void main(String[] args)
   {
      if (args.length != 3)
      {
```

```
            Console.WriteLine
                ("Usage: Transformer source.xml target.xml transform.xsl");
            Environment.Exit(1);
        }

        simpleTransform(args[0], args[1], args[2]);
    }

    private static void simpleTransform(String source,
        String target, String stylesheet)
    {
        XslTransform transformer = new XslTransform();
        transformer.Load(stylesheet);
        transformer.Transform(source, target);
    }
}
```

As you can see, a very small amount of code is required to perform simple transformations. You can try out the Transformer sample application yourself by passing the CakeCatalog.xml and CakeTransform.xsl files seen previously as the source XML and XSLT files, respectively. The sample project provides these files as inputs and indicates that the output should be stored in the file TxCatalog.xml.

Transformation Sources and Targets

You can pass an XSLT stylesheet to the *Load* method in various forms:

- A string specifying a URL (or filename) from which to obtain the document.
- An *XmlReader* wrapped around the source document.
- An *XPathNavigator*. Recall from the previous chapter that you can obtain an *XPathNavigator* from any *XmlNode* in a DOM using the *CreateNavigator* method. Typically, you would use the *CreateNavigator* method on an *XmlDocument* object that represents the XSLT stylesheet. Alternatively, you can pass in any object implementing the *IXPathNavigable* interface (such as *XmlNode*) and the *Load* method will obtain an *XPathNavigator* from it.

Access to the source and target XML document are both defined as parameters to the *Transform* method. The source XML document can be

- A *string* representing the URL from which to obtain the XML document.

- An *XPathNavigator* object representing the root of the source tree to be transformed. As with the *Load* method, any object implementing *IXPathNavigable* can be passed in and the *Transform* method will obtain the *XPathNavigator* it requires.

  The target document can be specified as

- A *string* URL representing the file location at which to store the resulting document.
- A *System.IO.Stream* to which the resulting document is written.
- A *TextWriter* to which the resulting document is written.
- An *XmlWriter* to which the resulting document is written.

There are also two forms of the *Transform* method that return an *XmlReader* that wraps up the resulting document. These are ideal when the resulting document must be processed in memory.

Note Not all combinations of source and target are supported. See the .NET Framework documentation for the different forms of the *Transform* method.

The following example shows how to use an *XmlDocument* as the input for a transformation. This approach works because the *XmlDocument* class implements *IXPathNavigable*:

```
XslTransform transformer = new XslTransform();
transformer.Load(stylesheet);

XmlDocument sourceDocument = new XmlDocument();
sourceDocument.Load(source);

transformer.Transform(sourceDocument, null, Console.get_Out());
```

You can find the full code for a DOM-based transformation in the DomTransformer.jsl sample file.

An XSLT stylesheet can include an *xsl:output* element that defines the preferred output format. The *method* attribute of this element can be set to *xml*, *html*, or *text* to specify the overall style of the output. The *xsl:output* element also has other attributes that determine the indentation of the output, the encoding, the document type to use, and so on. If you were to include the following line in the CatalogTransform.xsl file

```
<xsl:output method="text" />
```

the resulting output would simply be the text content of the document—it would have no tags or XML declaration. Note that this element has no effect on the transformation result when the output is done through an *XmlReader* or *XmlWriter*.

Transforming a *DataSet*

As you saw in the last chapter, it is possible to associate an XML document with an ADO.NET *DataSet* by using an *XmlDataDocument*. Because the *XmlDataDocument* class implements the *IXPathNavigable* interface, it can be used as a parameter to the *Transform* method. This means that data can be retrieved from a relational database into an ADO.NET *DataSet* and that data can then be transformed using an XSLT stylesheet using just a few lines of code:

```
DataSet ds = <data source>  // Obtain data from data source

XmlDataDocument dataDoc = new XmlDataDocument(ds);

XslTransform transformer = new XslTransform();
transformer.Load(stylesheet);

// Make the output pretty this time...
XmlTextWriter writer = new XmlTextWriter(Console.get_Out());
writer.set_Formatting(System.Xml.Formatting.Indented);

transformer.Transform(dataDoc, null, writer);
```

This code can be found in the sample file DataSetTransformer.jsl. Notice that it uses an *XmlTextWriter* to wrap standard output to set the formatting style to *Indented*. This adds line breaks and indentation, which makes the XML more human-readable.

Optimization and Partial Transformation

You have now seen how to perform basic transformations in J# applications using XSLT. These types of transformations can take input from various sources and transform it into the appropriate form—which is sufficient for many uses. But if the transformations form part of critical application logic, this approach can create a performance bottleneck because of the inefficiency of repeated file and string manipulation. To address this, optimizations are required.

Searching and Navigating Using XPath

In Chapter 5, you briefly encountered the *XPathNavigator* class, which provides read-only access to the nodes in an XML document. You can navigate through these nodes, moving forward and backward as required. An *XPathNavigator* can be obtained from an *XmlDocument*, an *XmlNode*, or from the specialized *XPathDocument* class. An example of the use of an *XPathNavigator*, taken from the sample file XPathNavigation.jsl, is shown here:

```
XPathDocument doc = new XPathDocument(source);
XPathNavigator nav = doc.CreateNavigator();
nav.MoveToFirstChild(); // Move from root to document element
nav.MoveToFirstChild(); // Move from document element to first CakeType
while (nav.MoveToNext())
{
   dumpCurrentNode(nav);
}

Console.WriteLine("And back again!");

while (nav.MoveToPrevious())
{
   dumpCurrentNode(nav);
}
```

The *XPathNavigator* class provides powerful XPath searching capabilities over the XML nodes of its associated document. You can query the XML document and retrieve a set of nodes that match the given query in the form of an *XPathNodeIterator*, with which you can walk through the retrieved nodes. The following code shows this technique as applied in the sample file XPathIteration.jsl:

```
private static void search(String source, String expression)
{
   XPathDocument doc = new XPathDocument(source);
   XPathNavigator nav = doc.CreateNavigator();
   XPathNodeIterator iterator = nav.Select(expression);
   while (iterator.MoveNext())
   {
      dumpCurrentNode(iterator.get_Current());
   }
}
```

At this stage, you might be thinking "So what?" This technique gives you similar functionality to the DOM navigation methods and the *SelectSingleNode* method you saw earlier as part of the *XmlDocument* class. Well, in terms of searching, the *XPathNavigator* offers one big advantage over the *XmlDocu-*

ment: you can compile the XPath expression being used to search the document. This offers great performance advantages when the same query is used repeatedly because you can parse the XPath string just once and then use the compiled expression again and again. The use of the *Compile* method on the *XPathNavigator* class is shown here:

```
XPathDocument doc = new XPathDocument(source1);
XPathNavigator nav = doc.CreateNavigator();

// Compile the expression to speed up subsequent navigation
XPathExpression compiledExpr = nav.Compile(expression);
XPathNodeIterator iterator = nav.Select(compiledExpr);

while (iterator.MoveNext())
{
   dumpCurrentNode(iterator.get_Current());
}

XPathDocument doc2 = new XPathDocument(source2);
XPathNavigator nav2 = doc2.CreateNavigator();

// Re-use the compiled expression
XPathNodeIterator iterator2 = nav2.Select(compiledExpr);
while (iterator2.MoveNext())
{
   dumpCurrentNode(iterator2.get_Current());
}
```

As you can see, the XPath query is compiled once and then used on both the first and second documents. The sample file CompiledXPathIteration.jsl uses the code above to search two cake catalogs using the same XPath expression.

Compiled XPath queries using an *XPathNavigator* are an efficient way of searching an XML document, but what does this mean for XSLT? Well, you can use the *XPathNavigator* and its optimizations to speed up XSLT transformations.

Optimizing XSLT Transformations

The *Load* and *Transform* methods of the *XslTransform* class allow you to specify the XML source document and the XSLT stylesheet in the form of *XPathNavigator* classes. You do this by passing an *XPathNavigator* or passing a class that implements the *IXPathNavigable* interface (which requires the class to implement a *CreateNavigator* method). Providing the source and stylesheet in this way greatly optimizes the transformation process.

As you've seen, the *XPathDocument* class is another way of representing an XML document. The *XPathDocument* class does not in itself provide methods for accessing parts of an XML tree. Instead, it allows you to obtain an *XPathNavigator* on the particular document so you can traverse it. The great advantage of the *XPathDocument* is that it is a lighter-weight object than a DOM-based *XmlDocument*. An *XPathDocument* does not maintain node identity information, nor does it perform all of the rule checking required by the W3C DOM standard. To use *XPathDocument* classes for both stylesheet and input documents, you can use code as shown in the XPathDocumentTransform.jsl sample file:

```
XPathDocument transform = new XPathDocument(stylesheet);

XslTransform transformer = new XslTransform();
transformer.Load(transform);

XPathDocument sourceDocument = new XPathDocument(source);

transformer.Transform(sourceDocument, null, Console.get_Out());
```

Partial Transformations

In some cases, you might want to simply transform part of a document. In our example, this could be a single *CakeType* element. However, the transformation of only part of a tree is trickier than you might expect.

For example, if you load the XML into an *XmlDocument*, an *XmlDataDocument*, or an *XPathDocument* and locate the node whose contents you want to transform, you might expect to be able to use the *XPathNavigator* obtained from this node to transform just the node and its descendents. However, the *XPathNavigator* obtained in such a way is still an *XPathNavigator* for the whole document to which this node pertains. Hence, to limit the scope of the *XPathNavigator*, you must clone the appropriate node, and its descendents, and place the subtree in its own *XmlDocumentFragment* as follows:

```
XPathDocument transform = new XPathDocument(stylesheet);

XslTransform transformer = new XslTransform();
transformer.Load(transform);

XmlDocument sourceDocument = new XmlDocument();
sourceDocument.Load(source);
XmlDocumentFragment partialTree = sourceDocument.CreateDocumentFragment();

partialTree.AppendChild(sourceDocument.SelectSingleNode(expression).Clone());
```

```
XPathNavigator nav2 = partialTree.CreateNavigator();

transformer.Transform(partialTree, null, Console.get_Out());
```

You use the *SelectSingleNode* method of the *XmlDocument* to find the required node, and this node (along with its descendents) is cloned. The cloned node is then appended to an empty *XmlDocumentFragment*, and an *XPathNavigator* is obtained from this fragment and passed to the *Transform* method.

The full code for this conversion can be found in the sample file PartialTransform.jsl.

Parameterization and External Functionality

If you've spent any time looking at XSLT stylesheets, you'll appreciate that even though they're a powerful transformation mechanism, they do not lend themselves easily to every situation. Some aspects of the way that stylesheets work make them difficult to adapt to "traditional" programming tasks. You might, for example, find it difficult to create code that relies on changing variable values because XSLT variables are read-only. This might encourage you to revert completely to procedural programming to perform this "difficult" part of the processing and thereby lose out on the benefits of stylesheet-based transformations. However, the Pareto Principle is still at work because stylesheets can do a lot of work with few lines of code. It can therefore be useful at times to combine stylesheets with function calls to other programming languages in which you can exploit alternative programming styles or external functionality.

Another traditional aspect of writing programs is working with information passed in from outside, such as properties or command-line parameters. XSLT stylesheets do not differ in this respect from other programs, and the stylesheet specification defines how parameters can be declared and applied within a stylesheet.

By using the *XsltArgumentList* with the *XslTranform* class, you can specify parameters and external functionality that can be used inside an XSLT stylesheet.

Passing in Parameters

XSLT stylesheets have common programming functionality, such as declaring and assigning variables. You can also call templates called *named templates* from other templates in much the same way that you call a method from within another method in the Java language. You can declare parameters to a named template and then specify parameter values when you call that template. In a typical Java program, you pass parameters internally to methods, but you also frequently pass in data from outside the program using command-line parameters or system properties. To make this functionality possible, you need a way to import external data into an XSLT stylesheet.

XSLT parameter declarations are scoped in much the same way as Java variables. Parameters can be declared inside a named template or within the scope of the *stylesheet* element (at the same level as the *template* elements themselves). Parameters declared in the scope of the *stylesheet* element have global scope and are populated with data passed into the stylesheet when it is invoked. For example, consider the transformation defined in the CatalogTransform.xsl stylesheet shown earlier. To pass in the particular vendor name, and possibly a unique vendor identifier, you can define two global parameters as follows:

```
<xsl:stylesheet xmlns:xsl="http://www.w3.org/1999/XSL/Transform" version="1.0">
   <xsl:param name="vendorId"/>
   <xsl:param name="vendor"/>
:
</xsl:stylesheet>
```

You can then use these global parameters to populate the *vendor* and *vendor_id* attributes of the *Catalog* element being created:

```
<xsl:template match="CakeCatalog">
   <Catalog type="Cake" vendor="{$vendor}" vendor_id="{$vendorId}">
      <xsl:apply-templates />
   </Catalog>
</xsl:template>
```

To pass in values for these parameters, you must instantiate an *XsltArgumentList* object and add parameter descriptions and values to it. You can specify the name, namespace, and value of each parameter. The following code shows how to set values for the *vendor* and *vendorId* attributes (which belong to the default namespace):

```
XsltArgumentList args = new XsltArgumentList();
args.AddParam("vendorId", "", "8293940");
args.AddParam("vendor", "", "Fourth Coffee");
```

You can then use the *XsltArgumentList* as a parameter into most of the overloaded forms of the *Transform* method:

```
transformer.Transform(sourceDocument, args, writer);
```

You'll find the full code for performing this parameterized transformation in the ParameterizedTransform.jsl sample file and the associated stylesheet in the ParamCatalogTransform.xsl sample file. The resulting output is shown in Figure 6-3.

ParamCatalogTransform.xsl

```
<xsl:stylesheet xmlns:xsl="http://www.w3.org/1999/XSL/Transform" version="1.0">
   <xsl:param name="vendorId"/>
   <xsl:param name="vendor"/>
   <xsl:output method="xml" />
   <xsl:template match="/">
      <xsl:apply-templates />
   </xsl:template>
   <xsl:template match="CakeCatalog">
      <Catalog type="Cake" vendor="{$vendor}" vendor_id="{$vendorId}">
         <xsl:apply-templates />
      </Catalog>
   </xsl:template>
   <xsl:template match="CakeType">
      <Entry>
         <EntryElement type="CakeStyle" value="{@style}" />
         <EntryElement type="Filling" value="{@filling}" />
         <EntryElement type="Shape" value="{@shape}" />
         <xsl:apply-templates />
      </Entry>
   </xsl:template>
   <xsl:template match="Message">
      <EntryElement type="Message" value="TEXT_CONTENT">
         <xsl:apply-templates />
      </EntryElement>
   </xsl:template>
   <xsl:template match="Description">
      <EntryElement type="Description" value="TEXT_CONTENT">
         <xsl:apply-templates />
      </EntryElement>
   </xsl:template>
</xsl:stylesheet>
```

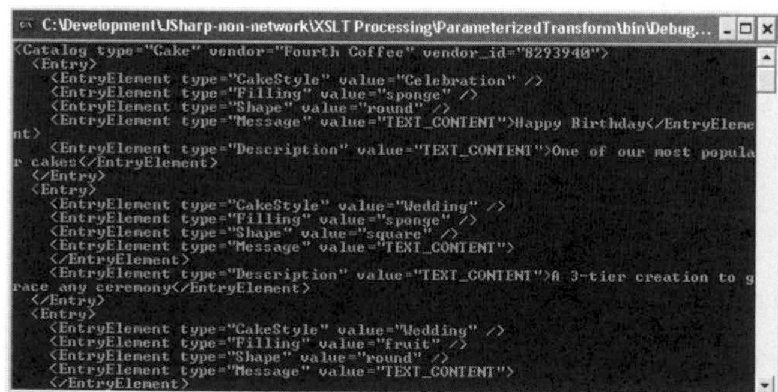

Figure 6-3 CakeCatalog transformed using a parameterized stylesheet to add vendor information

The *XsltArgumentList* will perform conversions on the parameters provided to prepare them for inclusion in an XML document. *Boolean* and *String* types convert directly to their XPath equivalents. Signed and unsigned integers, decimals, and floating-point numbers are all coerced into *System.Double* and then converted into the XPath *Number* type. All other types are converted into string representations using the *ToString* method, except for *XPathNavigator* and *XPathNodeIterator*. These two types allow you to create XPath *Node Fragments* and *Node Sets* that can be used in the XSLT stylesheet.

Consider creating a parameter that consists of the address information for the catalog vendor. This can be a hierarchy of elements and text that you already have in XML format and do not want to convert into individual parameters, such as the following:

```
<VendorInformation>
<Address>"999 Central Drive, Tickhill, CA"</Address>
</VendorInformation>
```

Given an *XmlDocument* or *XPathDocument* containing this partial XML tree, you can create an *XPathNavigator* and pass it as an argument as follows:

```
XmlDocument vInfo = ...; // Get the vendor information document

XPathNavigator nav = vInfo.CreateNavigator();
args.AddParam("vendorInfo", "", nav);

transformer.Transform(sourceDocument, args, writer);
```

In your XSLT stylesheet, you can then use this parameter as follows:

```
<xsl:stylesheet xmlns:xsl="http://www.w3.org/1999/XSL/Transform" version="1.0">
   <xsl:param name="vendorInfo"/>
⋮
     <xsl:template match="CakeCatalog">
      <Catalog type="Cake" vendor="{$vendor}" vendor_id="{$vendorId}">
         <xsl:copy-of select="$vendorInfo"/>
         <xsl:apply-templates />
      </Catalog>
   </xsl:template>
⋮
</xsl:stylesheet>
```

The parameter declaration is the same as the ones you've seen previously. However, when the parameter is evaluated, it becomes a document fragment. You can use the *xsl:copy-of* element to copy this fragment into the result tree; in this case, the element creates the *VendorInformation* element just below the *Catalog* element. The code for this transformation can be found in the sample file ParamFragmentTransform.jsl and the associated stylesheet in ParamFragmentCatalogTransform.xsl. The results of this addition are shown in Figure 6-4.

```
C:\Development\JSharp-non-network\XSLT Processing\ParamFragmentTransform\bin\Debu...
<Catalog type="Cake" vendor="Fourth Coffee" vendor_id="8293940">
  <VendorInformation>
    <Address>999 Central Drive, Tickhill, CA</Address>
  </VendorInformation>
  <Entry>
    <EntryElement type="CakeStyle" value="Celebration" />
    <EntryElement type="Filling" value="sponge" />
    <EntryElement type="Shape" value="round" />
    <EntryElement type="Message" value="TEXT_CONTENT">Happy Birthday</EntryEleme
nt>
    <EntryElement type="Description" value="TEXT_CONTENT">One of our most popula
r cakes</EntryElement>
  </Entry>
  <Entry>
    <EntryElement type="CakeStyle" value="Wedding" />
    <EntryElement type="Filling" value="sponge" />
    <EntryElement type="Shape" value="square" />
    <EntryElement type="Message" value="TEXT_CONTENT">
    </EntryElement>
    <EntryElement type="Description" value="TEXT_CONTENT">A 3-tier creation to g
race any ceremony</EntryElement>
  </Entry>
  <Entry>
    <EntryElement type="CakeStyle" value="Wedding" />
    <EntryElement type="Filling" value="fruit" />
```

Figure 6-4 CakeCatalog transformed, including additional vendor information

Invoking External Functionality

As noted earlier, XSLT is not as flexible or concise as a traditional procedural language when it comes to such things as calculation. You might therefore want to call an external function from within your XSLT stylesheet. We'll look at options for doing this next.

Extension Objects

One option for invoking external functionality is to define an extension object as part of the *XsltArgumentList* you pass into the *Transform* method. For example, you're required to state how many people each type of cake will feed. Building on the *ParameterizedTransform* class you saw previously in the ParameterizedTransform.jsl sample, we can add a simplified version of the *FeedsHowMany* method you saw in Chapter 2:

```
public class ExtensionTransform
{
    ⋮
public double FeedsHowMany(double diameter, String filling)
{
        boolean fruitFilling =
           (String.Compare(filling, "fruit") == 0) ? true : false;
        double munchSizeFactor = (fruitFilling ? 2.5 : 1);

        short numConsumers = (short)(diameter * munchSizeFactor);

        return numConsumers;
    }
}
```

The method takes a *double* value for the diameter of the cake in inches and a *string* stating the type of filling. The method returns the number of people that the cake feeds as a *double* value. You can then use this method from within the XSLT stylesheet by passing an instance of the *ExtensionTransform* class as an extension object. You do this by using the *AddExtensionObject* method of the *XsltArgumentList* class. You specify a namespace with which to associate the extension object and the object itself:

```
args.AddExtensionObject("http://www.fourthcoffee.com/xml",
   new ExtensionTransform());
```

The next step is to associate this namespace with a prefix in the stylesheet:

```
<xsl:stylesheet xmlns:xsl="http://www.w3.org/1999/XSL/Transform"
   version="1.0" xmlns:coffee="http://www.fourthcoffee.com/xml">
```

You can use this prefix and the method name to call the function. In this case, the function is called from within the template that matches *CakeType* elements, so the *filling* attribute is available to pass as a parameter:

```
<EntryElement type="Feeds">
   <!-- All cakes default to 10" in size -->
   <xsl:attribute name="value">
      <xsl:value-of select="coffee:FeedsHowMany(10.0, @filling)" />
   </xsl:attribute>
</EntryElement>
```

This addition to the stylesheet will cause a new *EntryElement* to be displayed for each cake showing how many people it will feed, as you can see in Figure 6-5. The full code for the *ExtensionTransform* class and the updated stylesheet are in the ExtensionTransform.jsl and ExtCatalogTransform.xsl sample files, respectively.

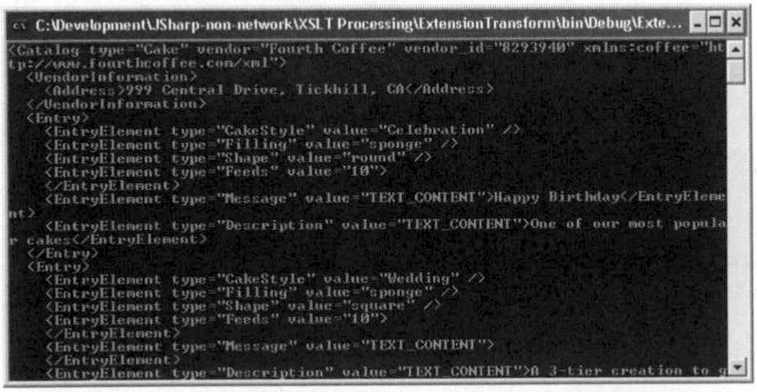

Figure 6-5 Using an extension object to call the *FeedsHowMany* method from within a stylesheet

ExtCatalogTransform.xsl

```
<xsl:stylesheet xmlns:xsl="http://www.w3.org/1999/XSL/Transform" version="1.0"
xmlns:coffee="http://www.fourthcoffee.com/xml">
   <xsl:param name="vendorId"/>
   <xsl:param name="vendor"/>
   <xsl:param name="vendorInfo"/>
   <xsl:output method="xml" />
   <xsl:template match="/">
      <xsl:apply-templates />
   </xsl:template>
   <xsl:template match="CakeCatalog">
      <Catalog type="Cake" vendor="{$vendor}" vendor_id="{$vendorId}">
         <xsl:copy-of select="$vendorInfo"/>
         <xsl:apply-templates />
      </Catalog>
   </xsl:template>
   <xsl:template match="CakeType">
      <Entry>
         <EntryElement type="CakeStyle" value="{@style}" />
         <EntryElement type="Filling" value="{@filling}" />
         <EntryElement type="Shape" value="{@shape}" />
         <EntryElement type="Feeds">
            <!-- All cakes default to 10" in size -->
            <xsl:attribute name="value">
               <xsl:value-of select="coffee:FeedsHowMany(10.0,
                  @filling)" />
            </xsl:attribute>
         </EntryElement>
         <xsl:apply-templates />
      </Entry>
   </xsl:template>
   <xsl:template match="Message">
      <EntryElement type="Message" value="TEXT_CONTENT">
         <xsl:apply-templates />
      </EntryElement>
   </xsl:template>
   <xsl:template match="Description">
      <EntryElement type="Description" value="TEXT_CONTENT">
         <xsl:apply-templates />
      </EntryElement>
   </xsl:template>
</xsl:stylesheet>
```

msxsl Script

An alternative approach to using extension objects is to use the embedded scripting capability available through the *urn:schemas-microsoft-com:xslt* namespace. This technique allows you to define your external functionality within the stylesheet. One advantage of this approach is that it keeps the two parts of the functionality together and makes it easier to take in the functionality "at a glance." However, be aware that using platform-specific extension functionality such as that provided by the *urn:schemas-microsoft-com:xslt* namespace will render your XSLT stylesheets less portable.

The first thing to do is to declare a prefix for the *urn:schemas-microsoft-com:xslt* namespace, which is usually set to *msxsl*. You should also declare a target namespace to be associated with the functionality, which in this case is *coffee*:

```
<xsl:stylesheet version="1.0"
  xmlns:xsl="http://www.w3.org/1999/XSL/Transform"
  xmlns:msxsl="urn:schemas-microsoft-com:xslt"
    xmlns:coffee="http://www.fourthcoffee.com/xml">
```

You can then define your function internally using the msxsl:script element, declaring the language of the code and associating the code with the namespace prefix:

```
<msxsl:script implements-prefix="coffee" language="C#">
  <![CDATA[
  public double FeedsHowMany(double diameter, string filling)
  {
    bool fruitFilling =
      (string.Compare(filling, "fruit") == 0) ? true : false;
    double munchSizeFactor = (fruitFilling ? 2.5 : 1);

    short numConsumers = (short)(diameter * munchSizeFactor);

    return numConsumers;
  }
  ]]>
</msxsl:script>
```

As you can see, this function is a C# form of the one used in the J# class. (There are only two differences: the J# *boolean* keyword is *bool* in C#, and our function uses the C# *string* type.) The function is written in C# because J# is not currently supported as a scripting language. Encapsulating the function in a CDATA section prevents it from being processed as if it were XML. The function is invoked in the same way as a method of an extension object:

```
<xsl:value-of select="coffee:FeedsHowMany(10.0, @filling)" />
```

The complete XSLT stylesheet is shown in the ScriptCatalogTransform.xsl sample file. The code to invoke the transformation from J#, contained in the sample file ScriptTransform.jsl, is no different (apart from not passing in the extension object because it is no longer needed).

ScriptCatalogTransform.xsl

```
<xsl:stylesheet version="1.0" xmlns:xsl="http://www.w3.org/1999/XSL/Transform"
   xmlns:msxsl="urn:schemas-microsoft-com:xslt"
xmlns:coffee="http://www.fourthcoffee.com/xml">

  <msxsl:script implements-prefix="coffee" language="C#">
     <![CDATA[
   public double FeedsHowMany(double diameter, string filling)
   {
      bool fruitFilling =
         (string.Compare(filling, "fruit") == 0) ? true : false;
      double munchSizeFactor = (fruitFilling ? 2.5 : 1);

      short numConsumers = (short)(diameter * munchSizeFactor);

      return numConsumers;
   }
      ]]>
   </msxsl:script>

   <xsl:param name="vendorId"/>
   <xsl:param name="vendor"/>
   <xsl:param name="vendorInfo"/>
   <xsl:output method="xml" />
   <xsl:template match="/">
      <xsl:apply-templates />
   </xsl:template>
   <xsl:template match="CakeCatalog">
      <Catalog type="Cake" vendor="{$vendor}" vendor_id="{$vendorId}">
         <xsl:copy-of select="$vendorInfo"/>
         <xsl:apply-templates />
      </Catalog>
   </xsl:template>
   <xsl:template match="CakeType">
      <Entry>
         <EntryElement type="CakeStyle" value="{@style}" />
         <EntryElement type="Filling" value="{@filling}" />
         <EntryElement type="Shape" value="{@shape}" />
         <EntryElement type="Feeds">
            <!-- All cakes default to 10" in size -->
            <xsl:attribute name="value">
               <xsl:value-of select="coffee:FeedsHowMany(10.0,
                  @filling)" />
            </xsl:attribute>
         </EntryElement>
```

```
            <xsl:apply-templates />
        </Entry>
    </xsl:template>
    <xsl:template match="Message">
        <EntryElement type="Message" value="TEXT_CONTENT">
            <xsl:apply-templates />
        </EntryElement>
    </xsl:template>
    <xsl:template match="Description">
        <EntryElement type="Description" value="TEXT_CONTENT">
            <xsl:apply-templates />
        </EntryElement>
    </xsl:template>
</xsl:stylesheet>
```

Summary

The ability to easily transform the contents of XML documents has been a key factor in the rise of XML as a data format. The .NET Framework provides all the functionality you need to incorporate such transformations into your applications or components. After reading this chapter, you should be able to use the *XslTransform* class to apply an XSLT transformation to XML documents from a variety of sources, including XML from ADO.NET *DataSet* objects.

To improve the efficiency of transformations, you can apply the *XPathDocument* and *XPathNavigator* classes. You can also pass parameters into an XSLT stylesheet using an *XsltArgumentList*. You can use this same mechanism to define external functionality that you can invoke from within your stylesheets.

7

ADO.NET

ActiveX Data Objects for the .NET Framework (ADO.NET) is a set of classes that allow data access within the Microsoft .NET Framework. It provides a rich set of APIs that let you manage data access for all types of components in a wide variety of situations. For example, XML sits at the heart of ADO.NET, so it allows simple transfer of data between an application and a Web service, and ADO.NET adopts a disconnected model that is ideally suited for data access when connectivity is unreliable, such as when you're accessing data across the Web.

Throughout the rest of this book we'll work with ADO.NET, so you'll be introduced to many new concepts as we go. This chapter provides the foundation you'll need for later chapters, and it will also enable you to start coding against ADO.NET immediately. You'll learn about the ADO.NET architecture, methods of data retrieval, how to manage transactions, and how to work with XML in ADO.NET.

The ADO.NET Architecture

ADO.NET provides the interface between applications written in Common Language Specification–compliant languages and data sources. These data sources include not only relational databases but other data sources such as the contents of an XML document or information contained in messages held in a Microsoft Exchange information store. In addition, ADO.NET allows you to manage data from multiple sources. For example, you might want to work with data from two different tables held in a SQL Server database in combination with XML data received from a remote component. The functionality provided under ADO.NET allows you to work with these diverse data sources as if they originated from a single source.

The ADO.NET model is based on disconnected access, unlike its predecessor ADO, which provided more limited support for disconnected working. Using the disconnected model, an application creates a connection to a data store and then keeps that connection open only for the time required to update or retrieve data. When the application retrieves data, you can choose whether to create a local cache of any data retrieved or access it in a read-only, forward-only manner. (We'll examine both of these methods later in this chapter.) If you keep a local cache of the data, the data is held in tables, which you can work with in a way that's similar to working with tables in a relational database. If you update the locally cached data, the application can once again create a connection to the data store and persist those changes to the database.

The disconnected data access model offers a number of advantages over the traditional connected data access model. The two primary advantages relate to scalability and the distributed nature of enterprise applications. The first advantage is that connections to a database are held open for a shorter time than in a connected model. Because resources are freed up quickly, they are available to other clients. Hence, more clients can share the same number of database connections, leading to improved application scalability.

The second advantage is that the disconnected model suits the disconnected, heterogeneous nature of enterprise applications. Many corporate applications cross over domain boundaries. In addition, clients on the Web, such as Web browsers, tend to work in a disconnected way to make the best use of available server resources and available bandwidth. The disconnected nature of ADO.NET makes it ideal for use in Web applications built with ASP.NET. (Chapter 16 explores ASP.NET and illustrates data access over the Web.)

ADO.NET Components

At a high level, the structure of a program that uses ADO.NET to manipulate data in a data store is similar to one that uses Java Database Connectivity (JDBC). Although the precise ordering might differ a little, the following sequence of steps is required:

1. Get a connection to the data store.
2. Create a command that packages an SQL statement or stored procedure.
3. Execute the command and retrieve the result.
4. Close the connection.

However, ADO.NET and JDBC differ at the object level. Figure 7-1 shows the major components of ADO.NET.

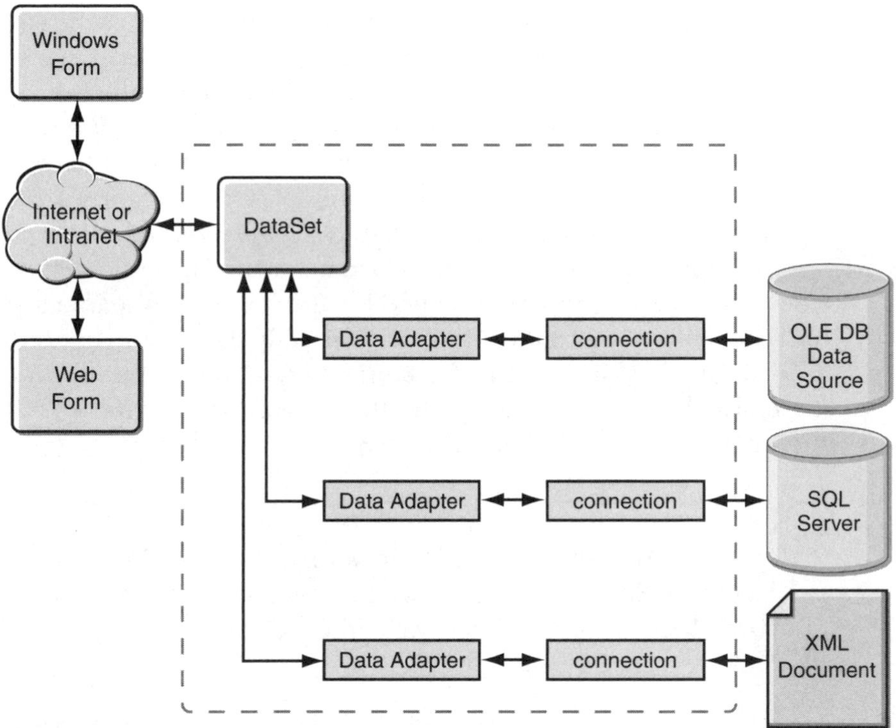

Figure 7-1 Major components of ADO.NET

ADO.NET revolves around the *System.Data* namespace and its four subnamespaces, which together contain the classes and interfaces that allow you to connect to data stores and manage those connections. The four subnamespaces are

- ***System.Data.Common*** Contains classes that are shared by the .NET data providers
- ***System.Data.OleDb*** Contains the classes that together allow access to and management of OLE DB data sources
- ***System.Data.SqlClient*** Contains the classes that allow access to and management of the SQL Server data source
- ***System.Data.SqlTypes*** Contains classes for native data types for SQL Server

As Figure 7-1 shows, the three main components are the *DataSet*, the data adapter, and the connection to the data source. The *DataSet* is an instance of *System.Data.DataSet*, and it provides a disconnected cache of data that is exposed in a format similar to a relational database. This cache contains tables, columns, and rows that you can navigate and perform operations against. The data adapter acts as a bridge between the *DataSet* and the actual data source. Because a data adapter must interact with the data source, it provides functionality specific to that data source (in the same way that you have specific JDBC drivers for different data sources). Therefore, a data adapter object will be an instance of a class that implements the *System.Data.IDataAdapter* interface, which defines the behavior common to all data adapter classes.

Third parties and Microsoft will make a range of adapters available that integrate with Visual Studio .NET, but currently the only adapters that ship with Visual Studio .NET are the *System.Data.OleDb.OleDbDataAdapter*, which accesses any OLE DB source, and the *System.Data.SqlClient.SqlDataAdapter*, which accesses SQL Server 7.0 or later.

Note You can access SQL Server by using the *OleDbDataAdapter*, but the *SqlDataAdapter* provides better performance because it is refined for use specifically with SQL Server and it also does not go through the OLE DB layer.

Connections, like data adapters, are specific to a data provider. Data adapter implementations must implement *IDataAdapter* to provide common access to their underlying data. Similarly, connection objects must implement *System.Data.IDbConnection*, which provides access to common control functionality for database connections. The two concrete connection classes that ship with Visual Studio .NET are *OleDbConnection* and *SqlConnection*.

Before we look at how you implement these components in code, let's take a more detailed look at the structures and roles of the *DataSet* and the data adapter.

DataSet Objects

As previously mentioned, a *DataSet* is a cache of data retrieved from one or more data sources. The *DataSet* is at the heart of the ADO.NET disconnected data access model. When you retrieve data from a data store, it becomes accessible through a table within a *DataSet*. The *DataSet* can contain multiple tables, and each of these tables can contain data retrieved from multiple data sources. Once the *DataSet* holds data for its tables, that data has no physical connection to the underlying data source—it is completely disconnected. The *DataSet* exposes an object hierarchy of tables, columns, and rows, which you can use to access and manage the data inside the tables. We'll explore this hierarchy later in the chapter.

Connections and Data Adapters

As noted earlier, a data adapter provides a bridge between a data source and a *DataSet*. The classes that represent a data adapter must implement the *System.Data.IDataAdapter* interface. You also learned that two implementations ship with Visual Studio—one for OLE DB data sources and one for SQL Server. Both implementations belong to their own subnamespaces of the *System.Data* namespace. Table 7-1 shows the main classes of these namespaces.

Table 7-1 The *OleDb* and *SqlClient* Namespaces

System.Data **Namespace Interface**	***OleDb*** **Namespace Implementation**	***SqlClient*** **Namespace Implementation**
IDbCommand	*OleDbCommand*	*SqlCommand*
IDbConnection	*OleDbConnection*	*SqlConnection*
IDataAdapter	*OleDbDataAdapter*	*SqlDataAdapter*
IDataReader	*OleDbDataReader*	*SqlDataReader*
IDataParameter	*OleDbParameter*	*SqlParameter*

To give you a taste of what functionality these classes expose, we'll discuss the common functionality the interfaces define and then start coding with these classes.

A data adapter requires a connection to connect to a data store; the ADO.NET connection object represents this connection. The connection object implements the *IDbConnection* interface, through which you can manipulate the connection. The connection object exposes properties that relate the underlying connection to the given data source—for example, the connection string used when you access the database. The object also exposes methods to open or close a connection and to manage transactions (as explained later in the chapter), and it exposes a method that returns a command object, which allows you to execute SQL statements against a database or invoke stored procedures within a database.

The command object is an instance of a class that implements the *IDbCommand* interface. This interface exposes properties that allow you to set items such as the command type, command text, and timeouts. The interface also exposes methods that allow you to execute SQL statements or stored procedures against a connection.

Note The *IDbCommand* interface exposes a *Prepare* method, which compiles a statement in advance of execution, like a JDBC *PreparedStatement* does.

Connecting to a Data Store

In the following sections, we'll use the Northwind database that ships with the .NET Framework SDK. To access this data source, we'll use the classes from the *SqlClient* namespace. We'll highlight any differences between the use of the classes in the SQL and OLE DB libraries where they are relevant.

Connecting to a Data Source (OLE DB and SQL)

To connect to a database, you must create a *SqlConnection* object. The simplest way to do this is to pass a connection string as a parameter to the *SqlConnection* constructor, as shown here:

```
String conString = "data source=(LOCAL);
   initial catalog=Northwind;
   integrated security=SSPI;
   persist security info=False;
   workstation id=(LOCAL);packet size=4096";
SqlConnection con = new SqlConnection(conString);
```

Many settings can be defined in the connection string. The most frequently used values are shown in Table 7-2. If you're using Visual Studio .NET, you can specify New Connection as the *ConnectionString* property of a connection (in the Properties window). The Data Link Properties dialog box that appears will, in effect, launch a wizard for creating a connection string.

Table 7-2 Elements of the *ConnectionString* Property for SQL Server Connections

Property	Description
Data source	The server name
Integrated security	The name of the authentication service to be used
Initial catalog	The database name
Persist security info	Indicates whether to persist security credentials
User ID	A SQL Server login
Connect timeout	The number of seconds within which a connection to the server must be established; an error is returned if the connection can not be made within this time

You can also create a *SqlConnection* object without passing any parameters. You can then set the *ConnectionString* property, which the *SqlConnection* object exposes, to specify the properties needed to connect to the database. Once you set the properties, you can connect to the database by calling the *SqlConnection* object's *Open* method. Note that the *Open* method might throw an *InvalidConnectionException* (which indicates that the connection is already open) or an *SqlException* (which is thrown when the underlying data provider returns an error or warning).

The following code example is taken from the sample file SimpleSqlConnection.jsl. As you can see, you should always invoke the *Close* method of the *SqlConnection* object. Alternatively, you can invoke the *SqlConnection* object's *Dispose* method, but as you'll see shortly, the *Close* method is the preferred approach.

```
SqlConnection connection = null;

// Connect to an SQL datasource
try
{
   connection = new SqlConnection();

   // We need to set the ConnectionString property
   connection.set_ConnectionString ("data source=(LOCAL);" +
      "initial catalog=Northwind;" +
      "integrated security=SSPI;" +
      "persist security info=False;" +
      "workstation id=(LOCAL);" +
      "packet size=4096");
```

```
    // The Open method uses the properties of the connection string
    connection.Open();
    Console.WriteLine("Opened connection successfully to " +
        connection.get_DataSource());
}
catch (System.Exception ex)
{
Console.WriteLine("Failed to open connection: " + ex);

// The finally block will close the connection
}
finally
{
    if (connection != null)
    {
        // Finally, close the connection
        connection.Close();
    }
}
```

Connections and Visual Studio .NET

Visual Studio .NET provides excellent support for ADO.NET components. To create a connection object and set its connection string properties, follow this simple procedure:

1. Drag an *OleDbConnection* or a *SqlConnection* control from the Data tab of the Toolbox onto the design area.
2. View the control's properties, and then select Connection String.
3. Select New Connection from the drop-down list to the right of the property name.
4. In the Data Link Properties dialog box, set the appropriate properties for the connection.

Some examples of connections created using Visual Studio .NET are provided in the sample project DataApplication. This sample has one *OleDbConnection* and two *SqlConnection* objects. One of the *SqlConnection* objects was created using the New Connection option, and the other was created by selecting an existing connection string from the list supplied in the Connection String drop-down list.

Connection Pooling

Pooling connections is one way to enhance the scalability of an application and improve its performance. Both the OLE DB and SQL providers support connection pooling, and in fact both provide connection pooling automatically. To disable connection pooling, you must add the following to the *ConnectionString* used to instantiate your connection:

```
Pooling=false
```

When you call the *Open* method of a connection, the connection pooler checks to see whether a connection pool exists for connections with exactly the same connection string as that of the connection you're working with. If no pool exists, the connection pooler creates one and fills it with connection objects. The number of connection objects added to the pool depends on the values of two properties: *Max Pool Size* and *Min Pool Size*. The default value for *Max Pool Size* is *100*, and the minimum is *0*. You can change the defaults by passing values in the *ConnectionString* to the connection constructor as key/value pairs. For example, the following code creates a connection string that defines a maximum pool size of 50 connection objects and a minimum of 1:

```
("data source=(LOCAL);
initial catalog=Northwind;
integrated security=SSPI;
persist security info=False;
workstation id=(LOCAL);packet size=4096
Max Pool Size=50; Min Pool Size=1);
```

If the connection string matches that of a connection pool, a connection object is served from the pool. As more connections are requested, they're also taken from the pool, and if necessary the number of connections in the pool is increased to match the demand for connections. Once the maximum number of connections is reached and requests for connections can no longer be honored, the requests are placed in a queue until they can be fulfilled by connections returning to the pool. To return a connection to the pool, you must explicitly call its *Close* method.

Consuming Connection Events

Connection objects can fire two types of events: *InfoMessage* and *StateChange*. You can use the *InfoMessage* event to retrieve messages from a database. You can also retrieve warnings from the database if these warnings do not result in an *OleDbException* or *SQLException* being thrown. The following code fragment shows an event handler that writes the details of the messages returned by the data source to the console:

```
private void sqlConnection_InfoMessage(Object sender,
   SqlInfoMessageEventArgs e)
{
   // get the errors collection
   SqlErrorCollection sec = e.get_Errors();

   // get the message count
   int msgCount = sec.get_Count();

   // iterate through messages
   for (int i=0; i < msgCount; i++)
   {
      Console.WriteLine("INFO: " + sec.get_Item(i).ToString());
   }
}
```

This code is provided as part of the ConnectionEvents.jsl sample file. It illustrates that the *System.Data.SqlClient.SqlInfoMessageEventsArgs* object exposes an *SqlErrorCollections* property. The object retrieved through this property contains a collection of error messages returned by the underlying data source. The example calls the *get_Count* method to get the total number of messages the *SqlErrorCollection* contains, and then it calls the *get_Item* method to get the next error message.

The second type of event, *StateChange*, occurs when the state of a connection changes, such as when it closes. The following code fragment, also from the ConnectionEvents.jsl sample file, illustrates the use of this event. The event handler in the code takes a *System.Data.StateChangeEventArgs* (for both SQL and OLE DB providers), which exposes two useful properties: *OriginalState* and *CurrentState*. In this example, the code prints out both the original and current states to the standard output:

```
private void connection_StateChanged(Object sender, StateChangeEventArgs e)
{
   Console.WriteLine("State Changed");
   Console.WriteLine("\tOriginal State: " + e.get_OriginalState());
   Console.WriteLine("\tCurrent State: " + e.get_CurrentState());
}
```

Executing Commands Against a Data Store

Once you've connected to a data store, you can execute commands against it. In this section, we'll look at how you can build command objects and execute these against a connection. Specifically, we'll look at how to invoke commands that return the following:

- A single value, such as an aggregate value
- A read-only data reader
- An updatable, scrollable *DataSet*

Building Commands

The *IDbCommand* interface defines the functionality of a command class. Its two implementations, *SqlCommand* and *OleDbCommand*, expose the same properties and methods, with the exception that *SqlCommand* provides support for reading XML. (We'll discuss this functionality later in this chapter). However, you use all command objects in the same way: You create an instance of the command class, and then you call one of its execute methods to invoke a stored procedure or execute a SQL statement.

The command classes' constructors are overloaded, so there are a number of ways you can create a new instance of a command. The following code shows the four constructor signatures for a *SqlCommand*:

```
public SqlCommand ()
public SqlCommand (String query)
public SqlCommand (String query, SqlConnection conn)
public SqlCommand (String query, SqlConnection conn, SqlTransaction tran)
```

As you can see, the fourth constructer accepts a third parameter of an *SqlTransaction*, which we'll discuss later in the chapter. Once you create a command class instance, each of the constructer parameters is exposed as a public property. For example, the following code is taken from the SimpleSqlCommand.jsl sample file. It shows how you can set the *CommandText* (an SQL statement) and the *Connection* properties of the command after it is instantiated as an alternative to passing them into the constructor:

```
// Create a command object
SqlCommand command = new SqlCommand();

// Associate with a Connection
command.set_Connection(connection);

// Set the command's text
command.set_CommandText("SELECT EmployeeID FROM Employees");
```

Once you've created a command object, you can use one of its execute methods to invoke a query on the underlying data store. Table 7-3 shows the execute methods exposed by the command classes. In the remainder of this chapter, we'll examine how to use these methods and how to work with the data they return. The sample file from which the preceding code is taken, SimpleSqlCommand.jsl, uses the *ExecuteScalar* method to retrieve a single value.

Table 7-3 *SqlCommand* and *OleDbCommand* Execute Methods

Method	*OleDbCommand/SqlCommand*	Description
ExecuteNonQuery	Yes/Yes	Executes a query and returns the number of rows affected. Used for update, insert, and delete commands.
ExecuteReader	Yes/Yes	Executes a query and returns a read-only *DataReader* object that contains the results of the query.
ExecuteScalar	Yes/Yes	Executes a query and returns only the first column of the first row from the result set returned by the underlying data source.
ExecuteXMLReader	No/Yes	Executes a query and returns a read-only *XmlDataReader* object.

Using Parameters in Statements

Earlier, you saw how to create a command that contains an SQL statement. The statement was really a one-shot deal because you couldn't modify it for reuse with different values. But in reality, you'll of course want to reuse statements because values are frequently derived at run time and you don't want to write hundreds of SQL statements that perform similar operations. ADO.NET supports parameterized statements, which allow you to create this type of reusable statement.

To create a parameterized statement, you use a placeholder within the statement to represent the location in which a parameter value can later be substituted. If you want to substitute multiple values in your statement, you can use multiple instances or forms of the placeholder in the statement. For SQL statements, the placeholder takes the form of a named parameter of the type *@parameterName*; for OLE DB, you simply use a *?* (question mark) as a placeholder. For example

```
// SQL Version
DELETE FROM Employees WHERE EmployeeID = @EmployeeID
```

```
// OLE DB Version
DELETE FROM Employees WHERE EmployeeID = ?
```

Once you define the statements with placeholders, you can create the parameters for use with the statements. To do this, you add the parameter name and data type to the collection of parameters associated with the command object. Parameters can be added through the *Add* method of the Sql*Parameter-Collection* object or the *OleDbParameterCollection* object. To get a parameter collection, you invoke the *get_Parameters* method of a command object. For example, the following code fragment, taken from the sample file SimpleParameterizedDelete.jsl, sets the parameters for an *SqlCommand* object:

```
// Create the SQL statement
String statementStr =
   "DELETE FROM Employees WHERE EmployeeID = @EmployeeID";

// Create a command object
SqlCommand command = new SqlCommand(statementStr, connection);

// Get the parameters collection
SqlParameterCollection parameters = command.get_Parameters();

// Add the parameters
SqlParameter parameter = parameters.Add("@EmployeeID", SqlDbType.Int);

// Set the value of the parameter
parameter.set_Value((System.Int32)num);

int rowsAffected = command.ExecuteNonQuery();

Console.WriteLine("Deleted " + rowsAffected + " rows");
```

When we added the parameter, we used the *Int* member of the *SqlDbType* enumeration, which specifies the data type of the parameter and is also specific to the underlying data provider. The data types are different for the SQL data provider and for the OLE DB data provider. Tables 7-4A through 7-4C show the permitted data types for each of these providers and shows how they map to the *System.Data.DbType* types and .NET Framework types.

Table 7-4A Data Type Mappings Between *SqlDbType* and .NET Framework

SqlDbType	**.NET Framework Type**
Bit	*bool*
TinyInt	*byte*
VarBinary	*byte[]*

Table 7-4A Data Type Mappings Between *SqlDbType* and .NET Framework

SqlDbType	.NET Framework Type
not supported	*char*
DateTime	*DateTime*
Decimal	*Decimal*
Float	*double*
Real	*float*
UniqueIdentifier	*Guid*
Int	*int*
SmallInt	*Int16*
Int	*Int32*
BigInt	*long*
BigInt	*Int64*
Variant	*object*
SmallInt	*short*
NVarChar	*string*
not supported	*UInt16*
not supported	*UInt32*
not supported	*UInt64*

Table 7-4B Data Type Mappings Between SqlDbType and OleDbType

SqlDbType	*OleDbType*
Bit	*Boolean*
TinyInt	*UnsignedTinyInt*
VarBinary	*VarBinary*
not supported	*Char*
DateTime	*DBTimeStamp*
Decimal	*Decimal*

Table 7-4B Data Type Mappings Between SqlDbType and OleDbType

SqlDbType	*OleDbType*
Float	*Double*
Real	*Single*
UniqueIdentifier	*Guid*
Int	*Integer*
SmallInt	*SmallInt*
Int	*Int*
BigInt	*BigInt*
BigInt	*BigInt*
Variant	*Variant*
SmallInt	*SmallInt*
NVarChar	*VarWChar*
not supported	*UnsignedSmallInt*
not supported	*UnsignedInt*
not supported	*UnsignedBigInt*
VarChar	*VarChar*
Money	*Currency*
DateTime	*DBDate*
TinyInt	*TinyInt*
DateTime	*DBTime*
not supported	*VarNumeric*

Table 7-4C Data Type Mappings between *OleDbType* and *System.Data.DbType*

OleDbType	*System.Data.DbType*
Boolean	*Boolean*
UnsignedTinyInt	*Byte*
VarBinary	*Binary*

Table 7-4C Data Type Mappings between *OleDbType* and *System.Data.DbType*

OleDbType	*System.Data.DbType*
Char	
DBTimeStamp	*DateTime*
Decimal	*Decimal*
Double	*Double*
Single	*Single*
Guid	*Guid*
Integer	
SmallInt	*Int16*
Int	*Int32*
BigInt	
BigInt	*Int64*
Variant	*Object*
SmallInt	
VarWChar	*String*
UnsignedSmallInt	*UInt16*
UnsignedInt	*UInt32*
UnsignedBigInt	*UInt64*
VarChar	*AnsiString*
Currency	*Currency*
DBDate	*Date*
TinyInt	*SByte*
DBTime	*Time*
VarNumeric	*VarNumeric*

Note The *Value* property of the *SqlParameter* and *OleDbParameter* classes is an object, so you must coerce any primitive types into objects to use them to set this value.

A parameter object exposes a number of public properties, which you can get and set by using the accessor methods it exposes. For a complete reference to these properties, you should see the product documentation, but for now we'll look at three of the most useful properties:

- *SourceColumn*
- *SourceVersion*
- *Direction*

The *SourceColumn* is the name of the column from which the value for a parameter will be loaded or retrieved. The *SourceVersion* indicates which version of this value to use because several versions might coexist simultaneously. For example, you might update the value of an entry within a *DataSet*, so the entry will have an original value that differs from its current value. There are four possible versions of any given data, and these are defined in the *System.Data.DataRowVersion* enumeration. Table 7-5 shows the members of this enumeration.

Table 7-5 *System.Data.DataRowVersion* Enumeration Members

Member	Description
Current	The current value within a column. This is the default value for a parameter.
Default	The value defined by the *DefaultValue* property of a *DataColumn*.
Original	The original, unmodified value of the column.
Proposed	The proposed value. This exists while the column is being edited.

The *Direction* property of the parameter object allows you to specify whether the parameter is used for input, for output, or as a return value. The output parameter is a special type of parameter that is used to transfer the value returned from a stored procedure or user-defined function. A return value is the result of some calculation or selection that is performed in the database. The *System.Data.ParameterDirection* enumeration defines the four possible values for this property, as shown in Table 7-6.

Table 7-6 ***System.Data.ParameterDirection*** **Enumeration Members**

Member	Description
Input	An input parameter
InputOutput	A parameter capable of both input and output
Output	An output parameter
ReturnValue	A parameter that represents a return value

For example, the following code fragment creates an SQL delete command, creates a parameter object, and then sets this object's *Direction* and *SourceVersion* properties:

```
// Create the SQL statement
String statementStr =
   "DELETE FROM Employees WHERE EmployeeID = @EmployeeID";

// Create a command object
SqlCommand command = new SqlCommand(statementStr, connection);

// Get the parameters collection
SqlParameterCollection parameters = command.get_Parameters();

// Add the parameters
SqlParameter parameter = parameters.Add("@EmployeeID", SqlDbType.Int);

// Set the direction and version
parameter.set_Direction(ParameterDirection.Input);
parameter.set_SourceVersion(DataRowVersion.Current);

// Set the value of the parameter
parameter.set_Value((Int32)num);

int rowsAffected = command.ExecuteNonQuery();

System.Console.WriteLine("Deleted " + rowsAffected + " rows");
```

Invoking Stored Procedures

Typically, a command is a string that contains an SQL statement, but a command can also invoke a stored procedure. In the context of ADO.NET, a stored procedure is a unit of SQL logic, or operations, encapsulated in a single command and stored within the underlying database. You can invoke a stored procedure simply by setting the *CommandType* property of a command object to

StoredProcedure (a member of the *System.Data.CommandType* enumeration) and then using the *ParametersCollection* object to define input and output parameters for the stored procedure. For more information on stored procedures and parameters, see the product documentation.

Retrieving a Single Record from a Data Source

Sometimes when you execute a query against a database, you expect to receive only a single result—for example, when you use aggregate functions. In such situations, you use the *ExecuteScalar* method of a command object. This method returns a single value of the type *System.Object*. If the database returns more than one value, only the first value in the result set is returned by the *ExecuteScalar* method.

The RetrieveSingleValue.jsl sample file shows how to use the *ExecuteScalar* method to return the aggregate value returned by the SQL *Count* function:

```
com.set_CommandText("SELECT Count(*) FROM Employees");

// ExecuteScalar return type System.Object
count = com.ExecuteScalar();
```

Using a *DataReader* Object for Read-Only Data Retrieval

You often need to retrieve data on a read-only basis—for example, when you're listing product details in an e-commerce application. In such situations, you do not need the ability to update the contents of a data source, and you definitely do not want to consume the resources associated with a read/write operation. The .NET Framework provides the *System.Data.IDataReader* interface for efficient, fast, read-only data access. Implementations of *IDataReader* are provided for both SQL Server and OLE DB providers. In addition to being read-only, a data reader provides forward-only navigation—in other words, you cannot navigate back and forth through data.

To create an implementation of *IDataReader*, you call the *ExecuteReader* method of a command object. For example

```
SqlDataReader sdr = myCommand.ExecuteReader();
```

If the *Command* object has an associated SQL *Select* statement, the *IDataReader* instance contains a table-like structure of data returned by the underlying data source. You can reference individual columns within this table, but the records (or rows) must be read sequentially, one at a time—you cannot move to a record at a given index. Before we look at how you can use the *IDataReader* interface to read data, we'll look at the properties you can access through the

IDataReader interface, which allow you to explore the structure and format of the data. Table 7-7 shows some of the most useful properties and methods a data reader object exposes.

Table 7-7 Useful *DataReader* Properties and Methods

Accessor Method	Parameters	Description
get_FieldCount	None	Returns an *int*, the number of columns.
get_RecordsAffected	None	Returns an *int*, the number of records affected by a *Command*. If the *Command* is an SQL *Select*, the method returns *-1*.
GetOrdinal	Column name as a *System.string*	Returns an *int*, the index of a named column. If the column does not exist, the method throws an *IndexOutOfRangeException*.
GetName	Column index as an *int*	Returns a *String*, the name of a column at a given index.

When an *IDataReader* instance is created, it is positioned directly before the first row in the retrieved data. To scroll through the rows, you call its *Read* method, which advances the data reader forward one record and returns *true* if there are further records:

```
while (sdr.Read())
{
   // Read the records
}
```

A data reader provides a number of methods to retrieve the contents of a particular column in the current record. If you want to get a value of a specific data type, you can invoke one of the *GetXXX* methods, where *XXX* is one of the .NET Framework data types (shown previously in Table 7-4). The *GetXXX* methods all take an integer as a parameter that represents the index of the column from which to retrieve the data.

You can invoke the *GetValue* method, which gets the value of a record in its native format, but to use this value you must still convert it into a valid type within the .NET Framework. Two useful methods that you can use in conjunction with the *Get* methods are *IsDBNull* and *GetDataTypeName*. The *IsDBNull* method returns *true* if the given column contains a nonexistent or missing value (in other words, if it is *Null* in database terms as represented by the *System.DBNull* class). The *GetDataTypeName* method returns the underlying SQL Server data type of the data. For example, the following code checks whether the record values for an employee's first name and last name are null, and if they are not, it writes their values to the standard output:

```
// Column 0 is the forename, column 1 is the
// middle initial, and column 2 is the surname
if (!sdr.IsDBNull(0) && !sdr.IsDBNull(2))
{
    Console.WriteLine(sdr.getValue(0).ToString() + ", ");
    Console.WriteLine(sdr.getValue(2).ToString() + "\n");
}
```

If your data consists of a large number of columns, retrieving individual column values can quickly result in verbose code. Fortunately, a data reader exposes a *GetValues* method, which returns the values of all the columns within the *IDataReader* instance. For example, the code shown in the DataReader.jsl sample uses the *GetValues* method to retrieve all the columns for a record, checks whether they are null, and if they are not it prints their values to the standard output.

Using *DataSet* Objects for Data Access

Earlier, we discussed the roles of data sets and data adapters—specifically, that a data set represents a cache of data that has a similar structure to that of a relational database, and that a data adapter acts as a bridge between a data source and a data set. In this section, we'll examine in more detail how to work with and manage data sets, and the role the data adapter plays. Specifically, we'll look at the following topics:

- Populating a table within a data set using a data adapter
- The structure of a data set and how to navigate this structure
- Defining relationships between tables within a data set
- The differences between a typed data set and an untyped data set
- Updating a data store from a data adapter

Populating a *DataSet* Table from a Data Adapter

Typically, a single data adapter populates a single table within a data set. The data set can contain multiple tables, each of which can be populated from different data sources. You can populate a data set in two ways: You can add data to an existing table, or you can allow the data adapter to automatically create a new table within the data set. To begin with, we'll examine code that automatically creates a table within a data set.

Before you can populate the data set, you must create an *IDataAdapter* instance. In this example, we'll use the *SqlDataAdapter* class. The *SqlDataAdapter* constructor is overloaded. It can accept no parameters, a command text string and a connection instance, a command text string and a connection string, or just a command instance. The following code fragment creates a new *SqlDataAdapter* instance by passing no parameters:

```
SqlDataAdapter da = new SqlDataAdapter();
```

Once we create the *SqlDataAdapter* object, we must associate a stored procedure or an SQL statement with it. The following code fragment associates an SQL statement with the *SqlDataAdapter* by calling its *set_SelectCommand* accessor method:

```
// Create a command
SqlCommand sqlCommand = new SqlCommand();
sqlCommand.set_CommandText("SELECT EmployeeID, FirstName, LastName
   FROM Employees");
sqlCommand.set_Connection(con);
// Set the data adapter's select command
da.set_SelectCommand(sqlCommand);
```

We used the *set_SelectCommand* method because the *SqlCommand* object represented an SQL select statement. However, if the SQL statement had represented an SQL update, insert, or delete command, we would have used one of the following accessor methods, as appropriate:

- *set_UpdateCommand*
- *set_InsertCommand*
- *set_DeleteCommand*

Once you associate the command with the *SqlDataAdapter*, you can call the *Open* method of the connection object. You're then ready to create a data set from this adapter.

The *DataSet* constructor has two overloads: one that accepts no parameters and one that accepts a string that represent the data set's name. The following code fragment demonstrates the use of the latter overload:

```
DataSet ds = new DataSet("myDataSet");
```

Once you create the *DataSet* object, you can populate it by calling the *SqlDataAdapter* object's *Fill* method. The *Fill* method returns an *int* that represents the number of rows retrieved or affected. The method has numerous overloads.

Most of these allow you to pass different combinations of *DataTable* and *DataSet* objects, named tables, and SQL commands. For a complete reference to these overloads, see the product documentation.

The following code fragment passes two parameters to the *Fill* command. The first is the *DataSet* object, and the second is a string that the command will use as a label for the table it will create within the *DataSet*. If we do not pass a name for the table, the *Fill* method will still automatically create a table, but it will call it *Table* (and then *Table1*, *Table2*, and so on, if you keep using the method without the parameter).

```
int i = da.Fill(ds, "Employees");
```

That's it. The *Fill* method has created a table containing data from the underlying database within the *DataSet*. You should now call the *Close* method of the *Connection* object, and you can then perform any operations you want on the data within the *DataSet*. The SimpleDataAdapter.jsl sample shows the full code for creating an *SqlDataAdapter* and using it to populate a table within a *DataSet*. Once we've populated the *DataSet*, we can print out how many lines the data adapter's *Fill* method retrieved:

The Structure of *DataSet* Objects and Navigation

So far in this chapter, we've looked at the *DataSet* purely at a table level, but as you might remember, we said that a *DataSet* has a structure like a relational database. This means that each table contains columns and rows to hold the data. Figure 7-2 shows the classes that form the structure of a *DataSet*.

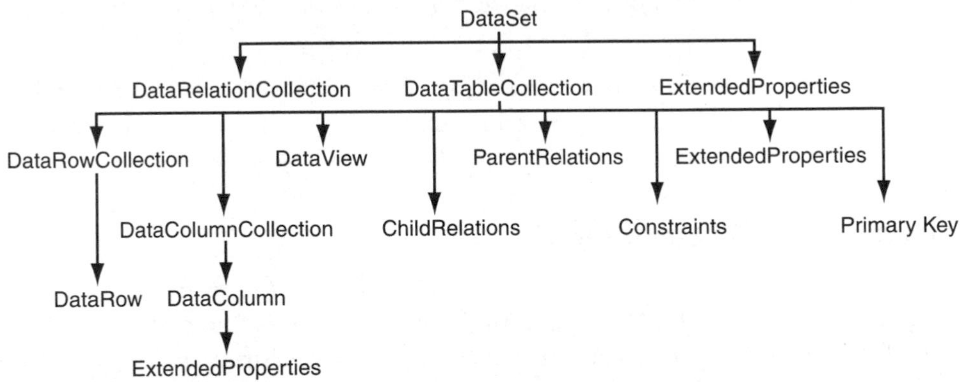

Figure 7-2 The *DataSet* object model

The first thing to note about Figure 7-2 is that all of the classes it shows belong to the *System.Data* namespace. The *DataSet* object contains multiple *DataTable* objects, and these are contained within the *DataTableCollection* object as the *Tables* property. Each *DataTable* contains a *DataRowCollection*, as a property called *Rows*, which contains multiple *DataRow* objects representing the rows in the table. The *DataTable* also contains a *DataColumnCollection*, as a property called *Columns*, which contains multiple *DataColumn* objects representing the columns in the table. In addition, the *DataSet* contains a *DataRelationsCollection*, which contains the relationships between the tables within the *DataSet*.

The *DataSet*, *DataColumn*, and *DataTable* can also have an *ExtendedProperties* object in which you can place customized information. For example, you can store the SQL statement you used to populate a table within the *DataSet* together with a timestamp indicating when the event occurred. For the moment, we'll concentrate on the *DataTable*, *DataColumn*, and *DataRow* objects. Later, we'll look at properties, constraints, and relationships.

A *DataSet* can be either typed or untyped, and this will govern how you navigate the *DataSet*. A typed *DataSet* is a class derived from *System.Data.DataSet* and generated from an XML schema. An untyped *DataSet* is an instance of the "out-of-the-box" *DataSet* class, with no associated XML schema. Using a typed *DataSet* makes coding an application much simpler because

- You can reference *DataTable* and *DataColumn* objects by a friendly name rather than by index, or by an item name represented as a string.
- Visual Studio .NET IntelliSense fully supports typed *DataSet* objects, so it will display the friendly names of the objects that comprise your *DataSet*.
- The structure of the data is defined by the XML schema, and this definition can be passed to another process, which will then automatically understand the structure and types of your data.

Navigating a Typed *DataSet*

The simplest way to create a typed *DataSet* is to use the tools provided by Visual Studio .NET: the XML Designer and the Component Designer. The XML Designer offers you precise control over the structure and content of the XML schema associated with the *DataSet*. We won't discuss this designer here—it was covered in Chapter 5. Instead, we'll look at how you can use the Component Designer to create an XML schema, and from that a new *DataSet* class that is derived from *System.Data.DataSet*.

To create a typed *DataSet* with Visual Studio .NET, you must first create a connection and then create any data adapter objects you want to use. In this example, we'll use a single data adapter. Looking at the IDE, the bottom section of the Designer window is the Component Designer. In the Component Designer, select the data adapter created earlier and then choose Generate Dataset from the Data menu. The Generate Dataset dialog box will appear, as shown in Figure 7-3.

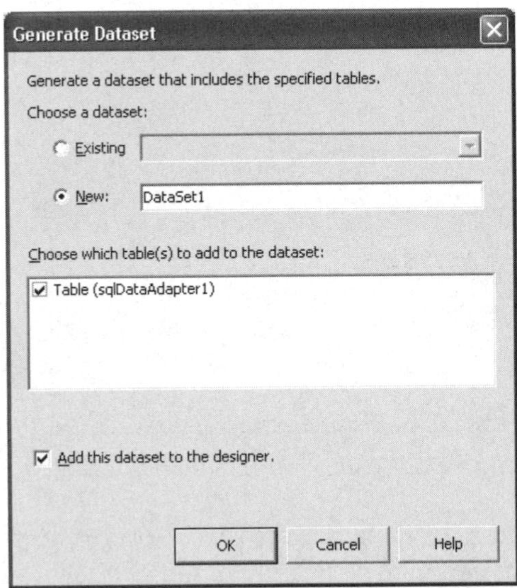

Figure 7-3 The Generate Dataset dialog box

Be sure that New is selected, and that the *DataSet* name is a meaningful one, such as *dsEmployees*. Visual Studio .NET will generate an XML Schema for the *DataSet*, and it will also generate a new class that inherits from *System.Data.DataSet* and is based on the information the XML Schema contains. That's it—you've created a typed *DataSet*. You can now populate this *DataSet* in the same way that you previously populated an untyped *DataSet*—by invoking the data adapter's *Fill* method.

Navigating a typed *DataSet* is simple because the objects that represent tables and columns are assigned friendly names. For example, to reference the *EmployeeID* column of the *Employees* table, you do not have to provide the names of the items as strings or integer indexes—instead, you reference their friendly names. The following code fragment shows how to do this, and Figure 7-4 shows Visual Studio IntelliSense providing support for the object's friendly names:

```
// Establish if the column can only accept unique values
bool b = employees1.get_Employees().get_EmployeeIDColumn().get_Unique();
```

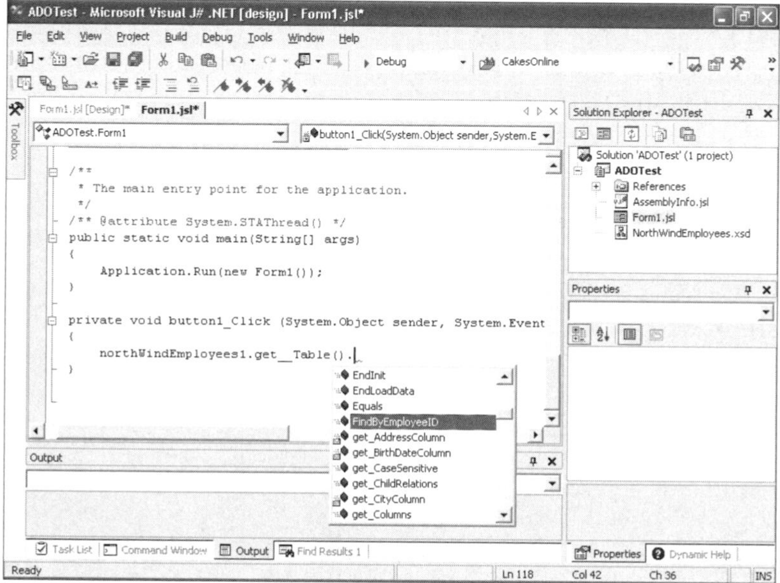

Figure 7-4 IntelliSense displaying a *DataColumn* object's friendly name

If you do not have access to Visual Studio .NET (or you have too much time on your hands), you can generate a strongly typed *DataSet* from the command line. To do this, you must first create an XML schema for your *DataSet*. The simplest way to do this is to create a small application that creates a *DataSet* populated from a query that you'll use to populate the *DataSet* at run time. After you create the *DataSet*, you invoke its *WriteXMLSchema* method, which generates an XML schema for the *DataSet* and writes this schema to file. You can then run xsd.exe (from the command line) to generate a *DataSet* class based on the schema, as in this example:

```
xsd.exe /d /l:J# MyXSDSchema.xsd /n MyXSDSchema.SomeNameSpace
```

The */d* flag instructs sxd.exe to generate a *DataSet*, */l* indicates the language, and */n* instructs xsd.exe to generate a namespace for the *DataSet* with a name of *MyXSDSchema.SomeNameSpace*. The code that's generated is placed by the tool in a file named MyXSDSchema.jsl. Now that you've created the *DataSet*, you must compile it into a library so you can consume it from your application. To do this, you simply use the Visual J# compiler with a command such as this:

```
vjc /t:library MyXSDSchema.jsl /r:System.dll /r:System.Data.dll
```

The */t* flag tells the compiler to output a library, and the */r* flags reference libraries on which there are dependencies. Once you've completed this compilation, you can use the typed *DataSet* from your applications. You use it in exactly the same way as shown in the previous section, but you must remember to import the newly created typed *DataSet*'s namespace, as in this example:

```
import MyXSDSchema.SomeNameSpace.*;
```

Navigating an Untyped *DataSet*

To navigate your way around an untyped *DataSet*, you must first get the tables contained within the *DataSet*. To do this, you call the *get_Tables* accessor method, which returns a *DataTableCollection* object:

```
DataTableCollection tables = ds.get_Tables();
```

Once the *get_Tables* method returns a *DataTableCollection*, you can use this object's *get_Count* accessor method to return the number of tables within the collection. If you want to check whether the collection contains a specific table, you can call the *Contains* method of the *DataTableCollection* object and pass it a table name as a string. The *Contains* method returns a *Boolean*, where a value of *true* indicates that the table is within the *DataTableCollection*, as in this example:

```
if (tables.Contains("Employees")==true)
{
    // Perform some processing on the table
}
```

To access a table within the *DataTableCollection*, you call the *get_Item* method. The *get_Item* method is overloaded: One form takes an integer index, and the other form takes a table name as a string. For example, to get the *Employees* table from the collection:

```
DataTable empTable = tables.get_Item("Employees");
```

Once you have a table, you can access its columns and rows through the *DataColumnCollection* and *DataRowCollection* objects. To get these collections, you simply call the *get_Columns* or the *get_Rows* method. Like the *DataTable*, the *DataColumnCollection* and the *DataRowCollection* both expose a *get_Count* method, which returns the number of rows or columns within the respective collections. To access a particular column within a *DataColumnCollection*, you can pass an integer index or a column name to the collection's *get_Item* method. Likewise, you can call the *get_Item* method of the *DataRowCollection* to get a specific row:

```
// Get the rows collection
DataRowCollection empRows = empTable.get_Rows();

// Get the first row of the collection
DataRow firstRow = empRows.get_Item(0);
```

Once you get a *DataRow* object, you can access individual records within it by calling its *get_Item* method, which is overloaded. The six signatures of this method are

```
get_Item(System.Data.DataColumn, System.Data.DataRowVersion)
get_Item(System.String <column name>, System.Data.DataRowVersion)
get_Item(int <column index>, System.Data.DataRowVersion)
get_Item(System.Data.DataColumn)
get_Item(System.String <column name>)
get_Item(int <column index>)
```

Instead of using the *get_Item* method, you can use the *get_ItemArray* method, which returns an *Object* array that contains all of the values within the *DataRow*. The NavigateDataSet.jsl sample file demonstrates the use of the *get_ItemArray* method, and it shows the complete code for navigating a *DataSet*.

Manipulating and Updating a Data Store from a Data Adapter

You can add and delete rows from a table within a *DataSet*, and when you have completed these changes you can commit the updates to the original data source. The important thing to note is that any local changes will not affect the underlying data source until you explicitly persist the updates through the data adapter.

You can add rows to a *DataTable* within a *DataSet* in a number of ways. All of these ways involve calling the *Add* method or the *InsertAt* method of the *DataRowCollection*. The *Add* method appends a row to the collection, and the *InsertAt* method inserts the new data at a specified index within the collection. The *Add* method is overloaded, so you can pass it an array of *Object* instances that form the row you want to insert or you can pass the method a *DataRow* object. To use the latter method, you must first create a new instance of the *DataRow* class. You cannot directly instantiate the *DataRow* class, so you must create a new instance by calling the *NewRow* method of the *DataTable*:

```
DataRow newRow = empTable.NewRow();
```

Once you create the *DataRow* instance, you can set individual records within it by calling its *set_Item* method, which takes two parameters: a column identifier, which can be the column name as a string, the column index as an integer, or a *DataColumn* object, and a value for the record passed as any subclass of *Object*, as shown here:

```
newRow.set_Item("LastName", "Roxburgh");
empRows.Add(newRow);
```

Alternatively, you can call the *DataRow* object's *set_ItemArray* method, which accepts an array of objects that represent the values for each of the records within the row. For example, to create a row with a *FirstName* of *Peter* and a *LastName* of *Roxburgh*, you would use the following code:

```
Object[] newValues = {"Peter", "Roxburgh"};
newRow.set_ItemArray(newValues);
empRows.Add(newRow);
```

As mentioned earlier, the *Add* method appends a row to the *DataRowCollection*; if you want to insert a row at a specific index, you must use the *InsertAt* method instead. This method has no overloads, and it accepts two parameters: a *DataRow* and an *int* index. If you specify an index that is greater than the length of the *DataRowCollection*, the new row will be inserted at the end of the collection. For example, this code snippet shows how to insert a row so that it is the second in the *DataRowCollection*:

```
DataRow newRow = empTable.NewRow();
Object[] newValues = {"Peter", "Roxburgh"};
newRow.set_ItemArray(newValues);
Rows.InsertAt(newRow,1);
```

If you want to delete a row, you can call the *Remove* method, which accepts a *DataRow* as a parameter. Alternatively, you can call the *RemoveAt* method, which accepts an *int* as a parameter, which indicates the index of the row to delete. If you want to the delete all the rows in the *DataRowCollection*, you can call the *Clear* method.

You can also add and delete columns within a *DataColumnCollection*. The *Add* method is overloaded; the most useful versions of this method have the following signatures:

```
Add(String <column name>)
Add(String <column name>, System.Type type)
Add(DataColumn)
```

In many cases, you'll use the final overload shown above because you'll need to define column properties, such as whether the column can contain only unique values, whether the column allows null data values, and the data type of the column. You can set many of these properties by passing them as arguments to the *DataColumn* column constructor. Alternatively, you can set them using appropriate accessor methods after you've created a *DataColumn* instance. When you create a new column in an existing table, the column's value of each row is set to the value of the column's *DefaultValue* property. If this property is not set, it has a default value of *DbNull*.

The following code fragment shows how to create a new instance of the *DataColumn* class, and it shows how to set some of the more frequently used public properties of the class. Table 7-8 describes these public properties.

```
DataColumn newColumn = new DataColumn();
dc.set_DataType(Type.GetType("System.Int16"));
dc.set_AllowDBNull = true;
dc.set_AutoIncrement(false);
dc.set_ColumnName("EmpoyeeShoeSize");
dc.set_Unique(false);
```

Table 7-8 Frequently Used *DataColumn* Public Properties

Property	Data Type	Description
AllowDBNull	*Boolean*	Indicates whether the column can contain null values. The default value is *true*.
AutoIncrement	*Boolean*	Indicates whether the value of a new row for the column automatically increments. The default value is *false*.
AutoIncrementSeed	*Long*	Indicates the starting value for *AutoIncrement*.
AutoIncrementStep	*Long*	Indicates the value by which incrementation occurs. The default value is 1.
ColumnName	*String*	The name of the column.
DataType	*System.Type*	The data type the column can contain.
DefaultValue	*Dependent on DataType*	The default value for a field within a column. The value is dependent on the data type of the column.
Expression	*String*	Represents an expression that is used to calculate, or generate, the value of the column. For example, you can create a calculated column such as a price including sales tax column, which is generated based on the values contained in other columns.
MaxLength	*Int*	Defines the maximum length of a column that contains textual data.

Table 7-8 Frequently Used *DataColumn* Public Properties

Property	Data Type	Description
ReadOnly	*Boolean*	Indicates whether the column will allow changes to a row once that row has been added to the *DataSet*. The default value is *false*.
Unique	*Boolean*	Indicates whether each record within the column must contain a unique value. The default value is *false*.

To remove a column from a *DataColumnCollection*, you call the collection's *Remove* method. The *Remove* method accepts either a *DataColumn* or the column name as a string. If the specified column does not exist, the method does not throw an exception.

Once you've implemented any change to the *DataSet*, you must call the data adapter's *Update* method to commit these changes to the underlying data source.

Warning The *Update* method will throw a *DBConcurrencyException* if it attempts to perform an operation against the database and you haven't set an appropriate select, insert, update, or delete command for it. For example, if you delete a row from a *DataSet*, you must set the value of the data adapter's *DeleteCommand* property with an appropriate SQL *Delete* statement.

The *Update* method is overloaded, but all overloads return an *int*, which indicates the number of rows affected. The four main variants of the method have the following signatures:

```
Update(System.Data.DataSet dataSet, String srcTable)
Update(System.Data.DataTable dataTable)
Update(System.Data.DataRow[] arrayOfDataRows)
Update(System.Data.DataSet dataset)
```

The UpdatingADataSet.jsl sample demonstrates modifying data within a *DataTable* and then committing the changes to the original data source. The code includes comments to help you navigate it. Briefly, the code connects to the database, uses the data adapter's *Fill* method to populate the *DataSet*, adds a new *DataRow* to the *DataTable* within the *DataSet*, adds a new *DataColumn*, and deletes a row from the *DataTable*. You should run this code and then run the TestUpdatingADataSet.jsl sample code to see the effect it has.

The TestUpdatingADataSet.jsl sample allows you to test whether the modifications have affected the underlying data source. When this code executes, it connects to the database and uses the data adapter's *Fill* method to populate a *DataSet*. The code then gets the *Employees* table from the *DataSet* and then iterates through the values contained within each row of the table, printing them to the console. The code then iterates through the table's columns and prints the name of each to the console. You'll find that the row of data added in UpdatingADataSet.jsl has been committed to the database. However, the additional column added to the in-memory *DataTable* has been lost. This should be expected since allowing dynamic schema changes to a database would be tricky!

Defining Relationships and Constraints

You can define a relationship between columns in different tables by using a *DataRelation* object. The intention of a *DataRelation* is to support parent-child relationships such as those between an order and its order lines, or a customer and her orders. This type of relationship in a relational database is typically implemented by using a primary key from one table as a foreign key in another. At its simplest, you create a *DataRelation* by passing its constructor a name for the relation, a parent *DataColumn*, and a child *DataColumn*, where both columns are of the same data type. For example, the following code from the DataRelationships.jsl sample file, shows how to set up a relationship between two tables:

```
// Get the tables from the DataTableCollection
DataTable employeeTable = dtc.get_Item("Employees");
DataTable employeeTerritoryTable = dtc.get_Item("EmployeeTerritories");

// Get the columns to relate
DataColumn parentColumn =
   employeeTable.get_Columns().get_Item("EmployeeID");
DataColumn childColumn =
   employeeTerritoryTable.get_Columns().get_Item("EmployeeID");

// Define the relationship
DataRelation relationship = new DataRelation("EmpIDRelation",
   parentColumn, childColumn);
```

Relations are stored in the *DataRelationCollection* of the *DataSet*. To get the *DataRelationCollection*, you call the *get_Relations* method of the *DataSet*. You can then add the *DataRelation* to the collection by invoking the collection's *Add* method:

```
DataRelationCollection drc = ds.get_Relations();
drc.Add(dr);
```

More often than not, when we define relationships, we want to define the behavior of one party in the relationship when changes to the other party might affect it. The *ForeignKeyConstraint* allows you to define this type of behavior. Specifically, it allows you to specify which one of the following changes will occur to a child row when a parent row is deleted or updated:

- A cascade delete (child rows are deleted) is performed.
- Child values are set to null.
- Child values are set to default values.
- An exception is thrown.

The *ForeignKeyConstraint* constructor is overloaded. For full details, you can see the SDK documentation. But in short, the overloads accept a mixture of constraint names, child columns, parent columns, and arrays of all these items. The following code fragment, taken from the Constraints.jsl sample file, illustrates calling the *ForeignKeyConstraint* constructor by passing a name for the constraint, a parent *DataColumn*, and a child *DataColumn*:

```
// Get the parent and child DataColumn objects
DataColumn parentColumn =
   employeesTable.get_Columns().get_Item("EmployeeID");
DataColumn childColumn =
   employeesTerritoriesTable.get_Columns().get_Item("EmployeeID");

// Create a foreign key constraint
ForeignKeyConstraint constraint =
   new ForeignKeyConstraint("EmpIDConstraint",
    parentColumn,  childColumn);
```

Once you create a *ForeignKeyConstraint* instance, you can use its *set_DeleteRule* and *set_UpdateRule* methods to define the behavior it defines. Both methods accept a single parameter, which must be a member of the *System.Data.Rule* enumeration.

```
constraint.set_DeleteRule(Rule.SetNull);
constraint.set_UpdateRule(Rule.Cascade);
```

The enumeration has four members, which Table 7-9 describes.

Table 7-9 *System.Data.Rule* Members

Member	Description
Cascade	Enforces cascaded deletes and updates. This is the default value for a constraint.
None	No action taken.
SetDefault	Sets affected row to a default value. You can define the default value of a column by setting its *DefaultValue* property to an appropriate value.
SetNull	Sets affected values to *DBNull*, which represents a record that has no value.

Each table in a *DataSet* has a *ConstraintsCollection* that contains its associated constraints. These constraints can be instances of *ForeignKeyConstraint* or *UniqueConstraint*; both descend from *System.Data.Constraint*. Once you set the rules for the *ForeignKeyConstraint*, you add the constraint to the *ConstraintsCollection* of the table that contains the foreign key. To add the constraint to the collection, you call the constraint's *Add* method. Like the other collections classes, the *ConstraintsCollection* class exposes the following methods:

- ***Add*** Adds a *Constraint* to the collection
- ***Clear*** Clears all constraints from the collection
- ***Contains*** Returns *true* if the named constraint is in the collection
- ***get_Item*** Returns a constraint referenced by name or index
- ***Remove*** Removes a constraint referenced by name or *Constraint* instance
- ***RemoveAt*** Removes a constraint at a specified index in the collection

Once you add the *ForeignKeyConstraint* to the *ConstraintsCollection*, you must set the *EnforceConstraints* property of the *DataSet* to *true*; otherwise, the constraints will not be applied to your data!

```
// Add the constraint to the table
employeesTerritoriesTable.get_Constraints().Add(constraint);

// Enforce constraints or it won't work
ds.set_EnforceConstraints(true);
```

The *UniqueConstraint* is used to specify that all the values in a column must be unique. Its extensively overloaded constructor allows you to specify whether the column is also the primary key of the table. You can check whether a *UniqueConstraint* is specified on a primary key by checking its *IsPrimaryKey* property, which returns *true* if the constraint is on the primary key. The *UniqueConstraint* constructor accepts a mixture of column names, arrays of column names, and Boolean values that indicate whether it is a primary key. The Constraints.jsl sample file demonstrates creating a *UniqueConstraint* that is not a primary key.

```
// Add a constraint that the combination of first name
// and last name must be unique.
DataColumn firstName = employeesTable.get_Columns().get_Item("FirstName");
DataColumn lastName = employeesTable.get_Columns().get_Item("LastName");
DataColumn[] columnsToConstrain = { firstName, lastName };
UniqueConstraint uConstraint = new UniqueConstraint("NameConstraint",
   columnsToConstrain, false);
employeesTable.get_Constraints().Add(uConstraint);
```

The code also creates a *ForeignKeyConstraint*, adds these constraints to a table, and ensures that the *DataSet* enforces the constraints.

Transaction Management

Most applications of any significance require you to provide transaction management. In this context, a transaction is any number of operations against a database that must all be performed together or not at all. This type of behavior is termed *atomic*, in that a transaction can group a set of database updates into one, atomic update. Just to be clear, let's take the example of a banking application. In this application, money can be transferred from A's account to B's account. In the normal course of operations, the money should be taken from A's account and then placed in B's account. However, if the money were taken from A's account and then the server were to crash, B would never receive the funds from A's account. Clearly, this is not the intended result. To get the required behavior, both the operations must be treated as if they were a single operation. Such an operation is called a *transaction*. By bundling the operations into one transaction, the transaction will not have succeeded until both of the basic operations are complete. If the server crashes before the second operation, the transaction will time out and the first update will not be committed to the database. Luckily, managing transactions for a situation such as this is simple using ADO.NET.

Beginning a database transaction with ADO.NET is a two-stage process. The first stage is to invoke the *BeginTransaction* method of the connection object. This method returns an instance of a class that implements the *IDbTransaction* interface, which you then assign to the *Transaction* property of a *Command* object:

```
// Create transaction object
SqlTransaction trans = conn.BeginTransaction();

// Assign Transaction to a Command
command.set_Transaction(trans);
```

Any operations you now execute using the command object will be associated with the *SqlTransaction*. Once you complete the operations, you can call the *SqlTransaction* object's *Commit* or *Rollback* method to commit or roll back the transaction.

The connection's *BeginTransaction* method is overloaded, and as such it allows you to optionally pass a member of the *IsolationLevel* enumeration, which specifies an isolation level for the transaction. You can check the isolation level of a transaction object by calling its *get_IsolationLevel* accessor method. The isolation levels supported by ADO.NET are slightly different than the five that JDBC supports. Table 7-10 describes the isolation levels that ADO.NET supports; note that higher isolation levels yield poorer performance than the lower levels.

Table 7-10 *System.Data.IsolationLevel* Enumeration Members

Member	Description
Chaos	Any changes that are pending from transactions with higher isolation levels can not be overwritten.
ReadUncommitted	Dirty reads are allowed—other transactions can read rows that contain uncommitted changes.
ReadCommitted	Dirty reads are not allowed—other transactions are prevented from reading rows that contain uncommitted changes. This is the default value for a transaction.
RepeatableRead	Protects against dirty reads and prevents nonrepeatable reads.
Serializable	The same as a *RepeatableRead* except that a lock is placed on the affected *DataSet* so updates and inserts are prevented.
Unspecified	Represents any isolation level different than those listed above.

Working with XML and ADO.NET

Chapter 5 introduced working with XML and ADO.NET. To refresh your memory, you learned that ADO.NET allows you to populate a DataSet from an XML document. You can read XML data into a DataSet, use an XML schema document to define the structure of the DataSet, or a combination of the two. Also in Chapter 5, you learned how to read an XML schema and XML data from files. To do this, you can invoke the ReadXml and ReadXmlSchema methods of a DataSet or use an XMLDataDocument object and invoke its Load and LoadXML methods. You also learned how an XMLDataDocument and DataSet synchronize, and you were briefly introduced to writing DataSet contents as XML and writing and retrieving XML Schema information. Here, we'll look at the following topics:

- Writing a *DataSet* as XML
- Loading *DataSet* Schema information from XML
- Writing *DataSet* Schema information as XML Schema

Writing a *DataSet* as XML

ADO.NET allows you to write a *DataSet* object's data as XML or write its structure as an XML schema. You can write either item to a file, a stream, or an *XMLWriter*, or write it as a string. Obviously, this functionality is useful for persisting *DataSet* information locally, but it is also useful for interacting with XML Web services (as you'll see in Chapter 17) and other means of sharing data within a distributed environment. If you simply want to get an XML representation of the *DataSet* that can be manipulated in memory, you can call the *DataSet* object's *GetXML* method, and to get the XML Schema, you call *GetXMLSchema*:

```
// Create and fill a DataSet
DataSet ds = new DataSet();
sqlDataAdapter.Fill(ds);

// Get the XML representations
String dsXML = ds.GetXML();
String dsSchema = ds.GetXMLSchema();
```

In contrast, if you want to write a representation of the *DataSet* as XML to a file, a stream, or an *XMLWriter*, you invoke the *WriteXML* method. This method can accept a single parameter, which is the output destination. Alternatively, you can pass two parameters, where the first is the output destination and the second is a member of the *System.Data.XmlWriteMode* enumeration.

This enumeration has three members, which define the format of the XML to be written. Table 7-11 describes these members.

Table 7-11 *System.Data.XmlWriteMode* Enumeration Members

Member	Description
IgnoreSchema	Writes the contents of the *DataSet* as XML but does not write a schema. This is the default value.
WriteSchema	Writes the contents of the *DataSet* as XML and writes the *DataSet* object's structure as an inline XSD Schema.
DiffGram	Writes the contents of the *DataSet* as a *DiffGram*, which is an XML representation that includes both the current and original versions of the *DataSet* object's data.

For example, the DataSetAsXML.jsl sample file writes a *DataSet* object's content and structure to a text file. The structure of the document is included within the XML document containing the data rather than as a separate document. The sample file DataSet.xml shows the type of output generated by the *WriteXML* method.

DataSet.xml

```
<?xml version="1.0" standalone="yes"?>
<EmployeesDS>
<!-- Inline Schema starts -->
<xs:schema id="NewDataSet" xmlns=""
xmlns:xs="http://www.w3.org/2001/XMLSchema"
xmlns:msdata="urn:schemas-microsoft-com:xml-msdata">
    <xs:element name="NewDataSet" msdata:IsDataSet="true"
msdata:Locale="en-GB">
      <xs:complexType>
        <xs:choice maxOccurs="unbounded">
          <xs:element name="Employees">
            <xs:complexType>
              <xs:sequence>
                <xs:element name="EmployeeID" type="xs:int"
                   minOccurs="0" />
                <xs:element name="LastName" type="xs:string"
                   minOccurs="0" />
                <xs:element name="FirstName" type="xs:string"
                   minOccurs="0" />
              </xs:sequence>
            </xs:complexType>
          </xs:element>
        </xs:choice>
```

```
      </xs:complexType>
    </xs:element>
  </xs:schema>
<!-- Inline Schema ends & data starts -->
  <Employees>
    <EmployeeID>1</EmployeeID>
    <LastName>Davolio</LastName>
    <FirstName>Nancy</FirstName>
  </Employees>

  <!-- Node sets cut for brevity-->

  <Employees>
    <EmployeeID>16</EmployeeID>
    <LastName>Peter</LastName>
    <FirstName>Roxburgh</FirstName>
  </Employees>
</EmployeesDS>
```

This chapter cannot provide a definitive guide to XML Schema, but a couple of items in the DataSet.xml sample file are worthy of our attention. The first is how the table and columns of the *DataSet* map to the XML elements. As you can see, the table is represented by an element, which has a child element for each of the columns the original *DataSet* contained. The second point to note is that XML Schema declares the data types of the elements that represent the original columns as two strings and an *int*. Of course, these are not the original data types, which were *System.String* and *System.Int32*. For a complete reference for how XML Schema types map to .NET types, see the product documentation.

In the previous example, we wrote an XML schema together with the data, but sometimes you'll want to write only an XML schema. To do this, you can invoke the *WriteXmlSchema* method of the *DataSet*. The method accepts a single parameter, which is the destination to write to. For example, the following code fragment writes an XML schema that represents the structure of a *DataSet* to a *StreamWriter*:

```
// Create a new StreamWriter instance
StreamWriter sw = new StreamWriter("mySchema.xsd");

// Write the DataSet's schema to the StreamWriter
myDataSet.WriteXmlSchema(sw);
```

Writing *DataRelation* Objects as XML

When you write XML to a destination or when you synchronize a *DataSet* with an *XmlDataDocument*, you can represent the relations between tables in the XML. When we wrote out the contents of a *DataSet* as XML earlier, in the DataRelationships.jsl file, you saw that the contents of each table appear in sequence within the XML. Therefore, only the data from the two tables is represented, and not the relationship between the two tables. Given the hierarchical nature of an XML document, you might want to use the relationship you've defined to have all of the elements representing child rows contained within their respective parent. To do this, you set the *Nested* property of the relationship to *true*.

```
// Set the Nested property
relationship.set_Nested(true);
```

The NestedDataRelationships.jsl sample file shows how to set the *Nested* property to *true* and then write an XML representation of the *DataSet* to a local file. The contents of the XML file are shown in the NestedDataRelationships.xml sample file.

Inferring the *DataSet* Structure from XML

You're likely to encounter a situation in which you have an XML data source but no XML schema. Luckily, ADO.NET provides a limited means of inferring the XML schema of an XML document. There are two main approaches to generating an XML schema from a *DataSet*. The first is to call the *InferXmlSchema* method of the *DataSet* (one that contains data derived from an XML source). The second approach is to pass the *InferSchema* member of the *System.Data.XmlReadMode* enumeration as a second parameter to the *ReadXml* method of the *DataSet*. The InferDataSetSchemaFromXml.jsl sample file demonstrates this technique, and it prints the derived schema to the console.

When the code executes, it populates the *DataSet* by reading the XML source in the sample file Sample.xml. At the same time, it infers the XML schema of the underlying data. Finally, the code prints the XML Schema by calling the *DataSet* object's *GetXmlSchema* method, which returns a string. The XML Schema appears as follows:

```
<?xml version="1.0" encoding="utf-16"?>
<xs:schema id="authors" xmlns=""
xmlns:xs="http://www.w3.org/2001/XMLSchema"
xmlns:msdata="urn:schemas-microsoft-com:xml-msdata">
  <xs:element name="authors" msdata:IsDataSet="true" msdata:Locale="en-GB">
    <xs:complexType>
```

```
      <xs:choice maxOccurs="unbounded">
        <xs:element name="author">
          <xs:complexType>
            <xs:sequence>
              <xs:element name="firstName" type="xs:string" minOccurs="0" />
              <xs:element name="lastName" type="xs:string" minOccurs="0" />
            </xs:sequence>
          </xs:complexType>
        </xs:element>
      </xs:choice>
    </xs:complexType>
  </xs:element>
</xs:schema>
```

That's pretty impressive, but how does ADO.NET generate this XML schema from the XML data? The *DataSet* will examine the incoming XML and decide which XML elements should become tables and which should become columns in tables. This inference process is governed by a number of rules, as described in detail in the .NET Framework documentation. Essentially, the *DataSet* looks for elements that have attributes and infers these as tables. In addition, any elements that have child elements are inferred as tables. Other elements, and attributes, are inferred as columns in one of the inferred tables. In the Sample.xml sample file, which follows, elements that become tables are marked as bold:

Sample.xml

```
<authors>
    <author>
        <firstName>
            John
        </firstName>
        <lastName>
            Sharp
        </lastName>
    </author>
    <author>
        <firstName>
            Andy
        </firstName>
        <lastName>
            Longshaw
        </lastName>
    </author>
    <author>
        <firstName>
            Peter
        </firstName>
```

```
        <lastName>
            Roxburgh
        </lastName>
    </author>
</authors>
```

The *DataSet* can also infer relationships through elements that are inferred as tables, which themselves are nested within elements that are inferred as tables. In this type of scenario, the *DataSet* creates a *DataRelation* between the two tables, and it also generates a new column in each table to help set up the relationship. An extra table is created in which this relationship is defined (thus linking the two tables based on the values in the new columns that have been added). The process then generates a *ForeignKeyConstraint* between the two tables. For more details about inferring relationships, and the limitations of the process, see the product documentation.

Summary

ADO.NET provides a disconnected data access model through classes in the *System.Data* namespace. In this chapter, we looked at many of the day-to-day tasks involved in developing .NET applications. You learned how to connect to a data store and execute SQL commands and stored procedures against it. At the heart of these operations is a *DataAdapter*, which acts as a bridge between a data source and a *DataSet*. The *DataSet* provides a local cache of data, which you can navigate much like you do a relational database. The *DataSet* consists of tables, columns, and rows that you can perform select, update, insert, and delete operations against. You also learned how ADO.NET embraces XML as a format for persisting and transferring data and for creating *DataSet* structures based on XML schemas.

Part III

Developing for the Enterprise

8

Multithreading with .NET

A thread is the unit of execution that the operating system uses to run an application. Every application running under Microsoft Windows requires at least one thread. Since its earliest days, the Win32 platform has supported multithreading, which allows multiple concurrent paths of execution through a process. The major benefit of using multiple threads in applications has been better performance, both perceived and real. Perceived performance can be enhanced, for example, by ensuring that a distinct thread handles the processing for user interactions in a GUI application. This user interaction thread can run at a slightly higher priority while background tasks are performed on lower-priority threads. This arrangement makes the application as a whole more responsive to user input and makes it appear to the user that the application is faster, although the overall real performance doesn't really change. Real performance improvement is realized on multiprocessor machines, when separate threads in the same process can be executed truly concurrently.

Using multiple threads can make the developer's life simpler. Many modern applications require that a number of simultaneous tasks be performed—gathering input from multiple sources (users, files, the network), processing data, formatting and outputting results, and so on. Without using multiple threads, a developer might be forced to use complicated logic and polling to perform these tasks.

On the other hand, the injudicious use of threads can make life difficult for a developer, especially if multiple threads need to access shared data. Synchronization can be a knotty problem if it's not approached correctly.

Threads themselves have become an integral part of the Windows operating system, and many parts of the Microsoft .NET platform rely on them for everyday tasks. In this chapter, we'll look at how the .NET Framework Class Library exposes the threading capabilities of Windows.

Threads and .NET

The Windows SDK makes threads available through a series of APIs such as *CreateThread*. These APIs form a relatively low-level interface, and you're expected to supply information about security, stack usage, and so on. (Some of this information might be *blank* if you want to use default values, but you still have to specify that it is *blank*!) Also, because the Windows SDK is based on C and C++, a lot of routine tasks, such as error trapping, are left to the developer. (Error handling is vitally important when you program with the Windows SDK but is too easily forgotten.)

The following sample, WinThread.cpp, is a C++ program that uses *CreateThread* to create and run a thread that executes the *ThreadFunc* function, passing it a parameter (variable *dwThrdParam*). The *ThreadFunc* procedure simply displays the value of this parameter in a message box. If you want, you can create a C++ Win32 project using Microsoft Visual Studio .NET (when the Win32 Application Wizard appears, click Application Settings, and set the Application type to Console application) and type this code (or simply use the sample code in the WinThread project)—it will compile and run. Notice that the function to be executed by the thread is passed to *CreateThread* as a pointer, as is the parameter, which is propagated through to *ThreadFunc*.

WinThread.cpp

```
#include "stdafx.h"


#include <windows.h>
#include <conio.h>


DWORD WINAPI ThreadFunc(LPVOID) ;

int _tmain(int argc, _TCHAR* argv[])
{
    DWORD dwThreadId, dwThrdParam = 1;
    HANDLE hThread;
    char szMsg[80];

    hThread = CreateThread(
        NULL,                        // no security attributes
        0,                           // use default stack size
        ThreadFunc,                  // thread function
        &dwThrdParam,                // argument to thread function
        0,                           // use default creation flags
        &dwThreadId);                // returns the thread identifier
```

```
    // Check the return value for success.

    if (hThread == NULL)
    {
       wsprintf( szMsg, "CreateThread failed." );
       MessageBox( NULL, szMsg, "main", MB_OK );
    }
    else
    {
       _getch();
       CloseHandle( hThread );
    }
    return 0;
}

DWORD WINAPI ThreadFunc( LPVOID lpParam )
{
    char szMsg[80];

    wsprintf( szMsg, "Parameter = %d.", *(DWORD*)lpParam );
    MessageBox( NULL, szMsg, "ThreadFunc", MB_OK );

    return 0;
}
```

There's plenty of room here for mayhem—for example, passing pointers to functions that don't match the signature required by *CreateThread*, or even passing an uninitialized pointer.

The model used by this API permits the method executed by the thread to take a single *LPVOID* parameter, although this parameter can actually contain almost any type of data. (*LPVOID* is C++-speak for "pointer to a generic blob of memory.") The thread function takes it on trust that the parameter has been populated with data of a type that it is expecting.

In the *System.Threading* namespace of the .NET Framework Class Library, Microsoft has implemented a convenient object-oriented abstraction for creating and managing Windows threads. The .NET Framework Class Library also offers automatic and manual synchronization mechanisms that allow you to control threads effectively. The threads that are created in this way run in managed space inside the common language runtime, which means that they can't maliciously or accidentally interfere with other unrelated threads that execute in other processes. However, threads can also originate from outside of the common language runtime and enter the managed environment, and managed threads fashioned by the common language runtime can call out to the unmanaged space (as discussed later in this and other chapters). Note that when you execute outside the bounds of the common language runtime, a thread is not protected in quite the same way.

Application Domains and Threads

Managed applications being executed by the common language runtime run in application domains. You'll recall from Chapter 2 that an application domain is the unit of isolation used by the common language runtime. Code that runs in one application domain cannot interact directly with code running in another application domain. A single real process that hosts the common language runtime might contain several application domains, each running a different application. One reason for this architecture is speed—several applications can run inside the same process, so the common language runtime can quickly switch from one application to another.

In execution environments prior to .NET, a thread belongs to a single application running in a single process; a thread running in one application cannot directly access a thread running in another. Instead, threads can make remote procedure calls, which involves marshaling parameters and any return values across application boundaries, and performing a process context switch, which is potentially quite expensive. In the common language runtime the situation is subtly different; threads belong to processes that host application domains. A single thread can span multiple application domains residing in the same process. This means that the same thread can be used to execute different applications at different times. In other words, there is no simple one-to-one relationship between application domains and threads; a single thread can cross application domain boundaries in the same host process, and a single application domain can use many threads. The common language runtime tracks which threads are currently executing in which application domains, and it manages and secures them accordingly.

Tip You can obtain a reference to the current application domain the current thread is executing in using the static method *System.Threading.Thread.GetDomain()*.

Creating Threads

The *System.Threading* namespace in the .NET Framework Class Library contains the *Thread* class and the *ThreadStart* delegate. The *Thread* class represents a thread of execution. As mentioned in Chapter 3, the class *System.Threading.Thread* performs functions similar to those of the *java.lang.Thread* class in the JDK, and the two can interoperate to some limited extent. The *ThreadStart* delegate is used to specify the name of a method to execute when a thread is created and starts running. Again, for purposes of comparison with the JDK, you can think of the method referred to by the *ThreadStart* delegate as somewhat functionally equivalent to the *run* method in the *java.lang.Runnable* interface or *java.lang.Thread* class.

To create and run a thread, you must create a *ThreadStart* delegate that refers to a method to be executed by the thread, create a *Thread* object using this delegate, and then start the thread object running. The *ThreadStart* delegate must refer to a void method that takes no parameters. In the sample CLRThread.jsl file in the CLRThreads project, the class *CLRThread* contains a single method called *ThreadProc* that displays the message" "Thread executing." The *main* method of the *ThreadRunner* class creates an instance of *CLRThread* called *threadObject* and instantiates a *ThreadStart* delegate called *startProc*, which refers to the *ThreadProc* method of *threadObject*:

```
CLRThread threadObject = new CLRThread();
ThreadStart startProc = new ThreadStart(threadObject.ThreadProc);
```

Next, a *Thread* object is created that will be used to run the *ThreadProc* method:

```
System.Threading.Thread runner = new System.Threading.Thread(startProc);
```

Note Notice the use of *System.Threading.Thread.* An unqualified *Thread* reference will refer to a *java.lang.Thread.* See Chapter 3 for an explanation.

Although the thread exists, it will not run until the *Start* method is invoked:

```
runner.Start();
```

At this point, the *ThreadProc* method runs. When *ThreadProc* finishes, the thread terminates.

Threads are asynchronous with respect to the code that creates them. If you want to wait for a thread to finish, you should invoke its *Join* method:

```
runner.Join();
```

If you compile and run the CLRThreads program, you should see output similar to that shown in Figure 8-1.

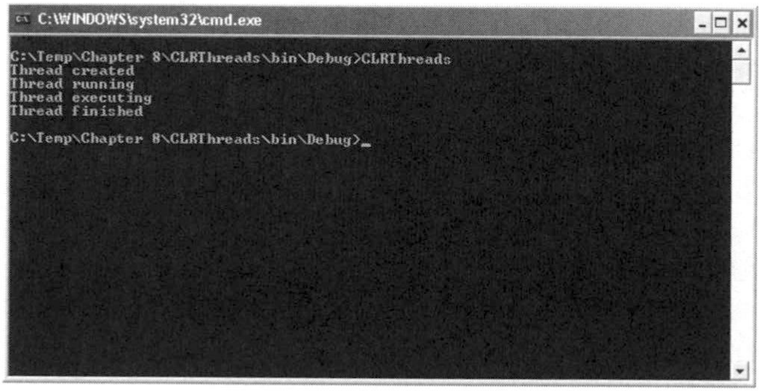

```
C:\WINDOWS\system32\cmd.exe

C:\Temp\Chapter 8\CLRThreads\bin\Debug>CLRThreads
Thread created
Thread running
Thread executing
Thread finished

C:\Temp\Chapter 8\CLRThreads\bin\Debug>_
```

Figure 8-1 The output of the CLRThreads program

Note that after you call *Start* to set a thread running, you cannot guarantee exactly when it will execute. In certain circumstances, the "Thread executing" message might appear before the "Thread running" message because of the way threads are scheduled (as explained later in this chapter).

Threads and Security

Multithreading is a powerful tool, but it can also be abused. It is not uncommon for a virus to spawn thousands of threads when it infects a host during a denial of service attack. For this reason, the *Start* method of the *Thread* class, along with many of the other methods documented in this chapter, requires that the application run with the *ControlThread* privilege. If this privilege has not been granted, the common language runtime will throw a *SecurityException*.

The *ControlThread* privilege is one of the flags that comprise the *Security* permission (described briefly in Chapter 2). By default, this privilege is granted only to assemblies originating from the My Computer zone. If you download an assembly from the Internet or your local intranet, or even from a shared drive over the local area network, you'll find that it cannot create or manage threads. However, you can change the code access security using the Microsoft .NET Framework Configuration tool, as described in Chapter 2. (But be careful!)

Passing Parameters to Threads

The first example in this chapter, WinThread.cpp, used a thread to execute a method that took a parameter. The model used by common language runtime threads does not permit you to point a *ThreadStart* delegate at a method that takes any parameters or returns a value, but you can achieve a similar result using a property). The sample project CLRThreadParam exposes a private *int* field in the *CLRThreadWithParam* class using the *get_Num* and *set_Num* property accessor methods.

If you compile and run this program, you'll see the message "Thread running" printed by the *ThreadRunner* class, as well as a message box displaying the value of *num* output by the thread itself, as shown in Figure 8-2.

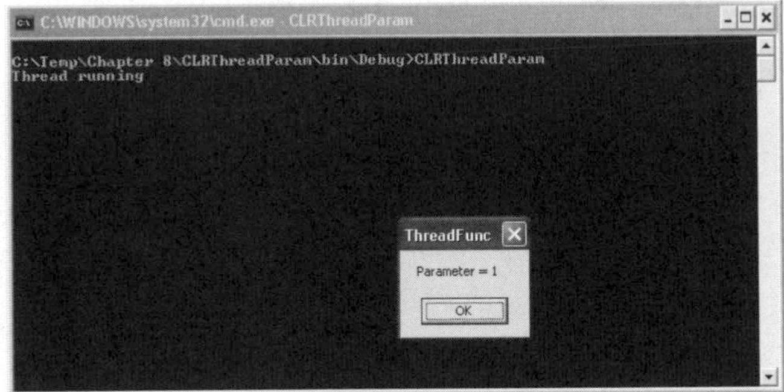

Figure 8-2 The output of the ClrThreadParam program

A word of warning: Although this solution is simple and does its job, it is not deterministic. Consider what happens if you change the value of *threadObject.num* after invoking the *Start* method:

```
System.Threading.Thread runner =
   new System.Threading.Thread(startProc);
runner.Start();
threadObject.set_Num(99);
Console.WriteLine("Thread running");
runner.Join();
```

Will the thread display the value 1 (the value that *num* had when the *Start* method was invoked) or 99? The answer depends on when the thread was scheduled, and the results can vary. If data can be accessed by more than one thread, you must ensure that any such updates are controlled and will not result in nondeterministic behavior or worse. We'll look at how to do this shortly when we discuss synchronization.

Thread States

A thread can be in one of several states at various stages in its lifecycle. When a thread is first created, it is in the *Unstarted* state. Once the *Start* method has been called, the thread moves into the *Running* state and can execute. When the thread has completed execution, it enters the *Stopped* state. Note that although the thread might have stopped running, the thread object itself still exists.

We saw earlier that you can cause a thread to wait for another thread to complete by using the *Join* method. In this case, the calling thread enters the *WaitSleepJoin* state. The following example causes the current thread to wait until the *runner* thread finishes:

```
System.Threading.Thread runner = new System.Threading.Thread(...);
runner.Start();
⋮
runner.Join();
```

If a thread joins another thread that has already stopped, the join operation completes immediately and the thread reverts to the *Running* state. You can determine the current state of a thread using the *get_ThreadState* method, as shown here. (*ThreadState* is a property.)

```
System.Threading.Thread runner = new System.Threading.Thread(...);
⋮
Console.WriteLine("State is " + runner.get_ThreadState());
```

The value returned by *get_ThreadState* is a member of the *ThreadState* enumeration and can be one of the following values: *Aborted*, *AbortRequested*, *Running*, *Stopped*, *Suspended*, *SuspendRequested*, *Unstarted*, or *WaitSleepJoin*.

Threads can be temporarily halted for a number of reasons, apart from waiting on a call to *Join*. For example, a thread that is performing an IO operation might be halted while waiting for data to arrive. You can explicitly suspend a thread by calling the *Suspend* method on that thread:

```
System.Threading.Thread runner = new System.Threading.Thread(...);
runner.Start();
⋮
runner.Suspend();
```

In this example, the *runner* thread is put into the *SuspendRequested* state but will continue executing until it reaches a safe point, whereupon it will suspend itself, entering the *Suspended* state. Calls to the *Suspend* method do not nest. Suspending a thread that is already in the *SuspendRequest* or *Suspended* state will have no effect.

You can resurrect a suspended thread using the *Resume* method:

```
runner.Resume();
```

You can resume only a suspended thread. If the target thread is not in the *Suspended* state, you'll trigger a *ThreadStateException* in the calling thread. (You cannot restart a *Stopped* thread, for example.)

Safe Points

A safe point is a point at which it is safe for the common language runtime to perform garbage collection. A safe point frequently occurs at the end of a method, when execution returns to the calling method. The common language runtime can intercept the flow of control by replacing the return address of the calling method with a different address that allows the runtime to take over and invoke the garbage collector or to perform any other runtime tasks required (such as suspending the thread). When these tasks have completed, the runtime returns control to the calling method and execution continues.

This interception and adjustment of the return address of a method on the stack is performed dynamically whenever the need arises. However, in some situations a method might execute for a long time or maybe even fail to terminate due to a logic error on the part of the programmer (an infinite loop, perhaps). The JIT compiler will detect such a situation before running the program. The JIT compiler will insert code to interrupt such loops if provoked by the need to perform garbage collection or suspend the thread. However, when the thread resumes so will the loop!

A thread can temporarily halt itself for a period of time with the *Sleep* method. This is a static method belonging to the *System.Threading.Thread* class. Executing *Sleep* causes the thread to enter the *WaitSleepJoin* state. You can specify the time to sleep as a number in milliseconds or as a time span using a *System.Timespan* argument. For example, to put the current thread to sleep for 2 days, 3 hours, 10 minutes, and 38 seconds, you can use the following:

```
TimeSpan ts = new TimeSpan(2, 3, 10, 38);
System.Threading.Thread.Sleep(ts);
```

Be aware that the parameter of the *Sleep* method actually specifies the minimum amount of time to suspend the process—it might actually sleep for longer depending on the load on the machine and the relative priorities of various threads (as discussed later). If you need to sleep for an indefinite period, you can specify the value *Timeout.Infinite* as the parameter of *Sleep*. You can execute *Sleep* with a very short timespan (or even 0) to voluntarily surrender the CPU and indicate that the scheduler should allow any other waiting threads to execute. This is also one way to manually insert a safe point in your code.

Terminating Threads

A thread terminates naturally when it finishes executing the method indicated by the *ThreadStart* delegate. Also, if a thread triggers an exception that it fails to catch, the exception will be propagated to the runtime which will kill the thread.

Interrupting a Thread

If a thread is in the *WaitSleepJoin* state (it is waiting for something to happen), you can wake it up, or even terminate it, by calling the *Interrupt* method:

```
System.Threading.Thread runner = new System.Threading.Thread(...);
⋮
runner.Interrupt();
```

If the target thread (*runner*) is asleep, the *Interrupt* method will throw a *ThreadInterruptException* and rouse the thread. (The thread will enter the *Running* state.) If the thread catches this exception, it can carry on processing. If not, the thread will terminate. If the target thread is not in the *WaitSleepJoin* state when the *Interrupt* method is invoked, the interrupt will remain pending until the thread moves into this state, at which point the interrupt will occur immediately. Although interrupting a thread is a good way to wake a sleeping thread, you should not rely on this approach to synchronize operations between threads because you can never be quite sure when the target thread will be interrupted! Later in this chapter, we'll look at better ways to synchronize threads.

Aborting a Thread

Another way to kill a thread is to use the *Abort* method:

```
System.Threading.Thread runner = new System.Threading.Thread(...);
⋮
runner.Abort();
```

The *Abort* method triggers a *ThreadAbortException* in the target thread, which enters the *AbortRequested* state. If you don't catch this exception in your thread, it will terminate. If you do catch this exception, the exception handler will run but the thread will still terminate, propagating the exception to any outer blocks in the same manner as an unhandled exception. You should use the exception handler to roll back any changes that need to be undone and to release any resources acquired by the thread. When processing has completed, the thread will be placed in the *Stopped* state. If you really don't want the thread to die, you can execute the static *System.Threading.Thread.ResetAbort()* method:

```
catch (System.Threading.ThreadAbortException e)
{
      ⋮
if (...)
{
            System.Threading.Thread.ResetAbort();
      }
}
```

The Aborted State

A race condition might occur if you start a thread and then abort it almost immediately. If the thread has not had a chance to run, you will not have entered any *try* blocks, so no exception handler will be active (you will not catch the *ThreadAbortException*) and no *finally* code will be executed. However, in this case the state of the thread is set to *Aborted*. To see what this means, look at the ThreadStates.jsl file in the ThreadStates project.

The *ThreadRunner* class creates a thread that executes the *ThreadFunc* method in a *CLRStateThread* object. This method sleeps for an infinite period of time. After the thread has been started, the *Sleep* method call temporarily suspends the thread that's running the *main* method and allows the *runner* thread to obtain the processor and execute. When the *main* method resumes, it aborts the *runner* thread and then waits for it to terminate before printing out its state. On a single processor computer, we obtained the output shown in Figure 8-3.

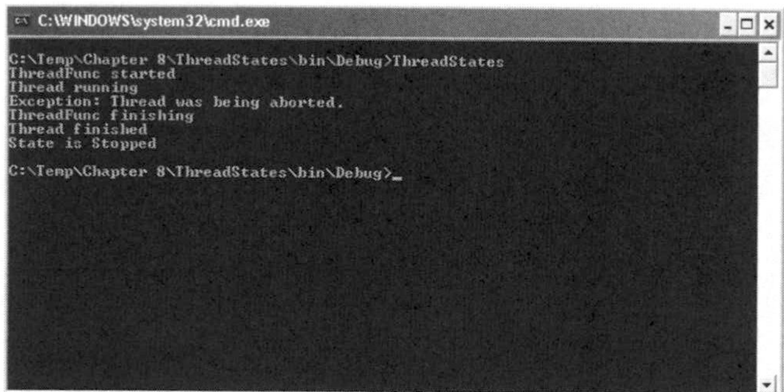

Figure 8-3 The output of the ThreadStates program

You can see the messages printed by the exception handler ("Exception: Thread was being aborted") and the *finally* block ("ThreadFunc finishing"). Also notice that the state of the *runner* thread was reported as *Stopped* after it was aborted.

When we commented out the *Sleep* statement in *main*, rebuilt the program, and ran it again (several times), we got different results, as shown in Figure 8-4.

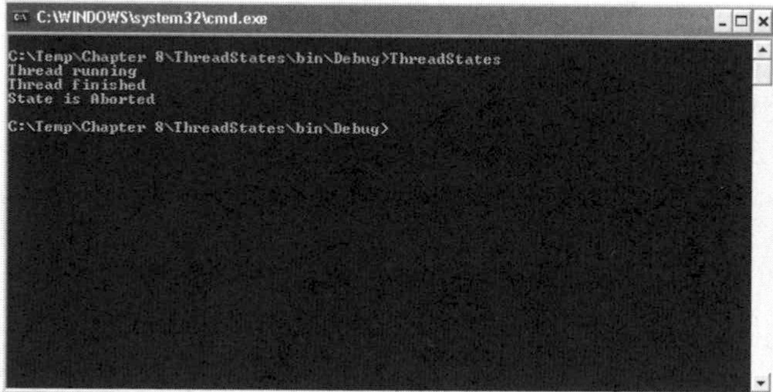

Figure 8-4 The ThreadStates program showing the aborted state

This time, the thread was aborted before it actually ran. Neither the exception handler nor the *finally* block were executed, and the state of the thread was reported as *Aborted*.

Depending on the speed of your computer and the number of processors, you might need to tinker with the duration of the *Sleep* statement in *main* and run the program several times to get similar results, but the important thing is to be aware that this problem can happen.

If you're calling unmanaged code inside a thread, the unmanaged code could trap and discard the *ThreadAbortException*. However, when the thread returns to the managed environment, the common language runtime will detect that the exception was discarded and throw it again.

Scheduling Threads

Every program that you write will use threads. When you execute a .NET application, the common language runtime will create an application domain, which will load the appropriate assemblies and then start a thread running at the entry point of your application. The static method *System.Threading.Thread.get_CurrentThread()* returns a reference to the currently running thread.

Thread Priorities

All threads have a priority assigned to them, which helps the operating system determine how to schedule them. Strictly speaking, thread priorities are just hints—the operating system doesn't have to honor them (although current versions of Windows ME, Windows 2000, and Windows XP do). You can examine the priority of a thread by querying the *Priority* property (call the *get_Priority* method). This returns a value in the *ThreadPriority* enumeration: *Highest, Above Normal, Normal, Below Normal, or Lowest.* You can use the following code to determine the priority of the current thread:

```
System.Threading.Thread me = System.Threading.Thread.get_CurrentThread();
ThreadPriority priority = me.get_Priority();
```

By default, the priority is *ThreadPriority.Normal.* You can change the priority of a thread (as long as it is not in the *Aborted* or *Stopped* state) using the *set_Priority* method. You specify a value from the *ThreadPriority* enumeration:

```
me.set_Priority(ThreadPriority.Lowest);
```

Assuming that the operating system does implement priorities, the scheduling mechanism should guarantee that a thread will be executed only if there are no higher-priority threads that have the *Running* state. Threads of the same priority will share the processor using algorithms determined by the operating system.

Note Windows 2000 and Windows XP dynamically boost the priority of a thread that has been waiting but whose wait condition has been recently satisfied. For example, a user interface thread that has been waiting for keyboard input will have a temporarily increased priority when input is received. This ensures that threads remain responsive. After executing for a period of time, Windows will drop the thread back to its original priority.

Tip When you're using an operating system that supports threads, changing the priority of a thread is a reliable way of ensuring that one thread will run before another. In the ThreadStates sample, rather than using *Sleep* to momentarily suspend the main program thread and allow *runner* to execute, it would be better to give the runner thread a higher priority:

```
⋮
System.Threading.Thread runner = new
   System.Threading.Thread(startProc);
   runner.Start();
runner.set_Priority(ThreadPriority.AboveNormal);
Console.WriteLine("Thread running");
runner.Abort();
⋮
```

You should avoid using the *Highest* priority for all but the most critical tasks. Even taking into account the dynamic boosting of thread priorities by Windows, high-priority threads can cause starvation among lower-priority threads, especially if they're long-lived and active (not suspended).

Background and Foreground Threads

The common language runtime further classifies threads as *background* or *foreground*. There is little difference between a background and a foreground thread. They are scheduled using the same strategies, and a high-priority background thread will override a lower-priority foreground thread. The difference between foreground and background threads becomes apparent when a multithreaded program finishes. Under normal circumstances, all threads that you create are designated as foreground, and an application keeps running as long as there is at least one foreground thread that has not completed. Background threads will be forcibly terminated (using the *Abort* method) when the last foreground thread in an application finishes. You can change a foreground thread to a background thread, and vice-versa, by setting the Boolean *IsBackground* property (use the *set_IsBackground* method) to *true* or *false*. (This is similar to executing *setDaemon* against a *java.lang.Thread* object.)

In the CLRThread.jsl file in the CLRSchedule project, the *CLRThread* class contains the usual *ThreadFunc* method, which is executed by a thread that is created and started by the *main* method of the *ThreadRunner* class. The *ThreadFunc* method contains an infinite loop that prints out a series of integers, starting at 0. The *main* method of *ThreadRunner* starts the thread running and then finishes. This will cause the thread that's running *main* to terminate, but the application will keep running because the thread created to run *ThreadFunc* is a foreground thread.

If you uncomment the statement *runner.set_IsBackground(true)* in the *main* method, build the application again, and run it, you'll find that the *runner* thread starts and then stops quickly when the main application thread terminates. This is because the common language runtime automatically kills all background threads when the last foreground thread for an application completes. Run the program a few times—sometimes the background thread will not even get to start running! In these circumstances the exception handler does not run either (neither would a *finally* block)—the thread is zapped without mercy.

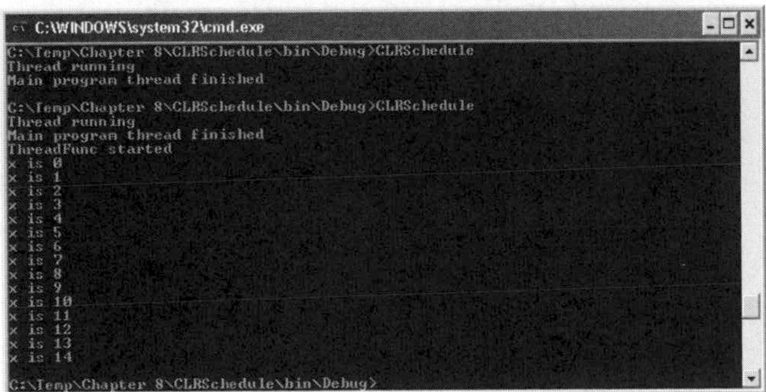

Figure 8-5 The output of the CLRShedule program (two runs)

Threads and Unmanaged Code

It is possible for code running in the common language runtime to transition to the outside world and continue executing in an unmanaged environment. This occurs, for example, when your code calls COM objects and libraries.

COM Apartments

COM has its own threading concerns, and many volumes have been written about the joys of apartment threading (single threaded and multithreaded apartments), whose details are beyond the scope of this book. Under normal circumstances, the common language runtime does not use apartments as such. However, when a managed object calls into COM, it will create an apartment to hold the requested COM object. (Behind the scenes, the common language runtime calls the *CoInitializeEx* API.) You can specify whether this apartment should be single-threaded or multithreaded by setting the *ApartmentState* property of the thread that is calling COM to the *ApartmentState.STA* or *ApartmentState.MTA* method, respectively. You should set the *ApartmentState* property of a thread to match the threading model used by any COM objects that the thread will invoke; otherwise, COM will have to perform cross-apartment marshaling with all its attendant performance penalties.

Here is an example of setting the apartment state:

```
System.threading.Thread runner = new System.Threading.Thread(...);
⋮
runner.set_ApartmentState(ApartmentState.MTA);
```

You can set this property only once for a thread—any subsequent attempts to change the *ApartmentState* property will have no effect. You should also set this property early if you suspect that you'll need it; the thread does not have to have started—it only needs to exist. If you haven't set this property, the first call to COM will result in the creation of a multithreaded apartment.

You can set the *ApartmentState* property of the main application thread using the *System.STAThreadAttribute* or *System.MTAThreadAttribute* at the entry point of the application (the *main* method). If you use Visual Studio .NET to create a Console or Windows application, you'll notice that this attribute is applied automatically to the *main* method:

```
/** @attribute System.STAThreadAttribute() */
public static void main(String[] args)
{
    ⋮
}
```

Note Console and Windows application default to the STA apartment state primarily because threads that perform interactive IO with a user should not run in a multi-threaded apartment.

Calling Managed Code

Threads can also cross into the common language runtime from outside; you can make common language runtime objects and classes available to unmanaged code. This crossover is also achieved using COM Interop and the common language runtime exposes managed objects as if they were COM objects. Unmanaged code accesses common language runtime objects using proxy objects called COM-Callable Wrappers (CCWs). (See Chapter 13 for details.) Apartment issues are less important in this scenario because common language runtime objects act like free-threaded objects—they can be called from single-threaded and multithreaded COM apartments. There is one major exception to this rule: Serviced Components, which are covered in detail in Chapter 14.

Synchronization

Earlier, when we discussed a technique for passing parameters to threads using a property, you learned that problems can occur, mainly due to uncertainty about how threads are executed. You can never guarantee the order in which threads are run (unless they all have different priorities), so if one thread sets some shared data to a value that is read by another, the reading thread might run before the writing thread has actually written the data. In situations in which the running order matters, threads must be carefully synchronized.

As a simple example, consider the *Stock* and *StockController* classes shown in the StockControl.jsl file in the StockControl project. The *Stock* class models stock items held in a fictitious warehouse. The private variable *numInStock* holds the volume of the item currently in stock. You can use the property *get_numberInStock* to query the current stock level. The method *addToNumInStock* increases the volume of the item in the warehouse when it is restocked, and the *reduceNumInStock* is used when customers order that item. If the stock is insufficient to satisfy the order, *reduceNumInStock* throws an exception.

The *StockController* class is a test harness that creates two concurrent threads that manipulate the same *Stock* object, called *widgets*. The *TakeOrders* method actually performs the deed, ordering seven widgets and adjusting the stock level in the warehouse accordingly. The method displays messages indicating its progress—you can use the *Name* property (available through the *set_Name* and *get_Name* methods in J#) to associate an identifying string with a thread. The *main* method populates the *Stock* object with 10 widgets and then creates and starts two threads that run the *TakeOrders* method.

When this program is built and executed, a number of scenarios are possible. One is that the *main* thread creates the *sc1Runner* and *sc2Runner* threads and executes their *Start* methods, setting their status to *Running*. In the ideal situation, once one of the threads starts, it executes the *TakeOrders* method to completion, deducting seven widgets from the available stock before the second thread runs and trips the exception in *reduceNumInStock* because there are no longer enough widgets available to fulfill the second order. The ideal output is shown in Figure 8-6.

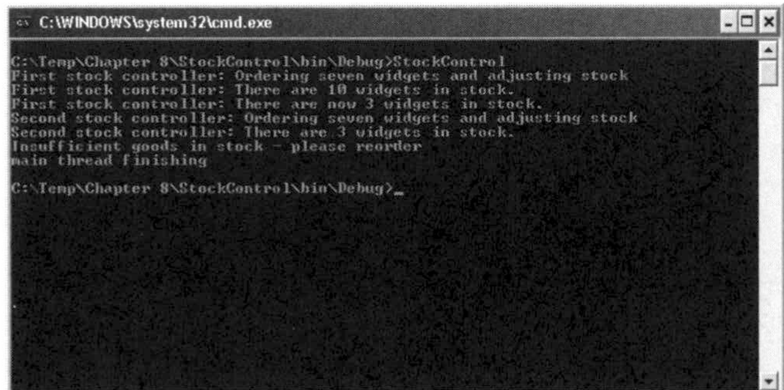

Figure 8-6 The ideal output of the StockControl program

In alternative scenario, the *TakeOrders* method is interrupted partway through its execution and the *sc2Runner* thread starts executing before the *sc1Runner* completes. (This can even occur without *sc1Runner* being interrupted if you're using a multiprocessor machine.) Both threads might conceivably execute the *reduceNumberInStock* method simultaneously. If you examine this method closely, you'll see a looming problem:

```
if (numInStock >= byHowMany)
{
      numInStock -= byHowMany;
      return numInStock;
}
else
{
      throw new System.Exception
         ("Insufficient goods in stock - please reorder");
         }
```

There is a very real possibility that a race condition will occur. If *sc1Runner* performs the test in the *if* statement first, it will find that *numInStock* (10) is greater than *byHowMany* (7). Execution will then proceed to the next statement. If *sc2Runner* performs the same test at the same time but before *sc1Runner* has actually updated the stock level, it will get the same results. Both threads will deduct 7 from *numInStock*, resulting in the same goods being ordered twice and the *numInStock* variable becoming corrupted—it will end up containing the value -4! Figure 8-7 shows the output.

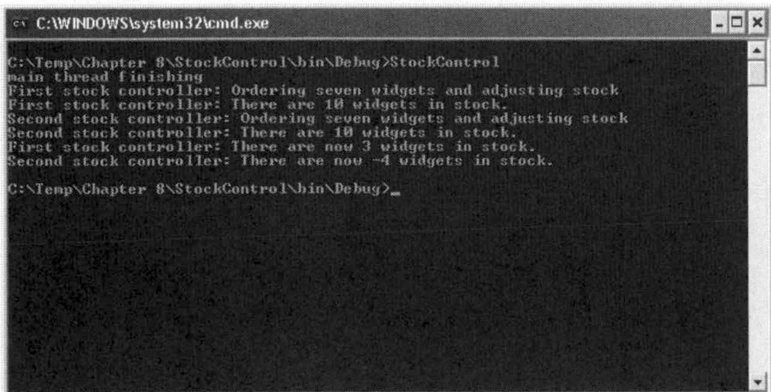

Figure 8-7 A race condition in the StockControl program

Tip We simulated this problem by adding the statement *System.Threading.Thread.Sleep(1)* inside the *if* statement in *reduceNumInStock* before deducting from *numInStock*. This might not always work (using *Sleep* to force the execution order of threads is not guaranteed), but if you run the program a few times, you should get these results at least once.

The issue is really one of atomicity. In a multithreaded environment, it is vitally important that sequences of test and set operations form an indivisible unit. But when you write code in a high-level language such as Visual Basic .NET, C#, or J#, even single statements are not guaranteed to be atomic. For example, look at the *addToNumInStock* method in the *Stock* class. It contains the following statement:

```
numInStock += howMany;
```

If you open StockControl.EXE using the Intermediate Language Disassembly tool (ILDASM) and examine the Microsoft Intermediate Language (MSIL) code for this method, you'll see this sequence of instructions:

```
.method public hidebysig virtual instance int32
            addToNumInStock(int32 howMany) cil managed
{
    // Code size 25 (0x19)
    .maxstack  3
    .locals init ([0] int32 V_0)
```

```
    IL_0000:    ldarg.0
    IL_0001:    ldarg.0
    IL_0002:    ldfld        int32  ReaderWriter.Stock::numInStock
    IL_0007:    ldarg.1
    IL_0008:    add
    IL_0009:    stfld        int32  ReaderWriter.Stock::numInStock
    IL_000e:    ldarg.0
    IL_000f:    ldfld        int32  ReaderWriter.Stock::numInStock
    IL_0014:    stloc.0
    IL_0015:    br.s         IL_0017
    IL_0017:    ldloc.0
    IL_0018:    ret
} // end of method  Stock::addToNumInStock
```

1. Push the current value of the static field *numInStock* onto the stack.
2. Push the value of argument 1 (the *howMany* parameter) onto the stack.
3. Add the two items at the top of the stack together, pushing the result onto the stack
4. Pop the item at the top of the stack back into the static field *numInStock*.

The important instructions are from address *IL_0002* to *IL_0009*. The sequence of operations is as follows:

This sequence could be suspended partway through. Another thread running the same method at the same time might corrupt the *numInStock* variable in a manner similar to the corruption you saw caused by concurrent execution of the *reduceNumInStock* method. And these are not the only combinations of sequences that can lead to this state of affairs—one thread running *addToNumInStock* while another is executing *reduceNumInStock* can be equally disastrous.

The key to writing thread-safe code (code that will operate in a correct and well-defined manner when executed by multiple concurrent threads) is to use an appropriate synchronization technique.

Manual Synchronization

There are many ways to synchronize access to data. Some are more expensive than others in terms of resources used and other overhead, and some are more appropriate than others for a given scenario. Writing thread-safe applications is a matter of appreciating the options available and then applying them effectively.

You should ask yourself, "What code should I make thread-safe?" If you're building class libraries, you never know exactly how the methods in your classes will be invoked—they might be executed concurrently from multiple threads. So all code that you write should be thread-safe—or carefully documented with a big red warning label if it is not.

However, this does not mean that you must always implement expensive synchronization techniques. You can achieve a high level of thread safety by designing your classes carefully or using algorithms that can tolerate race conditions. Classes that expose static methods or static data are *always* vulnerable in a multithreaded environment and require synchronization. Restricting classes to instance methods and data does not guarantee thread safety (the *Stock* class shown earlier is an example of this), but such classes are less prone to problems with multithreading, and weak points can be isolated and protected more easily.

Note The ability to mark a method as thread-safe or otherwise would certainly be a useful feature—possibly using a *ThreadSafe* attribute that takes a Boolean parameter indicating whether the author intended the method to be available to a multithreaded environment. Naturally, the default value of this attribute would be *false*. The common language runtime (which knows all about the threads being used) could examine this attribute before executing each method and take appropriate action—throwing an exception if a non-thread-safe method is invoked from anything other than the primary thread running an application, or enforcing the serialization of all non-thread-safe methods. The cost would be a few extra instructions executed before each method call, but the benefits could be enormous.

.NET Class Library Thread Safety

For reasons of performance, Microsoft has adopted the "big red warning label" approach and many of the classes in the .NET Class Library are not thread-safe. For instance, Microsoft created a number of classes in the *System.Collections* namespace for handling collections of data—hash tables, array lists, queues, and so on. However, you can make many classes thread-safe by creating a static thread-safe wrapper and accessing the class exclusively through this wrapper. Microsoft has implemented such a wrapper for most of the collection classes.

For example, the *ArrayList* class provides the *Synchronized* method. You pass this method an *ArrayList*, and it returns a thread-safe reference to the same object:

```
import System.Collections.*;
⋮
ArrayList al = new ArrayList();
ArrayList sal = ArrayList.Synchronized(al);
sal.Add(...); // Use sal like an ordinary ArrayList
⋮
```

Note that the *System.Array* class does not have a *Synchronized* method, and arrays are not thread-safe by default. For classes such as this, you must implement your own wrappers. In a number of cases, the .NET Framework Class Library provides the *SyncRoot* property, which returns an object that can be used to provide synchronized access. You can use this property with some of the synchronization primitives described in this chapter to implement thread safety for those classes.

Sync Blocks

Behind the scenes, each object running using the common language runtime contains a data structure that you can use to synchronize access to that object. This data structure is referred to as the *sync block*. Object-level synchronization primitives, such as the *Monitor* class, use it.

The *Monitor* Class

You can use the *System.Threading.Monitor* class to control access to shared resources and critical sections of code (code that should be executed by only one thread at a time). A *Monitor* object can obtain an exclusive lock over the sync block of an object specified by the developer when the static *Enter* method is used. An attempt to execute *Enter* by another thread will result in that thread being blocked. You release the lock by executing *Monitor.Exit* over the same object. If any threads are blocked, one of them will be selected and granted the lock, and then it can continue processing. Any remaining threads will remain blocked and continue waiting.

Note The *Monitor* object operates in a manner similar to that used by *synchronized* methods in Java. The implementation of a synchronized method in J# actually executes *Monitor.Enter(this)* when the method starts and *Monitor.Exit(this)* when the method completes.

For example, if you need to restrict concurrent access to a resource such as the *numInStock* variable shown in the StockControl sample discussed earlier, you can use the technique shown here (this version of the code is available in the ConcurrentStockControl project):

```
private int numInStock = 0;
⋮
// Restock the warehouse
public int addToNumInStock(int howMany)
{
    try
    {
        Monitor.Enter(this);
        this.numInStock += howMany;
        return this.numInStock;
    }
    finally
    {
        Monitor.Exit(this);
    }
}


// Remove stock from warehouse
public int reduceNumInStock(int byHowMany) throws System.Exception
{
    try
    {
        Monitor.Enter(this);
        if (this.numInStock >= byHowMany)
```

```
            {
                this.numInStock -= byHowMany;
                return this.numInStock;
            }
            else
            {
                throw new System.Exception(
                    "Insufficient goods in stock - please reorder");
            }
        }
        finally
        {
            Monitor.Exit(this);
        }
    }
```

When a method calls *Monitor.Enter*, the common language runtime will attempt to lock the sync block for the specified object (*this* in the example above). If the sync block is already locked by another thread, *Monitor.Enter* will be suspended until it is released. The method call *Monitor.Exit* over the same object releases the sync block. Invocations of *Monitor.Enter* and *Monitor.Exit* must be balanced—if you call *Monitor.Enter* over the same object twice, you must call *Monitor.Exit* twice to release the sync block. Failure to do this can result in the sync block never being released, leading to some long waits by blocked threads!

You should consider your exception handling strategy carefully when you use a monitor. Unhandled exceptions in a thread will cause the thread to terminate, and all its locks will be released automatically. However, if you catch exceptions, you must be prepared to release locks manually as part of the exception handling process. The code shown above uses a *try...finally* construct to guarantee that *Monitor.Exit* is executed before the methods finish.

Note If *Monitor.Enter* blocks, the thread will enter the *WaitSleepJoin* state. The thread can be woken using the *Interrupt* method, or it can be aborted.

When you use a monitor, you should consider carefully the object whose sync block you're going to use. The same object must be available to all the threads you intend to coordinate; otherwise, they'll have nothing in common to synchronize on. But you should avoid using a wide-ranging global object as a generic locking object because this can lead to sync block contention. Ideally, when you use monitors for synchronization, each protected resource (or group of resources) should have its own associated lock object (probably the object itself).

You should also ensure that you avoid deadlock. Deadlock commonly happens when threads require several locks over the same resources but acquire those locks in a different sequence—for example, when two threads that have obtained one lock each attempt to obtain the lock held by the other and end up waiting indefinitely for each other. To reduce the likelihood of deadlock, you should always lock resources in the same order.

Tip You might find the Execute Around pattern (not one of the GoF patterns) useful in deadlock situations. This pattern involves creating a *synchronizer wrapper* object that performs all the locking and can take a delegate that refers to a method to be executed after the necessary locks have been acquired.

The *Monitor* class also has the *TryEnter* method, which will attempt to grab the sync block for the selected object but will terminate if the lock cannot be obtained. *TryEnter* returns a Boolean value indicating whether the lock was obtained successfully:

```
if (Monitor.TryEnter(this))
{
try
    {
        // lock obtained - do processing
        ⋮
}
finally
    {
        Monitor.Exit(this);
    }
}
else
{
// failed to obtain lock
⋮
}
```

The *TryEnter* method is overloaded, and you can optionally specify a timeout as a second parameter. The method will wait until the lock is obtained (returning *true*) or until the timeout occurs (returning *false*):

```
TimeSpan ts =
   new TimeSpan(0, 0, 30); // 0 hours, 0 minutes, 30 seconds
if (Monitor.TryEnter(this, ts))
{
      ⋮
}
```

The *Interlocked* Class

The *Monitor* class is general-purpose—it allows you to implement a variety of short and long-lived locking strategies (although long-lived locks are not always recommended as they can adversely affect the concurrency and throughput of your applications). For example, you can perform *Monitor.Enter* in one method and execute the corresponding *Monitor.Exit* method in another—as long as the same thread invokes both methods. A monitor can be too heavy and coarse-grained for some operations, however, so the .NET Framework Class Library provides some specialized alternatives in the *Interlocked* and *ReaderWriterLock* classes.

The *Interlocked* class provides synchronized access to variables shared by multiple threads. It implements the *CompareExchange*, *Decrement*, *Exchange*, and *Increment* methods. These methods comprise atomic operations—for example, *Increment* will increment an *int* or a *long* variable and will not be preempted partway through its execution:

```
int i = 100;
Interlocked.Increment(i); // atomic
```

Similarly, the *Interlocked.Decrement* method will atomically decrement an *int* or *long* variable.

The *Interlocked.Exchange* method performs an atomic query and assignment operation. The value of the second argument overwrites the first, but the method returns the original value of the first argument before the assignment occurred. It will operate on *int*, *float*, and *Object* types

---

Tip If you use *Exchange* over *Object* types, make sure you have overridden the *Equals* method to make comparisons meaningful.

```
int i = 100;
int j = 120;
int oldValue = Interlocked.Exchange(i, j);   // oldValue = i; i = j;
```

The *Interlocked.CompareExchange* method is an atomic test and set operation that compares the first and third arguments. If they are equal, the variable specified by the first argument is set to the value specified by the second; otherwise, the first argument is left unchanged. The value returned is the original value of the first argument (whether or not it has been changed):

```
int i = 100;
int j = 120;
int k = 100;
int oldValue =
  Interlocked.CompareExchange(i, j, k);   // oldValue = i;

     // if (i == k)

     //         i = j;
```

Like *Interlocked.Exchange*, *Interlocked.CompareExchange* will operate on *int*, *float*, and *Object* types. (All three parameters must be of the same type.)

The *ReaderWriterLock* Class

Just as the *Interlocked* class is a highly specialized beast optimized for performing a defined set of operations, so the *ReaderWriterLock* class is aimed at a particular set of problems. The *ReaderWriterLock* class caters for the "single writer, multiple readers" scenario. In this situation, a resource can be read by many threads concurrently with impunity, but a thread writing to the resource needs exclusive access. You can contrast this with the more draconian monitor approach, which enforces mutual exclusion regardless of whether the protected resource is being read or written to.

The algorithm used by the *ReaderWriterLock* class is based on fairness. Under normal circumstances, concurrent read requests can overlap. However, if a writer requests access, all further read requests will be queued behind the writer. This prevents the writer from potentially being blocked indefinitely.

The *ReaderWriterLock* class exposes a variety of methods for acquiring reader and writer locks, for releasing locks held, and for determining whether the current thread is actually holding a lock. These are instance methods, so to use them you must create a *ReaderWriterLock* object. The following code fragment shows implementations of the *get_numberInStock* and *reduceNumInStock* methods, which employ a *ReaderWriterLock* called *stockLock*. (This code is available in the ReaderWriterStockControl project.)

You should note several important points. First, you obtain a lock by calling *AcquireReaderLock* or *AcquireWriterLock* as appropriate. An attempt to obtain a writer lock will block if reader locks currently exist over the same *ReaderWriterLock* object, as will attempts to acquire a reader lock if a writer lock is currently held or has been requested. Remember that even though reader locks can be obtained concurrently, they will be held in a queue once a writer lock has been requested. Both methods expect a timeout parameter. If the lock has not been gained when the timeout expires, the common language runtime will throw a *System.ApplicationException* containing the message "This operation returned because the timeout period expired." You can specify a value of 0 for the timeout if you do not want to wait, or *Timeout.Infinite* if you're prepared to wait indefinitely. Here's the code:

```
private int numInStock = 0;
private ReaderWriterLock stockLock = new ReaderWriterLock();
⋮
// How many in stock
/** @property */
public int get_numberInStock() throws System.Exception
{
      try
      {
            stockLock.AcquireReaderLock(new TimeSpan(0, 0, 5));
            return this.numInStock;
      }
      finally
      {
            if (stockLock.get_IsReaderLockHeld())
            {
                  stockLock.ReleaseReaderLock();
            }
      }
}
⋮
// Remove stock from warehouse
public int reduceNumInStock(int byHowMany) throws System.Exception
{
      try
      {
            stockLock.AcquireWriterLock(new TimeSpan(0, 0, 5));
            if (this.numInStock >= byHowMany)
            {
                  this.numInStock -= byHowMany;
                  return this.numInStock;
            }
            else
```

```
            {
                throw new System.Exception(
                    "Insufficient goods in stock - please reorder");
            }
        }
        finally
        {
            if (stockLock.get_IsWriterLockHeld())
            {
                stockLock.ReleaseWriterLock();
            }
        }
    }
```

You release locks using the *ReleaseReaderLock* or *ReleaseWriterLock* method. If you're currently holding a writer lock as well as a reader lock, *ReleaseReaderLock* will actually release them both. *ReleaseWriterLock* will release only a writer lock, however (it will also throw an exception if the thread is holding a reader lock). An error will result if you release a lock that you don't hold, which is why the *finally* blocks in the sample code shown above execute the property accessor methods *get_IsReaderLockHeld* and *get_IsWriterLockHeld*. These methods return *true* if the thread currently holds a lock of the designated type, *false* otherwise.

What constitutes a read or write operation (requiring a reader or a writer lock) is up to the developer. It's normally taken for granted that a read operation reads some data value, and that a write operation modifies it in some way, but what you actually do is your decision. The *ReaderWriterLock* class provides the methods *UpgradeToWriterLock* and *DowngradeFromWriterLock* to allow you to convert a reader lock to a writer lock and back again if needed.

Warning The common language runtime does not care whether you write when you hold a reader lock, or vice-versa. Reading with a writer lock is no big deal, but writing with only a reader lock can be dangerous if others have reader locks also.

Reader and writer locks implement nested semantics. If you acquire a reader lock using *AcquireReaderLock* five times, you should release it using *ReleaseReaderLock* five times. An alternative is to use the method *ReleaseLock*, which will release all the locks that a thread holds on a *ReaderWriterLock* object regardless of how many times it grabbed them.

Automatic Synchronization

The Java language provides a *synchronized* method modifier that can be used to perform automatic synchronization of method calls. Similarly, the .NET Framework Class Library contains a pair of attributes that you can use to synchronize access to methods and objects. The first of these is *System.Runtime.CompilerServices.MethodImplAttribute*.

Method Synchronization

The *MethodImplAttribute* class has many uses. It is commonly employed by compiler writers, which is why it is in the *CompilerServices* namespace. Its purpose is to supply metadata indicating how a method is actually implemented—for example, whether it was developed using managed or unmanaged code. One option you can specify is *Synchronized*. This indicates to the common language runtime that the method should be accessed by only one thread at a time. The runtime will automatically serialize access to the method in a particular object, and will block a thread that attempts to execute the method if another thread is currently executing it.

The following code shows another version of the *reduceNumInStock* method, which uses *MethodImplAttribute*:

```
import System.Runtime.CompilerServices.*;
⋮
/** @attribute MethodImplAttribute(MethodImplOptions.Synchronized) */
public int reduceNumInStock(int byHowMany) throws System.Exception
{
      if (numInStock >= byHowMany)
      {
            numInStock -= byHowMany;
            return numInStock;
      }
      else
      {
               throw new System.Exception(
                  "Insufficient goods in stock - please reorder");
      }
}
```

This synchronization approach makes access to the method itself thread-safe (two threads will not be able to execute *reduceNumInStock* in the same object concurrently), but it does not prevent other methods (such as *addToNumInStock*) from running, so this technique is appropriate only for protecting data manipulated by a single method. You can apply *MethodImplAttribute* to static and instance methods.

Object Synchronization

Managed objects live in application domains. An application domain can be divided into contexts. A context groups objects that share the same features, or context attributes. Each application domain has a default context, which is created when the application domain is created, but additional contexts might be created automatically as new objects with specific requirements are instantiated.

Objects themselves can be marked as being context-bound or context-agile. A context-agile object can be accessed freely from any other context in the same application domain. Context-bound objects can be accessed directly by other objects in the same context, but objects in other contexts must use proxies to access a context-bound object. (You will learn more about context-bound and context-agile objects in Chapter 11.) Much of the time, you don't need to be concerned whether an object is context-agile or context-bound because proxy generation and marshaling of method calls across context boundaries occurs automatically. (Marshaling across a context boundary in the same application domain is not as expensive as it sounds because everything is performed in process.) The exception to this rule, however, is if you want to apply context attributes to a class. All objects that have the same set of context attribute values reside in the same context and must be explicitly marked as being context-bound. One such attribute is *System.Runtime.Remoting.Contexts.SynchronizationAttribute*, which is used for performing object-level synchronization.

The *SynchronizationAttribute* is applied to a class. The class must inherit from *System.ContextBoundObject* for this attribute to have any effect. You can specify one of four synchronization options (listed below). If you've ever designed COM+ classes, these options might have a familiar feel.

- **REQUIRED** The object must execute in a synchronized context. If necessary, a new context will be created. If the object is invoked by another object that is already in a synchronized context, the existing context will be used. All method calls to the object and any other objects sharing the same context will be serialized.
- **REQUIRES_NEW** A new synchronized context will be created for the object. All method calls to this instance of the object (and any other synchronized objects it creates) will be serialized. Other instances of the object will be created in their own contexts.
- **SUPPORTED** The object can execute in the current context, regardless of whether the context is synchronized. Method calls to the object are not serialized.

- **NOT_SUPPORTED** The object will not execute in a synchronized context. If necessary, a new nonsynchronized context will be created. Method calls are not serialized.

The implementation of the *Stock* class shown below, available in the SynchronizedStockControl project, uses the *REQUIRES_NEW* option to create a synchronized context that serializes all method calls to the same instance of each *Stock* object (different instances still operate independently and can be accessed concurrently). Notice that the methods themselves require no additional logic for handling multithreading:

```
import System.*;
import System.Runtime.Remoting.Contexts.*;

// Stock class - models stock items in a warehouse
/ ** @attribute
    SynchronizationAttribute(SynchronizationAttribute.REQUIRES_NEW)
  */
public class Stock extends ContextBoundObject
{
      private int numInStock = 0;

      // How many in stock
      public int get_numberInStock()
      {
            return this.numInStock;
      }

      // Restock the warehouse
      public int addToNumInStock(int howMany)
      {
            this.numInStock += howMany;
            return this.numInStock;
      }

      // Remove stock from warehouse
      public int reduceNumInStock(int byHowMany) throws System.Exception
      {
            if (this.numInStock >= byHowMany)
            {
                  this.numInStock -= byHowMany;
                  return this.numInStock;
            }
            else
            {
                  throw new System.Exception(
                     "Insufficient goods in stock - please reorder");
```

```
            }
        }
}
```

Object synchronization is a powerful concept and is relatively easy to apply, but it does come with a penalty. In particular, as with the use of monitors, it locks an object for exclusive access and makes no distinction between read and write operations. Also, object synchronization does not apply to static methods.

Static and Thread Data

Static fields usually belong to a class rather than individual objects or sets of objects. When you use multithreading, however, you can create different instances of a static variable in different threads by applying the *ThreadStaticAttribute* to the variable in question. These are known as *thread-relative* static fields:

```
/** @attribute ThreadStaticAttribute() */
private static int threadVar = 100; // initialization may not occur
```

In this example, each thread will receive its own copy of the variable *threadVar*. Each instance created by a thread will automatically be assigned the value 0 regardless of whether the variable declaration contains any initialization. (This does *not* apply if the main program thread instantiates the object containing the variable—normal initialization will occur in this case.) You can apply this attribute only to static variables.

Under the covers, thread-relative static fields are implemented using managed thread local storage (TLS). The *Thread* class exposes the *AllocateDataSlot*, *SetData*, and *GetData* methods that allow you to interact with managed TLS directly, creating and releasing TLS data slots dynamically:

```
private LocalDataStoreSlot ldss;
⋮
public void doWork()
{
      ⋮
      ldss = System.Threading.Thread.AllocateDataSlot();
      System.Threading.Thread.SetData(ldss, " "Some data");
      ⋮
}

public void doSomeMoreWork()
{
      ⋮
```

```
        String msg = (String)System.Threading.Thread.GetData(ldss);
    ⋮
}
```

The class *System.LocalDataStoreSlot* is the .NET abstraction for a piece of TLS. The static method *AllocateDataSlot* creates a new chunk of TLS and returns a reference to it. You can use the static *SetData* method to store information in a slot. The information stored can be almost anything—the parameter is passed in as an *Object*. Later, the data can be read back using the *GetData* method, which passes a reference to the same slot. The result must be cast to the type of data held in that slot. Data slots are private to a thread, and no other thread can access them.

You can also create named data slots. This gives you increased flexibility—the name of a slot can be a string variable, and you do not have to retain static references to slots allocated in one method for use by another:

```
public void doWork()
{
        ⋮
LocalDataStoreSlot ldss =
        System.Threading.Thread.AllocateNamedDataSlot("Slot 1");
System.Threading.Thread.SetData(ldss, " "Some data");
⋮
}

public void doSomeMoreWork()
{
        ⋮
    LocalDataStoreSlot ldss =
        System.Threading.Thread.GetNamedDataSlot("Slot 1");
    String msg = (String)System.Threading.Thread.GetData(ldss);
⋮
}
```

If you call *GetNamedDataSlot* on a nonexistent slot, it will be created automatically and its contents will be initialized to *null*. (It would be nicer if the runtime threw an exception, but you can't have everything!) If you try to create two slots with the same name, the common language runtime will throw a *System.ArgumentException* with the message "Item has already been added." You can release named slots using the *FreeNamedDataSlot* method.

A final variation on the static variable theme is the context static variable. All threads executing in the same context share static variables marked with *System.ContextStaticAttribute*. Different contexts see different instances of static data marked in this way.

```
/** @attribute ContextStaticAttribute() */
private static int contextData;
```

Interthread Communication

We've examined some basic synchronization techniques, but they are not appropriate for every situation when you're handling multiple threads. Let's look at some additional techniques you can use for implementing more advanced cooperation and communication between threads.

Thread Notification

You've learned how to use the *Monitor* class to perform exclusive locking using a sync object. But consider a common scenario from the world of computer science: that of *producers* and *consumers*.

A producer is an object that creates resources. A consumer is an object that obtains resources from a producer. A simple producer might implement an iterative process, creating one resource after another. A consumer will wait until a resource is ready, and then retrieve it from the producer and exercise it in some way. When the consumer has finished, it will wait for the next resource to become available, and so on.

The producer and the consumer should both run concurrently, but the consumer cannot access a resource until the producer has finished building it, and the producer cannot modify the resource once the consumer has started to use it. The producer and consumer could run at different speeds—the producer might be able to create resources faster than the consumer can gobble them up. In this situation, the resources must not be lost, but somehow queued for processing. There might also be a variable number of consumers, and no resource can be accessed by more than one consumer. Figure 8-8 shows the architecture of a typical producer-consumer system.

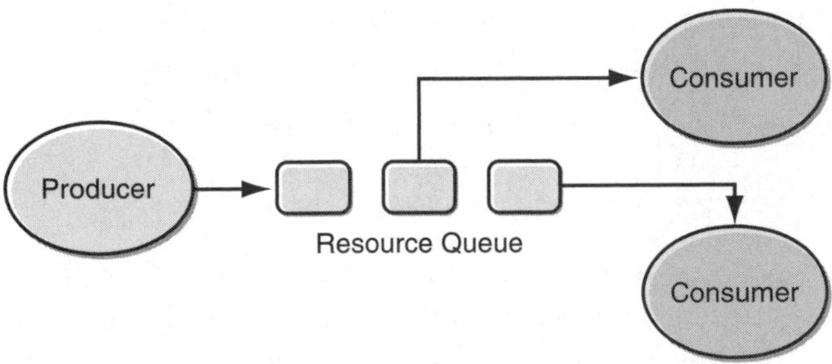

Figure 8-8 The producer-consumer architecture

To manage access to resources, you could guarantee exclusive access to the resource queue by locking it with *Monitor.Enter*. However, if a consumer locks the queue and there is nothing for the consumer to process, the consumer will have to unlock the queue immediately; otherwise, the producer will not be able to place anything in it. The consumer could poll for items on the queue, but this would be expensive—the consumer would have to lock the queue, examine it, and then release the lock if nothing is there. Another problem is how long the consumer should sleep between polls. If the interval is too short, the system will spend its time obtaining and releasing locks and not doing any real work. If the interval is too long, the consumer might be overwhelmed with data when it processes the queue, the producer might have to wait for a long time while the consumer uses the queue, and the system as a whole might become fitful.

A better solution is to use the *Monitor.Wait* and *Monitor.Pulse* methods.

Waiting

The *Wait* method of the *Monitor* class is used in conjunction with *Monitor.Enter* and *Monitor.Exit*. As you'll recall, *Monitor.Enter* exclusively locks a resource. *Monitor.Wait* releases the lock on the resource but puts the thread into the *WaitSleepJoin* state. The thread will be woken up when another thread executes *Monitor.Pulse* over the same resource, and it will attempt to reacquire the lock (effectively automatically performing another *Monitor.Enter* command).

The sample program ProducerConsumer.jsl in the ProducerConsumer project shows an implementation of a producer and a consumer based on this model. The producer is the *Calculator* class. *Calculator* exposes a public *System.Collections.Queue* object called *power2Queue* and a method called *calcPowersOfTwo*. The purpose of *calcPowersOfTwo* is to calculate powers of two for all integers from 1 to 20. Each result is posted to *power2Queue* as it is generated. The method initially locks the queue:

```
Monitor.Enter(Calculator.power2Queue);
```

The program then enters a *while* loop to generate the various powers of two. As each value is generated, it is placed on the queue:

```
power2Queue.Enqueue(new  Integer(currPos  *  currPos));
```

Note You can queue any type that descends from *Object*. However, unlike the hierarchy defined in .NET Framework Class Library, the

Java primitive types (such as *int*) are not freely convertible to *Object*. The solution is to use an appropriate wrapper—*Integer*, in this case.

Having queued the value, the method signals to any waiting consumer that some data is ready, using *Monitor.Pulse*:

```
Monitor.Pulse(Calculator.power2Queue);
```

Before the consumer can continue, the producer must release the lock on the queue:

```
Monitor.Exit(Calculator.power2Queue);
```

If a consumer is waiting and is scheduled to run, it can obtain the lock. The producer calls *Monitor.Enter* again and blocks until the lock is granted before generating the next power of two.

The consumer is the *Printer* class. The *printPowersOfTwo* method does the work—it grabs the lock on the queue:

```
Monitor.Enter(Calculator.power2Queue);
```

The method then executes *Monitor.Wait* on the *power2Queue*, which releases the lock and puts the thread into a *WaitSleepJoin* state. The reason for calling *Monitor.Enter* first is that you cannot execute *Monitor.Wait* on an object unless you currently hold a lock on that object, which is obtained using *Monitor.Enter*. (If you attempt to wait without getting the lock first, the common language runtime will throw a *SynchronizationLockException*.) The *Wait* method specifies the object to wait on, and optionally a timeout parameter. The example will wait for a maximum of 10 seconds (approximately). The value returned by *Wait* indicates whether the wait was successful (it was released by a pulse from another thread) or not (a timeout occurred). The *while* loop shown in the *printPowersOfTwo* method terminates if the *Wait* operation times out:

```
while (Monitor.Wait(Calculator.power2Queue, new TimeSpan(0, 0, 10)))
{
      ⋮
}
```

Inside the loop, the code iterates through all the available items on the queue, extracting them and printing them. Remember that you cannot control when threads will execute, and there is no guarantee that when the *Calculator* object executes the *Pulse* method, the *Printer* will get a chance to run before the *Calculator* gets the lock again and adds another value to the queue. So, when the *Printer* runs, more than one item might be waiting to be processed.

Returning to the *calcPowersOfTwo* method in the *Calculator* class, after all the powers of two have been generated and dispatched, the method executes the *PulseAll* command:

```
Monitor.PulseAll(Calculator.power2Queue);
```

If several threads are in the *WaitSleepJoin* state, *Pulse* will wake just the first thread that happens to be waiting. The others will remain waiting. Another method, *PulseAll*, is available that wakes all threads waiting on the object, and each one will attempt to obtain the lock when it is released. (Only one will succeed—the others will block.) This is useful in a multithreaded environment if you're not sure how many threads are waiting on an object and you want to release them all. An illustration of when you might want to use *PulseAll* is shown in the example.

Monitor Queues

Internally, a monitor contains two queues—the *Waiting* queue and the *Ready* queue. (Do not confuse these with the *System.Collections.Queue* object used by the ProducerConsumer example.) When a thread executes *Monitor.Enter* and gets blocked, it is placed in the *Ready* queue. When the lock is released, a subsequent thread switch will cause the next available thread to be extracted from the *Ready* queue and run. If a thread executes *Monitor.Wait*, it will be placed instead in the *Waiting* queue. When the *Pulse* method is executed by another thread, the first thread in the *Waiting* queue will be moved to the *Ready* queue and become available to run. If the *PulseAll* method is invoked, all threads in the *Waiting* queue will be moved to the *Ready* queue.

To make life more interesting, the *main* method in the *Runner* class in the ProducerConsumer program creates two *Printer* threads, which compete for output from the *Calculator*. The *Printer* class exposes the *printerName* field, which the *Runner* class sets to a different value for each thread. Each *Printer* thread displays its name as it prints data. If you run this program several times, you'll observe the nondeterministic nature of thread scheduling. One thread might dominate another, or the output might be shared evenly. Figure 8-9 shows the output of one run on a single-processor computer. Occasionally, you might find that the *Printer* threads do not output anything—they just sit idle for 10 seconds and then terminate. We'll explain the reason for this in a moment.

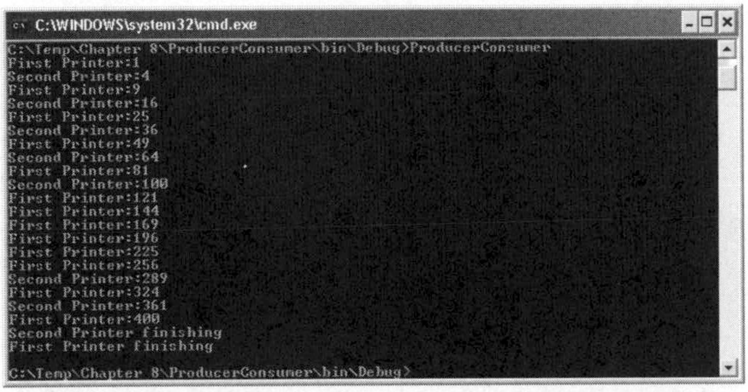

```
C:\WINDOWS\system32\cmd.exe
C:\Temp\Chapter 8\ProducerConsumer\bin\Debug>ProducerConsumer
First Printer:1
Second Printer:4
First Printer:9
Second Printer:16
First Printer:25
Second Printer:36
First Printer:49
Second Printer:64
First Printer:81
Second Printer:100
First Printer:121
First Printer:144
First Printer:169
First Printer:196
First Printer:225
First Printer:256
Second Printer:289
First Printer:324
Second Printer:361
First Printer:400
Second Printer finishing
First Printer finishing

C:\Temp\Chapter 8\ProducerConsumer\bin\Debug>
```

Figure 8-9 The output of the ProducerConsumer program

Using Events

The reason you occasionally get no output from the *Printer* objects is due to a race condition that can occur when you use *Pulse* and *Wait*. The problem is that if you execute a *Pulse* when there are no waiting objects, the pulse will be lost. *Pulse* and *Wait* rely on the fact that a thread is waiting before another thread sends a *Pulse*. A more reliable approach to using a monitor to pass signals between threads is to employ events. The common language runtime provides two specialized event classes for signaling threads: *System.Threading.ManualResetEvent* and *System.Threading.AutoResetEvent*. An event object can be in one of two states: signaled or unsignaled. The event classes provide methods that allow a thread to wait until an event enters the signaled state, blocking while it is unsignaled. Additional methods are available that you can use to change the state.

The technique for using a *ManualResetEvent* object is quite straightforward. When you create one, you specify an initial state—*true* means signaled and *false* means unsignaled:

```
import System.Threading.*;
⋮
ManualResetEvent dataReady = new ManualResetEvent(false);
```

To wait for a *ManualResetEvent* object to become signaled, you invoke the *WaitOne* method. This method will block the current thread until the event is signaled. You can specify an optional timeout parameter: *WaitOne* returns *true* if the wait was successful, *false* on a timeout:

```
dataReady.WaitOne();
```

Another thread can set the state of the event to signaled by executing the *Set* method:

```
dataReady.Set();
```

When the event is signaled, it will release *all* threads that are waiting for it. What's more, the event will remain in a signaled state—if you wait again, the wait operation will complete immediately. If a thread has successfully waited for an event, it should set the event back to the unsignaled state using the *Reset* method:

```
dataReady.Reset();
```

The following code shows an implementation of the *Calculator* class based on *ManualResetEvent* objects rather than on monitors. This version is available in the EventProducerConsumer project. The class creates two *ManualResetEvent* objects called *dataReady* and *queueReady*, initializing them both to the unsignaled state. The *calcPowersOfTwo* method simply signals the *dataReady* event when the next power of two is available on the queue, and then it waits for the *queueReady* event before continuing. The *Printer* class signals this event when it has retrieved the data from the queue. After receiving the signal, the *calcPowersOfTwo* method resets the *queueReady* signal before looping and generating the next power of two.

```
public class Calculator
{
    public static Queue power2Queue = new Queue();
    public static ManualResetEvent dataReady =
       new ManualResetEvent(false);
    public static ManualResetEvent queueReady =
       new ManualResetEvent(false);

    public void calcPowersOfTwo()
    {
        int currPos = 1;

        // Calculate powers of 2 up to 20
        while (currPos <= 20)
        {
            power2Queue.Enqueue(new Integer(currPos * currPos));

            // Inform the next consumer that some data is available
            dataReady.Set();

            // Wait for the consumer to signal that the queue is empty
```

```
            queueReady.WaitOne();
            queueReady.Reset();
            currPos += 1;
        }

        dataReady.Set();
    }
}
```

The *Printer* class makes use of the two *ManualResetEvent* objects defined in the *Calculator* class. The *printPowersOfTwo* method waits for the *dataReady* event to be signaled, resets it, and then retrieves the next item from the queue if there is one. (The queue might be empty because the *calcPowersOfTwo* method also signals the *dataReady* event when it has finished.) Once it has extracted the item from the queue, the method signals the *queueReady* event, releasing the *Calculator* thread to generate the next value:

```
public class Printer
{
    public String printerName;

    public void printPowersOfTwo()
    {
        // Wait for the data ready signal from the producer
        Calculator.dataReady.WaitOne();
        Calculator.dataReady.Reset();

        // Retrieve and display as many values as are on the queue
        while (Calculator.power2Queue.get_Count() > 0)
        {
            Integer data = (Integer)Calculator.power2Queue.Dequeue();
            Console.WriteLine(printerName + " ":" + data);

            // Signal that the queue is empty
            Calculator.queueReady.Set();

            // Wait for more data
            Calculator.dataReady.WaitOne();
            Calculator.dataReady.Reset();
        }

        Console.WriteLine(printerName + " " finishing");
    }
}
```

This solution appears to be more natural than using a monitor, and it works well for a single producer with a single consumer. However, the inherent nature of *ManualResetEvents* can lead to race conditions, mainly because when an event is signaled it releases all threads that are waiting on it. Both threads can run concurrently. Applying the *Reset* method immediately after waiting, as both classes shown above do, might not prevent this. You can solve this problem using an *AutoResetEvent*.

The *AutoResetEvent* class is remarkably similar to the *ManualResetEvent* class, but with one vital difference: When an *AutoResetEvent* object is signaled, it releases only one waiting object and resets itself to the unsignaled state automatically. This eliminates the need to perform separate *Reset* calls, and the operation is atomic, removing the race condition. You can use *AutoResetEvents* in the *Calculator* and *Printer* class—you just change the types of *dataReady* and *queueReady* in the *Calculator* class:

```
public static AutoResetEvent dataReady = new AutoResetEvent(false);
public static AutoResetEvent queueReady = new AutoResetEvent(false);
```

You should also hunt down every call to *Reset* and remove it. With this modification, the code will look like this:

```
public void calcPowersOfTwo()
{
    int currPos = 1;

    // Calculate powers of 2 up to 20
    while (currPos <= 20)
    {
        power2Queue.Enqueue(new Integer(currPos * currPos));

        // Inform the next consumer that some data is available
        dataReady.Set();

        // Wait for the consumer to signal that the queue is empty
        queueReady.WaitOne();

        currPos += 1;
    }

    dataReady.Set();
}
⋮
public void printPowersOfTwo()
{
    // Wait for the data ready signal from the producer
    Calculator.dataReady.WaitOne();

    // Retrieve and display as many values as are on the queue
```

```
        while (Calculator.power2Queue.get_Count() > 0)
        {
            Integer data = (Integer)Calculator.power2Queue.Dequeue();
            Console.WriteLine(printerName + ":" + data);

            // Signal that the queue is empty
            Calculator.queueReady.Set();

            // Wait for more data
            Calculator.dataReady.WaitOne();
        }

        Console.WriteLine(printerName + " finishing");
    }
    ⋮
```

Again, this works fine with a single consumer thread, but a different problem arises if two or more consumers are required. You'll find that one consumer terminates normally, but the remaining consumers hang. This is because they're all waiting for the *dataReady* event. At the end of the *calcPowersOfTwo* method, the *Calculator* class signals this event, but as it is now an *AutoResetEvent* it will release only one waiting thread. The others will remain blocked indefinitely. The solution is to use a *ManualResetEvent*, called *finished*, to indicate that the *calcPowersOfTwo* method has finished rather than overloading the *dataReady* event. Being a *ManualResetEvent*, it will release all threads that are waiting for it. The *printPowersOfTwo* method in the consumer should then wait for the *dataReady* or *finished* event to be signaled. Fortunately, this is possible as I will now describe.

The *AutoResetEvent* and the *ManualResetEvent* classes both inherit directly from a third class called *WaitHandle* (where much of their common processing is implemented). The *WaitHandle* class has a static method called *WaitAny*, which takes an array of *WaitHandle* objects (which can be a mixture of the two event types) and waits until one of them is signaled:

```
public static AutoResetEvent dataReady = new AutoResetEvent(false);
public static ManualResetEvent finished = new ManualResetEvent(false);
⋮

WaitHandle.WaitAny(new WaitHandle[] {Calculator.dataReady,
    Calculator.finished});
```

Another method, *WaitAll*, takes an array of *WaitHandle* objects but completes only when they have all been signaled. Completed event-based versions of the *Calculator* and *Printer* classes are shown here (the completed code is available in the AutoResetProducerConsumer project):

```
public class Calculator
{
      public static Queue power2Queue = new Queue();
      public static AutoResetEvent dataReady = new AutoResetEvent(false);
      public static AutoResetEvent queueReady = new AutoResetEvent(false);
      public static ManualResetEvent finished =
            new ManualResetEvent(false);

      public void calcPowersOfTwo()
      {
            int currPos = 1;

            // Calculate powers of 2 up to 20
            while (currPos <= 20)
            {
                  power2Queue.Enqueue(new Integer(currPos * currPos));

                  // Inform the next consumer that some data is available
                  dataReady.Set();

                  // Wait for the consumer to signal that the queue is empty
                  queueReady.WaitOne();
                  currPos += 1;
            }

            finished.Set();
      }
}

public class Printer
{
      public String printerName;

      public void printPowersOfTwo()
      {
            // Wait for the data ready or finished signals from the producer
            WaitHandle.WaitAny(new WaitHandle[] {Calculator.dataReady,
                  Calculator.finished});

            // Retrieve and display as many values as are on the queue
            while (Calculator.power2Queue.get_Count() > 0)
            {
                  Integer data = (Integer)Calculator.power2Queue.Dequeue();
```

```
                Console.WriteLine(printerName + ":" + data);

                // Signal that the queue is empty
                Calculator.queueReady.Set();

                // Wait for more data
                WaitHandle.WaitAny(new WaitHandle[] {Calculator.dataReady,
                    Calculator.finished});
            }

            Console.WriteLine(printerName + " finishing");
        }
    }
```

Mutexes

Mutexes are lightweight objects that guarantee mutually exclusive access to a resource. (The name mutex is a contraction of the phrase "mutual exclusion"). Like the event classes, the *Mutex* class inherits from *WaitHandle*, so much of its functionality should now be familiar to you. Semantically, mutexes operate on the concept of *ownership* rather than events, but the signaling mechanism is the same as that used by events. The general idea is that to access a shared resource, a thread should first issue the *WaitOne* method of a mutex:

```
Mutex resourceMutex = new Mutex();
⋮
resourceMutex.WaitOne();
```

If the mutex is free, access to it is granted to the requesting thread, and it is said to be *owned* by that thread. Another thread that issues *WaitOne* over the same mutex will be blocked. A thread relinquishes ownership of a mutex using the *ReleaseMutex* method:

```
resourceMutex.ReleaseMutex();
```

If any other threads are waiting, *one* of them will be unblocked and granted ownership. The others will remain blocked. If a thread terminates while it owns a mutex, ownership will be granted to the next waiting thread.

Perhaps the main reason for using a mutex instead of some of the other mechanisms you've seen in this chapter is that mutexes can be used across processes. All the other synchronization mechanisms you've seen so far operate only inside a single process. When you create a mutex, you can give it a name:

```
Mutex resourceMutex = new Mutex(true, "MyResource");
```

The Boolean parameter to the constructor indicates whether the thread owns the named mutex. Only the thread that actually creates the mutex should specify a value of *true*. Other threads in other processes can attach to the same mutex by specifying the same name (you must adopt a naming scheme that prevents unintentional clashes of mutex names) but setting the ownership parameter to *false* in the constructor.

Timers

Besides allowing you to create threads manually, the common language runtime will create threads for you automatically when you employ various .NET features—including Web services, Remoting, and timers. We'll cover Web services and Remoting later in this book, but it's worth taking a brief look at timers here.

The *System.Threading.Timer* class allows you to execute a method at defined intervals. To do this, it makes use of a *TimerCallback* delegate that refers to a method that you specify, and it creates a thread to run this method whenever the timer expires.

The ClockTick project offers a simple example of using the *Timer* class to execute a method every five seconds. The *Timer* constructor expects a *TimerCallback* delegate that points to the method to be invoked every time the timer is triggered. This method must return *void* and take a single *Object* parameter containing user-defined state information. The second parameter to the *Timer* method is the data that will be passed as the parameter to the callback method every time it runs. This should be an *Object* (that is, almost anything can be passed in) or *null* if you don't want to use this parameter. The third argument indicates when the timer should first run. It is specified as an interval relative to the current time. The final parameter is the period to wait between invocations of the timer. Here's an example:

```
System.Threading.Timer ticker =
    new System.Threading.Timer(new TimerCallback(tickTock), null,
    new TimeSpan(0, 0, 0), new TimeSpan(0, 0, 5));
```

Each time the indicated period has elapsed, a new thread is created that runs the *tickTock* method. The method itself prints out the current date and time:

```
private void tickTock(Object state)
{
    Console.WriteLine("It is now " + System.DateTime.get_Now());
}
```

Once the thread is created, you cannot change the timer interval or suspend the timer. You can kill the thread by calling its *Dispose* method or by terminating the entire program. The ClockTick program runs until you press the Enter key.

Figure 8-10 shows the output generated by this program.

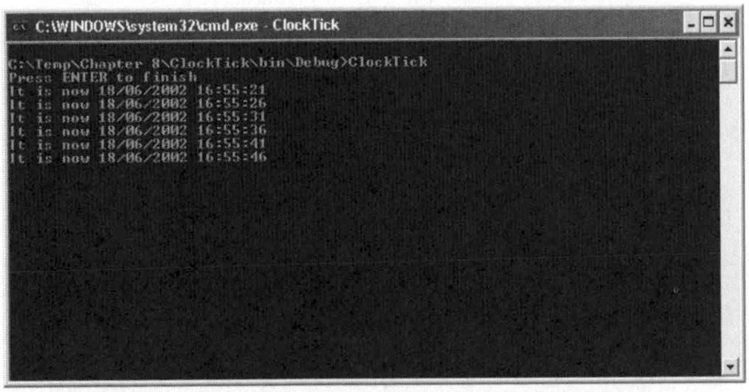

```
C:\WINDOWS\system32\cmd.exe - ClockTick
C:\Temp\Chapter 8\ClockTick\bin\Debug>ClockTick
Press ENTER to finish
It is now 18/06/2002 16:55:21
It is now 18/06/2002 16:55:26
It is now 18/06/2002 16:55:31
It is now 18/06/2002 16:55:36
It is now 18/06/2002 16:55:41
It is now 18/06/2002 16:55:46
```

Figure 8-10 The output of the ClockTick program

Thread Pooling

In a client/server system, a single server process frequently has to handle requests from multiple clients. Ideally, the server will handle these requests in a concurrent manner, using threads. (Single-threaded servers tend to form bottlenecks and do not survive long in a commercial environment.)

But how many threads should a server create? This is a little like asking how long is a piece of string. One solution would be to create a new thread for every client request, process the request, and then destroy the thread when processing has completed. However, this approach has at least two drawbacks. The first is that thread creation and destruction is a moderately expensive operation. The second drawback concerns the number of threads: If 5,000 clients submit requests at the same time, how practical is it to create 5,000 concurrent threads?

A more scalable solution is to create a pool of threads (called *worker threads*) in the server. When a request arrives, an idle worker thread from the pool can be dispatched to handle it. When it's finished, the thread will return to the pool. If no worker threads are available when a request arrives, the server can create a new worker thread or queue the request until a worker thread becomes free. The strategy can be dynamic, taking into account resources such as the number of threads already running, the number of CPUs, and the memory available. This sounds like a lot of work to put together, but the development team at Microsoft has already done it for you in the *System.Threading.ThreadPool* class. This act was not as philanthropic as its sounds because the team had to build this functionality for other parts of the

.NET Framework Class Library anyway—timers, sockets, and asynchronous I/O all use it.

The *ThreadPool* Class

If you examine the documentation for the *ThreadPool* class, you might be intrigued to discover that it comprises a few static methods but does not have a constructor. This is because a *ThreadPool* object is created automatically on demand the first time you need it. A process can contain at most one thread pool.

The threads that a thread pool contains have default properties, such as the priority, which you should not attempt to change. Pooled threads are designated as background threads. You must also leave thread management to the thread pool; do not cancel or abort threads that are running under the auspices of the thread pool. (There is no simple way to cancel a thread request once it has been queued in the thread pool.) Threads are created as required by the thread pool, and you have little control over how many threads there are because the thread pool uses its own heuristics to determine the optimum size based on the machine load, the work being performed, and the number of processors. (Actually, the thread pool has a default limit of 25 threads for each available processor, but this can be changed—although I am not going to show you how!)

A thread pool contains a queue of work items. As clients submit requests, work items are added to the queue. An internal thread inside the thread pool takes items of this queue and assigns them to worker threads, which it then invokes. The simplest way to create a work item is by using the *QueueUserWorkItem* method. This method expects a *WaitCallback* delegate (which you saw in the section on timers) that refers to the method to be executed by a worker thread, together with an optional parameter (an *Object*) any supplying additional user-defined information for that method. The delegated method must have a *void* return type and take a single *Object* parameter:

```
private void doWork(Object state)
{
    ⋮
}
⋮
int data = ...;    // example user-defined data
ThreadPool.QueueUserWorkItem(new WaitCallback(doWork), new Integer(data));
⋮
```

If the thread pool does not exist, it will be created at this juncture. At some point, when a worker thread becomes available, the *doWork* method will run.

You can also queue requests for methods to be executed once a resource becomes available. In the threaded world, you wait for resources using a *WaitHandle* object (a *ManualResetEvent*, *AutoResetEvent*, or *Mutex*). With a thread pool, you can use the *RegisterWaitForSingleObject* method to specify a *WaitHandle*, a *WaitOrTimerCallback* delegate that refers to a method (with optional parameter), and a timeout interval. When the *WaitHandle* object is signaled, a worker thread will execute the designated method. If a timeout occurs, the target method will also be run. The target method must supply two parameters—the inevitable *Object* and a *boolean* that will be set to *true* if the wait has timed out or *false* otherwise:

```
private AutoResetEvent evt = new AutoResetEvent(false);
⋮
private void waitAndDoWork(Object state, boolean timedOut)
{
    ⋮
}
⋮
ThreadPool.RegisterWaitForSingleObject(evt,
    new WaitOrTimerCallback(waitAndDoWork), null,
    new TimeSpan(0, 0, 10), true);
    ⋮
```

In the preceding example, a thread will be executed that runs the *waitAndDoWork* method when the *AutoResetEvent evt* is signaled or when the 10-second timeout expires. (As with the other synchronization methods, you can specify a 0 value if you do not want to wait—this is not wise with a thread pool—or *Timeout.Infinite* if you're willing to wait forever.) The *null* value in the middle is the argument passed to *waitAndDoWork*. The final Boolean parameter (*true*) indicates whether the worker thread should wait again when the method completes or just finish. In this case, the thread will wait once more and run the *waitAndDoWork* method again the next time the event is signaled, and then wait again, and so on. Be careful: If you wait on a *ManualResetEvent*, be sure to reset it in the delegated method before it finishes; otherwise, you might trigger a fast-running infinite loop in the worker thread!

Asynchronous I/O

As mentioned earlier, other areas of .NET use the thread pooling mechanisms. The technique used to perform asynchronous I/O is worth a brief mention because it employs patterns that are used in many aspects of .NET that rely on asynchronous operations and that you can use in your own classes.

If you examine the *System.IO.Stream* class, you'll see that it contains methods for sending and receiving streams of bytes to or from a source. The *Stream* class is used as a basis for more specialized streams, such as the *System.IO.FileStream* class and *System.Net.Sockets.NetworkStream*. Two methods in the *Stream* class, *BeginRead* and *BeginWrite*, are of particular interest. These methods initiate an I/O operation asynchronously, employing worker threads from the thread pool. The signature of both methods is the same. You must provide a buffer indicating the source or destination for the data, an offset into the buffer at which to begin reading or writing, the number of bytes to read or write, and an *AsyncCallback* delegate that points to a method that will be executed when the read or write operation has completed. (There is also a final *Object* parameter which represents a user-defined state. See Chapter 9 for some examples that use it.)

The following example uses a *FileStream* object to write approximately 10 MB of data to a file asynchronously, calling the *writingDone* method when it has finished. This example is available in the PoolThreads project:

```
private void writingDone(IAsyncResult ar)
{
    ⋮
}
⋮
FileStream fs = new FileStream("C:\\temp\\MyFile", FileMode.OpenOrCreate);
ubyte [] fileData = new ubyte[10000000];
⋮
IAsyncResult result = fs.BeginWrite(fileData, 0, 10000000,
    new AsyncCallback(writingDone), null);
```

The *Begin* methods return an *IAsyncResult* object that contains status information about the operation, including a reference to the final *Object* parameter submitted earlier, which is accessible through the *AsyncState* (*get_AsyncState*) property. Another useful property is *IsCompleted*, which you access by calling the *get_IsCompleted* method from J#. This method returns a Boolean value indicating whether the operation has finished. Incidentally, the method targeted by the *AsyncCallback* delegate in the *Begin* methods must also take an *IAsyncResult* parameter, which will be populated with a reference to this same object.

If you need to wait for the asynchronous operation to complete before continuing (assuming you've performed some other tasks in the meantime), you can use the *EndRead* or *EndWrite* methods, which are also exposed by the *Stream* class. These methods expect the *IAsyncResult* value returned from the corresponding *Begin* method call as a parameter, and they block until the worker thread has completed its task:

```
fs.EndWrite(result);
```

If the operation has already completed, the *End* method will finish immediately.

Summary

This chapter provided an extensive tour of threads in the .NET platform. You learned how to create and manage threads using the *Thread* class in the *System.Threading* namespace. You also learned how to synchronize threads using the various objects available in the .NET Framework Class Library—in particular, the *Monitor* class, the *Interlocked* class, and the *ReaderWriterLock* class. The chapter also explained how to notify threads about significant events using the *ManualResetEvent* and *AutoResetEvent* classes and how to use the *Mutex* class to achieve lightweight exclusive locking between threads and across processes. Finally, you learned to use the .NET thread pooling mechanisms when performing background tasks with threads.

9

Basic Network Programming

Network programming in one shape or form is an essential aspect of building distributed systems. It involves enabling communication over a network and the passing of data between processes running on different computers. Numerous technologies and paradigms have emerged to take the grunge work out of building distributed systems and encapsulating repetitive low-level boilerplate code into higher-level abstractions. Examples include COM+ in the Microsoft world and Enterprise JavaBeans (EJB) in the Java arena. These technologies have allowed developers to concentrate on the business logic of their applications rather than having to worry about how individual bytes of data travel from one machine to another.

High-level paradigms have their limitations, however. Even though they're excellent for constructing systems in which all computers run the same software and are based on the same platform, they do not cope as well in less homogenous environments, which might force the developer to rely on lower-level concepts.

Microsoft .NET is a wonderful example of a development environment that exposes a rich variety of APIs for handling network programming. Because integrating with other systems often involves resorting to lower-level services, this chapter will look at using sockets over TCP/IP with .NET. We'll also discuss the implementation of HTTP in .NET and how you can exploit it for building portable Internet and intranet systems. In later chapters, we'll look at some of the upper layers of functionality that .NET provides, including the Remoting architecture and Web services.

Sockets Essentials

The two main aspects of network programming define where data is actually transmitted to (or sent from) and transmitting that data in a manner that a receiving application can understand. Data transmission is concerned with formats and protocols. This chapter (and the rest of this book, actually) will assume that the underlying network protocol being used is TCP/IP, the protocol of the Internet. Other protocols might be layered over it—HTTP and SOAP, for example—but TCP/IP is the lowest common denominator of many modern networked systems.

Even though TCP/IP is the underlying protocol, the format of the data broadcast over TCP/IP is largely up to the applications doing the sending and receiving. Any scheme that is used must be portable, taking into account such issues as binary data and big endian versus little endian computers. Defining the source and destinations of data is all about managing and creating *endpoints*. Endpoints are the metaphorical software plugs and sockets that connect computers together. Because they can identify the source of any request, endpoints can also feature in the implementation of security.

The Sockets API was created many years ago for C programmers who were building applications running under UNIX. Since then, sockets have been ported and adapted for use by a variety of other operating systems, including the Microsoft Windows family. Microsoft's latest incarnation of the socket library can be found in the *System.Net.Sockets* namespace in the .NET Framework Class Library. Even if you're familiar with sockets and socket programming, it's still worthwhile to look at how to use them with .NET because Microsoft has added a selection of features, type safety, and object-oriented wrappers.

As mentioned earlier, the protocol underpinning sockets is TCP/IP. However, TCP/IP is actually a family of transport protocols that are often used in conjunction with other transport protocols. The protocol type requested at run time by the processes at both ends of the wire determines the specific protocol used. (The sending and receiving process must use the same protocol type.) Examples of transports that sockets can use include Transmission Control Protocol (TCP), User Datagram Protocol (UDP), Internetwork Packet Exchange (IPX), Sequenced Packet Exchange (SPX), Gateway-to-Gateway Protocol (GGP), and Internet Control Message Protocol (ICMP). TCP is the most common transport protocol used for handling connection-oriented sockets, and UDP is its counterpart in the connectionless world, so we'll concentrate on these two.

The JDK has its own socket library in the java.net package. Microsoft has provided an implementation of this package in vjslib.dll. If you're careful, you can use JDK sockets and .NET sockets in the same class, but be sure to use the appropriate namespace qualifiers—*System.Net.Sockets.Socket* and *java.net.Socket.*

Connection-Oriented Sockets

Sockets support two modes of operation: connection-oriented and connectionless. We'll examine connectionless sockets shortly. Connection-oriented sockets operate by establishing a virtual circuit, or continuous connection, between a process that sends data (referred to as the *client* in this model) and the process that receives and processes the data (referred to as the *server*).

In a typical connection-oriented configuration, the server process attaches to a well-known endpoint and waits for clients to contact it. An endpoint has two elements: the Internet Protocol (IP) address of the computer running the process and a port number. (See the IP Addresses and Ports sidebar if you're not familiar with these concepts.) The server sleeps until a client calls. When a call occurs, the server can optionally examine the identity of the computer executing the client process, which is transmitted as part of the client request by TCP. If it determines that the client computer is valid, it can spawn a dedicated thread to service the client. The main server thread continues to wait for the next client to connect, and so on.

IP Addresses and Ports

TCP/IP uses IP addresses to identify computers. IP addresses have four parts and are often described using *dotted-quad* notation—for example, 192.168.1.1. If you think of the Internet as a network of networks, an IP address has to specify two things: which local network a machine belongs to and the address of that machine on that local network. An IP address has four parts instead of two because of the different network and computer numbering schemes that are available—the network can be identified using one, two, or three of the parts, and the machine is identified using the remainder. The more parts of the address that are dedicated to identifying the network, the fewer unique machine addresses are available on that network, and vice versa.

IP addresses are maintained centrally by the Internet Network Information Center (InterNIC) and its local subsidiaries. Organizations that want to connect to the Internet must obtain an IP address (or, more commonly, a range of addresses) from InterNIC. In many cases, however, organizations access the Internet through an Internet service provider (ISP). An ISP has a pool of IP addresses obtained from InterNIC, and it leases an address to each client computer that connects to the Internet through it. The duration of the lease is determined by the ISP, but it is often limited to a few hours. On expiration, the client computer can disconnect and reconnect if necessary. Most ISPs charge a small fee for this service.

One implication of this mechanism is that the IP address of a given client computer is not always the same, and conversely two different computers might be assigned the same IP address at different points in time. This is fine for client computers, but it's not so good for servers. (It makes it difficult for a client to locate a server if its address changes frequently.) For this reason, some ISPs also offer hosting facilities on their computers, renting space and processing power for server applications that need to reside at an IP address that does not vary.

The IP address uniquely identifies the computer, but many server processes might be running on that computer, so there must be a means of discovering a process as well as a computer. For connections that use sockets, each server process listens on a port. You can think of a port as an integer that identifies the server process to a client. To communicate with a server, a client must specify the IP address of the server computer and the port the server process is listening on. The TCP/IP specification reserves a number of well-known ports for specific system processes. For example, port 23 is usually occupied by the Telnet service, which provides remote terminal connection services to the host computer, and port 80 is reserved for the HTTP service, which receives Web requests from clients. In fact, the TCP specification reserves all ports below 1024, so you should not use these for your own server applications.

Connection-Oriented Servers

The *CakeServer* class (available in the file CakeServer.jsl in the CakeSizeServer project) is an example of a simple connection-oriented server. It is an extension of the example shown in earlier chapters that figures out how many people a cake of a given size, shape, and filling will feed. This time, however, the server performs the service remotely, using sockets. The *main* method creates a socket for clients to connect to.

```
Socket serverSocket = new Socket(AddressFamily.InterNetwork,
   SocketType.Stream, ProtocolType.Tcp);
```

The parameters of the *Socket* constructor include an *AddressFamily*, a *SocketType*, and a *ProtocolType*. These are all enumerations, and there are many combinations that you can specify, but not all combinations are legal. The *AddressFamily* parameter indicates the addressing scheme used by the socket. This affects how addresses will be interpreted. Options include *NetBios*, *DecNet*, *Banyan*, *Sna*, and *InterNetwork*, among a plethora of others. The *CakeServer* class uses *InterNetwork*, which indicates that it will specify an IP (version 4.0) address. (An *InterNetworkV6* option is also available for IP version 6.0 addresses, but it is not fully supported by version 1.0 of the .NET Framework Class Library.)

The *SocketType* parameter specifies how the socket will be used. The value *Stream* indicates that the socket should support a reliable two-way continuous connection between the client and the server. The *ProtocolType* parameter helps to determine which of the many transport protocols in the TCP/IP suite will be used. The example uses *Tcp*. You can use only a protocol that is valid for the specified address family and protocol type; otherwise, the common language runtime will throw a *System.Net.Sockets.SocketException* at run time. We won't describe every possible combination of parameters in this book; we'll simply create a connection-oriented Internet socket over TCP using the values *InterNetwork*, *Stream*, and *Tcp*.

After you fashion a socket, you establish an endpoint that you can bind it to. In theory, different address families can use different formats to specify an endpoint. The .NET Framework Class Library defines the generic *EndPoint* class in the *System.Net* namespace, which holds the functionality common to endpoints for all address families. You're unlikely to ever use an *EndPoint* object directly. You're more likely to use a specialized class that inherits from it and contains the additional functionality peculiar to an address family. *IPEndPoint* is just such a class; you use it to manage IP endpoints. (In fact, it is currently the only specialized *EndPoint* class, although others might be added in the future.)

An *IPEndPoint* comprises an IP address and a port number. The IP address used by a server is typically that of the computer the server process is running on. You might know the name of your computer, but the name is not the same as its IP address. Remember that an IP address can change, so it's not a good idea to hard-code it into an application. In contrast, the name is less likely to change. The .NET Framework Class Library offers the ability to look up the IP address of a computer given its name, using the Domain Name System (DNS)—a DNS server maintains a dynamic database of computer names and IP addresses.

The *Dns* class in the *System.Net* namespace contains a selection of useful methods, one of which is *Resolve*. This returns an *IPHostEntry* object for a specified computer, from which you can extract its IP address. If you want to make the application independent of the computer name as well, you can also invoke *Dns.GetHostName*, which returns the name of the local computer. An added complication of DNS is that a single computer can have several aliases, so the *IPHostEntry* class actually contains an array of addresses in a property called *AddressList* (which is accessed using *get_AddressList* from J#).

The *CakeServer* class uses the first matching IP address that it finds:

```
IPHostEntry ipHostInfo = Dns.Resolve(Dns.GetHostName());
IPAddress ipAddress = ipHostInfo.get_AddressList()[0];
```

Note If you've used sockets in the past, you might be more familiar with the *GetHostByName* method than with the *Resolve* method. (*GetHostByName* is available as *getByName* in *java.net* in the JDK.) The *Resolve* method is actually a wrapper around *GetHostByName* and the *GetHostByAddress* method (which looks up an IP address using dotted-quad notation). You can use *Resolve* to return an *IPHostEntry* object that represents a computer given either its name or to return a string containing its address in dotted-quad format. *Resolve* calls the appropriate *GetHostByName* or *GetHostByAddress* method for you.

The port number is a positive integer. The *IPEndPoint* class exposes two static fields called *MinPort* (0) and *MaxPort* (65535). These fields indicate the lower and upper values that you can use for the port number. You can use any value in this range that is not already in use on the local computer, but you should refrain from using any value less than 1024 if you want to avoid clashing with any of the reserved system ports. Our example uses the static value *cakePort (4000)* defined in the *CakeServerUtils* class (in the CakeUtils.jsl sample file in the CakeUtils project, which has been added to the CakeSizeServer solution for your convenience):

```
public class CakeServerUtils
{
   public static final int cakePort = 4000;
   ⋮
}
```

Note The original Berkeley UNIX socket libraries, on which most subsequent versions are based, let you associate a port number with a service name and store it in a system file, along with other service/port pairs. You could then execute the *getservbyname* method, which took the name of a service as its argument and returned the corresponding port. Sadly, this feature is also not currently available with .NET (or with the JDK, for that matter).

The IPEndPoint constructor creates an endpoint that you can attach to the socket using the Bind method:

```
IPEndPoint ipEp = new IPEndPoint(IPAddress.Loopback,
   CakeServerUtils.cakePort);
serverSocket.Bind(ipEp);
```

Next, the socket has to be placed in the listening state. In this mode of operation, the socket can start to wait for incoming client requests. These requests are held in an internal queue until the application services them. You must specify the maximum length of this queue when you put the socket into listening mode using the *Listen* method:

```
serverSocket.Listen(5);
```

This statement sets the queue length to 5. If more clients try to connect at a rate that causes the queue to overflow, their connection attempts will be aborted with a *SocketException*.

Note The queue length is not the same as the maximum number of clients that the server can handle at the same time; it is the number of clients that have tried to connect but that the server has not yet accepted. Clients that are currently being handled aren't included in this number.

Having placed the socket in listen mode, the server has nothing else to do until a client sends a request. It can sit and wait for a client request by executing the *Accept* method:

```
CakeServer server = new CakeServer();
```

```
// Wait for a client to connect
server.clientSocket = serverSocket.Accept();
```

The *Accept* method sleeps until a client connects. The original socket is reserved for clients to connect to, so when a client contacts the server, a new private communications channel is opened up just for that client. (In JDK terms, this is a *java.net.ServerSocket* object.) The value returned by *Accept* is a reference to a new socket created especially for conversing with the client. When the client transmits data to the server, it will appear on this new socket. The server should send any response to the client through this socket.

In our example, the application creates a new instance of the *CakeServer* class before issuing the call to *Accept*. The *CakeServer* class contains a *Socket* instance variable called *clientSocket*, and the value returned by *Accept* is used to populate this variable:

```
public class CakeServer
{
   private Socket clientSocket;
   ⋮
}
```

Selective Client Access

If you want to restrict access to the server for clients originating from certain computers, you can examine the endpoint attached to the socket created for the client; it will contain the IP address of the client. You can compare this address to the addresses of clients that you want to allow or deny access, and then you can take appropriate action—closing the socket to deny access or continuing.

For example, to reject requests from the computer named MOCKTURTLE on our network, you can use the following code fragment:

```
Socket clientSocket;
Socket serverSocket;
⋮
clientSocket = serverSocket.Accept();
IPEndPoint clientEndPoint = (IPEndPoint)clientSocket.get_RemoteEndPoint();
IPAddress clientAddress = clientEndPoint.get_Address();
if (clientAddress.Equals(Dns.Resolve("MOCKTURTLE").get_AddressList()[0]))
{
   // Deny access
```

```
    clientSocket.Close();
}
else
{
    // Process the request
}
```

If you have a list of computers that you want to allow or deny access to, another strategy is to use a hash table (*System.Collections.Hashtable*) of computer names and query that hash table to look for a match.

The *CakeServer* class also contains a method called *handleClientRequest*:

```
private void handleClientRequest()
{
    ⋮
}
```

The server uses this method as the callback for a thread that it creates to service the client:

```
System.Threading.Thread runner = new
    System.Threading.Thread(new ThreadStart(server.handleClientRequest));
runner.Start();
```

In this way, the server can handle multiple clients simultaneously. The main server thread loops back, creates another *CakeServer* object, and then waits for a new client to connect. In the meantime, the *handleClientRequest* method running on the new thread takes care of the client.

The *handleClientRequest* method is where the business logic of the server lies. A client application transmits three items of data to the server, which describe the size, shape, and filling of a prospective cake, respectively. These are passed as integers over the socket. However, a minor issue arises here. Sockets act as conduits for unstructured streams of data. You can read the data sent down a socket using the *Receive* method, but this data appears as an array of unsigned bytes:

```
ubyte[] data = new ubyte[4];
clientSocket.Receive(data, 4, SocketFlags.None);
```

The parameters of the *Receive* method include an array to read the data into, and two optional parameters: the number of bytes to read, and a flag. The *Receive* method will block if insufficient data is available to satisfy the request—in this case, waiting until 4 bytes (the length of an integer) have been sent. If you omit this parameter, the *Receive* call will use the size of the array specified as the first parameter. The *SocketFlags* parameter determines the nature of the receive operation. Normally, reads from a socket are destructive and function on a queued basis—that is, when you read from a socket, the data you've read is removed and the data is read in the same order in which it was written.

The *SocketFlags* parameter lets you change this policy. If you specify *SocketFlags.Peek*, the data will be copied from the socket but not removed. A client can send urgent data that jumps to the head of the queue by using the *SocketFlags.OutOfBand* flag, and a server can read this urgent data with the same *SocketFlags.OutOfBand* value. If no out-of-band data is available, the receive operation will block. You can combine flags using the bitwise or operator. Our example specifies *SocketFlags.None*, which clears all flags and uses the default behavior.

The application itself is responsible for parsing the raw data received into meaningful information. The server uses the static *buildInt* method of the *CakeServerUtils* class to convert the array of 4 bytes into an integer:

```
public static int buildInt(ubyte [] data) throws System.Exception
{
   return data[0] + 256 * data[1] + 65536 * data[2] + 16777216 * data[3];
}
```

Note The implementation of the *FeedsHowMany* method in the previous chapters used *short* parameters. In this chapter, we'll temporarily switch to using *int* parameters because doing so will make the *buildInt* and *buildArray* (shown below) methods more interesting.

The *handleClientRequest* method repeats this process two more times, extracting the shape and filling of the cake from the socket before calling the static *FeedsHowMany* method of the *CakeInfo* class. This is the same method we used in earlier chapters:

```
int numEaters = CakeInfo.FeedsHowMany(diameter, shape, filling);
```

The value returned, *numEaters*, is sent back to the client. In the same way that data can be read from a socket only as an array of bytes, you can transmit only an array of bytes down a socket. The application uses the static *CakeServerUtils.buildArray* method to convert the *numEaters* integer into an array of four *ubyte* values:

```
data = CakeServerUtils.buildArray(numEaters);
```

The *buildArray* method itself performs the converse operation of *buildInt* using a combination of modulus, division, and right-shift operations to split an integer into its constituent bytes:

```
public static ubyte[] buildArray(int intData)
{
   ubyte [] data = new ubyte[4];
   data[0] = (ubyte)(intData % 256);
   intData >>= 8;
   data[1] = (ubyte)(intData % 256);
   intData >>= 8;
   data[2] = (ubyte)(intData % 256);
   data[3] = (ubyte)(intData / 256);
   return data;
}
```

The server transmits the data back to the client using the *Send* method. The parameters are the same as those used by *Receive*:

```
clientSocket.Send(data, 4, SocketFlags.None);
```

You'll observe that when the method terminates (or an exception occurs), it executes the *Shutdown* method:

```
clientSocket.Shutdown(SocketShutdown.Both);
```

This method disables sending and/or receiving data over a socket in a graceful manner. (The underlying protocol causes an exchange of messages between both ends of the socket, allowing the server to notify the client that the socket is about to disappear.) Using the value *SocketShutdown.Both* disables sending and receiving, but you can be more selective by specifying *SocketShutdown.Send* or *SocketShutdown.Receive* to simply prevent sending or receiving data. If you've totally shut down a socket, you should also close it and release any resources held:

```
clientSocket.Close();
```

If the client attempts to send or receive any more data over a socket that has been successfully closed, the common language runtime will throw a *SocketException*.

Socket Options for Sending Data

To maximize throughput and make the most efficient use of network resources, most implementations of sockets buffer data as it is sent. This sometimes means that several short messages will be delayed slightly and combined into a single network packet (a technique referred to as *Nagle coalescing*, after the inventor of the algorithm used). This is implemented within the operating system, and most applications are not even aware that it is occurring. The result is that even if a *Send* method call has completed and returned, the data itself might not have actually been physically transmitted.

You can change this behavior by setting the *NoDelay* option of the socket using the *SetSocketOption* method:

```
clientSocket.SetSocketOption(SocketOptionLevel.Socket,
   SocketOptionName.NoDelay, 1);
```

The arguments to the *SetSocketOption* method are a level, an option, and a value. The level determines how the option is applied. Many options operate on the socket as a whole; others are used by specific protocols. If you specify an invalid level for a given option, the common language runtime will throw a runtime exception. Our example sets the *NoDelay* option to 1, which enables it and prevents packet sharing. Setting it to 0 disables it.

On other occasions, you might find that a large send operation blocks while data packets are assembled and transmitted to the receiver. It is possible for the *Send* method to block, especially if the server has previously sent data to the client but the client has not yet received it. (It might be busy doing something else, causing a backlog in the internal processing of its network buffers.) You can prevent an indefinite delay by setting the *SendTimeout* option:

```
clientSocket.SetSocketOption(SocketOptionLevel.Socket,
   SocketOptionName.SendTimeout, 1000);
```

This example sets the timeout for the socket to 1000 ms (1s). If the timeout occurs, the sending application will receive a *SocketException*.

Like the *Send* method, the *Close* method of a socket can also block. Normally, a socket will not close until all its data has been sent. You can force the socket to close after a given period of time by setting its *linger* option. You do this by creating a *System.Net.Sockets.LingerOption* object and populating it with information about the specified timeout, and then calling the *SetSocketOption* method to apply it:

```
LingerOption socketOpt = new LingerOption(true, 5);
clientSocket.SetSocketOption(SocketOptionLevel.Socket,
   SocketOptionName.Linger, socketOpt);
```

These statements create a *LingerOption* object that enables lingering for 5 seconds before timing out. At that point, any data that has not been sent will be lost. You can specify a timeout of 0 to close the socket immediately and discard all untransmitted data. By default, lingering is disabled. This is not as dangerous as it sounds: Even though the *Close* method will terminate immediately, the socket itself will be closed gracefully in the background and data that has already been transmitted should not be lost.

Sockets and Security

Chapter 8 described issues related to security and threads and explained that the ability to create threads is a potentially powerful privilege and that applications that use threading require the ControlThread code access privilege. A similar situation arises with sockets. A malicious assembly can open a socket from your computer and start sending all your sensitive data to a competitor. Assemblies that make or accept connections with sockets must be granted System.Net.SocketPermission. By default, assemblies that you download from the Internet or an intranet or that you load from a network share do not have this privilege, although you can modify the code access security policy to grant it to them. The .NET Framework Configuration tool shown below allows you to selectively grant access to individual hosts and ports.

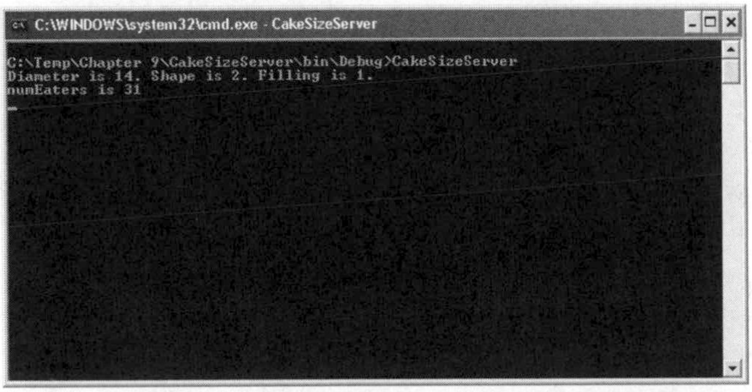

If you're planning to use DNS, the assembly must also be granted *System.Net.DnsPermission*. By default, local and Intranet zone assemblies can use DNS, but assemblies downloaded from the Internet cannot.

Connection-Oriented Clients

Writing a client application that uses sockets is less involved than writing a server. A typical client application will create a socket and connect it to the server. Once the connection is established, the client can send the server any data it needs and then wait for a response. The *CakeClient* class in the sample file CakeClient.jsl in the CakeSizeClient project is just such a client for the *CakeServer* class.

The *CakeClient* class is a simple test harness that asks the *CakeServer* class how many people a 14-inch hexagonal fruit cake will feed:

```
int requestedSize = 14;
int requestedShape = CakeShape.Hexagonal;
int requestedFilling = CakeFilling.Fruit;
```

Like the server, the client creates a connection-oriented socket based on TCP:

```
Socket cakeServerSocket = new Socket(AddressFamily.InterNetwork,
   SocketType.Stream, ProtocolType.Tcp);
```

The next task is to connect this socket to the appropriate endpoint on the server machine. To do this, you first need the IP address of the server computer. The program asks the user for the name of the computer in question and stores it in the variable *serverComputer*. The *CakeClient* looks up the IP address of the server computer, using a similar technique to that used by the server for finding its own address:

```
IPHostEntry serverAddresses = Dns.Resolve(serverComputer);
IPAddress serverAddress = serverAddresses.get_AddressList()[0];
```

Dns.Resolve raises the *SocketException* "No such host is known" if the named computer cannot be located.

To connect to the server, the client can create an endpoint structure that specifies the address and port of the server process and then call the *Connect* method using this endpoint as the parameter:

```
IPEndPoint ipEndpoint = new IPEndPoint(serverAddress,
   CakeServerUtils.cakePort);
cakeServerSocket.Connect(ipEndpoint);
```

If the server has not yet executed a *Listen* call, the common language runtime will throw a *SocketException*, informing the client that "No connection could be made because the target machine actively refused it." If the server is accepting calls, the *Connect* method will block until the *Accept* method in the server has instantiated the new socket as described earlier. At this point, the client can send data to the server.

In the *CakeClient*, the data transmitted comprises three integers: the size of the cake, the shape, and the filling. These integers are converted into *ubyte* arrays by the same *buildArray* utility method used by the server, and then sent to the server in sequence:

```
ubyte [] data = new ubyte[4];
data = CakeServerUtils.buildArray(requestedSize);
cakeServerSocket.Send(data, 4, SocketFlags.None);
```

As you might recall, when the server has received all three integers, it calls the *FeedsHowMany* method and passes the value returned back to the client through the socket. The client waits for this reply using the *Receive* method:

```
cakeServerSocket.Receive(data, 4, SocketFlags.None);
```

The data passed back is converted to an integer and displayed, and then the client closes the socket and terminates.

To execute these applications, you start the server (execute the CakeSizeServer.exe program) and then run the client (CakeClient.exe). When you're prompted by the client, type the name (or IP address) of the computer running the server program. The results are shown in Figures 9-1 and 9-2.

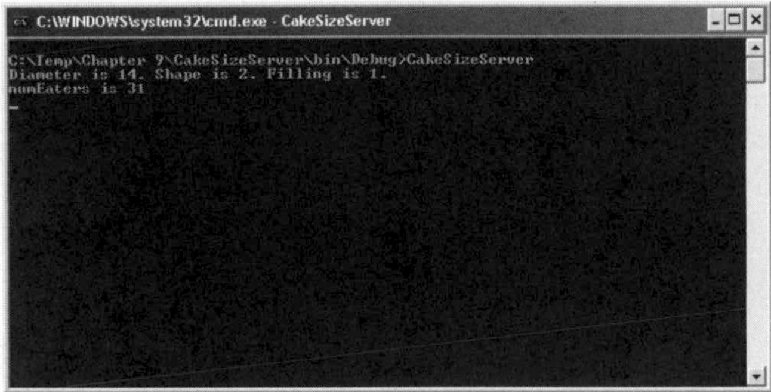

Figure 9-1 Output of the CakeServer program

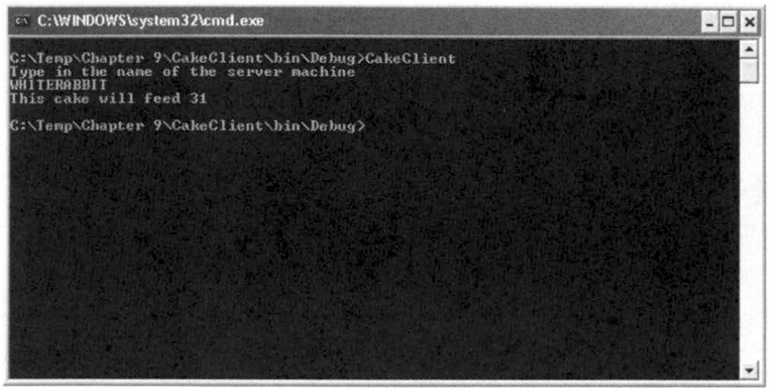

```
C:\WINDOWS\system32\cmd.exe
C:\Temp\Chapter 9\CakeClient\bin\Debug>CakeClient
Type in the name of the server machine
WHITERABBIT
This cake will feed 31

C:\Temp\Chapter 9\CakeClient\bin\Debug>
```

Figure 9-2 Output of the CakeClient program

The *TcpListener* and *TcpClient* Classes

The *Socket* class provides an implementation of sockets that is reasonably faithful to the original UNIX model, except that it is based on objects and methods rather than functions. However, if you find yourself writing a lot of socket code, you'll be repeatedly implementing the same common idioms—creating a socket using a valid set of arguments, creating an endpoint comprising a machine address and a port number, binding the socket to the endpoint, setting the request queue length, waiting for requests. Also, if you're approaching J# from a pure Java angle and have never before programmed sockets using C or C++, you might find the *Socket* class a little low-level compared to what you're used to—after all, the JDK has the *java.net.ServerSocket* class, which hides all of this stuff.

To give you the same convenience in J#, Microsoft has created a pair of classes named *TcpListener* and *TcpClient* that abstract out much of this routine work. They are located in the *System.Net.Sockets* namespace. These classes are basically just wrappers around the *Socket* class. The *TcpListener* class is used for creating socket server applications, and the *TcpClient* is its counterpart for building socket clients. In many ways, the *TcpListener* class is analogous to the *ServerSocket* class of the JDK.

The following code shows the *main* method of the *CakeServer* class, which is written using a *TcpListener* rather than a raw socket. (This code is available in CakeServer.jsl in the TcpCakeSizeServer project.) The *TcpListener* constructor expects a port number as its argument. The constructor creates an Internet, connection-oriented, TCP socket (IP version 4.0) and binds it to an endpoint comprising the IP address of the local machine and the specified port. If you need more control, you can use the *TcpListener* class, which offers a second constructor that takes a handcrafted *IPEndPoint* parameter or a third constructor that takes an *IPAddress* and a port number. The *Start* method puts the *TcpListener* into listen mode.

One difference between a *TcpListener* and a *Socket* is that you cannot set the queue length, although you can query the *Pending* property (use *get_Pending* from J#), which returns a Boolean indicating whether there are any pending connections. The *AcceptSocket* method blocks the listener until a client connects, returning a socket for communicating with the client when it does so. The *Stop* method, in the *finally* block, closes down the listener and stops it from accepting any more requests:

```
public static void main(String[] args)
{
   // Use a TCP listener rather than a socket
   TcpListener serverListener = null;

   try
   {
      // Create a TCP socket, and bind it to an endpoint comprising
      // the IP address of the local machine, and cakePort
      serverListener = new TcpListener(CakeServerUtils.cakePort);

      // Start listening
      serverListener.Start();

      // Loop forever, waiting for and servicing clients
      while (true)
      {
         CakeServer server = new CakeServer();

         // Wait for a client to connect
         server.clientSocket = serverListener.AcceptSocket();

         // Spawn a thread to handle the client request
         System.Threading.Thread runner = new System.Threading.Thread(
            new ThreadStart(server.handleClientRequest));
         runner.Start();
      }
   }
   catch(System.Exception e)
   {
      Console.WriteLine("Exception: " + e);
   }
   finally
   {
      // Tidy up
      if (serverListener != null)
         serverListener.Stop();
```

```
    }
}
```

You cannot directly access the socket contained in a *TcpListener* object. The *TcpListener* class exposes the *Server* property, which returns a reference to the underlying socket, but this method is protected and is available only to code inside classes that are inherited from *TcpListener*. However, you can query the endpoint created for the socket using the *LocalEndpoint* property, which is returned as a generic *EndPoint* object. You should cast it to an *IPEndPoint* if you want to examine address and port information:

```
TcpListener serverListener;
⋮
IPEndPoint ipEndpoint = (IPEndPoint)serverListener.get_LocalEndpoint();
```

This new version of the CakeServer will operate perfectly well with the existing client, which was developed using sockets. However, for the sake of completeness, the following fragment shows another implementation of the *main* method of the client that uses a *TcpClient* object to replace the socket. This code is available in the file CakeClient.jsl in the TcpCakeClient project.

A *TcpClient* is closer to what a programmer familiar with the JDK would think of as a *java.net.Socket*. The *TcpClient* has three constructors. The one used here specifies the name of the server computer to attach to and the port that the server process is listening on. This constructor will create a client socket and then use DNS to obtain the IP address of the server, create an endpoint, and connect the socket to that endpoint.

The *TcpClient* class uses a *NetworkStream* object to actually send and receive data. This is one of the stream classes discussed in Chapter 8 that can perform asynchronous I/O using a thread from the thread pool. Our example performs synchronous I/O because there is little else the client can do while it's waiting to receive a reply from the server, but in serious client applications you might find it beneficial to use the asynchronous *BeginRead* and *BeginWrite* methods of this object. The *GetStream* method of the *TcpClient* class returns a reference to this stream. The client code executes the *Write* method to send data to the server. (The parameters are a buffer containing the data, an offset into the buffer indicating the starting point of the data, and the length of the data.)

Similarly, the client uses the *Read* method to perform a blocking read of the response from the server. The *Close* method of the *TcpListener* class closes the client socket and terminates the connection to the server:

```
public static void main(String[] args)
{
   // Find out how many people a 14" hexagonal fruit cake will feed
```

```
int requestedSize = 14;
int requestedShape = CakeShape.Hexagonal;
int requestedFilling = CakeFilling.Fruit;

TcpClient cakeClient = null;

try
{
   Console.WriteLine("Type in the name of the server machine");
   String serverComputer = Console.ReadLine();

   // Create a TcpClient to communicate with CakeServer
   cakeClient = new TcpClient(serverComputer, CakeServerUtils.cakePort);

   // Get a handle on the stream for transmitting and receiving data
   NetworkStream dataStream = cakeClient.GetStream();

   // Transmit the parameters for the cake down the socket
   // First the size
   ubyte [] data = new ubyte[4];
   data = CakeServerUtils.buildArray(requestedSize);
   dataStream.Write(data, 0, 4);

   // Then the shape
   data = CakeServerUtils.buildArray(requestedShape);
   dataStream.Write(data, 0, 4);

   // And finally the filling
   data = CakeServerUtils.buildArray(requestedFilling);
   dataStream.Write(data, 0, 4);

   // Wait for the reply from the server
   dataStream.Read(data, 0, 4);

   // Convert the reply into an integer
   int numEaters = CakeServerUtils.buildInt(data);

   // Display the result
   Console.WriteLine("This cake will feed " + numEaters);

   // Close the socket, and finish
   cakeClient.Close();
}
catch (System.Exception e)
{
   Console.WriteLine("Exception communicating with server: " + e);
   if (cakeClient != null)
      cakeClient.Close();
}
}
```

Interoperability with JDK Sockets

JDK sockets and .NET sockets are noninterchangeable. For instance, you cannot cast a JDK socket to a .NET socket, or vice versa. However, at the network level there is a high degree of interoperability. A .NET *TcpClient* object can use its *NetworkStream* to transmit data to a JDK *ServerSocket*, and a JDK client socket can communicate with a *TcpListener* object without any problem.

The sample *JDKCakeClient* class (in the JDKCakeClient project) illustrates a sample JDK client that will work with the *TcpListener* implementation of the CakeServer application (in the TcpCakeSizeServer project). For convenience, the class also contains the various constants and utility methods that were previously supplied by the CakeUtils assembly, mainly because you cannot access .NET assemblies when you use the JDK compiler. The main method is remarkably similar to the *TcpClient* implementation of the *CakeClient* class. The main difference, apart from using a *java.net.Socket* object, is that the I/O is performed using *DataInputStream* and *DataOutputStream* objects rather than the single *NetworkStream* object implemented by .NET. Although a Visual J#.NET project is supplied, you can also compile the *JDKCakeClient* class and execute it using the JDK.

Data Transmission Issues

Even though .NET sockets and JDK sockets can work together, whether the data transmitted from one socket is actually understood by the application at the other end is another matter.

You might wonder why the *JDKCakeClient* class jumps through various hoops, converting integers into byte arrays and vice versa when the *DataOutputStream* class has a perfectly good *writeInt* method that will transmit a 4-byte integer without further ado. Well, the answer is that the *writeInt* method sends an integer as 4 bytes, with the most significant byte first. When the *CakeServer* class reads the data from the socket and converts it back to an integer, it expects the least significant byte first. This is the classic big endian/little endian problem. We could arguably have said that the *buildInt* and *buildArray* methods expect the data in big endian format, which would fix the problem for JDK clients, but other operating systems and languages use little endian encoding, and programs developed on those platforms would not be able to pass data to the *CakeServer* class.

For both ends of the socket to interpret the data passed over the network in the same way, they should agree on a common representation for that data. In the CakeServer example, this is achieved by using the same routines to encode and decode the data at each end of the wire. The original UNIX sockets library includes a set of four functions that convert long and short integers to and from a neutral representation called the *network byte order*. These functions are *htonl* (host to network long), *htons* (host to network short), *ntohl* (network to host long), and *ntohs* (network to host short). If you transmit native integer data over a socket, you should first convert it to network-byte ordering. The receiving end should convert it back to host-byte ordering. The .NET Framework Class Library has implementations of these as static methods in the *IPAddress* class. They're called *HostToNetworkOrder* and *NetworkToHostOrder*; they're overloaded and can operate on *long*, *short*, and *int* values.

Note The network-byte ordering used by the sockets library is actually big endian. This means that the implementations the *htons*, *ntohs*, *htonl*, and *ntohl* functions on a UNIX machine that also uses a big endian architecture are actually null operations. The same functions on a computer running Windows might need to do some real work because Windows is a little endian operating system (the JDK excepted).

Note, however, that unlike the JDK *DataInputStream* and *DataOutputStream* classes, neither the *System.Net.Sockets.Socket* class nor the *System.Net.Sockets.NetworkStream* class provides a prepackaged means of sending or receiving any type of data other than raw arrays of *ubyte*. You're welcome to subclass the *NetworkStream* class and implement your own methods for transmitting other types. Microsoft is not being lazy: It omitted this functionality because there's a better way to send chunks of data in a safe manner.

Binary data has often posed a problem for socket-based systems. Some organizations have actually forbidden developers from sending binary numeric data over a socket, so everything has to be converted to an agreed Unicode character representation (that is, to a string), transmitted, and then decoded at the other end. If you're considering doing this, bear in mind that the sending operation is not necessarily atomic and that transmitting a large block of data might require several receives at the other end to retrieve it all.

Similarly, if Nagle coalescing has not been disabled, several small data items might be retrieved with a single receive operation. You must clearly define the data boundaries—in essence, what you must do is define your own type marshaling mechanism. While this can occasionally be fun to do, life is too short to spend a lot of time writing libraries of marshaling routines. (Ask anyone on the COM development team at Microsoft.) Java has its own in-built means of bundling data and unbundling it again: serialization. Serialization is a mechanism for converting objects into a format that can be transmitted over a data stream and then reassembled into a copy of the original object at the other end. Native Java serialization can be used only by native Java applications—a program written in C# will not understand the format of a Java serialized stream. The .NET Framework Class Library implements a more extensible mode of serialization that can be used by any language that executes under the auspices of the common language runtime, as well as some other selected environments. We'll discuss serialization in more detail in Chapter 10.

Connectionless Sockets

Connection-oriented sockets are essential if you want to make certain that data that is sent is actually received. The TCP protocol is quite good at ensuring that packets of data are not lost and that large multipacket data items are assembled in the correct order before being handed over to a receiving socket. This reliability comes at a cost, though, and establishing a TCP connection can consume considerable resources and time.

In some situations, speed is more important than 100 percent accuracy. Take audio streaming, for example. Not every packet of audio data has to arrive at the receiving application that's outputting the resulting sounds, as long as most of the packets do. Missing packets will result in an occasional glitch or crackle. A human listener should be able to cope with this and would certainly find the result more pleasing than if the audio player were to halt while the retransmission of missing packets is requested—or worse still, if the audio player were to report an exception every time a packet appeared out of sequence.

Connectionless sockets are based on UDP. In this protocol, a sending application does not establish a direct connection to a receiving application. (This model uses the terms *sender* and *receiver* to identify the processes because it is more peer-to-peer-oriented than the client/server form implemented by connection-oriented sockets.) Instead, the sender just fires off a packet of data to an endpoint on a computer that it hopes is listening. If a receiver is listening, a process connected to that endpoint will receive the data, although the sender will not necessarily know it. Likewise, if the packet disappears without a trace or if no process is connected to the destination endpoint—or even if the computer that should be listening is down—the sender will be unaware. The sender just dispatches the data in the hope that it will arrive. This mechanism is sometimes referred to as "Send and Pray."

Caution Do not confuse connectionless sockets with asynchronous communication mechanisms such as message queues. With connectionless sockets, if no process is listening on an endpoint, any data sent to that endpoint will evaporate into the ether. The data will not be held pending in any queue and will not be retrievable if the listening process starts up later.

The *PriceSender* class (in the sample file CakePriceSender.jsl in the CakePriceSender project) is an example of a sending application. It periodically generates a message with information about offers on cakes, which it sends to a receiving application called *PriceListener* (in the file CakePriceListener.jsl in the CakePriceListener project). If the receiving application is listening, it will display the data in the message.

Looking at the *PriceSender* class first, the initial difference between this and the original *CakeServer* class is the statement that creates the socket:

```
Socket sender = null;
⋮
sender = new Socket(AddressFamily.InterNetwork, SocketType.Dgram,
   ProtocolType.Udp);
```

Although the address family is the same as before, the type of socket is different, as is the transport protocol. Connectionless sockets send individual *datagrams* (which are like telegrams but contain data) rather than establishing a continual stream, and they use UDP. The statements that create a local endpoint and bind the socket to that endpoint are identical to the earlier example (although the variables have different names):

```
IPHostEntry senderHostInfo = Dns.Resolve(Dns.GetHostName());
IPAddress senderAddress = senderHostInfo.get_AddressList()[0];
IPEndPoint senderEndpoint = new IPEndPoint(senderAddress, senderPort);
sender.Bind(senderEndpoint);
```

Datagrams should to be sent to a named destination. The program prompts for the name of the computer running the receiving process, uses DNS to obtain its IP address, and then constructs an endpoint comprising this address and a port that the receiving process will be listening on. The endpoint is stored in variable *receiverEndpoint*. The program then enters a loop, simulating the periodic generation of messages and sending them out. In this case, all the program does is sleep for 10 seconds and then send the same string out each time.

Tip The program shows a convenient way to convert a string into an array of bytes using Unicode encoding. The *System.Text* namespace contains several classes you can use for encoding text in different ways. The *UnicodeEncoding* class has the *GetBytes* method, which will convert a string into an array of Unicode byte-pairs (UTF-16). This is similar to the *getBytes* method of the *java.lang.String* class in the JDK. The various encoding classes also provide a *GetString* method that will convert an encoded byte array back into a string.

You use the *SendTo* method to send a datagram. The parameters include the data to be sent, as a *ubyte* array (there is no direct equivalent to the *java.net.DatagramPacket* class of the JDK), and the endpoint to send the data to. *SendTo* is overloaded, and you can optionally specify the length of the data and a starting offset into the array as well as a selection of socket flags (just like the *Send* method).

The *PriceListener* class in the CakePriceListener project creates a UDP socket and binds it to an endpoint on the local computer, using the same port that the sending process dispatches messages to. Having created the socket, the *PriceListener* class enters a loop, waiting for messages to appear and then printing them on the console.

You wait for UDP messages by executing the *ReceiveFrom* method. This method is overloaded in a similar manner to *SendTo*, but at a minimum you should specify a *ubyte* array big enough to hold the received data (the common language runtime will throw an exception if the array is too small to hold the entire datagram) and an endpoint. The endpoint will be filled in with the details of the sending computer—the IP address and the port. You must instantiate this endpoint variable before calling *ReceiveFrom*.

The *PriceListener* class uses the values *IPAddress.Any* for the IP address and 0 for the port—they will be overwritten when data is received, but you have to specify values for these parameters in the constructor, and these are good placeholders. Also notice that the variable is declared as an *EndPoint* rather than as an *IPEndPoint* (although it is instantiated using an *IPEndPoint* constructor). This is because the *ReceiveFrom* method expects an *EndPoint* and not an *IPEndPoint*, and in this situation the common language runtime cannot downcast the variable.

```
EndPoint senderEndpoint = new IPEndPoint(IPAddress.Any, 0);
```

The *ReceiveFrom* method will block until a datagram arrives. Remember that datagrams are not queued; any datagrams that arrive while the *PriceListener* program is not listening will be lost. It is also possible for the sender to send an empty message. The *ReceiveFrom* method returns the number of bytes actually received (as does the *Receive* method, actually). You should check this value before processing the results because there might not be any! Assuming that some data actually does arrive, the program will convert it into a string (the sender sent it as an array of Unicode bytes, so the receiver must convert it back again) and prints it:

```
Console.WriteLine(
   System.Text.Encoding.get_Unicode().GetString(cakePriceData));
```

Even though this example shows the principles of sending and receiving using UDP, it is not very realistic. A receiving application is much more likely to perform some task or other while waiting for data to arrive rather than sit in a blocked state waiting for data. We'll describe techniques for addressing this situation shortly.

If you compile and run the *CakePriceSender* application, you'll be prompted for the name of the receiving computer, and then the program will go off in its loop of sleeping and generating messages. It doesn't matter that the receiving application isn't running—the messages will just fall into the proverbial black hole. When you execute the *CakePriceListener* application, it will receive any messages that are sent after it started listening, as shown in Figure 9-3. (You might get a couple of messages immediately, but that would be due to the internal buffering used by sockets.)

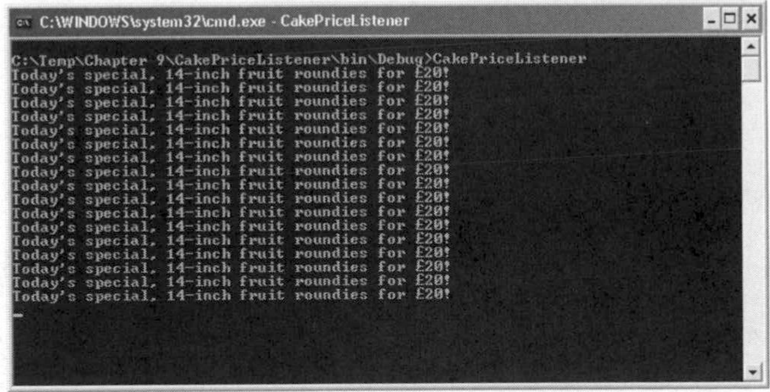

Figure 9-3 The CakePriceListener application

The *System.Net.Sockets* namespace also contains the *UdpClient* class. This is analogous to the *TcpClient* class, but it is for handling UDP sockets. Its counterpart in the JDK world is the *java.net.DatagramSocket* class. Like the *TcpCli-*

ent class, *UdpClient* automates much of the work involved in setting up a UDP socket and binding it to an endpoint. The overloaded constructor allows you to bind to an endpoint attached to a port on a local or remote machine. Once the endpoint has been created, you can use the *Receive* method to wait for data from a sender. *Receive* returns an array of *ubyte* and expects an *IPEndPoint* (*not* an *EndPoint*) parameter that identifies the sender.

The *main* method shown below shows an alternative implementation of the *PriceListener* class. (This is available in the file UdpListener.jsl in the UdpListener project.)

```
public class PriceListener
{
   // Local port for receiving
   private static int receiverPort = 4002;

   // Maximum length of messages that can be received
   private static int messageLength = 100;


   public static void main(String[] args)
   {
      // Define a UdpClient for receiving
      UdpClient receiver = null;

      try
      {
         // Create the UDP listener
         receiver = new UdpClient(receiverPort);

         // Loop forever, waiting for messages and printing them
         while (true)
         {
            ubyte[] cakePriceData = new ubyte[messageLength];

            // Create an endpoint which will be populated with the address
            // of the sender
            IPEndPoint senderEndpoint = new IPEndPoint(IPAddress.Any, 0);

            // Receive data from the sender (this may block or return zero
            // bytes)
            cakePriceData = receiver.Receive(senderEndpoint);
            if (cakePriceData.length > 0)
            {
               // Convert the ubyte array of Unicode characters into
               // a String and display it
               Console.WriteLine(System.Text.Encoding.get_Unicode().
                  GetString(cakePriceData));
```

```
                }
            }
        }
        catch(System.Exception e)
        {
            Console.WriteLine("Exception: " + e);
        }
        finally
        {
            // Tidy up
            if (receiver != null)
                receiver.Close();
        }
    }
}
```

There is no *UdpListener* class (to match *TcpListener*) because it is unnecessary. Instead, you can use the *Connect* method of *UdpClient* to attach to a remote endpoint and use the *Send* method to transmit data.

Blocking and Nonblocking Sockets

When you keep them simple, sockets are suspiciously easy to program against. However, as everyone knows, the world is not a simple place, and many real-world situations will be more complex than the *CakeSizeServer* and *CakeClient* scenario. Also, networks are fragile. Even though the TCP transport used by connection-oriented sockets does all it can to guarantee delivery of data, and in the correct sequence, the protocol cannot recover from situations such as a broken network or a computer crash. However, an application will know when such a failure has occurred because of errors raised in the sending or receiving application if a connection is unexpectedly terminated.

For example, if a process is blocked while waiting to receive data on a socket and the sending process (or something else, such as a network failure) breaks the circuit, the receiver will trip a socket exception with the message "An existing connection was forcibly closed by the remote host." The same exception will occur if you try to send data down a socket when the receiver has closed it. The message is not specific enough to figure out exactly what the problem is, but at least you know that something nasty has happened at the other end of the wire, and the application can perform some sort of error recovery—or at least record a diagnostic somewhere!

A more interesting situation occurs if the client and server somehow get out of synch. When a server is executing the *Receive* method, it will block until the specified number of bytes of data have arrived. If they do not arrive, the *Receive* method might block indefinitely. There is also the issue of variable-length data: Sometimes there will be a need for a client or a server to send data of unspecified length, so a mechanism must be agreed upon that allows the receiving end of a socket to determine when all the data has been received. If the client gets itself into the state in which it is performing a receive operation on the same socket at the same time as the server (because it thinks it has sent all the data that the server is expecting and is waiting for a reply, but the server has not realized this and is still waiting for more data), both ends will wait for each other forever.

To prevent such a situation from occurring, sockets have a *Blocking* property, which you can access using the *set_Blocking* and *get_Blocking* methods from J#. By default, this property is set to *true*. You can change it to *false* to create a nonblocking socket:

```
Socket clientSocket = ...;
clientSocket.set_Blocking(false);
```

The socket will no longer block if there is no data for it to read. Instead, calls to the *Receive* method will terminate immediately, sucking whatever data is available from the socket. The *Receive* method passes back the number of bytes read as the return value:

```
int numBytes = serverSocket.Receive(...);
```

While this approach looks promising, it can lead to problems. For example, what should a server do if it reads zero bytes? Should it just loop until something does appear? What if it receives an incomplete message from the client? (The *Send* operation is not guaranteed to be atomic, especially if the client is sending a large amount of data.) How would the server know? Another problem is that issuing an *Accept* method call on a nonblocking socket will throw a *SocketException* with the message "A non-blocking socket operation could not be completed immediately" if no client is attempting to connect at that precise instant. And a client that connects to a server socket that is not currently open and accepting requests will also get an exception: "No connection could be made because the target machine actively refused it."

An alternative to using a nonblocking socket is to set a receive timeout, in milliseconds, using *SetSocketOption*:

```
Socket clientSocket;
⋮
clientSocket.SetSocketOption(SocketOptionLevel.Socket,
   SocketOptionName.ReceiveTimeout, 5000);
```

If a timeout occurs, the common language runtime will throw a *SocketException*: "A connection attempt failed because the connected party did not properly respond after a period of time, or established connection failed because connected host has failed to respond." If you're using timeouts, you must be prepared to catch exceptions such as this, handle them elegantly, and recover if possible.

Using Sockets Asynchronously

You should use the connection-oriented TCP protocol if you're building synchronous clients and servers and you want to ensure that data is transmitted successfully between them. TCP comes at a price, though—sometimes you'll simply want to use the datagram approach of UDP because of its inherently asynchronous nature, despite the lack of guarantees. Let's look at some of the features of sockets under .NET that you can use to build reliable, asynchronous applications and get the best of both worlds.

The *Poll* and *Select* Methods

The TCP examples shown earlier created a thread for each client that connected to the server. Threads consume resources, and lots of threads consume lots of resources. Do you know how many concurrent clients a server will be handling at any one moment? A better way is to use the *Poll* and *Select* methods of the *Socket* class, which you can bring into play to multiplex on a single thread.

The *Poll* method allows you to query the status of a socket to determine what will happen if you attempt to send or receive data using it. You can use it to determine whether an attempt to read or write from the socket will succeed immediately, block, or result in an error. It is primarily useful for TCP sockets. To use it, you specify a timeout in microseconds (you cannot use a *TimeSpan* with this method) and a *mode*. The *Poll* method will wait until the timeout expires, or an operation indicated by the specified mode will not block. For example, to wait for up to two seconds for data to arrive on a socket, you can use this:

```
Socket mySocket;
⋮
boolean readyToRead = mySocket.Poll(2000000, SelectMode.SelectRead);
```

The Boolean value *readyToRead*, which the *Poll* method returns, indicates whether some data is available to be read (*true*) or the operation timed out (*false*). The volume of data is not disclosed, however, so a subsequent receive operation might still block if it attempts to read more data than is available. *SelectRead* can also be used by a server socket to establish whether an accept operation will block—it will return *true* if a client is attempting to connect to a socket that is in listen mode. The other values you can specify are *SelectWrite* and *SelectError*. The *SelectWrite* option returns *true* if data can be sent down the socket without being blocked, and *SelectError* returns *true* if the connection has been broken or unexpected out-of-band data is available. If you want to wait indefinitely, set the timeout interval to –1 when you call *Poll*. Alternatively, you can use 0 to obtain the current status of a socket and return immediately.

The *Poll* method lets you examine the status of a given socket. You can use the static *Select* method to determine the condition of a set of sockets. It expects four parameters: a list of sockets to check for readability, a list of sockets to check for writability, a list of sockets to check for errors, and a timeout (again in microseconds). The lists are passed in as *IList* interfaces; *IList* is implemented by many of the collection classes of .NET. Here's an example of how you can use the *Select* method:

```
Socket sender1 = ...;
Socket sender2 = ...;
ArrayList sendList = new ArrayList();
sendList.Add(sender);
sendList.Add(sender2);
Socket receiver1 = ...;
Socket receiver2 = ...;
ArrayList receiveList = new ArrayList();
receiveList.Add(receiver1);
receiveList.Add(receiver2);
ArrayList errorList = new ArrayList();
errorList.Add(sender);
errorList.Add(sender2);
errorList.Add(receiver1);
errorList.Add(receiver2);
Socket.Select(sendList, receiveList, errorList, 2000000);
```

This example creates and populates three *ArrayList* objects (*ArrayList* implements *IList*), with references to various sockets used for sending and receiving, and then it invokes *Select*. The call to *Select* returns after two seconds. The method always waits for the specified duration. When it returns, the contents of the *receiveList* collection will be populated with sockets from the original array that are ready to be read from. Similarly, the *sendList* collection will contain only those sockets from the original list that can be written to without blocking, and the *errorList* collection will contain all the sockets that reported errors. You can specify *null* for any of the *IList* parameters, but not for all of them at the same time!

Network Streams

The *Select* and *Poll* methods give you a great deal of control over how and when individual sockets are serviced. In many cases, however, they might be too low-level for what you need; code that uses them can become tortuous and involved. The common language runtime does provide a middle ground between spawning a thread dedicated to each socket connection and using *Select* and *Poll* on a single thread: the thread pool and stream mechanism (described in Chapter 8).

The *Socket* class exposes asynchronous versions of many of its methods. For example, you can issue the *BeginAccept* method to execute *Accept* asynchronously on a thread from the thread pool. *BeginAccept* expects an *AsyncCallback* that references a method to be run when a client connects. This callback should execute *EndAccept* to obtain the socket created to communicate with the client. (This will block until the accept operation has completed.) Here's an example of using *BeginAccept*:

```
serverSocket.BeginAccept(new AsyncCallback(handleAsyncClientRequest),
   serverSocket);
⋮
private void handleAsyncClientRequest(IAsyncResult ar)
{
   // Get the server socket, passed as the AsyncState property
   Socket serverSocket = (Socket)ar.get_AsyncState();

   // Wait for client to connect
   clientSocket = serverSocket.EndAccept(ar);

   // Issue BeginAccept again to allow more clients to connect
   serverSocket.BeginAccept(new AsyncCallback(handleClientRequest),
      serverSocket);

   // Send/Receive data using clientSocket
   ⋮
}
```

When the client has connected, the request can be handled using the same thread obtained from the thread pool to wait for the client. If you want to allow additional clients to connect, you should execute *BeginAccept* again (in the callback), which will allocate another thread from the pool if one is available. Incidentally, in the preceding code we passed the socket as the last parameter to *BeginAccept*. This is the user-defined state object that can be examined in the callback using the *AsyncState* property (*get_AsyncState*) of the *IAsyncResult* parameter, and provides a convenient way for the new thread to get a handle on the socket being used.

A socket client has the *BeginConnect* and *EndConnect* methods available, to create a thread that connects to a socket server asynchronously:

```
Socket clientSocket = ...;
IPEndPoint ipEndpoint = ...;
⋮
clientSocket.BeginConnect(ipEndpoint, new AsyncCallback(connectCallback),
   clientSocket);
⋮
private void connectCallback(AsyncResult ar)
{
   // Wait for the connect to complete
   Socket clientSocket = (Socket)ar.get_AsyncState();
   clientSocket.EndConnect(ar);

   // Send and receive data
   ⋮
}
```

In addition, a client and a server can employ the *BeginSend*, *EndSend*, *BeginReceive*, and *EndReceive* methods. The parameters of the *Begin* methods are similar to their synchronous cousins, with the addition of an *AsyncCallback* argument, which indicates the method to be executed when data is sent or received, and the usual user-defined state object:

```
⋮
ubyte [] data = ...;  // data to be sent
clientSocket.BeginSend(data, 0, data.length, SocketFlags.None,
   new AsyncCallback(sendCallback), clientSocket);
⋮

private void sendCallback(IAsyncResult ar)
{
   // Wait for the send to complete
   Socket clientSocket = (Socket)ar.get_AsyncState();
   int numBytesSent = clientSocket.EndSend(ar);
   ⋮
}
```

The *End* methods block until the operation has completed, and they return the number of bytes sent or received as appropriate.

For connectionless socket applications, there are the methods *Begin-SendTo* and *BeginReceiveFrom*, as well as *EndSendTo* and *EndReceiveFrom*.

Web Network Programming

Sockets are the foundation of many higher-level APIs for building distributed applications that communicate over the Internet (or an intranet). They're lean and mean—they're fast because they offer the minimum functionality needed to transport data from one computer to another. In this section, we'll examine some of the classes that Microsoft has layered on top of sockets for building systems that use upper-layer protocols, such as HTTP for handling Web requests and providing additional features not available to raw sockets. You'll learn about the approach that the .NET Framework Class Library adopts for defining the HTTP classes and about how the model can be extended to implement other application-defined protocols.

If you've built Web-based systems, you should be familiar with the cycle of operations for a typical exchange of messages between a client and a server. In a Web environment, the client is often a browser such as Microsoft Internet Explorer and the server is a Web server such as Microsoft Internet Information Services (IIS). For the moment, we'll ignore Web services in which the client might be another custom application.

The server resides on a computer that usually listens for incoming client requests using a server socket connected to a well-known port. (Port 80 is reserved for ordinary HTTP requests.) A Web server offers resources that can be accessed by a client that issues an appropriate Uniform Resource Identifier (URI). A URI comprises several pieces: the protocol or scheme for communicating with the server, the address of the server computer itself, and an optional string identifying the particular resource needed. For example, the URI *http://www.contentmaster.com/pages/framesets/mainex_fr.asp* specifies the protocol as HTTP, the name of the server computer as *www.contentmaster.com*, and the requested resource as */pages/framesets/mainex_fr.asp*.

How the resource request is interpreted is entirely up to the server—in this case, the resource is an Active Server Pages (ASP) page. The server processes the request and sends back a reply, which in the case of an HTTP server is most likely encoded as an HTML or XML response. In the case of HTTP, the protocol might be connectionless and use TCP/IP services such as DNS to discover the IP address of the destination server. The client fires off a request, which the server can accept or deny—or even not bother answering. If no reply is received within a reasonable period of time, most browsers will time out and display a default error page. If a reply is sent back, it might arrive as a single packet or many, depending on the nature of the resource requested. The browser receives all this data, pieces it together, and displays the result.

Connection-oriented protocols might also be used when you access data over the Web—File Transfer Protocol (FTP), for example. By using higher-level protocols, you can also add features that are not available with the lower-level protocols. For example, even though sockets can identify the source of a request, they carry no information about the credentials of the process on the client computer that issued that request. Protocols such as HTTP and HTTPS can transmit information about the identity of the requesting process to a server, which is transported through the underlying socket as ordinary data. (HTTPS works with Secure Sockets Layer (SSL) to encrypt this data; more on this later in the chapter.)

Pluggable Protocols

Besides HTTP, HTTPS, and FTP, client applications might want to use other protocols such as Gopher, News, or NNTP, and more protocols might be added in the future (and some might disappear). However, the basic model used is often the same—the client requests a URI and waits for a server response that (it hopes) is in a format it expects. Rather than tie a structure to a specific protocol, the .NET Framework Class Library uses a system of pluggable protocols, which is flexible and extensible.

The *System.Net* namespace contains two abstract classes—*WebRequest* and *WebResponse*—that you can use as a basis for implementing the request/response model of the Web. The *WebRequest* class defines the basic framework needed to issue a request for a URI. The *WebResponse* class specifies the essential functionality exposed by the response to a Web request. Both classes are protocol-independent. The intention is that a developer can derive specialized versions of the classes to handle each required protocol, although the .NET Framework Class Library already contains the *HttpWebRequest* and *HttpWebResponse* classes, which implement HTTP versions of these classes. They are located in the *System.Net* namespace. Also, the *FileWebRequest* and *FileWebResponse* classes provide a file system implementation of these two classes (using the *file:* scheme).

Note Do not confuse the *HttpWebRequest* and *HttpWebResponse* classes in *System.Net* with the *HttpRequest* and *HttpResponse* classes in *System.Web*. The *System.Web* classes are used primarily by ASP.NET code running on the Web server and are intended to process requests from clients and construct responses to send to clients. ASP.NET is covered in detail in Part V of this book.

When you define your own request class, you must register the scheme (such as *http* or *ftp*) that it handles by executing the static *RegisterPrefix* of the *WebRequest* class. The *WebRequest* class maintains a mini in-memory database of registered prefixes and request classes. A given prefix (such as *ftp*) can be registered only against a single request class. The return value from *WebRequest.RegisterPrefix* is *true* if the prefix was successfully registered, *false* otherwise.

Note The prefixes *http*, *https*, and *file* are automatically registered by .NET. The *http* and *https* prefixes are handled by the *HttpWebRequest* class, and the *file* prefix is handled by the *FileWebRequest* class. You cannot reregister these prefixes against your own request classes.

Registering Request Classes

An alternative to using *WebRequest.RegisterPrefix* to register a request class is to use the application configuration file. This file has an optional *<webRequestModules>* section in which you can specify prefixes and associated request classes. The default configuration setting is shown here:

```
<configuration>
   <system.net>
      ⋮
      <webRequestModules>
         <add prefix = "http"
            type = "System.Net.HttpRequestCreator"
         />
         <add prefix = "https"
            type = "System.Net.HttpRequestCreator"
         />
         <add prefix = "file"
            type = "System.Net.FileWebRequestCreator"
         />
      </webRequestModules>
   ⋮
   </system.net>
   ⋮
</configuration>
```

You create an instance of the request class by executing the static *Create* method of the *WebRequest* class, passing it the URI, including the scheme name, of the requested resource. (*WebRequest* acts as a factory for different request types.) For example, if you've defined your own class for processing FTP requests called *FtpRequest*, the following lines of code will register it with the *ftp* prefix and instantiate it to handle an FTP request to a server at the Fourth Coffee company:

```
WebRequest.RegisterPrefix("ftp", new FtpRequest());
WebRequest request = WebRequest.Create("ftp://ftp.fourthcoffee.com");
```

The *Create* method examines the prefix specified in the URI and builds an instance of the request class registered against that prefix. It is common practice to use a *WebRequest* variable to refer to the underlying request object. The *WebRequest* class contains most of the functionality you're likely to need, and writing code in this way decouples it from the underlying protocol, making it easier to switch if the need arises. If a derived request object exposes additional properties and methods, you can cast the return value of *Create* to the appropriate type to access them:

```
FtpRequest request =
   (FtpRequest)WebRequest.Create("ftp://ftp.fourthcoffee.com");
```

Requesting and Receiving Data Using HTTP

Creating an HTTP connection is simply a matter of using a valid URI containing the http prefix to create a *WebRequest* object. The *PageReader* class in the PageReader.jsl sample below (available in the BasicWeb project) illustrates how to connect to an HTTP server, request a page of data, and process the response (this code is available in the BasicWeb project). The *main* method contacts the server at *www.microsoft.com* and requests the home page *ms.htm*:

```
WebRequest request = WebRequest.Create("http://www.microsoft.com/ms.htm");
```

This statement actually creates an *HttpWebRequest* object and fires off the request for the page. You retrieve the reply from the server using the *GetResponse* method of the request object. This method will block until the server replies (or the client times out), and then it will create a *WebResponse* object. By default, an *HttpWebRequest* object will wait up to 100 seconds for a reply. The program changes the timeout to 10 seconds by modifying the *Timeout* property, which is specified in milliseconds:

```
request.set_Timeout(10000);
⋮
WebResponse response = request.GetResponse();
```

Strictly speaking, the *response* variable in this example is an *HttpWebResponse* object, and you can cast the return value from *GetResponse* if you need to. (There are a few additional properties and methods specific to HTTP that you can access.) To retrieve the reply from the server, you read the data using the *Stream* object returned by the *GetResponseStream* method. A word of warning: Because you can use the *Stream* class's *Read* method to populate a *ubyte* array and you can determine how long the response is by querying the *ContentLength* property, you might be tempted to create a *ubyte* array big enough to hold the entire response and issue a single *Read* request to fetch it. But depending on the volume of data in the response, this approach might not succeed because the Web server may struggle to transmit data to the underlying socket at a sufficient rate. You can end up losing a lot of data!

A more tolerant approach is to create a *StreamReader* based on the response stream and read the data a line at a time:

```
StreamReader reader = new StreamReader(response.GetResponseStream());
String pageData = reader.ReadLine();
while (pageData != null)
{
   Console.WriteLine(pageData);
   pageData = reader.ReadLine();
}
```

Once all the data has been extracted, you should close the response object, as shown here:

```
response.Close();
```

If you compile and run the program, it will display the HTML text for the Microsoft home page.

An HTML page can link to other resources, such as images and sounds. You must request these resources as well, using the URIs embedded in the HTML response received from the server. These resources usually consist of binary data, so you should not use a text-based stream to read them—use a *BinaryReader* instead. Alternatively, you can use the *DownloadFile* method of a *WebClient* object. (The *WebClient* class will be described shortly.)

In addition, a single response from a server might be broken into several pieces. After the first part of the response has been returned, subsequent fragments will be sent as HTTP 100-continue responses (part of the HTTP 1.1 protocol). You can handle these responses in your applications by assigning *HttpContinueDelegate* to the *ContinueDelegate* property of the *HttpWebRequest* object. (Use *set_ContinueDelegate* in J#.) The method referenced by the delegate will be automatically invoked for each *continue* response received.

If you connect to the Internet using a Web proxy, you should create a *WebProxy* object and attach it to the request object so the request is routed correctly. The following code fragment creates a *WebProxy* that routes requests through the proxy server listening on port 80 at the address *http://myproxy*. The Boolean value (*true*) indicates that the proxy should not be used for URIs on the local intranet.

```
WebRequest request = ...;
WebProxy proxy = new WebProxy("http://myproxy:80", true);
request.set_Proxy(proxy);
WebResponse response = request.GetResponse(); // uses the proxy
```

The *WebProxy* class has a highly overloaded constructor, and you can specify a range of different values and settings. One useful constructor allows you to provide an array of URIs that will bypass the proxy. If you want to ensure that the same proxy is used by all Web requests, instead of setting the *Proxy* object for each *WebRequest* object you can use the *GlobalProxySelection* class. This class specifies global proxy settings for use by all requests in the application. It exposes a public static property called *Select* that you can use to get or set the global proxy:

```
WebProxy proxy = ...;
GlobalProxySelection.set_Select(proxy);
```

Note that setting the *Proxy* property for a *WebRequest* object overrides the global proxy setting. You can also indicate that a proxy should not be used by setting the *Proxy* property to the value returned by the static *GetEmptyWebProxy* method of the *GlobalProxySelection* class:

```
WebRequest request = ...;
Request.set_Proxy(GlobalProxySelection.GetEmptyWebProxy());
```

Note The *System.Net* namespace also includes the classes *FileWebRequest* and *FileWebResponse*. These are used for accessing local files using the *file://* scheme. The methods you use to request and retrieve a file are similar to those described in this section for handling HTTP requests. We won't discuss these classes further.

Web Access and Security

As with sockets, using the Web classes requires the appropriate permission. Assemblies that work with the Web classes must be granted *System.Net.WebPermission*. Again, as with sockets, assemblies that you download from the Internet or an intranet or that you load from a network share do not have this privilege. You can, however, modify the code access security policy to grant it to them. The .NET Framework Configuration tool also allows you to selectively grant assemblies access to individual Web sites.

Posting Data

By default, the *HttpWebRequest* class uses the HTTP *GET* method when submitting a request to a URI. You can switch the nature of the request by setting the *Method* property of an *HttpWebRequest* object before retrieving any response. (If you try to change it afterwards, you'll trip an *InvalidOperationException*.) Valid values you can use include *HEAD*, *POST*, *PUT*, *DELETE*, *TRACE*, and *OPTIONS*. We won't describe all these methods here, but we'll look at how to use the *POST* verb to submit data to a Web server.

The *POST* verb is commonly used when sending large volumes of data. (Large in this case means more than can be handled in the query string of a *GET* command.) It is often used with HTML forms. Data is sent to the Web server as a stream. The Web server often executes a program to read this stream, process it, and send back any results. This program might be a CGI script, an ASP page, or just about any other type of executable that can handle streamed input.

The server must be informed of the type of data in the stream and how much data to expect. The HTTP protocol does this by setting fields in the header at the start of the request with this information. The HTTP header is transmitted first, followed by the data stream. The *WebRequest* class exposes the HTTP header fields as properties. The following code fragment transmits the contents of the string variable *data* using an HTTP *POST* operation. The *Method*, *ContentType*, and *ContentLength* properties set the fields in the HTTP header with appropriate values. (For details on HTTP content types, see the HTTP 1.1 specification.)

The *GetRequestStream* method returns a stream that you can use for sending the data to the Web server. If you want to send a string, it makes sense to create a *StreamWriter* wrapper around this stream. Certain characters have special meanings in URIs and streams posted to Web servers. These characters must be filtered out and replaced with an appropriate escape sequence. For example, spaces should be replaced with +, and the *&* character should be replaced by the sequence *%26*. The static *UrlEncode* method of the *System.Web.HttpUtility* class does this, and it returns an encoded string, which can be submitted safely to a Web server. In this example, the *data* string is encoded for transmission before being sent. You should close the stream when all the data has been output.

```
String data = ...;
WebRequest request = ...;
request.set_Method("POST");
request.set_ContentType("application/x-www-form-urlencoded");
String encodedData = HttpUtility.UrlEncode(data);
request.set_ContentLength(data.length());
StreamWriter writer = new StreamWriter(request.GetRequestStream());
writer.Write(encodedData);
writer.Close();
```

Tip The classes in the *System.Web* namespace are implemented in the assembly System.Web.dll. Be sure to reference this assembly when you compile an application that uses this namespace. From the command line, use the */reference* flag, as described in earlier chapters. If you're using Visual Studio .NET, choose Add Reference from the Project menu; in the Add Reference dialog box, select System.Web.dll and then click OK.

If all is well and the Web server understands the request, you can open the response stream using the *GetResponseStream* method of the request object and process any reply as before. If the server does not understand the request, the content length indicated does not match the actual length of the content, or some other sort of error occurs, an attempt to read the response form the server will throw a *WebException* containing an HTTP error code.

The *HttpWebRequest* and *HttpWebResponse* Objects

Most of the time, ordinary vanilla *WebRequest* and *WebResponse* objects will provide an adequate interface for interacting with the Web using HTTP. However, the *HttpWebRequest* and *HttpWebResponse* classes contain some additional methods and properties that you can use if you're writing specialized code. In particular, the *Cookies* property lets you get or set a collection of cookies associated with a response or request, and the *ClientCertificates* property lets you retrieve X509 certificate information for a request.

Processing Requests Asynchronously

The examples shown so far send a request and receive a response synchronously. In the world of unreliable connections and indeterminate response times that is the Internet, sending and receiving data in this manner can tie up an application for a long time. The solution, as ever, is to use the thread pool and perform these operations asynchronously. (You can then set a long timeout period to give requests a chance to succeed!)

The *WebRequest* class supplies the methods *BeginGetRequestStream* and *BeginGetResponse* methods, which follow the familiar asynchronous pattern: Both methods return an *IAsyncResult* object and expect an *AsyncCallback* delegate that refers to a method to be executed by a thread from the thread pool, along with a user-defined state object. The *EndGetRequestStream* method blocks until the request stream has been established, and it returns a stream handle. The *EndGetResponse* method also blocks until a reply is received from the Web server, and it returns a *WebResponse* object you can use to read and process the reply:

```
WebRequest request = ...;
// Wait for a response asynchronously
request.BeginGetResponse(new AsyncCallback(waitForResponse), request);
⋮
private void waitForResponse(IAsyncResult ar)
{
// Extract the WebRequest object from the async. state property
   WebRequest request = (WebRequest)ar.get_AsyncState();

   // Wait for response. Block the thread if necessary
   WebResponse response = request.EndGetResponse(ar);
```

```
    // Read the response and process it a line at a time
    StreamReader reader = new StreamReader(response.GetResponseStream());
    ⋮
}
```

You can cancel an asynchronous call to *BeginGetResponse* by calling the *Abort* method of the request object.

Using a *WebClient* Object

Just as the *TcpClient* class wraps the code for setting a client socket and setting its properties, the *WebClient* class does the same for a *WebRequest*. The *WebClient* class exposes methods that let you upload and download data to and from a Web server—for example, to hide the complexities of setting the properties needed to perform a POST operation. You can send data to a server using the *UploadData*, *UploadFile*, and *UploadValues* methods. You can use the *OpenWrite* method to open the request stream to send data to the server. (You still need to encode the data to make sure it is not misinterpreted by the server.) The *DownloadData* and *DownloadFile* methods retrieve data from a Web server to a byte array or a local file on the client, and the *OpenRead* method returns a handle to the response stream.

The following code shows an alternative implementation of the main method of the *PageReader* class that uses a *WebClient* rather than a *WebRequest* to read the *ms.html* page at *www.microsoft.com*:

```
public static void main(String[] args)
{
    WebClient client = new WebClient();

    // Send a request for the home page at www.microsoft.com
    StreamReader reader =
        new StreamReader(client.OpenRead("http://www.microsoft.com/ms.htm"));

    // Read the response and display it a line at a time
    String pageData = reader.ReadLine();
    while (pageData != null)
    {
        Console.WriteLine(pageData);
        pageData = reader.ReadLine();
    }

    // Close the stream
    reader.Close();
}
```

HTTP Connection Management and Pooling

HTTP was originally designed to be a connectionless protocol because of the nature of client requests and the overall fragility of the Internet. Just because a client had issued a request, there was no guarantee that it would stay connected and issue another, or that the connection between the client and the server would not evaporate because of a switching error somewhere! These were valid concerns, but the overall cost of connecting and disconnecting each time a client sent a request to the same server became prohibitive. Consider a Web page containing embedded images and other resources—it requires a number of requests to transmit the entire content of the page to the client. Continual connecting and disconnecting began to affect the rate at which data could pour through the Internet as a whole—a large proportion of the packets flowing around the Internet dealt with handling connections and routing rather than sending real data.

The HTTP 1.1 protocol addressed these issues and provided persistent connections. This involved the client setting a flag in the HTTP header of the initial request asking for a persistent connection, and when the client had finished it would send another HTTP header containing a *close* flag. (In fact, the default in HTTP 1.1 is to assume a persistent connection unless the client requests otherwise.) A server does not have to honor the request to keep a persistent connection open, however. (This doesn't result in an error, but a new connection must be established the next time the client communicates.) Also, most servers will time out and close a connection that has been inactive for a period of time.

HTTP 1.1 also supports pipelining. A client can send a series of requests without waiting for a response each time. The server should process these requests and send back responses in the same order that the requests were received. The client can then stream through the responses as they are received.

You can indicate that an *HttpWebRequest* object should use a persistent connection by setting its *KeepAlive* property (*set_KeepAlive* in J#) to *true* (which is the default value). Setting this property to *false* will send an HTTP header with the close flag set. You can ask that a request be pipelined by setting the *Pipelined* (*set_Pipelined*) property of the request object to true. Pipelining requires that *KeepAlive* also be set to *true*. These properties are not available through the *WebRequest* class.

Persistent connections are a potentially expensive resource. The .NET Framework Class Library implements persistent HTTP connection pooling. When an *HttpWebRequest* object connects to a URI, a *ServicePoint* object is created that caches the connection. If another *HttpWebRequest* object accesses the same server (the resource could be different), the same connection will be used and shared by this second request. You can query the *ServicePoint* object used by an *HttpWebRequest* object using the *ServicePoint* property (*get_ServicePoint*). Remember that the connection is established only after a request object attempts to actually send data to or retrieve data from a Web server. You can also obtain a handle on a *ServicePoint* by calling the static *FindServicePoint* method of the *ServicePointManager* class, passing in a URI that specifies the Web server in question:

```
ServicePoint pooledConnection = ServicePointManager.FindServicePoint(
   new Uri("http://www.microsoft.com"));
```

If there is currently no existing *ServicePoint* for the specified Web server, *FindServicePoint* will create one.

The HTTP 1.1 protocol currently allows up to two concurrent requests to share a connection. If a third request is made to the same Web server, the request will block until one of the first two is closed or a timeout occurs. However, you can increase the *ConnectionLimit* property of a *ServicePoint* object to prevent this behavior:

```
// Increase the connection limit to 4
pooledConnection.set_ConnectionLimit(4);
```

You can change the default connection limit for all *ServicePoint* objects by setting the *DefaultConnectionPointLimit* property of the *ServicePointManager* class. This will affect only service points created after the property has been changed.

To examine the number of active connections a *ServicePoint* has, you can query its *CurrentConnections* property. As requests disconnect, the number of active connections using a *ServicePoint* can drop to zero. If a *ServicePoint* has not been used for a period of time, it will be recycled. The default value is actually *900000ms* (15 minutes). You can modify this idle time setting using the *MaxIdleTime* property:

```
// Set the idle time to 30s (30000ms)
pooledConnection.set_MaxIdleTime(30000);
```

You can limit the size of the *ServicePoint* pool by setting the *MaxServicePoints* property of the *ServicePointManager* class. This value defaults to zero, which means that there is no limit on the size of the pool.

Security over the Internet

Security in distributed applications is always an issue, and even more so with applications that use the Internet. We'll cover two important aspects of security in this section. The first aspect concerns restricting access to resources and applications running on the Web server to certain applications and individuals. You need a way to identify the source of any requests (authentication) and check that the source is allowed to perform any requested action (authorization)—you don't want any old hacker to upload files onto your Web server or download sensitive data.

The second aspect concerns securing the data as it flows over the Internet. You never know who is listening and monitoring the packets flowing over the network. So another requirement is that sensitive data should not make sense if intercepted by an unauthorized third party. This means encrypting data.

Authentication and Authorization

The HTTP protocol defines a challenge/response mechanism for handling security. A client application attempting to access a resource will be challenged by the Web server hosting that resource to prove its identity. The client must reply with a token of some sort that identifies it and one that the Web server can verify. Once the client has been identified, the server can grant or deny access to resources on that server. The .NET Framework Class Library supports a variety of Internet authentication mechanisms—Basic, Digest, Negotiate, NTLM, and Kerberos.

Tip If you're accessing an ASP.NET resource running under IIS, the ASP.NET application should be configured to run using the Windows ASP.NET authentication provider. Configuration of IIS and ASP.NET applications is covered in more detail in Chapter 16.

In this model, when a *WebRequest* is issued to a Web server, the server will require the client to verify its identity. The common language runtime uses the *System.Net.AuthenticationManager* class to do this, and the Web client might not be aware of what is happening behind the scenes. This class delegates much of its work to *authentication modules*, which are classes that implement the *System.Net.IAuthenticationModule* interface and perform the actual authentication of requests.

.NET is preconfigured with modules that handle Basic, Digest, Negotiate, NTLM, and Kerberos authentication. Authentication modules must be registered with the authentication manager. When a client request requires authentication, the common language runtime invokes the authentication manager, which in turn calls the *Authenticate* method of each registered authentication module in turn until one of the modules returns a positive response (request allowed) or the list of modules is exhausted (request denied).

Some authentication modules permit preauthentication. Preauthentication allows an authentication module to preemptively authenticate a Web client in the expectation that the server will require this to happen anyway—this can save time when the client contacts the Web server and can also conserve bandwidth by not sending a request to the server in the first place if the authentication fails. Authentication modules are registered with the authentication manager using the static *AuthenticationManager.Register* method or in the *<authenticationModules>* section of the application configuration file:

```
<configuration>
   <system.net>
      ⋮
      <authenticationModules>
         <add type = "System.Net.DigestClient" />
         <add type = "System.Net.NegotiateClient" />
         <add type = "System.Net.KerberosClient" />
         <add type = "System.Net.NtlmClient" />
         <add type = "System.Net.BasicClient" />
      </authenticationModules>
      <webRequestModules>
         ⋮
      </webRequestModules>
      ⋮
   </system.net>
   ⋮
```

The *Authenticate* method parameters include the *WebRequest* object submitted by the client, which identifies the URI being accessed, and an *ICredentials* object that contains the credentials that help identify the client. A client request must therefore provide a set of credentials for the authentication system to validate. How these credentials are gathered depends on the authentication method the server expects when the client accesses a given resource. For example, if the URI demands Basic authentication, the client request must supply a username and password and store this information in the *Credentials* property of the *WebRequest* before submitting it. This can be achieved using a *System.Net.NetworkCredential* object:

```
HttpWebRequest request =
   (HttpWebRequest)WebRequest.Create("http://www...");
NetworkCredential credentials =
   new NetworkCredential("user name", "password");
request.set_Credentials(credentials);
WebResponse response = request.GetResponse();
⋮
```

Note that if the requested URI does not authenticate users, any credential information supplied by the client will be ignored. Also, some authentication mechanisms (Digest, for example) expect a domain as well as a username and a password. The *NetworkCredential* constructor is overloaded, and one implementation takes an additional domain parameter.

You can also create a credential cache using the *CredentialCache* class, associating credentials with one or more URIs and authentication schemes (Basic, Digest, Kerberos, and so on). You can then attach this cache to *WebRequest* objects—the same cache can be associated with multiple requests. The authentication module on the server can obtain the credentials associated with a particular URI and authentication scheme by calling the *GetCredentials* method of the cache dispatched with the request and validate them. Using a credential cache is useful for applications that need to access multiple Internet resources.

```
// Create a credential cache
CredentialCache cache = new CredentialCache();

// Add credentials to the cache
cache.Add(new Uri("http://www..."),"Basic",
   new NetworkCredential("user name", "password"));
cache.Add(new Uri("http://www.../"),"Digest",
   new NetworkCredential("user name", "password", "digest domain"));
⋮
HttpWebRequest request =
   (HttpWebRequest)WebRequest.Create("http://www.microsoft.com/ms.htm");

// Attach the cache to the WebRequest
request.set_Credentials(cache);

// Submit the request, with credential cache
WebResponse response = request.GetResponse();
⋮
```

Kerberos and NTLM authentication can also specify user details, but a default set of credentials based on the Windows identity of the process running the application will also be generated. This information is accessible through the *DefaultCredentials* property of the *CredentialCache* object.

When authentication has completed, the *Authenticate* method returns a *System.Net.Authorization* object. The authorization object contains an authorization token in its *Message* property. The Web server examines this token when granting or denying access to protected resources. The contents of the *Message* property depend on the type of authentication performed—different schemes generate different format messages. Authorization is essentially a task performed by the Web server once a client has been authenticated. (Authorization in ASP.NET applications will be covered in Chapter 16.)

Encryption

For data to be transmitted securely, it must be encrypted. One of the simplest ways to do this is to use SSL or Transport Layer Security (TLS). *TLS/SSL* uses public key encryption to secure the exchanges between the client and the Web server. If a Web server supports SSL, you can simply issue URIs of the form *https://www*.... The WebRequest class will automatically manufacture an appropriate object that you can use to communicate over SSL. SSL comes at a cost, though; performance tends to be slower due to the amount of encryption/decryption required. You might not notice this on a Web client (the Internet is almost always slow!), but you might find that the Web server requires additional processing power and memory to maintain speed. If you're using IIS, you must obtain and install a server certificate if you want to support SSL.

An alternative to using SSL to encrypt the channel communicating between the client and the server is to simply encrypt the payload of each message. The .NET Framework supports private-key encryption using encryption service providers in the System.Security.Cryptography namespace. Providers are available for a number of algorithms, including DES, Triple DES, RC2, and Rijndael. Public-key encryption is also available using providers for the RSA and DSA algorithms. The public-key algorithms can also be used to generate digital signatures, guaranteeing the identity of the sender of a message and its contents.

Hashing is another mechanism used to form digital signatures, and a variety of common hashing algorithms are supported, including MD5, SHA1, SHA256, SHA384, and SHA512, depending on the length of the hash key you require. The longer the hash, the more secure it will be, but the longer it will take to generate and decode. For more information on using the cryptographic services in .NET, see the .NET Framework SDK documentation.

Summary

This chapter covered many of the low-level techniques you can use for building networked applications. You saw how to use connection-oriented sockets for transporting data in a reliable way between a client and a server, and you learned how to use connectionless sockets for implementing peer-to-peer style applications. The sockets library can operate with the thread pool to allow you to build applications that work with sockets asynchronously.

You also saw how to create applications that communicate with Web servers using HTTP. In particular, you learned how to use the *WebRequest* and *WebResponse* classes to submit a request to a Web server and retrieve a reply. We looked at how to manage HTTP connections and the techniques needed to access secure resources over the Internet.

10

Serializing Objects

The previous chapter highlighted the problems associated with transporting data of varying lengths and formats over a network. The main issue is using a structure to represent the data that a sender and a receiver both agree on and that is unambiguous—to avoid little endian vs. big endian questions, for example. The same problems can arise when you persist objects to a data store: Applications that write data must use a format that other applications can interpret correctly. (The term *data store* in this context can mean a database, a collection of files, or some other set of data.)

Often, you'll need to convert an object from the internal format used in an application to a format suitable for persistence or transportation. The process of converting an object into such a form is called *serialization*. The reverse process is called *deserialization*. Serialization is an important part of any distributed system. For example, in the Microsoft .NET Framework, serialization is employed when you use the .NET Remoting architecture (covered in Chapter 11) or access Web services (described in Part V).

The Java language supports serialization as a mechanism for marshaling objects between processes, and it uses its own internal format. Java serialization is used by Remote Method Invocation (RMI) to pass objects by value across process boundaries. You can serialize and deserialize objects manually through the *readObject* and *writeObject* methods of the *ObjectInputStream* and *ObjectOutputStream* classes, respectively, in the java.io package of the JDK. You can exploit native Java serialization from J# to consume and produce serialized streams that can be written or read by other Java applications. However, the .NET Framework offers its own serialization technologies that can you can use from any of the languages that execute in the common language runtime. These are

- **Binary serialization** A compact format that's useful for sharing data between managed applications.
- **XML serialization** A more open but less dense format that is typically used when you don't want to restrict the applications that can read the data to those built using the .NET Framework SDK. XML serialization is the method of choice when you build Web services, for example.

In this chapter, we'll examine how serialization works and how to use the classes and features of the .NET Framework to implement binary and XML serialization. You'll also learn how to customize how data is serialized.

Serializing and Deserializing Data

The serialization architecture of the .NET Framework is highly customizable. The basic mechanism is simple, but at several points you can override the default behavior and extend it with your own code. In essence, an object is converted into a series of bytes, which is sent down a stream. The stream can be directed toward persistent storage (a file stream), sent over a network, or dispatched to some other destination. Whatever the ultimate target, eventually this stream of bytes must be reconstructed into a copy of the original object.

Formatting Data

The format of the byte stream emitted by the serialization process is governed by a formatter object. The .NET Framework Class Library supplies two formatters that you can use off the shelf: the *BinaryFormatter* class (located in the *System.Runtime.Serialization.Formatters.Binary* namespace) and the *SoapFormatter* class (located in the *System.Runtime.Serialization.Formatters.Soap* namespace). You can also create your own custom formatter objects by implementing the *System.Runtime.Serialization.IFormatter*. The *BinaryFormatter* and *SoapFormatter* classes both implement the *IFormatter* interface.

Implementing the *IFormatter* Interface

If you want to implement the *IFormatter* interface yourself, the preferred technique is to extend the *System.Runtime.Serialization.Formatter* class and override its methods and properties. The *Formatter* class is abstract, but it provides some helper methods that you can use to interact with the .NET Framework during the serialization and deserialization processes. You should provide your own implementation of the *Serialize* and *Deserialize* methods. The *Serialize* method is passed an output stream and an object; the method should write a serialized version of the object (which can be complex, containing subobjects) to the stream. Conversely, the *Deserialize* method is passed an input stream, and the method should extract the object data from this stream and use it to reconstitute the object. (Again, this can be a complex object.)

If you implement *IFormatter* in this way, you must also supply implementations of the following abstract methods inherited from the *Formatter* class, which are not actually part of the *IFormatter* interface: *WriteArray*, *WriteBoolean*, *WriteByte*, *WriteChar*, *WriteDateTime*, *WriteDecimal*, *WriteDouble*, *WriteInt16*, *WriteInt32*, *WriteInt64*, *WriteObjectRef*, *WriteSByte*, *WriteSingle*, *WriteTimeSpan*, *WriteUInt16*, *WriteUInt32*, *WriteUInt64*, and *WriteValueType*. This looks like a lot of work but is not as bad as it appears. All of these methods are similar, and their task is to write data of the appointed type (passed in as a parameter, together with the name of the data) in a serialized form to the output stream. You can use these methods when you implement *Serialize*.

You must also implement the *Binder*, *Context*, and *SurrogateSelector* properties (which *are* part of the *IFormatter* interface). Other helper classes are available in the *System.Runtime.Serialization* namespace. You'll learn more about binding, streaming contexts, and serialization surrogates later in this chapter.

The *SoapFormatter* class generates an XML stream that can contain simple and complex objects. This class is often used for describing parameters and return values, and forms a fundamental part of the infrastructure needed to support Web services. We'll examine it further in Part V of this book. For the time being, we'll concentrate on the *BinaryFormatter* class.

The formatter will check that the object to be serialized actually supports serialization. An object can be serialized if it is marked with the *SerializableAttribute* (which is somewhat similar to applying the *Serializable* tag interface in the JDK). A class can also control the serialization process by implementing the *System.Runtime.Serialization.ISerializable* interface. If the object does implement the *ISerializable* interface, the formatter will call the *GetObjectData* method of the object at the appropriate juncture (*GetObjectData* is the only method defined in the *ISerializable* interface), and this method should convert the object into a stream of bytes. If the object is simply marked with the *SerializableAttribute*, the formatter will use its own default mechanism for converting the object into a stream of bytes. Either way, the resulting stream can be sent to a file, over the network, or wherever!

The Serializer.jsl sample file (in the NETSerialization project) shows how to use a *BinaryFormatter* to store a *Cake* object (see the sample Cake.jsl in the Cake project, which has been added to the NETSerialization solution) to a file. A *Cake* object has four properties: filling, shape, size, and message. The *filling*, *shape*, and *size* properties are *short* values, and the message property is a *String*. The *Cake* class is marked with the *SerializableAttribute*:

```
/** @attribute SerializableAttribute() */
public class Cake
{
⋮
}
```

The *main* method of the *Serializer* class creates a test *Cake* object and sets its properties:

```
Cake cake = new Cake();
cake.set_Filling(Cake.Fruit);
cake.set_Shape(Cake.Round);
cake.set_Size((short)12);
cake.set_Message("Happy Birthday");
```

The *main* method then creates a *BinaryFormatter* object and a *Stream* for writing data to the file CakeInfo.bin:

```
BinaryFormatter formatter = new BinaryFormatter();
Stream stream = new FileStream("CakeInfo.bin", FileMode.Create,
   FileAccess.Write, FileShare.None);
```

The *Serialize* method of the *IFormatter* interface (which *BinaryFormatter* implements) serializes its second argument (the *Cake* object), sending the result down the stream specified by its first argument (the file stream):

```
formatter.Serialize(stream, cake);
```

If you want to send a serialized *Cake* object over a network, the principle is exactly the same. The only difference is that you should use a network stream rather than a file stream. The *System.Net.Sockets.TcpClient* class provides the *GetStream* method, returning a *NetworkStream* object:

```
TcpClient client = new TcpClient(...);
formatter.Serialize(client.GetStream(), cake);
```

If you're using raw sockets or the *UdpClient* class, which send arrays of bytes, you can employ a *System.IO.MemoryStream* to serialize an object into a *ubyte* array:

```
Socket sender = new Socket(...);
⋮

// The array must be big enough to hold the serialized data.
ubyte [] data = ...;
MemoryStream memStream = new MemoryStream(data);

// Serialize the object to the MemoryStream.
// The result will be stored in the data array.
formatter.Serialize(memStream, cake);
memStream.Close();

// Transmit the data
sender.Send(data);
```

Note that the automatic serialization mechanism requires that the class being serialized not only be designated as serializable but that all ancestor classes be serializable as well. (Native Java serialization has the same requirement.) This is not a problem for types such as the *Cake* class shown above because it descends from *Object,* which is also serializable. But be aware of this issue if you're implementing your own class hierarchy. If your class can be subclassed, mark it with the *SerializableAttribute* unless you want to prevent it from being serialized.

Note If you examine the CakeInfo.bin file generated by the *Serializer* class, you should notice that the *final* member variables (the cake fillings and shapes) are not serialized. This is because the values for these variables are defined by the values specified in the class definition itself (stored with the metadata of the class), and these variables cannot be assigned to in code. When the *Cake* object is deserialized, these variables will be populated from the metadata as the *Cake* object is instantiated, and not from the serialization stream.

Deserialization

Deserialization is a matter of reading a binary stream and using it to reconstitute an object. When an object is serialized using a binary formatter, the resulting stream contains the name of the class, the identity of the assembly, and the name and value of every member of the object. When a stream is deserialized into an object, the binary formatter (which handles deserialization as well as serialization) must have access to the assembly defining the class specified in the stream so it can build an instance of the required object. The formatter can then populate the members of the object using the data in the stream.

It's worth noting that the formatter accesses the member variables directly and does not execute constructors or use object properties when it assigns the data values—this is for reasons of speed. The *Deserializer* class in the Deserializer.jsl sample file (in the NETDeserialization project) rebuilds a *Cake* object from the CakeInfo.bin file and displays its values. The method in the formatter that does the work is *Deserialize*. This method expects a *Stream* as its parameter, which it reads and uses to construct the object. The result of the *Deserialize* method is actually an *Object*, which you must cast appropriately:

```
BinaryFormatter formatter = new BinaryFormatter();
Stream stream = new FileStream("CakeInfo.bin", FileMode.Open,
   FileAccess.Read, FileShare.Read);
Cake cake = (Cake) formatter.Deserialize(stream);
```

As with the *Serialize* method, you can deserialize data that appears on almost any stream. For example, to read *Cake* data arriving on a *TcpClient*, you can use the following:

```
TcpListener server = new TcpListener(...);
server.Start();
TcpClient client = server.AcceptTcpClient();
Cake cake = (Cake)formatter.Deserialize(client.GetStream());
```

Alternatively, if you're using the low-level Sockets API or the *UdpClient* class, where the data arrives as an array of bytes, you can wrap the data inside a *MemoryStream* object and deserialize it:

```
Socket receiver = new Socket(...);
ubyte [] data = ...
⋮
receiver.Receive(data);
MemoryStream memStream = new MemoryStream(data);
Cake receivedCake = (Cake)formatter.Deserialize(memStream);
```

The principal advantages of using the *BinaryFormatter* class over the XML alternatives are speed and compactness. As mentioned earlier, the *BinaryFormatter* quickly accesses the internals of objects directly and doesn't bother with niceties such as whether that data is public, private, or protected. This guarantees that all member variables in an object will be saved to the serialization stream and populated correctly when being deserialized. This sounds like an obvious requirement for serialization, but there are obvious security implications—if you understand the format used by the serialization process, you can forge your own objects! This is even easier if you're using XML serialization to transmit data in XML format over the Web. For this and other reasons, which will be described in due course, the default XML serialization mechanisms supplied with .NET will read and populate only public member variables and members that are reachable through publicly accessible properties. Totally private data (members not directly accessible and not exposed through properties) will not be serialized.

As far as compactness is concerned, you've seen that the *BinaryFormatter* class does not store much information about the structure of the data itself—it just records the identity of the class and assembly in the serialized output stream. In contrast, the XML formatter builds an XML representation of the object being serialized, which is more verbose but more portable—any application that can consume XML can read and process this representation. Speed and compactness become more important as you serialize and deserialize larger and larger objects—you might not notice much difference in performance between the formatters when you serialize a single *Cake* object, but if you're serializing a collection of 10,000 of them, the distinction will become a lot more obvious.

Note The format used by native Java serialization is even more compact than that used by the *BinaryFormatter* class, but it is less able to cope with versioning issues.

Versioning

Deserializing a stream into an object using a binary formatter relies on having the definition of the class available. The binary formatter uses the assembly and class name found in the serialized stream to locate the assembly required to instantiate an *empty* object of the appropriate type. The mechanism used for locating the assembly is the same as that used by the loader (as described in Chapter 2). The class can be contained in a local private assembly or in an assembly in the Global Assembly Cache (GAC). The binding policy used to redirect requests for one version of an assembly to another, and any codebases specified in the application configuration file (if it has one), will be applied. This means that it is possible to serialize an object using one version of its implementation and then attempt to deserialize it using another. This might or might not work, depending on the nature of the changes between the two versions.

Once an empty object has been created, the deserialization process will attempt to fill its members using the information specified in the serialization stream. This information comprises the name of each member, along with its type and value. The binary deserialization process is therefore not affected by the following modifications to the class:

- A change in the order of the member variables of a class. (This is also true of native Java serialization performed using the JDK.
- A change in the type of any member variable, as long as it is possible to cast from the old type to the new (not true of Java serialization).

Note A class can implement the *System.IConvertible* interface to define custom conversions to primitive common language runtime base types. Deserialization will exploit these conversions if it needs to.

- Changes to the names of any methods (not true of Java serialization).
- The addition or removal of methods (not true of Java serialization).
- Changes to the signatures of any methods and constructors (not true of Java serialization).

Versioning in the JDK

For the JDK purist, you can indicate that a Java class is serialization-compatible with an older version. This allows you to add, remove, and change the signatures of methods in much the same way that you can with .NET serialization.

The serialization format used by native Java serialization identifies the class with a *serial version unique ID*. This is a unique hash based on the methods, variables, types, class, parent class, and other features of the serialized object. If a class changes in any way, the contents will hash to a different value. When an object is deserialized, the JVM will generate the hash for the target class and compare it to the hash in the serialized stream. If they're different, the JVM will throw an exception (*java.io.InvalidClassException*).

However, you can override the generated serial version unique ID for a class with your own value by adding a *static final long* variable called *serialVersionUID* to the class:

```
public class Cake
{
   static final long serialVersionUID = 4832732748870872134L;
   ⋮
}
```

The value should be the same as that of the version of the class you want to be compatible with. You can obtain the serial version of a class using the serialver utility supplied with the JDK:

```
C:\> serialver Cake
Cake:    static final long serialVersionUID = 4832732748870872134L;
```

Note that if you force the serial version unique ID in this way, you must ensure that the collection of member variables in the class have not changed. Otherwise, you might have problems when deserializing—if the type of a variable has changed (the JDK will attempt to cast data if it can), the class will be deemed incompatible and the JDK will throw an exception. Any new variables added to a class will be set to *null* or zero (depending on their type), and the data for variables that are no longer present will be discarded.

Binary deserialization in .NET will permit the addition of new member variables, although they'll be left in an unassigned state after deserialization has occurred. (There will be no corresponding values in the serialized stream.) However, if you change the name of any member variable, deserialization will fail and throw an exception. Similarly, if you remove a member variable deserialization will also fail, although if you know that a member has been removed since an object was serialized, you can take certain steps to recover data from the original stream. This involves performing selective deserialization by defining your own custom serialization/deserialization mechanism and handling the differences between the stream and the expected data manually. We'll look at custom serialization shortly.

Note Strictly speaking, if you add a member variable to an existing serializable class, you should mark that variable with the *System.NonSerializedAttribute*. This will result in the new member being omitted from any future serialization and will maintain compatibility with code that might use serialized instances of older versions of this class. Of course, hardly anyone does this because they don't want to have to cope with the resulting lost state! Just be aware that once you've created and published a class, you can ensure absolute compatibility with existing code only by never adding or removing anything. We'll look at the *NonSerializedAttribute* later in this chapter.

By default, the serialization stream contains the version number, strong name, and culture of the assembly containing the serialized object, and this information is used to ensure that the correct version of the assembly is used when the stream is deserialized back into an object (notwithstanding any binding policy specified by the application configuration file). If you examine the CakeInfo.bin file generated by the *Serializer* class shown earlier, you'll see something similar to this embedded in the binary data. (Your version number and public key token might differ from those shown here.)

```
...... Cake, Version=1.0.849.23238, Culture=neutral, PublicKeyToken=5cebc9b2f5e
65f60......CakeInfo.Cake.....
```

Note If the assembly defining the serialized object class is not signed, the *PublicKeyToken* will be null.

If you're absolutely certain that member variables will never change their names and member variables will never be added or removed, you can save some time (and space) and turn off this version checking before serializing or deserializing data. (But be careful!) The *BinaryFormatter* class has an *AssemblyFormat* property that you can set to the value *FormatterAssemblyStyle.Simple*. The only other option is *FormatterAssemblyStyle.Full*, which happens to be the default. The *FormatterAssemblyStyle* enumeration is defined in the *System.Runtime.Serialization.Formatters* namespace:

```
BinaryFormatter formatter = ...;
formatter.set_AssemblyFormat(FormatterAssemblyStyle.Simple);
```

When an object is serialized, the binary formatter will not emit any assembly version, strong name, or culture information—just the unqualified namespace and class:

```
CakeInfo.Cake...
```

When the stream is deserialized, the *BinaryFormatter* will use whatever version of the specified assembly happens to be available. This feature allows you to deploy the latest version of an assembly on a computer without worrying about which versions were used when any data was serialized.

The Serialization Binder

During deserialization, the formatter actually uses a serialization binder object to determine which assembly to load and which class to instantiate. A serialization binder is a class that extends the *System.Runtime.Serialization.SerializationBinder* abstract class. The default binder performs the actions described in the text, but you can change the binding mechanism used by implementing your own binder. For example, you might want to have finer control over which version of an assembly is used, or you might want to load a different class altogether. You can do this by extending the *SerializationBinder* class and overriding the *BindToType* method. This method takes the identity of the assembly (a string that includes the name, version, culture, and public key—for example, *"Cake, Version=1.0.849.23238, Culture=neutral, PublicKeyToken=5cebc9b2f5e65f60"*) and class (including namespace), which are retrieved from the serialization stream by the formatter. The *BindToType* method can examine these parameters, parse them, and return the type of an object that the formatter should create (as a *System.Type*):

```
public class CustomBinder extends SerializationBinder
{
   public Type BindToType(String assemblyName, String, typeName)
   {
      // Parse and examine the assembly name and type
      // If a different type should be used then ...
      if (...)
      {
         // ... deserialize into a MyNameSpace.MyClass object
         // from the MyAssembly.dll assembly
         return Type.GetType("MyNameSpace.MyClass, MyAssembly");
      }
```

```
        else
        {
            // otherwise use the default type passed in
            return Type.GetType(typeName + "," + assemblyName);
        }
    }
}
```

To use a custom serialization binding, you must instantiate a binder object and attach it to the formatter being used through its *Binder* property:

```
BinaryFormatter formatter = new BinaryFormatter();
SerializationBinder binder = new CustomBinder();
formatter.set_Binder(binder);
```

Being Selective

You can perform selective serialization of member variables in a class. This is most useful for member variables that are used purely for calculations or that do not maintain meaningful state over time. An example could be a variable that refers to a file stream. A file stream is really just a reference to an internal structure managed by the operating system; it might be valid when an object is serialized, but it is likely to be invalid when the object is deserialized at some unspecified point in the future. (In general, this behavior is true of most objects that are accessed through handles.) Selective serialization is also useful if a member variable is of a type that is not itself serializable; this member can be omitted.

The simplest way to perform selective serialization is to use the *NonSerializedAttribute* class to tag members that you do not want to serialize, as shown below. This is somewhat analogous to marking a field as *transient* when you use the JDK.

```
/** @attribute SerializableAttribute() */
public class Widget
{
    private int size; // Serialized

    /** @attribute NonSerializedAttribute()    */
    private FileStream fs; // Not serialized
    ⋮
}
```

You must prefix each member variable that you do not want to be serialized with this attribute. After deserialization occurs, the member variable will be uninitialized and should be assigned before use.

Advanced Serialization

You've seen how basic serialization is performed and controlled using attributes. But at times you'll need more control over how an object or a collection of objects is serialized and deserialized. We'll look at this next.

Customizing Serialization

You can influence the format of the serialization stream used to serialize an object by implementing the *System.Runtime.Serialization.ISerializable* interface. This is useful if you need to perform some additional or nonstandard processing as part of the serialization process. A large number of classes in the .NET Framework Class Library implement the *ISerializable* interface.

For example, consider the *FileStream* member variable in the *Widget* class discussed in the previous section. By default, it is pointless to preserve the state of variables such as this because the state is transitory—once the context changes (when the object is deserialized into another process), file handles and the like become meaningless. For this reason, the member variable was tagged with *NotSerializedAttribute*. On the other hand, using custom serialization, you could instead save the name of the file that the *FileStream* member was using as part of the serialization stream. On deserialization, you could read the name of this file back in from the stream, open the file, and point the *FileStream* member variable at it (all with some suitable error checking, of course). The *Widget* class (in the Widget.jsl sample file in the CustomSerialization project) illustrates one way of providing this functionality.

The *Widget* class wraps a *FileStream* object in such a way that it can be used to manipulate a file and be serialized, and when the object is deserialized the *FileStream* is recreated and restored to the state it was in; if you read from the *FileStream* after deserialization, read operations will carry on from the point at which they left off prior to serialization. (You might see some interesting phenomena if the file itself changes in the intervening period, however!)

You should note a few key points about the *Widget* class. The first is that it is tagged with *SerializableAttribute*, just like any other serializable class. Second, it implements the *ISerializable* interface. The class contains three private member variables: a *FileStream* variable called *fs*, a *String* that holds the filename, and a *long* variable called *offset* that records the position in the *FileStream* when serialization occurs:

```
import System.*;
import System.IO.*;
import System.Runtime.Serialization*;
```

```
/** @attribute SerializableAttribute() */
public class Widget implements ISerializable
{
   private FileStream fs;
   private String filename;
   private long offset;
   ⋮
}
```

The *Widget* class provides methods for opening a file stream over a named file (*OpenStream*), returning a handle to the file stream (*GetStream*), and closing the file stream (*CloseStream*). These methods are simply there to give the *Widget* class some functionality and play no part in the serialization process.

The *ISerializable* interface comprises a single method called *GetObjectData*, which is called by the formatter when it decides to serialize the object. Before invoking *GetObjectData*, the formatter will have performed some initialization, set up some data structures, and written out data such as the assembly information to the serialization stream. Two parameters are passed to *GetObjectData*: a *SerializationInfo* object and a *StreamingContext* structure:

```
public void GetObjectData(SerializationInfo info, StreamingContext context)
{
⋮
}
```

The *SerializationInfo* parameter provides controlled access to the serialization stream. It exposes methods for writing to this stream and reading data back from it (for deserialization). For serialization, the most useful method is *AddValue*. This method, which is heavily overloaded, writes a name and data pair out to the stream. For example, the following statement outputs the member variable *fileName* and associates it with the name "*File Name*":

```
Info.AddValue("File Name", fileName);
```

You can send whatever data you need to the serialization stream—you simply give each item a unique but meaningful name (which does not have to be the same as the name of the variable) so you can identify it when the object is deserialized. The *Widget* class also calculates the offset of the current position in the *FileStream* and serializes it with the name "*Offset*":

```
offset = fs.get_Position();
info.AddValue("Offset", offset);
```

The *FileStream* variable, *fs*, is not saved because it can be re-created from the filename and the offset when deserialization occurs. The *StreamingContext* parameter to *GetObjectData* passes context information that can be useful to the serialization process. The *StreamingContext* structure also contains a *State* property. You can query this property to determine the destination of the serialization stream—it could be a local file, an application in another application domain, an application on a remote machine, or someplace else. The way you perform serialization might vary depending on the ultimate destination (such as transforming the name of the file to reference a network share if the *Widget* object is being sent to a process running on another computer).

It might seem odd that *ISerializable* contains only a method for serializing an object and not a corresponding method for deserializing the object. In fact, deserialization is performed by providing a constructor that takes a *SerializationInfo* parameter and a *StreamingContext* parameter, just like the *GetObjectData* method. Conventionally, this constructor is private. (You're unlikely to ever want to call it explicitly.) If you omit this constructor, the object cannot be deserialized.

```
private Widget(SerializationInfo info, StreamingContext context)
{
⋮
}
```

Serialization Surrogates

It is possible for one class to take responsibility for serializing and deserializing objects of another class. Such classes are referred to as *serialization surrogates*. A serialization surrogate must implement the *System.Runtime.Serialization.ISerializationSurrogate* interface. This interface contains two methods, *GetObjectData* and *SetObjectData*:

```
public void GetObjectData(Object obj, SerializationInfo info,
   StreamingContext context)
{
   ⋮
}

public Object SetObjectData(Object obj, SerializationInfo
   info, StreamingContext context, ISurrogateSelector selector)
{
   ⋮
}
```

The *GetObjectData* method is similar to that of the *ISerializable* interface, except that it takes an additional *Object* parameter that indicates the object to be serialized. *SetObjectData* is called during deserialization. It is passed an empty object and can use the data in the *SerializationInfo* parameter to populate this object.

A *SerializationSurrogate* is discovered and invoked through an *ISurrogateSelector* object, which is attached to the *SurrogateSelector* property of the formatter. (By default, this property is *null.*) *ISurrogateSelector* is an interface located in the *System.Runtime.Serialization* namespace, and the .NET Framework Class Library provides a default implementation in the *System.Runtime.Serialization.SurrogateSelector* class that you can use as-is or extend for your own purposes. An *ISurrogateSelector* links surrogates together in a list and can iterate through this list to search for a surrogate that is capable of serializing and deserializing an object of the type specified by the formatter object. You can add a *SerializationSurrogate* to this list by calling the *Add* method of the *SurrogateSelector* class (which is not part of the *ISurrogateSelector* interface). This method's parameters include the type of data the surrogate can handle:

```
public void AddSurrogate(Type type, StreamingContext context,
   ISerializationSurrogate surrogate);
```

You can remove a surrogate from the list by using the *RemoveSurrogate* method. You can even chain *SurrogateSelectors* together using the *ChainSelector* method of the *SurrogateSelector* class. (Again, this is not part of the *ISurrogateSelector* interface.) This allows the selector to forward queries for a matching surrogate to other selectors if it cannot find a match itself.

In the deserialization constructor, you read the contents of the serialization stream, extracting items using the names specified when the object was serialized. (You do not have to read the data back in the same order it was written.) You can also perform any other initialization needed. For example, the constructor in the *Widget* class populates the *offset* and *fileName* member variables and then creates a *FileStream* over the specified file, setting the read/write position to the location indicated by the offset variable. (There should be some error checking, but it is omitted here for clarity.)

```
private Widget(SerializationInfo info, StreamingContext context)
{
   offset = info.GetInt64("Offset");
   fileName = info.GetString("File Name");
```

```
    fs = new FileStream(fileName, FileMode.OpenOrCreate,
        FileAccess.ReadWrite);
    fs.set_Position(offset);
}
```

The *SerializationInfo* class provides a whole raft of *GetXXX* methods that you can use to extract data of different types from the serialization stream. The *Widget* constructor uses *GetString* and *GetInt64* (which returns a Java *long*).

Handling Object Graphs

The examples shown so far have been simple, inasmuch as the objects being serialized have been small and straightforward. However, you can serialize entire graphs of related objects using the same mechanism—as long as you're aware of some possible complications. A collection of objects, possibly of different types, might contain dependencies. For example, consider the extended version of the *Cake* class and the *Baker* class shown in the Cake.jsl and Baker.jsl sample files (in the GraphSerialization project), respectively. A *Baker* object encapsulates the details of the chef (currently just the name) that is responsible for creating and delivering the cake:

Baker.jsl

```
package GraphSerialization;
import System.*;

// Cake Baker class - each cake is assigned to a single Baker

/** @attribute SerializableAttribute() */

public class Baker
{
    private String name;

    public Baker(String bakerName)
    {
        this.name = bakerName;
    }

    /** @property */
    public String get_Name()
    {
        return this.name;
    }
}
```

The *Cake* class has two additional properties: an *ID* that allows a cake to be uniquely identified and a reference to the *Baker* who is baking it. The constructor populates the member variables that back these properties. Both properties are immutable: No self-respecting baker would consider assuming control of a partially baked cake started by another baker.

```
public class Cake
{
    ⋮
    // Cake data
    private String message;
    private int filling;
    private float size;
    private int shape;
    private String id;

    // Who baked the cake?
    private Baker baker;

    // Set defaults for size, shape, filling, and message
    // gives the cake the specified ID,
    // and assigns it to the specified Baker
    public Cake(String cakeID, Baker cakeBaker)
    {
        this.filling = Sponge;
        this.shape = Square;
        this.size = 8;
        this.message = "";
        this.id = cakeID;
        this.baker = cakeBaker;
    }

    // Properties
    /** @property */
    public Baker get_Baker()
    {
        return this.baker;
    }

    /** @property */
    public String get_ID()
    {
        return this.id;
    }
    ⋮
}
```

A typical application that manages information concerning *Bakers* and *Cakes* could employ a collection object such as a *System.Collections.Hashtable* to assemble them together. The *Kitchen* class (in Kitchen.jsl) is an example of just such an application:

```
public class Kitchen
{
   /** @attribute System.STAThread() */
   public static void main(String[] args)
   {

      // Create some bakers
      Baker diana = new Baker("Diana");
      Baker francesca = new Baker("Francesca");
      Baker james = new Baker("James");

      // Get the bakers to make some cakes
      Cake cake1 = new Cake("Cake1", diana);
      Cake cake2 = new Cake("Cake2", diana);
      Cake cake3 = new Cake("Cake3", francesca);
      Cake cake4 = new Cake("Cake4", james);

      // Store the baker and cake information in a Hashtable
      Hashtable kitchenData = new Hashtable();
      kitchenData.Add(diana.get_Name(), diana);
      kitchenData.Add(francesca.get_Name(), francesca);
      kitchenData.Add(james.get_Name(), james);
      kitchenData.Add(cake1.get_ID(), cake1);
      kitchenData.Add(cake2.get_ID(), cake2);
      kitchenData.Add(cake3.get_ID(), cake3);
      kitchenData.Add(cake4.get_ID(), cake4);
      ⋮
   }
}
```

The application can then serialize the *Hashtable* to a file to persist all this data:

```
// Serialize the hashtable to a file
BinaryFormatter formatter = new BinaryFormatter();
FileStream stream = new FileStream("Kitchen.bin", FileMode.Create,
   FileAccess.Write, FileShare.None);
formatter.Serialize(stream, kitchenData);
stream.Close();
```

Note You can serialize any collection as long as two conditions are met: first, the collection class itself is serializable, and second, the objects you have placed in it are all serializable. In our example, the *Hashtable* class implements *ISerializable*, so the first condition is met. Both the *Baker* and the *Cake* classes are tagged with *Serializable-Attribute* so the second condition is met also.

Rebuilding the hash table from the serialized stream is simply a matter of deserializing from the Kitchen.bin file. However, behind the scenes the deserialization process has a little more work to do. The issue lies with the *Baker* references in the *Cake* objects. Prior to serialization, the contents of the *kitchenData* hash table would have looked similar to the layout shown in Figure 10-1.

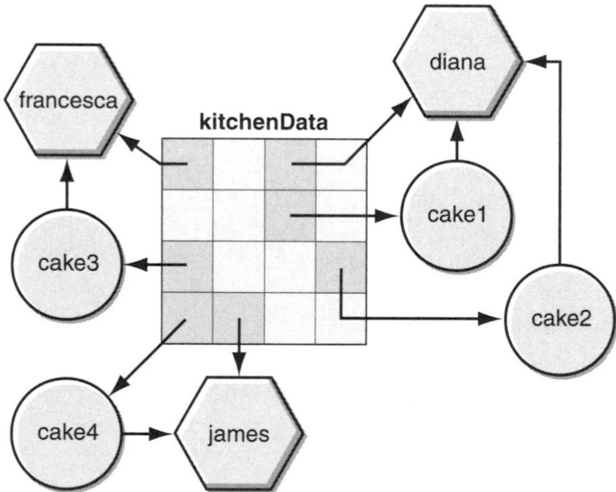

Figure 10-1 The layout of the *kitchenData* hash table

Notice the multiple references to the various *Baker* objects. Each cake stores a reference to the associated baker. On deserialization, the formatter must be clever enough to realize that once a *Baker* object has been instantiated, the references in the *Cake* objects should be fixed up to refer to this object and not cause the creation of new duplicate *Baker* objects, as shown in Figure 10-2.

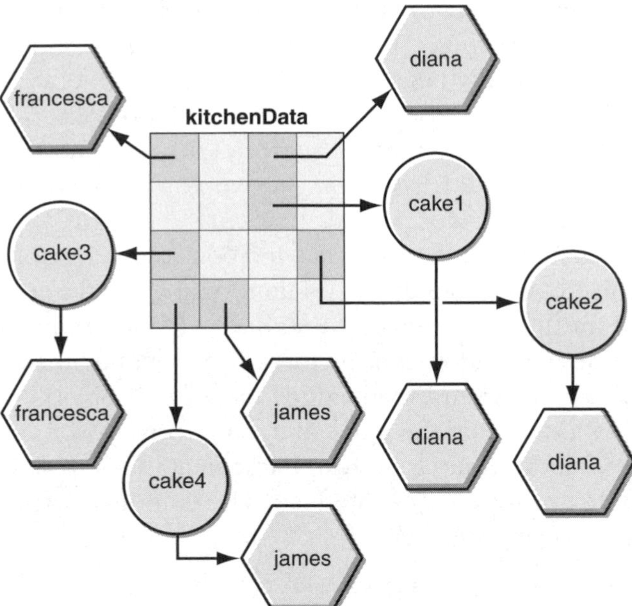

Figure 10-2 Chaos in the kitchen!

Fortunately, the default deserialization mechanism implemented by the .NET Framework classes has a degree of intelligence. As mentioned earlier, all formatters must implement the *IFormatter* interface. Although this interface is small (it has two methods, *Serialize* and *Deserialize*, along with three properties), you'll appreciate that any class implementing this interface has to do a lot of work, but much of this effort is the same regardless of the format being used. For this reason, the serialization architecture involves not just the formatter but also a number of helper objects. (You've already seen one—the *SerializationBinder* class.)

Two additional classes that are used throughout binary deserialization are *System.Runtime.Serialization.ObjectIDGenerator* and *System.Runtime.Serialization.ObjectManager*. During deserialization, the formatter calls the *ObjectManager* to determine whether a given object reference refers to an object that has already been deserialized or to an object that is still in the stream. The *ObjectManager* operates in conjunction with the *ObjectIDGenerator*. The *ObjectIDGenerator* generates a unique serial number for each object in the stream (keep in mind that such a serial number is not globally unique, only unique for the stream) as it is presented, but it can also determine whether the object has already been seen; if so, it passes back an indication that the object has been previously rebuilt. Determining the object's deserialization status is possible because the *ObjectIDGenerator* maintains an internal hash table of object references and serial numbers. If the *ObjectManager* indicates that the referenced object has already been deserialized, the formatter will resolve the reference immediately. Otherwise, it will register a fixup with the *ObjectManager* indicating that resolution must be performed later, after the referenced object has been read in. (The *ObjectManager* exposes a *DoFixups* method that the formatter can call to resolve these references.)

There is no guarantee of the order in which objects in a graph will be serialized or deserialized. Also note that at no time during the deserialization process will any default constructors be called. (If an object implements *ISerializable*, the deserialization constructor will be invoked, however.) There might well be occasions when the interdependencies of objects require some additional initialization beyond the scope of that performed by the formatter. To help you in this situation, your classes can implement the *System.Runtime.Serialization.IDeserializationCallback* interface. This interface specifies a single method with the following signature:

```
public void OnDeserialization(Object sender)
{
   // Place your initialization code here
   ⋮
}
```

At the end of the deserialization process, after every object has been reconstructed, the *ObjectManager* will call this method (which is actually an event delegate and is invoked by the formatter calling the *RaiseDeserializationEvent* method of the *ObjectManager*) on each object that implements the *IDeserializationCallback* interface.

There's a lot more to this process than we have space to cover here, but most of the time you don't need to know exactly what's happening as long as you're aware that the default deserialization mechanism should construct an object graph that's the same as the original. However, in case you ever feel the need to implement your own custom formatter, Microsoft has created the *System.Runtime.Serialization.Formatter* abstract class to assist you (as mentioned earlier in this chapter, in the sidebar titled "Implementing the *IFormatter* Interface"). This class contains much of the logic needed to interact with the *ObjectManager*, but remember that you must supply your own implementation of the *WriteXXX* helper methods that will handle outputting data to the serialization stream as well as the *Serialize* and *Deserialize* methods.

XML Serialization

Previous chapters have described the rationale behind XML and explained its benefits, such as portability, interoperability, and so on. Although version 1.1.4 of the JDK predates much of the XML support now available for Java, many recent packages developed by the Java Community Process program provide mechanisms for applications written in Java to convert objects into XML representations and back again. Perhaps the best known of these is the Java Architecture for XML Binding (JAXB), which is intended as a mechanism for serializing Java objects into an XML format. Related specifications include the Java API for XML-Based RPC (JAX-RPC) and the Java API for XML Messaging (JAXM). Both of these allow applications written in Java to send and receive XML messages using SOAP, either RPC-style or document-oriented. As of this writing, JAXB and JAX-RPC are works in progress, but they should be released by the end of 2002; JAXM 1.0 was finalized in the fall of 2001.

The .NET Framework Class Library has built-in support for converting objects to and from an XML format through the *XmlSerializer* class of the *System.Xml.Serialization* namespace. The *XmlSerializer* allows you to serialize and deserialize objects into XML documents while providing you with a fine degree of control over the shape of the output. Next, we'll look at how to use the *XmlSerializer* class and the supporting classes in the *System.Xml.Serialization* namespace.

XML Formatting

Chapter 5 showed you how to manually convert objects into XML and back again using Microsoft's implementation of DOM. The XmlSerializer class can automate much of this work, generating a default XML representation of an object or a graph of objects. The XMLSerialization class (in file XMLSerialization.jsl in the XMLSerialization project) shows a simple example of using an XmlSerializer object to serialize the CakeInfo.Cake class used earlier in this chapter to an XML file called CakeInfo.xml. By the way, the XmlSerializer class does not require that the object being serialized implement ISerializable or that it be tagged with SerializableAttribute (although you won't get an error if it is).

The two key lines in the *XMLSerialization* class are the statements that instantiate the *XmlSerializer* and serialize the object. The *XmlSerializer* class has several constructors, the simplest of which takes a *System.Type*. You can then use the *XmlSerializer* object to create XML documents that comprise serialized instances of this type. (The constructor uses reflection to determine the constitution of the type and initialize some internal data structures.) There are several ways to obtain type information from an object; the example uses the

GetType method, which is inherited from *System.Object*. The class being serialized must provide a default (no parameters) constructor:

```
Cake cake = new Cake();
⋮
XmlSerializer serializer = new XmlSerializer(cake.GetType());
```

You can then use the *Serialize* method of the *XmlSerializer* class to send an XML representation of an object to the appointed stream, much as you would the *BinaryFormatter* class:

```
Stream stream = new FileStream(...);
⋮
serializer.Serialize(stream, cake);
```

The *Serialize* method is overloaded, and you can serialize to a *TextWriter* or an *XmlWriter* as well as to a generic *Stream*.

If you're thinking that this all looks just a bit too easy, your suspicions might be justified. If you build and run the XMLSerialization project and then examine the results in the CakeInfo.xml file, you'll see the following:

```
<?xml version="1.0"?>
<Cake xmlns:xsd="http://www.w3.org/2001/XMLSchema"
xmlns:xsi="http://www.w3.org/2001/XMLSchema-instance" />
```

The serializer has written a perfectly valid XML document, but all it contains is the XML header and the namespace declaration. So what went wrong? The problem is that the *Cake* class contains no public instance member variables—XML serialization will output only public accessible instance data. (Static member variables are not considered part of the object's data and are omitted even if they're public, as they are with binary serialization.) As you'll recall, this is what the *Cake* class looks like:

```
public class Cake
{
   ⋮

   // Cake data
   private String message;
   private short filling;
   private short size;
   private short shape;
   ⋮
}
```

Although the *XMLSerializer* class will not read private data, it will make use of properties. If you edit the *Cake* class and uncomment the *@property* directives (the XMLSerialization project contains a copy of the *Cake* class that you can edit), rebuild the *Cake* project, and execute the *XMLSerialization* class again, you should notice the difference in the CakeInfo.xml file that is produced:

```
<?xml version="1.0"?>
<Cake xmlns:xsd="http://www.w3.org/2001/XMLSchema"
xmlns:xsi="http://www.w3.org/2001/XMLSchema-instance">
   <Filling>1</Filling>
   <Message>Bon Voyage</Message>
   <Shape>1</Shape>
   <Size>12</Size>
</Cake>
```

The key point to learn from this little lesson is that XML serialization will serialize public member variables and data that's accessible through properties, but it will not serialize data that can be read only by using regular methods. The XML deserialization process is similar—it will reconstitute an object only through its public member variables and properties. What happens if a property is read-only? XML serialization will allow data to be serialized, but it cannot be used by XML deserialization when populating an object.

Tip Don't expose a public field as a property or it will be serialized twice!

Serializing Graphs as XML

You can also serialize graphs of multiple objects, such as the list of *Cakes* and *Bakers* discussed earlier, using the *XmlSerializer* class. The contents of a container object, such as a collection (an object that implements the *ICollection* interface), will be serialized automatically as long as some conditions are met; the *Add* method must take a single parameter, and the *Item* method must take a single integer parameter. This is true for many of the collection types, but not for the *Hashtable* class because the *Add* method takes multiple parameters and the *Item* method takes an *Object* rather than an integer. This means you cannot initialize an *XmlSerializer* using a *Hashtable*. (You'll get an *InvalidOperationException* when the *XmlSerializer* class attempts to reflect the *Hashtable* object.) Instead, you can use an *ArrayList*, which is less functional but allows you to at least collect objects of different types together.

In addition to selecting an appropriate collection type, you must of course ensure that the contents of the collection themselves meet the XML serialization requirements described in the previous section. Each class *must supply a default constructor*, and you should provide a means of accessing the contents of the class through publicly available members or properties. You can control the format of the output and the namespaces used by applying the various *Xml Attribute* classes to your code. Some of these will be described later in this chapter.

To serialize a collection or array, you must also supply information to the *XmlSerializer* object about the type of the collection and the type or types of the contents. For example, consider the situation where the object being serialized is an *ArrayList* and the contents are *Cake* and *Baker* objects. The *XmlSerializer* class supplies a constructor for just such an eventuality—it expects the type of the containing class and an array of types describing the classes comprising the contents:

```
Type[] extraTypes = new Type[2];
extraTypes[0] = Type.GetType("Baker");
extraTypes[1] = Type.GetType("Cake");
XmlSerializer serializer = new
   XmlSerializer(Type.GetType("System.Collections.ArrayList"), extraTypes);
```

You can then create a stream and serialize to that stream, much as before.

Namespace and Type Handling

The default namespaces added to the XML generated by the *XmlSerializer* are *xmlns:xsd* (*http://www.w3.org/2001/XMLSchema*) and *xmlns:xsi* (*http://www.w3.org/2001/XMLSchema-instance*). You can override this behavior by creating an *XmlSerializerNamespaces* object and populating it with a list of namespaces and aliases. To attach the namespace *http://www.fourthcoffee.com/xmlcakes* to the XML output and give it the alias *fc*, you would create the following *System.Xml.Serialization.XmlSerializerNamespace* object:

```
XmlSerializerNamespaces nameSpaces = new XmlSerializerNamespaces();
nameSpaces.Add("fc", "http://www.fourthcoffee.com/xmlcakes");
```

An *XmlSerializerNamespace* can contain a list of several namespaces. The *Add* method simply appends a namespace to the list it holds. To emit the namespace information when the XML is generated, you must invoke a variant of the *Serialize* method:

```
serializer.Serialize(stream, cake, nameSpaces);
```

The third parameter is the list of namespaces. The result of this command is an XML file containing the following:

```
<?xml version="1.0"?>
<Cake xmlns:fc="http://www.fourthcoffee.com/xmlcakes">
  <Filling>1</Filling>
```

```
  <Message>Bon Voyage</Message>
  <Shape>1</Shape>
  <Size>12</Size>
</Cake>
```

For this effort to be totally meaningful, you must also tag the elements of the XML document with the namespace prefix. You can do this using a *System.Xml.Serialization.XmlTypeAttribute* applied to the *Cake* class:

```
/** @attribute XmlTypeAttribute(Namespace=
"http://www.fourthcoffee.com/xmlcakes")
 */
public class Cake
{
⋮
}
```

The *Namespace* parameter should be the same as one of the namespaces added to the *XmlSerializerNamespace* object in order for the appropriate alias to be applied. Otherwise, the full namespace specified in the *XmlTypeAttribute* will be output. The result should look like this:

```
<?xml version="1.0"?>
<Cake xmlns:fc="http://www.fourthcoffee.com/xmlcakes">
  <fc:Filling>1</fc:Filling>
  <fc:Message>Bon Voyage</fc:Message>
  <fc:Shape>1</fc:Shape>
  <fc:Size>12</fc:Size>
</Cake>
```

You can also change the name of the XML type itself. This is especially useful if the class name is not a legal XML identifier, as defined by W3C. If you want the type to be named *FondantArt* rather than *Cake*, you can use the *TypeName* parameter of the *XmlTypeAttribute*:

```
/** @attribute XmlTypeAttribute(TypeName="FondantArt",
Namespace="http://www.fourthcoffee.com/xmlcakes") */
public class Cake
{
    ⋮
}
```

As a further step, you can override the name, namespace, and other information for an individual element in a class using a *System.Xml.Serialization.XmlElementAttribute*. You can apply this attribute to public member variables and to property accessor methods. For example, to change the element name and namespace for the *Message* element of the *Cake* class, you can use the following code:

```
/** @attribute XmlTypeAttribute(TypeName="FondantArt",
Namespace="http://www.fourthcoffee.com/xmlcakes") */
public class Cake
{
    ⋮
    /** @property */
    /** @attribute XmlElementAttribute(ElementName="Greeting",
    Namespace="http://www.fourthcoffee.com/greeting")    */
    public String get_Message()
    {
        return this.message;
    }
⋮
}
```

The results of these changes are shown below:

```
<?xml version="1.0"?>
<FondantArt xmlns:fc="http://www.fourthcoffee.com/xmlcakes">
  <fc:Filling>1</fc:Filling>
  <fc:Greeting>Bon Voyage</fc:Greeting>
  <fc:Shape>1</fc:Shape>
  <fc:Size>12</fc:Size>
</FondantArt>
```

Controlling Serialization

Besides the *XmlTypeAttribute*, the *System.Xml.Serialization* namespace contains a couple of other attributes that you can use to govern the format of the XML generated by the serialization process. The *XmlRootAttribute* allows you to identify a class as forming the root element of an XML document, which is useful primarily if you're defining classes that contain nonprimitive public members, effectively defining a data hierarchy. The class at the top of the hierarchy can be tagged with *XmlRootAttribute*, and you can specify a namespace and an element name. (The default is the same as the name of the class.) You can also indicate the XSD data type that should be used when generating an XML document. This set of possibilities is illustrated by the various classes in the XMLGraph project, which serializes a graph of cakes and bakers (like the binary example shown earlier).

The *KitchenData* class (in KitchenData.jsl) exposes pairs of the *Baker* and *Cake* classes through public properties. The *Baker* class is available in Baker.jsl, and the *Cake* class is found in Cake.jsl. Both classes have been modified for this project. The *KitchenData* class is shown here:

```
/** @attribute XmlRootAttribute(Namespace="http://www.fourthcoffee.com/
xmlcakes", ElementName="Kitchen") */
public class KitchenData
```

```
{
   private Baker baker;
   private Cake cake;

   /** @property */
   public void set_Baker(Baker baker)
   {
      this.baker = baker;
   }

   /** @property */
   public Baker get_Baker()
   {
      return this.baker;
   }

   /** @property */
   public void set_Cake(Cake cake)
   {
      this.cake = cake;
   }

   /** @property */
   public Cake get_Cake()
   {
      return this.cake;
   }
}
```

The following code fragment from the *main* method of the *Kitchen* class creates, populates, and serializes a *KitchenData* object to a file called Kitchen.xml:

```
// Create a baker
Baker diana = new Baker("Diana");

// Get the baker to make a cake
Cake cake1 = new Cake("Cake1", diana);
cake1.ID = "cake1";
cake1.message = "Happy Birthday";

// Store the baker and cake in a KitchenData object
KitchenData kitchen = new KitchenData();
kitchen.baker = diana;
kitchen.cake = cake1;

// Serialize the KitchenData object to a file
FileStream stream = new FileStream("Kitchen.xml", FileMode.Create,
```

```
   FileAccess.Write, FileShare.None);
XmlSerializerNamespaces nameSpaces = new XmlSerializerNamespaces();

XmlSerializer serializer = new
   XmlSerializer(Type.GetType(kitchen.ToString()));
nameSpaces.Add("fc", "http://www.fourthcoffee.com/xmlcakes");
serializer.Serialize(stream, kitchen, nameSpaces);
stream.Close();
```

The resulting XML file should resemble the following:

```
<?xml version="1.0" ?>
<fc:Kitchen xmlns:fc="http://www.fourthcoffee.com/xmlcakes">
  <fc:Baker>
    <fc:Name>Diana</fc:Name>
  </fc:Baker>
  <fc:Cake>
    <fc:Baker>
      <fc:Name>Diana</fc:Name>
    </fc:Baker>
    <fc:Filling>0</fc:Filling>
    <fc:Id>cake1</fc:Id>
    <fc:Message>Happy Birthday</fc:Message>
    <fc:Shape>0</fc:Shape>
    <fc:Size>8</fc:Size>
  </fc:Cake>
</fc:Kitchen>
```

You can use the *XmlIgnoreAttribute* to specify that a field or property (the *get* accessor) in a class should not be included in the serialization stream. For example, the following code will cause the *Id* property to be omitted when the *Cake* class is serialized:

```
public class Cake
{
   private String id;
   ⋮

   /** @attribute XmlIgnoreAttribute()    */
   /** @property */
   public String get_Id()
   {
      return this.id;
   }
   ⋮
}
```

Deserializing an XML Stream

The *XmlSerializer* class provides a *Deserialize* method that you can invoke to read an XML stream and use to create and populate objects. You can deserialize from a generic stream, a *TextReader*, or an *XmlReader*. To deserialize a *KitchenData* object containing the nested *Baker* and *Cake* objects from the file Kitchen.xml (created in the previous example), you can simply open a file stream, instantiate an *XmlSerializer*, and call *Deserialize*:

```
FileStream stream = new FileStream("Kitchen.xml", FileMode.Open, FileAccess.Rea
d, FileShare.Read);
XmlSerializer serializer = new
   XmlSerializer(Type.GetType("XMLGraph.KitchenData"));
KitchenData kitchen = (KitchenData)serializer.Deserialize(stream);
stream.Close();
```

When you get it right, XML deserialization is almost trivial, but getting it right relies on you having a valid XML file and making sure that the class or classes you're attempting to deserialize into are compatible with the contents of that file. If you take care of the first requirement (you might have to manually edit the file if it needs fixing!), you can meet the second one by using the XSD.exe command-line tool supplied with the .NET Framework Class Library. You can use the XSD utility to reverse-engineer a schema from an XML file and then create a class definition from the resulting XSD file.

The simplest way to generate an XSD schema is to use Microsoft Visual Studio .NET. You can add the XML file to a project, display it, and choose Create Schema from the XML menu on the toolbar. Figure 10-3 shows the schema created for the Kitchen.xml file (Kitchen.xsd).

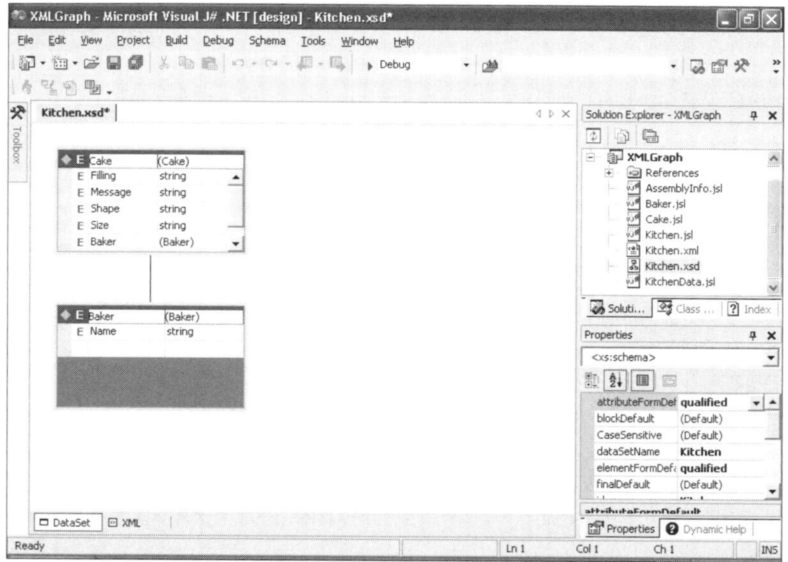

Figure 10-3 Kitchen.XSD schema in Visual Studio .NET

Having created an XML Schema, you can use the command following line to generate a class that corresponds to this schema.

```
xsd Kitchen.xsd /c /l:cs
```

If you're programming in Java, you'll face a slight problem—the XSD utility will output code in a limited choice of languages: Visual Basic .NET, C#, or JScript. Java is not yet an option! Just to prove that XSD works, we generated the file below from Kitchen.xsd using the C# option. (It looks a bit like Java if you squint.)

Kitchen.cs

```
//------------------------------------------------------------------------------
// <autogenerated>
//     This code was generated by a tool.
//     Runtime Version: 1.0.3705.209
//
//     Changes to this file may cause incorrect behavior and will be lost
//     if the code is regenerated.
// </autogenerated>
//------------------------------------------------------------------------------

//
// This source code was auto-generated by xsd, Version=1.0.3705.209.
//
using System.Xml.Serialization;
```

```
/// <remarks/>
[System.Xml.Serialization.XmlTypeAttribute(Namespace="http://www.fourthcof-
fee.com/xmlcakes")]
[System.Xml.Serialization.XmlRootAttribute("Kitchen", Namespace="http://
www.fourthcoffee.com/xmlcakes", IsNullable=false)]
public class Kitchen {

    /// <remarks/>
    [System.Xml.Serialization.XmlElementAttribute("Cake")]
    public KitchenCake[] Items;
}

/// <remarks/>
[System.Xml.Serialization.XmlTypeAttribute(Namespace="http://www.fourthcof-
fee.com/xmlcakes")]
public class KitchenCake {

    /// <remarks/>
    public string Filling;

    /// <remarks/>
    public string Message;

    /// <remarks/>
    public string Shape;

    /// <remarks/>
    public string Size;

    /// <remarks/>
    [System.Xml.Serialization.XmlElementAttribute("Baker")]
    public KitchenCakeBaker[] Baker;
}

/// <remarks/>
[System.Xml.Serialization.XmlTypeAttribute(Namespace="http://www.fourthcof-
fee.com/xmlcakes")]
public class KitchenCakeBaker {

    /// <remarks/>
    public string Name;
}
```

If the input stream does not match what is expected, the deserialization process will attempt to recover as best it can, but as a result one or more objects might be set to *null* when the procedure has completed. To help you handle these situations, the *XmlSerializer* class publishes four events that you can trap. These events are raised when certain conditions arise. They are

- ***UnknownAttribute*** This occurs if an attribute whose type is not known is presented in the input stream.
- ***UnknownElement*** Likewise, this occurs if an unknown element appears in the input stream.
- ***UnknownNode*** This occurs if an unexpected node appears.
- ***UnreferencedObject*** This applies only to SOAP messages and occurs when the *XmlSerializer* finds a type definition in the input stream that is not actually used anywhere else in the input stream.

You can catch these events by creating an appropriate delegate and referencing a method to be executed when the event is raised. The *System.Xml.Serialization* namespace supplies a delegate for each of these events: *XmlAttributeEventHandler*, *XmlElementEventHandler*, *XmlNodeEventHandler*, and *UnreferencedObjectEventHandler*.

You subscribe to an event by calling the apposite *add* event method of the *XmlSerializer* object. The following code shows how to intercept the *UknownElement* event:

```
private void handleXmlElementEvent(Object sender,
   XmlElementEventArgs e)
{
   ⋮
}
⋮
XmlSerializer serializer = new XmlSerializer(...);
serializer.add_UnknownElement(new
   XmlElementEventHandler(handleXmlElementEvent));
KitchenData kitchen = (KitchenData)serializer.Deserialize(stream);
```

The *EventArgs* parameter passed to the event handler contains information about the unexpected element and the position in the input stream at which it occurred. You can use this information to take some corrective action or record the fact that some unexpected input was received.

Summary

This chapter provided insight into how to use the serialization and deserialization features of the .NET Framework to construct representations of objects that can be transported in a portable manner. The *BinaryFormatter* is useful for creating compact replicas of objects, including all private members, and the *XmlSerializer* is valuable for generating XML representations of objects. You saw the different components that comprise the binary serialization architecture, and you should now understand how to effect your own customized binary serialization by implementing the *ISerializable* interface.

The XML serialization mechanisms are convenient and quick and can also be tailored by applying the various XML attribute classes.

11

.NET Remoting

The Microsoft .NET Remoting architecture lets you construct distributed solutions based on high-level network abstractions such as remote procedure calls (RPCs), serialization, and messaging. You can create and deploy server applications almost anywhere on your network, or even over the Internet, and connect to them from client applications reliably and securely using the infrastructure supplied by the .NET platform.

Remoting uses the familiar concept of proxy objects. Clients communicate with proxies, which in turn communicate with real server objects. The proxy hides the complexities of distributed activation from the client, making a remote object as easy to access as a local one. You can modify the way in which proxies send requests from a client to a server by implementing a custom marshaling strategy. Server objects can be hosted by .NET applications or by Microsoft Internet Information Services (IIS) version 6.0 or later. The implementation of the .NET Remoting infrastructure uses TCP and HTTP as transport protocols. If you need to use a different protocol—for communicating with a legacy server, for example—you can implement your own communications channel.

The mechanisms used by .NET Remoting are very flexible. You can extend them if the default implementation of the various components does not match your requirements. In this chapter, we'll look at how you can use the .NET Remoting architecture for communicating between clients and remote servers and how you can customize it.

The Common Language Runtime Remoting Architecture

The Remoting architecture of the common language runtime allows you to make remote method calls and access remote objects. Before we look at how remoting works, we first need to consider exactly what .NET means by a *remote object*.

Remote Objects

In the traditional programming model, a remote object is an object that's running in a different process than the one invoking it. The two processes can be on the same machine or on different machines. The RPC infrastructure provided by many environments hides the fact that an object is remote through the use of proxies and stubs (as described in Chapter 1). But .NET uses application domains to isolate applications, and several application domains might be contained in the same process. In .NET, any method call that crosses an application domain boundary is considered an RPC.

Another complication is the *context*, which is used to group objects that share certain common properties—synchronization attributes, transactions, and thread affinity, for example. Chapter 8 discussed how objects can be marked as being context-bound or context-agile. A context-agile object can be accessed freely from any other context in the same application domain. Context-bound objects can be accessed directly by other objects in the same context, but objects in other contexts must use proxies to access a context-bound object—even if they reside in the same application domain.

The designers at Microsoft decided to build a generic remoting architecture that employs the same basic principles whether a remote method being invoked is in the same application domain but different context as the caller, in a different application domain in the same process, in a different process, or on a completely different machine. The architecture uses pluggable, customizable components that can be optimized for these scenarios.

As we discussed in 'sc, remote objects come in two varieties: those that can change their state and those that are immutable. You might argue that all objects can change their state, but sometimes what you want is a copy of an object for analysis or reporting purposes. For example, an automated teller machine (ATM) might be asked to display the details of recent transactions applied to a customer's bank account, and the ATM will not modify this data (you hope!). Once the copy has been created, the original data can change to its heart's content (a pending account transaction can be cancelled, for example), but these changes will not be reflected in the copy. A new, updated copy would have to be generated for you to see the most recent version of the data.

Similarly, if the local copy somehow changes, the original data will not change (just as writing "deposit $1,000,000" on your bank statement will not suddenly add $1,000,000 to your account, no matter how much you'd like it to).

In the .NET Remoting architecture, local object copies are called *marshal-by-value objects*. They represent a snapshot of the state of an object at a given point in time.

Note Copies of objects are useful, but their usefulness depends on how they are used. Some design patterns (such as those used when you program with ADO.NET *DataSet* objects) use what are essentially marshal-by-value objects to perform batch updates. Chapter 7 explained how an ADO.NET *DataSet* can contain several rows of data retrieved from a database and how this data can be modified by an application. When the application has finished making the changes, it can send the updates back to the database *en masse*. This approach can be efficient in terms of network bandwidth, but the logic involved when you propagate the updates to the database can be tortuous because you have to take into account that another application might have already modified the data. You should not blindly overwrite such updates.

As an alternative to the marshal-by-value object, you can use the *marshal-by-reference object*. A marshal-by-reference object is an object whose value can be dynamic, and all applications that use it will see (or be able to make) changes to its state. Applications do not hold a copy of the object; instead, they retain a reference to the original object living in its own application domain. Every time an application needs to modify the object, it must access it through the reference. A proxy object that hides the underlying mechanics usually provides the reference.

You can compare Figures 11-1 and 11-2 to see the differences between marshal-by-value and marshal-by-reference objects. In Figure 11-1, an object created in the server application domain is accessed using a marshal-by-value object in the client application domain. This causes a complete copy of the object to be instantiated in the client, including all of its fields. If the value of *field1* changes in the object in the server application domain, the value of *field1* will remain unchanged (at 99) in the object in the client application domain.

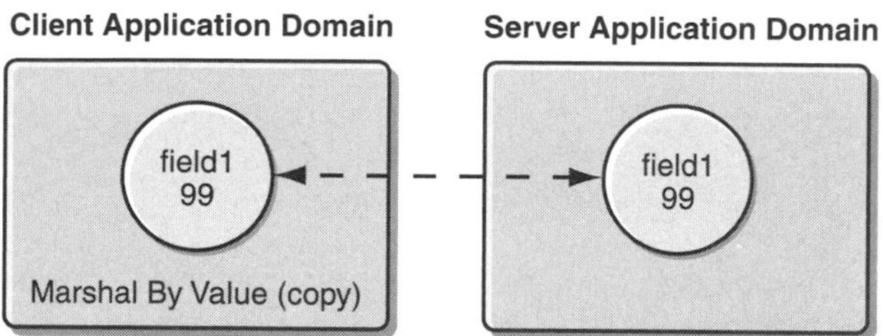

Figure 11-1 A marshal-by-value object

In Figure 11-2, a similar object in the server application domain is accessed by using a marshal-by-reference object in the client application domain. This time, the object is not copied to the client application domain; instead, a proxy object is created that can be used to access the original object in the server application domain. If the value of *field1* changes in the object in the server application domain, this new value will be visible through the proxy in the client application domain.

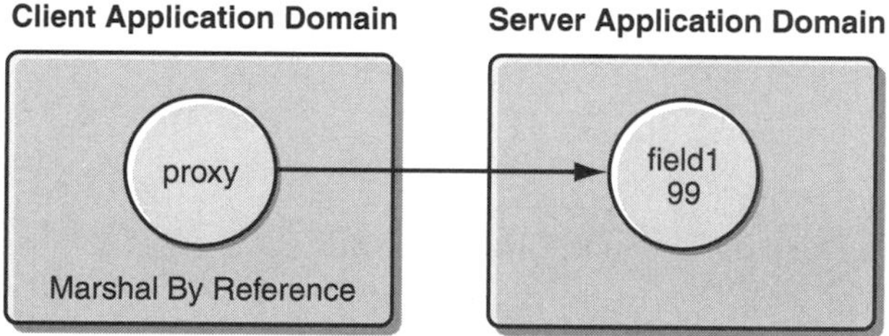

Figure 11-2 A marshal-by-reference object

Performing updates by using reference objects is less involved (at the application programming level, at least) than updating by using value objects, but the drawback is that every access to a reference object involves using the proxy, which can in turn require transmitting data over a network (depending on the relative location of the application domains involved). Even accessing other objects in the same application domain can require a proxy if the objects in question occupy different contexts, although the .NET infrastructure performs a number of optimizations to minimize the overhead in this situation.

Marshal-by-value objects must be serializable—that is, they must be marked with the *SerializableAttribute*, and they can implement the *ISerializable* interface. (See Chapter 10 for details.) Marshal-by-reference objects extend the *System.MarshalByRefObject* class, which is an abstract class that provides default implementations of some of the mechanisms required for managing remote references. (The nearest functional equivalent in the JDK is the *java.rmi.server.RemoteObject* class.)

Marshal-by-reference objects are a common feature in .NET Remoting. The sample file CakeUtils.jsl (in the CakeUtils project) shows a variation on the *CakeInfo* class used in earlier chapters. The class exposes the single method, *FeedsHowMany*, which establishes how many people a cake of given dimensions, shape, and filling will serve. The class extends the *MarshalByRefObject* class, allowing it to be remoted.

If you download and examine this sample, you'll notice that the *FeedsHowMany* method is no longer static. This is because static methods behave differently from instance methods in a remoting environment. We'll explore the reasons for this later in the chapter. The method also prints a message ("Calculating...") on screen while it's running so you can observe where objects of this type are actually instantiated.

The .NET Remoting Model

Remote objects require a context and an application domain to execute in. You can create your own server application to act as a host, or you can use IIS. For the time being, we'll look at building your own server application and consider IIS hosting later.

A host server application registers a channel for listening to incoming client requests. A channel transports messages between the server application and clients. The .NET Framework Class Library has two basic types of channel available, but you can also define your own custom channels. The two built-in channels are *System.Runtime.Remoting.Channels.Tcp.TcpChannel,* which uses TCP for transmitting and receiving messages, and *System.Runtime.Remoting.Channels.Http.HttpChannel,* which is based on HTTP. You must add a reference to the assembly System.Runtime.Remoting.dll to use the objects of the *System.Runtime.Remoting* namespace (and its child namespaces).

By default, TCP channels package messages and data using binary encoding and HTTP channels use SOAP (but you can override this behavior). These channels are two-way—you can use them to both send and receive messages. Specialized versions are also available: *TcpClientChannel*, *TcpServerChannel*, *HttpClientChannel*, and *HttpServerChannel.* These are intended for use only at the client or the server end, as their names imply.

The server application registers a channel with the static *RegisterChannel* method of the *System.Runtime.Remoting.Channels.ChannelServices* class. The following code fragment creates and registers a TCP channel that listens to port 6000. Note that you cannot create more than one TCP channel using the same port on the same computer at the same time.

```
import System.Runtime.Remoting.Channels.*;
import System.Runtime.Remoting.Channels.Tcp*;
:
ChannelServices.RegisterChannel(new TcpChannel(6000));
```

The next step depends on whether the objects being remoted are instantiated by the server or by the client. (The reasons for choosing one option over the other will be discussed shortly.) In the case of server-activated objects, the server application must register the type or types of objects that it can create and manage, together with an activation mode. We'll also look at activation modes in more detail later in the chapter. For now, suffice it to say that when you use server-activated objects, the server governs the lifetimes of those objects and multiple clients can share such objects; client-activated objects, in contrast, are managed by a single client and are private to that client—they cannot be shared.

The server registers object types using the static *RegisterWellKnownServiceType* method of the *System.Runtime.Remoting.RemotingConfiguration* class. This method also expects a unique URI to identify the object type. Any client that knows the URI can instantiate objects of the specified class on the server. (This is what we mean when we say that a service type is *well-known.*) Internally, the remoting infrastructure maintains a table of types, URIs, and activation modes. Each type that is registered is added to this table. This table is consulted by the remoting infrastructure when a client attempts to gain access to a well-known object.

The following code registers the *CakeInfo* class of the *CakeUtils* namespace. This namespace is implemented in the CakeUtils.dll assembly. The URI specified is *CakeInfo.rem*; it is customary to attach the suffix *rem* to remote object URIs. The final parameter is the activation mode. You should specify one of the values from the *System.Runtime.Remoting.WellKnownObjectMode* enumeration. (More on this later.)

```
import System.Runtime.Remoting.*;
:
RemotingConfiguration.RegisterWellKnownServiceType(
   Type.GetType("CakeUtils.CakeInfo, CakeUtils"),
   "CakeInfo.rem", WellKnownObjectMode.Singleton);
```

If the objects are client-activated, the client takes responsibility for creating and managing them and the server simply provides an environment in which they can execute. The types still have to be registered with the server, but the server does not publish a URI (the service types available are not well-known—a client must know which classes can be activated on the server) or specify an activation mode for them. The server can invoke the *RemotingConfiguration.RegisterActivatedServiceType* method to perform this task:

```
RemotingConfiguration.RegisterActivatedServiceType(
   Type.GetType("CakeUtils.CakeInfo, CakeUtils"));
```

Note You can register the same class as a well-known server-activated type and a client-activated type on the same server.

That is all the server host application needs to do. However, if the server terminates, the registered channel and service type information will be lost and the client will not be able to use it to activate remote objects. The main thread of a typical server application will therefore suspend itself quietly in some way until an administrator shuts it down. A completed host server application that implements server-activation is shown in the CakeServer.jsl sample file in the ServerActivatedTCPCakeSizeServer project.

A client application that wants to access a remote object must also create a channel and register it. The type of the channel should be the same as that used by the server. The client does not need to specify a port number for the TCP channel. Behind the scenes, the .NET Remoting infrastructure will create a client socket and dynamically allocate it a port number. If you do specify a port, you should select one that is not already in use; otherwise, an exception will be thrown by the Remoting infrastructure:

```
ChannelServices.RegisterChannel(new TcpChannel());
```

The client activates the remote object by using one of the static methods of the *System.Activator* class. The *GetObject* method is used to create a proxy that references a server-activated remote object. You specify the URI that was created when the type was registered on the server. The proxy itself is actually constructed on the client using the type information specified by the first parameter of the *GetObject* method, and it does not need to contact the server at this time, so no network traffic will be generated. The validity of the object URI is not checked until the first method call to the remote object occurs. Also, note that the proxy type returned by *GetObject* is *Object*, so you should cast it as appropriate.

```
CakeInfo ci =
   (CakeInfo)Activator.GetObject(Type.GetType("CakeUtils.cakeInfo,
   CakeUtils"), "tcp://localhost:6000/CakeInfo.rem");
```

Note If the server is running on a different computer than the client, you should replace *localhost* with the name of the server computer.

You use the *GetObject* method to access a server-activated object. On the other hand, the *CreateInstance* method of the *Activator* class constructs a new instance of a client-activated object on a remote server. *CreateInstance* is heavily overloaded. The version shown below specifies the type of the remote object, an array of constructor values, and an array of activation attributes. The array of constructor values is *null* in this case, which will cause the default constructor (with no parameters) to be invoked when the object is created on the server. If you supply real values in this array, the best-matching constructor that takes parameters of the same types as your list will be used instead. (For example, if you populate the array with an *int* and a *String*, the server will look for a constructor that takes an *int* and a *String*, in that order.) If no usable constructor can be found, a *MissingMethodException* will be thrown. The array of activation attributes should include a *UrlAttribute* specifying the address of the remote server. The *UrlAttribute* class is located in the *System.Runtime.Remoting.Activation* namespace.

```
CakeInfo ci = (CakeInfo)Activator.CreateInstance(
   Type.GetType("CakeUtils.CakeInfo, CakeUtils"), null,
   new System.Object[] {new UrlAttribute("tcp://localhost:6000")});
```

The *CreateInstance* method contacts the specified server, instantiates an object of the appropriate type, and returns a proxy that can be used to access that object. Once again, the value returned must be cast.

Whether *GetObject* or *CreateInstance* is used, the result is a proxy that exposes the same methods as the remote object. You can invoke these methods on the proxy, and they will be executed on the remote object. The listing in the CakeClient.jsl sample file in the ServerActivatedTCPCakeClient project is a client application that invokes a server-activated *CakeInfo* object. It calls the *FeedsHowMany* method using the proxy and prints the result.

You can verify that the *CakeInfo* object is executing remotely from the client by observing where the "Calculating…" message printed by the *CakeInfo* object is output—it should be displayed on the host server, as shown in Figure 11-3.

Figure 11-3 The console screen showing the host server output

Remote Exceptions

If the host application throws an exception while activating an object or executing one of its methods on behalf of a client, the client application will be notified of the exception and will also be supplied with a stack trace indicating where the error occurred on the server. This stack trace will often be lengthy, but it can make for interesting reading if you're keen to follow how messages are propagated from a server back to the client and see the various parts of the remoting infrastructure involved.

The stack dump shown below is an example of the error output of the client. The error was caused by the server not being able to locate the assembly containing the remote object class. To achieve this, we deliberately deleted the copy of the CakeUtils assembly in the ConfigTCPCakeSizeServer\bin\Debug folder (you'll see more of this example later) after compiling the remote server class. If you want to try this yourself, you must then run the server from the command line, because if you execute it in Visual Studio .NET, the IDE will notice that the assembly has been deleted and copy it again.

```
Exception communicating with server: System.IO.FileNotFoundException: File or
assembly name CakeUtils, or one of its dependencies, was not found.
File name: "CakeUtils"
```

```
Server stack trace:
   at System.Reflection.Assembly.nLoad(AssemblyName fileName, String codeBase,
Boolean isStringized, Evidence assemblySecurity, Boolean throwOnFileNotFound,
Assembly locationHint, StackCrawlMark& stackMark)
   at System.Reflection.Assembly.InternalLoad(AssemblyName assemblyRef, Boolean
 stringized, Evidence assemblySecurity, StackCrawlMark& stackMark)
   at System.Reflection.Assembly.InternalLoad(String assemblyString, Evidence
assemblySecurity, StackCrawlMark& stackMark)
   at System.Reflection.Assembly.Load(String assemblyString)
   at System.Runtime.Remoting.RemotingConfigInfo.LoadType(String typeName,
String assemblyName)
   at System.Runtime.Remoting.RemotingConfigInfo.StartupWellKnownObject(String
asmName, String svrTypeName, String URI, WellKnownObjectMode mode, Boolean
fReplace)
   at System.Runtime.Remoting.RemotingConfigInfo.StartupWellKnownObject(String
URI)
   at System.Runtime.Remoting.RemotingConfigHandler.CreateWellKnownObject(
String uri)
   at System.Runtime.Remoting.IdentityHolder.CasualResolveIdentity(String uri)
   at System.Runtime.Remoting.Messaging.MethodCall.ResolveType()
   at System.Runtime.Remoting.Messaging.MethodCall.ResolveMethod(Boolean bThrow
IfNotResolved)
   at System.Runtime.Remoting.Messaging.MethodCall..ctor(Object handlerObject,
BinaryMethodCallMessage smuggledMsg)
   at System.Runtime.Serialization.Formatters.Binary.BinaryMethodCall.ReadArray
(Object[] callA, Object handlerObject)
   at System.Runtime.Serialization.Formatters.Binary.ObjectReader.Deserialize(
HeaderHandler handler, __BinaryParser serParser, Boolean fCheck,
IMethodCallMessage methodCallMessage)
   at System.Runtime.Serialization.Formatters.Binary.BinaryFormatter.
Deserialize(Stream serializationStream, HeaderHandler handler, Boolean fCheck,
IMethodCallMessage methodCallMessage)
   at System.Runtime.Remoting.Channels.CoreChannel.DeserializeBinaryRequest
Message(String objectUri, Stream inputStream, Boolean bStrictBinding)
   at System.Runtime.Remoting.Channels.BinaryServerFormatterSink.ProcessMessage
(IServerChannelSinkStack sinkStack, IMessage requestMsg, ITransportHeaders
requestHeaders, Stream requestStream, IMessage& responseMsg, ITransportHeaders&
 responseHeaders, Stream& responseStream)

Exception rethrown at [0]:
   at System.Runtime.Remoting.Proxies.RealProxy.HandleReturnMessage(IMessage
reqMsg, IMessage retMsg)
   at System.Runtime.Remoting.Proxies.RealProxy.PrivateInvoke(MessageData&
msgData, Int32 type)
   at CakeUtils.CakeInfo.FeedsHowMany(Int16 diameter, Int16 shape, Int16
filling)
   at CakeSizeClient.CakeClient.main(String[] args) in C:\Temp\Chapter 11\
ConfigTCPCakeClient\CakeClient.jsl:line 25
```

```
Fusion log follows:
=== Pre-bind state information ===
LOG: DisplayName = CakeUtils
 (Partial)
LOG: Appbase = C:\Temp\Chapter 11\ConfigTCPCakeSizeServer\bin\Debug\
LOG: Initial PrivatePath = NULL
Calling assembly : (Unknown).
===

LOG: Policy not being applied to reference at this time (private, custom,
partial, or location-based assembly bind).
LOG: Post-policy reference: CakeUtils
LOG: Attempting download of new URL file:///C:/Temp/Chapter 11/ConfigTCPCake-
SizeServer/bin/Debug/CakeUtils.DLL.
LOG: Attempting download of new URL file:///C:/Temp/Chapter 11/ConfigTCPCake-
SizeServer/bin/Debug/CakeUtils/CakeUtils.DLL.
LOG: Attempting download of new URL file:///C:/Temp/Chapter 11/ConfigTCPCake-
SizeServer/bin/Debug/CakeUtils.EXE.
LOG: Attempting download of new URL file:///C:/Temp/Chapter 11/ConfigTCPCake-
SizeServer/bin/Debug/CakeUtils/CakeUtils.EXE.
```

The *ObjRef* Object and Proxies

The .NET Remoting architecture uses a pair of proxies on the client called the *TransparentProxy* and the *RealProxy*, each of which has a well-defined purpose. The reference returned to the client application when an object is activated is actually a *TransparentProxy* object. The *TransparentProxy* packages up a method call and its parameters into an *IMessage* object (an object that implements the *System.Runtime.Remoting.Messaging.IMessage* interface and is essentially a serializable representation of the method call) and passes it to the *RealProxy* object, which handles the actual marshaling and transmission of data. The proxy objects are constructed by the *GetObject* or *CreateInstance* method, using the type information supplied as parameters to these methods.

In the case of a well-known server-activated object, the client call to the *GetObject* method creates the proxy objects without needing to contact the server. However, if the remote object is client-activated, the *CreateInstance* method executed by the client will result in a message being transmitted to the server, which will then create and activate an object of the required type (assuming the server has registered the requested type). Depending on any context attributes specified in the metadata of the object type, the server might also need to create a new context to house the object. The remoting infrastructure on the server will then create an *ObjRef* object; this is a serializable representation of a remote object reference that can be passed from one context and application domain to another. An *ObjRef* contains the information needed to locate a remote object and create the appropriate proxy objects. The *ObjRef* is returned from the server to the *CreateInstance* method in the client, which uses it to create the *RealProxy and TransparentProxy* objects for communicating with the server before handing the *TransparentProxy* back to the client as the return value from *CreateInstance*.

The *TransparentProxy* object contains a list of all the methods and interfaces implemented by the remote object. When a method call is made through the *TransparentProxy*, the runtime intercepts and examines the call to determine whether it is valid and how remote the referenced object really is. If the remote object is in the same application domain and context as the client, it is not really remote, and the *TransparentProxy* will route the request directly to a local instance of the object. If the remote object is in the same application domain as the client but in a different context, the *TransparentProxy* will determine whether the remote object is context-agile. A context-agile remote object residing in the same application domain as the client can also be accessed directly. (By default, classes that directly inherit from *MarshalByRefObject* are context-agile.)

A remote object class can extend the *System.ContextBoundObject* class (which itself inherits from *MarshalByRefObject*), but such classes are not context-agile. Neither are classes whose metadata restricts them to a particular context, such as those that are tagged with *SynchronizationAttribute* (which was described in Chapter 8). Method calls to these objects will be forwarded on to the *RealProxy* object, as will calls to objects that are located in a different application domain. The *TransparentProxy* packages the method invocation, with its parameters, into an *IMessage* object and calls the *Invoke* method on the *RealProxy* object, passing this message as a parameter. The *RealProxy* does the real work of arranging for the data to be transported to its ultimate destination, which might be another context in the same application domain or in a different application domain, possibly over the network.

Messages, Channels, and Channel Sinks

Besides the proxies and the *ObjRef*, other items are involved in remoting that are mainly concerned with the physical transportation of data between the client and server application domains. Once the *RealProxy* object has been created, its task is to arrange for the requested method to be called on the remote object, using the information supplied by the *IMessage* object passed as a parameter to its *Invoke* method. (The *TransparentProxy* actually creates a *System.Runtime.Remoting.Messaging.MethodCall* object and passes it to the *RealProxy*; the *MethodCall* class implements the *IMessage* interface.) The *RealProxy* will route the message over the channel to the server, but before the message is transmitted it must be transformed into a format that the channel can handle.

Message transformation is achieved using *channel sinks*. A channel sink is a class that implements the *IClientChannelSink* or *IServerChannelSink* interface, depending on whether the sink is used to send or receive messages. The purpose of a channel sink is to examine the message object passed in, process it, and then forward the result to another sink for further processing or transmission. Channel sinks are linked into sink chains. The first sink in the sink chain on the client side is often the formatter sink. It is installed by the channel, and the type of the sink is determined by the type of the channel.

The *TcpChannel* class uses a *BinaryClientFormatterSink* object, which serializes data into a binary format using a *BinaryFormatter* object, as described in Chapter 10. The *HttpChannel* class employs a *SoapClientFormatterSink* object, which serializes data into XML using a *SoapFormatter* object. You can create your own custom sinks and arrange for them to be inserted into the sink chain, usually before the formatter sink (it is easier to manipulate the message before it is formatted), although you can insert them after the formatter sink if needed. Later in the chapter, we'll look at some scenarios showing why you might want to do this and how to customize the remoting infrastructure.

After the message has been formatted and processed by various channel sinks, it can be passed to a *transport sink*. The transport sink is the last sink in the chain on the client side, and it is responsible for physically sending the transformed data to the appropriate endpoint on the server using the protocol indicated by the channel (TCP or HTTP). The transport sink is an integral part of the channel object and cannot be extended or replaced (unless you create your own custom channel class). On the server side, the transport sink is the first in the chain, and it is responsible for receiving the message sent by the client.

Sinks are chained together on the server side much as they are on the client, and again you can inject your own custom sinks into the chain. The sink chain will also include a formatter sink, which is responsible for deserializing the message back into a recognizable *IMessage* object. The formatter sink will usually be a *BinaryServerFormatterSink* object or a *SoapServerFormatterSink* object, depending on the type of the channel.

The final sink on the server side is called the *stack builder sink*. (Strictly speaking, the stack builder sink is not a channel sink, and there might be other objects between the channel sink chain and the stack builder, as described later in this chapter.) The stack builder sink takes the deserialized *IMessage* object and uses it to construct a stack frame for the target method of the remote object. It then invokes the target method, and the remote object reads its parameters from the stack, just as it would if it were the subject of a local method call. (If you're familiar with CORBA or RMI, you can think of the stack builder sink as the server stub or skeleton.)

You cannot override or extend the stack builder sink. Any return values and output parameters from the method are intercepted by the stack builder sink, which sends the results back through the server sink chain in reverse order, serializing them, and eventually submitting the resulting data to the transport sink at the end of the chain. The message is transmitted to the transport sink on the client, which passes the data through the client sink chain, deserializing the message, and returning it to the *RealProxy* object. The *RealProxy* object passes the results to the *TransparentProxy*, which returns them to the client object.

Figure 11-4 shows the components of the basic remoting infrastructure.

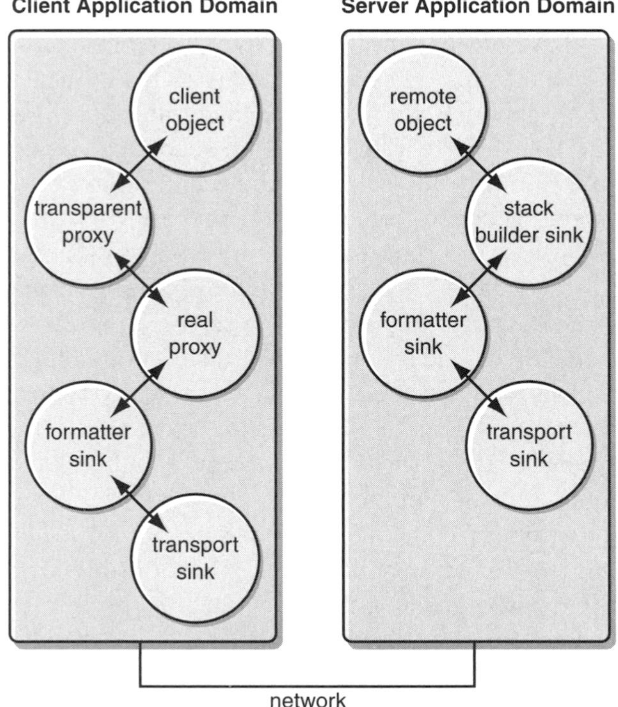

Figure 11-4 The basic remoting infrastructure

Programming with TCP Remoting

The remoting infrastructure enables you to use different models of processing and activation. Let's look at the different options available and how you can implement distributed systems using them. We'll initially concentrate on remoting using the TCP channel and a custom server host process. In subsequent sections, we'll look at the HTTP channel and discuss how to host remote objects in IIS.

Server-Activated Object Remoting

Server-activated object types must be registered with the host server application. We did this earlier using the static *RegisterWellKnownServiceType* method of the *RemotingConfiguration* class. An alternative to hard-coding the details of individual types and channels into the host server is to use a configuration file. (We discussed configuration files in Chapter 2.) The schema used by application configuration files includes a *system.runtime.remoting* element, which supports various child elements and attributes used for specifying remoting configuration information.

The following listing, CakeSizeServer.exe.config, is a configuration file for the CakeServer application. The *<application>* element contains information about the remote objects that an application hosts or consumes. The *<application>* element holds a number of child elements. The two most important ones for host server applications are *<channels>* and *<service>*. (The order of the child elements is unimportant.)

CakeSizeServer.exe.config

```
<?xml version="1.0"?>
<configuration>
  <system.runtime.remoting>
    <application>
      <channels>
        <channel port="6000" displayName="CakeServerChannel"
            type="System.Runtime.Remoting.Channels.Tcp.TcpChannel,
            System.Runtime.Remoting, Version=1.0.3300.0, Culture=neutral,
            PublicKeyToken=b77a5c561934e089" />
      </channels>
      <service>
        <wellknown type="CakeUtils.CakeInfo, CakeUtils"
            objectUri="CakeInfo.rem" mode="Singleton" />
      </service>
    </application>
  </system.runtime.remoting>
</configuration>
```

The *<channels>* element specifies the channels that the host application uses. It comprises one or more *<channel>* elements containing the details for each channel. A host server can listen on multiple channels, but each channel type can be used only once. (You cannot listen on two TCP channels, for example, but you can listen on a TCP channel and an HTTP channel.) The attributes of a channel are the port to listen on, the type of the channel (which is specified as a fully qualified class and assembly), and an optional display name (which is used by programs such as the .NET Framework Configuration Tool to identify the channel for display purposes only).

Configuration File Schema Templates

The entry specifying the assembly that provides the *TcpChannel* class shown in the preceding CakeSizeServer.exe.config file uses a fully qualified assembly name, including version, culture, and public key token. This is a bit of a mouthful and can be painful to maintain (especially if you have a lot of configuration files) if a new version of the *System.Runtime.Remoting* assembly is released. For this reason, the configuration file schema also supports templates.

A template is a predefined set of attributes each of which is named with a unique string identifier (the *id* attribute) that can be referenced elsewhere simply by using this identifier. The machine.config file (located under \WINDOWS\Microsoft.NET\Framework\<*version*>\Config) contains a number of useful templates at the end. The final part of the machine.config file is reproduced here:

```
<system.runtime.remoting>
   ⋮
   <channels>
      <channel id="http" type=
         "System.Runtime.Remoting.Channels.Http.HttpChannel,
         System.Runtime.Remoting, Version=1.0.3300.0, Culture=neutral,
         PublicKeyToken=b77a5c561934e089"/>
      <channel id="http client" type=
         "System.Runtime.Remoting.Channels.Http.HttpClientChannel,
             System.Runtime.Remoting, Version=1.0.3300.0, Culture=neutral,
             PublicKeyToken=b77a5c561934e089"/>
      <channel id="http server" type=
         "System.Runtime.Remoting.Channels.Http.HttpServerChannel,
          System.Runtime.Remoting, Version=1.0.3300.0, Culture=neutral,
          PublicKeyToken=b77a5c561934e089"/>
      <channel id="tcp" type=
         "System.Runtime.Remoting.Channels.Tcp.TcpChannel,
          System.Runtime.Remoting, Version=1.0.3300.0, Culture=neutral,
          PublicKeyToken=b77a5c561934e089"/>
```

```
      <channel id="tcp client" type=
         "System.Runtime.Remoting.Channels.Tcp.TcpClientChannel,
          System.Runtime.Remoting, Version=1.0.3300.0, Culture=neutral,
          PublicKeyToken=b77a5c561934e089"/>
      <channel id="tcp server" type=
         "System.Runtime.Remoting.Channels.Tcp.TcpServerChannel,
         System.Runtime.Remoting, Version=1.0.3300.0, Culture=neutral,
         PublicKeyToken=b77a5c561934e089"/>
   </channels>
   <channelSinkProviders>
      <clientProviders>
         <formatter id="soap" type=
            "System.Runtime.Remoting.Channels.SoapClientFormatterSinkProvider,
            System.Runtime.Remoting, Version=1.0.3300.0, Culture=neutral,
            PublicKeyToken=b77a5c561934e089"/>
         <formatter id="binary" type=
            "System.Runtime.Remoting.Channels.BinaryClientFormatterSinkProvider,
            System.Runtime.Remoting, Version=1.0.3300.0, Culture=neutral,
            PublicKeyToken=b77a5c561934e089"/>
      </clientProviders>
      <serverProviders>
         <formatter id="soap" type=
            "System.Runtime.Remoting.Channels.SoapServerFormatterSinkProvider,
            System.Runtime.Remoting, Version=1.0.3300.0, Culture=neutral,
            PublicKeyToken=b77a5c561934e089"/>
         <formatter id="binary" type=
            "System.Runtime.Remoting.Channels.BinaryServerFormatterSinkProvider,
            System.Runtime.Remoting, Version=1.0.3300.0, Culture=neutral,
            PublicKeyToken=b77a5c561934e089"/>
         <provider id="wsdl" type=
            "System.Runtime.Remoting.MetadataServices.SdlChannelSinkProvider,
            System.Runtime.Remoting, Version=1.0.3300.0, Culture=neutral,
            PublicKeyToken=b77a5c561934e089"/>
      </serverProviders>
   </channelSinkProviders>
</system.runtime.remoting>
```

The template with the *id* of *tcp* contains the information required by the server configuration file, which can be updated to use a *ref* to this template:

```
<channels>
  <channel port="6000" displayName="CakeServerChannel" ref="tcp" />
</channels>
```

If the version number of the *System.Runtime.Remoting* assembly changes, only the machine.config file needs to be updated.

The *<service>* element identifies the types that the host server application exposes and specifies the activation mode for each type. The *<service>* element can contain *<wellknown>* elements describing server-activated types and *<activated>* elements that provide information about client-activated types. For server-activated types, the *<wellknown>* element comprises attributes specifying the type (class and assembly, including locale, version, and public key token information if the assembly is in the GAC), the activation mode, and the published URI for objects of this type. As with the *<channel>* element, an optional display name is provided.

After creating a configuration file, you can make the host server application read the remoting information and configure itself, using the static *RemotingConfiguration.Configure* method. You specify the name of the configuration file as the parameter:

```
RemotingConfiguration.Configure("CakeSizeServer.exe.config");
```

This should replace any calls made to *ChannelServices.RegisterChannel* and *RemotingConfiguration.RegisterWellKnownServiceType*. You can modify the configuration file, changing channel information and adding or removing types without having to rebuild the host application. The result of these changes is a reasonably generic server application that can host almost any type of remote object, although the server still needs to be linked with the assembly that provides the remote object class.

Although there is no direct reference to the assembly or class within the code, the runtime still needs to know about the remote object assembly to activate the appropriate version of the object, so the metadata for the server application must include this information. An alternative is to use reflection in the host server application to dynamically load the required assembly when the server executes. The *RemotingConfiguration* class provides methods that allow you to extract the details of the configuration file that would be useful in this situation. We'll cover some of these methods later. To see the completed code for the nonreflected server, consult the CakeServer.jsl sample file in the ConfigTCP-CakeSizeServer project.

Tip A generic host server is a prime example of an application that you should consider making into a Windows service. See Chapter 15 for details.

You can also use a configuration file with the client. In this case, the important elements are *<channels>* (again) and *<client>*. A client channel does not need to specify a port number. The *<client>* element can contain

<wellknown> child elements describing server-activated remote objects and *<activated>* elements that provide information about client-activated remote objects. The *<wellknown>* element has *url* and *type* attributes, which should be set to match those of the remote object, plus an optional *displayName* attribute. The file CakeClient.exe.config, which follows, shows the client configuration file for the CakeClient application:

CakeClient.exe.config

```
<?xml version="1.0"?>
<configuration>
  <system.runtime.remoting>
    <application>
      <channels>
        <channel displayName="CakeClientChannel" ref="tcp" />
      </channels>
      <client>
        <wellknown type="CakeUtils.CakeInfo, CakeUtils"
           url="tcp://localhost:6000/CakeInfo.rem" />;
      </client>
    </application>
  </system.runtime.remoting>
</configuration>
```

As with the server, when a client has a configuration file such as this, it can dispense with the call to *ChannelServices.RegisterChannel*, replacing it with a call to *RemotingConfiguration.Configure* that specifies the configuration file as its parameter. Furthermore, you can replace the call to *Activator.GetObject* with the *new* operator, making the remote object reference appear just like a local object:

```
RemotingConfiguration.Configure("CakeClient.exe.config");
CakeInfo ci = new CakeInfo();
```

The complete code sample, CakeClient.jsl in the ConfigTCPCakeClient project, shows the client application updated to use the configuration file.

Activation Modes

The .NET Framework provides two activation modes for server-activated objects: *Singleton* and *SingleCall*. The activation mode is specified when the object type is registered, either in the configuration file or using the *RegisterWellKnownServiceType* method. (If you're using the *RegisterWellKnownServiceType* method, you should specify one of the values in the *System.Runtime.Remoting.WellKnownObjectMode* enumeration.)

When a client invokes a method on a server-activated remote object, the sequence of operations that follows depends on the activation mode. If the remote object is activated in *Singleton* mode, the remoting infrastructure will consult the internal tables of the host server to determine whether an object of the appropriate type has already been created. If so, the request will be directed to that object; if not, the remoting infrastructure will create a new instance. In this arrangement, it is possible that many clients will be executing methods on the same instance of the remote object at the same time, in different threads.

Caution Be sure that all methods defined by classes that can be remoted in *Singleton* mode are thread-safe.

If the remote object is activated in *SingleCall* mode, the remoting infrastructure will create a new instance of the remote object for each client method call. The object will be destroyed after the method call completes and will not be reused. No two clients will share the same object. In this case, thread safety becomes an issue only if the remote class defines static data.

From the preceding discussion, you might infer that you can use a singleton remote object to share global data between client applications. While this is feasible, you should be aware of some caveats. The major issue is that even though the singleton mode ensures that no more than one instance of the remote object will be active at any time in the host server application, the remoting infrastructure might destroy the object if it has not been used for a while and re-create a new instance when a client needs it. As a result, you cannot guarantee to the client that it will always have access to the same instance of the singleton object, and you cannot rely on the values of any instance variables being retained. The purpose of this approach is to conserve resources—memory, especially—on the server computer. We'll look in detail at how object lifetimes are managed later.

Even though objects might be continually created and destroyed, the remoting infrastructure does maintain the semantics of static data—but again, you must be aware of how static data access is managed in .NET. Static data is preserved even as objects are torn down and re-created by the runtime. However, static data and methods are regarded as context-agile regardless of the contextual requirements of the defining class. This means that they are always accessed from within the same context as the caller and are never actually remoted—the client must have access to the assembly defining the remote class, and this information is used to create local copies of static data and execute static methods.

In the case of a remote method, the remote object's copy of the static data will be used, but a client application running in a different context will have its own local static data, probably with different values! Similarly, if the client invokes a static method on a remote object, the *TransparentProxy* will instead direct the method call to a local copy running in the same context as the client.

Finally, when a host server application instantiates a server-activated object on behalf of a client, it will build the object using its default constructor. It is therefore vitally important to be sure that it has one and that it performs whatever initialization is required. Failure to provide such a constructor will result in the runtime throwing a *System.MissingMethodException* when a client makes the first method call. (This can be confusing because it is the constructor that is missing rather than the method being called.) The runtime does not currently provide a mechanism for invoking other constructors on server-activated objects (unlike client-activated objects).

Using Interfaces

For a client to use a remote object, it must have access to the metadata describing that object. One way to make the metadata available is to provide the assembly containing the remote object class to the client, but this is wasteful and can lead to versioning issues, especially if the host server application is updated to use a later release of the assembly. A more flexible approach is to define an interface for the remote object. The server should instantiate an object that implements this interface, and the client should activate the object through the interface. For example, in the CakeServer scenario, the *CakeInfo* class in the *CakeUtils* assembly can be represented by the *ICakeInfo* interface, packaged up in the *CakeInterface* assembly, as shown here:

```
package CakeInterface;

public interface ICakeInfo
{
   public short FeedsHowMany(short diameter, short shape, short filling);
}
```

The *CakeInfo* class can be amended to implement this interface. (This version of the *CakeInfo* class is available in the InterfaceCakeUtils project.)

```
package CakeUtils;
import CakeInterface.*;
⋮
public class CakeInfo extends MarshalByRefObject implements ICakeInfo
{
⋮
}
```

Note If the *CakeUtils* assembly is strongly named and stored in the GAC, the *CakeInterface* assembly (holding the *ICakeInfo* interface) must also be strongly named and placed in the GAC.

The code in the host server application can be left untouched (although you might need to recompile it against the new version of the *CakeInfo* class—a relinked version is available in the InterfaceTCPCakeSizeServer project), but you should modify the client to use this interface. If you're using a client configuration file, this involves changing the *<wellknown>* element:

```
<wellknown type="CakeInterface.ICakeInfo, CakeInterface"
   url="tcp://localhost:6000/CakeInfo.rem" />;
```

Also, if you've replaced the *Activator.GetObject* method call in the client code with the *new* operator, you'll unfortunately have to put it back because you cannot use *new* to instantiate an interface using the Java language. However, you can make use of the information supplied in the client configuration file to avoid hard-coding any assembly and remote server URL information. The *RemotingConfiguration* class supplies the static *GetRegisteredWellKnownClientTypes* method, which retrieves an array of *WellKnownClientTypeEntry* objects that contain the contents of the *<wellknown>* elements. You can find the type and URL of an object by querying the *ObjectType* and *ObjectUrl* properties. The following code fragment shows how to activate a remote *CakeInfo* object using the *ICakeInfo* interface and a configuration file:

```
import CakeInterface.*;
⋮
RemotingConfiguration.Configure("CakeClient.exe.config");
WellKnownClientTypeEntry [] entry =
   RemotingConfiguration.GetRegisteredWellKnownClientTypes();
ICakeInfo ci = (ICakeInfo)Activator.GetObject(
   entry[0].get_ObjectType(), entry[0].get_ObjectUrl());
```

When you build the client application, you must reference the *CakeInterface* assembly containing the interface, but you no longer need access to the *CakeUtils* assembly. The code sample CakeClient.jsl in the InterfaceTCPCakeClient project shows the updated version of the *CakeClient* class. (The *CakeShape* and *CakeFilling* classes have been moved to the *CakeInterface* assembly to allow continued access by the client.)

Client-Activated Object Remoting

A client-activated object, as its name suggests, is a remote object that is created and managed by a client application. The host server application simply provides an environment in which such objects can execute. The client is passed a reference to the remote object in the usual way—through a *RealProxy/TransparentProxy* pair (as described earlier).

Configuration File Settings

Client-activated object types have to be registered with the host server application, using either the *RemotingConfiguration.RegisterActivatedServiceType* method or a configuration file that uses the *<activated>* element rather than the *<wellknown>* element to define the service. We discussed the *RegisterActivatedServiceType* method earlier, but for completeness, the following fragment shows the *<service>* entry that you can place in the server configuration file if you prefer to use the *RemotingConfiguration.Configure* method:

```
<service>
   <activated type="CakeUtils.CakeInfo, CakeUtils"/>
</service>
```

The client configuration file should be adjusted in a similar manner. The *<wellknown>* child element of the *<client>* element should be replaced with an *<activated>* element that specifies the remote object type. Also, the *<client>* element itself must have a *url* attribute added that indicates the protocol and port that the server is listening on to wait for activation requests. This information corresponds to the *<channel>* attributes specified in the server configuration file. The modified *<client>* element is shown here:

```
<client url="tcp://localhost:6000">
   <activated type="CakeUtils.CakeInfo, CakeUtils"/>
</client>
```

Activating Objects

A client can activate an object using the *Activator.CreateInstance* method. This was also described earlier, but bear in mind that one major advantage of client activation over server activation is that client-activated objects can be built using nondefault constructors. The *CreateInstance* method can take an array of constructor parameters as one of its arguments, and the constructor that best matches this parameter list will be used when the object is instantiated on the server (or a *MissingMethodException* will be thrown if no matching constructor can be found). Correspondingly, a disadvantage is that *CreateInstance* cannot be used to create an instance of an interface—you can apply it only to object types. (A purist would argue that a client should not attempt to create a client-activated object using an interface anyway, but a workaround is shown below.)

To create an object using its default constructor, you need only specify the object type when you use *CreateInstance*. The remaining details—URL and channel information—are all discovered from the configuration file. You can also query the configuration file to obtain the registered type of the object. Again, this is useful if you want to avoid hard-coding type information into your programs. You saw earlier that the *RemotingConfiguration* class had static methods that allow you to query type information for well-known server-activated objects. It also has the equivalent functionality for obtaining information about client-activated objects: the *GetRegisteredActivatedClientTypes* method. This method returns an array of *ActivatedClientTypeEntry* objects (one for each *<activated>* element in the configuration file), and you can determine type and assembly information using properties exposed by the *ActivatedClientTypeEntry* class.

The following code fragment shows how to activate a *CakeInfo* object using a configuration file. This example uses the *ICakeInfo* interface, although the configuration file actually specifies the *CakeInfo* class. This is legal as long as the *CakeInfo* class implements the *ICakeInfo* interface.

```
// Configure the client channel and remote object activator
RemotingConfiguration.Configure("CakeClient.exe.config");

// Extract the type of the registered remote interface
ActivatedClientTypeEntry [] entry =
   RemotingConfiguration.GetRegisteredActivatedClientTypes();

// Create a reference to a remote CakeInfo object through
// the remote interface
ICakeInfo ci =
   (ICakeInfo)Activator.CreateInstance(entry[0].get_ObjectType());
```

Once a client-activated object has been instantiated, it will remain alive on the server until the client destroys it by removing its last reference (possibly when the client application terminates) or the remoting infrastructure determines that the object has been inactive for too long and decides to remove it (a strategy discussed in the next section). All the time the remote server object is alive, any variables it contains will have their values preserved between method calls; this is another major difference between client-activated and server-activated objects. However, systems that rely heavily on client-activated objects might not scale well as a result.

Note If you're familiar with the Enterprise JavaBeans (EJB) model of Java 2 Enterprise Edition (J2EE), you can think of the .NET client-activated object as being roughly analogous to the stateful session bean. A .NET server-activated single-call object is equivalent to a stateless session bean, and a .NET server-activated singleton object is similar to an entity bean. If you're a "COM head," you can think of a .NET client-activated object as similar to the model used by classical DCOM; a .NET server-activated single-call object also bears more than a passing resemblance to the stateless COM+/MTS model.

Managing Object Lifetimes and Leases

A key issue in distributed systems is balancing the need to keep objects available between client requests and conserving the resources required to keep a large number of objects in memory. The problem is how to determine whether an idle object will remain idle (in which case it can be destroyed) or might suddenly be activated by a client (in which case it will need to be created again shortly after it is destroyed). Although this issue affects singleton server-activated objects, in the case of client-activated objects, which are guaranteed to retain state between calls, the issue is even more acute because a host server application might not be aware that a client application has terminated and that its remote objects should be destroyed.

Architectures such as DCOM use reference counting to keep track of the number of clients holding references to a remote object, and they destroy objects when the number of references drops to zero, but this relies on the client applications themselves being written correctly. (If you're a DCOM hack, you'll undoubtedly have spent many happy hours trying to work out whether your *AddRef* and *Release* calls balance.) Even if the client code is correct, issues such as network failure can wreak havoc on such a system because clients can no longer inform host server applications that they've finished with a remote object. To try to counter the effects of this, DCOM implements periodic pinging of clients over the network, sending an "are you still alive" message—the DCOM infrastructure on the client responds in the affirmative if the client application is still running and sends no response otherwise). This uses network bandwidth—a noticeable overhead in a system that comprises many thousands of objects and client applications executing concurrently.

With .NET, Microsoft has implemented a more scalable and fault-tolerant mechanism that places less reliance on the client code and that can cope with network failure. Remote object lifetimes are governed using a system of *leases*, a *lease manager*, and a series of *sponsors*. When a remote object is created, it is granted a lease that allows it to reside in memory for a designated period of time. When an object becomes idle, its lease starts ebbing away. If the object is not reactivated, its lease will eventually expire and the object can die.

Every application domain has a *lease manager* object. The purpose of the lease manager is to periodically examine the list of expired leases in its domain and determine whether to arrange for the corresponding objects to be garbage collected. Before this happens, the lease manager will ask any sponsors that have registered with the remote object whether they want to renew the lease for that remote object. Only if the lease is not renewed will the object be destroyed.

A sponsor is an object that implements the *System.Runtime.Remoting.Lifetime.ISponsor* interface. You can define your own custom sponsor class by implementing this interface; a default sponsor class is available in *System.Runtime.Remoting.Lifetime.ClientSponsor*. The only method in the *ISponsor* interface is *Renewal*, which takes a lease as a parameter and returns a *TimeSpan* that indicates the length of any renewal period granted. A sponsor is associated with a particular object and can extend the lease for that object when the lease manager calls its *Renewal* method. (It might decide not to do so, depending on the policy the sponsor implements.)

A remote object does not have to have any sponsors, in which case it will be terminated when its lease first expires. (The lease will be renewed whenever a client calls a method on the object, however, so as long as an object is reasonably active it will not disappear.) Sponsors are typically created by the client application, which then registers them with a remote object's lease. This gives the client a degree of control over how the lifetime of the remote object is managed.

You can use the static *RemotingServices.GetLifetimeService* method to obtain the default lease for a remote object (which is returned as an *ILease* object):

```
import System.Runtime.Remoting.*;
import System.Runtime.Remoting.Lifetime*;
⋮
// Create a reference to a remote CakeInfo object
ICakeInfo ci = (ICakeInfo)Activator.GetObject(...);

// Obtain the lifetime service lease for the remote CakeInfo object
ILease lease = (ILease)RemotingServices.GetLifetimeService(ci);
```

Internally, this method calls the *GetLifetimeService* of the remote object itself. The *GetLifetimeService* method is implemented by the *MarshalByRefObject* class, but a class can override it to change the terms of the default lease. The *ILease* interface supplies the *Register* method, which a client uses to specify a sponsor. Although the sponsor object is often created by the client, the sponsor object itself should also be remote, executing in the same application domain as the remote object, because the sponsor object must be directly available to the runtime on the remote server:

```
// Create a new custom sponsor object
ISponsor sponsor = (MyCustomSponsor)Activator.CreateInstance(...);

// Associate the sponsor with the lease for the remote object
lease.Register(sponsor);
```

A lease has a number of properties that you can query to determine its state, and you can modify some of these properties. The *CurrentLeaseTime* property (*get_CurrentLeaseTime* in J#) returns a *TimeSpan* indicating the amount of time left on the lease, and the *CurrentState* property (*get_CurrentState*) returns the current state of the lease (initial, active, expired, and so on). You can use the *InitialLeaseTime* property to set the initial period for the lease. This is useful for client-activated objects that are instantiated before (possibly a long time before) the first method call. You can prevent the lease from expiring by setting this property to *TimeSpan.Zero*. Be careful, though—remote objects with leases that do not expire can become memory hogs.

Each time a method is invoked on a remote object, its lease period is reset using the value specified by the *RenewOnCallTime* property. When a lease becomes due for renewal through inactivity and the lease manager asks a sponsor to renew the lease on an object, it will wait for the time specified by the *SponsorshipTimeout* property for the sponsor to reply. If the sponsor fails to respond in this period, it is assumed to have died and is removed from the lease's list of sponsors. Setting this property to *TimeSpan.Zero* will effectively disable all sponsors for this lease. These properties can be changed only on a lease that is in the *initial* state (before the corresponding object has been activated). The following code fragment shows how to set these properties:

```
lease.set_InitialLeaseTime(new TimeSpan(0, 2, 0));    // 2 minutes
lease.set_RenewOnCallTime(new TimeSpan(0, 3, 0));     // 3 minutes
lease.set_SponsorshipTimeout(new TimeSpan(0, 0, 10)); // 10 seconds
```

You can set these properties globally for the lease manager in an application domain using the *System.Runtime.Remoting.Lifetime.LifetimeServices* class (the individual lease properties override those of the lease manager), which also exposes the *LeaseTime*, *RenewalOnCallTime* and *SponsorshipTimeout* static properties. You should set these properties from the host server application because that is where the lease manager that controls the remote object lifetime executes. In addition, the *LeaseManagerPollTime* property specifies how frequently the lease manager checks for expired remote object leases. These properties can also be set using a server application configuration file: You add a *<lifetime>* child element to the *<application>* element, as shown below. The suffixes determine the unit of time—2M means 2 minutes, and 10S indicates 10 seconds, for example. You can also specify MS for milliseconds, H for hours, and even D for days:

```
<?xml version="1.0"?>
<configuration>
  <system.runtime.remoting>
    <application>
      ⋮
      <lifetime leaseTime="2M" sponsorshipTimeout="10S"
         renewOnCallTime="3M" leaseManagerPollTime="2M"/>
    </application>
  </system.runtime.remoting>
</configuration>
```

TCP Remoting Security

Remote objects and assemblies are subject to the same security constraints as locally accessed objects. Security policies for code access dictate what a remote object can and cannot do, based on the location (or zone) of the client (remember that code executes on a server computer when requested by a client) and the degree of trust the client assembly has been granted. The remoting infrastructure performs security checks when it invokes methods in the *RemotingConfiguration* and *ChannelServices* classes, as well as when it activates objects. By default, a client can create a TCP channel to a host server, activate a remote object on that server, and execute its methods if the client assembly is located on the local intranet or on the same computer as the host server application. A client cannot activate a host object over the Internet unless the host server computer explicitly trusts the client assembly (or the zone permissions are adjusted on the server computer).

Securing the data sent from a client to a server requires encrypting the data before it is transmitted by the channel and decrypting it after the transmission. With the TCP channel, this involves adding a custom sink to the sink chain to perform the encryption and decryption on both the client and server ends of the channel. It makes sense to encrypt messages after they have been serialized and decrypt them again before they are deserialized. But authenticating clients based on identity and authorizing them to execute selected methods on a remote object would be a nontrivial task over the TCP channel because the TCP channel does not provide any built-in support for attaching credentials to messages. An additional custom sink to perform this task would be required on the client side of the channel before the data is serialized and encrypted. A corresponding sink on the server side would examine these credentials and accept or reject the method request. Such a strategy would also involve enrolling users and creating, storing, and managing credential information on the server, possibly in a secure database.

Security management is far easier using the HTTP channel and IIS as the host server application. The TCP channel was designed to be lean and mean, so you should use the TCP channel for applications executing using a local area network (LAN), where speed is the main issue, but employ the HTTP channel for wide area networks (WANs), intranets, and the Internet, where security is more important.

Remote Method Parameters

The examples you've seen so far in this chapter have shown how to invoke the *FeedsHowMany* method of the *CakeInfo* class. The parameters of this method are three short integers. Integers, like all the primitive types of J#, are marshaled by value when they're sent as parameters to a remote server. If the remote method changes any of these parameters, it simply changes a local copy in the server process. The new values will not be copied back when the method completes. In this respect, the semantics of a remote method call are similar to those of a local call in Java.

The fun starts when a remote method expects a nonprimitive object as a parameter. In this situation, you have a choice: You can marshal the parameter either by reference or by value, depending on how the object type is defined. Types that are marked with *SerializableAttribute* will always be marshaled by value, and the data will be copied to the server. For a parameter to be passed by reference, the type of the parameter must descend from *MarshalByRefObject*. Any changes that the server makes to the contents of this parameter will be treated by the server as a remote method call back to the client.

Also, when the client registers the channel, the client must create a port that the server can use for communicating back to the client application. This can be any unused port. It is often a good idea to let the remoting infrastructure itself pick a port; you can do this by specifying zero when you define the channel programmatically (or when you specify the *<channel>* element in a configuration file):

```
// Register a channel and create a port on the client
ChannelServices.RegisterChannel(new TcpChannel(0));
```

Remote Events

Recall that the event-handling mechanism of .NET uses delegates to refer to methods that subscribe to events. To provide a little variation and to prove that remoting clients and servers can be written in different languages, we wrote a version of the *CakeInfo* class in C# that publishes an event (available in the *CSharpCakeUtils* namespace sample shown below and also downloadable as the CSharpCakeUtils project).

Recall from Chapter 3 that a class that publishes an event should expose a method that allows subscribers to register delegates for this event. (The example uses the *AddOnFeedsHowManyEvent* method for this purpose.) When the event is raised, the methods referred to by any subscribing delegates are executed. It is also possible for remote objects to raise events that a client application can subscribe to, and the mechanism used is similar. However, one difference is that a delegate registered with a remote server object will point to a method executing in the client. When an event is raised, the server will submit a remote call back to the client to execute this method, temporarily reversing the roles of the client and the server.

Delegates themselves are marshal-by-value objects and will always be serialized when they are passed from a client to a remote object server. However, the method referred to by a delegate can be located in the client as long as some requirements are met, both in terms of the subscribing client and any arguments returned by an event when it is raised.

In the *CSharpCakeUtils* assembly shown below, the *FeedsHowMany* method is nearly identical to the J# implementation used in earlier examples in this chapter, with the exception that it raises an event called *FeedsHowManyEvent* before the method finishes. This method takes a parameter indicating the number of consumers the cake will serve and passes it to any registered handler that subscribes to this event.

The assembly also contains the *FeedsHowManyEventArgs* event arguments class, which defines the data returned to the client when the event is raised. This class must be marked as *Serializable*. (The data is marshaled from the server back to the client.) The *CakeInfo* class exposes the *FeedsHowManyEventHandler* delegate, which defines the callback that a client wanting to subscribe to the *FeedsHowManyEvent* should use. The public *AddOnFeedsHowManyEvent* method binds a delegate to the event. The *OnFeedsHowManyEvent* method raises the event when it is invoked from *FeedsHowMany*.

Although this version of the *CakeInfo* class is written in C#, it can still be hosted by a J# application that uses the same techniques shown earlier in this chapter. (The ClientActivatedTCPCakeSizeServerWithEvent project does just that.)

CSharpCakeUtils.cs

```
using System;
using System.Runtime.Remoting;
using System.Runtime.Serialization;
using CakeInterface;

namespace CSharpCakeUtils
{
   /// <summary>
   /// C# implementation of the CakeInfo class, with events
   /// </summary>


   // Event args class for the FeedsHowManyEvent.
   // This data is returned when FeedsHowManyEvent is raised by the
   // FeedsHowMany method of the CakeInfo class
   [Serializable()]
   public class FeedsHowManyEventArgs : EventArgs
   {
      private int numEaters;

      public FeedsHowManyEventArgs(int num)
      {
         numEaters = num;
      }

      public int NumberOfEaters
      {
         get
         {
            return numEaters;
         }
      }
   }

   public class CakeInfo : MarshalByRefObject, ICakeInfo
   {
      // Define delegate and event
      public delegate void FeedsHowManyEventHandler(object sender,
         FeedsHowManyEventArgs arg);
        private event FeedsHowManyEventHandler feedsHowManyEvent;

      //Method that raises the FeedsHowManyEvent
      protected void OnFeedsHowManyEvent(FeedsHowManyEventArgs e)
      {
         if (feedsHowManyEvent != null)
            feedsHowManyEvent(this, e);
      }
```

```
        // Public method allowing clients to subscribe to
        // the FeedsHowManyEvent
        public void AddOnFeedsHowManyEvent(FeedsHowManyEventHandler handler)
        {
           feedsHowManyEvent += handler;
        }

        public CakeInfo()
        {
           Console.WriteLine("Hello!");
        }

        // Work out how many people a cake of a given size, shape,
        // and filling will serve
        public short FeedsHowMany(short diameter, short shape, short filling)
        {
           Console.WriteLine("Calculating...");
           double munchSizeFactor = (filling == CakeFilling.Fruit ? 2.5 : 1);
           double deadSpaceFactor;

           switch (shape)
           {
              case CakeShape.Square:    deadSpaceFactor = 0;
                 break;
              case CakeShape.Hexagonal: deadSpaceFactor = 0.1;
                 break;
              case CakeShape.Round:     deadSpaceFactor = 0.15;
                 break;
              default:                  deadSpaceFactor = 0.2;
                 break;
           }

           short numConsumers =
             (short)(diameter * munchSizeFactor * (1 - deadSpaceFactor));

           // Raise the FeedsHowManyEvent passing back the number
           // of consumers
           OnFeedsHowManyEvent(new FeedsHowManyEventArgs(numConsumers));

           // Also return the number of consumers the regular way
           return numConsumers;
        }
    }
}
```

A subscribing object should instantiate a *FeedsHowManyEventHandler* delegate and then call the *AddOnFeedsHowMany* method of the remote *CakeInfo* object. The delegate can refer to a method in the client or even another remote method. The CakeClient.jsl sample in the ClientActivatedTCP-

CakeClientWithEvent project uses the local *EventHandler* method of the *CakeClient* class. Because the *CakeClient* class will be accessed from the remote server, it must also fulfill the requirements of a remote object: It must either be *Serializable* or inherit from *MarshalByRefObject*. If you mark the class as serializable, it will be marshaled by value and a copy will be created at the remote server. The delegate method will be invoked in this copy at the server, which is probably not what you want in this case. Therefore, this example uses *MarshalByRefObject*; the client will be accessed by reference using a proxy from the server, and the delegated method will execute locally at the client.

Tip If you want to see the difference between the two types of client marshaling, you can remove the *MarshalByRefObject* inheritance and instead mark the class with the *Serializable* attribute. When the event handler runs, the message output will be displayed on the server console screen and not the client.

A reference to the assembly containing the client code (CakeClient) must also be added to the host server application. The J# compiler does not allow you to reference executables (EXE files), only libraries (DLLs). Therefore, the *CakeClient* class has been wrapped up inside a DLL. The configuration file should be updated to use the *CakeInfo* class in the *CSharpCakeUtils* assembly. (We also changed the name of the configuration file to CakeClient.dll.config for consistency.) Furthermore, the client must specify a port that the server can use for communicating back to the client as part of the channel configuration. You can use the value 0 to allow the remote infrastructure to select an unused port. The configuration file must be deployed with each client application using this library:

```
<?xml version="1.0"?>
<configuration>
  <system.runtime.remoting>
    <application>
      <channels>
        <channel ref="tcp" displayName="CakeClientChannel" port="0"/>
      </channels>
      <client url="tcp://localhost:6000">
        <activated type="CSharpCakeUtils.CakeInfo, CSharpCakeUtils" />
      </client>
    </application>
  </system.runtime.remoting>
</configuration>
```

Apart from adding the reference to the *CakeClient* assembly and changing the reference to the *CakeUtils* assembly to *CSharpCakeUtils* (and updating the *<activated>* element in the configuration file in the same way as the client), you don't have to change any code in the host server application. Figures 11-5 and 11-6 show the console for the server application and the client test harness (in the ClientActivatedTestHarness project), respectively. Notice that the event message is displayed at the client.

Figure 11-5 The console screen showing the output of the host server application

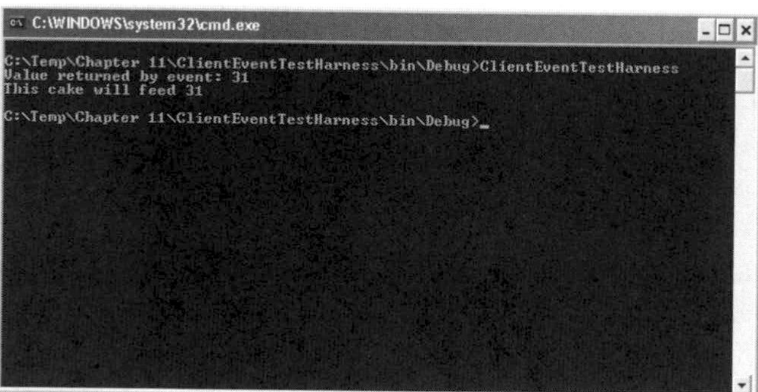

Figure 11-6 The console screen showing the output of the client test harness

HTTP Remoting

The TCP channel provides basic reliable end-to-end communication and transmission of messages based on low-level sockets. It is ideally suited for use on a LAN. The HTTP channel, on the other hand, being based on the HTTP protocol, is ideal for transmitting data over longer distances. You can use many of the same techniques that you've already seen in this chapter, but the HTTP channel provides some additional functionality. Specifically, you can use IIS as a host server application and publish remote methods on the Web. The HTTP channel also provides better cross-platform interoperability.

Remoting Server Hosting

HTTP remoting uses the *System.Runtime.Remoting.Channels.Http.HttpChannel* class to transport messages between a client and a server. In a manner similar to TCP remoting, HTTP remoting has specialized *HttpClientChannel* and *HttpServerChannel* classes designed for the client or server. The *HttpChannel* provides the functionality required by an HTTP client and an HTTP server and is the variant that is used most often.

Using the HTTP channel in its simplest form is almost identical to using the TCP channel. (But be sure you don't use the same port as an existing TCP server.) The CakeServer.jsl sample file in the ServerActivatedHTTPCakeSizeServer project shows the basic CakeServer, which implements server-activated objects over the HTTP channel. Notice that this class now creates an *HttpChannel* and that the published URI has the suffix *.soap*, which is the convention when you use SOAP.

The changes necessary for the client are similar. Notice also that the URI requested by the *Activator.GetObject* method specifies the HTTP protocol. For completeness, the HTTP version of the basic *CakeClient* is available in CakeClient.jsl in the ServerActivatedHTTPCakeClient project.

As with TCP remoting, you can also use a configuration file to specify channel (use the *ref="http"* template in the *<channel>* element) and type information. Remote objects that are accessed using the HTTP channel and a custom host server application can be client-activated or server-activated.

By default, the *HttpChannel* inserts a *System.Runtime.Serialization.Formatters.Soap.SoapFormatter* object into the message sink chain to serialize requests as XML and add the necessary SOAP headers. (SOAP is covered in detail in Part V of this book.) This has some advantages over the *BinaryFormatter* used by the TCP channel. In particular, because the format emitted by the *SoapFormatter* follows the SOAP standard for remote procedure calls, a remoting client application based on the HTTP channel can interact with almost any server that accepts SOAP method calls. The server does not have to be written using Visual Studio .NET or even be running on a Microsoft platform. Most Web services are SOAP-based, and with a little care an HTTP remoting client can interoperate with a Web service. Microsoft supplies the SOAPSUDS tool (in the \Program Files\Microsoft Visual Studio .NET\FrameworkSDK\bin folder) for generating runtime assemblies that client applications can use to access Web services.

You should bear in mind, however, that the *SoapFormatter* has some disadvantages compared to the *BinaryFormatter*. Firstly, the size of a SOAP message is often bigger than its binary cousin. You'll especially notice this if a remote method takes object parameters, which brings us to the second drawback.

In Chapter 10, we looked at how binary and XML serialization work. Binary serialization writes the entire contents of a serializable object—private as well as public data—to a serialization stream. XML serialization, on the other hand, outputs only publicly accessible data (public data members and properties), and totally private data is not emitted. The same rule applies when you use the *SoapFormatter* class (which uses the XML serializer to do some of its dirty work). Hence, objects marshaled by value as parameters across an HTTP channel will have only their publicly accessible data transmitted. This will affect how you design and implement remote services over HTTP. This restriction does not apply to objects marshaled by reference because their data is not actually transmitted. (Only an *ObjRef* that is used to build a proxy at the server end is transmitted.)

Note There is a small difference between XML serialization as described in Chapter 10 and the *SoapFormatter*. Classes serialized using an *XmlSerializer* object do not have to be tagged as serializable, but classes serialized as parameters using the *SoapFormatter* must be (if they are not marshal-by-reference types).

It is possible to combine the *HttpChannel* with binary serialization by changing the formatter used by the channel. This will still use HTTP as the transmission protocol, but the data sent will be binary rather than XML. The simplest way to do this is to use a configuration file and specify a *<formatter>* element as part of the channel. On the client side, this should be contained in a *<clientProviders>* element:

```
<application>
  <channels>
    <channel ref="http">
      <clientProviders>
        <formatter ref="binary"/>
      </clientProviders>
    </channel>
  </channels>
  ⋮
</application>
```

In a server configuration file, you should use a *<serverProviders>* element. The syntax is the same as the *<clientProviders>* element. Be sure that if you change the formatter at one end, you change it at the other end as well. (A binary formatter at the client does not mix well with a SOAP formatter at the server.)

Tip You can also change the formatter when you use the *TcpChannel*. Use *<formatter ref="soap"/>* to switch to the SOAP formatter. The values *binary* and *soap* are actually templates defined in the machine.config file. (See the sidebar titled "Configuration File Schema Templates" earlier in this chapter.)

Hosting with IIS

If you're using the HTTP channel, an alternative to building a custom server application is to host remote objects using IIS. This enables you to make use of the security features that IIS exposes and reduces the amount of security checking you have to do in your own code (as described in the next section). Remote objects hosted by IIS must be server-activated. For the sake of response time, you should also minimize the use of events calling back to the client as well as the number of parameters that are marshaled by reference.

If you want to host remote objects in IIS, you must follow some fairly strict rules. First, you must create a virtual directory alias that refers to a physical folder. This folder holds the assembly that defines the remote object. You can do this from the Internet Information Services tree in the Computer Management console, under Administrative Tools in Control Panel. Use the default access permissions. You then create a folder called *bin* under the physical folder and place the assembly in that folder. Any other private assemblies used by your remote objects should also be placed in the bin folder. Finally, you must create a configuration file called Web.config and place it in the folder that corresponds to the virtual directory. (This will be the folder that holds the bin folder.) For example, to host the CakeUtils.dll assembly under IIS, you can use the following procedure. (You do not have to call the folder CakeUtils or the IIS virtual directory CakeServer, but these are the names we'll use in this section.)

1. Create a folder called C:\CakeUtils.
2. Create an IIS virtual directory called CakeServer that maps to this physical folder.

3. Create a folder called C:\CakeUtils\bin.
4. Copy CakeUtils.dll into C:\CakeUtils\bin.
5. Create the Web.config file in C:\CakeUtils.

The Web.config file is an ordinary server configuration file. The following example publishes the *CakeInfo* class of the *CakeUtils* assembly using the URI *CakeInfo.soap*, over an ordinary HTTP channel. No port is necessary because IIS will listen for incoming requests on port 80 by default, although you can specify a different port if you want to keep remote object traffic separate from ordinary Web traffic. (This will start a new thread in IIS that listens to the specified port, so if you use a different port for each application you might create many additional listener threads in IIS—be aware of scalability issues.)

```
<?xml version="1.0"?>
<configuration>
  <system.runtime.remoting>
    <application>
      <service>
        <wellknown type="CakeUtils.CakeInfo, CakeUtils"
           objectUri="CakeInfo.soap" mode="SingleCall"/>
      </service>
      <channels>
        <channel ref="http" />
      </channels>
    </application>
  </system.runtime.remoting>
</configuration>
```

A client can use a remote object hosted by IIS just as it can use any other server-activated object. The main requirements are that the client must register an HTTP channel and the URL specified must refer to the URI of the remote object in conjunction with the name and virtual directory of the remote server and the port it is listening on (port 80 by default).

The following configuration file is for the *CakeClient* class you saw earlier in this chapter. (You should replace *localhost* in the *<wellknown>* element with the name of the server that's running IIS.) The *useDefaultCredentials* attribute of the channel is a custom property that applies only to HTTP channels. It causes the credentials of the process that's executing the client application to be transmitted to IIS as part of the request. IIS can be configured to allow or deny access to the remote object based on this information. You might be denied access when you attempt to activate the remote object if you omit this attribute, depending on how IIS security is configured on your system.

```
<?xml version="1.0"?>
<configuration>
  <system.runtime.remoting>
    <application>
      <channels>
        <channel ref="http" useDefaultCredentials="true"/>
      </channels>
      <client>
        <wellknown type="CakeUtils.CakeInfo, CakeUtils"
           url="http://localhost:80/CakeServer/CakeInfo.soap"/>
      </client>
    </application>
  </system.runtime.remoting>
</configuration>
```

HTTP Remoting Security

The TCP channel provides almost no support for encrypting messages and authenticating method requests. On the other hand, the HTTP channel, when used with IIS to host remote objects, supports encryption using SSL as well as integrated Windows authentication and even Kerberos. You can implement these options using little or no code—it's simply a matter of configuring IIS appropriately and ensuring that client applications transmit their credentials if required, as shown in the previous section.

The Web.config file in an IIS virtual directory can specify security information. The optional *<system.web>* child element, under *<configuration>*, can contain *<authentication>* and *<authorization>* elements. The *<authentication>* element indicates the authentication mode, which dictates how users should be authenticated (using forms-based security, Microsoft Passport, Integrated Windows security or no security). The *<authorization>* element determines which users and roles should be permitted or denied access.

The following example file is an extended version of the server Web.config file shown earlier. It configures IIS to use Integrated Windows security to authenticate users to permit access only to JSharp and ALongshaw from the WONDERLAND domain, and to deny access to everyone else (the unauthorized users will receive a 401 "Unauthorized" message from the server, which will be trapped by the remoting infrastructure as an exception).

```
<?xml version="1.0"?>
<configuration>
  <system.runtime.remoting>
    <application>
      <service>
        <wellknown type="CakeUtils.CakeInfo, CakeUtils"
```

```
          objectUri="CakeInfo.soap" mode="SingleCall"/>
      </service>
      <channels>
        <channel ref="http"/>
      </channels>
    </application>
  </system.runtime.remoting>
  <system.web>
  <authentication mode="Windows"/>
  <authorization>
    <allow users="WONDERLAND\JSharp, WONDERLAND\ALongshaw"/>
    <deny users="*" />
  </authorization>
  </system.web>
</configuration>
```

Many more configuration options are available with IIS, some of which will be covered in Part V of this book.

Customizing Remoting

By now, you should appreciate that the remoting services implemented by .NET are comprehensive and for the most part pretty simple to program against. Much of the complexity of marshaling objects, creating proxies, and transmitting data is hidden in a set of system-defined classes. However, the remoting infrastructure is highly extensible; the .NET Framework Class Library provides a set of helper classes and interfaces that you can use if you want to examine or modify the default behavior of the remoting system. There's much more to remoting than we have the time or space to cover in this chapter, so here we'll concentrate on a few of the less esoteric options.

One-Way Remoting

On some occasions, a remote method might not return a value and might have no output arguments of any description, only inputs. Such methods are sometimes termed "fire and forget." They can be executed asynchronously because there is no need for the client to wait until the method completes. This is especially useful over the HTTP channel, where the remote object can be very distant (especially if it's hosted by IIS). You can tag remote object methods that follow this pattern with *System.Runtime.Remoting.Messaging.OneWayAttribute* when they're defined:

```
import System.Runtime.Remoting.*;
import System.Runtime.Remoting.Messaging.*;
```

```
⋮
public class RemoteObject extends MarshalByRefObject
{
/** @attribute OneWayAttribute() */
public void RemoteAsyncMethod(...)
{
⋮
}
⋮
}
```

A one-way method must be declared as a void, must use only marshal-by-value parameters, and cannot throw any exceptions. When the client calls a one-way method, it *might* execute asynchronously. There is no absolute guarantee, and the runtime might elect to execute the method synchronously if it determines that this would be more efficient.

The *RemotingServices* Class

Much of the time, you'll be content to use the remoting infrastructure as is. However, if you require more detailed control, you can use the *System.Runtime.Remoting.RemotingServices* class (not to be confused with the *System.Runtime.Remoting.Services.RemotingService* class), which contains a collection of useful helper methods.

The *RemotingServices.Marshal* method can be used by a server application to dynamically publish an object that extends *MarshalByRefObject*. It returns an *ObjRef* that can be passed back to a client when it connects. (There's also an *Unmarshal* method that converts an *ObjRef* into a proxy, but this is used less frequently because the *Connect* method is preferable, as explained shortly.) You can optionally specify a URI that a client can request. You should register a channel before marshaling an object. One reason for adopting this approach is that it allows a server to create and activate an object using any available constructor. (The standard mechanism allows only the default constructor to be used by server-activated objects.)

The following code fragment creates and publishes an instance of the programmer-defined class *MyRefObjectType*. Be aware, however, that the object (*publishedObject*) is still subject to the lifetime policies implemented by the remoting infrastructure and might be garbage collected if its lease expires.

```
MyRefObjectType publishedObject = new MyRefObjectType(...);
ChannelServices.RegisterChannel(new TcpChannel(6000));
ObjRef wellKnownRef = RemotingServices.Marshal(publishedObject,
   "MyRefObjectURI");
```

A client, aware of the channel and URI published by the server, can connect to this object using either the *GetObject* method (as shown earlier) or the *RemotingServices.Connect* method, which returns a proxy:

```
ChannelServices.RegisterChannel(new TcpChannel());
MyRefObjectType proxy =
   (MyRefObjectType)RemotingServices.Connect(Type.GetType(
   "MyRefObjectTypeAssembly.MyRefObjectType, MyRefObjectTypeAssembly"),
   "tcp://MyServer:6000/MyRefObjectURI");
```

Any method calls made using the *proxy* variable will actually be remote method calls, which are dispatched to the application that's hosting the remote object (*MyServer*).

A server can cease publishing an object using the *Disconnect* method. This method returns a B*oolean* value indicating whether the operation was successful:

```
boolean success = RemotingServices.Disconnect(MyRefObjectType);
```

The *Disconnect* method does not destroy the object, and it can be registered again later, either on the same or a different channel or URI using the *Marshal* method. Do not try to call *Disconnect* on a client-side proxy—the result will be a *RemoteException* and the message "Cannot call disconnect on a proxy."

You can use the *RemotingServices.ExecuteMessage* method to connect to a remote object, execute a method, obtain any return value, and disconnect from the remote object. The method expects the message data to be passed in as a *System.Runtime.Remoting.Messaging.IMethodCallMessage* object, and it returns an implementation of *System.Runtime.Remoting.Messaging.IMethodReturnMessage*. (These are both subtypes of *System.Runtime.Remoting.Messaging.IMessage*.) It would not be usual for a client to create its own *IMessage* objects, but this method is useful for a server that receives a method call on a custom message sink (as described later). Messages enter the message sink chain as *IMessage* objects, and a custom sink can use this method to scrutinize the message and forward it to another server.

Tip You can extract the details of an *IMethodCallMessage* object by assigning it to a *System.Runtime.Remoting.MethodCall* object (this is the concrete type of the object) and examining its properties. Useful properties include *MethodName* (*get_MethodName*), *TypeName* (*get_TypeName*), and *Uri* (*get_Uri*).

The *RemotingServices* class interacts with the remoting infrastructure and exposes methods that a client can use to determine the nature of useful aspects of a remote object, including these:

- ***IsObjectOutOfAppDomain*** This method takes a transparent proxy (returned by *Connect or GetObject*) and returns a Boolean value indicating whether the proxy refers to an object in a different application domain.
- ***IsObjectOutOfContext*** This method takes a transparent proxy and returns a value indicating whether the proxy refers to an object in a different context.
- ***IsOneWay*** This method expects a *System.Reflection.MethodBase* that contains the metadata for a method (obtained using reflection) and indicates whether the method is one-way.
- ***IsTransparentProxy*** This method takes an object reference and returns a Boolean value indicating whether the reference refers to a transparent proxy or a real object.

Tracking Handlers

Another interesting feature supplied by the remoting infrastructure is the ability to track when objects are marshaled and unmarshaled. You can use this feature to log object accesses. It can also give you insight into how the remoting services perform their task. Whenever objects are marshaled, unmarshaled, or disconnected, the remoting infrastructure can notify one or more registered tracking handlers about the event, passing them information about the remote object in question.

A tracking handler is a class that implements the *System.Runtime.Remoting.Services.ITrackingHandler* interface. This interface defines three methods:

- ***DisconnectedObject(System.Object obj)*** This method is called when the specified object is disconnected by a host server application. (It can longer accept requests.)
- ***MarshaledObject(System.Object obj, ObjRef ref)*** This method is called whenever a remote object (*MarshalByRefObject* or *Serializable*) is marshaled and an *ObjRef* is created.
- ***UnmarshaledObject(System.Object obj, ObjRef ref)*** Similarly, this method is called whenever a remote object has been unmarshaled.

The *CakeTracker* class shown in the following listing (available in the TrackedCakeUtils project) shows a simple implementation of a tracking handler. All it does is print the details of the object being disconnected, marshaled, or unmarshaled, to the console. The *ObjRef* class has properties that supply some details about the remote object reference. The *CakeTracker* class uses the *URI* property (*get_URI*) to display the URI of the remote reference:

```
package CakeUtils;
import System.*;
import System.Runtime.Remoting.*;
import System.Runtime.Remoting.Services.*;


// Tracking handler that monitors how the CakeInfo class is used
public class CakeTracker implements ITrackingHandler
{
   public void DisconnectedObject(System.Object obj)
   {
      Console.WriteLine("Object disconnected: " + obj.ToString());
      Console.WriteLine();
   }

   public void MarshaledObject(System.Object obj, ObjRef ref)
   {
      Console.WriteLine("Object Marshaled: " + obj.ToString() +
           " URI:" + ref.get_URI());
      Console.WriteLine();
   }

   public void UnmarshaledObject(System.Object obj, ObjRef ref)
   {
      Console.WriteLine("Object unmarshaled: " + obj.ToString() +
           " URI: " + ref.get_URI());
      Console.WriteLine();
   }
}
```

To track remote objects, you create an instance of the *CakeTracker* class and register it with the remoting infrastructure. The *System.Runtime.Remoting.Services.TrackingServices* class contains the static method *RegisterTrackingHandler* for this purpose. You can register tracking handlers on clients and host server applications. (The following example shows a client; the two lines of code that create and register a tracking handler will be the same on the server.)

```
⋮
import System.Runtime.Remoting.Services.*;
import CakeUtils.*;

// Test client for the CakeSizeServer class
public class CakeClient
{
   public static void main(String[] args)
   {
      ⋮
      try
      {
         ITrackingHandler trackingHandler = new CakeTracker();
         TrackingServices.RegisterTrackingHandler(trackingHandler);

         // Configure the client channel and remote object activator
         RemotingConfiguration.Configure("CakeClient.exe.config");
⋮
      }
   }
}
```

If you register more than one tracking handler, each one will be called in turn as tracking events occur. Figures 11-7 and 11-8 show the server console for tracked versions of the CakeServer and CakeClient applications, respectively, which implement client-activated remote objects. (These applications are available in the projects TrackedClientActivatedTCPCakeSizeServer and TrackedClientActivatedTCPCakeClient.)

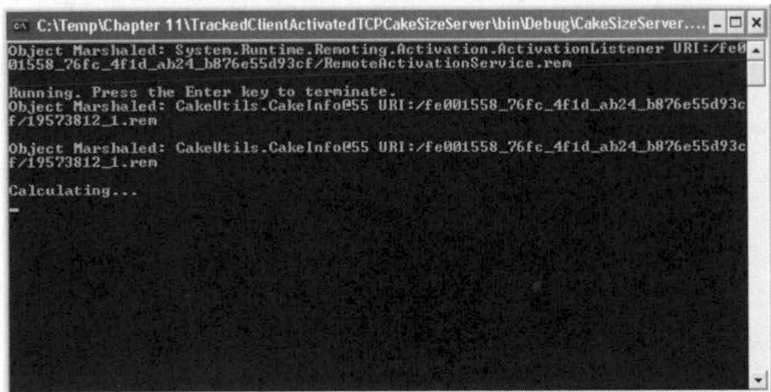

Figure 11-7 The server console screen showing tracking messages for a client-activated object

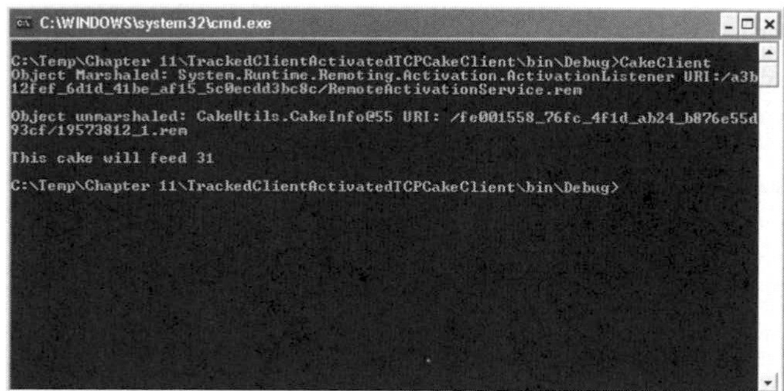

Figure 11-8 The client console screen showing tracking messages

If you change the configuration to use server-activated objects (see the projects TrackedServerActivatedTCPCakeSizeServer and TrackedServerActivatedTCPCakeClient), you'll notice fewer marshaling messages (none on the client), highlighting the differences in the remoting protocol and the timing of marshaling calls used by the two different models. Server-activated remote objects do not create an *ActivationListener*, for example—the *ActivationListener* object waits for activation requests from clients and then instantiates remote objects as demanded by the client. You can also see the internal URIs generated for each remote object. A further interesting exercise is to change the *CakeInfo* class from *MarshalByRefObject* to *Serializable*; in this case, a copy of the object is transferred from the server application to the client when it is marshaled, and thereafter the client uses the local copy.

Custom Channel Sinks and Channels

Occasionally, you might find it useful to customize the channel sink chain, such as when you need to encrypt data or add security credential information when you use the TCP channel—scenarios described earlier in the chapter. You can also build custom channel sinks that log remote requests or track the activity of remote objects.

Creating a custom channel sink is a matter of implementing the *IClientChannelSink* interface or *IServerChannelSink* interface (both are in the *System.Runtime.Remoting.Channels* namespace) and optionally the *IMessageSink* interface. The channel sink interfaces contain a *NextChannelSink* property that you can use to obtain a reference to the next sink in the chain, and they contain methods for processing an *IMessage* object, synchronously or asynchronously, before handing it off to the next sink in the chain.

You must also define a custom channel sink provider object that can create your custom sink. You implement the *IClientChannelSinkProvider* or

IServerChannelSinkProvider interface (also in *System.Runtime.Remoting.Channels*). Both these interfaces contain the *CreateSink* method, which should instantiate a custom sink object. Channel sink providers are also chained together, so when a provider has finished building its custom sink, the infrastructure can invoke the next provider in the chain to build its own sinks. Both sink provider interfaces therefore include a *Next* property for linking sink providers together.

The simplest way to install a custom channel sink is to add the custom sink provider class to the list of providers loaded by the remoting infrastructure in the configuration file. The following example loads a server channel sink provider class called *CredentialServerChannelSinkProvider* in the *Credentials* assembly:

```
<configuration>
  <system.runtime.remoting>
    ⋮
    <channelSinkProviders>
      <serverProviders>
        <provider type="Credentials.CredentialServerChannelSinkProvider,
          Credentials" />
      </serverProviders>
    </channelSinkProviders>
  </system.runtime.remoting>
</configuration>
```

You can also create custom channels if you need to send data using a protocol other than TCP or HTTP or if you want to implement some rudimentary form of load balancing and redirect client requests to different servers based on their load. To do this, you implement the *IChannelSender*, *IChannelReceiver* and *IChannel* interfaces (which are in *System.Runtime.Remoting.Channels*) to communicate with the channel sink chains and physically transmit or receive data. At run time, you load a custom channel using the *ChannelServices.RegisterChannel* method or using the configuration file:

```
<?xml version="1.0"?>
<configuration>
  <system.runtime.remoting>
    <application>
      <channels>
        <channel type="NewProtocolAssembly.NewChannel, NewProtocolAssembly,
          ... ", ... />
      </channels>
      ⋮
    </application>
```

```
  </system.runtime.remoting>
</configuration>
```

Summary

This chapter took you on a grand tour through the world of .NET Remoting. You should now understand the remoting architecture and how to build host server applications and client programs. You learned how to implement client-activated and server-activated remote objects, and you learned about the available server activation modes. The chapter also explained how remote object lifetimes are managed using leases. You learned how to subscribe to events published by remote objects, and you learned the requirements of marshal-by-value and marshal-by-reference parameters of remote methods.

The chapter explained how to use the TCP and the HTTP channels and described the differences between them in terms of marshaling and serialization. You also learned how to use IIS as a host for remote objects that are accessed using HTTP.

The chapter concluded with a description of the ways in which you can customize the remoting infrastructure, using the methods available in the *RemotingServices* class as well as using more intricate techniques such as building custom message sinks and channels.

12

Using Message Queues

You learned in the last few chapters how to send messages between processes that are running concurrently, either on the same computer or on different computers. But sometimes a client application might need to send a message to a server process that is not executing at that time. Rather than have the message be rejected and raise an exception, it might be better to store the message and forward it to the target server process when it eventually does start running. In a similar scenario, you might need to send a message to a server process when the client is disconnected from the network. Again, it would be useful to store and forward the message once a network connection has been established.

Consider the example of a traveling salesperson who visits clients and places orders for goods using a local application running on a laptop computer. The order details can be stored on the laptop and then downloaded to the server process that handles orders when the salesperson arrives back in the office and connects the laptop to the LAN.

Of course, applications that use this model of processing must be structured not to expect an immediate response from a server when a request is sent. Instead, such applications can periodically poll for a reply, use some sort of event infrastructure to subscribe to an event that's raised when a reply arrives, or even be designed to not expect a response at all. These strategies imply a need for reliability and the assurance that once a client application has dispatched a message it will be received by a server process or that the client will at least be informed if the message is not delivered within a given period of time. Security is another issue. Messages should not be compromised while they're waiting to be sent, or during transmission.

Building the infrastructure needed to handle the myriad situations that can arise when you design asynchronous distributed applications would be a time consuming and expensive process. Fortunately, this functionality is already available when you base your applications on Microsoft Windows, through Microsoft Message Queuing.

Message queuing has been an available in Windows since the days of the Windows NT Option Pack, which supplied Microsoft Message Queue (MSMQ) version 1.0. With the advent of Windows 2000, MSMQ became an integral part of the operating system, and version 3.0, officially called Message Queuing 3.0, is available as part of the Windows XP platform. Other vendors have also produced their own message queuing solutions, many of which predate MSMQ. IBM's WebSphere MQ (formerly MQSeries) is an example.

When you build distributed applications, it's important to be able to integrate across vendor platforms, so a selection of bridging components are also available from third-party integrators. Microsoft recommends the Envoy MQ Client from Envoy Technologies (*http://www.envoytech.com*) for connecting MSMQ and Message Queuing 3.0 services to non-Windows platforms. (Envoy Technologies also supplies implementations of MSMQ for operating systems other than Windows, such as Linux and Sun's Solaris.)

In this chapter, we'll look at how to write J# applications that use Message Queuing 3.0 for communicating between processes. In particular, we'll examine the architecture of Message Queuing 3.0 and look at how to program against message queues using the classes available in the .NET Framework Class Library.

The Architecture of Message Queuing 3.0

If you're familiar with MSMQ running under Windows NT and Windows 2000, you should be aware that the architecture of Message Queuing 3.0 under Windows XP and Windows .NET Server includes some subtle changes.

Queues, Servers, and Active Directory

The Message Queuing 3.0 architecture is based on queues, Message Queuing 3.0 Servers, and Message Queuing 3.0 Clients. Message Queuing 3.0 Servers and Clients (capitalized) are services that run on Windows XP and Windows .NET Server computers; they are distinct from the client and server (lowercase) applications that are built using them.

Applications developed using Message Queuing 3.0 submit messages to queues or receive messages from queues. A queue can be public or private. A *public queue* is created and managed by a single computer, and the details of the queue (but not its messages) are published in the Active Directory database. Active Directory is managed by the domain controller, which is usually also a

Message Queuing 3.0 Server. Other computers in the same domain can use the Message Queuing 3.0 APIs to query Active Directory and obtain information about the public queues in that domain. Applications can submit messages to public queues, subject to any security that is enforced. Depending on where the queues are located, messages might be routed through a Message Queuing 3.0 Server.

Messages sent by a Message Queuing 3.0 Client are temporarily cached in local *outgoing queues* until they have been transmitted. Outgoing queues are created automatically as needed, and they disappear when they're no longer required—you cannot create or delete them yourself. If a Message Queuing 3.0 Client computer becomes detached from the network, it can still be used to send messages, but the messages will be retained in an outgoing queue and transmitted only after a connection to the domain is reestablished. The Message Queuing 3.0 Server can also provide routing services to queues in other domains and remote sites, although it's better if routing servers are not installed on primary domain controllers. (Use a secondary domain controller instead.)

Note Message Queuing 3.0 Client computers in the same domain can have direct connectivity with each other (if they use the same network protocol) and can bypass the Message Queuing 3.0 Server when they send messages to each other, but ideally you should configure Message Queuing 3.0 on these computers to send messages through the Message Queuing 3.0 Server for routing. This can help to control the flow of messages around the network and reduce the amount of bandwidth needed, by concentrating the message traffic.

Of course, the use of public queues depends on all participating computers being members of a domain. A computer that is not part of a domain cannot create or access a public queue and must use private queues instead. (This restriction also applies when you use a workgroup.) Like a public queue, a private queue is created and managed by a single computer, but its details are not published in Active Directory. A computer cannot access a private queue on a second computer unless the first computer knows the name of the private queue and has been granted appropriate access rights by the second computer. Computers that are not part of a domain must have a direct connection to one another because routing facilities will not be available either.

You can use private queues in a domain environment if you need to keep queue information secret.

Transactional Message Queues

When a message is posted to a queue, you can never be quite sure when it will be received. In some applications, you might want to post a message, or a series of related messages, to a queue as part of a single greater atomic operation. You'll also want to ensure that if something goes wrong partway through the operation, any messages already posted can be "unsent"—that is, removed from the queue before being received. Achieving this manually can be a taxing process that involves locking and synchronizing access to the queue along with any other resources involved in the operation. Fortunately, this requirement occurs so often that Microsoft has provided a built-in a mechanism to support it: transactions.

A message queue can be marked as transactional. You probably associate transactions with updates to databases, but the same principle can be applied to any operation that reads and writes data. In the case of a message queue, an application can start a transaction that reads the message from the queue and processes it, and then the application can commit the transaction. In the event of a failure, the transaction will be rolled back and the message will be returned to the head of the queue, ready to be read again.

Transactions can be complex, involving the sending and receiving of multiple messages in conjunction with modifications to other resources such as a database. In the event of a rollback, every send and receive operation performed and every modification made during the transaction must be undone. The Message Queuing 3.0 services work in conjunction with the Microsoft Distributed Transaction Coordinator (MS DTC) to achieve this.

Transactions consume resources, so you should mark a queue as transactional only if it is absolutely necessary.

Managing Queues

You can create and manage queues using code (as described later in this chapter) or manually using the Computer Management snap-in, which is available under Administrative Tools in Control Panel. The Message Queuing service is listed in the Services And Applications folder. You can use the Action menu commands to create, view, and delete messages and message queues when the appropriate folder or queue is selected.

Figure 12-1 shows the Message Queuing configuration on one computer. There's a single public queue called *CakeQueue* (what else?), as well as a pair of private queues called msmqtriggernotifications (which was created automatically and handles message queuing triggers) and MyQueue (which I created manually).

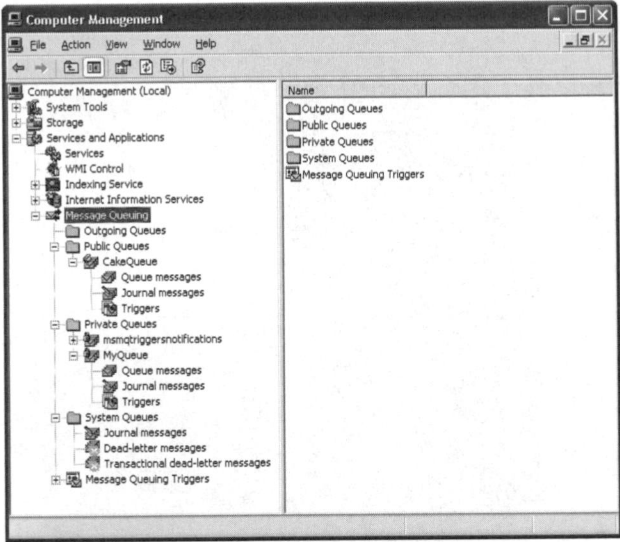

Figure 12-1 The computer management console showing the Message Queuing configuration

If you have the Professional or Enterprise edition of Visual Studio .NET, you can also use Server Explorer to create, examine, and modify message queues, as shown in Figure 12-2.

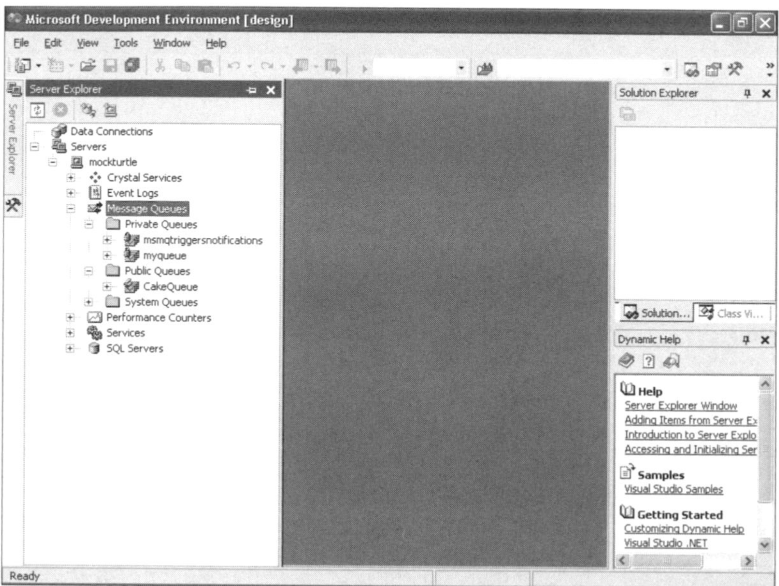

Figure 12-2 Server Explorer in Visual Studio .NET displaying message queues

System Queues

Besides public and private queues, the Message Queuing 3.0 architecture also uses a number of system queues.

The system queues you're most likely to notice are the journal queues and the dead-letter queues. Each computer that's configured to support Message Queuing 3.0 will contain a single outgoing journal queue, which is sometimes referred to as the *computer journal queue*. (It's in the System Queues folder, under Message Queuing in the Computer Management console). When a message is *sent* from the computer, a copy can be retained in this queue, specified on a message-by-message basis. Each message queue, private or public, also has an associated journal queue that records copies of messages *received* on that queue. This feature is disabled by default but can be enabled on a queue-by-queue basis. Each journal is configured with a finite amount of storage. Once this storage is exceeded, new messages will no longer be journaled. (No errors will occur, however.) It's up to the administrator to purge the journal queues periodically.

The dead-letter queues hold messages that failed to be delivered because the destination queue did not exist or the message expired, because it was not delivered within a reasonable time, or because of some other unforeseen error that rendered the message undeliverable. There are two dead-letter queues in the System Queues folder, which are often referred to as the *computer dead-letter queues*. The *Dead-letter messages* queue holds failed nontransactional messages, and the *Transactional dead-letter messages* queue holds failed transactional messages. Again, an administrator should monitor and purge these queues periodically.

Message Delivery

Messages posted to a queue can be assigned a priority that determines how quickly they'll proceed to the head of the queue to be read by a receiving application. The priority can be set to a value between 0 and 7. The value 0 indicates the lowest priority, and 7 is the highest priority (the default is 3). You can specify the priority when you submit a message. Transactional messages always have the same priority (0) because they must be received in the same order in which they were sent, and any priority specified by the developer will be ignored.

Queues can also be assigned a priority between –32768 and 32767. (The default is 0.) Queues with a higher priority will be serviced by the message queuing software in the operating system to deliver messages to applications before those of a lower priority. You should be careful when you modify queue priorities because a low-priority queue can easily be starved by a group of higher-priority ones.

Messages themselves can be delivered to a message queue using one of two modes: express or recoverable. An express message is stored in memory during routing and delivery and consequently can be processed very quickly. The drawback is that if a system failure occurs that causes a machine to shut down, any express messages in the memory of that computer will be lost. Express messages are resistant to network failure, however—they'll simply sit in the memory of the routing server that's attempting to deliver them to the destination until the network connection is restored.

Recoverable messages are written to temporary files on disk as they're transmitted and are thus tolerant to many forms of machine failure and premature shutdown. When the computer restarts, the message queuing service can resume processing recoverable messages. Recoverable messages are also resistant to network failure.

You specify the delivery mechanism as part of the message. (The default is to use recoverable delivery.) Only nontransactional messages can be marked for express delivery; transactional messages must be recoverable.

Message Queuing Triggers

Message queues can be monitored using message queue triggers. A message queue trigger allows you to specify automatic processing when messages are submitted to a queue. A trigger analyzes messages that appear on the queue by applying one or more rules. A rule can specify a match based on criteria such as the message priority, the message contents, or the source of the message. If a rule matches the message, an action indicated by the trigger will be executed. An action can invoke a COM component or run a standalone executable. The trigger itself can leave the message on the queue for a receiving application or remove it, acting as a filter.

You can apply message queue triggers to system queues such as the computer journal queue, as well as to ordinary public and private queues.

Programming Message Queues

Now that you have an understanding of how Message Queuing 3.0 operates, we'll look at how to use it when you build J# applications. The .NET Framework Class Library provides a comprehensive API for interacting with Message Queuing 3.0 in the *System.Messaging* namespace.

Posting and Receiving Messages

We'll adapt the by-now familiar example of the *CakeSizeServer* and *CakeSizeClient* used in many of the preceding chapters to show the use of message queues. Briefly, the *QueuedCakeClient* class (which is contained in the file QueuedCakeClient.jsl in the CakeSizeClient project) constructs a request comprising the details of a cake (size, shape, and filling) and submits it to a public message queue called *CakeQueue* on the computer running the QueuedCakeSizeServer application. (See the file QueuedCakeSizeServer.jsl in the CakeSizeServer project.)

Tip The example described below is spread across four projects. The CakeSizeClient solution file (CakeSizeClient.sln) contains all four projects. If you open this solution using Visual Studio.NET, you'll be able to access all four projects together.

You should create the public, nontransactional *CakeQueue* message queue manually using the Computer Management console before proceeding further. (It is not transactional.)

Note Although a path is specified for the queue, Active Directory will be used to resolve this path and send the message to the appropriate queue. We'll discuss this more later.

The *QueuedCakeSizeServer* reads the *CakeQueue*, validates the request, and then calls the *FeedsHowMany* method of the *CakeInfo* class (in CakeUtils.jsl, in the CakeUtils project), which returns a value indicating how many people the specified cake will feed. This value is packaged up into another message and sent back to the client before the server cleans up and terminates. The client tells the server which queue to reply to as part of the data in the original request (a private queue called *CakeResponse* on the client computer). When the client receives the reply, it unpacks it, displays the result, tidies up, and finishes.

Messages and Serialization

Now for the details. The *FeedsHowMany* method of the *CakeInfo* class expects three parameters of type *short* that indicate the diameter, filling, and shape of the cake. Rather than send this data as three small packages, the client makes use of a new class, *CakeRequest* (in CakeClasses.jsl, in the CakeClasses project) that acts as a wrapper for this information. This class is in the *CakeClasses* namespace, along with the *CakeFilling* and *CakeShape* classes used in earlier chapters.

The contents of messages posted to a message queue are serialized, either as XML or using a binary format. (The programmer can specify which.) For this reason, the *CakeRequest* class is kept simple—it holds public data (properties would have been overkill for this example) so it can be easily serialized as XML, but it is also tagged with *SerializeableAttribute* to support binary serialization.

Note The Message Queuing API also supports the sending and receiving of primitive types if you're developing in C# or Visual Basic .NET, but not if you're developing in J#. The reason for this is the way that the primitive types are handled. In C# and Visual Basic .NET, the primitive types are actually aliases for structures defined in the *System* namespace. C# and Visual Basic .NET support the automatic boxing of structures, which allows structures (value types) to be used like regular objects (reference types). Remember, however, that both J# and Java distinguish between the primitive types and objects, and primitive types cannot be converted automatically to objects or vice-versa. For more details, see Chapter 3.

Attaching to a Queue and Creating a Message

The *main* method of the *QueuedCakeClient* class creates a *System.Messaging.MessageQueue* object that connects to the public queue *CakeQueue* on the computer called WhiteRabbit (the computer running the *QueuedCakeSizeServer* program). Notice that the syntax of a public message queue is *<machine>**<queue>*:

```
import System.Messaging.*;
import CakeClasses.*;
⋮
public class QueuedCakeClient
{
   private static String serverQueuePath = "WhiteRabbit\\CakeQueue";
⋮
   public static void main(String[] args)
   {
      ⋮
// Connect to the public CakeQueue on the server computer
MessageQueue cakeQueue = new MessageQueue(serverQueuePath);
⋮
}
}
```

Note You must reference the assembly *System.Messaging.dll* to use the *System.Message* namespace.

Note Instantiating a new *MessageQueue* object in an application simply creates an object in memory that can be used to access an existing queue—it does not create a physical message queue. If you want to create a message queue programmatically, you must use the *MessageQueue.Create* method, which is described later.

The *main* method creates a *CakeRequest* object and populates it with some sample data that describes a 12-inch square fruit cake. This object is then packed up into a *System.Messaging.Message* object. In addition to the object to be serialized, you can optionally supply the *Message* constructor with an instance of a serializer class. This serializer class instance will be used to serialize the message object into the message body when it is posted to the queue. The *System.Messaging* namespace supplies two ready-made serializers called *BinaryMessageFormatter* and *XmlMessageFormatter* (the default formatter) but you can also define your own by implementing the *IMessageFormatter* interface if you prefer. Note that if you do define your own serializer, you must make it available to the server process that deserializes the message as well as to the client.

Note A third formatter is also available: *ActiveXMessageFormatter*. Previous versions of MSMQ supplied ActiveX components for posting and receiving messages. The format of messages sent using the ActiveX components was different from that emitted by the *BinaryMessageFormatter* and the *XmlMessageFormatter* classes. If you need to interoperate with MSMQ systems that employ the MSMQ ActiveX components, you should use the *ActiveXMessageFormatter* to serialize and deserialize messages:

```
// Create a new cake size request:
// How many people will a 12" square fruit cake feed?
   CakeRequest request = new CakeRequest();
   request.diameter = 12;
   request.shape = CakeShape.Square;
   request.filling = CakeFilling.Fruit;

   // Create a message containing the cake size request
   // Format the message using binary serialization
   Message msg = new Message(request, new BinaryMessageFormatter());
```

Tip Do not confuse the *System.Messaging.Message* class, which defines a message for posting to a message queue, with classes that implement the *System.Runtime.Remoting.Messaging.IMessage* interface, which define messages for transmission using .NET Remoting.

Next, the client sets some selected properties of the message. The *Recoverable* property determines whether the message uses express (in-memory) or recoverable (on-disk) delivery. A value of *false* indicates express delivery which consumes fewer resources. (This is the default.) The *Priority* property should be self-explanatory. You can set the priority value to any of the values in the *MessagePriority* enumeration. The *QueuedCakeClient* class sets the priority to *Low*, indicating that this is not the most urgent of messages. The default priority is *MessagePriority.Normal*, but eight values are available ranging, from *MessagePriority.Lowest* (priority 0) to *MessagePriority.Highest* (priority 7):

```
// Set the message properties - use express delivery (in-memory),
// and set the priority to low
msg.set_Recoverable(false);
msg.set_Priority(MessagePriority.Low);
```

Using a Response Queue

In this example, the client sending a message expects a reply from the server. In theory, the reply could be posted back to the same queue to which the original message was submitted, and this would most likely work if there were only a single client and the client and server coordinated their work with each other. However, as soon as multiple clients started submitting requests and expecting replies, the situation would become untenable—clients could end up reading requests posted by other clients instead of replies to their own requests. The system would soon degenerate into chaos.

To avoid this situation, a client should create its own private message queue and pass the details of that message queue to the server along with the original message. The server should post its reply to this message queue. (This is analogous to the scheme used by connection-oriented sockets, whereby a server listens for requests on a publicly advertised endpoint, but when a client connects to that endpoint a private port is created for sending any replies back to the client.)

To support this protocol, the *Message* class provides the *ResponseQueue* property. You can create a message queue and store a reference to it in this property. The server can extract the value of this property when it reads the message and send the reply back using the specified queue. The *QueuedCakeClient* class uses the local private queue *CakeResponse* for this purpose. Notice that the syntax for a private message queue is <*machine*>\private$\<*queue*>. (You can use "." to refer to the local computer.) The code checks whether the queue already exists using the static *MessageQueue.Exists* method. If the queue does not exist, it is created using *MessageQueue.Create*. (Your application must be running with sufficient privileges—*MessageQueuePermissionAccess.Admin-*

ister—to perform this operation.) Otherwise, a reference to the existing queue is created:

```
private static String responseQueuePath = ".\\private$\\CakeResponse";
⋮
// Create a local, private response queue that the server
// can send the reply to
// Check that the queue does not already exist
// If it doesn't, create it
MessageQueue responseQueue;
if (!MessageQueue.Exists(responseQueuePath))
{
   responseQueue = MessageQueue.Create(responseQueuePath);
}
// If the queue already exists, open it
else
{
   responseQueue = new MessageQueue(responseQueuePath);
}

// Set the ResponseQueue property of the message to this queue
msg.set_ResponseQueue(responseQueue);
```

Posting a Message

Once the response queue has been created, the message can then be sent to the *CakeQueue* using the *Send* method. The parameters to *Send* include the message itself and an optional label—a text string that can be used to identify the message, or filter the message using a queue trigger. The contents of the label are entirely up to the programmer (but make it meaningful). The *QueuedCakeClient* class creates a label comprising the text "Cake Size Request" with the current timestamp appended to the end:

```
// Send the message, with the label
cakeQueue.Send(msg, "Cake Size Request: " + DateTime.get_Now());
```

If you set a breakpoint in the *QueuedCakeClient* class at this point and run the program, you can see the message appearing in the *CakeQueue* on the server computer after the *Send* method is executed. Figure 12-3 shows the Computer Management console on the server computer (WhiteRabbit) with the Queue Messages folder of *CakeQueue* displayed:

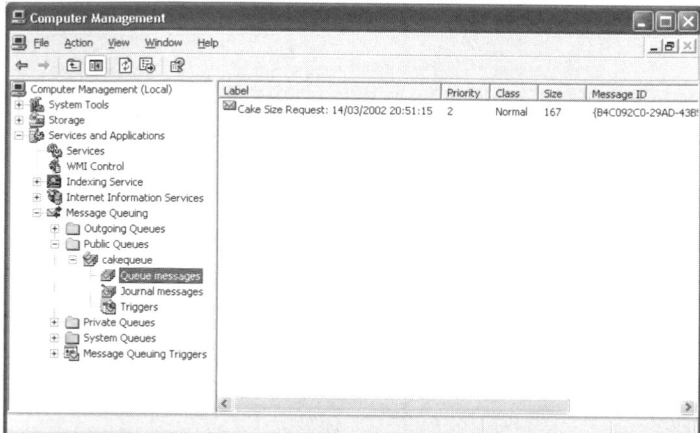

Figure 12-3 The Computer Management console showing the contents of *CakeQueue*

If you double-click on a message, you can display its properties, including the body, as shown in Figure 12-4. If you're concerned about confidentiality, you should encrypt messages (as described later in the chapter).

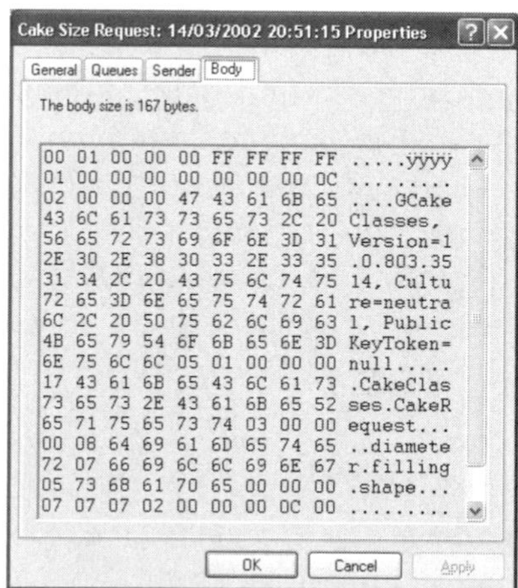

Figure 12-4 The body of a cake size request message

Receiving a Message

Having submitted the request, the *QueuedCakeClient* class waits for the reply to be sent back on the response queue. You do this using the *Receive* method, which will block until a message is available. You can optionally specify a time-out value. (The *QueuedCakeClient* class will wait for a maximum of two minutes.) If a timeout occurs, a *MessageQueueException* will be thrown, which you should be prepared to catch.

```
// Wait for the reply - up to two minutes
msg = responseQueue.Receive(new TimeSpan(0, 2, 0));
```

At this point, it's worth switching our attention to the *QueuedCakeSizeServer* class, which handles the request sent by the *QueuedCakeClient*. The *main* method of the *QueuedCakeSizeServer* class connects to the local public *CakeQueue* (the *QueuedCakeSizeServer* runs on the computer called WhiteRabbit on my network) and then simply calls *Receive*. This time, no timeout parameter is specified, so the method will block until the client posts the request message to the queue, whereupon it will be removed from the queue and returned in the *Message* object (*cakeMessage*) specified as the return value from the *Receive* method:

```
public class QueuedCakeSizeServer
{
   private static String queuePath = ".\\CakeQueue";

   public static void main(String[] args)
   {
      ⋮
      // Connect to the local public CakeQueue
      MessageQueue cakeQueue = new MessageQueue(queuePath);

      // Receive the next request from the queue
      // - this will block until a message arrives
      Message cakeMessage = cakeQueue.Receive();
      ⋮
   }
}
```

Once the message has been received, the message body containing the *CakeRequest* object sent by the client must be extracted. Recall that the message body was serialized using a *BinaryMessageFormatter* object by the client. You should use the same class to deserialize the body. You can do this by setting the *Formatter* property of the message object and then querying the *Body* property. (Even though the *Formatter* property for the message was specified when the message was created, the formatter itself is not actually transmitted with the message, so you must create one when the message is received.)

```
// Get the body of the message
// - deserialize using a BinaryMessageFormatter
cakeMessage.set_Formatter(new BinaryMessageFormatter());
System.Object cakeData = cakeMessage.get_Body();
```

Theoretically, the body of the message can be almost any type of data, so the *Body* property returns an *Object*. You can try to cast this directly into an object of the type you're expecting, but this strategy is not wonderfully safe. Remember that a public message queue is public, so other applications might have posted data to it, possibly containing all sorts of weird and wonderful information. A better approach is to examine the type of the body and cast it only if you can guarantee that it has the appropriate type. In Java, you can use the *instanceof* operator to verify the type of a Java object; a similar approach will also work with J# and the *System.Object* class.

```
// Verify that the message is in the correct format
// Report an error and discard it if not
if (!(cakeData instanceof CakeRequest))
{
   Console.WriteLine("Bad message - discarding");
}
// Otherwise extract the details from the CakeRequest object
// and call FeedsHowMany to generate an answer for the request
else
{
   CakeRequest cakeRequest = (CakeRequest)cakeData;
   :
}
```

After retrieving the *CakeRequest* object from the message body, you can use its contents to invoke the static *FeedsHowMany* method of the *CakeInfo* class. Remember that the value returned (a Java *short*) will be wrapped up into another message and passed back to the client. Also remember that Java and J# do not support the boxing of primitive types into objects, so a Java *short* cannot be placed directly into the body of a message (which must be an *Object*). The value returned from *FeedsHowMany* is used to construct a *java.lang.Short* instead:

```
Short numEaters = new Short(CakeInfo.FeedsHowMany(cakeRequest.diameter,
   cakeRequest.shape, cakeRequest.filling));
```

The next task is to create a message containing this *Short* value and send it back to the client using the response queue specified by the client. You can determine the response queue by querying the *ResponseQueue* property of the original message:

```
// Extract the response queue from the original message
MessageQueue responseQueue = cakeMessage.get_ResponseQueue();
```

The body of the message sent back to the client will comprise the return value from FeedsHowMany—this is held in the Short variable numEaters. Short variables are Object types, but they are sadly not serializable either as XML or using the BinaryMessageFormatter class. One simple solution is to convert the Short into a string using the toString method. (This is the main reason for using a Short rather than a short—you cannot build a string directly from a Java short.) Strings *are* serializable.

The Recoverable flag and the formatter used to serialize the string are also set:

```
// Construct the reply to be sent back to the client
Message reply = new Message(numEaters.toString());
reply.set_Recoverable(false);
reply.set_Formatter(new BinaryMessageFormatter());
```

Note Although you cannot build a string directly from a Java short, you can use a little coercion, as in this example:

```
short s = 10;

String myString = "" + s;
```

However, this code is not particularly clear or elegant, and it can become a maintenance headache, so document it carefully if you choose to use it.

The message can now be sent to the client. Nothing else needs to be placed on the response queue, so it will be closed after the message is sent. This will release whatever resources the queue object was occupying in memory:

```
// Send the reply
responseQueue.Send(reply);
responseQueue.Close();
```

Let's switch our attention back to the client now. The client waiting to receive this reply on the response queue will wake up. The message body received should be scrutinized to make sure it is a string. If all is well, the value returned can be displayed before the client closes the *CakeQueue* and deletes the private response queue using the static *Delete* method of the *MessageQueue* class:

```
// Wait for the reply - up to two minutes
msg = responseQueue.Receive(new TimeSpan(0, 2, 0));
msg.set_Formatter(new BinaryMessageFormatter());
System.Object replyData = msg.get_Body();

// The reply should contain a String value representing a short
// - the number of people the cake will feed
if (!(replyData instanceof String))
{
   Console.WriteLine("Bad reply - discarding");
}
else
{
   // Display the result
   String numEaters = (String)replyData;
   Console.WriteLine("The cake will feed " + numEaters);
}

// Tidy up and free resources
cakeQueue.Close();
MessageQueue.Delete(responseQueuePath);
```

Using Message Queues in Windows Forms and Web Forms Applications

The *QueuedCakeClient* and *QueueCakeSizeServer* examples are console applications. If you're building Windows Forms or Web Forms applications (as described in Chapter 16), you can use the features of Visual Studio .NET to automate some of the programming tasks. Server Explorer allows you to drag-and-drop a message queue onto a form, as shown in Figure 12-5.

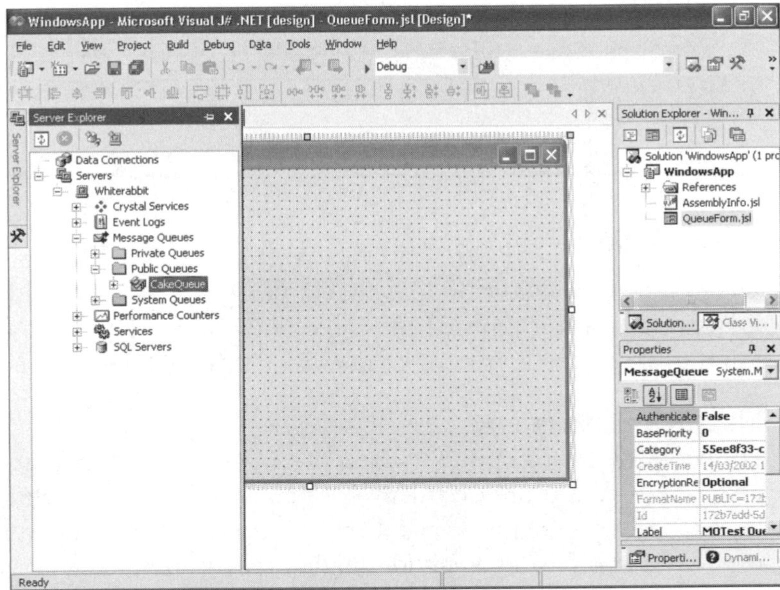

Figure 12-5 Server Explorer showing the *CakeQueue* selected, ready to be dragged onto the form

This will create a *MessageQueue* object and add it to the application, as shown in Figure 12-6.

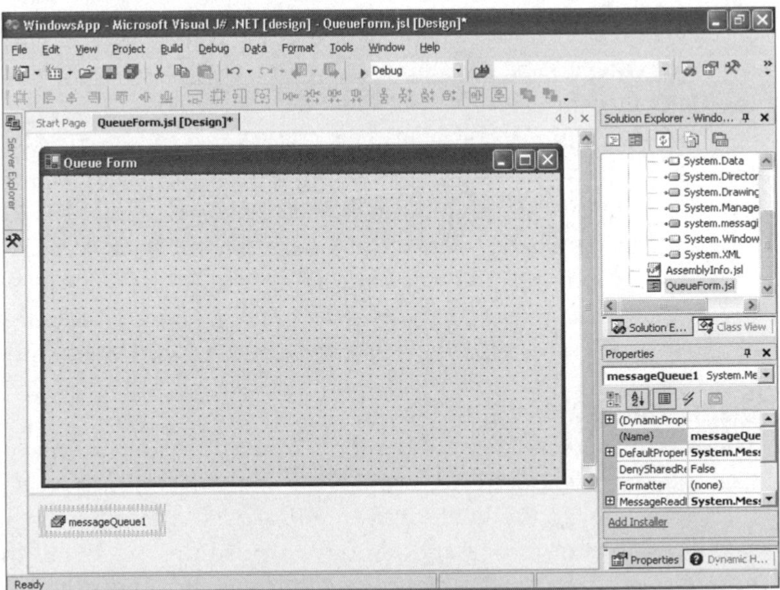

Figure 12-6 The form showing the *MessageQueue* object (*messageQueue1*) underneath

A default name for the *MessageQueue* object will be generated automatically, but you can use the Properties window to view or change it and any other properties of the message queue at design time.

Handling Messages

The *QueuedCakeClient* and *QueuedCakeServer* classes show the essential programming constructs needed to build applications based on message queues, but they also raise a number of questions that we'll address now.

Message Peeking

Perhaps the most important concept to grasp about message queues is that receive operations are destructive. When you execute the *Receive* method of a message queue, the first available message will be removed from the queue and returned to you. (The operation might block if the queue is empty, depending on any timeout specified.) Sometimes you might want to examine a message before removing it in case it is not for you! In this situation, you should use the *Peek* method of the message queue, which returns a copy of the message at the head of the queue while leaving the original message still queued:

```
MessageQueue cakeQueue = ...;
Message cakeMessage = cakeQueue.Peek();
```

The *Peek* method will block if the queue is empty, but as with the *Receive* method, you can specify a timeout. A *MessageQueueException* will be thrown if the timeout expires.

You should also bear in mind that a message queue is a prioritized, first-in-first-out data structure. When you send a message, you have little control over how it flows through the queue, other than being able to specify its priority. You cannot place a message at a particular position in a queue, for example. Likewise, receiving and peeking using the *Receive* and *Peek* methods will involve only the message at the head of the queue (although there are ways of accessing messages elsewhere in the queue, as you'll see in the next section).

Enumerating Messages

The *MessageQueue* class implements message enumeration, which allows you to iterate nondestructively through the messages in a queue. As you access a message, you can modify it or even remove it, although you cannot use an enumerator to insert a message in a given position. To list all the messages in a queue, you can call the *GetMessageEnumerator* method on the queue. This method returns a *System.Message.Messaging.MessageEnumerator* object. You can then use this enumerator to access each message in turn.

The following code fragment creates an enumerator over the public *CakeQueue* and displays the label of each message found in the queue. An enumerator provides access to messages on a message-by-message basis. Chapter 5 described how to use an enumerator, but here's a recap: To access a message, you must advance to it using the *MoveNext* method. You can read the message using the *Current* property. You can then move on to the next message by executing *MoveNext* again. The *MoveNext* method returns a Boolean value—*true* if the operation was successful and another message is available, *false* if you've reached the end of the enumeration. The *Close* method discards the enumerator and frees any resources it occupied:

```
MessageQueue cakeQueue = new MessageQueue(".\\CakeQueue");
MessageEnumerator enumerator = cakeQueue.GetMessageEnumerator();

Message msg = null;
while (enumerator.MoveNext())
{
   msg = enumerator.get_Current();
   Console.WriteLine(msg.get_Label());
}
enumerator.Close();
```

Remember two important points when you use a message enumerator. First, you can proceed forward through the list of messages, but you cannot go back to an earlier message. However, you can invoke the *Reset* method to go right back to the beginning of the enumeration and start over. The second point is that any changes you make to messages or the message queue using an enumeration are dynamic and will have instant effect. For example, if you change the *Priority* of a message to a high value, the message might suddenly be shifted to the head of the queue. A concurrent application receiving from the same queue might then read this message. Similarly, you can delete a message from the queue using the *RemoveCurrent* method of the enumeration, but this can lead to a range of concurrency issues if another application is currently receiving this message. We'll look at how to handle such issues next.

Message Queue Concurrency

Message queues are shared objects, and they can be accessed by multiple applications simultaneously. Although the Message Queuing infrastructure prevents two receive requests from obtaining the same message, it is possible for two peek requests to read the same object, which might be undesirable. The problem is exacerbated when concurrent applications access the same queue at the same time and one of them tinkers with the message queue using an enumerator (as previously described).

An application can request exclusive read access to a message queue when opening it. The message queue constructor has an optional Boolean parameter that defaults to *false* but when set to *true* will obtain exclusive read access when the application reads the message queue using *Receive* or *Peek* or creates an enumerator over the queue:

```
MessageQueue cakeQueue = new MessageQueue(".\\CakeQueue", true);
```

A read lock is not obtained on the queue until the first read operation occurs, but then the read lock will be retained until the queue is closed (using the *Close* method). If a *Receive* or *Peek* method call blocks, the queue can potentially be read-locked for a long time. A second application that attempts to read from the queue at the same time will throw a *MessageQueueException* and access will be denied. Note that this restriction does not apply to *Send* operations. (It would be awkward if an application waiting on an empty queue were also to block all attempts to post a message to that queue!) Similarly, an enumerator can block read access to queue for a lengthy period. An alternative to using an enumerator to iterate through all the messages in a queue is to use the *GetAllMessages* method of the queue. This returns a copy of the contents of the queue as an array of *Message* objects. The queue is read-locked while the array is constructed, but then the queue can be closed and the lock released.

```
Message [] list = cakeQueue.GetAllMessages();
```

Message Aging

When you post a message to a queue, you can never be quite sure when, or even if, it will be received. In some circumstances, if a message is not processed within a particular timeframe it will become obsolete or out of date and should be discarded. Message objects have two properties that can affect the lifespan of a message: *TimeToReachQueue* and *TimeToBeReceived*.

The *TimeToReachQueue* property is a *TimeSpan* indicating the maximum permissible time that can elapse before reaching the destination queue. This property is used most commonly when the destination queue is at a remote site and the message requires routing, if the sender (or the destination queue) is currently disconnected from the network, or if the message will be cached either on the sending machine or on a routing server. If this time expires before the message reaches the destination queue, the message will be deleted. If the *UseDeadLetterQueue* property of the message is set to *true*, a copy of the message will be recorded in the local dead-letter queue. Otherwise, it will be silently discarded, although it might generate a negative acknowledgment message (as explained later).

Note The *TimeToReachQueue* property depends on the system clocks of machines in the network being accurately synchronized.

The *TimeToBeReceived* property is similar, except that it specifies how long the message can live once it reaches the destination queue before being discarded (unless it is received before the time interval elapses):

```
⋮
Message msg = ...;

// Give the message 10 minutes to reach the destination queue
msg.set_TimeToReachQueue(new TimeSpan(0, 10, 0));

// Allow the message to live for an hour if the server process
// is not active
msg.set_TimeToBeReceived(new TimeSpan(1, 0, 0));

// Record the message in the dead-letter queue if it is discarded
msg.set_UseDeadLetterQueue(true);
⋮
```

Correlating Messages

If you're sending a message that expects a reply, you can employ the response queue strategy used in the earlier examples. In a more complex situation, a client might send a number of messages to a server, or to different servers, and expect a response for each message sent. It would therefore be useful to be able to correlate the replies received with the original messages sent.

Each *Message* object has a string *Id* property (which you can examine using the *get_Id* method in J#). This property is read-only and is populated with a message identifier when the *Message* object is sent. The identifier has two parts: the globally unique identifier (GUID) of the sending computer and a unique identifier for the message on that computer. These are fairly meaningless strings to the average human, but if you're interested you can display them. A typical message identifier looks like this:

```
b4c092c0-29ad-43b5-8e73-0f7909f40114\12293
```

The actual value of the message identifier is not important, but the fact that it's unique can be useful. Incidentally, if you examine the *Id* property of a message before sending it, it will consist entirely of zeros; the *Send* method populates the *Id* property.

When a server receives the message from a queue, it can examine the *Id* property of the message and use it to set another property called the *CorrelationId* of the reply message to the same value:

```
// Server, receiving request and sending reply to client
Message cakeMessage = cakeQueue.Receive();
⋮
Message reply = ...;
reply.set_CorrelationId(cakeMessage.get_Id());
⋮
```

When the client receives the reply, it can compare the *CorrelationId* of the reply message against the *Id* of the messages it has sent (assuming the client recorded them somewhere) to determine which message the reply is for. But one tiny little gotcha can occur.

If you examine the *Message* class in the Visual Studio .NET documentation, you'll see that it has a large number of properties, many of which are useful only in certain situations. To save time during a receive operation, not every property belonging to a message is retrieved when the message is received. Instead, message properties are filtered using the *MessageReadPropertyFilter* property object of the message queue they're posted to. The *MessageReadPropertyFilter* property object is really just a collection of Boolean flags that indicate which properties should be read and which should be omitted. By default, the flag corresponding to the *CorrelationId* property is *false*. (The documentation erroneously states that it is *true*, but you can easily verify for yourself that it is not.) If you want to read the *CorrelationId* property of a message, you must set the *CorrelationId* flag of the *MessageReadPropertyFilter* for the queue to *true* before receiving the message:

```
// Client, reading reply from server
MessagePropertyFilter props =
   responseQueue.get_MessageReadPropertyFilter();
props.set_CorrelationId(true);
msg = responseQueue.Receive(...);
⋮
```

If you attempt to read the correlation ID of a message without setting the property filter first, an InvalidOperationException will be thrown.

Peeking, Receiving, and Message IDs

Under normal circumstances, you can receive or peek at only the first available message at the head of a message queue. But if you're correlating messages, the *MessageQueue* class allows you to receive and peek at a message with a specified message ID or correlation ID using the *ReceiveById*, *ReceiveByCorrelationId*, *PeekById*, and *PeekByCorrelationId* methods. These methods expect the appropriate identifier as a parameter, passed in as a string. Message IDs are unique, so the *ReceiveById* and *PeekById* methods will match at most one message. However, several messages can use the same correlation ID. The *ReceiveByCorrelationId* and *PeekByCorrelationId* methods return the first matching message found.

These methods are overloaded. Unless you specify a timeout, they will throw an exception if a message with the specified identifier is not immediately available in the queue. If you do specify a timeout, an exception will be thrown only if a matching message does not appear during the specified interval.

Journaling Messages

Messages have a *UseJournalQueue* property. If this property is set to *true*, the message will be journaled on the originating computer—a copy of the message will be recorded in the journal messages system queue:

```
Message msg = ...;
msg.set_UseJournalQueue(true);
⋮
```

Note that the message will not appear in the journal messages queue until it has been delivered to the destination queue if the destination queue is on a remote computer or until the message has been received if the destination queue is on the local computer.

You can also set the *UseJournalQueue* property of a queue. In this case, the message will be recorded in the journal queue attached to the message queue when the message is delivered to the queue. In other words, setting the *UseJournalQueue* property of a message records the message in the system journal queue on the sending computer, and setting the *UseJournalQueue* property of a message queue records the message in the local journal queue on the destination computer when the message arrives in the queue.

Managing Queues

You've learned how to create and delete queues using the static *Create* and *Delete* methods of the *MessageQueue* class and how to determine whether a given message queue exists using the *Exists* method. Of course, you can also create and delete message queues using the Computer Management console in Control Panel. But in addition to creating and removing queues, you'll often need to perform other administrative tasks with message queues, which we'll look at now.

Message Queue Capacity

By default, message queues have an unlimited capacity, which means, in theory, that they can be asked to hold an infinite number of messages of indeterminate length. (This would require a lot of disk storage!) Under normal circumstances, most commercial applications based on message queues tend to process messages at fairly regular intervals, and message queues never quite reach infinite length. But a rogue situation could arise whereby a process continually posts messages to a queue that is never read.

The *MessageQueue* class exposes two properties that you can use to limit the storage space occupied by a queue: *MaximumQueueSize* and *MaximumJournalSize*. The units for these properties are kilobytes. For example, to limit the size of the *CakeQueue* to 500 KB, you can use the following:

```
cakeQueue.set_MaximumQueueSize(500);
```

A word of warning: Be sure to set the maximum queue size to a value big enough to accommodate the day-to-day processing of the system. If a backlog of messages in a queue grows faster than a server application reading those messages can handle, the queue will fill up. When the maximum size is reached, further messages posted to that queue will be discarded without your realizing it. However, if the sender requests message acknowledgments, a negative acknowledgment for each lost message will be posted to the administration queue specified in the message (as explained later in this chapter).

You can empty a message queue by purging it. You can execute the *Purge* method of the *MessageQueue* object, which discards all messages that are in the queue. This is a nonreversible operation—messages are not sent to the dead-letter queue or the journal queue.

```
cakeQueue.Purge();
```

Message Queue Connection Caching

You're probably aware that when you connect to a shared resource such as a database, a certain amount of checking must be performed and some data structures will have to be initialized to handle the connection. The checks involved ensure that the requested resource actually exists and that the identity of the principal executing the connection request has sufficient privileges. If the shared resource is located remotely, this work can involve a significant burst of network traffic.

When an application has finished using the resource, a close operation often discards all this information. Another connection request by the same application will cause the checking and initialization to be repeated. To reduce this overhead, many shared resources provide connection pooling, whereby a pool of connection handles is created and cached in memory. Connection requests are redirected transparently to the pool. Some checking still needs to be performed, but much of the information required is cached, so a connection is retrieved much more quickly.

Message queue connections can be cached by an application. Whenever you execute *Send*, *Peek*, or *Receive*, a connection handle is used, so pooling can considerably improve performance. The *MessageQueue* class provides the static property *EnableConnectionCache*. When this is set to *true* (the default), message queue connections will be pooled; when set to *false*, pooling will be disabled. Here is how you set this property:

```
MessageQueue.set_EnableConnectionCache(true);
```

When the cache is full, the *MessageQueue* class discards entries from the pool on a least-recently-used basis. However, the size of the pool is managed by the *MessageQueue* class, and you have little control over how big it is, although you can clear the connection pool using the static *ClearConnectionCache* method:

```
MessageQueue.ClearConnectionCache();
```

Message Queue Security

You might want to restrict access to message queues by limiting the identities of principals that can post or read messages on a queue. You use the *SetPermissions* method of a queue for this purpose. This method is overloaded and allows you to indicate the privileges required to manipulate a message queue by using an access control list or by explicitly assigning access rights to individual groups and users.

For example, to permit the user *WONDERLAND\JSharp* to send and receive messages from *CakeQueue*, you can use the code shown in this fragment:

```
cakeQueue.SetPermissions("WONDERLAND\\JSharp",
   MessageQueueAccessRights.WriteMessage |
   MessageQueueAccessRights.ReceiveMessage,
   AccessControlEntryType.Set);
```

Using this form of the *SetPermissions* method, you can grant any of the privileges listed in the *System.Messaging.MessageQueueAccessRights* enumeration, and you can combine privileges, as shown above. Note, however, that this form of *SetPermissions* is absolute—the flag *AccessControlEntryType.Set* will set the specified permissions but eliminate any others previously granted to the selected principal.

Note Granting *ReceiveMessage* access implicitly grants the *PeekMessage* privilege, which allows the user to peek at as well as receive messages.

The alternative is to use *AccessControlEntryType.Allow*, which adds the specified privileges to any that already exist. You can also specify *Revoke* to remove all privileges granted directly to a principal (the *MessageQueueAccessRights* parameter is ignored, and the result can be a little confusing for the unwary), or you can specify *Deny* to actively deny any rights specified.

The following line of code removes the *PeekMessage* privilege from *WONDERLAND\JSharp*. (The *ReceiveMessage* privilege granted earlier will remain, but the user will only be able to receive messages, not peek at them.)

```
cakeQueue.SetPermissions("WONDERLAND\\JSharp",
   MessageQueueAccessRights.PeekMessage,
   AccessControlEntryType.Deny);
```

You can examine the privileges assigned to a message queue using the Computer Management console in Control Panel. Select the message queue, right-click, choose Properties, and then click on the Security tab. Figure 12-7 shows the Security page for *CakeQueue* after the Receive Message privilege has been granted, but the Peek Message privilege has been denied to the user WONDERLAND\JSharp. (The Send Message privilege was also granted—you'd have to scroll down to see it in the dialog box.)

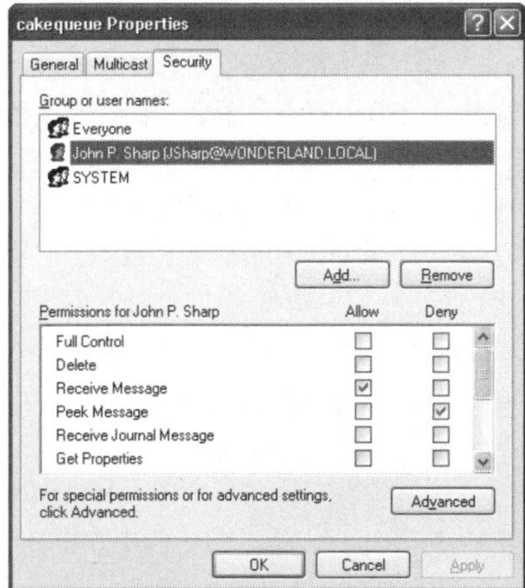

Figure 12-7 The permissions on the *CakeQueue* message queue for the user WONDERLAND\JSharp

If you revoke a user's privileges, the user might still be able to use the message queue if she is a member of one or more groups that still has access. On the other hand, if you explicitly deny a privilege, that user will not be able to perform the associated operation no matter what groups she belongs to.

The owner of the queue (the principal who first created it) has full rights over the queue and does not need to be granted any other privileges to use it, although it is remarkably easy to revoke privileges, even those of the owner—so beware! You can change the permissions applied to the message queue back to the default values supplied by the operating system using the *ResetPermissions* method (assuming you still have sufficient privileges to do so).

Also note that even though any changes you make to the properties of a message queue will be propagated back to Active Directory on the domain controller, message queue properties are also cached in *MessageQueue* objects in the applications that are using them. If you've instantiated a *MessageQueue* object and suspect that its permissions have since been changed (by another application), you can invoke its *Refresh* method to obtain its updated properties from Active Directory.

Enumerating Message Queues

The message queuing infrastructure provides methods that allow you to enumerate the queues available in your domain or workgroup (security permitting, of course). The static method *GetPublicQueues* of the *MessageQueue* class returns an array containing all the public message queues found in Active Directory. The following line of code creates a list of public queues and stores it in the *queues* array:

```
MessageQueue [] queues = MessageQueue.GetPublicQueues();
```

You can iterate through this array, querying each queue as required. The *GetPublicQueues* method is overloaded, and its other variant allows you to specify a selection of criteria that can be matched against properties of message queues. Only queues whose properties match these criteria will be retrieved. You create a *System.Messaging.MessageQueueCriteria* object to hold this information. You can specify a limited number of criteria: *CreatedAfter*, *CreatedBefore*, *ModifiedAfter*, *ModifiedBefore*, *MachineName*, *Label*, and *Category*. (The *Category* property of a message queue allows you to attach the same user-generated GUID to a set of related queues.)

The following example filters the list to return only the queues created before January 1, 2002, on the machine called Alice (my domain controller).

```
MessageQueueCriteria criteria = new MessageQueueCriteria();
criteria.set_CreatedBefore(new DateTime(2002, 1, 1));
criteria.set_MachineName("Alice");
MessageQueue [] queues = MessageQueue.GetPublicQueues(criteria);
```

Note The *MessageQueue* class also contains shorthand versions of *GetPublicQueues* that save you from creating a *MessageQueueCriteria* object. These methods are *GetPublicQueuesByCategory*, *GetPublicQueuesByLabel*, and *GetPublicQueuesByMachine*.

The *GetPublicQueues* method family returns a copy of the message queues identified. Although you can use these copies for sending and receiving messages, you cannot change their properties. If you want to modify the properties of a message queue, you should instead invoke the *GetMessageQueueEnumerator* of the *MessageQueue* class, which returns a *MessageQueueEnumerator*. The enumerator is used in much the same way as a *MessageEnumerator*—you call the *MoveNext* method to iterate through message queues and read the *Current* property to obtain a reference to the current message queue. The *GetMessageQueueEnumerator* method can optionally take a *MessageQueueCriteria* parameter.

Note The *GetPublicQueues* method family and the *GetMessageQueueEnumerator* method obtain message queue information from Active Directory. If the domain controller is down or Active Directory is not available, these methods will fail.

In addition to iterating through public message queues, you can obtain lists of private message queues on a particular computer. The *GetPrivate-QueuesByMachine* method expects the name of a computer as its parameter and returns an array of *MessageQueue* objects:

```
MessageQueue [] queues = MessageQueue.GetPrivateQueuesByMachine("Alice");
```

Unlike the *GetPublicQueues* method family, the *GetPrivateQueuesByMachine* method contacts the specified machine directly to obtain the list of private queues and will therefore function correctly even if a domain controller is not available and Active Directory is not operational.

Asynchronous Operations

The examples presented so far have assumed that receive and peek operations are synchronous. The applications have issued method calls that might block if the requested message queue is empty. One key strength of message queuing solutions is that they're designed for asynchronous operations, and blocking is a feature that should be designed out of any such systems. We'll examine some of the issues involved in asynchronous operations next.

Receiving Messages Asynchronously

The receive and peek operations of the *MessageQueue* class support the asynchronous programming model used elsewhere in the .NET Framework Class Library. The *BeginPeek* and *BeginReceive* methods start a receive or peek operation asynchronously, using a thread from the thread pool. In their simplest form, they raise *PeekCompleted* or *ReceiveCompleted* events as appropriate. An application can subscribe to these events to obtain the information retrieved from the message queue.

Before subscribing to the *ReceiveCompleted* event, you must define a method to act as a callback when the event is raised. This method must conform to the usual requirements of an event handler method: It should take an *Object* parameter that holds the sender of the object, as well as an *EventArgs* parameter that holds event-specific information. In the case of the *ReceiveCompleted* event, the *EventArgs* parameter should be a *System.Messaging.ReceiveCompletedEventArgs* object. The *ReceiveCompletedEventArgs* class exposes the message received through its *Message* property.

The *MessageReceived* method shown on the next page is an example that you can use to subscribe to the *ReceiveCompleted* event:

```
private void MessageReceived(System.Object sender,
   ReceiveCompletedEventArgs args)
{
   // Extract the message
   Message cakeMessage = args.get_Message();

   // Specify the formatter
   cakeMessage.set_Formatter(new BinaryMessageFormatter());

   // Deserialize the message
   CakeRequest cakeData = (CakeRequest)cakeMessage.get_Body();

   // Process the message body
   ⋮
}
```

To subscribe to the *ReceiveCompleted* event, you must set the *ReceiveCompleted* event property of the message queue to a *ReceiveCompletedEventHandler* delegate that refers to the *MessageReceived* method. You can then invoke the *BeginReceive* method:

```
MessageQueue cakeQueue = ...;
⋮
cakeQueue.add_ReceiveCompleted(
   new ReceiveCompletedEventArgs(MessageReceived));
cakeQueue.BeginReceive();
⋮
```

Execution will continue after *BeginReceive*, but when a message has been received, the *MessageReceived* method will run (on its own thread). There is a corresponding event (*PeekCompleted*) and a delegate (*PeekCompletedEventArgs*) for performing an asynchronous peek.

Both the *BeginReceive* and *BeginPeek* methods are overloaded. You can optionally specify a *TimeSpan*. If a message does not become available in the intervening period, the waiting thread will terminate silently (without throwing an exception), and the event handler will not be invoked if a message subsequently arrives in the queue. Further overloads allow you to specify an *AsyncCallback* delegate rather than subscribing to an event, and a programmer-defined state object. In these cases, you should execute the *EndReceive* or *EndPeek* method to obtain the message retrieved from the queue. (If the corresponding *BeginReceive* or *BeginPeek* method timed out, you *will* receive an exception this time).

Note Multithreaded peeking is limited to ordinary peek operations. If you want to call *PeekById* and *PeekByCorrelationId* asynchronously, you must create your own thread to do it.

Disconnected Queues

In the traveling salesperson scenario described at the start of this chapter, the application running on the salesperson's laptop computer submits messages to a queue. These messages are cached locally and then dispatched to the destination queue when the laptop computer is connected to the corporate network. Message Queue 3.0 supports this mode of operation, but there is one issue: Normally, when an application sends a message to a queue the underlying infrastructure must be able to locate the target queue. (Message Queue 3.0 takes the view that if the queue does not exist, it would be useful to throw some sort of exception rather than silently lose messages!) If the target queue is a private queue on another machine, the message queuing infrastructure will attempt to contact the destination machine, fail, and throw an exception almost immediately. If the target queue is a public queue, the message queuing infrastructure will instead try to contact the domain controller so it can query Active Directory for the details and routing information of the target queue. Again, if the laptop is disconnected from the network, this will fail and throw an exception (but not immediately—the underlying mechanisms will allow a little time for the domain controller to respond before timing out).

Sending a message to a message queue when you're disconnected from the network therefore requires a little cunning. You can identify a message queue when you instantiate a *MessageQueue* object in a few ways. The techniques shown so far have specified the pathname of the message queue (*WhiteRabbit\\CakeQueue*, for example), and these need to be resolved either by contacting the target machine in the case of a private message queue or through Active Directory if the message queue is public (as just described). An alternative is to use a format name. Format names do not require any further resolution, so if the named queue is not immediately accessible it doesn't matter.

Several types of format name are available, but the simplest and most portable simply specifies the GUID of the destination message queue with a *PUBLIC* or *PRIVATE* prefix. The GUID of a public message queue is assigned when the queue is created, and you can find it by using the Computer Management console and examining the *ID* property, as shown in Figure 12-8.

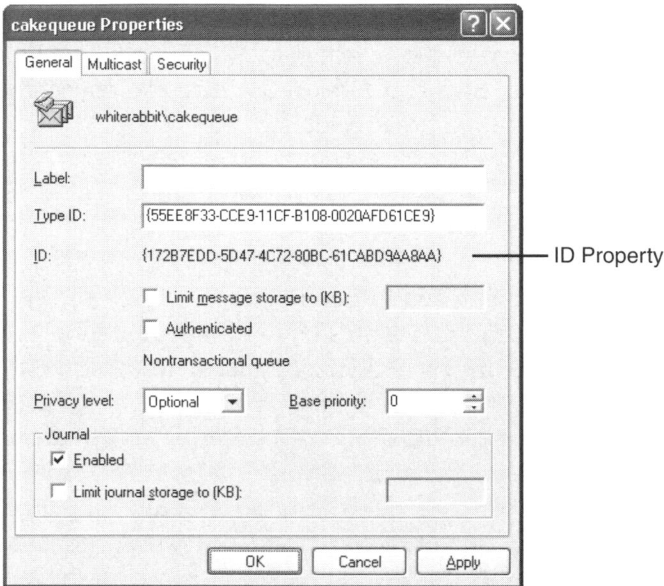

Figure 12-8 The properties of the *CakeQueue* message queue

Once you know the GUID of a public message queue, you can create a *MessageQueue* object that's capable of supporting a disconnected send operation:

```
private static String serverQueuePath =
   "FORMATNAME:PUBLIC=172B7EDD-5D47-4C72-80BC-61CABD9AA8AA";
⋮
MessageQueue cakeQueue = new MessageQueue(serverQueuePath);
```

When a message is sent to this queue, if the laptop computer is connected to the network the message will be transmitted. If the laptop computer is disconnected, the message will be cached locally in an outgoing queue and transmitted automatically once a network connection is reestablished. Remember that if the *TimeToReachQueue* property of the message is specified, the message will start to age when it is sent and might expire while still cached locally if the period is too short. Also notice that if the public queue is dropped and re-created, its GUID will change, rendering the format name useless! In other words, once you've created the public queues needed for processing messages in your system, you should keep them —don't drop them and rebuild them unless you're prepared to reset any disconnected clients that access them.

An alternative is to use a direct format name that comprises the address of the computer that holds the destination message queue and the name of the queue. The address can be specified in the form of an IP address, a machine name, or an HTTP URL. For example, the *CakeQueue* public queue on the computer called WhiteRabbit can be referenced as follows:

```
private static String serverQueuePath =
   "FORMATNAME:DIRECT=OS:WhiteRabbit\\CakeQueue";
```

Then again, if you know the IP address of the destination computer, you can use it for referencing the queue. (Do not use this approach if the destination computer's address is obtained using DHCP because the address might change.)

```
private static String serverQueuePath =
   "FORMATNAME:DIRECT=TCP:192.168.1.2\\CakeQueue";
```

A private message queue does not have a GUID, so a different type of format name must be used for disconnected operations. Again, several options are available, including the ability to use direct format names, as shown in this example:

```
private static String responseQueuePath =
   "FORMATNAME:DIRECT=TCP:192.168.1.2\\PRIVATE$\\CakeResponse";
```

The simplest format comprises the GUID of the target machine and the number of the queue on that machine. The machine GUID is created when message queuing is installed on a computer, and you can find the GUID allocated to a computer by calling the static *MessageQueue.GetMachineId* method and passing the name of the machine as a string parameter. You can do this only while you're connected to the network, but once you've obtained the GUID for a computer, it will not change unless message queuing is reinstalled on that computer. The queue number is an eight-digit identifier.

Determining the queue number for a private queue is a convoluted process—use Windows Explorer to navigate to the folder \WINDOWS\System32\MSMQ\Storage\Lqs, look through the names of the files to locate the storage file corresponding to your private message queue, and find the eight-digit prefix. For example, the storage file named 00000043.6ab7c4b8 is for private message queue number 00000043. (Storage files that comprise a GUID without a prefix are for public queues, and you can ignore those.) After establishing the GUID of the target computer and the number of the message queue, you can string them together and specify them as the format name. A typical format name for a private message queue looks like this:

FORMATNAME:PRIVATE=B4C092C0-29AD-43B5-8E73-0F7909F40114\00000003

Tip You can also find the format name of a private message queue by creating a *MessageQueue* object using a pathname (such as .\private$\CakeResponse) while you're connected to the domain (so the Active Directory lookup will operate) and then querying the *FormatName* property of the *MessageQueue* object. You can then replace the path in your code with the format name, recompile the program, and execute it while you're disconnected from the network.

Again, note that if a private message queue is deleted and rebuilt, its queue number will probably change, with all that this implies for client applications.

Some restrictions apply when you use format names: You cannot test for the existence of, create, or delete a queue that's specified using a format name, for example.

Requesting an Acknowledgment

When you send a message to a queue, you can arrange for information messages to be dispatched to another message queue whenever something significant happens to the original message, such as safe delivery to the destination queue or successful receipt by the server application. These messages are generated by the underlying message queuing infrastructure and are referred to as *positive acknowledgments*. You can also request that messages be generated if a failure is detected, such as a message expiring before it is delivered. These are examples of *negative acknowledgments*. If you want to see the different acknowledgments, positive and negative, that are available, you can look up the *System.Messaging.AcknowledgeTypes* enumeration in the Visual Studio .NET documentation.

To request an acknowledgement, you set the *AdministrationQueue* property of a message to a queue for receiving the acknowledgement messages. This queue is referred to as an *administration queue*, and it is often created specifically for holding acknowledgment messages, although any public or private queue can be used:

```
private static String adminQueuePath = ".\\private$\\AdminQueue";
⋮
Message msg = ...;
// Create or open the Admin queue to hold the acknowledgement messages
MessageQueue adminQueue;
```

```
if (!MessageQueue.Exists(adminQueuePath))
{
   adminQueue = MessageQueue.Create(adminQueuePath);
}
// If the queue already exists, open it
else
{
   adminQueue = new MessageQueue(adminQueuePath);
}
msg.set_AdministrationQueue(adminQueue);
```

You must also indicate which acknowledgements you want to receive by setting the *AcknowledgeType* property of the message. You can set this property to any of the values in the *AcknowledgeTypes* enumeration, and if you require acknowledgements for more than one event as the message passes through the network, you can combine values. The following code fragment requests acknowledgement when the message is delivered to the destination queue and when the server process has received the message:

```
msg.set_AcknowledgeType(
   AcknowledgeTypes.FullReachQueue | AcknowledgeTypes.FullReceive);
```

When the message, *msg*, is sent to a queue, the various acknowledgment messages will appear in the administration queue specified by the message. An application can read the administration queue and track the message. Messages posted to the administration queue have no body; instead, they provide information about the message they refer to through properties. The two most important properties are *Acknowledgment* and *CorrelationId*. The *Acknowledgment* property indicates the acknowledgment event that generated the message and is one of the values in the *System.Messaging.Acknowledgment* enumeration (not to be confused with the *AcknowledgeTypes* enumeration). The value *ReachQueue* indicates that the message reached the destination queue, and the value *Receive* specifies that the message was successfully received. The *CorrelationId* contains the *Id* of the original message but is available only if you set the *CorrelationId* property of the *MessageReaderPropertyFilter* of the queue to *true*, as described earlier.

The following code fragment reads and processes a message from the administration queue to determine whether it is acknowledging delivery or receipt of the message:

```
⋮
adminQueue.get_MessageReadPropertyFilter().set_CorrelationId(true);
Message adminMsg = adminQueue.Receive();
if (adminMsg.get_Acknowledgment().Equals(Acknowledgment.ReachQueue))
{
```

```
    Console.WriteLine("Message " + adminMsg.get_CorrelationId() +
    " reached its destination queue");
}
if (adminMsg.get_Acknowledgment().Equals(Acknowledgment.Receive))
{
    Console.WriteLine("Message " + adminMsg.get_CorrelationId() +
        " received by destination application");
}
⋮
```

Note Peeking at a message does not count as receiving it because the message is not actually removed from the queue. Therefore, a peek operation will not generate a *Receive* acknowledgment.

Messaging in the Real World

Many commercial applications have stringent requirements regarding reliability, security, and connectivity. The remainder of this chapter will examine how Message Queuing 3.0 addresses these issues.

Reliability and Transactions

Earlier, you learned the basic theory behind using transactions with message queues. The practical implementation of this theory is quite straightforward. First and foremost, transactions can be used only with transactional message queues. (Message queues are nontransactional by default.) You specify whether a message queue supports transactions when you create it. If you're using the Computer Management console in Control Panel or Server Explorer in Visual Studio .NET, the dialog box that specifies the queue details includes a check box that you should select if you want to make the queue transactional. Figure 12-9 shows the Create Message Queue dialog box of Server Explorer.

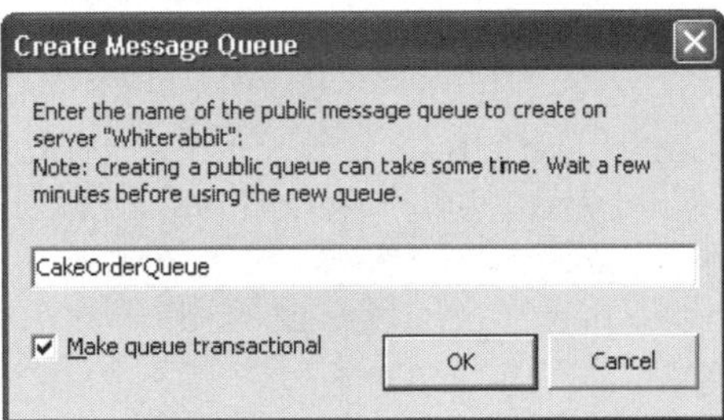

Figure 12-9 The Create Message Queue dialog box in Visual Studio .NET

Alternatively, you can execute the static *MessageQueue.Create* method and use the optional second parameter. A value of *true* indicates that the queue is transactional:

```
MessageQueue.Create("WhiteRabbit\\CakeOrderQueue", true);
```

You can query the *Transactional* property of a message queue to determine whether it supports transactions, but once the message queue is built you cannot change this property.

To post a message to a transactional queue, you should either create a new transaction or join an existing one. Before going any further, you should understand that message queuing supports two categories of transactions, internal and external. Internal transactions are created using the *MessageQueueTransaction* class in the *System.Messaging* namespace, and they are implemented by the message queuing service. External transactions are transactions created and managed by software and services that are not part of the message queuing service—SQL Server or COM+, for example.

External transactions and internal transactions offer similar functionality, but internal message queuing transactions are independent of external transactions. A COM+ component or a SQL Server stored procedure cannot join a transaction created by the message queuing service. However, the message queuing service can join some transactions that were created externally depending on how they're defined. Confused? Let's consider both types of transaction and discuss how to use them.

Using Internal Transactions

To use an internal transaction to send a message, you create a *MessageQueueTransaction* object, initiate the transactions using the *Begin* method of the transaction object, perform one or more transactional send operations, and then execute the *Commit* method of the transaction object. The *Send* method includes an optional *MessageQueueTransaction* parameter that specifies the transaction that the *Send* method call belongs to. The messages become available to a receiver only after the transaction has been successfully committed. The messages will be delivered in the same sequence in which they were sent. If the sender detects an error while posting messages, it can execute the *Abort* method of the transaction object. This method will remove all messages from the queue that have been sent since the *Begin* method was executed.

The following code fragment shows two send operations to the transactional *CakeOrderQueue*, which are performed as part of the same transaction:

```
// Sending application
MessageQueue cakeOrderQueue = ...;
MessageQueueTransaction transact = new MessageQueueTransaction();
transact.Begin();
Message message1 = ...;
Message message2 = ...;
try
{
   cakeOrderQueue.Send(message1, "Message Label1", transact);
   cakeOrderQueue.Send(message2, "Message Label2", transact);
   transact.Commit();
}
catch (System.Exception e)
{
   transact.Abort();
}
```

Note Transactions can be nested, and inner transactions will not complete until the outermost transaction either commits or aborts. If the outermost transaction aborts, all inner transactions that indicated that they would commit will be aborted instead. Furthermore, a nested transaction that aborts will ultimately cause the outermost transaction to abort as well, along with all other nested transactions belonging to the outermost transaction. Also note that if you fail to commit a transaction, it will be aborted when the *MessageQueueTransaction* object is destroyed.

You cannot use the transactional version of the *Send* method to post a message to a nontransactional queue. (It will throw an exception.) However, you can post a message to a transactional queue without defining a transaction. In this case, the message queuing service will automatically create a transaction for you, begin it, send the message, and commit it when the send operation is complete. This is referred to as a *singleton transaction* because it comprises a single operation only. One exception to this rule is especially important if you're building applications designed to function in a disconnected environment: If you send a single, nontransactional message to a transactional message queue on a remote computer identified using a direct format name, a transaction will not be created and the message will be posted to the local transactional dead-letter queue instead (provided that you set the *UseDeadLetterQueue* property of the message—otherwise, it will disappear silently).

You receive messages from a transactional queue using a similar approach. You create a transaction, execute *Begin*, perform one or more transactional *Receive* method calls (*Receive* can optionally take a *MessageQueueTransaction* as a parameter), and then execute *Commit* when all the messages have been successfully received. If an error occurs, you can execute *Abort*, and all messages received since the *Begin* method call will be returned to the queue:

```
// Receiving application
MessageQueue cakeOrderQueue = ...;
MessageQueueTransaction transact = new MessageQueueTransaction();
transact.Begin();
try
{
   Message message1 = cakeOrderQueue.Receive(transact);
   Message message2 = cakeOrderQueue.Receive(transact);
   transact.Commit();
⋮
}
catch (System.Exception e)
{
   transact.Abort();
}
```

Although transactions guarantee the atomicity of multiple send and receive operations and ensure that messages are received in precisely the same order that they were sent, the programmer is responsible for ensuring that everything that is sent is received. In other words, if a sender posts four messages as a transaction, the receiver should receive four messages—not three, not five. How does a sender know how many messages comprise a transaction? Each message has a *TransactionId* property that contains the 16-bit identifier of the sending computer and a 4-byte transaction sequence number. All messages that belong to the same transaction will have the same *TransactionId*. A receiving application can peek at each message in the queue, examine its *TransactionId*, and determine whether it is part of the same transaction as the previous message received. (Peeking is nondestructive and does not count as a transactional operation.) If the *TransactionId* matches, the message should be received; if not, the final message has been received, so the receive transaction should commit.

Alternatively, you can examine the *IsFirstInTransaction* and *IsLastInTransaction* properties of a message, which will be *true* if the message is the first or the last message, respectively, in a transaction. If the transaction contains a single message only, both of these properties will be *true* at the same time.

Caution The *TransactionId, IsFirstInTransaction* and *IsLastInTransaction* properties are further examples of message properties that are not retrieved by default. You must set the *TransactionId, IsFirstInTransaction* and *IsLastInTransaction* flags of the *MessageReadPropertyFilter* of the message queue to *true* before peeking at or receiving messages if you want to query these properties.

A final point to consider: Message queue transactions are apartment-aware, so if the apartment state of your application is single-threaded, you will not be able to access the same transaction from multiple threads. Chapter 8 describes how to change the apartment state of a thread.

Using External Transactions

An external transaction is created outside the scope of the message queuing service. When you use the .NET Framework, classes that employ external transactions must inherit from the *System.EnterpriseServices.ServicedComponent* class. External transactions can then be defined declaratively (as described in Chapter 3). For example, you can tag the *QueuedCakeClient* class with a *TransactionAttribute* that forces the creation of a new external transaction when its methods are executed:

```
import System.EnterpriseServices.*;
⋮
/** @attribute TransactionAttribute(TransactionOption.RequiresNew) */
public class QueuedCakeClient extends ServicedComponent
{
    ⋮
}
```

The *Send* and *Receive* methods of the *MessageQueue* class allow you to specify that the send or receive operation should be part of the external transaction, as in this example:

```
cakeOrderQueue.Send(message1, "Message Label1",
   MessageQueueTransactionType.Automatic);
```

You can commit the transaction using the static *SetComplete* method of the *System.EnterpriseServices.ContextUtil* class:

```
ContextUtil.SetComplete();
```

Alternatively, you can use the *SetAbort* method to roll back the transaction. (External transactions, the *ContextUtil* class, and serviced components will be described in detail in Chapter 14.)

Message Authentication and Encryption

An earlier section described how to query and modify the access control privileges associated with an individual message queue. An application can send or receive messages from a message queue only if the principal executing the application has been granted the appropriate access rights. However, in addition to controlling who has access to message queues, it is also important to be able to authenticate the sender of a message and to guarantee the integrity of that message. These considerations become critical when you perform messaging over a WAN or the Internet.

Authenticating Messages

Authenticating the sender of a message is a slightly more complex process than authenticating principals when you use other technologies because of the asynchronous nature of message queues. The security mechanisms cannot assume that the sender is always connected to the computer that holds the destination message queue. To be authenticated, therefore, messages themselves must contain information about the sender. This information takes the form of a digital signature and a certificate.

To send an authenticated message, the principal sending the message must have previously obtained a certificate and registered it in Active Directory in the domain that holds the destination queue, associating it with the Windows Security ID (SID) of the principal. A certificate is generated automatically for each user of a computer after message queuing has been installed, and this internal certificate can be registered with Active Directory using the Computer Management console in Control Panel. You select the Message Queuing service, choose Properties from the Action menu, and then click on the User Certificate tab in the Message Queuing Properties dialog box, as shown in Figure 12-10. Click Register to register the current user certificate.

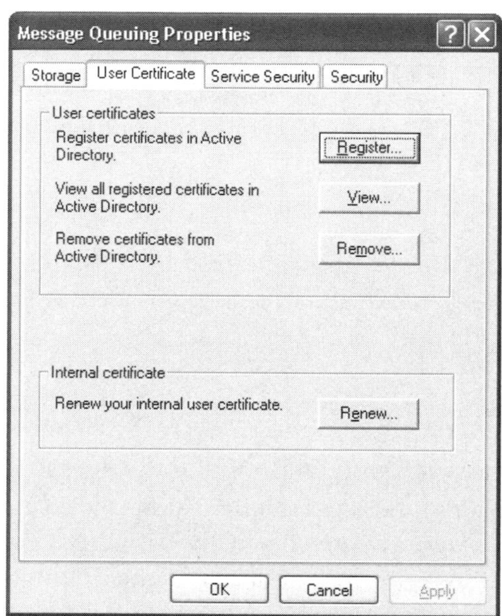

Figure 12-10 The User Certificate tab of the Message Queuing Properties dialog box

Certificates created and stored in this way are referred to as *internal certificates*. If you require a higher level of security, you can also obtain external certificates issued by a certification authority and register them manually in Active Directory.

When an authenticated message is posted to a queue, the sender creates a digital signature for the message based on its contents and a private cryptographic key. The sender attaches its SID, the public certificate (containing the public key needed to decrypt the digital signature), and the digital signature to the message as it is sent to the message queue. A receiver can compute its own digital signature for the message, decrypt the signature sent with the message using the public key supplied with the message, and compare the two signatures. If they are the same, the message has not been tampered with. The receiver can then examine the user certificate held in Active Directory for the SID supplied with the message, and if it matches the certificate posted with the message, the receiver can also be reasonably sure that the sender is authentic.

Sending and Receiving an Authenticated Message

Once users have been certified and registered, you can enable authentication when you use a message queue by setting the *Authenticate* property of the queue. You can do this in code (call *set_Authenticate(true)* on the appropriate *MessageQueue* object) or from the Computer Management console. Just select the queue to use and choose Properties from the Action menu. In the Properties dialog box, select the Authenticated check box, as shown in Figure 12-11.

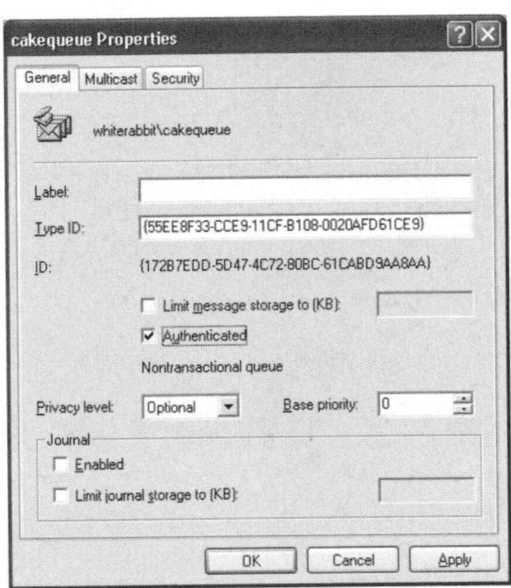

Figure 12-11 The Properties dialog box for the *CakeQueue* message queue

When this property is set, all messages sent to the queue must be authenticated; otherwise, they'll be rejected. (They'll be redirected to the sender's dead-letter queue if the *UseDeadLetter* property of the message is set to *true*, or they will just vanish). You can arrange for a message to be authenticated by setting the *UseAuthentication* property to *true* (call *set_UseAuthentication(true)* in J#). When the message is posted, it will be signed as described above, and the digital signature and SID of the sender will be attached automatically. When the message is received, the authentication process will check the contents of the message and the attached certificate. Again, this will happen automatically.

If you want to use a different mechanism, you can set the *AuthenticationProvider* and *AuthenticationProviderType* properties of the message to the name of an authentication provider and the type of authentication it performs, respectively. (Registering alternative authentication providers is beyond the scope of this book.)

Encrypting a Message

Authentication guarantees that the sender and the message are both valid, but the message can still be intercepted and read by a third party. To secure a message, you must encrypt it. Encryption is optional by default, but you can enforce it on a message queue by setting the *EncryptionRequired* property to *EncryptionRequired.Body* in code or by setting the Privacy Level to Body in the message queue Properties dialog box in the Computer Management console (shown earlier in Figure 12-11). After you set this message queue property, you should set the *UseEncryption* property for all messages to *true* and set their *EncryptionAlgorithm* property to one of the supported encryption algorithms.

Messaging over HTTP

A neat new feature of Message Queuing 3.0 is the ability to access message queues over the Internet. You can address a message queue using a format name comprising a URL that specifies the host computer and the name of the message queue. For example, to access the public *CakeQueue* message queue on *WhiteRabbit* over HTTP, you can use the following:

```
FORMATNAME:DIRECT=HTTP://WhiteRabbit/msmq/CakeQueue
```

A format name is required because Active Directory does not hold the details of message queues available over the Internet. The *msmq* element is important because it specifies that the URL is that of a message queue rather than some other type of resource. It will always occur after the computer name but before the name of the queue. Messages sent to an HTTP destination will be transmitted using SOAP. Note that you cannot send messages that have the *UseEncryption* property set to *true* over HTTP—an exception will be thrown if you try. If you want to encrypt messages over the Internet, you should use Secure Sockets Layer (SSL) and specify the HTTPS transport in the format name.

Summary

In this chapter, you learned how to use message queues to build distributed applications. We covered the architecture of Message Queuing 3.0, how to create queues, and how to implement security. You also learned how to write J# programs that connect to a queue, post a message, receive a message, and reply using a response queue. You saw how to employ the asynchronous programming model and exploit events and threads to maximize throughput when you wait for messages to appear on a queue. Finally, you learned techniques such as how to use disconnected queues for applications that are only periodically attached to a network.

Part IV

Integrating with Windows

13

Integrating with Unmanaged Components

In an ideal world, you'd be able to combine components in a seamless manner without having to worry about how they were implemented, which languages they were created with, which tools were used to build them, or even the platform they execute on. The Java programming language was designed to be portable and all-pervasive, and even though it has not lived up to the hype of the early days, it is available on almost every common computing platform. Java applications created on one computer will run unchanged on a totally different computer and processor architecture as long as the developer remains within the confines of the standard libraries supplied with the JDK. What's more, Java applications can consume Java components (JavaBeans and Enterprise JavaBeans) that were compiled on any computer and developed using any of the commercially available Java compilers—as long as they emit standard Java bytecodes. Interoperability between components created using the Java programming language is, by definition, easy.

Microsoft .NET has a similar aim in terms of interoperability, but the common language runtime takes things a step further. You saw in Chapter 2 how components can be written in one .NET-compliant language and consumed by applications written in another. The main requirement for this feat is that both languages be compiled to produce assemblies that are executed by the common language runtime.

While the seamless integration of components and applications is fine for new development, a large base of existing, heritage (legacy) code is still out there. For the foreseeable future, in many enterprise applications you'll be confronted with the challenge of integrating software into your systems that was created using technologies other than .NET. For example, you might have a number of COM components that you've purchased or that you've expended a great deal of effort to produce, and you might not want to discard them. You might need to use heritage library routines implemented as functions in regular DLLs. You might also want to make use of certain specialized services of Microsoft Windows XP, such as the System Restore API or the Background Intelligent Transfer Service. These services do not currently have .NET interfaces available, so you have to use alternative means. In still another scenario, you might find yourself needing to integrate with Java 2 Enterprise Edition (J2EE) applications or even CORBA components.

In this chapter, we'll examine some of the more common options for meeting these challenges. In particular, you'll learn how to invoke functions implemented in DLLs and how to use various techniques for integrating COM components into .NET. (I'll assume that you're already familiar with COM.) We'll also look at how to make .NET components available to COM clients. Finally, we'll consider some ideas for integrating existing J2EE and CORBA objects into a .NET application.

Managed and Unmanaged Code

Before proceeding further, let's review part of the.NET architecture, along with some terminology. As you'll recall from Chapter 2, code built for .NET executes in an application domain, which runs under the auspices of the common language runtime. This code uses the facilities of the .NET platform to provide features such as type safety, code verification, memory allocation and deallocation, and other runtime management. Such code is therefore said to be *managed*. On the other hand, COM components, DLLs, and other heritage objects are not designed to operate in such a cozy, safe environment. They can freely stamp all over memory allocated to the application in which they are running, leak memory like a sieve, do freaky things such as invalid type casting, and generally make a mess. This kind of code is said to be *unmanaged*.

To further contrast these two modes, consider the following:

- The common language runtime executes machine code, not Microsoft Intermediate Language (MSIL). The JIT compiler converts MSIL into machine code before the common language runtime runs it. The common language runtime is itself a set of unmanaged DLLs (mscoree.dll, mscorwks.dll, mscorsvr.dll, and others) that provide memory management, protection, and garbage collection (referred to as the *managed heap*). It relies on tools such as compile-time verification (which can be turned off!) to ensure that the code does not do anything bad.

- Unmanaged code executes in the same process as managed code. The common language runtime can load an unmanaged DLL and invoke its methods. An unmanaged DLL cannot be verified, like MSIL can. As a result, unmanaged methods can do anything to the process, as described above. Furthermore, although unmanaged code uses its own unmanaged heap and stack space, it can access the managed heap of the common language runtime through methods exposed by the .NET Framework Class Library. It is thus vitally important that any unmanaged code that you execute from the common language runtime be trustworthy and correct! Security constraints relating to unmanaged code are described later in this chapter.

At this juncture, a couple of points are worth noting. First, even though managed and unmanaged code function as part of the same process, they are said to execute in different spaces, mainly because managed code is executed by common language runtime DLLs and unmanaged code isn't. The managed and unmanaged spaces have their own heaps, and managed and unmanaged code sometimes use different data formats. Second, calling unmanaged code from the managed environment requires a transition from the managed to the unmanaged space. This procedure involves the marshaling of data, passing information to convey how method parameters and return types should be interpreted in the two different spaces, and indicating how the unmanaged code should be located and invoked. The situation is conceptually similar to performing cross-apartment method calls in COM, and some of the techniques used are also similar.

Invoking Methods in Unmanaged DLLs

Despite its aim of being a globally portable platform, the Java language has always acknowledged the potential need to interact with non-Java code. The Java platform defines the Java Native Interface (JNI), which allows a developer to create native language adapters (typically written in C or C++) for interfacing with non-Java libraries. JNI provides tools and defines language bindings, allowing you to pass Java objects and types to a native language adapter, which can then convert them to native language types before forwarding them to the target library. Although JNI can generate skeleton code for an adapter, you must implement the adapter yourself. Thus, although the scheme used is highly flexible, you must have a good understanding of how to map Java types to native types and vice versa to use it successfully.

The JNI is not available in J#, but if you want to access functions implemented in native DLLs, all is not lost. J/Direct, a feature that Microsoft provided with Visual J++ 6.0, is also available with J#.

Using J/Direct

J/Direct uses compiler directives to define native methods declaratively. The common language runtime loads the target DLL and performs any data marshaling indicated automatically without your having to write an adapter. All you have to do is specify which functions in which DLLs you want to call, and then you can call those functions as if they were regular methods in the common language runtime. The common language runtime provides the .NET interop marshaler that converts data from managed J# formats and passes them to the unmanaged space as the corresponding unmanaged types. It converts output parameters and return values back to managed J# types.

Isomorphic and Nonisomorphic Types

Managed types that have directly equivalent unmanaged types can be passed from managed to unmanaged space without the marshaler having to perform any work. This is because the layout of these types in memory is the same in managed and unmanaged space. Such types are referred to as *isomorphic* (or *blittable*). In other instances, the marshaler might need to perform some rearrangement of data in memory. These types are referred to as nonisomorphic. In the simplest cases, the compiler and the runtime can establish how to map J# types into their unmanaged equivalents automatically. Table 13-1 lists the mappings that are implemented automatically when you use J/Direct with J#. In more complex cases, such as when you pass complex data types or interfaces as parameters, you might need to provide explicit information to the marshaler about the various conversions required.

Table 13-1 Java and Windows Native Type Mappings

Java Type	Native Type
byte	*BYTE* or *CHAR*
short	*SHORT* or *WORD*
int	*INT, UINT, LONG, ULONG, HWND* or *DWORD*

Table 13-1 Java and Windows Native Type Mappings

Java Type	Native Type
Char	*TCHAR*
Long	*__int64*
Float	*Float*
Double	*Double*
boolean	*BOOL*
java.lang.String, *System.String* (immutable)	*LPCTSTR* (ANSI) or *LPCWSTR* (Unicode); not allowed as a return type
java.lang.StringBuffer (mutable)	*LPTSTR* (ANSI) or *LPWSTR* (Unicode); not allowed as a return type
java.lang.Integer	*4-byte integer*
java.lang.Boolean	4-byte *BOOL*
java.lang.Char	*CHAR* (ANSI) or *WCHAR* (Unicode)
java.lang.Short	2-byte *SHORT*
java.lang.Float	4-byte *FLOAT*
java.lang.Object, *System.Object*	Pointer to a *struct*
Void	*VOID*; allowed only as a return type
byte[]	*BYTE* *
short[]	*WORD* *
char[]	*TCHAR* *
int[]	*DWORD* *
float[]	*float* *
double[]	*double* *
long[]	*__int64* *

Warning The Java language does not have any unsigned types, so an *int* marshaled as a *UINT* might contain a negative value and be misinterpreted by the unmanaged function that is called. Therefore, you must perform all possible range checking on parameters before passing them to DLLs if you want to avoid potentially confusing results.

Declaring Native Methods

You declare a native method and bring its name into scope in J/Direct using the *@dll.import* directive. For example, the *MessageBeep* function, which is used to output the various burps and other noises emitted by Windows and implemented in \WINDOWS\System32\User32.dll, is defined in the Platform SDK in this way:

```
BOOL MessageBeep(
  UINT uType   // sound type
);
```

The corresponding J/Direct definition that you can create in J# is as follows:

```
/** @dll.import("USER32.DLL") */
private static native boolean MessageBeep(int uType);
```

Notice the use of *@dll.import* before the method declaration, which indicates the DLL supplying the native method. The method itself must be declared as *static native*. Having declared the method, you can invoke it as if it were a regular Java method.

Note You can omit the *.dll* extension from the filename in the *@dll.import* directive as long as the file actually has the extension *.dll*. (Some earlier versions of Windows had EXE files that were really DLLs, so we always prefer to be explicit.)

Marshaling *Struct* Objects

Many native methods take complex parameters, which are usually implemented as *struct* objects. Java doesn't have *struct* objects—instead, you have to define classes that have the same public fields as these structures. For example, consider the *FlashWindowEx* method, which is also implemented in User32.dll. This method lets you flash the title bar and taskbar button for a window to attract the user's attention. Windows itself often uses this feature if an application that has been minimized suddenly requires the user's attention, but you can also exploit it for other ends.

The C++ definition of the *FlashWindowEx* function is shown here:

```
BOOL FlashWindowEx(
  PFLASHWINFO pfwi  // flash status information
);
```

The parameter is a pointer to a *FLASHWINFO* structure, which is defined like this:

```
typedef struct {
  UINT  cbSize;     // The size of the struct
  HWND  hwnd;       // The handle of the Window to flash
  DWORD dwFlags;    // How to flash the window
  UINT  uCount;     // How many times to flash the window
  DWORD dwTimeout;  // Time between flashes
} FLASHWINFO, *PFLASHWINFO;
```

To use *FlashWindowEx* from J#, you must first define a class that matches the *FLASHWINFO* structure:

```
/** @dll.struct(pack=4) */
public class FLASHWINFO
{
   int cbSize;
   int hWnd;
   int dwFlags;
   int uCount;
   int dwTimeout;
}
```

The *@dll.struct* directive identifies the class to the marshaler. The actual names used by the fields (and the class itself) do not have to be the same as the original structure, although it makes things easier to understand and maintain if they are.

You must take care of one complication when you marshal J# classes as *struct* objects: field packing and alignment. By default, in the common language runtime, fields in classes are aligned on 8-byte boundaries. Therefore, in the *FLASHWINFO* class there will be 4 bytes of dead space between each field, (An *int* is 4 bytes in size.) However, the corresponding structure in the Windows API will align these same fields on 4-byte boundaries, resulting in a mismatch between the *FLASHWINFO* class and the *FLASHWINFO* struct. To fix this problem, you can specify the *pack* modifier for the *@dll.struct* directive. Using a value of 4, as shown above, causes fields to be aligned on 4-byte boundaries with no dead space in between.

Caution Packing is quite a complex topic, and the way in which fields in a *struct* are packed depends to some extent on how the *struct* is defined and the compiler options that were used to build the native DLL. Do not blindly use the value *4* as a magic number everywhere—it might not always work. You must understand a little about the native structure that's being mapped to. For more information about the relationship between field alignment and packing levels, see the Windows Platform SDK documentation or the ANSI C draft 3.5.2.1.

After you define the class and declare the native method, you can use them. The JDirect project, which is included in the book's sample files, shows a simple Windows-based application written in J# that uses the *FlashWindowEx* method in the constructor of the main form (called *CakeForm*, in the file CakeForm.jsl). Part of the code is shown here:

```
public class CakeForm extends System.Windows.Forms.Form
{
    ⋮
   /**
    * Constants used by the FlashWindowEx function
    */
   private final int FLASHW_STOP = 0x00000000;
   private final int FLASHW_CAPTION = 0x00000001;
   private final int FLASHW_TRAY = 0x00000002;
   private final int FLASHW_ALL = (FLASHW_CAPTION | FLASHW_TRAY);
   private final int FLASHW_TIMER = 0x00000004;
   private final int FLASHW_TIMERNOFG = 0x0000000C;

   public CakeForm()
   {
       ⋮
// Get the handle of the window
       IntPtr hWnd = this.get_Handle();

       // Create and populate a FLASHWINFO object
       FLASHWINFO windowInfo = new FLASHWINFO();

       // The size of the windowInfo object
```

```
        windowInfo.cbSize = 20;

        // The handle of the current window
        windowInfo.hWnd = hWnd.ToInt32();

        // Flash the caption and taskbar button continuously until stopped
        windowInfo.dwFlags = FLASHW_TIMER | FLASHW_ALL;

        // Number of times to flash - ignored if flashing continuously
        windowInfo.uCount = 0;

        // Flash twice a second
        windowInfo.dwTimeout = 500;

        // Call FlashWindowEx to start the window flashing
        FlashWindowEx(windowInfo);
    }
    ⋮
}
```

The Platform Invoke Service

Strictly speaking, J/Direct is provided with J# for backward compatibility with existing Visual J++ projects, and you should not try to use it from languages other than J#. However, the .NET Framework provides its own generic mechanism for invoking unmanaged code: the Platform Invoke Service (P/Invoke). P/Invoke is more powerful and flexible than J/Direct, and you should prefer it over J/Direct if you're developing code from scratch.

As with J/Direct, using P/Invoke involves creating a method definition (or prototype) for each unmanaged function and specifying whether any special marshaling of parameters is required. Let's look at an example.

Calling the System Restore API

If you're familiar with Windows XP, you might have come across the System Restore API. This feature, which is commonly used by application installation programs, provides a facility to undo any changes made to the system if it becomes unstable as a result of the installation. Using the System Restore API, you can record the current state of the operating system and installed applications. If any subsequent changes—installed applications or devices, for example—cause instability in the system, you can roll them back. The System Restore API was designed to be called from applications developed using C++ or C. The current release of the .NET Framework Class Library does not provide direct access to the System Restore API, so if you want to employ it from J#, you must use P/Invoke.

The System Restore API works by monitoring selected files on a drive-by-drive basis and making copies of these files before changing them when the system is updated. Toward this end, a driver in the Windows XP operating system intercepts operations on files. The copies are compressed to save space. Each set of saved files is referred to as a *restore point*. A user can revert the system to the state determined by any restore point captured on the computer using the System Restore tool, which is available from the System Tools folder in the Accessories program group.

In the following example, we'll examine how to invoke the System Restore API from a J# program. The application itself will create a restore point, install a dummy application, and then commit the restore point. You can then use the System Restore tool to show that the restore point was successfully created and then roll back the application installation and uninstall it.

Tip For the System Restore API to work, you must make sure that System Restore is enabled. In Control Panel, select Performance and Maintenance, and click System. In the System Properties dialog box click the System Restore tab and make sure that the Turn Off System Restore check box is deselected.

To use the System Restore API, you must define the J# equivalent of the data structures used by the various System Restore methods, and provide information on how to marshal any nonisomorphic data that will not be automatically converted by P/Invoke. You must also declare the System Restore API methods to bring them into scope in the J# application and to direct P/Invoke to the appropriate unmanaged DLL. A common strategy is to create a J# class to act as a wrapper for the unmanaged method calls and data structures. This class can be deployed in its own reusable library, although to keep this example simple, we have defined it in the same project as the code that calls it.

The System Restore API contains two important methods, *SRSetRestorePoint* and *SRRemoveRestorePoint*, along with two data structures, *RESTOREPOINTINFO* and *STATEMGRSTATUS*. The API is implemented in the unmanaged library Srclient.dll. The file SrRestorePtApi.h, which is supplied with the Platform SDK (not Visual Studio .NET), contains C++ definitions of these functions and data structures, as shown next.

Note The System Restore API actually defines two versions of the *SRSetRestorePoint* function and the *RESTOREPOINTINFO* data structure—for ANSI and Unicode implementations. The function and structure are distinguished by different suffixes in their names—*A* for ANSI and *W* for Unicode. We'll restrict our discussion to the Unicode version here, mainly because the common language runtime uses Unicode.

SrRestorePtApi.h

```
/*************************************************************************

Copyright (c) 2000 Microsoft Corporation

Module Name:
    SRRestorePtAPI.h

Abstract:
    This file contains the declarations for the SRRESTOREPT_API

*************************************************************************/

#if !defined( _SRRESTOREPTAPI_H )
#define _SRRESTOREPTAPI_H

//
// Type of Event
//

#define MIN_EVENT                   100
#define BEGIN_SYSTEM_CHANGE         100
#define END_SYSTEM_CHANGE           101
#define BEGIN_NESTED_SYSTEM_CHANGE  102    // for Whistler only - use this
                                           // to prevent nested restore pts
#define END_NESTED_SYSTEM_CHANGE    103    // for Whistler only - use this
                                           // to prevent nested restore pts
#define MAX_EVENT                    103

//
// Type of Restore Points
//

#define MIN_RPT                 0
#define APPLICATION_INSTALL     0
```

```
#define APPLICATION_UNINSTALL   1
#define DESKTOP_SETTING         2     /* Not implemented */
#define ACCESSIBILITY_SETTING   3     /* Not implemented */
#define OE_SETTING              4     /* Not implemented */
#define APPLICATION_RUN         5     /* Not implemented */
#define RESTORE                 6
#define CHECKPOINT              7
#define WINDOWS_SHUTDOWN        8     /* Not implemented */
#define WINDOWS_BOOT            9     /* Not implemented */
#define DEVICE_DRIVER_INSTALL   10
#define FIRSTRUN                11
#define MODIFY_SETTINGS         12
#define CANCELLED_OPERATION     13    /* Only valid for END_SYSTEM_CHANGE */
#define BACKUP_RECOVERY         14
#define MAX_RPT                 14


#define MAX_DESC                64
#define MAX_DESC_W              256   // longer for Whistler

//
// for Millennium compatibility
//

#pragma pack(push, srrestoreptapi_include)
#pragma pack(1)

//
// Restore point information
//

typedef struct _RESTOREPTINFOA {
    DWORD   dwEventType;                // Type of Event - Begin or End
    DWORD   dwRestorePtType;            // Type of Restore Point - App
                                        // install/uninstall
    INT64   llSequenceNumber;           // Sequence Number - 0 for begin
    CHAR    szDescription[MAX_DESC];    // Description - Name of
                                        // Application / Operation
} RESTOREPOINTINFOA, *PRESTOREPOINTINFOA;

typedef struct _RESTOREPTINFOW {
    DWORD   dwEventType;
    DWORD   dwRestorePtType;
    INT64   llSequenceNumber;
    WCHAR   szDescription[MAX_DESC_W];
} RESTOREPOINTINFOW, *PRESTOREPOINTINFOW;
```

```
//
// Status returned by System Restore
//

typedef struct _SMGRSTATUS {
    DWORD   nStatus;            // Status returned by State Manager Process
    INT64   llSequenceNumber;   // Sequence Number for the restore point
} STATEMGRSTATUS, *PSTATEMGRSTATUS;

#pragma pack(pop, srrestoreptapi_include)


#ifdef __cplusplus
extern "C" {
#endif

//
// RPC call to set a restore point
//
// Return value  TRUE if the call was a success
//               FALSE if the call failed
//
// If pSmgrStatus nStatus field is set as follows
//
// ERROR_SUCCESS        If the call succeeded (return value will be TRUE)
//
// ERROR_TIMEOUT        If the call timed out due to a wait on a mutex for
//                      for setting restore points.
//
// ERROR_INVALID_DATA   If the cancel restore point is called with
//                      an invalid sequence number
//
// ERROR_INTERNAL_ERROR If there are internal failures.
//
// ERROR_BAD_ENVIRONMENT If the API is called in SafeMode
//
// ERROR_SERVICE_DISABLED If SystemRestore is Disabled.
//
// ERROR_DISK_FULL              If System Restore is frozen (Windows
//                              Whistler only)
//
// ERROR_ALREADY_EXISTS    If this is a nested restore point

BOOL __stdcall
SRSetRestorePointA(
   PRESTOREPOINTINFOA  pRestorePtSpec,  // [in] Restore Point specification
   PSTATEMGRSTATUS     pSMgrStatus      // [out] Status returned
   );
```

```
BOOL __stdcall
SRSetRestorePointW(
   PRESTOREPOINTINFOW  pRestorePtSpec,
   PSTATEMGRSTATUS     pSMgrStatus
   );

DWORD __stdcall
SRRemoveRestorePoint(DWORD dwRPNum);

#ifdef __cplusplus
}
#endif


#ifdef UNICODE
#define RESTOREPOINTINFO        RESTOREPOINTINFOW
#define PRESTOREPOINTINFO       PRESTOREPOINTINFOW
#define SRSetRestorePoint       SRSetRestorePointW
#else
#define RESTOREPOINTINFO        RESTOREPOINTINFOA
#define PRESTOREPOINTINFO       PRESTOREPOINTINFOA
#define SRSetRestorePoint       SRSetRestorePointA
#endif

#endif // !defined( _RESTOREPTAPI_H )
```

Defining Constants

The first task is to map the constants into J# syntax. In the previous example using J/Direct, we converted these definitions into private static final constants. This is OK, and it works, but it might be useful to make them more widely available in case the same constants need to be used in other classes or projects. The most obvious way to do this is to create a wrapper class and expose these constants as public static final values, as shown in the *SystemRestoreWrapper* class below (which is supplied in the SystemRestore project). This class can then be packaged as a library assembly, which allows it to be used elsewhere:

```
/**
 * Class that wraps the System Restore API constants and functions
 * Definitions are taken from srrestoreptapi.h, supplied with the Platform
 * SDK, and converted to J# syntax
 */
public class SystemRestoreAPIWrapper
{
```

```
    // Type of Event

    public static final int MIN_EVENT = 100;
    public static final int BEGIN_SYSTEM_CHANGE = 100;
    public static final int END_SYSTEM_CHANGE = 101;
    public static final int BEGIN_NESTED_SYSTEM_CHANGE = 102;
    public static final int END_NESTED_SYSTEM_CHANGE = 103;
    public static final int MAX_EVENT = 103;

    // Type of Restore Points

    public static final int MIN_RPT = 0;
    public static final int APPLICATION_INSTALL = 0;
    public static final int APPLICATION_UNINSTALL = 1;
    public static final int DESKTOP_SETTING = 2;
    public static final int ACCESSIBILITY_SETTING = 3;
    public static final int OE_SETTING = 4;
    public static final int APPLICATION_RUN = 5;
    public static final int RESTORE = 6;
    public static final int CHECKPOINT = 7;
    public static final int WINDOWS_SHUTDOWN = 8;
    public static final int WINDOWS_BOOT = 9;
    public static final int DEVICE_DRIVER_INSTALL = 10;
    public static final int FIRSTRUN = 11;
    public static final int MODIFY_SETTINGS = 12;
    public static final int CANCELLED_OPERATION = 13;
    public static final int BACKUP_RECOVERY =14;
    public static final int MAX_RPT = 14;

    public static final int MAX_DESC_W = 256;

⋮
}
```

Mapping Data Structures

The next task is to define the J# versions of the *RESTOREPOINTINFO* and *STATEMGRSTATUS* structures. You can accomplish this as before, by creating J# classes to represent these structures. The type of each field should match the corresponding type in the original structures. Remember that some types are isomorphic or are transformed automatically (for example, J# *int* and *long* fields are automatically converted into the equivalent 32-bit and 64-bit integer quantities when they're passed across to the unmanaged space) and others might require some explicit conversion. Taking the *STATEMGRSTATUS* structure (the simpler of the two) first, the equivalent J# class looks like this:

```
public class STATEMGRSTATUS
{
   public System.UInt32 nStatus;
   public long llSequenceNumber;
}
```

Note that the Java language does not have unsigned types. For example, the closest Java type to *DWORD* in Windows is *int*, as you saw when we used J/Direct. However, the *System* namespace defines the *UInt32* structure, which is used as the basis for unsigned 32-bit integer values in other .NET languages. You can also use this structure from J#. The marshaler recognizes this type and knows how to convert it to an unsigned 32-bit unmanaged value. The *System* namespace also contains the *Int64* structure, which is equivalent to a Java language *long*, and *Int32*, which is the same as a Java language *int*. However, the J# compiler will forbid you from exposing value types such as *Int64* and *Int32*, for which there are corresponding Java language types in the metadata of an assembly (although you can use them internally within classes). The only exceptions to this rule are the value types that have no Java language equivalent, such as *UInt32*.

One additional piece of information is required. Because you have the same data packing and alignment issues mentioned previously, the marshaler needs to know how to lay out the data in memory when it is passed between managed and unmanaged space. You indicate this by tagging the class with the *System.Runtime.InteropServices.StructLayoutAttribute*. This attribute expects a *System.Runtime.InteropServices.LayoutKind* parameter to its constructor. *LayoutKind* is an enumeration containing three values: *Explicit*, *Sequential*, and *Auto*. Using the explicit option allows you to define exactly where each field in the class starts. (We'll look at this shortly.) The auto option allows the common language runtime to lay out the contents of the structure as it sees fit. The sequential option causes the fields to be laid out sequentially in the order in which they appear in the class.

The *StructLayoutAttribute* class also defines the *Pack* member, which you can use to control the alignment of sequential fields by specifying the byte-boundary where a field starts after the previous one finishes. Although *Pack* is an integer, you should set it to the value 0, 1, 2, 4, 8, 16, 32, 64, or 128. (0 specifies use of the default packing alignment.) A compiler error will be generated if you specify a value other than one of those in this set. By default, fields are aligned on 8-byte boundaries. To work properly, the fields in the *STATEMGRSTATUS* structure must be aligned on 4-byte boundaries. (See the earlier discussion on packing with J/Direct.) The completed *STATEMGRSTATUS* class is shown here:

```
/** @attribute StructLayoutAttribute(LayoutKind.Sequential, Pack=4) **/
public class STATEMGRSTATUS
{
   public UInt32 nStatus;
   public long llSequenceNumber;
}
```

The *RESTOREPOINTINFO* structure requires a little more thought. The fields *dwEventType*, *dwRestorePtType*, and *llSequenceNumber* are straightforward enough. (They're similar to the fields in *STATEMGRSTATUS*.) But the *szDescription* field needs careful handling. If you look at the original C++ definition of *RESTOREPOINTINFO*, you'll see that the *szDescription* field is described as an array of Unicode characters:

```
WCHAR szDescription[MAX_DESC_W];
```

Arrays in the common language runtime are totally different from arrays in C++. It is actually more convenient in J# to define the *szDescription* field as a *String* and specify explicitly how the value should be marshaled into unmanaged space. To do this, you apply the *System.Runtime.InteropServices.MarshalAsAttribute* to the *String*. The constructor for *MarshalAsAttribute* expects a *System.Runtime.InteropServices.UnmanagedType* value as its parameter. This parameter indicates the target type in unmanaged space. The *UnmanagedType* enumeration contains values covering most basic unmanaged types. You can create your own custom marshaler if you need to marshal data in a different manner.

Table 13-2 describes the members of the *UnmanagedType* enumeration. Note that you can also apply the *MarshalAsAttribute* to individual method parameters that are being passed to unmanaged space, so some of the members in the table are not applicable to data structures.

Table 13-2 Members of the *UnmanagedType* Enumeration

Member	Description
AnsiBStr	An ANSI character string prefixed with a single-byte length count.
AsAny	Uses reflection to dynamically determine the source type and performs automatic marshaling of the result.
Bool	A 4-byte Boolean value; *false* is indicated by 0, and *true* is indicated by any nonzero value.
BStr	A Unicode character string prefixed with a 2-byte length count.

Table 13-2 Members of the *UnmanagedType* Enumeration

Member	Description
ByValArray	A fixed-length array that appears in a structure and whose size is specified by the *SizeConst* field of the *MarshalAsAttribute*. You can determine the type of the individual target elements by using automatic marshaling from managed space, or you can specify the type explicitly using the *ArraySubType* field of the *MarshalAsAttribute*.
ByValTStr	A fixed-length character array that appears in a structure. The *CharSet* member of the *StructLayoutAttribute* containing this field indicates the type of characters (ANSI or Unicode) in the target array. As with *ByValArray*, you specify the length of the target array using the *SizeConst* field of the *MarshalAsAttribute*.
Currency	A COM currency type that is intended to be used primarily to convert *System.Decimal* values.
CustomMarshaler	Indicates that a custom marshaler should be used. The *MarshalType* field of the *MarshalAsAttribute* specifies the fully qualified name (assembly, class, version, and so on) of the custom marshaler class.
Error	This is applied to a method parameter rather than to a field in a structure. It is attached to a 32-bit integer parameter to indicate that the parameter should be marshaled as the *HRESULT* of a COM method call.
FunctionPtr	A function pointer.
I1	A 1-byte signed value.
I2	A 2-byte signed value.
I4	A 4-byte signed value.
I8	An 8-byte signed value.
IDispatch	A COM *IDispatch* interface pointer.
Interface	A COM interface pointer. The interface must provide metadata specifying the GUID that identifies it.
IUnknown	A COM *IUknown* interface pointer.

Table 13-2 Members of the *UnmanagedType* Enumeration

Member	Description
LPArray	A C-style array. You specify the length by using the *SizeConst* field of the *MarshalAsAttribute* if the array is fixed length, or you indicate a parameter that holds the length of the array using the *SizeParamIndex* field (for method calls only—this is analogous to using the *size_is* modifier with COM).
LPStr	An ANSI character string (single-byte characters, null terminated).
LPStruct	A pointer to a C-style *struct*.
LPTStr	A platform-dependent character string that is based on the character type the operating system uses. For example, in Windows 98 this is an ANSI string, but in Windows XP it is a Unicode string.
LPWStr	A Unicode character string.
R4	A 4-byte floating point number.
R8	An 8-byte floating point number.
SafeArray	A COM *SafeArray*. This is a self-describing type that includes the number of dimensions, the bounds of each dimension, and the type of data held in the array.
Struct	A C-style *struct* that is used primarily with common language runtime value types.
SysInt	A platform-dependent integer that is based on the data width used by the operating system. For example, in Windows 98 this is a 4-byte integer, and in 64-bit Windows it is an 8-byte integer.
TBStr	A platform-dependent, length-prefixed string. For example, the string will comprise ANSI characters in Windows 98 and Unicode characters in Windows XP.
U1	A 1-byte unsigned integer.
U2	A 2-byte unsigned integer.
U4	A 4-byte unsigned integer.
U8	An 8-byte unsigned integer.

Table 13-2 Members of the *UnmanagedType* Enumeration

Member	Description
VariantBool	A 2-byte COM Boolean value (*false* = 0, *true* = –1).
VBByRefStr	A Microsoft Visual Basic string that is passed by reference.

Returning to the *RESTOREPOINTINFO* class, the *szDescription* field should be a *String* marshaled as a *ByValTStr*, with the *SizeConst* property set to the *MAX_DESC_W* constant exposed by the *SystemRestoreAPIWrapper* class. The completed class is shown below. The characters in the string will be Unicode, and this is indicated using the *CharSet* member of the *StructLayoutAttribute*. Also, to add a bit of variation (and to show you how to use the feature), the layout of the class is specified using *LayoutKind.Explicit*. Each field is tagged with a *System.Runtime.InteropServices.FieldOffsetAttribute* that indicates the position of the start of the field from the beginning of the class.

```
/** @attribute StructLayoutAttribute(LayoutKind.Explicit,
   CharSet=CharSet.Unicode) **/
public class RESTOREPOINTINFO
{
   /** @attribute FieldOffsetAttribute(0) **/
   public UInt32 dwEventType;

   /** @attribute FieldOffsetAttribute(4) **/
   public UInt32 dwRestorePtType;

   /** @attribute FieldOffsetAttribute(8) **/
   public long llSequenceNumber;

   /** @attribute FieldOffsetAttribute(16) **/
   /** @attribute MarshalAsAttribute(UnmanagedType.ByValTStr,
      SizeConst=SystemRestoreAPIWrapper.MAX_DESC_W) **/
   public String szDescription;
}
```

Defining the System Restore API Methods

The final step is to define the *SRSetRestorePoint* and *SRRemoveRestorePoint* functions. You do this by declaring them with *System.Runtime.InteropServices.DllImportAttribute*, which specifies the name of the native DLL that implements the function. A convenient place to put these definitions is in the *SystemRestoreAPIWrapper* class. Both methods are implemented in Srclient.dll (located in the Windows\System32 folder). Like the *FlashWindowEx* function shown earlier, these methods should be declared as *native static*. They are also declared as *public* to make them accessible to the outside world.

Remember that the *SRSetRestorePoint* method contains a character string in its second parameter. The *CharSet* field of the *DllImportAttribute* should be set to indicate the type of characters used—it's Unicode in our example. Furthermore, if you examine the original C++ file, SrRestorePtApi.h, you'll see that there is actually no method called *SRSetRestorePoin*t. Instead, there are two versions called *SRSetRestorePointA* (the ANSI version of the function) and *SRSetRestorePointW* (the Unicode version). The C++ header file uses a macro to alias the name *SRSetRestorePoint* to whichever of these two functions is appropriate for the current platform. The *DllImportAttribute* also allows you to alias methods, using the *EntryPoint* field. Set it to the name of real function inside the DLL.

Choosing Between ANSI and Unicode Methods Automatically

The alias used by the *SRSetRestorePoint* method is actually redundant—we've included it primarily to show you how to use the *Alias* field. All Win32 API functions that handle strings are supplied in two versions: one that takes ANSI arguments, and one that takes Unicode arguments. The name of the ANSI version of a function must end with an *A*, while the name of the Unicode version of the same function must end with a *W*. When an unmanaged function that uses strings is invoked, the common language runtime will perform a match using an algorithm that depends on the character type used by the platform.

In the case of an ANSI platform (such as Windows 98), the common language runtime will first try to call the function using the name specified in the managed declaration. If this fails, the common language runtime will look for a function with an *A* suffix. If the platform is Unicode based, the common language runtime will first try the *W* suffix and will search using the declared name only if this fails (as you can see, the search sequence is different for ANSI and Unicode). In both cases, if the search is unsuccessful, the common language runtime will look for a mangled version of the function name (such as *_SRSetRestorePoint@32*) based on the size of the parameter list. If this fails as well, the common language runtime will throw an exception (*java.lang.UnsatisfiedLinkError*).

An alternative approach is to specify the *CharSet* field for *DllImportAttribute*. If this field is set to *CharSet.Unicode*, the common language runtime will automatically attempt to execute the W version of a function if it cannot locate a function with the original name. This saves the common language runtime from having to examine the platform. Similarly, specifying *CharSet.Ansi* will direct the common language runtime to use the A version of the function. (The default, *CharSet.Auto*, causes the common language runtime to look for one or the other version, depending on the platform.)

Using an alias is faster than making the common language runtime work out the name of the method, but there's one major drawback: If you hard-code an alias to refer to the Unicode version of a function, the call will not work on an ANSI platform. Specifying *CharSet.Unicode* or *CharSet.Ansi* can be equally restrictive. If you want the maximum portability, let the common language runtime figure out whether to use ANSI or Unicode.

SRSetRestorePoint returns a *BOOL* in the C++ implementation; this is mapped to a Java language *boolean* by the marshaler. The two parameters are defined in C++ as pointers. The Java language does not have explicit pointers, but objects are always marshaled by reference when you pass them as parameters, and the marshaler will automatically convert an object reference into a *struct* pointer. However, if you want to make this marshaling explicit, you can apply a *MarshalAsAttribute* that specifies *UnmanagedType.LPStruct* as the native data type, as shown in the following code

The *SRRemoveRestorePoint* method is simpler. It is also located in Srclient.dll, but it does not require any aliasing. The return value from *SRRemoveRestorePoint* is a *DWORD* in C++. This is a 4-byte unsigned quantity that corresponds to a *System.UInt32* in the .NET Framework. The parameter is also a *UInt32*.

```
public class SystemRestoreAPIWrapper
{
   ⋮
   /** @attribute DllImportAttribute("srclient.dll",
      CharSet=CharSet.Unicode,
      EntryPoint= "SRSetRestorePointW") **/
   public static native boolean SRSetRestorePoint(
      /** @attribute MarshalAsAttribute(UnmanagedType.LPStruct) **/
      RESTOREPOINTINFO pRestorePtSpec,

      /** @attribute MarshalAsAttribute(UnmanagedType.LPStruct) **/
STATEMGRSTATUS pSMgrStatus);/** @attribute DllImportAttribute("srclient.dll")
**/

public static native UInt32 SRRemoveRestorePoint(int dwRPNum);
}
```

Invoking the System Restore API

The *Installer* class available in the book's sample files in the SystemRestore project is a simple test harness that exercises the System Restore API from J#. The code creates a restore point by calling *SRSetRestorePoint*. The *RESTOREPOINT-INFO* parameter is populated with information about the restore point to be created, the *dwEventType* field is set to the *BEGIN_SYSTEM_CHANGE* constant to indicate that a new restore point is being created, and the *dwRestorePtType* field is set to *APPLICATION_INSTALL* to indicate the type of the restore point. (You can also create restore points before you perform other operations, such as installing a new device driver or changing desktop settings.) The *szDescription* field is set to a text string that indicates the purpose of the restore point. This description is displayed by the System Restore tool when the user wants to select a restore point to roll back, so it's helpful to users to make it meaningful. The *STATEMGRSTATUS* parameter to *SRSetRestorePoint* is filled in by the operating system when the method is called and returned to the application. It will contain information such as a unique sequence number used to identify the restore point internally and a status field that's filled in with a reason code if the call to *SRSetRestorePoint* fails. The return value from *SRSetRestorePoint* indicates whether the call was successful.

If the restore point is created successfully, the code will continue by installing a dummy application consisting of an EXE file, a DLL, and an INI file residing under a new folder called Cake Application. (We had to get cakes in here somewhere!) This code uses classes and methods found in the *System.IO* namespace of the .NET Framework Class Library and has nothing to do with the System Restore API.

Once the new application has been installed, the method *SRSetRestore-Point* is called again to complete the restore point and commit the changes made to your hard disk. The *dwEventType* field of the *RESTOREPOINTINFO* parameter is set to *END_SYSTEM_CHANGE*, and the *llSequenceNumber* field is set to the sequence number that was returned when the restore point was created. If all is well, *SRSetRestorePoint* will return *true* and the program will finish with the new application having been successfully installed. If *SRSetRestore-Point* returns *false*, an error must have occurred, so the application is deleted and the restore point is removed by calling the *SRRemoveRestorePoint*.

There is a slight anomaly in the System Restore API at this point. The *SRRemoveRestorePoint* function expects the sequence number of the restore point to be removed as its parameter. The type specified in the System Restore API for this parameter is *DWORD* (*UInt32* in J#). However, the type of the sequence number returned in the *STATEMGRSTATUS* class is an *INT64* (*Int64* in J#). C++ will allow you to assign an *INT64* to a *DWORD* without a murmur. But J#, having

Java-like semantics, is a lot fussier and won't let you commit such a heinous crime. Instead, you must explicitly cast from a *long* to a *UInt32*.

Viewing the Results

If you compile and run the program, you should get output similar to that shown in Figure 13-1.

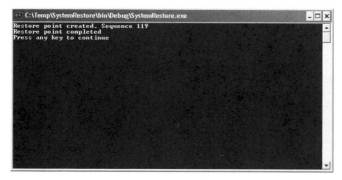

Figure 13-1 The output of the SystemRestore program

Notice that the folder C:\Cake Application was created. It contains Application.exe, along with the Library subfolder that contains the files Application.dll and Application.ini, as shown in Figure 13-2.

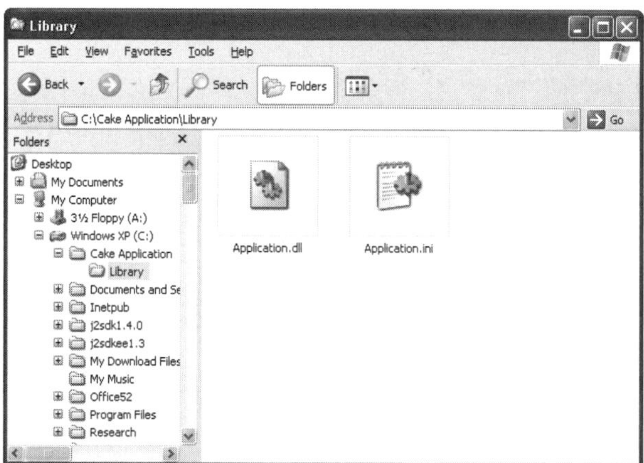

Figure 13-2 Windows Explorer showing the Cake Application folder

You can verify that the restore point was created using the System Restore tool. From the Start menu, choose All Programs, Accessories, System Tools, and then select System Restore to launch the program. The Welcome To System

Restore dialog box will appear. Click Next to display the restore points that were created on your system, as shown in Figure 13-3.

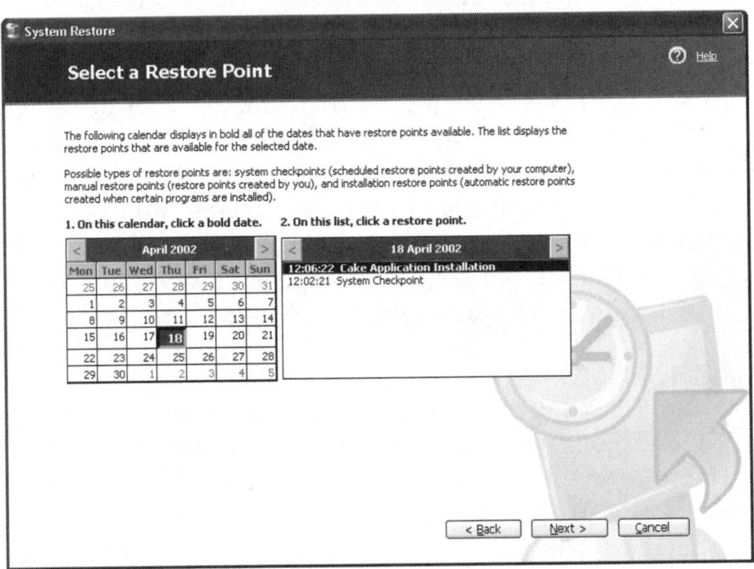

Figure 13-3 The System Restore user interface

The calendar will default to the current date, and you should see the text *Cake Application Installation* listed as a restore point. You can uninstall the Cake Application by selecting this restore point and clicking Next. The computer will restart in maintenance mode, roll back the application installation, and then reboot. (Afterwards, you can undo this undo operation and restore the application if you want to!)

Other P/Invoke Issues

You can put P/Invoke to many interesting uses, which this chapter cannot thoroughly cover in the space available. However, before leaving the subject let's look at a few important wrinkles, issues, and other tips.

Using Callbacks

Unmanaged code can call back into managed space using a delegate. Delegate parameters are automatically marshaled as function pointers by P/Invoke, although it doesn't hurt to be explicit and provide the *MarshalAsAttribute* with the argument *UnmanagedType.FunctionPtr*. (It's good documentation.) The *Enumerator* class shown below (available in the file Enumerator.jsl in the sample project EnumWindows) uses a delegate as the parameter to the native

EnumWindows function found in User32.dll. This is the classic function that enumerates the top-level windows on the screen by calling a specified routine and passing the handle of each window visited in turn to that routine.

In this example, the method *VisitWindow* is supplied as the method to be called. The important point to grasp in this example is the use of the delegate *EnumWindowsCallback*. (Note the use of *@delegate*.) This delegate matches the signature of the method used by the *EnumWindows* function. (See the Platform SDK for details about *EnumWindows*.) You specify *EnumWindowsDelegate* as the type of the callback function when you declare *EnumWindows*. When the Enumerator program is executed, it will display the handle of every top-level window that appears on the desktop. Completed code for this example is available in the file Enumerator.jsl, in the EnumWindows project.

Calling Conventions

Before the advent of the common language runtime, one of the joys of performing cross-language method calls was the game called "Who will clean up the stack?" The rules are quite simple: The caller creates some parameters and puts them on the stack and then calls a function; the callee examines the contents of the stack and performs the requisite operations defined by the function using this information. The fun comes when the function finishes and returns to the caller. Who will clean up the stack?

In the good old days of UNIX, when programmers wrote only in C, they created interesting functions that could take variable numbers of parameters using a technique known as *varargs*. (Go ask your grandfather to explain.) Only the caller would know for certain what it had placed on the stack, so it was the caller's responsibility to clean up the stack when the function call completed. This is referred to as the *Cdecl* calling convention. Then along came a more disciplined breed of programmers who felt that *varargs* was a step too far and decided, for optimization reasons, to banish it and allow the callee to clean up the stack instead. This is referred to as the *StdCall* calling convention. To muddy the waters further, along came C++, some of whose compilers implicitly pass a reference to the current object (*this*) as the first parameter to a method, using a calling convention termed *ThisCall*.

As mentioned in Chapter 2, the common language runtime takes a massive leap forward by ensuring that all .NET-supported languages use the same calling convention. So normally who cleans up the stack is not an issue. However, when you call unmanaged code, it can be a very big issue indeed. If you fail to clean up the stack, or the caller and the callee both attempt to clean up the stack, the result can be some nasty exceptions (but not as nasty as things used to get before the days of the common language runtime). So, when you call an unmanaged function in a DLL, check the documentation to determine the calling convention required, and make sure you use the same. You can specify the calling convention to use with *DllImportAttribute*:

```
/** @attribute DllImportAttribute("mylibrary.dll",
   CallingConvention=CallingConvention.Cdecl) **/
public static native int MyFunction(int someData);
```

You should use one of the values in the *System.Runtime.InteropServices.CallingConvention* enumeration, but don't try the *FastCall* option because it is not yet implemented by the common language runtime. If you're calling ordinary Windows API methods (such as those implemented in the various Windows DLLs and the Platform SDK), the safest option is to use *Winapi* (which is the default). *Winapi* uses the calling convention that's applicable to the platform—*StdCall* in Win32, and *Cdecl* in WinCE. As mentioned, you should bear in mind that *DllImportAttribute* is metadata and is interpreted at runtime. If you specify *Winapi*, you won't need to recompile an assembly built using Windows XP if you deploy it on Windows CE.

Handling Polymorphic Parameters

C and C++ allow you to write functions whose parameters can have different meanings at different times, depending on the value of other parameters. For example, the *WinHelp* function in User32.dll interacts with the Windows Help system. The function is defined in the Platform SDK as follows:

```
BOOL WinHelp(
   HWND hWndMain,
   LPCTSTR lpszHelp,
   UINT uCommand,
   DWORD dwData
);
```

At first glance, the function appears innocuous enough. But in the documentation, you'll discover that the *dwData* parameter, which is loosely described as "additional data," can be a pointer to a *MULTIKEYHELP* structure, a pointer to a *HELPWININFO* structure, an integer, or a string, depending on the value supplied for the *uCommand* parameter! The Java language doesn't allow such functions. How, therefore, should you invoke *WinHelp* using P/Invoke from J#? You have two options: You can cheat unsafely or you can cheat safely.

Let's look at the unsafe cheating method first. You declare the method as shown here:

```
/** @attribute DllImportAttribute("user32.dll") **/
public static native boolean WinHelp(UInt32 hWndMain,
    String lpszHelp,
```

```
    UInt32 uCommand,
    Object dwData);
```

If you indicate that the fourth parameter is an *Object*, any object type can be marshaled. (If you want to pass an integer, you must pass it as a *System.Int32* because a primitive *int* cannot be converted to a *Object*.) This is the unsafe method because not only can you pass an integer, string, *MULTIKEYHELP*, or *HELPWININFO*, you can pass anything you like, valid or not! At run time, the marshaler will examine the type of the object passed in and perform the conversion as described earlier in Table 13-1.

A safer solution is to use overloading. You define the *WinHelp* function four times, with a different fourth parameter each time. (You'll also need to define J# versions of the *MULTIKEYHELP* and *HELPWININFO* classes.)

```
/** @attribute DllImportAttribute("user32.dll") **/
public static native boolean WinHelp(UInt32 hWndMain,
    String lpszHelp,
    UInt32 uCommand,
    int dwData);

/** @attribute DllImportAttribute("user32.dll") **/
public static native boolean WinHelp(UInt32 hWndMain,
    String lpszHelp,
    UInt32 uCommand,
    String dwData);

/** @attribute DllImportAttribute("user32.dll") **/
public static native boolean WinHelp(UInt32 hWndMain,
    String lpszHelp,
    UInt32 uCommand,
    MULTIKEYHELP dwData);

/** @attribute DllImportAttribute("user32.dll") **/
public static native boolean WinHelp(UInt32 hWndMain,
    String lpszHelp,
    UInt32 uCommand,
    HELPWININFO dwData);
```

You have no guarantee that the developer who calls the *WinHelp* method will use the correct version for a given value of *uCommand*, but at least the J# compiler can perform some type checking and reduce the opportunity for errors.

Handling Exceptions

Unmanaged code can throw exceptions. If the unmanaged code explicitly throws an exception using structured exception handling (SEH), the common language runtime will map this to a managed *System.Runtime.InteropServices.SEHException* object when the unmanaged code finishes. You must be prepared to catch and handle exceptions in your J# applications whenever you invoke an unmanaged function.

Some unmanaged functions provide additional information if they detect an error, using the unmanaged methods *SetLastError* or *SetLastErrorEx*. In an unmanaged environment, you call the *GetLastError* function to obtain this information. In managed space, you can indicate that an unmanaged function sets the last error code by setting the *SetLastError* field of *DllImportAttribute* to *true* when you declare the function. If the unmanaged code sets the last error code, the common language runtime will cache the value when the function returns. The caller (in managed space) can invoke the static method *GetLastWin32Error* of the *System.Runtime.InteropServices.Marshal* class to retrieve the error code.

Security Constraints

Unmanaged code is not subject to the same verification as managed code, and it can basically do almost anything it likes. All managed code that makes use of P/Invoke, either directly or indirectly, must be granted the *UnmanagedCode* privilege. The *UnmanagedCode* privilege is one of the flags comprising the *Security* permission, as described in Chapter 2. By default, this privilege is granted only to assemblies loaded from the My Computer zone. This prevents untrusted code in assemblies downloaded from the Internet or even a shared network drive from calling unmanaged functions that might reformat your hard drive.

Calling COM Components

COM has been around for a number of years, and a large base of useful COM components is now available. COM components execute in unmanaged space, but you can integrate these components into your .NET applications using COM Interop.

You can create, manage, and communicate with a COM component from managed code by using a Runtime Callable Wrapper (RCW). The RCW acts as a proxy to the COM object. It hides the differences between the COM and the .NET component models, how objects are activated, and how object lifetimes are managed. The overall aim of the RCW is to make the COM object appear just like any other ordinary .NET object (if there is such a thing!).

Note Behind the scenes, COM Interop uses P/Invoke to execute unmanaged code, and COM Interop is subject to the same security constraints.

Creating and Using an RCW

If you're using Visual Studio.NET, you can create an RCW automatically by adding a reference to a COM component by using the COM tab of the Add Reference dialog box (shown in Figure 13-4).

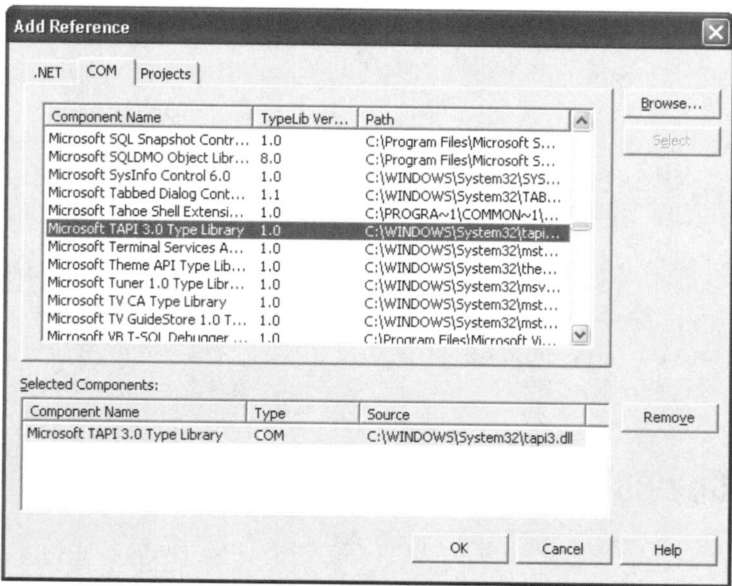

Figure 13-4 The COM tab of the Add Reference dialog box

The COM page lists the COM components and type libraries that are recorded in the Windows Registry of the local machine. You can select any of these items or click Browse to hunt for a component on the hard disk. If you select a component (such as the Microsoft TAPI 3.0 Type Library—the telephony API—as shown in the figure) and click OK, an RCW will be created for this component and added to the list of references in your project. The RCW will be implemented in an assembly and namespace whose name is based on that of the DLL implementing the original COM component, with the suffix *Lib*. In the case of the Microsoft TAPI 3.0 Type Library (which is implemented in

Tapi3.dll), the namespace is called *TAPI3Lib* and is implemented by the assembly *Interop.TAPI3Lib.dll*. You can bring the contents of this assembly into scope in the normal way, using an *import* statement:

```
import TAPI3Lib.*;
```

The contents of the *TAPI3Lib* namespace will be made available through Intellisense in the usual manner. You can create and manipulate TAPI3 objects just as you would ordinary .NET objects, and you can invoke methods on them in the same way as you would invoke methods on .NET components. The RCW converts and marshals the .NET types and method calls into their COM equivalents.

The RCW Implementation

The RCW performs some small naming transformations when it provides access to COM. Each coclass defined in the original type library is made available as a .NET class and an interface. The name of the class is the same as the original coclass, with the suffix *Class* appended to it, while the name of the interface is the same as the original coclass without the *Class* suffix.

For example, the TAPI coclass, which is the main entry point into the TAPI object model, is made available in the RCW as the *TAPIClass* type and the *TAPI* interface. The *TAPIClass* actually implements the *TAPI* interface in the RCW. The rationale behind this approach is that you should access the *TAPI* coclass through the *TAPI* interface in your .NET code. However, you cannot instantiate an interface, so the *TAPI* object must be created using *TAPIClass*, as shown here:

```
TAPI tapiObject = new TAPIClass();
```

If you have the Platform SDK available, you can examine the original definition of the TAPI coclass by looking at the file Tapi3.idl (supplied in the *Include* folder of the Platform SDK). The definition is reproduced here:

```
[
        uuid(21D6D48E-A88B-11D0-83DD-00AA003CCABD),
        helpstring("TAPI 3.0 TAPI Object")
    ]
    coclass TAPI
    {
        [default] interface ITTAPI;
        [default, source] dispinterface ITTAPIDispatchEventNotification;
        [defaultvtable, source] interface ITTAPIEventNotification;
        interface ITTAPICallCenter;
    };
```

The TAPI coclass implements several interfaces, and all of these are also available through the RCW. Figure 13-5 shows part of the *TAPIClass* definition in the RCW, Interop.TAPI3Lib.dll, using the Visual Studio .NET Object Browser.

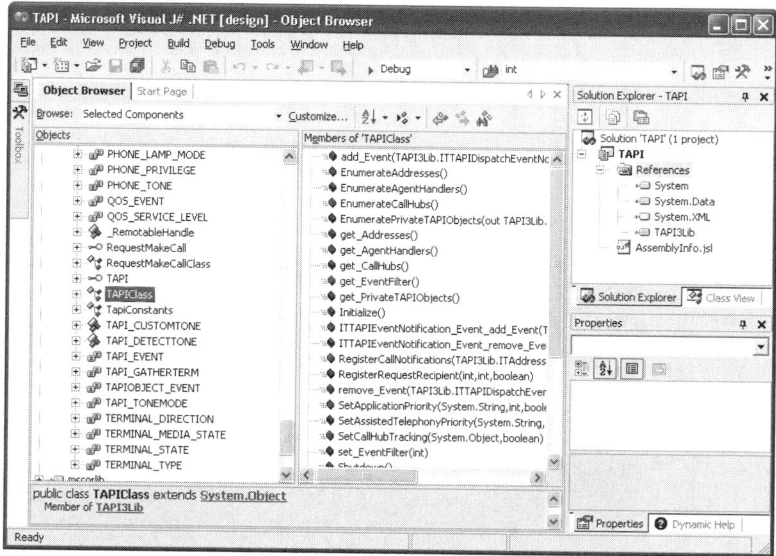

Figure 13-5 The definition of the *TAPIClass* type in the RCW

You can access all of these interfaces through the *TAPIClass* type, in much the same way as you would the TAPI interface. For example, to create an *ITTAPICallCenter* object, you would use the following statement:

```
ITTAPICallCenter callCenterObject = new TAPIClass();
```

Handling *HRESULT* Values

Like native code executed using P/Invoke, methods of COM components can report error conditions. The usual way for a COM method to do this is through the value returned by the method, which is invariably an *HRESULT*. Traditional C++ code checks this value to ensure that it is *S_OK* (which means the method call was successful). Any other value indicates an error, and the value itself specifies the reason for the error. The common language runtime does not pass *HRESULT* values back to managed clients as return values. Instead, managed COM method calls return either a void or the value of any parameter marked as *[retval]* in the original COM method. (*[retval]* is a COM attribute used by the MIDL compiler to indicate that a parameter should be marshaled as the return value.) If a COM method call attempts to pass back an *HRESULT* other than *S_OK*, the common language runtime will trap it and raise an exception.

The exception object created will be of a type that maps to the value of the *HRESULT*. For example, the COM *HRESULT* value *E_NOTIMPL* (the method is not implemented) will be signaled with a *System.NotImplementedException* object. You can of course trap all exceptions as a *System.Exception* object. Note that not all COM exceptions have corresponding managed exceptions. (This observation is especially true if you're calling a COM component that defines its own set of exception codes.) Unmapped exceptions are translated into *System.Runtime.InteropServices.COMException* objects, and you can obtain the *HRESULT* value that generated the exception by examining the *ErrorCode* (*get_ErrorCode* in J#) property. In addition, if the COM object supports the *IErrorInfo* interface, the *Message* (*get_Message*) property of the exception will be filled in with the string returned by *IErrorInfo.GetDescription*, the *Source* (*get_Source*) property will be populated with the return value from *IErrorInfo.GetSource*, and the *HelpLink* (*get_HelpLink*) property will contain information returned by the *IErrorInfo.GetHelpFile* and *IErrorInfo.GetHelpContext* methods.

Marshaling and Apartments

The RCW uses the .NET interop marshaler to marshal data between the managed and unmanaged spaces, including COM. Although apartments are not an issue when you use P/Invoke, they can become important when you consider COM Interop.

COM objects execute in apartments. When the common language runtime instantiates a COM object, it creates an apartment for it, which by default is multithreaded. You might recall the use of the *STAThread* attribute, which is often inserted automatically by Visual Studio into your code, especially when you create console and Windows Forms applications. This setting fixes the value of the *Thread.ApartmentState* property, causing the current thread to run using the specified apartment state. (See Chapter 8.) The *STAThread* attribute directs COM Interop to create a single-threaded apartment. (Threads that handle the user interface must reside in a single-threaded apartment.) If the thread affinity of a COM server (specified by the *ThreadingModel* setting in the Windows Registry) that's dishing out components to a .NET client matches that of the .NET client, the common language runtime will create the COM component in the same apartment as the .NET client code and the .NET interop marshaler will perform all the necessary marshaling. If the *ThreadingModel* setting does not match that of the .NET client, the COM component will be created in a separate apartment. The .NET interop marshaler will marshal data from managed space to unmanaged space and then use COM to perform cross-apartment marshaling.

Cross-apartment marshaling can be expensive and time-consuming, so you should try to ensure that calls to COM components made by managed code are performed in the same apartment. However, this might not always be feasible. The *Thread.ApartmentState* property can be set only once for a thread—thereafter, it cannot be changed. If the same managed thread makes calls to single-threaded apartment COM components and multithreaded apartment COM components, some cross-apartment COM marshaling will be unavoidable. As a workaround, you have at least two choices: You can create a new thread for each COM component you want to use and set its *ApartmentState* property appropriately (this might prove to be more expensive than performing cross-apartment marshaling if you use it to excess!). Or you can try to ensure that the COM components you use support the both-threading model (so that they will execute in both single and multithreaded apartments).

Creating an RCW from the Command Line

If you're not using Visual Studio .NET as your programming environment, you can still create an RCW for a COM component, but you must do it manually. The main requirement is that you have access to the type library of the COM component, which might be held in a TLB file or it could be packaged with the component in its DLL file.

The Type Library Importer (Tlbimp.exe) will create an assembly containing the RCW, from the type library for a COM component. The type library does not have to be registered in the Windows Registry for Tlbimp to work; it is sometimes used in conjunction with the MIDL compiler, which can generate a type library from an IDL definition of a COM component.

Tip MIDL and Tlbimp are especially useful if you want to access some of the very recent functionality of Windows XP from managed code. An example is the Background Intelligent Transfer Service (BITS). You can use BITS to upload and download files to or from a file server over the Web. It operates as a service, executing in the background, and is accessed using DCOM. The BITS API is available to C++ programmers using the Microsoft Platform SDK. BITS does not provide a type library, but the Platform SDK does include an IDL file (called Bits.idl), which defines the interfaces and methods of BITS. Using MIDL, you can create the type library and then use Tlbimp to generate the RCW.

You execute Tlbimp from the command line. When you create the RCW in this way, you can sign it to generate an assembly with a strong name. The RCW assembly can then be copied to the GAC and be made globally available.

Note The ability to sign RCWs is one compelling reason for using Tlbimp rather than Visual Studio .NET to create them. RCWs generated by Visual Studio .NET are inherently private assemblies. RCWs generated by Tlbimp can be placed in the Global Assembly Cache (GAC) and shared by multiple applications if they are signed.

For example, the following commands create a public/private key pair in a file called Bits.snk (using the Sn.exe utility described in Chapter 2), generate an RCW in an assembly called Bits.dll from the type library called Bits.tlb, sign it with the key pair found in Bits.snk, and deploy the assembly to the GAC:

```
sn -k Bits.snk
tlbimp Bits.tlb /out:Bits.dll /keyfile:Bits.snk
gacutil /i Bits.dll
```

Tip If the type library is embedded in a DLL, you must specify the name of the DLL as the source to the *Tlbimp* command. If the DLL contains several type libraries, you can specify which one you want to import into an RCW by appending a resource identifier to the source. For example, to create an RCW based on the first type library in the component file MyComponent.dll, you would use this command:

```
tlbimp MyComponent.dll\1 /out:MyComponentLib.dll
```

Sinking COM Events

COM components can publish events. Managed components can subscribe to these events, registering their own methods as event handlers. When such an event is raised, COM is effectively calling back into managed space from the unmanaged environment. Event handler parameters must be marshaled from the unmanaged space by the .NET interop marshaler. When an RCW is generated, it provides .NET delegates that you can specify as callbacks into your code from the COM component, for subscribing to COM events. (COM+-savvy readers: The RCW generates interfaces compatible with COM connection points.) The names generated for these delegates are combinations of the COM sink event interface and the name of the event, and they have the word *EventHandler* appended to the end.

For example, consider the *ExplorerDemo* class, available in the ExplorerDemo.jsl sample file in the ExplorerDemo project, which demonstrates how to create and manage a Microsoft Internet Explorer window from J#. To access Internet Explorer, you can add a reference to the Microsoft Internet Controls library (in \WINDOWS\System32\shdocvw.dll), as shown in Figure 13-6.

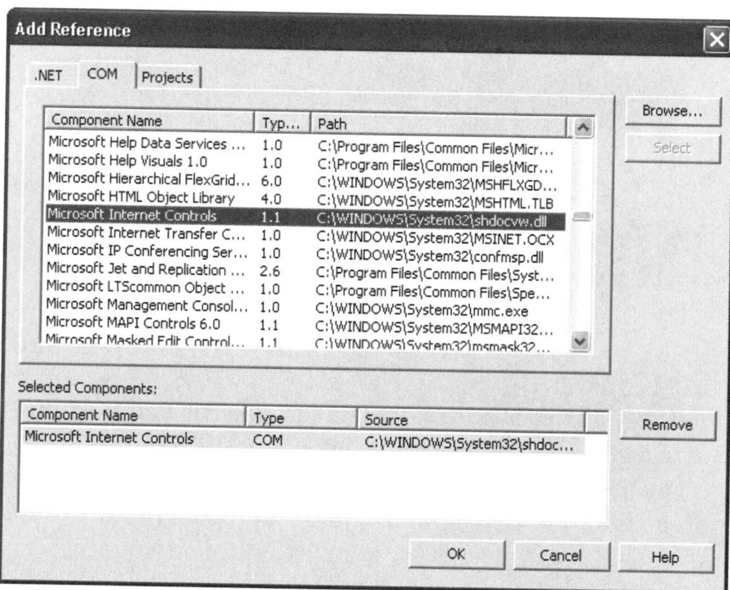

Figure 13-6 Adding a reference to the Microsoft Internet Controls library

This action will create an RCW called SHDocVw in the assembly Interop.SHDocVw.dll. The *SHDocVw* namespace contains a selection of objects, interfaces, delegates, and constants. The *InternetExplorerClass* exposes the *InternetExplorer* interface. The *doWork* method shown below creates an instance of *InternetExplorerClass* and references it using the *InternetExplorer* variable, *ie*:

```
private void doWork()
{
    ⋮
InternetExplorer ie = new InternetExplorerClass();
```

The *InternetExplorer* interface supplies methods that allow you to subscribe to the various events that can occur, using the *add_<XXX>* methods (where <XXX> is the name of the event). The corresponding *remove_<XXX>* methods allow you to unsubscribe from an event. To subscribe to an event, you must first create a delegate that refers to the method to be invoked when the event is raised. As described earlier, each event has its own delegate class defined by the RCW for this purpose. For instance, the *OnVisible* event expects a *DWebBrowserEvents2_OnVisibleEventHandler* delegate. (*DWebBrowserEvents2* is the name of the event interface in the Internet Explorer COM library.) This delegate must refer to a method that takes a single *boolean* parameter indicating whether the Internet Explorer window is visible and returns a void. The *ExplorerDemo* class provides just such a method, called *ieVisible*:

```
ie.add_OnVisible(new DWebBrowserEvents2_OnVisibleEventHandler(ieVisible));
```

In much the same way, the *TitleChange* event requires a *DWebBrowserEvents2_TitleChangeEventHandler* delegate, which refers to a method that returns a void and takes a single *String* parameter containing the new title displayed when a page is loaded into Internet Explorer. The *ExplorerDemo* class contains the *ieTitleChange* method for this purpose:

```
ie.add_TitleChange(new
    DWebBrowserEvents2_TitleChangeEventHandler(ieTitleChange));
```

To test these event handlers, the *doWork* method makes the Internet Explorer window visible and navigates to the user's selected home page. At this point, Internet Explorer should burst into life on the user's desktop. If the user navigates to other URLs, the *TitleChange* event will fire and you'll see the text output by the *ieTitleChange* method in the console window. (The *doWork* method waits for the user to press the Enter key before terminating because when this method finishes so does the program, and all the event handlers will be lost even though the Internet Explorer window will remain). Figure 13-7 shows the console window after navigating to the author's home page (the MSN UK Homepage) and then moving to the Microsoft Press Web site.

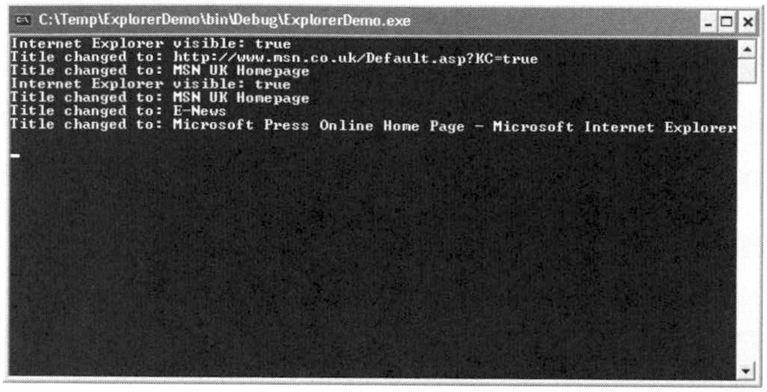

```
C:\Temp\ExplorerDemo\bin\Debug\ExplorerDemo.exe
Internet Explorer visible: true
Title changed to: http://www.msn.co.uk/Default.asp?KC=true
Title changed to: MSN UK Homepage
Internet Explorer visible: true
Title changed to: MSN UK Homepage
Title changed to: E-News
Title changed to: Microsoft Press Online Home Page - Microsoft Internet Explorer
```

Figure 13-7 The console window showing the messages output by the event handlers

Using COM Objects Without Type Libraries

Not all COM objects provide nicely wrapped type libraries. In these cases, you cannot create a static RCW using Tlbimp or the Add Reference dialog box in Visual Studio .NET. Instead, you have at least two choices: late binding or manual marshaling.

Using Late Binding

Late binding is commonly used when you access COM objects that implement *IDispatch*. The COM *IDispatch* interface defines methods that allow a client to query the interfaces an object implements at run time, and discover its methods and properties. Late binding offers an advantage over using a static RCW because the client is not tied to any particular implementation or version of a COM server. (Versioning still is an issue in COM.) The disadvantages are the additional overhead needed to make method calls and the extra complexity required in your J# code.

Late binding is based on reflection and the type system employed by the common language runtime. When used in conjunction with COM Interop, the common language runtime interacts with a dynamically created RCW, which in turn uses the methods of the *IDispatch* interface to dynamically invoke methods and access properties of the underlying COM object.

To see how late binding works, consider the following example. The Fourth Coffee company has an existing COM component that exposes two classes called *CakeFactory* and *Cake*. This component was developed using Visual Basic 6, but the developers at Fourth Coffee want to access it from J#. For reasons best known to them, the developers wish to use late binding. (This component will support early binding as well, but we're looking for a demonstration of late binding here). The Visual Basic code for the *Cake* class is shown here (it is available in the FourthCoffee Visual Basic 6.0 project):

Cake.cls

```
Option Explicit

Private size As Integer
Private filling As Integer
Private shape As Integer

Public Property Let CakeFilling(ByVal fill As Integer)
    filling = fill
End Property

Public Property Get CakeFilling() As Integer
    CakeFilling = filling
End Property

Public Property Let CakeShape(ByVal shp As Integer)
    shape = shp
End Property

Public Property Get CakeShape() As Integer
    CakeShape = shape
End Property

Public Property Let CakeSize(ByVal sz As Integer)
    size = sz
End Property

Public Property Get CakeSize() As Integer
    CakeSize = size
End Property
```

This class has been kept deliberately simple. All it does is expose the *CakeFilling*, *CakeShape*, and *CakeSize* properties, each of which is implemented as a Visual Basic 6.0 *Integer*. The *CakeFactory* class is also straightforward. It provides two methods: *CreateCake*, which takes parameters describing the properties of a cake and creates a new *Cake* object using them, and *FeedsHowMany*, which is another implementation of the method we've seen so often in this book!

CakeFactory.cls

```
Option Explicit

' Cake Fillings
Const CF_FRUIT = 0
Const CF_SPONGE = 1
```

```
' Cake Shapes
Const CS_SQUARE = 0
Const CS_ROUND = 1
Const CS_HEXAGONAL = 2

' Make a cake using the supplied details
Public Function CreateCake(ByVal size As Integer, ByVal shape As Integer,
   ByVal filling As Integer) As Cake

    Dim theCake As Cake

    Set theCake = New Cake
    theCake.CakeSize = size
    theCake.CakeShape = shape
    theCake.CakeFilling = filling

    Set CreateCake = theCake

End Function

' How many people does a cake of a given size, shape, and filling feed
Public Function FeedsHowMany(ByVal diameter As Integer,
   ByVal shape As Integer, ByVal filling As Integer) As Integer

    Dim munchSizeFactor As Double
    Dim deadSpaceFactor As Double
    Dim numConsumers As Integer

    munchSizeFactor = IIf(filling = CF_FRUIT, 2.5, 1)

    Select Case shape
        Case CS_SQUARE
            deadSpaceFactor = 0
        Case CS_HEXAGONAL
            deadSpaceFactor = 0.1
        Case CS_ROUND
            deadSpaceFactor = 0.15
        Case Else
            deadSpaceFactor = 0.2
    End Select

    numConsumers = diameter * munchSizeFactor * (1 - deadSpaceFactor)
    FeedsHowMany = numConsumers

End Function
```

The component is deployed as FourthCoffee.dll (an unmanaged DLL). The J# *CakeClient* class, available in the COMCakeClient project, shows how to access the *CakeFactory* and *Cake* classes through late binding. If you examine the project, you'll notice that no explicit RCW has been created or imported; everything is done through reflection. The key line of code is actually the first statement in the *main* method:

```
Type cakeFactoryType = Type.GetTypeFromProgID("FourthCoffee.CakeFactory");
```

This piece of magic creates a *System.Type* object based on information found in the Windows Registry, which was located through the specified ProgID using the static method *GetTypeFromProgID* of the *System.Type* class. (There's also a static *GetTypeFromCLSID* method that takes a CLSID of a component, which is specified as a *System.Guid* and creates a *System.Type* object in the same manner.) In this case, the ProgID used is that of the *CakeFactory* class. (ProgIDs generated by Visual Basic 6.0 are usually of the form *project.class*, although you can use the OLE/COM Object Viewer available from the Tools menu of Visual Studio.NET, and the Platform SDK, to verify the ProgID of any registered component.) Assuming that the statement is successful (the value returned will be *null* if it wasn't), the *cakeFactoryType* variable will be populated with type information about the COM object. (In case you're interested, the actual value returned is *System.__ComObject*, which is an opaque representation of a COM object.)

The next task is to create the RCW itself. You can do this using the static *CreateInstance* method of the *System.Activator* class. (You saw this method before, when we used Remoting.)

```
Object cakeFactory = Activator.CreateInstance(cakeFactoryType);
```

The *CreateInstance* method dynamically creates an instance of the object indicated by its *System.Type* parameter—in this case, a *System.__ComObject*. Information about exactly which COM class the *cakeFactory* object represents is retained deep within the RCW and is not easily accessible. (*System.__ComObject* is opaque, remember.) You can assume that because you instantiated this object using the ProgID *FourthCoffee.CakeFactory*, you can treat it as a COM *CakeFactory* object.

Remember that you created this object using late binding, so the only way you can access its methods is through *IDispatch*. The *System.Type* class defines the *InvokeMember* method, which is useful on such occasions as this. The *InvokeMember* method is used to access a member of a type. A member can be a method, a property, or a field. The arguments to *InvokeMember* are the name of the member, a *System.Reflection.BindingFlags* value indicating what sort of member it is, binding information that can be used to choose between overloaded members that have the same name, the object over which the member should be invoked, and an array of parameters taken by the member. The value returned by the *InvokeMember* method is the value resulting from accessing the member. An exception will be thrown if the member does not exist or the parameters are wrong or the return value is miscast.

The following statements create an array of three *System.Int16* values. (Visual Basic *Integers* are 16-bit values, and the data must be convertible to *Objects*, so you cannot use Java language primitive types such as *short*.) The values denote a 12-inch hexagonal sponge cake and then call the *FeedsHowMany* method of the *cakeFactory* object. In this example, the method call will be intercepted by the RCW (the *cakeFactory* object) and executed as a COM method call. The return value will be marshaled from COM back to your managed code. The result will be the number of people this cake will serve.

```
Object [] params = new Object[]{(Int16)12, (Int16)2, (Int16)1};
Int16 numEaters = (Int16)cakeFactoryType.InvokeMember("FeedsHowMany",
   BindingFlags.InvokeMethod, null, cakeFactory, params);
Console.WriteLine("This cake will feed " + numEaters);
```

You can use the same technique to execute the *CreateCake* method and return a COM *Cake* object. This time, the value returned is another *System.__ComObject*:

```
Object cake = cakeFactoryType.InvokeMember("CreateCake",
   BindingFlags.InvokeMethod, null, cakeFactory, params);
```

Once the *Cake* object has been created, you can verify that its properties are set correctly by querying the *CakeSize*, *CakeShape*, and *CakeFilling* properties—you set the *BindingFlags* parameter to *GetProperty*. (You can also use *SetProperty* to change a property value as long as the property is not read-only.)

```
Int16 size = (Int16)cakeFactoryType.InvokeMember("CakeSize",
   BindingFlags.GetProperty, null, cake, null);
Int16 shape = (Int16)cakeFactoryType.InvokeMember("CakeShape",
   BindingFlags.GetProperty, null, cake, null);
Int16 filling = (Int16)cakeFactoryType.InvokeMember("CakeFilling",
   BindingFlags.GetProperty, null, cake, null);
Console.WriteLine("Size is " + size + ", Shape is " + shape +
   ", and Filling is " + filling);
```

The CakeClient.jsl sample file in the COMCakeClient project contains the complete code.

Note You might be wondering how (or maybe even why) we're using the *cakeFactoryType* object to invoke *Cake* properties. After all, the *cakeFactoryType* variable was created using the ProgID of the *CakeFactory* class. You're welcome to create a *Type* variable using the ProgID *FourthCoffee.Cake* and execute *InvokeMember* using this variable instead, but this would be a waste of effort. The fourth parameter of *InvokeMember* (the *cakeFactory* and *cake* objects in the examples presented) is the key—it specifies exactly which COM object should be used. You can actually use any *Type* variable you like for this purpose, as long as it represents a *System.__ComObject*. We even tried using the *FlexGrid* control (with a ProgID of *MSFlexGridLib.MSFlexGrid*), and it all worked beautifully.

Manual Binding and Marshaling

An alternative to using late binding in the absence of a type library is for you to define the metadata required by the RCW yourself. The *System.Runtime.InteropServices* namespace contains a number of attributes that you can use to define classes and interfaces and specify that they're implemented by COM. The most important attributes are *ComImportAttribute*, which marks an interface or class as being externally implemented through COM, and *GuidAttribute*, which specifies the GUID of the interface or class. In the case of an *IDispatch* interface, the individual members should be tagged with their DispIds using *DispIdAttribute*. You can specify the directionality of individual method parameters using *InAttribute* and *OutAttribute*. If any of the parameter types requires additional marshaling (strings, for example), you can apply *MarshalAsAttribute*, as shown earlier when we discussed P/Invoke.

Using the *CakeFactory* and *Cake* classes from the previous example, here are .NET definitions of interfaces for these classes. We deliberately used the same naming scheme that the RCW uses—the interfaces are named after the original implementations, and the coclass has the suffix *Class* appended to the end. The code for this example is available in the file CakeClient.jsl in the ManualCOMCakeClient project.

```
/** @attribute ComImportAttribute() */
/** @attribute GuidAttribute("2F2A5381-B1DB-4828-9982-A77DA2470237") */
public interface Cake
{
/** @attribute DispIdAttribute(0x68030002) */
void CakeFilling(/** @attribute InAttribute() */ short filling);
```

```
/** @attribute DispIdAttribute(0x68030002) */ short CakeFilling();

/** @attribute DispIdAttribute(0x68030001) */
void CakeSize(/** @attribute InAttribute() */ short filling);

/** @attribute DispIdAttribute(0x68030001) */
short CakeSize();

/** @attribute DispIdAttribute(0x68030000) */
void CakeShape(/** @attribute InAttribute() */ short shape);

/** @attribute DispIdAttribute(0x68030000) */
short CakeShape();
}

/** @attribute ComImportAttribute() */
/** @attribute GuidAttribute("977BAB34-FB20-4884-B73D-8A63E73DA8F4") */
public interface CakeFactory
{
/** @attribute DispIdAttribute(0x60030000) */
Cake CreateCake(/** @attribute InAttribute() */ short size,
    /** @attribute InAttribute() */ short shape,
    /** @attribute InAttribute() */ short filling);

/** @attribute DispIdAttribute(0x60030001) */
short FeedsHowMany(/** @attribute InAttribute() */ short diameter,
 /** @attribute InAttribute() */ short shape,
 /** @attribute InAttribute() */ short filling);
}

/**
 * .NET definition of the CakeFactory class
 */

/** @attribute ComImportAttribute() */
/** @attribute GuidAttribute("28915B3A-DC8A-4780-AFF5-0C6136AF4496") */
public class CakeFactoryClass {}
```

Note The GUIDs for the interfaces and the class were generated by Visual Basic. If you rebuild the Visual Basic component, the GUIDs might change.

Common Managed COM Interfaces

COM objects that do not have type libraries almost inevitably implement horrendously complex interfaces, usually incorporating methods that return other interface pointers. You can end up having to work out how to map a number of COM interfaces to their managed equivalents. To save you a bit of time, the .NET Framework Class Library provides managed definitions of some of the standard COM interfaces in the *System.Runtime.InteropServices* namespace. Their names all take the form *UCOM<XXX>*, where *<XXX>* is the name of the underlying COM interface.

For example, *UCOMIPersistFile* is the managed version of the COM *IPersistFile* interface. The other interfaces available are *UCOMIBindCtx*, *UCOMIBindConnectionPoint*, *UCOMIBindConnectionPointContainer*, *UCOMIEnumConnectionPoints*, *UCOMIEnumConnections*, *UCOMIEnumMoniker*, *UCOMIEnumString*, *UCOMIEnumVARIANT*, *UCOMIMoniker*, *UCOMIRunningObjectTable*, *UCOMIStream*, *UCOMITypeComp*, and *UCOMITypeLib*. To obtain a reference to a specific interface exposed by an RCW, you just cast to the appropriate interface. The following statements create an *InternetExplorer* object (see the *ExplorerDemo* class shown earlier) and retrieve a reference to its *IConnectionPointContainer* interface:

```
InternetExplorer ie = new InternetExplorerClass();
UCOMIConnectionPointContainer icpc =
   (UCOMIConnectionPointContainer)ie;
```

The definition of *CakeFactoryClass*, for accessing the *CakeFactory* coclass that implements the *CakeFactory* interface, is worthy of further mention. The class does not actually contain any methods because the methods are implemented by the underlying COM class. Additionally, the class does not explicitly implement the *CakeFactory* interface. If you try to attach an *implements CakeFactory* clause, your code will not compile because you'll also have to provide implementations of the *CreateCake* and *FeedsHowMany* methods. (These are the general rules of interface implementation.)

To create a *CakeFactory* object, you use this statement:

```
CakeFactory cakeFactory = (CakeFactory)new CakeFactoryClass();
```

This looks mighty suspect! Under normal circumstances, you'd expect the J# compiler to reject any attempt to cast an object as an interface that it does not explicitly implement. However, in the case of classes tagged with *ComImportAt-*

tribute, the compile-time checking of such casts is temporarily suspended. It will be performed instead at run time, when the RCW generated for the *CakeFactoryClass* attempts to obtain a pointer to the specified interface (*CakeFactory*) through *QueryInterface*, in the classic COM manner. If *QueryInterface* fails, the RCW will throw an exception.

Having obtained an interface pointer to a *CakeFactory* object, you can execute the *FeedsHowMany* and *CreateCake* methods as before. This time, however, you do not have to use *InvokeMember*:

```
// How many people will a 12" hexagonal(2) sponge(1) cake feed?
short numEaters = cakeFactory.FeedsHowMany((short)12, (short)2, (short)1);
Console.WriteLine("This cake will feed " + numEaters);

// Call the CreateCake method to create a new Cake object
Cake cake = cakeFactory.CreateCake((short)12, (short)2, (short)1);
Console.WriteLine("Cake created");

// Verify the properties of the new cake
short size = cake.CakeSize();
short shape = cake.CakeShape();
short filling = cake.CakeFilling();
Console.WriteLine("Size is " + size + ", Shape is " + shape +
   ", and Filling is " + filling);
```

The Marshal Class

The *System.Runtime.InteropServices.Marshal* class is a utility class containing a range of static methods for managing the transition from managed to unmanaged space and vice-versa. Methods are available for copying blocks of memory between the two spaces and interacting with the COM infrastructure, including managed implementations of the *IUnknown* methods (*QueryInterface*, *AddRef*, and *Release*). Furthermore, methods are available that allow you to obtain pointers to the *IDispatch* (*GetIDispatchForObject*) and *IUnknown* (*GetIUnknownForObject*) interfaces of a COM object accessed through an RCW. With one exception, you're unlikely to use many of the methods of the *Marshal* class on a day-to-day basis, mainly because much of the functionality is automatically available through an RCW anyway. But on occasion you might need to delve more deeply than the RCW will allow, so it's nice to know that the *Marshal* class is there.

The method that you might find useful is *ReleaseComObject*, which implements the *Release* method of the COM *IUnknown* interface. You can use this method if you want to release a reference to a COM object earlier than the common language runtime would have (and maybe save some resources). If you try to access an object after having released it, you'll cause a *NullReferenceException* to be thrown.

Many of the methods in the *Marshal* class make heavy use of the *System.IntPtr* type, which is a managed implementation of a pointer to unmanaged memory. Unmanaged pointers are marshaled as *IntPtr* values by many of the *Marshal* methods.

Integrating .NET Components into COM

In addition to calling COM components from managed space, you can expose .NET components to unmanaged code using COM Interop. To do this, you must create a COM Callable Wrapper (CCW) for your managed component. Like an RCW, the CCW hides the differences between the .NET model and COM, making the .NET component appear as a regular COM component to COM clients. A COM client activates and accesses a .NET component through a CCW in the same way as it would use any other COM component.

A CCW is a nontrivial piece of code. It has to create and manage a .NET component on behalf of a COM client, keeping track of the number of references and arranging for the .NET component to be garbage collected when the last reference disappears. In other words, it provides the functionality of the *IUnknown* interface. The CCW might also need to implement other interfaces, such as *IDispatch* and *IConnectionPoint*, which will return information obtained using reflection to query the metadata of the .NET component. In addition to these interfaces, your .NET component might expose its own custom interfaces, and the CCW must map these to COM as well.

Designing .NET Components for COM Interop

The tools supplied by Microsoft can create CCWs from most .NET components, but it's good practice to follow a few guidelines when you design classes to be exposed to COM:

- Stick to automation-compliant data types. Do not create methods that take nonautomation types as parameters or pass them back as return values. Not all COM clients will be able to consume COM interfaces exporting types that are not automation-compliant.

- Try to use isomorphic types. This is less crucial than the previous point and might not always be possible, but it will help improve marshaling performance. You should provide marshaling information using *MarshalAsAttribute* for nonisomorphic types that are passed to COM clients.
- Do not create static methods.
- Do not define parameterized constructors.
- Define and implement interfaces explicitly. This is good practice and means that the CCW will not have to generate its own interfaces for accessing your classes.
- Implement event sink interfaces to provide access to managed events from COM. (See the following example.)

For example, consider the *Cake* class (in Cake.jsl in the CakeComponent project). This class implements three interfaces called *ICake*, *IBaker*, and *IBakerEvents*. The *ICake* interface defines four properties: *Size*, *Shape*, *Filling* (the usual suspects), and *Message* (such as "Happy Anniversary"). The *IBaker* interface contains the method *BakeCake*, which takes a parameter indicating how long the cake should be baked and then raises the *CakeBaked* event when this period has expired. The *CakeBaked* event is defined through the event sink interface *IBakerEvents*.

Starting with the *ICake* interface, setting *ComVisibleAttribute* to *true* makes this interface visible to COM. In fact, interfaces and classes will be visible to COM by default, but it is still worthwhile to be explicit and use this attribute, if only for documentation purposes. Each interface must be tagged with a unique GUID (the COM IID), using *GuidAttribute*. Use the GuidGen utility that's supplied with Visual Studio .NET (and that's available in the Tools menu as the Create GUID command) to generate unique GUIDs.

Each property defined by the *ICake* interface is implemented as a pair of getter and setter methods. Remember that with J#, you must explicitly call these methods *set_<XXX>* and *get_<XXX>* and provide the *@property* directive. This interface is converted into a COM dual interface, and you can optionally specify dispatch IDs for each method and property using *DispIdAttribute*. The parameters of each setter method are input parameters and are tagged with *InAttribute* (the default). For methods that return output values, you should tag each output parameter with *OutAttribute*. The *set_Message* method takes a *String* parameter, and a *MarshalAsAttribute* is applied to ensure that it is marshaled correctly as a COM *BSTR*. The *ICake* interface is reproduced here:

```
/** @attribute ComVisibleAttribute(true) */
/** @attribute GuidAttribute("EDEDB0B2-82CB-4120-B6F6-0633913C46B8") */
public interface ICake
{
   /** @property */
   public void set_Size(/** @attribute InAttribute() */ short size);

   /** @property */
   public short get_Size();

   /** @property */
   public void set_Shape(/** @attribute InAttribute() */ short shape);

   /** @property */
   public short get_Shape();

   /** @property */
   public void set_Filling(/** @attribute InAttribute() */ short filling);

   /** @property */
   public short get_Filling();

   /** @property */
   public void set_Message(/** @attribute InAttribute() */
      /** @attribute MarshalAsAttribute(UnmanagedType.BStr) */ String msg);

   /** @property */
   public String get_Message();
}
```

The *IBaker* interface is likewise tagged with *ComVisibleAttribute* and *GuidAttribute*. Its single method, *BakeCake*, takes one input parameter:

```
/** @attribute ComVisibleAttribute(true) */
/** @attribute GuidAttribute("9A0C6B4B-2D1F-4d42-983D-E9E84AFD7868") */
public interface IBaker
{
   public void BakeCake(/** @attribute InAttribute() */ short howLongFor);
}
```

The *IBakerEvents* interface is the COM event sink interface, which effectively defines the COM connection points that clients can use to subscribe to events. Each event should define one method, providing the connection point for that event. When a COM client subscribes to an event, it attaches to this connection point and supplies an implementation of the named method (known as the *event sink*). In this example, the *BakeCake* method of the *IBaker* class raises the *CakeBaked* event when the cake is baked. The *IBakerEvents* event sink interface therefore defines a method called *CakeBaked*. How this method is actually hooked up to the corresponding event will be revealed shortly. Methods that define event sinks can take parameters, although they should not return values. In addition, the event sink interface must be tagged with *InterfaceTypeAttribute*, specifying a parameter of *ComInterfaceType.InterfaceIsIDispatch*—an event sink interface must be exposed to COM as an *IDispatch* interface.

```
/** @attribute ComVisibleAttribute(true) */
/** @attribute GuidAttribute("6DF0B938-37D5-490b-8AF6-C285720F1DB2") */
/** @attribute InterfaceTypeAttribute(ComInterfaceType.InterfaceIsIDispatch) */
public interface IBakerEvents
{
   // Event sink method
   public void CakeBaked();
}
```

The *Cake* class contains the code that implements these three interfaces. It is tagged with *ComVisibleAttribute* and is given a COM CLSID using *GuidAttribute*. The class is also given a human-readable ProgID using *ProgIdAttribute*. The *ClassInterfaceAttribute* specifies the type of interface the class exposes to COM. You can generate an *IDispatch* interface only, using the setting *ClassInterfaceType.AutoDispatch*, or a dual interface using the setting *ClassInterfaceType.AutoDual*. However, the recommended setting is *ClassInterfaceType.None*. This prevents an interface being automatically generated for the class and ensures that the class is accessible only through any interfaces it explicitly implements.

In this example, the *Cake* class implements *ICake* and *IBaker*. No class interface is generated, so the class can be accessed only through the *ICake* and *IBaker* interfaces. Also note that the order in which the interfaces are specified is significant: the first interface listed (*ICake*) will be the default interface for the class.

```
/** @attribute ComVisibleAttribute(true) */
/** @attribute GuidAttribute("DA8ADFF6-22C4-4513-9E82-64B7CE3305C1") */
/** @attribute ProgIdAttribute("CakeComponent.Cake") */
/** @attribute ClassInterfaceAttribute(ClassInterfaceType.None) */
⋮
// ICake is the default interface
public class Cake implements ICake, IBaker
{
   ⋮
}
```

"But," you scream, "what about the *IBakerEvents* interface?" Event interfaces are indicated by using *ComSourceInterfacesAttribute*. You list the name of the interface and the assembly for each event interface the class implements—in this case, the *CakeComponent.IBakerEvents* interface in the *CakeComponent* assembly (the name of the assembly created by the project):

```
/** @attribute ComSourceInterfacesAttribute("CakeComponent.IBakerEvents,
   CakeComponent") */
```

Much of the *Cake* class is reasonably straightforward—it implements the properties of the *ICake* interface. The *BakeCake* method of the *IBaker* interface is a little more interesting. When invoked, this method uses a thread from the thread pool (see Chapter 8 for details) and uses it to execute the private method *CakeBaker*, passing the time to wait as a parameter:

```
public void BakeCake(short howLongFor)
{
   //   Spawn a thread that waits for the specified period of time
   //   and then raises the CakeBaked event
   ThreadPool.QueueUserWorkItem(new WaitCallback(CakeBaker),
      new Short(howLongFor));
}
```

We'll come back to the *CakeBaker* method shortly. First, let's look at how the event mechanism works.

You should remember that an event in J# is implemented using a delegate (marked with the *@delegate* directive) and a pair of *add_<XXX>* and *remove_<XXX>* methods (marked with the *@event* directive) to allow a client to subscribe to and unsubscribe from the event. For the COM event sink mechanism to work with .NET, the name of the event must be the same as the name of the method in the event sink interface. In this example, the event sink method is called *CakeBaked*, so the name of the event is also *CakeBaked*, which is published in J# through a pair of methods called *add_CakeBaked* and *remove_CakeBaked*. The delegate type itself can be called almost anything—here it's *CakeBakedEventHandler*—but its signature must match that of the event sink method (no parameters, void return value in this case). The *Cake* class creates a private delegate variable called *bakedEventHandler* to hold the subscriptions to the event.

```
/** @delegate */
private delegate void CakeBakedEventHandler();
private CakeBakedEventHandler bakedEventHandler = null;

/** @event */
public void add_CakeBaked(CakeBakedEventHandler handler)
```

```
{
   bakedEventHandler =
      (CakeBakedEventHandler)Delegate.Combine(bakedEventHandler, handler);
}


/** @event */
public void remove_CakeBaked(CakeBakedEventHandler handler)
{
   bakedEventHandler =
      (CakeBakedEventHandler)Delegate.Remove(bakedEventHandler, handler);
}
```

Returning to the *CakeBaker* method, you can see that it sleeps for the designated period of time. (The current implementation actually waits for seconds rather than minutes, but you can change it if you want to wait 20 minutes for an event when you test the code!) When the method wakes up, it raises the *CakeBaked* event by calling *Invoke* on the delegate variable (*bakedEventHandler*). At this point, any clients acting as sinks will have their sink methods executed:

```
private void CakeBaker(Object bakeTimeObject)
{
   Short bakeTimeSeconds = (Short)bakeTimeObject;
   int bakeTimeMilliseconds = bakeTimeSeconds.shortValue() * 1000;
   // Use 60000 for minutes

   // Wait for the cake to bake
   System.Threading.Thread.Sleep(bakeTimeMilliseconds);

   // Raise the CakeBaked event
   bakedEventHandler.Invoke();
}
```

One final point: .NET classes that are exposed as COM servers must be placed where a COM client can find them. You can either deploy the COM server in the same folder as the client or you can place it in the GAC. If you want to go for the GAC option, you must sign the assembly—by generating a key pair using the Sn utility and applying *AssemblyKeyFileAttribute* to the assembly.

The complete code for the Cake.jsl sample file can be found in the downloadable CakeComponent project.

Creating a COM Callable Wrapper

The *Cake* class is implemented as a class library, and the project is compiled into the file CakeComponent.dll. To make the *Cake* class available to COM, you must create the CCW. You can do this in two ways: by using the type library export utility (Tlbexp.exe) to create a COM type library or by using the assembly registration utility (Regasm.exe), which can also create a type library but also registers the component in the Windows Registry. The following command registers the component and creates the type library CakeComponent.tlb:

```
Regasm CakeComponent.dll /tlb:CakeComponent.tlb
```

You should then either copy CakeComponent.dll to the folder containing your COM client executable or place it in the GAC.

Note If your COM clients are built using Visual Basic 6.0 or earlier, you should place the component DLL in the same folder as the Visual Basic runtime (\Program Files\Microsoft Visual Studio\VB98).

It is instructive to examine what the CCW actually produces for your component: You can place the CakeComponent.dll assembly in the GAC and use the OLE/COM Object Viewer from the Tools menu of Visual Studio .NET. If you expand the All Objects folder, you can look for the component with the ProgID *CakeComponent.Cake* and expand it. You'll see the various interfaces implemented through the CCW, as depicted in Figure 13-8.

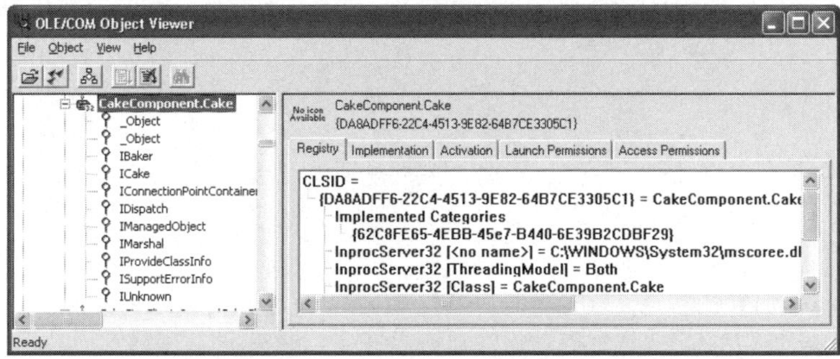

Figure 13-8 The OLE/COM Object Viewer showing the CCW for CakeComponent.dll

You should have been expecting the *IBaker* and *ICake* interfaces because you defined these yourself. You can also see that the CCW created the standard COM *IUnknown*, *IConnectionPointContainer*, *IProvideClassInfo*, *ISupportErrorInfo*, and *IMarshal* interfaces. The *IManagedObject* interface, which is also created automatically as part of the CCW, provides what's called the Managed Object Interface. This interface defines two methods: *GetSerializedBuffer*, which you can use to obtain a serialized version of the object (as a *BSTR*) if the object supports serialization, and *GetObjectIdentity*, which returns a three-part unique identifier (a GUID, the ID of the application domain, and the ID of the CCW) for the object if you need to perform a managed object equality test in your COM code. The IDL definition for *IManagedObject* is shown here:

```
[
  odl,
  uuid(C3FCC19E-A970-11D2-8B5A-00A0C9B7C9C4),
  helpstring("Managed Object Interface"),
  oleautomation
]
interface IManagedObject : IUnknown {
    HRESULT _stdcall GetSerializedBuffer([out] BSTR* pBSTR);
    HRESULT _stdcall GetObjectIdentity(
                    [out] BSTR* pBSTRGUID,
                    [out] int* AppDomainID,
                    [out] int* pCCW);
};
```

The *_Object* interface provides access to the *System.Object* methods available to all managed objects—*ToString*, *Equals*, *GetHashCode*, and *GetType*, as shown below. (The *ReferenceEquals* method is omitted because it does not translate to COM very well—if you need to determine whether two references refer to the same managed COM object, use the *GetObjectIdentity* method of the *IManagedObject* interface.) The *java.lang.Object* methods are not exposed. A COM client can use this interface to execute *System.Object* methods against a managed COM component.

```
[
  odl,
  uuid(65074F7F-63C0-304E-AF0A-D51741CB4A8D),
  hidden,
  dual,
  nonextensible,
  oleautomation,
  custom(0F21F359-AB84-41E8-9A78-36D110E6D2F9, System.Object)

]
interface _Object : IDispatch {
    [id(00000000), propget,
      custom(54FC8F55-38DE-4703-9C4E-250351302B1C, 1)]
    HRESULT ToString([out, retval] BSTR* pRetVal);
    [id(0x60020001)]
    HRESULT Equals(
       [in] VARIANT obj,
       [out, retval] VARIANT_BOOL* pRetVal);
```

```
    [id(0x60020002)]
    HRESULT GetHashCode([out, retval] long* pRetVal);
    [id(0x60020003)]
    HRESULT GetType([out, retval] _Type** pRetVal);
};
```

Finally, the two interfaces *ICake* and *IBaker* contain the methods and properties you implemented in the *Cake* class. Figure 13-9 shows the *ICake* interface in the OLE/COM Object Viewer. You'll be comforted to see that the J# properties have been translated into COM. (The *get_* and *set_* prefixes of the J# methods have disappeared, and instead the *propget* and *propput* IDL attributes have been applied, together with paired DispIDs.)

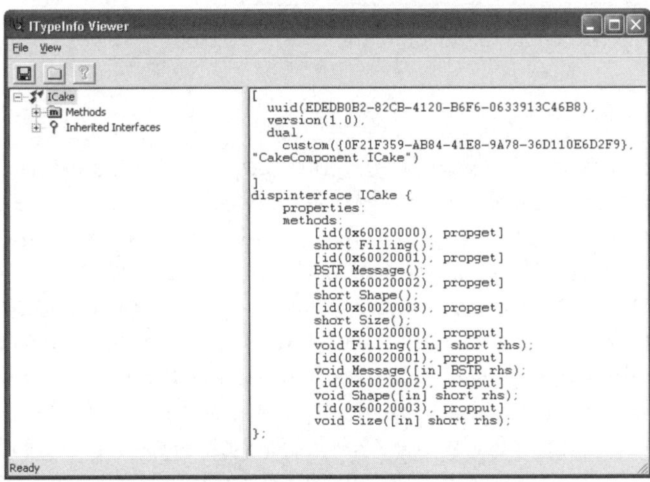

Figure 13-9 The IDL implementation of the *ICake* interface

For completeness, Figure 13-10 shows the *IBaker* interface, which comprises the single method *BakeCake*.

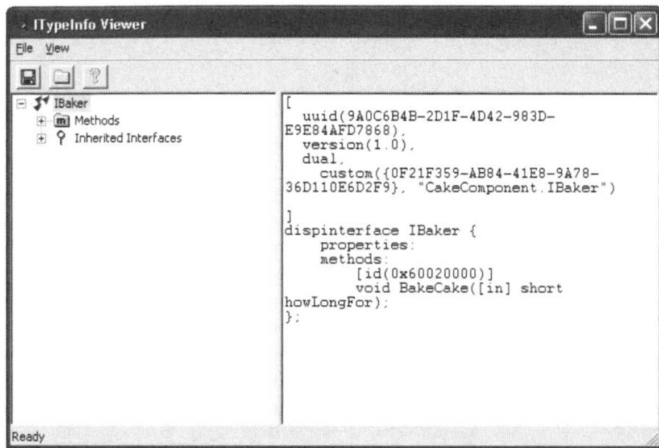

Figure 13-10 The IDL implementation of the *IBaker* interface

Testing the CCW

To test that the CCW works as expected, the *CakeClient* Visual Basic 6.0 project contains a form that instantiates a *Cake* object, sets its properties, calls the *BakeCake* method through the *IBaker* interface, and registers an event handler for the *CakeBaked* event. The *Cake* object is defined using the Visual Basic *WithEvents* keyword. (This allows an object to use the COM connection point mechanism without having to manually query the various interfaces and connect them together; the object instead defines methods of the form *object_event* that the Visual Basic runtime will automatically connect as COM event sinks.) The *CakeBaked* event is handled by the *CakeObject_CakeBaked* method.

To use the *CakeComponent*, you must set a reference to the type library in the References dialog box. (Choose References from the Project menu, scroll down to CakeComponent, and select it, as shown in Figure 13-11.)

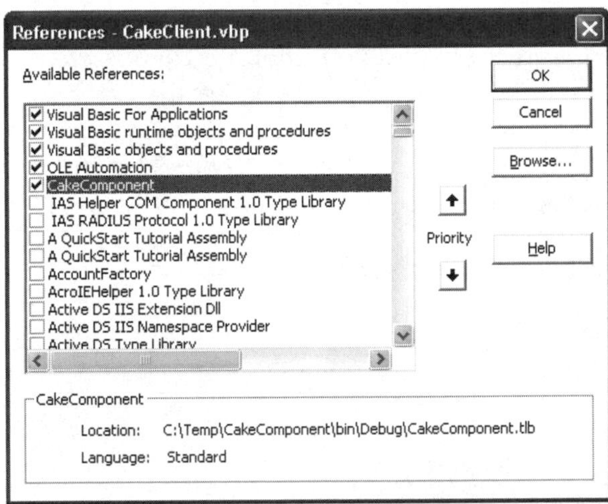

Figure 13-11 The Visual Basic 6.0 Project References dialog box

If you compile and run the program, the Cake Client form will appear. You can set the size of the cake, its shape, and the filling, and you can type a message to be iced on the cake. The Order button invokes the *cmdOrder_Click* method, which instantiates a new *Cake* object, sets its properties, and then retrieves them again to display the results in a message box, as shown in Figure 13-12.

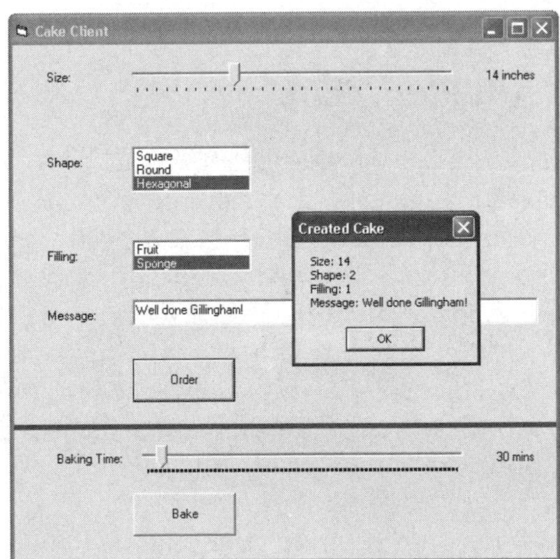

Figure 13-12 The Cake Client program after you create a new cake

At this point, you can set the time required to bake the cake and click the Bake button. (These controls are disabled until the cake is created.) After the designated number of minutes (or seconds, if you left the *Cake* class unchanged earlier), the sleep operation in the *Cake* component will expire and raise the *CakeBaked* event, triggering the *CakeObject_CakeBaked* method in the Visual Basic code and displaying a message box (as shown in Figure 13-13).

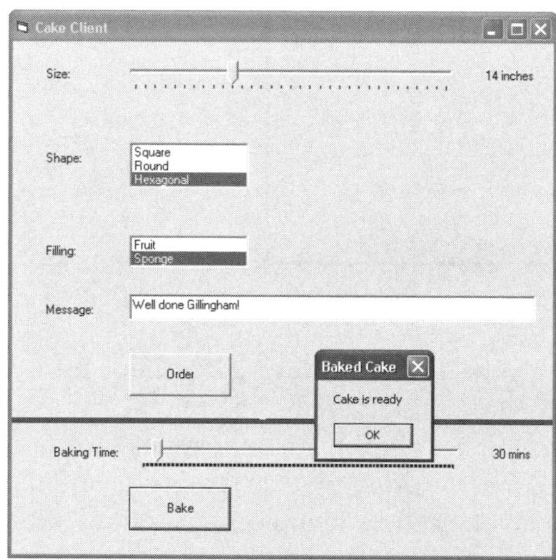

Figure 13-13 The cake has been baked.

Interoperability with Other Technologies

You've seen how Microsoft provides tools that allow you to build applications in J# (and other .NET-supported languages) that can interoperate with components created using other technologies. However, Microsoft has concentrated on defining mechanisms for communicating between components built and running using Microsoft's own infrastructure—primarily because this is what Microsoft knows best and because so many other technologies are out there that it would be impossible for Microsoft to provide interfaces to them all. This state of affairs also leads to a healthy market for third-party integration tools, so it should be seen as an opportunity rather than a shortcoming on Microsoft's part.

However, at times you'll need to integrate with other systems. In the Java arena, this will primarily involve communicating with J2EE servers running Enterprise JavaBeans (EJBs) and services running under CORBA. Depending on your level of ingenuity and what you're willing to spend on third-party software, a number of solutions are available, including (in no particular order):

- Using a COM/CORBA bridge. The Object Management Group (OMG), recognizing the ubiquitous nature of COM on Windows, has defined a mechanism for COM/CORBA interworking. A number of vendors have produced COM/CORBA bridging middleware based on this mechanism. You can use COM Interop to access bridging components from .NET.
- Using a COM/J2EE bridge. You can use CORBA as a stepping stone to a J2EE server, but method calls have to pass through several layers of software to reach their destination. Internally, J2EE clients and servers communicate using RMI. Although RMI is not directly supported by J#, the specification of the wire protocol is freely available. (See *http://java.sun.com/products/jdk/1.1/docs/guide/rmi/spec/rmi-protocol.doc.html.*) The protocol is based on HTTP and Java Object Serialization. Commercial products are available that will translate from the protocol used by COM to RMI. Once again, you can access these components from .NET through COM Interop.
- Building a .NET/J2EE bridge. If you're feeling brave, you can implement your own custom serialization mechanism along with your own Remoting protocol to communicate with an RMI server. Remember that the architecture of these two aspects of the .NET Framework are highly customizable for just such situations. This solution is more direct than using COM and should yield better performance.

Note Microsoft itself uses a similar approach for interoperating between .NET and COM+. See Chapter 14 for details.

- Using an MSMQ connector. J2EE defines its own message queuing infrastructure in the Java Messaging Service (JMS). JMS is an integrated part of the J2EE specification and can be used to communicate with EJBs. The available MSMQ connectors allow you to combine MSMQ and JMS. Or, if you prefer, you can use the JMS service provider for MSMQ.

- Taking advantage of .NET cross-language interoperability. For example, even though no tools are available that implement J# language bindings for CORBA, there are plenty for C++. You can combine managed and unmanaged C++ fairly seamlessly using Visual Studio .NET, and you can create managed C++ components that act as bridges to CORBA and that you can integrate with J#.
- Using a low-level networking solution, such as sockets. Nothing will stop you from building applications in J# that send and receive data using sockets. Indeed, the .NET Framework Class Library provides good coverage of sockets—see Chapter 8 for details. Most operating systems have intrinsic support for sockets, and it is relatively easy to establish a connection to a process that's listening on an endpoint if you know the address to use and have the appropriate access rights.

The Real Solution: XML Web Services

The list in the previous section was intentionally short on details. These days, if you ask any of the major software and platform vendors about the best way to integrate disparate systems of varying architecture, you'll get the same answer: Use XML Web services.

In the final chapters of this book, we'll cover XML Web services as implemented by the current release of .NET, so we won't go into much detail here. The major computing platform vendors are often at each other's throats, so when they all agree on something it is a significant event. Such is the case with Web services. Based on XML and HTTP, the fundamental Web service architecture is platform neutral and vendor independent. Before we get too carried away, though, be warned that the Web services available now are not the finished article—they're merely a good starting point. For example, Web services do not provide much support for transactions, security, remote events, and so on. (Some vendors provide implementations of these features, but they are by no means accepted across the board.) The next step is the Global XML Web Services Architecture (GXA). Microsoft, along with other vendors and organizations, is working to define a series of standards that cover the requirement to implement high-performance, distributed, fault-tolerant messaging across heterogeneous networks. If you want more information about GXA, a good starting point is the paper published by Microsoft at *http://msdn.microsoft.com/library/default.asp?url=/library/en-us/dngxa/html/gloxmlws500.asp*.

Summary

This chapter showed you how to make use of unmanaged code from a J# application that executes using the common language runtime. You learned how to use P/Invoke to execute code residing in an unmanaged DLL and how to marshal data between the managed and unmanaged spaces using attributes. You also learned how to consume COM components from .NET clients, using a variety of techniques to create an RCW. Finally, you learned how to expose .NET components to COM by creating a CCW.

Although you learned how to invoke COM components from J#, the one technology notably absent from this chapter is COM+. This subject warrants a chapter of its own—the next one.

14

Serviced Components and COM+

COM is a powerful technology. In the old days, to build COM components successfully you had to understand how the "plumbing" worked—you were forced to spend time worrying about building implementations of *IUnknown*, *IDispatch*, and other common interfaces before you could even begin to worry about implementing your business logic. Microsoft Visual Basic 6.0 changed that to some extent, generating much of the required boilerplate code for you automatically. The Microsoft .NET Framework goes a step further by generating COM callable wrappers (CCWs) for your classes if you want to expose them to COM clients. If you read the previous chapter, this is old news.

COM had its critics—it was difficult to build scalable systems or manage distributed transactions or pool resources using COM. So Microsoft developed Microsoft Transaction Server (MTS), which became amalgamated with the Microsoft Windows 2000 operating system family as COM+. COM+ provides a range of features that are aimed squarely at developers who need to create high-performance, easily maintainable systems, including these:

- **Declarative transaction processing** You can specify how a method published by a COM+ component should participate in a transaction—whether it should create a new transaction, join an existing one, or be nontransactional. You can also indicate whether the transaction should commit or abort depending on the success or failure of the method. You achieve this using attributes rather than code.

- **JIT activation** Objects can be deactivated when not in use. This feature conserves resources on the host server computer. When a client accesses a deactivated object, the COM+ runtime will silently activate a new instance of the object.
- **Object pooling** The COM+ runtime can provide a pool of preinstantiated objects. An object can be obtained from the pool and activated on an as-needed basis when called by client code and then returned to the pool when the client has finished using it.
- **Role-based security** You can specify the roles that are permitted to activate an instance of a component and use its methods. You can define these roles using attributes and query them in code. An administrator can assign users to these roles when the component is deployed.
- **Queuing** A request to a COM+ component can be placed in a queue and executed asynchronously.
- **Loosely coupled events** A COM+ component can raise events. Clients can select which events they want to be informed about. The coupling between a COM+ component's events and the clients that want to be notified is held in a database in the COM+ catalog. When an event is raised, the COM+ Event System queries the database, creates an instance of each client interested in the event, and then invokes the event sink method on each client object.

COM+ also has other features, such as the ability to import transactions from an outside environment (known as "Bring Your Own Transaction," or BYOT), compensating resource managers that allow you to implement transactional semantics with nontransactional resources, and interoperability with other processing models that are executing on other platforms through the COM Transaction Integrator. These features are beyond the scope of this chapter, which will instead concentrate on the core features previously listed.

If you're approaching J# development as an experienced Java 2 Enterprise Edition (J2EE) programmer, you'll notice many functional similarities between COM+ and the Enterprise JavaBeans (EJB) model. However, there are a number differences (some subtle, others not so subtle) that this chapter will make you aware of.

The use of declarative attributes in COM+ to request functionality from the component runtime should be familiar to you because these mechanisms are also used by the .NET Framework. There is good reason for this: Even though COM+ predates .NET, it was designed with .NET in mind.

The .NET Framework Class Library contains the *System.EnterpriseServices* namespace, which defines classes, attributes, and enumerations for interacting with COM+. You can build COM+ components and COM+ clients quickly and easily using the contents of this namespace. In the .NET world, COM+ components are referred to as *serviced components*.

Out of necessity, COM+ had to define its own infrastructure for managing issues such as security. Although the mechanisms used are similar to those of .NET, they are not the same, and they operate independently. This means you have to do a bit of work when you implement COM+ security from managed code. However, COM+ and .NET will merge seamlessly and become one in the not-too-distant future, eliminating such issues.

In this chapter, we'll take a good look at how to build COM+ clients and serviced components in J#. You'll learn how to invoke methods on a serviced component synchronously and asynchronously. We'll discuss how to use transactions and take advantage of COM+ object pooling, and we'll look at how to implement COM+ security.

Note This chapter assumes that you have some familiarity with COM+ concepts (but you do not need to be an expert).

Using an Existing COM+ Component

We'll begin our odyssey through the world of serviced components by demonstrating how easy it is to consume a COM+ component from J#. A COM+ component can be written in almost any language, but our example will use Visual Basic 6.0 because it is quick and easy to do so.

Note If you don't have Visual Basic 6.0 or don't want to follow along, skim through this section and resume reading closely at the section titled "Building a Serviced Component," where you'll learn how to create a serviced component using J#.

The FourthCoffee Components Revisited

Calling a COM+ component from managed code is not much different from using a regular COM component, at least as far as the programmer is concerned. You create a runtime callable wrapper (RCW) that acts as a proxy for the COM+ component, and you use the objects and methods exposed by the RCW just as you would ordinary managed components and methods.

The Visual Basic 6.0 project group FourthCoffee.vbg in the FourthCoffee folder contains an updated version of the Visual Basic FourthCoffee components used in Chapter 13. The *CakeFactory* class supplies the methods *FeedsHowMany* and *CreateCake*, and the *Cake* class exposes the size, shape, and filling of the cake as properties. This version of the project also uses enumerations for the cake filling and shape (just to prove that it can be done). An extra feature is the *Baker* class, shown below, which contains the *BakeCake* method. (We implemented a simpler version of this method in the J# example at the end of Chapter 13.)

```
Public Sub BakeCake(ByVal howLongFor As Integer, ByVal cake as Cake)
```

The *Cake* and *CakeFactory* classes are held in the FourthCoffee project, generating the ActiveX DLL FourthCoffee.dll. For reasons that we'll describe later, the *Baker* class is held in a separate project called FourthCoffeeBaker, generating FourthCoffeeBaker.dll.

Configuring the Fourth Coffee COM+ Application

If you examine the properties of the *CakeFactory*, *Cake*, and *Baker* classes, you'll notice that the *MTSTransactionMode* property is set to *NoTransactions*. (The default setting is *NotAnMTSObject*, which prevents an object from being able to use many of the COM+ services.) If you build the FourthCoffee and FourthCoffeeBaker projects, you can use the Component Services console to create a COM+ application and install and configure the FourthCoffee components.

A COM+ application is simply a container that hosts COM+ components and provides a configurable environment in which they can execute. As such, its role is similar to that of the EJB container in the J2EE platform. To save you a little time and effort, the FourthCoffee folder contains a Windows Installer package called FourthCoffee.msi. You can execute this package to create the Fourth Coffee COM+ application and install the FourthCoffee components.

Note If you prefer to create the Fourth Coffee COM+ application by hand, you're most welcome to. The Component Services console is accessible through Control Panel. (Select Performance and Maintenance, and then select Administrative Tools). You can create a new COM+ application by expanding the Component Services tree to display the COM+ Applications folder and then choosing New, Application from the Action menu. You can install components in a COM+ application by expanding the Components folder and choosing New, Component from the Action menu. For the Fourth Coffee application, you should create components using FourthCoffee.dll (in the FourthCoffee folder) and FourthCoffeeBaker.dll (in the CakeBaker folder).

Figure 14-1 shows the components installed in the Fourth Coffee COM+ server.

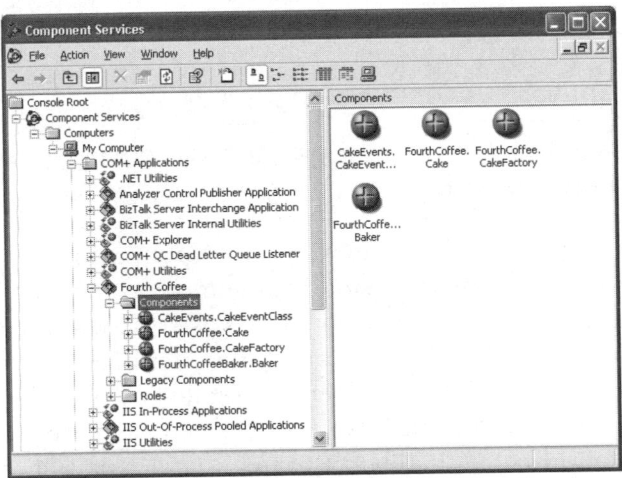

Figure 14-1 The Component Services console showing the FourthCoffee components

COM+ allows you to configure component interfaces as supporting asynchronous, queued operations. Queued calls to methods defined by a queued interface are serialized and posted to an MSMQ message queue. (You must have message queuing installed on your computer for this to operate.) A listener component (part of the COM+ infrastructure) can be alerted when a message arrives so that it can deserialize the method call information contained in the message and invoke the appropriate method on the designated COM+ component. You don't have to write any extra code to support this functionality—you simply set the appropriate properties using the Component Services console.

Figure 14-2 shows the Properties dialog box for the Fourth Coffee COM+ application, with queuing enabled. Selecting the Queued option will cause COM+ to create message queues (one public and several private—their names are unimportant) for the component.

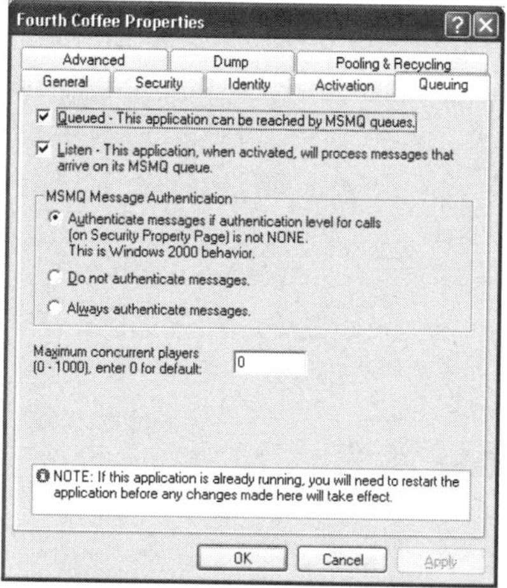

Figure 14-2 The Properties dialog box for the Fourth Coffee COM+ application, showing the queuing configuration properties

Methods of queued interfaces can take only input parameters and cannot have a return value. The *BakeCake* method of the *Baker* component is just such a method, so the *_Baker* interface generated by Visual Basic can be marked as a queued interface. To do this, you expand the interfaces folder under the *Baker* component, select the *_Baker* interface, right-click on it, select Properties, click on the Queuing tab, and make sure Queued is selected, as shown in Figure 14-3. (If you installed the Fourth Coffee COM+ application using the Windows Installer package, the *Queued* property will already be set.)

Note When you create a component using Visual Basic 6.0, Visual Basic will automatically generate an interface for each component that has the same name as the underlying class but is prefixed with an underscore.

If the *Queued* property for an interface is disabled, this means that one or more methods in the interface do not meet the requirements for queued operations (no output parameters or return values are allowed, as you'll recall) and the interface will not support queuing.

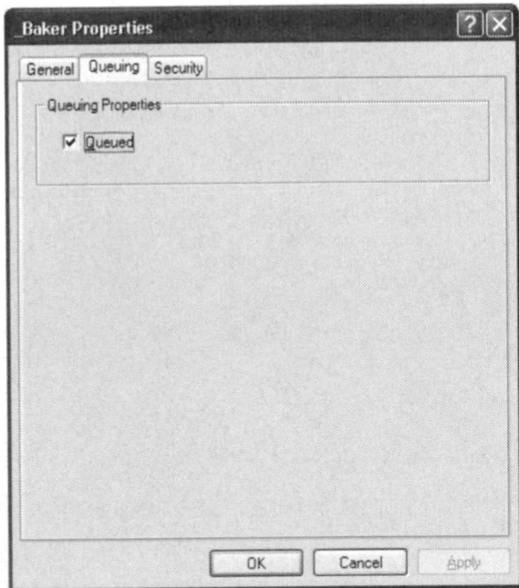

Figure 14-3 The properties of the *_Baker* interface

You must consider one other important factor when you mark interfaces for queued operations: the serializability of method parameters. The *BakeCake* method takes a Visual Basic 6.0 *Integer* and a *Cake* object as arguments. For a queued method call to be bundled up into a serializable package and posted to a queue, the method call's parameters must also be serializable. The primitive automation-compliant data types (such as *Integer*) are serializable, so they do not pose a problem and require no further thought. Classes, on the other hand, do require attention. A class created using the .NET Framework Class Library can be tagged with the *Serializable* attribute. However, in this example, the *Cake* class is implemented in Visual Basic 6.0, so the *Serializable* attribute cannot be applied. The solution is to enable the *Persistable* property of the *Cake* class and to implement the *Class_ReadProperties* and *Class_WriteProperties* subroutines. (We won't go into the details here.)

Once you've configured the Fourth Coffee application, it will be accessible through COM+ on the machine on which it is installed. If you want to use it from another computer, you must export the COM+ application to create a deployment package that can be copied and installed elsewhere. You can either export the entire COM+ application or create an application proxy (as shown in Figure 14-4) that can be installed on a remote client and used to access the application.

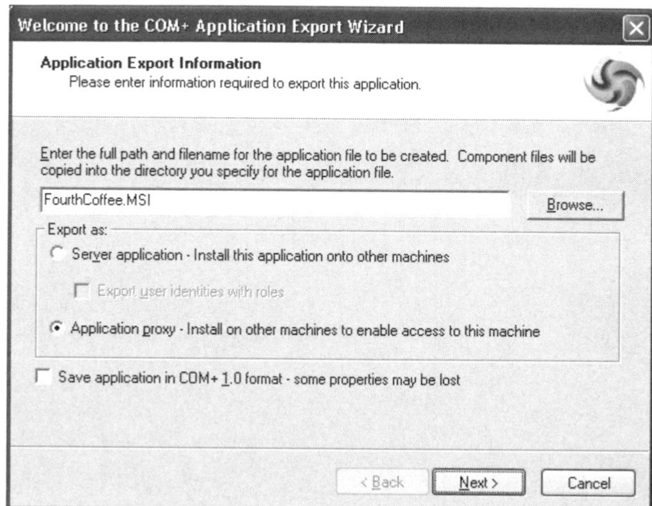

Figure 14-4 Creating a deployment package for the Fourth Coffee application

---

Note If you want to create a package for installation on a computer running Windows 2000, you must select the Save Application In COM+ 1.0 check box.

Using the Fourth Coffee COM+ Application

The *CakeClient* class (which is available in the file COMPlusCakeClient.jsl in the COMPlusCakeClient project) shows a J# test harness that exercises the FourthCoffee components. To compile this class, you must create RCWs for the FourthCoffee and FourthCoffeeBaker DLLs. (You can use the COM tab of the Add Reference dialog box to do this, as we did in Chapter 13.)

The *main* method of the *CakeClient* class creates a new *CakeFactory* object and then calls the *FeedsHowMany* method, displaying the results in the console. (This is a synchronous method call.) The program continues, executing *CreateCake* to create a new *Cake* object using the cake factory and verifying that the size, shape, and filling properties of the cake have been set appropriately. Finally, the program creates a *Baker* object and executes its *BakeCake* method. However, the program makes use of the queued configuration of the *Baker* class, so the call to *BakeCake* is performed asynchronously. (The program will not be blocked while the cake is baking.) To access the *Baker* class through its queued interface, you must instantiate it using a queue moniker.

The *System.Runtime.InteropServices.Marshal* class has the static *BindToMoniker* method for occasions such as this:

```
Baker baker = (Baker)Marshal.BindToMoniker(
    "queue:ComputerName=WHITERABBIT/new:FourthCoffeeBaker.Baker");
```

We'll refrain from describing the full syntax of COM+ monikers because it is beyond the scope of this book. Suffice it to say that the moniker specified will attempt to create a new *FourthCoffeeBaker.Baker* object and access it through a message queue on the computer called Whiterabbit (the name of the computer on which we installed and configured the *Baker* component—you'll need to change this unless you have a computer with the same name). When the *BakeCake* method is invoked through the *baker* variable, the call will be queued and executed asynchronously.

Subscribing to a Loosely Coupled Event

Executing the *BakeCake* method asynchronously is fine, but it would be useful to know when the cake is ready. The usual mechanism would be for the *Baker* class to publish an event that is raised when the cake is ready, and allow clients to subscribe to this event. But the distributed, message-based nature of the COM+ interaction renders the original COM *IConnectionPoint* event model unsuitable. When using connection points, clients and servers have to query each other for information about events and sinks that might generate an unacceptable level of network traffic, and the mechanisms used require that the subscribing client must be running when the publishing server raises the event (which might not be the case when you use a COM+ queued interface). Instead, COM+ provides loosely coupled events (LCEs).

In the LCE model, you raise events by executing methods on a specially constructed event class, which is recorded in the COM+ catalog. (Each method will raise a different event.) A subscriber implements an interface that matches the event class and provides the code that the client will execute when the event is raised. Multiple subscribers can each have their own implementations of the event class. The subscriber must also be registered in the COM+ catalog as a COM+ application. An administrator can then use the Component Services console to tie a subscribing client to one or more event classes. The information about which clients subscribe to which event classes is held in the event store in the COM+ catalog. When a publisher calls a method defined by the event class, the COM+ events subsystem will query the event store to locate any subscribers. Each subscriber will then be instantiated, and the corresponding method will be invoked.

In the FourthCoffee example, the *CakeEvents* Visual Basic project defines an event class called *CakeEventClass*. This class has a single method named *CakeBaked*, which takes a *Cake* object as an input parameter. This method is used to raise the *CakeBaked* event from the *BakeCake* method in the *Baker* class. The method body itself is actually empty because the implementation will be supplied by each subscribing client.

The *BakeCake* method instantiates a *CakeEventClass* object and calls its *CakeBaked* method, passing the *Cake* object (which should now be cooked) as the parameter:

```
Dim cakeBakedEvent as CakeEventClass
Set cakeBakedEvent = new CakeEventClass
cakeBakedEvent.CakeBaked cake
```

If you build the CakeEvents component (CakeEvents.dll), you can install it in the Fourth Coffee application using the Component Services console. You should install it using the Install New Event Class(es) option, as shown in Figure 14-5. (If you ran the Windows Installer package FourthCoffee.MSI earlier, this component will have already been created and installed for you.)

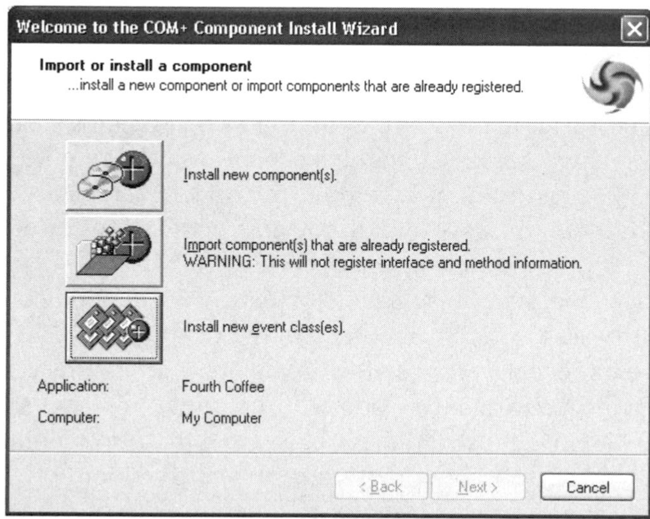

Figure 14-5 Installing a new event class in a COM+ application

Note The FourthCoffeeBaker project, which contains the *Baker* class, contains a reference to the *CakeEvents* component defined by the *CakeEvents* project. The *CakeEvents* project in turn contains a reference to the FourthCoffee components in the FourthCoffee project. Visual Basic 6.0 forbids circular references between projects, so the *Baker* class must be placed in a separate Visual Basic 6.0 project from the *Cake* and *CakeFactory* classes.

Once the event class has been installed, expand the Interfaces folder under the *CakeEvents.CakeEventClass* component, right-click on the *_CakeEventClass* interface, and view its properties. You'll see the unique interface ID (IID) assigned to this interface (similar to the one shown in Figure 14-6—the IID generated might vary if you did not use the installer package to install the event class). Make a note of the IID because you'll need it when you implement a subscriber.

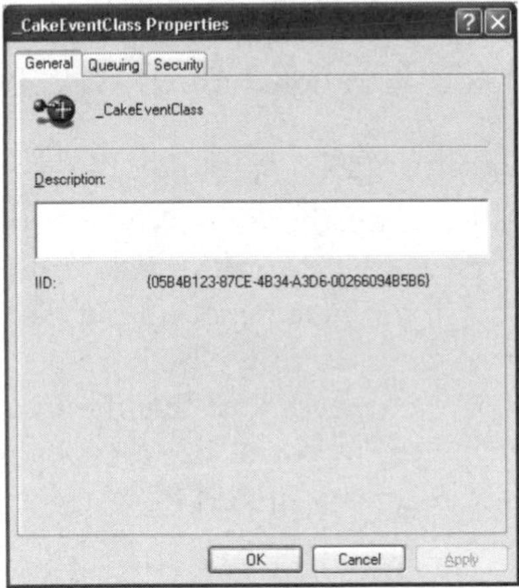

Figure 14-6 The properties of the *_CakeEventClass* interface, showing the IID

To subscribe to the *CakeBaked* event in J#, you must create a component that implements an interface with the same IID as the interface exposed by the event class. The *CakeBakedEventSink* class (available in EventSink.jsl in the COMPlusCakeEventSink project—we added it to the same solution as the COMPlusCakeClient project for convenience) shows an example. The *CakeBakedEventSink* class implements the *ICakeEventClass* interface, which is also defined in EventSink.jsl. The *ICakeEventClass* interface contains the *CakeBaked* method (as specified by the *CakeEventClass*, created earlier in Visual Basic). Also, the *ICakeEventClass* is tagged with *ComVisibleAttribute* (this interface will be exposed to COM+ when the component is registered in the COM+ catalog) and has a *GuidAttribute* that is the same as that of the IID of the *_CakeEventClass*. (If the IID you saw earlier is different from ours, replace the *GuidAttribute* with your own value.) The COM+ infrastructure uses this IID to determine which classes can subscribe to the *CakeBaked* event (as explained later).

All .NET components that are deployed in COM+ applications must inherit from the *System.EnterpriseServices.ServicedComponent* class. You must add a reference to the System.EnterpriseServices.dll assembly to access the classes in the *System.EnterpriseServices* namespace. The *ServicedComponent* class provides the infrastructure that a .NET component will need when it interacts with COM+. (We'll come back to this later.)

The *CakeBaked* method takes a *Cake* object as its input parameter. This component was defined in Visual Basic and compiled as the FourthCoffee.dll ActiveX DLL. You might be tempted to add a reference to the DLL by using the COM tab of the Add Reference dialog box, as we did in earlier examples, but this approach has a problem: It generates an RCW that operates as a private assembly. When a .NET serviced component is registered in the COM+ catalog, all assemblies that it references must be signed with strong names; otherwise, registration will fail. So you must create a strongly named RCW manually and reference that instead.

You can build a strongly named RCW in several ways, but one approach I often take is to create a pair of keys using the Sn utility and then execute Tlbimp with the appropriate type library, specifying the *keyfile* option, which signs the resulting RCW using the keys in the designated file. It just so happens that the Visual Basic FourthCoffee project generates a type library called FourthCoffee.tlb that can be used by Tlbimp. Make a copy of this file in a convenient place (the WINDOWS\Temp folder for example) and execute the following commands from the command line to create the signed RCW called FourthCoffee.dll:

```
sn -k FourthCoffee.snk
tlbimp FourthCoffee.tlb /keyfile:FourthCoffee.snk
```

Note If the FourthCoffee components are running, you'll be denied access when you execute Tlbimp. Stop the FourthCoffee components using the Component Services console: Right-click on the Fourth Coffee COM+ application and choose Shut Down from the shortcut menu.

If you're going to reference this RCW from several applications, you might want to place it in the Global Assembly Cache (GAC):

```
gacutil /i FourthCoffee.dll
```

For consistency, you can create a signed version of the FourthCoffeeBaker RCW, using the FourthCoffeeBaker.tlb type library generated by Visual Basic (which you'll find in the CakeBaker folder):

```
sn -k FourthCoffeeBaker.snk
tlbimp FourthCoffeeBaker.tlb /keyfile:FourthCoffeeBaker.snk
gacutil /i FourthCoffeeBaker.dll
```

Back in the COMPlusCakeEventSink project, you should add a reference to the signed version of the FourthCoffee assembly. (In the References dialog box, click on the .NET tab and use the Browse button to locate FourthCoffee.dll in the WINDOWS\Temp folder.) You should also update *COMPlusCakeClient* project to remove any references to the unsigned RCWs (FourthCoffee and FourthCoffeeBaker) and reference the signed versions instead.

The *COMPlusCakeEventSink* assembly itself should also be strongly named. The assembly is signed using the keys in the file CakeEventSink.snk, as indicated by the assembly level *AssemblyKeyFileAttribute*. By convention, this attribute is specified in the AssemblyInfo.jsl file created with each project by Visual Studio .NET (the purpose of this file is to provide a convenient place to specify assembly-level attributes), but we added it to EventSink.jsl and removed AssemblyInfo.jsl to keep everything in one place.

The implementation of the *CakeBaked* method in the *CakeBakedEventSink* class displays a message box indicating that the cake has been baked and outputs the details of the cake. The call to *ReleaseComObject* ensures that the *cake* object is released in a timely manner. You can compile this class, which produces the assembly COMPlusCakeEventSink.dll.

Note Message boxes can be useful for providing some visual feedback when you test serviced components, but you should not use them in a production environment—mainly because they might be displayed on the computer that's hosting the serviced component rather than on the client that's calling the serviced component. (It depends on how the hosting COM+ applications are configured.) Even if the message box is displayed on the client computer, this approach is still not good practice for production applications because the COM+ application might be configured to run as a service and operate without a GUI. Furthermore, if the event class is not configured to fire events in parallel (the default situation), a message box that's waiting for user acknowledgement might block other subscribers from being notified!

The next step is to create a new COM+ application using the Component Services console and install the CakeBakedEventSink component. (We haven't supplied a package for this, so you'll have to do it yourself!) To keep resource use to a minimum, create a COM+ Library application. You can name the application anything you like. (We used "Fourth Coffee Client.") Once you've created the application, you can install the CakeBakedEventSink component from COMPlusCakeEventSink.dll.

You can then attach this component to the *CakeBaked* event. To do this, expand the *COMPlusCakeEventSink.CakeBakedEventSink* component to display the Subscriptions folder, right-click on it, and choose New, then Subscription (as shown in Figure 14-7) to launch the COM+ New Subscription Wizard.

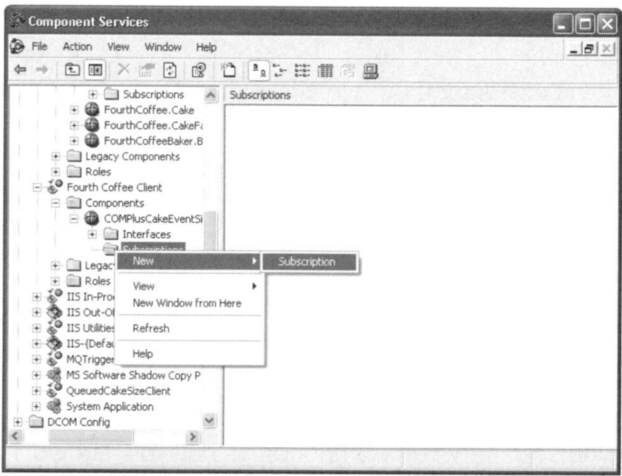

Figure 14-7 Adding a new subscription to the *CakeBakedEventSink* component

On the wizard's Select Subscription Method(s) page, you'll see a list of the interfaces and methods implemented by the *CakeBakedEventSink* component. Scroll to the bottom of the list and select the *CakeBaked* method in the *ICakeEventClass* interface, as shown in Figure 14-8. Click Next to continue.

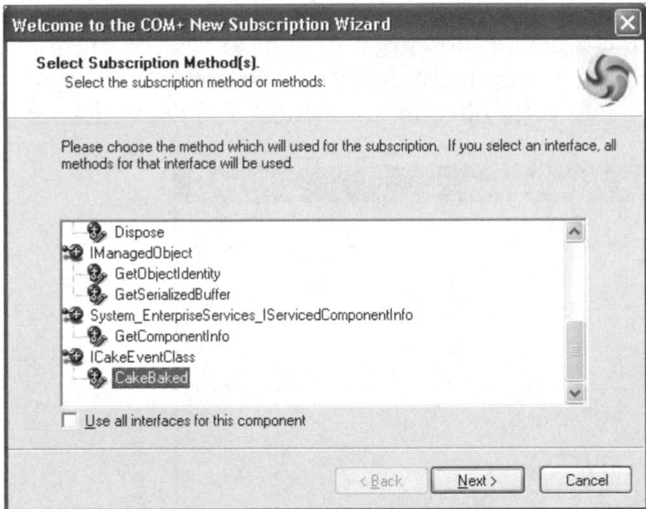

Figure 14-8 The interfaces and methods implemented by the *CakeBakedEventSink* component

On the Select Event Class page, you'll see every event class that implements an interface with the same GUID as that used by the *ICakeEventClass* interface—*CakeEvents.CakeEventClass* in this case, as shown in Figure 14-9. To subscribe to the events represented by an event class, select it and click Next.

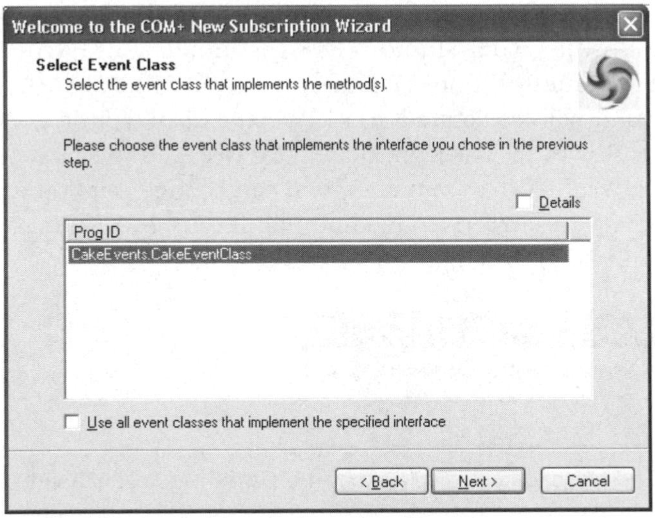

Figure 14-9 The Select Event Class page

The final page of the wizard allows you to give the subscription a meaningful name and enable the subscription. (You can also enable and disable subscriptions using the Component Services console.) Figure 14-10 shows the Subscription Options page filled in. Click Next, and then click Finish.

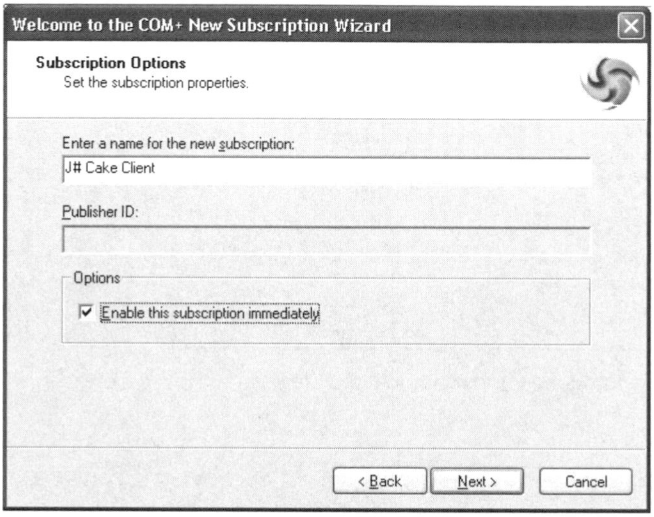

Figure 14-10 The Subscription Options page

The *COMPlusCakeEventSink* assembly needs to be available to the Visual Basic runtime, so copy the file COMPlusCakeEventSink.dll to the folder \Program Files\Microsoft Visual Studio\VB98 (assuming you have Visual Basic installed in the default location). When you execute the COMPlusCakeClient program, the cake will be created and its details displayed in a console window, as before. However, 30 seconds later (we tweaked the *BakeCake* method to wait in seconds rather than minutes—you can change it if you really want to wait half an hour!) the *BakeCake* method will raise the *CakeBaked* event and the message box shown in Figure 14-11 will appear.

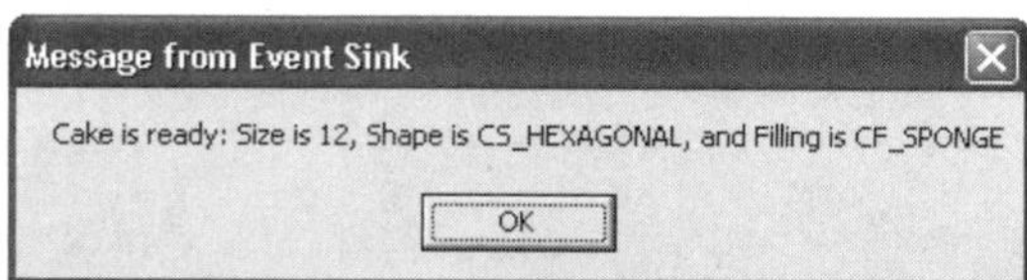
Message from Event Sink
Cake is ready: Size is 12, Shape is CS_HEXAGONAL, and Filling is CF_SPONGE
OK

Figure 14-11 The message box displayed by the *CakeBaked* event handler

Note that the event handler ran and displayed the message box even though the COMPlusCakeClient application already finished. The COM+ event subsystem creates a new instance of the *CakeBakedEventSink* object in the COM+ process that executes the *Baker* object whenever the event occurs.

Note A subscribing component will receive every notification of an event raised by the publisher, no matter which client invoked the action that caused the publishing component to raise the event. (There is no direct link between a client application and a subscriber.) However, once you've created a subscription, you can adjust the properties of that subscription and apply a filter so that the subscriber is notified of an event only if it is relevant. (The details of event filtering are beyond the scope of this chapter.)

Building a Serviced Component

You've learned how to consume a serviced component from J# and how to subscribe to a loosely-coupled event. It's now time to look at how a serviced component can be implemented in J#.

To provide a little relief from cakes, the upcoming examples use data from the Northwind Traders database that ships with the .NET Framework SDK and that was described in Chapter 1. This database holds information about products supplied by Northwind Traders, registered customers that can place orders for those products, and the details of those orders. Information about the goods ordered is held in two tables called Orders and Order Details. When a customer places an order, a new entry is added to the Order table and the individual order lines are inserted into the Order Details table. Both tables are linked using the OrderID column. Customer information is recorded in the Customers table and is linked to the Orders table using the CustomerID column. Figure 14-12 shows the structure of the relevant tables.

Figure 14-12 The Orders, Order Details, and Customers tables from the Northwind Traders database

We'll look at how to create a serviced component that exposes methods for performing the following operations:

- **Placing an order** The component will insert one row in the Orders table and one or more rows in the Order Details table.
- **Querying an order** The component will return the details of an order given the OrderID.
- **Canceling an order** The component will delete information in the Order Details and Order tables, given the OrderID.

To preserve the integrity of the database, all of these methods will require the use of COM+ transactions.

Serviced Component Basics

You saw earlier that a serviced component must inherit from the *System.EnterpriseServices.ServicedComponent* class. In fact, this is all that a serviced component needs to do if it is to operate with COM+. The *ServicedComponent* class provides a default implementation of the methods that comprise the COM+ *IObjectControl* interface. (Strictly speaking, it doesn't actually implement *IObjectControl*—it just looks like it does, for reasons we don't have space to fully explain here.) You can apply a selection of attributes to a serviced component to modify the way in which it interacts with the COM+ environment.

When you design a serviced component, you should remember the basic rule of COM: Use interfaces. Yes, you can simply create a serviced component and deploy it in a COM+ application, and the .NET Framework will generate a default class interface for you, but the component will support only late binding for unmanaged clients. (Managed clients reference the assembly that holds the serviced component and will still be able to use early binding.) If you define interfaces, you have far more control over the methods exposed to clients, and the .NET Framework will generate a COM custom interface that supports early binding. The *IOrderComponent* interface, shown below, is the interface implemented by the *OrderComponent* serviced component. It defines the methods for manipulating orders, as described previously. (Complete code for this example is available in the file OrderComponent.jsl in the NorthwindOrders project.)

```
/** @attribute ComVisibleAttribute(true) */
/** @attribute GuidAttribute("FA068D1B-D61C-4c54-A68E-16CA49EB7872") */
public interface IOrderComponent
{
   public int PlaceOrder(String CustomerId, ICollection details)
      throws System.Exception;
   public ICollection QueryOrder(int orderId) throws System.Exception;
   public void CancelOrder(int orderId);
}
```

The *PlaceOrder* method expects a customer ID (which is held as a string in the database) and a collection of order lines that define the goods that comprise the order. If successful, *PlaceOrder* will return the integer ID of the newly created order; if not, it will throw an exception. The *QueryOrder* method takes an order ID and returns a collection containing the order lines that comprise the order. Again, if something nasty happens, the method will throw an exception. The *CancelOrder* method is used to remove an order from the database. For reasons that will be explained shortly, this method does not explicitly throw an exception if an error occurs.

The interface is tagged as being visible to COM (it will be visible anyway, but it is good practice to be explicit), and a GUID has also been assigned, which saves the .NET Framework from having to assign one itself. So far, there is nothing special to see.

The definition of the *OrderComponent* serviced component is shown here:

```
/** @attribute TransactionAttribute(TransactionOption.Required) */
/** @attribute ClassInterfaceAttribute(ClassInterfaceType.None) */
public class OrderComponent extends ServicedComponent
   implements IOrderComponent
{
```

```
    ⋮
}
```

The class inherits from *ServicedComponent* and implements the *IOrderComponent* interface, as expected. However, the *OrderComponent* class is also tagged with a couple of attributes. The *ClassInterfaceAttribute*, which was described in Chapter 13, indicates which interfaces should be generated for the class (if any). In this case, all functionality is exposed through the *IOrderComponent* interface, so the option *ClassInterfaceType.None* is used.

Of more interest is *TransactionAttribute*. One fundamental feature of COM+ and serviced components is the way in which they operate with transactional resource managers such as database management systems (DBMSs). (Chapter 7 described the use of transactions with Microsoft SQL Server.) The *TransactionAttribute* is used to indicate how the component will use transactions when its methods are called. The possible values are summarized in Table 14-1. The *OrderComponent* class specifies *TransactionOption.Required*, which indicates that each method should be called in the context of a transaction. If no transaction is currently active, a new one will be created. *TransactionAttribute* can be applied only to a class and not to individual methods, and it is meaningful only when applied to serviced components.

Serviced Components and Context

You encountered the concept of *context* in Chapter 8, when we discussed multithreading, and in Chapter 11, when we looked at the .NET Remoting architecture. As you'll recall, a context is a set of properties that provide an environment for objects. For example, a context can determine the scope of a transaction (all objects executing in the same context can belong to the same transaction) as well as provide for synchronization between objects. An application domain can contain multiple contexts.

In Chapter 11, we also discussed context-agile and context-bound objects. A context-agile object can be accessed directly from any context in an application domain. Access to a context-bound object from outside the object's context is achieved through a proxy. All COM+ objects are context-bound, and the *System.EnterpriseServices.ServicedComponent* class inherits from *System.ContextBoundObject*.

Serviced components can be tagged with attributes (such as *TransactionAttribute*, which we just described) that define the context for that component. When you instantiate a serviced component, either it will join the current context or a new context will be created if the current context is incompatible with the attributes specified for the new component. If a serviced component demands that it be executed in a new transaction (see the options described in Table 14-1) or a new synchronization unit (see later), a new context will be created to house the component. Access to the component from another context will involve marshaling data through a proxy. In an ideal world, you should minimize the number of cross-context transitions when you build serviced components. (Cross-context marshaling is a little more expensive for serviced components than it is for regular .NET components.) Therefore, to maximize performance you should carefully consider the transaction and synchronization options for a component when you design it.

One final word of warning: Contexts used by serviced components are specialized versions of contexts used by nonserviced components because they must be propagated into the COM+ runtime environment. The concepts are similar, but the implementation is different. For example, when you attach the *Synchronization* attribute to a regular .NET context-bound class, you use the *System.Runtime.Remoting.Contexts.SynchronizationAttribute* class. When you apply synchronization to a serviced component, you must use the *System.EnterpriseServices.SynchronizationAttribute* class instead.

Table 14-1 Transaction Options for Serviced Components

Option	Description
TransactionOption.Disabled	No transaction is used. If a transaction already exists, the component will not use it. The component executes in the current context.
TransactionOption.NotSupported	No transaction is used. If a transaction already exists, a new context is created without a transaction and the component is executed in the new context.
TransactionOption.Required	If a transaction already exists, it will be used. If not, a new transaction in a new context will be created.

Table 14-1 Transaction Options for Serviced Components

Option	Description
TransactionOption.RequiresNew	A new transaction and context will always be created.
TransactionOption.Supported	If a transaction already exists, it will be used. If not, execution will proceed without a transaction.

The *System.EnterpriseServices* namespace defines a selection of assembly-level attributes that you can use to configure the COM+ application that hosts the serviced components. The *ApplicationNameAttribute* specifies the name of the COM+ application to be created, the *ApplicationIDAttribute* is the GUID that identifies the application, and *ApplicationActivationAttribute* indicates whether the COM+ application is a library or a server application. The *Description* attribute provides a text description of the application and can also be attached to individual classes as well as the assembly. These attributes are applied when a serviced component uses automatic installation; if the component is manually installed, an administrator can override these values (although it is considered bad etiquette to do so, and in some cases this can cause the component to malfunction—the component author usually has a good reason for specifying particular settings).

If you examine the *PlaceOrder* and *QueryOrder* methods in the *OrderComponent* class, you'll see that they both adopt a similar strategy:

1. Connect to the database.
2. Perform some updates.
3. Save the changes.
4. Disconnect from the database.

In the event of an error, the changes will be rolled back. Data access is performed using ADO.NET. (See Chapter 7 for details.) The key point to notice is how changes are saved or rolled back. Remember that these methods execute in the context of a transaction. The *ContextUtil* class supplies static methods that you can use to query and manipulate the COM+ context. The two methods used by this example are *SetComplete* (which commits the transaction) and *SetAbort* (which causes the transaction to be rolled back). Both methods also indicate that the component instance can be discarded when the method completes. (More about activation shortly.) If you're familiar with COM+ development, note that the *ContextUtil* class is an implementation of the COM+ *IObjectContext* interface.

The *CancelOrder* method is slightly different because it does not explicitly call *ContextUtil.SetComplete* or *ContextUtil.SetAbort*. Instead, the method is tagged with *AutoCompleteAttribute*, as shown here:

```
/** @attribute AutoCompleteAttribute() */
public void CancelOrder(int orderId)
{
    ⋮
}
```

The use of *AutoCompleteAttribute* causes an implicit call to *ContextUtil.SetComplete* if the method returns normally, but it invokes *ContextUtil.SetAbort* if the method throws an unhandled exception. You'll notice that the method itself does not perform any exception trapping; this is intentional. If you catch an exception in the method, it will no longer be unhandled, and the method will complete successfully and call *ContextUtil.SetComplete*.

Warning At first glance, it might seem that the *PlaceOrder*, *QueryOrder*, and *CancelOrder* methods perform a lot of unnecessary work in connecting to the database and disconnecting when they finish. Connecting and disconnecting from a database have a reputation for being time-consuming operations because user credentials are passed to the DBMS and checked, and then various data structures are set up to handle the connection internally by the DBMS software. You might therefore be tempted to create a constructor that connects to the database and exposes the database connection to the other methods in the class. *Do not adopt this approach.* True, each instance of the component will have its own private connection to the database, but this is not a scalable solution and will ultimately lead to resource contention in the DBMS and sluggish performance as more and more concurrent instances of the serviced component are created. You'll have little or no control over how many connections are established (which might also have some licensing implications), and eventually the DBMS will hit its limit and prevent any further connections from being established.

In Chapter 7, we looked at how ADO.NET supports connection pooling. This is the preferred approach. The OLE DB and SQL providers that Microsoft provides as part of the .NET Framework Class Library support connection pooling automatically, based on the connection string used to access the data source. All connections that use the same connection string will be pooled. Thus, once the pool has been populated with connections, the act of opening a connection will simply cause an existing connection to be retrieved from the pool, and closing a connection will cause it to be returned to the pool. (Do be sure to close connections rather than rely on the common language runtime to tidy them up for you.) Remember that you can configure the minimum and maximum size of the pool in the ADO.NET connection string and thus maintain control over the number of concurrent connections established.

The details for each order passed into *PlaceOrder* and returned by *QueryOrder* are held in an *ICollection* object that contains a set of *OrderDetails* objects. The *OrderDetails* class is also defined in OrderComponent.jsl, and it implements the *IOrderDetails* interface. The *IOrderDetails* interface exposes the contents of each order line as a series of properties, which are implemented as private variables in the *OrderDetails* class. The *IOrderDetails* interface is tagged as being visible to COM and has a GUID:

```
/** @attribute ComVisibleAttribute(true) */
/** @attribute GuidAttribute("E65F6A55-C7F9-43af-B6CE-D693878A0596") */
public interface IOrderDetails
{
   /** @property */
   public int get_OrderId();

   /** @property */
   public void set_OrderId(int orderId);

   /** @property */
   public int get_ProductId();

   /** @property */
   public void set_ProductId(int productId);

   /** @property */
   public Decimal get_UnitPrice();

   /** @property */
   public void set_UnitPrice(Decimal unitPrice);

   /** @property */
   public short get_Quantity();
```

```
    /** @property */
    public void set_Quantity(short quantity);

    /** @property */
    public double get_Discount();

    /** @property */
    public void set_Discount(double discount);
}
```

The *OrderDetails* class is a serviced component. However, it has no *TransactionAttribute* specified, so it will not participate in any COM+ transactions. The default value for *TransactionAttribute* is *TransactionOption.Disabled*, which permits a component to execute in the current context regardless of whether any transaction is active:

```
/** @attribute ClassInterfaceAttribute(ClassInterfaceType.None) */
public class OrderDetails extends ServicedComponent
    implements IOrderDetails
{
    private int orderId;
    private int productId;
    private Decimal unitPrice;
    private short quantity;
    private double discount;

    ⋮
}
```

At this point, you can compile the *OrderComponent* file and place the resulting assembly, NorthwindOrders.dll, in the GAC.

Registering and Using the Serviced Component

The *OrderTest* class (in the file OrderTest.jsl in the OrderTest project, which has been added to the NorthwindOrders solution for your convenience) exercises the *OrderComponent* and *OrderDetails* classes. The project contains a reference to the *NorthwindOrders* assembly held in the GAC. (You cannot reference the *NorthwindOrders* component through COM because it was written in managed code—you're not allowed to create an RCW that directly references a CCW.) If you have rebuilt the NorthwindOrders project, you should update the reference to point to the correct version of the assembly. (Drop and re-create the reference.)

The *main* method of the *OrderTest* class creates an *OrderComponent* object and an array of *OrderDetails*. The method then populates the order details array and places an order. The number of the new order is returned from

PlaceOrder and displayed by the *main* method. The *QueryDetails* method is then called to check that the order has been placed, and the details of the order are displayed in the console. The order is then canceled by calling the *CancelOrder* method. Finally, *QueryOrder* is executed again, with the same order number as before. This time, the details collection returned should be empty because the order no longer exists.

If you run the *OrderTest* application, two things will happen. The second thing (we'll come to the first in a moment) is that a console window will display the number of the newly created order (returned by *PlaceOrder*), the details of the order (returned by *QueryOrder*), and the details again (returned by *QueryOrder* after *CancelOrder* is called). The second set of details should be empty (the order was canceled), as shown in Figure 14-13.

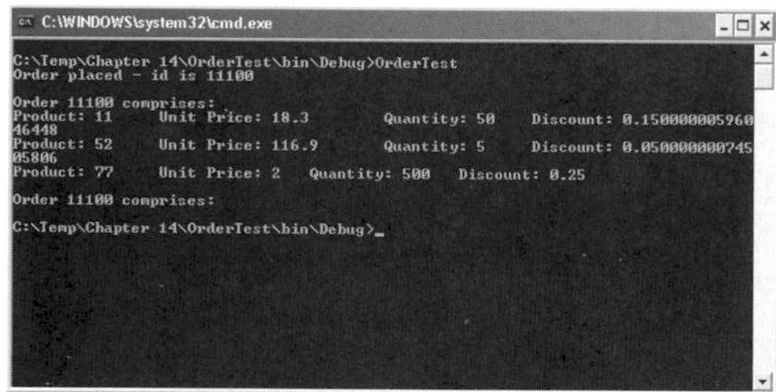

Figure 14-13 The output of the OrderTest program

The first thing that happens is that the Northwind Orders COM+ application is created in the COM+ catalog, and the *OrderComponent* and *OrderDetails* components are added. The configuration settings used for the Northwind Orders application are taken from the various attributes attached to the classes (along with some default values for settings whose values were not specified). This is known as *dynamic registration*.

When a managed client invokes a serviced component, the runtime will check to make sure that the serviced component is available in the COM+ catalog. If not, the runtime will create a *System.EnterpriseServices.RegistrationHelper* object and execute its *InstallAssembly* method, which will examine the metadata of the serviced component, create the COM+ application, and register the components. You can also use the *RegistrationHelper* class from your own code. The *InstallAssembly* method performs the following tasks:

- It registers the assembly in the Windows Registry by calling *RegisterAssembly* method of a *System.Runtime.InteropServices.Registration-*

Services object. Managed classes registered in this way have their *InprocServer32* key set to MSCOREE.DLL (the entry point to the common language runtime). Other keys will be added to indicate the name of the managed class implementing the serviced component, the assembly and version, and the codebase. Figure 14-14 shows the keys added to the Registry for the *OrderDetails* component.

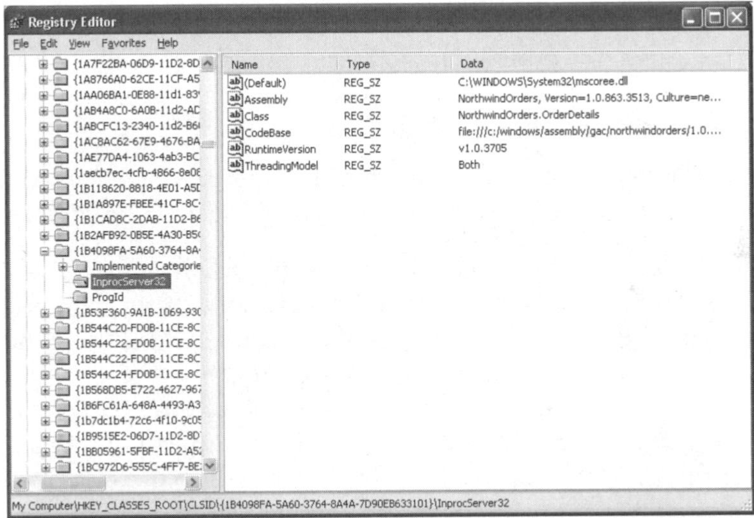

Figure 14-14 The Windows Registry showing the keys for the *OrderDetails* component

---

Note Although serviced components must be signed, they do not have to be deployed as shared assemblies in the GAC—they can be private and use *XCOPY* deployment. This approach is not recommended, however. Once a serviced component has been registered, it is potentially available to every application running on that computer (and elsewhere, if the application is exported). Each client would have to have its own local copy of the same version of the assembly implementing the serviced component; otherwise, the common language runtime would not be able to locate it and the client application would fail.

- It generates a type library, using the *ConvertTypeLibToAssembly* method of a *System.Runtime.InteropServices.TypeLibConverter* object, and registers it in the Windows Registry.
- It creates a new COM+ application, using the values specified in attributes of the assembly that holds the serviced component. This is achieved using the unmanaged COM+ administrative APIs (details of which you can find in the Platform SDK).
- It uses the type library to install and configure the serviced components in the COM+ application, again using unmanaged COM+ administrative API calls.
- Finally, it examines any custom attributes attached to the components and applies them to the components in the COM+ catalog.

Note that this process happens only when a *managed* client attempts to access an *unregistered* serviced component. If the component is called by unmanaged code, it must already be registered. You can either write the registration code yourself (using the *RegistrationHelper* class—an example is available in the OvenInstaller project at the end of this chapter) or an administrator can manually create a COM+ application and install the components. If you adopt the latter approach, be sure that you have documented the settings required by the COM+ application and each component so that the administrator will configure them correctly.

The *RegistrationHelper* class also contains the method *UninstallAssembly*, which you can call to remove a COM+ application from the catalog.

GUIDs and Versioning

The *OrderComponent* and *OrderDetails* components shown in the previous example use fixed GUIDs, which are generated by the developer. This is fine for the production version of a component, but if you're in the development phase of a project, you might find it more convenient to omit the GUID and instead let the runtime generate one for you automatically.

Each time you invoke a serviced component from a managed client, the common language runtime will load information about the serviced component from the assembly used when the client was compiled or follow any versioning policy specified by the client's configuration file (if available). If a GUID is supplied explicitly by the serviced component, the COM+ runtime will use the GUID to activate the appropriate serviced component as indicated by the Registry. If the version of the serviced component referenced by the client is different from that indicated in the Registry, you might get a mismatch between the two versions of the serviced component (the client-referenced serviced component might be more recent and implement an interface that has been modified from that recorded in the Registry), possibly resulting in some rather obscure errors.

If a serviced component does not specify a GUID, a new GUID will be generated for each version of the serviced component. The new version of the serviced component will be installed in the COM+ application, and the client will access the correct version through COM+. However, the serviced component will be registered multiple times—once for each version. This means that existing clients, built using earlier versions of the serviced component, will still function. (The version that a client references is specified in the manifest in the client assembly that's generated when the client is compiled.)

Features of Serviced Components

Now that we've covered the bare essentials of implementing a serviced component, it's worth taking a look at the other features surrounding COM+ development.

Synchronization, Activities, and Context

As you might recall from Chapter 8, multithreaded objects can use synchronization to prevent two concurrent threads from accessing a shared resource simultaneously, possibly corrupting data. This is achieved by controlling, and possibly prohibiting, concurrent calls to methods of the same object. The same feature is available to serviced components, through *System.EnterpriseServices.SynchronizationAttribute* (not to be confused with *System.Runtime.Remoting.Contexts.SynchronizationAttribute*, which offers similar functionality but does not operate with COM+). The situation in COM+ is more complex than the cases examined in Chapter 8, however, because multiple threads can execute across multiple computers. (COM+ components can be remote.) If synchronizing multiple threads is hard, synchronizing multiple distributed threads is 10 times as hard. Fortunately, COM+ and serviced components provide a mechanism to ease the burden on the poor developer.

In COM+ parlance, a set of objects performing work on behalf of the same client is referred to as an *activity*. Synchronization is used to control how objects that are part of the same activity interleave their execution.

Note A client can have several concurrent activities, but components do not have to execute in the context of an activity. (See Table 14-2 for an explanation.)

The SynchronizationAttribute class uses values from the System.EnterpriseServices.SynchronizationOption enumeration. SynchronizationAttribute is applied to a component, as shown here:

```
/** @attribute SynchronizationAttribute(SynchronizationOption.Required) */
public class MyComponent extends ServicedComponent implements IMyInterface
{
    ⋮
}
```

Synchronization is accomplished by the COM+ runtime through locks. Each activity has a lock, and when a call is made into an activity from outside, the calling thread might make an attempt to obtain this lock, depending on how synchronization is configured. If the lock is currently held by another thread, the calling thread might block until the lock becomes available. When the lock is released, a blocked thread can acquire it and continue processing. You should note that there are no features such as timeouts—once a thread requests the activity lock, it will block indefinitely until the lock is available.

Table 14-2 summarizes the *SynchronizationOption* values available and how they affect the concurrency and context hosting a serviced component. A context belongs to at most one activity, but an activity can contain multiple contexts. As with transactions, if a serviced component is instantiated in a context whose synchronization settings are incompatible with the component's requirements, a new context will be created to hold the serviced component.

Table 14-2 Synchronization Options for Serviced Components

Option	Description
SynchronizationOption.Disabled	No synchronization is used. Threads executing methods in the component will not acquire the activity lock. The component will operate in the current activity regardless of the synchronization settings used by other components already existing in this context. The current context will also be used, unless the *TransactionAttribute* setting is incompatible with the current context when a new context will be created.
SynchronizationOption.NotSupported	No synchronization is used, and the component will not form part of any activity. Threads executing methods of the component will not acquire the activity lock. You can use this setting only if the component is not transactional and does not use COM+ JIT activation (see later in this chapter).
SynchronizationOption.Required	If a synchronized activity already exists, it will be used. (A new context might need to be created in this activity, depending on the transactional attributes of the class.) If not, a new activity containing a new context will be created. Method calls to the component will acquire the activity lock.
SynchronizationOption.RequiresNew	A new synchronized activity and context will always be created. Method calls to the component will acquire the activity lock.
SynchronizationOption.Supported	If an activity already exists, it will be used and method calls will acquire the activity lock. If not, method calls to the component will proceed without synchronization. (You might need to implement your own locking scheme if you want to protect data encapsulated within the component!)

An example using synchronization is supplied in the *Stock* class (in the file StockControl.jsl in the project COMPlusStockControl). The *Stock* class available in this project is a variation on the *Stock* class used in the examples in Chapter 8, but it is implemented as a serviced component that implements the *IStock* interface defined in the same project. A *Stock* object keeps track of how many items of a particular type are available in a supplier's warehouse. The *IStock* interface defines methods for increasing the number in stock, reducing the number in stock, or just querying the number in stock:

```
// IStock interface - models stock items in a warehouse
/** @attribute ComVisibleAttribute(true) */
public interface IStock
{
   /** @property */
   public int get_numInStock();
   public int addToNumInStock(int howMany);
   public int reduceNumInStock(int byHowMany) throws System.Exception;
}
```

The *Stock* class itself uses a private instance variable called *numberInStock* to hold the volume of the stock item available in the warehouse. (In a production application, this information would be held in a database rather than being maintained as internal state in the *Stock* class—the reasons for this will be explained later.) The *addToNumInStock* and *reduceNumInStock* methods manipulate this variable:

```
public class Stock extends ServicedComponent implements IStock
{
   private int numberInStock = 0;

   ⋮

   // Restock the warehouse
   public int addToNumInStock(int howMany)
   {
      this.numberInStock += howMany;
      return this.numberInStock;
   }

   // Remove stock from warehouse
   public int reduceNumInStock(int byHowMany) throws System.Exception
   {
      if (this.numberInStock >= byHowMany)
      {
         this.numberInStock -= byHowMany;
         return this.numberInStock;
      }
```

```
        else
        {
           throw new System.Exception
             ("Insufficient goods in stock - please reorder");
        }
    }
    ⋮
}
```

If the *addNumInStock* and *reduceNumInStock* methods were allowed to execute concurrently over the same instance of the *Stock* class, the *numberInStock* variable could become corrupted. (Remember that the += and -= operators comprise several MSIL instructions and are not atomic.) This can also occur if *reduceNumInStock* is executed concurrently by two separate threads, and the same is true for the *addNumInStock* method. The *Stock* class is therefore tagged with *SynchronizationAttribute*, using the value *SynchronizationOption.RequiresNew*. This setting creates a new synchronized context for each instance of the *Stock* component. Concurrent calls to the same instance of the object will be serialized, but calls to other instances (and to other objects) can proceed in parallel:

```
/** @attribute SynchronizationAttribute(SynchronizationOption.RequiresNew) */
/** @attribute ClassInterfaceAttribute(ClassInterfaceType.None) */
public class Stock extends ServicedComponent implements IStock
{
    ⋮
}
```

The *StockController* class, in the same project, is a test harness that creates a *Stock* object and then spawns two threads that manipulate the *Stock* object. (A COM+ application called Stock Control Demo, which contains the *Stock* serviced component, will be created automatically if you build and execute the project.)

Static Methods

When we looked at the .NET Remoting architecture in Chapter 11, you learned that the static methods of an object are never executed remotely—instead, they're run locally, in the client. The same is true of static methods exposed by serviced components. To be honest, you should really avoid using them if possible. The reason is that they're not available through COM+ (they don't appear in the Component Services console) or through a type library and cannot be exposed through an interface—they can therefore be invoked only by managed clients because you need a reference to the managed assembly to see them.

Serviced Component Activation

One good reason to build serviced components is the inherent support they provide for scalability. Serviced components can be JIT-activated and pooled. Well-designed serviced components are highly reusable objects.

JIT Activation

You should not confuse JIT activation of a serviced component with JIT compilation used by the common language runtime—they are distinct concepts that both happen to be performed "just in time." JIT activation is used to conserve resources required by a serviced component on a computer that can potentially host thousands of instances of the same component.

A typical client application can instantiate a serviced component and invoke its methods. There might be a significant period of time between method calls, and keeping a serviced component active in the intervening time can be expensive in terms of the memory required. The alternative is to force client applications to instantiate serviced components as required and then destroy them after each method call, creating and destroying further instances as each method call is made. This approach might save memory on the host computer, but at the cost of increased client complexity and the overhead of continually creating and destroying objects (not to mention the volume of extra network traffic generated).

JIT activation permits an inactive serviced component to be destroyed but transparently re-created if the client invokes one of its methods. This act of deception is achieved through the proxies and stubs used by COM+. When a client instantiates a serviced component, the COM+ runtime creates a proxy that is handed to the client and a stub that executes on the server. Method calls issued by the client pass through the proxy and are marshaled (possibly over the network if the serviced component is remote) to the stub. The stub unmarshals the method call and invokes the real serviced component. Return values and output parameters are sent back from the serviced component, through the stub and proxy, and eventually end up in the client.

So far, this is not much different from the generic RPC architecture employed by COM, CORBA, RMI, and even .NET Remoting. The trick with JIT activation comes when the method call completes. If the serviced component has finished its work and does not need to maintain any state information, the COM+ runtime *might* destroy the serviced component. (If and when this occurs is actually up to the runtime.) However, the server-side stub and the client-side proxy will remain intact. If the client invokes another method on the serviced component, the method call will pass through the proxy to the stub, which will create a new instance of the serviced component if the previously used instance was destroyed—otherwise the existing instance will be used, and then call the requested method. When the method call completes, the serviced component instance might be destroyed again. The client will not be aware of any of this chicanery.

Note The COM+ server-side stub also includes context information; the context is retained between method calls on the server-side even though the objects contained by the context can disappear.

You can indicate that a serviced component supports JIT activation by tagging it with *System.EnterpriseServices.JustInTimeActivationAttribute*, as shown in the *Widget* class below:

```
/** @attribute JustInTimeActivationAttribute(true) */
public class Widget extends ServicedComponent
{
    ⋮
}
```

State Management

JIT activation sounds great, but there's one question that we need to answer: How does the COM+ runtime know that a serviced component has completed its work and has no state that needs to be preserved? A serviced component might define methods that populate and query data held inside the component, and a client might rightfully expect that if it stores a value in an object, that value will still be there when the object is next accessed.

To solve this problem, each serviced component contains a flag called the *done bit*. You can arrange for this flag to be set when you've finished with an object and are happy for it to be discarded, or you can leave the flag clear if you want the object to remain active. Typically, you either set or clear the done bit during each method for a JIT activated component.

The done bit is not directly accessible, however. You can manipulate and query the done bit by using the static Boolean *DeactivateOnReturn* property (*get/set_DeactivateOnReturn* in J#) of the *ContextUtil* class:

```
ContextUtil.set_DeactivateOnReturn(true); // Indicate "doneness"
```

Note Serviced components that use transactions are automatically JIT-activated. The static *SetComplete* and *SetAbort* methods of the *ContextUtil* class set the done bit and will deactivate a JIT-activated object when the calling method completes. Tagging a method with *AutoCompleteAttribute* will also set the done bit.

The *Widget* class (in Widget.jsl in the JITWidget project) shows an example of a JIT activated serviced component. A widget is a highly prized piece of mock-Medieval earthenware, produced only by the skilled craftsmen of Trottiscliffe Moor in West Lumockshire. During the manufacturing process, the craftsmen take a lump of grey Lumockshire clay and model it into a widget of a specified length and breadth. The widget is then painted, and optionally varnished, before being delivered to the customer.

The *Widget* class contains methods (*SetWidgetDimensions*, *PaintWidget*, and *VarnishWidget*) that model the manufacturing process. A *Widget* object has some internal state (length, breadth, color, varnished flag) that must be maintained between method calls as the widget is created. These methods set the done bit to *false*. (This is actually the default state, but it does not hurt to be explicit.) Only when the widget has been completed and dispatched to the customer can the state information be discarded. (The *PrintWidget* method is used to create the dispatch note; it also sets the done bit to *true*.)

The completed *Widget* class is shown here:

```
/** @attribute ComVisibleAttribute(true) */
public interface IWidget
{
   public void SetWidgetDimensions(int length, int breadth);
   public void PaintWidget(String color);
   public void VarnishWidget(boolean varnished);
   public String PrintWidget();
}

/** @attribute ClassInterfaceAttribute(ClassInterfaceType.None) */
/** @attribute JustInTimeActivationAttribute(true) */
public class Widget extends ServicedComponent implements IWidget
{
   private int length, breadth;
   private String color;
   private boolean varnished;

   public void SetWidgetDimensions(int length, int breadth)
```

```
    {
        this.length = length;
        this.breadth = breadth;
        ContextUtil.set_DeactivateOnReturn(false);
    }

    public void PaintWidget(String color)
    {
        this.color = color;
        ContextUtil.set_DeactivateOnReturn(false);
    }

    public void VarnishWidget(boolean varnished)
    {
        this.varnished = varnished;
        ContextUtil.set_DeactivateOnReturn(false);
    }

    public String PrintWidget()
    {
        ContextUtil.set_DeactivateOnReturn(true);
        return this.color + " widget, size " + this.length +
            " x " + this.breadth + " ready for delivery";
    }
}
```

The *WidgetClient* class is a test harness that creates a *Widget* object, invokes the methods needed to manufacture a widget, and then calls the *PrintWidget* method to display the details. Because the *WidgetClient* and *Widget* classes are part of the same project, you don't need to deploy the *Widget* class to the GAC to build and run the test harness.

An interesting exercise is to invoke *PrintWidget* twice. The first time, you'll see a message indicating the state of the widget. The second time, the state will have been discarded and you'll see the default values for the widget's state instead, as shown in Figure 14-15.

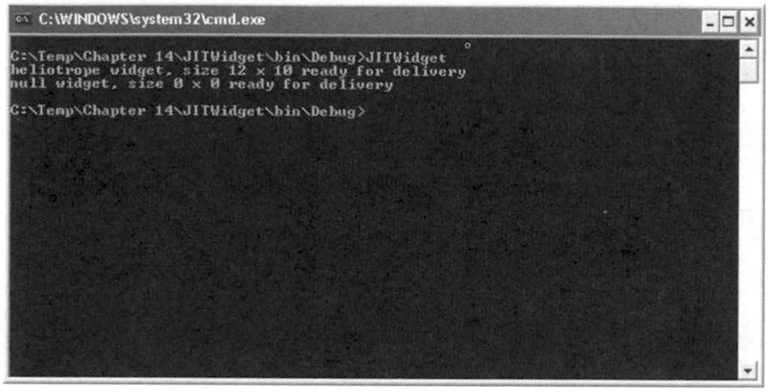

Figure 14-15 The output of the *WidgetClient* class

Object Pooling

By default, when a serviced component is deactivated, it is destroyed. If another instance of the same component is required, it must be constructed from scratch. Object construction can be an expensive process—the common language runtime has to obtain a chunk of memory from its heap, locate the assembly that defines the class to be instantiated, load the assembly, create the new object, execute its default constructor, and perform any other initialization required.

A more scalable solution is to use object pooling. A pool of objects can be created by the COM+ application, and objects from this pool can be handed to clients as needed. When an object is deactivated, rather than being destroyed it can be returned to the pool. You can specify that a serviced component should support pooling, as well as control the size of the pool, by using *System.EnterpriseServices.ObjectPoolingAttribute*. For example, to indicate that the *Widget* component should be pooled, you can use the following code. (A pooled version of the *Widget* class is available in the PooledWidget project.)

```
/** @attribute ObjectPoolingAttribute(true, MinPoolSize=100,
MaxPoolSize=200) */
public class Widget extends ServicedComponent implements IWidget
{
    ⋮
}
```

An initial pool of 100 *Widget* objects will be created. Additional objects will be created and added to the pool on demand, up to a limit of 200. When the upper limit is reached, requests for *Widget* objects will be queued and widgets will be served up to clients as they are deactivated by other clients. You can specify an optional timeout parameter by using the *ObjectPoolingAttribute* to indicate how long a client can be queued waiting for an object before giving up and throwing an exception; the default value is 6000 milliseconds (1 minute). As objects are deactivated and clients become quiescent, the number of objects in the pool will gradually drop down to 100.

For pooling to function, you must also implement an instance method called *CanBePooled*. (If you're familiar with COM+ development, you'll recognize *CanBePooled* as part of the *IObjectControl* interface.) If this method returns *true*, the object will be returned to the pool when it is deactivated; if it returns *false*, the object will be discarded. A default implementation of *CanBePooled* that returns *false* is supplied as part of the *ServicedComponent* class. A minimal version of *CanBePooled* for the *Widget* component is shown here:

```
public class Widget extends ServicedComponent implements IWidget
{
   ⋮
   protected boolean CanBePooled()
   {
      return true;
   }
   ⋮
}
```

If an object contains state variables, you might want to initialize them before handing the object to the client when the object is first activated. The usual place to perform initialization is the object's constructor. However, the constructor for a pooled object is executed when the object is created and added to the pool. If an object is returned to the pool, its state variables will be left intact. Another client receiving this same object from the pool will find the object populated with the data from its previous use. (This feature might be useful under some circumstances—see the sidebar titled "Stateless vs. Stateful Objects.") For this reason, the *ServicedComponent* class defines two additional methods called *Activate* and *Deactivate*. (Again, for those of you who are familiar with COM+, these are also part of the *IObjectControl* interface.) The *Activate* method is executed when an object is handed to a client, and *Deactivate* is executed when the client has finished with the object. If you implement *CanBePooled*, you should always override *Activate* and *Deactivate* as well. Place any client-specific initialization code you require in the *Activate* method, and use the *Deactivate* method to tidy up and remove any sensitive information. The following code shows implementations of *Activate* and *Deactivate* for the pooled *Widget* component:

```
public class Widget extends ServicedComponent implements IWidget
{
   private int length, breadth;
   private String color;
```

```
    private boolean varnished;

    ⋮

    protected void Activate()
    {
        this.length = 1;
        this.breadth = 1;
        this.color = "puce";
        this.varnished = false;
    }

    protected void Deactivate()
    {
        this.length = 0;
        this.breadth = 0;
        this.color = null;
        this.varnished = false;
    }
    ⋮
}
```

The *CanBePooled*, *Activate*, and *Deactivate* methods are called on behalf of the client by the runtime at the appropriate junctures during a pooled object's lifecycle. A client should not be able to call these methods directly. (You should make the methods protected, as shown in the examples above, or expose the serviced component through an interface, as all the examples have done so far, and ensure that *CanBePooled*, *Activate*, and *Deactivate* are not part of the interface so they'll be hidden from the client.) However, under some circumstances, a client might have good cause to want to actively destroy a serviced component and ensure that it is not returned to the pool. You can achieve this using the *Dispose* method. The *ServicedComponent* class exposes *Dispose*, and a client can call it to destroy an object. If a serviced component needs to perform any additional cleaning up, you should override the *Dispose* method and place the cleanup code there. Do not put cleanup code in a finalizer because you'll have no control over when it will be called. The *Dispose* method will be available through the *IDisposable* interface. (This interface is registered automatically when the serviced component is installed into its host COM+ application.)

Stateless vs. Stateful Objects

Developers who build distributed systems have an ongoing debate about the pros and cons of stateless and stateful objects. Most developers argue that holding state for any length of time can affect the scalability of a system that's based on serviced components—and that you should therefore minimize the amount of state an object needs to hold between method calls. This argument is valid much of the time, but there will always be exceptions, and occasionally using a component that maintains state can make sense.

In fact, the key issue is not holding state per se, but holding state on behalf of a client. If a pooled component needs a bundle of non-client-specific information before it can service any client, it makes sense for the component to obtain this when it is instantiated and to retain it during its time in the pool (as long as this state is not too volatile).

Furthermore, holding state does not in itself affect scalability. Holding resources always affects scalability. By storing state, you can cause the object to stay in memory and thus use up a resource (one of the objects in the pool). Holding state in memory affects your ability to load balance between servers because your client becomes linked to the particular server/component instance. This can frequently affect your ability to scale because some servers become unduly loaded due to state-based client affinity.

The viability of state holding will always depend on the volatility and consistency requirements of the data. If you have writable data that needs a high level of consistency, don't store it in an object between calls. For read-mostly data that does not have critical consistency, store away!

To summarize: Stateless objects are the preferred model for many implementations, but stateful objects have their uses.

Caching Shared State

You should think carefully about the type and amount of internal state held by any serviced components you write. However, sometimes you'll need to share state information *between* objects. You can hold shared state in a variety of ways—in a file on disk, using a Windows service such as the ASP.NET State Service (see Chapter 15 for more information about interacting with Windows Services from J#), or through a resource manager such as a DBMS. (The Northwind

Traders database is really just an example of persistent shared state.) However, schemes such as these might be impractical or too heavyweight if the amount of shared information to be held is small or does not need to persist indefinitely. COM+ provides the Shared Property Manager (SPM) for occasions such as this.

The SPM acts as a middle-tier cache, allowing you to store and retrieve data by name through user-defined shared properties. Data is stored in memory on the COM+ server on a per-process basis—all serviced components executing in the same COM+ host process can share property values. Shared properties are transient, however; when the host process shuts down, all shared properties in that process will be lost.

Note When you're considering whether to use the SPM, you should bear two things in mind. First, the SPM is not transactional—any changes you make to data held in the SPM will not be rolled back if a transaction aborts, for example. Second, using the SPM ties a client to a particular instance of a COM+ application and makes load-balancing more difficult.

To create a shared property, you must first create a shared property group. You do this by instantiating a *SharedPropertyGroupManager* object and invoking its *CreatePropertyGroup* method. The *SharedPropertyGroupManager* class is located in the *System.EnterpriseServices* namespace. The following code fragment, which can be executed as part of a method in a serviced component, creates a new shared property group called GroupName:

```
SharedPropertyGroupManager spgm = new SharedPropertyGroupManager();
boolean exists = false;
PropertyLockMode lock = PropertyLockMode.SetGet;
PropertyReleaseMode release = PropertyReleaseMode.Process;
SharedPropertyGroup spg = spgm.CreatePropertyGroup("GroupName", lock,
   release, exists);
```

The parameters of *CreatePropertyGroup* are the name of the new group, a lock mode, a release mode, and a Boolean flag. The lock mode specifies the degree of concurrency supported by the property group. The value *PropertyLockMode.SetGet* will lock a property as it is accessed, but concurrent threads in this and other components that execute in the same host process will be able to access other properties. You can specify an alternative value, *PropertyLockMode.Method*, which will lock all properties in the property group. You should use this value if there are interdependencies between properties. In this case, the lock on the property group will be retained until the method that's acquiring the lock completes.

The release mode parameter indicates the lifetime of the shared property group. The value *PropertyReleaseMode.Process* ties the lifetime of a shared property group to the lifetime of the host process, and the shared property group will not be destroyed until the host process terminates. You can also specify *PropertyReleaseMode.Standard*, which causes the shared property group to disappear when the last reference to the group is released.

You execute *CreatePropertyGroup* both to create a property group and to obtain a handle on an existing property group. The Boolean flag parameter (*exists* in the example) will be filled in with a value indicating whether the call to *CreatePropertyGroup* created a new group (*false*) or returned a reference to an existing group (*true*).

Note Although the Boolean *exists* parameter is a primitive type and would normally be passed by value to a regular Java method, you should notice that *CreatePropertyGroup* is a .NET Framework method that expects an output parameter. The J# compiler will generate code that passes the Boolean variable by reference. If you were writing this code in C#, you wouldn't need to initialize the *exists* variable before calling *CreatePropertyGroup* either!

Having established the property group, you can use it to create and access properties. The *CreateProperty* method does this. You pass the name of the property to be created or accessed, and a Boolean flag. A reference to the named property will be returned, and the Boolean flag will indicate whether the property has just been created (*false*) or previously existed (*true*):

```
SharedProperty myProperty = spg.CreateProperty("PropertyName", exists);
```

Finally, you can read and write the property using *get_Value* and *set_Value*. The property data is held as an *Object*, so you must cast it to the appropriate type when you retrieve the data using *get_Value*:

```
String someData = ...;
myProperty.set_Value(someData);    // write the property
⋮
someData = (String)myProperty.get_Value(); // read the property
```

Serviced Components, COM+, and Remoting

The Enterprise Services infrastructure that .NET uses as the front for COM+ is actually heavily based on the .NET Remoting architecture. (See Chapter 11 for details about Remoting.) Serviced components can be hosted in process (library components) or out of process (server components).

When a managed client instantiates an in-process serviced component, .NET Enterprise Services uses a modified version of the .NET Remoting object activation chain and invokes the COM *CoCreateInstance* method through a managed wrapper (written in managed C++). This allows COM+ to initialize the COM+ context for the serviced component. As you might recall, the Windows Registry *InprocServer32* key for a serviced component actually refers to MSCOREE.DLL, so *CoCreateInstance* calls on the common language runtime to actually create the serviced component (the class name and assembly are also supplied as keys in the Windows Registry) in the same application domain as the managed client. The common language runtime creates a transparent proxy and a customized real proxy to provide access to the serviced component from the client. The customized real proxy is known as a *serviced component proxy* (SCP). The SCP contains information about the COM+ context created for the serviced component. The transparent proxy and the SCP are marshaled through COM+ back to the managed client. This infrastructure is shown in Figure 14-16.

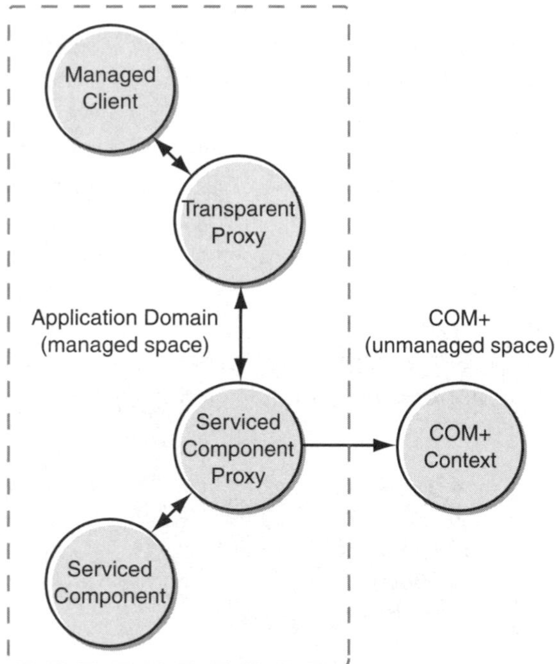

Figure 14-16 The infrastructure created for an in-process serviced component

The managed client and the serviced component execute in the same application domain. The client executes methods through the transparent proxy and the SCP. When a method call is made, the SCP examines the current COM+ context (the context ID is cached in the SCP) and compares it to the context hosting the serviced component. If they are the same, the SCP simply forwards the method call to the serviced component. If the contexts are different, the SCP calls the COM+ runtime to perform a context switch.

The SCP supplies a callback function for the COM+ runtime that refers back to the SCP. After COM+ has switched contexts, it invokes the callback which returns control to the SCP. The SCP executes the serviced component using the new context (and it also caches the ID of the new context, replacing the previously held value). Notice that COM+ is used only to provide the context and COM+ services; the serviced component itself is still executed by the common language runtime. This means that parameters passed from a managed client to a serviced component do not have to be marshaled as unmanaged COM types and back again.

Server-based serviced components execute out of process, and an extended form of the in-process infrastructure is created. When a managed client instantiates an out-of-process serviced component, the remoting activation chain initially operates as before, using a wrapper to call *CoCreateInstance*. This time, however, the common language runtime creates the serviced component in a new process. An SCP and a transparent proxy are created as before, but communication with the client is achieved through DCOM. (The common language runtime executing the server process does not know whether the client is managed or unmanaged.) Therefore, a CCW is also created to marshal method calls from DCOM into the transparent proxy. If the client is managed, it receives a transparent proxy and a specialized version of the SCP called a *remote serviced component proxy* (RSCP) that communicates with DCOM through an RCW. An unmanaged client will communicate with the serviced component through DCOM as if it were an ordinary COM+ component. Figure 14-17 shows the infrastructure created when a managed client invokes a serviced component.

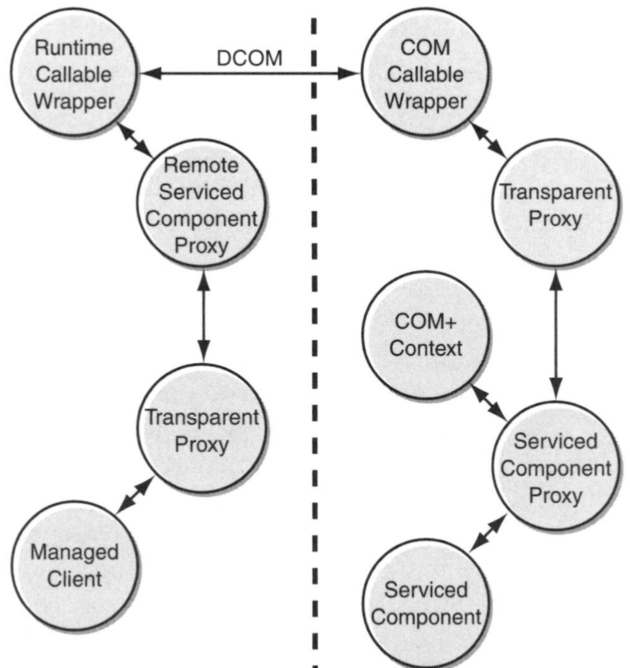

Figure 14-17 The infrastructure created for an out-of-process serviced component

More About Transactions

We discussed some aspects of transactions earlier in this chapter, when we described the use of *TransactionAttribute*. However, it's worth taking a closer look at how transactions interact with serviced components and the runtime environment.

> Note Chapter 7 showed you how to use explicit transactions with ADO.NET through SqlTransaction objects. These are referred to as imperative transactions because they're defined and managed by the program code written by the developer. Serviced components use declarative transactions, which are implemented using TransactionAttribute. The COM+ runtime manages declarative transactions in conjunction with the Microsoft Distributed Transaction Coordinator (MS DTC). You should not mix imperative and declarative transactions in the same code.

You use transactions to define the atomicity of a series of operations performed against resource managers. When the transaction commits, the results of the operations are made permanent. If the transaction aborts, the results are rolled back. The power of transactions managed by COM+ is that they can span multiple resource managers. The COM+ runtime uses the facilities of the MS DTC to propagate the outcome of a transaction to every resource manager participating in the transaction, using the Two-Phase Commit (2PC) protocol to ensure consistency everywhere. (The details of the MS DTC and 2PC are beyond the scope of this book.) A resource manager interacts with the MS DTC through a series of standard interfaces implemented by the resource manager.

Bear in mind that a resource manager might be accessed through a number of different applications, not just serviced components, and these applications might need to be protected from one another. For example, SQL Server (a resource manager that provides access to a database) can be accessed through tools such as SQL Server Enterprise Manager. Concurrent applications must be protected from one another. Otherwise, you can just imagine what could happen if two applications (COM+ and otherwise) try to manipulate the same data at the same time.

Specifying an Appropriate Isolation Level

In the following discussion, a resource manager is anything that provides controlled access to a shared, persistent resource—not just a DBMS. For example,

MSMQ is a nondatabase resource manager; the protected resources are message queues.

When you specify the transactional requirements of a serviced component, you can indicate the degree of transactional concurrency (also known as the *isolation level*) you want to allow by using the *Isolation* property of *TransactionAttribute*. Isolation is typically achieved by a resource manager through a series of locks. Two types of lock are used—*shared* and *exclusive*. A shared lock is often acquired when data is read, and other concurrent applications and threads might also acquire a shared lock over the same data at the same time. An exclusive lock is required when an application is modifying, inserting, or deleting data. Other applications cannot access the data until the lock is released. This is for consistency—if the transaction in which the data is modified, inserted, or deleted is rolled back, the changes will be undone, so it might not be safe for another application to have access to the modified data until any changes are made permanent.

The following code fragment shows how to specify the isolation level for a serviced component. You specify a value from the *System.EnterpriseServices.TransactionIsolationLevel* enumeration. Table 14-3 describes the available isolation options.

Caution Note that the isolation level describes only the degree and duration of shared locking that occurs when a serviced component reads data. When data is modified, it the locking used is *always* exclusive (although the serviced component might be blocked if other applications hold a shared lock on that data), and the exclusive lock is always held until the transaction completes (commits or aborts). Generally speaking, the more data that is locked (with either type of lock), the greater the effect on the concurrency of other applications. You should seek to minimize the volume of data you lock while balancing this requirement against the need to maintain a consistent view of the data.

```
/** @attribute TransactionAttribute(TransactionOption.Required,
   Isolation=TransactionIsolationLevel.Serializable) */
public class MyComponent extends ServicedComponent implements ...
{
   ⋮
}
```

Table 14-3 Isolation Levels for Serviced Components

Option	Description
TransactionIsolationLevel.ReadCommitted	The serviced component acquires a shared lock over data as it is read. If another application already holds an exclusive lock over the same data, the serviced component will be blocked until the exclusive lock is released. Once a data item has been retrieved, the shared lock is released (which often is *before the transaction completes*). Another application can then update this data. If the serviced component reads the same data again as part of the same transaction, it might therefore obtain different values.
TransactionIsolationLevel.ReadUncommitted	This isolation level is similar to *ReadCommitted*, except that if another application holds an exclusive lock over data when a serviced component attempts to read it, the exclusive lock will be ignored and the data will be retrieved. This prevents a thread from being blocked, but this situation is potentially dangerous and provides no guarantees about the consistency of data!
TransactionIsolationLevel.RepeatableRead	This isolation level is similar to *ReadCommitted*, except that shared locks are retained until the transaction completes. Another application cannot modify the locked data, so if the same data is read again, it will have the same values.
TransactionIsolationLevel.Serializable	This isolation level is an extended form of *RepeatableRead*. The entire resource being accessed (a table in a relational database, for example) is share-locked, not just the data (rows) being read. This prevents any modifications from being made to any other data in the resources until the transaction completes. The rationale behind this approach is that if the query that identifies the data is executed again as part of the same transaction, it should return exactly the same data items—with no new "phantom" additions.
TransactionIsolationLevel.Any	If a serviced component is invoked by another serviced component, the calling serviced components isolation level will be used. If the calling serviced component is not transactional, the *Serializable* isolation level will be used.

The default isolation level is *Serializable*. This is the safest in terms of consistency, but you might find that it decreases concurrency and therefore performance. For a component that only writes data, you might find *ReadCommitted* (or even *ReadUncommitted*) more useful. Similarly, if a component does not repeatedly read the same data in the same transaction, *ReadCommitted* should be perfectly acceptable. Use the *RepeatableRead* or *Serializable* isolation levels only if you *must* perform repeated reads in the same transaction *and* guarantee that the same data will be fetched each time.

Transaction Duration

The isolation level determines the circumstances under which data is locked. How long the data remains locked can depend on the duration of the transaction. Remember that some shared locks, and all exclusive locks, that are acquired during a transaction will be retained until the transaction completes. Concurrent requests by other components might be blocked until the transaction finishes. Therefore, to avoid lengthy waits and to maximize throughput, you must design serviced components to keep transactions as short as possible.

In our discussion of JIT activation, we drew your attention to the *done bit*, which indicates that a serviced component has completed its work and can be deactivated. Serviced components also have a *consistent bit* (often called the *happy bit*), which indicates whether the serviced component wants to commit or abort the current transaction. The done bit and happy bit are used together at the end of each method call to determine the ultimate outcome of the transaction, as follows. (This is a simplified version of what happens—if a new transaction is created while an existing transaction is active, the algorithm gets more involved!)

- If the done bit is set and the happy bit is set, the transaction can be committed and the serviced component deactivated.
- If the done bit is set and the happy bit is clear, the transaction will be aborted and the serviced component deactivated.
- If the done bit is clear, the component will still be active (it will not be deactivated) and so the transaction outcome can't yet be determined.

You can set the happy bit using the *ContextUtil.SetComplete* method, and you can unset it using the *ContextUtil.SetAbort* method. These two methods also set the done bit, as you saw earlier. If you want to set or clear the happy bit without changing the done bit, you can invoke *ContextUtil.EnableCommit* or *ContextUtil.DisableCommit*. Remember, however, that until a method completes with the done bit set, the transaction outcome will not be determined.

Therefore, a method that invokes *DisableCommit* can be overridden if a subsequent method call in the same context executes *EnableCommit*.

You can also access the happy bit using the static *MyTransactionVote* property of the *ContextUtil* class. You can query the current state of the happy bit and change it. The values you use (*Commit*, *Abort*) are specified in the *System.EnterpriseServices.TransactionVote* enumeration:

```
ContextUtil.set_MyTransactionVote(TransactionVote.Abort);
```

Of course, the other way to complete a transaction is to tag methods with *AutoCompleteAttribute*. This attribute sets the done bit (again, as you saw earlier) and sets the happy bit if the method finishes successfully, or it clears the happy bit if the method terminates due to an unhandled exception.

.NET and COM+ Security

COM+ defines its own security mechanisms, mapping the identity of the client process to its own custom roles. The scheme used by .NET is similar, but it is implemented by the common language runtime. The *System.EnterpriseServices* namespace provides classes and enumerations that allow you to bridge the gap between the two systems. Before we look at how to implement COM+ security from managed code in a serviced component, it is worth reviewing the requirements and models used by .NET and COM+.

Code Access Security Requirements

Despite the fact that you use the .NET Framework Class Library to build serviced components, an application that instantiates a serviced component must be granted the *UnmanagedCode* privilege. This means that assemblies downloaded from the Internet, an intranet, or a local area network will not be able to instantiate serviced components unless they are explicitly trusted.

The .NET Role-Based Security Model

Chapter 2 described how .NET role-based security works. To recap, you can tag classes and methods with System.Security.Permissions.PrincipalPermissionAttribute, as shown here:

```
/** @attribute PrincipalPermissionAttribute(SecurityAction.Demand,
   Role="WONDERLAND\\Bakers") */
/** @attribute PrincipalPermissionAttribute(SecurityAction.Demand,
   Name="WONDERLAND\\JSharp") */
public static short FeedsHowMany(short diameter, short shape,
```

```
    short filling)
{
        ⋮
}
```

When an application executes the *FeedsHowMany* method, the common language runtime examines the identity of the process calling the method to ensure that it is either *WONDERLAND\JSharp* or a member of the *WONDERLAND\Bakers* role.

The .NET Framework Class Library also provides the *System.Security.Permissions.PrincipalPermission* class, which you can use to implement imperative security if you prefer. (See Chapter 2 for the details.)

The COM+ Role-Based Security Model

COM+ also provides role-based declarative security. COM+ security can be configured by an administrator through the Component Services console in Control Panel. An administrator can create roles and add Windows users and groups to those roles, as shown in Figure 14-18.

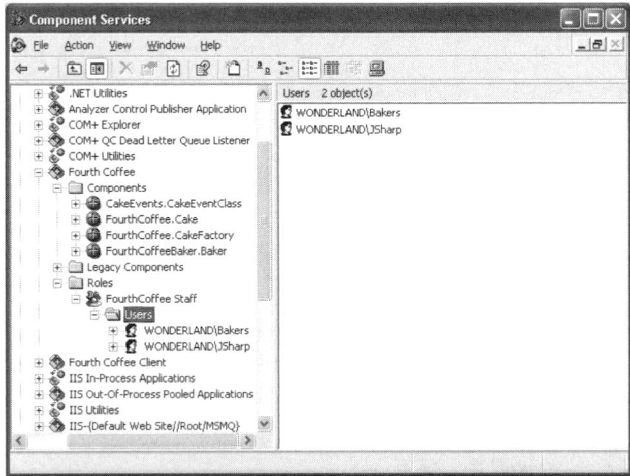

Figure 14-18 Adding users to roles in the Component Services console

Roles can be granted access to an entire component, specific interfaces, or individual methods. (You must first enable authorization in the COM+ application.) Figure 14-19 shows an example of granting the members of the *FourthCoffee Staff* COM+ role access to the *CakeFactory* component (and implicitly removing access for all other users).

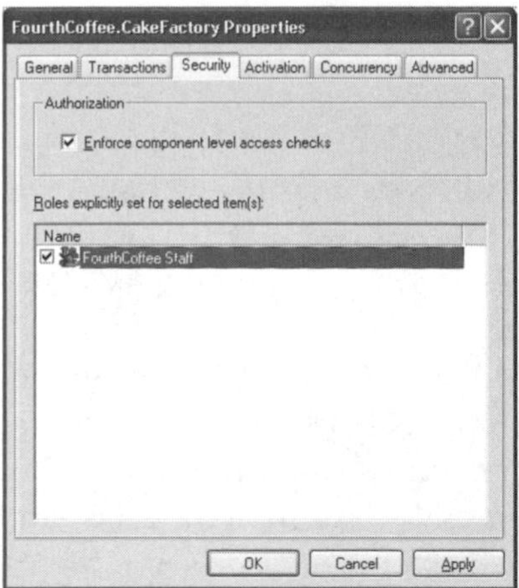

Figure 14-19 Granting access to the members of the *FourthCoffee Staff* role

You can enforce security at the process level only or at the process and component level (the preferred option). At execution time, when a client application invokes a COM+ component, the COM+ runtime examines the identity of the client process and uses it to grant or deny access to the component, interface, or method. The frequency with which the client will be authenticated can be specified, ranging from once when the client first connects to the component to every time a packet of data is sent from the client to the COM+ application.

If a COM+ component requires access to secure resources, such as a DBMS, an administrator can configure the identity to be used. By default, the COM+ component will impersonate the caller, passing the identity of the caller to the resource manager. The caller must have been granted permission by the resource manager for this strategy to be successful. A preferred technique is to configure the COM+ application to run as a particular fixed identity. All access to resource managers will use this identity instead, which means that individual users do not have to be granted direct access.

Implementing COM+ Security from .NET

If you're building a serviced component, you can preconfigure much of the COM+ security information using attributes.

The *System.EnterpriseServices.ApplicationAccessControlAttribute* class allows you enable COM+ security and specifies the COM+ application-level security attributes such as the frequency of authentication and the impersonation level. You apply this attribute at the assembly level, as shown here:

```
/** @assembly ApplicationAccessControlAttribute(true,
   AccessChecksLevel=AccessChecksLevelOption.ApplicationComponent,
   Authentication=AuthenticationOption.Packet,
   ImpersonationLevel=ImpersonationLevelOption.Identify) */
```

The *AccessChecksLevelOption, AuthenticationOption*, and *ImpersonationLevelOption* enumerations contain values corresponding to each of the possible settings that an administrator can select when configuring a COM+ application manually.

To implement COM+ role-based security, you should define roles using *SecurityRoleAttribute* and secure components using *ComponentAccessControlAttribute*. (You should not use *PrincipalPermissionAttribute*.) You can use the *SecurityRoleAttribute* class to tag an entire assembly, a class, and individual methods. When a role is applied to an assembly, any user in the role will have access to every component in the assembly. When applied to a class or method, the security role will have access to that class or method only. The following example enables access control at the class level for the *CakeFactory* class, creates a COM+ role called *Bakers*, and then applies this role to the *CakeFactory* class. An administrator can then populate the *Bakers* role with users by using the Component Services console. (The *Bakers* role will initially be empty.) If you want to create multiple roles, you must apply *SecurityRoleAttribute* multiple times:

```
/** @attribute ComponentAccessControlAttribute(true) */
/** @attribute SecurityRoleAttribute("Bakers") */
public class CakeFactory extends ServicedComponent implements ...
{
⋮
}
```

If you examine the serviced component using the Component Services console and look at the security settings for the *CakeFactory* component, you'll see that authorization has been enabled and that the *Bakers* role has been created and applied to the *CakeFactory* component, as shown in Figure 14-20.

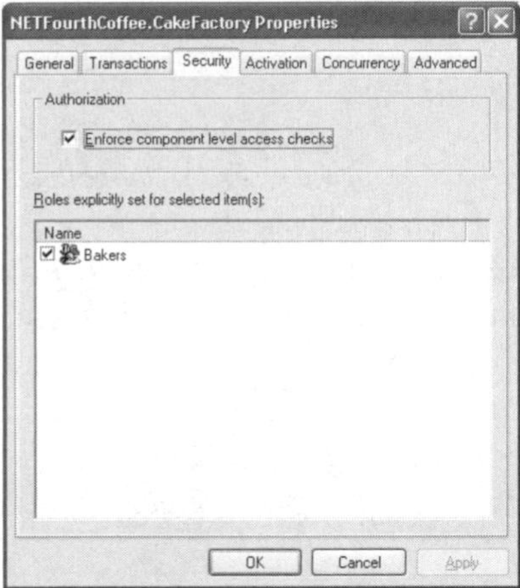

Figure 14-20 The security settings for the *CakeFactory* component

To secure a single method, you attach a *SecurityRoleAttribute* to the method as shown below. If you want to apply the same role to several methods, you must repeat the *SecurityRoleAttribute* for each method.

```
/** @attribute SecurityRoleAttribute("Master Bakers") */
public ICake CreateCake(short size, short filling, short shape)
{
⋮
}
```

Note If you implement method-level security, the .NET Framework will automatically create an extra role called *Marshaler* and attach it to the *IDisposable* and *IManagedObject* interfaces generated for the serviced component. This role allows clients to execute the methods defined by these interfaces. For example, if users need to execute the *Dispose* method, you should add them to the *Marshaler* role.

From our earlier discussions, you should recall that if you do not implement an interface, a serviced component will support only late binding and will not directly expose any methods to unmanaged COM+ clients. Therefore, you can provide method-level security only if you create serviced components that implement interfaces. However, rather confusingly, the *SecurityRoleAttribute* is applied to the method implementations in the serviced component, not to the method declarations in the interface!

COM+ Imperative Security

You can query security information programmatically and obtain details such as the account name used by the client that's executing code in a serviced component. The static property *CurrentCall* of the *System.EnterpriseServices.SecurityCallContext* class returns a *SecurityCallContext* object containing the security information relating to the current method call. The *SecurityCallContext* class itself defines a raft of additional methods and properties that you can use to determine whether security is actually enabled for the current context (the *IsSecurityEnabled* property), as well as determine the identities used by the process that's directly calling the serviced component (*DirectCaller*) and determine the process that originally made the method call (*OriginalCaller*). These might well be different.

The *OriginalCaller* and *DirectCaller* properties return a *SecurityIdentity* object, which contains information about the identity of the calling process, including the account name. The *SecurityCallContext* class provides the method *IsCallerInRole*, which you can use to determine whether the identity of the calling process matches a specified role. (The *ContextUtil* class also supplies *IsCallerInRole* as a static method). The *IsUserInRole* method allows you to specify an account name and a role and determines whether that account name is assigned to the role.

You can use this information to control access to sensitive code sequences in a method of a serviced component, which gives you a finer degree of control than can be achieved using declarative security alone. For example, in the *CreateCake* method shown below, declarative security attributes limit access to members of the Master Bakers group. The code examines the details of the original caller, and if the identity is WONDERLAND\JSharp (a newly recruited master chef who needs close monitoring), the method will write a record to the Windows event log recording the date and time the cake was created.

```
/** @attribute SecureMethodAttribute() */
/** @attribute SecurityRoleAttribute("Master Bakers") */
public ICake CreateCake(short size, short filling, short shape)
{
   SecurityCallContext context = SecurityCallContext.get_CurrentCall();
   if (context.get_IsSecurityEnabled())
   {
      SecurityIdentity caller = context.get_OriginalCaller();
      if (caller.get_AccountName().Equals("WONDERLAND\\JSharp"))
      {
         System.Diagnostics.EventLog appLog =
            new System.Diagnostics.EventLog("Application", ".",
            "Fourth Coffee");
```

```
            String logMessage = "WONDERLAND\\JSharp is creating a new cake. "
             + DateTime.get_Now();
            appLog.WriteEntry(logMessage,
               System.Diagnostics.EventLogEntryType.Warning);
        }
    }

    // Create the cake
    ⋮
}
```

Asynchronous Components

Earlier, you saw how to build a J# client application that accesses the Fourth-Coffee components hosted within COM+. The components themselves were written in Visual Basic and supported queued method execution and loosely coupled events. Next, we'll look at how to provide the same functionality using serviced components.

Creating a Queued Component

The *Oven* class (in the file Oven.jsl in the Oven project) models an oven for baking cakes. Before you place a cake in the oven, you must set the oven to the correct temperature and wait for the oven to reach that temperature. The *Oven* class implements the *IQueuedOven* interface, which defines the *SetTemperature* method. This method takes a temperature as a parameter and sets the oven to that temperature, finishing only when the specified temperature has been reached. The method does not return a value and is a prime candidate for queued execution. The interface is tagged with the *System.EnterpriseServices.InterfaceQueuingAttribute* class, which allows the interface to support queued method calls. The constructor for this attribute takes a Boolean parameter that indicates whether to enable queuing (*true*) or disable queuing (*false*). You can add methods to the *IQueuedOven* interface as long as you obey the golden rule that they don't return values. (The J# compiler doesn't enforce this rule, but the component won't install in the COM+ catalog if you break it.)

```
/** @attribute InterfaceQueuingAttribute(true) */
public interface IQueuedOven
{
   public void SetTemperature(short temperature);
}
```

The COM+ application that hosts the *Oven* class must be configured to support queuing. You do this by applying the *System.EnterpriseServices.Appli-*

cationQueuingAttribute class at the assembly level. This attribute provides three properties that you can specify to enable queuing, enable the queue listener, and specify the maximum number of concurrent queued requests that can be processed. You use *ApplicationQueuingAttribute*, as shown here:

```
/** @assembly ApplicationQueuingAttribute(Enabled=true,
   QueueListenerEnabled=true, MaxListenerThreads=10) */
```

A client that wants to call the *SetTemperature* method of the *IQueuedOven* interface can do so synchronously by instantiating an *Oven* object in the same way you would an ordinary COM+ component:

```
IQueuedOven oven = new Oven();

// Wait for the oven to reach the correct temperature before continuing
Oven.SetTemperature((short)200);
```

If you want to invoke *SetTemperature* asynchronously, you use a queue moniker to instantiate the *Oven* object, you can see in the following code. (You should replace *WHITERABBIT* in the moniker with the name of your own computer.) This client code is available in the file OvenClient.jsl in the OvenClient project.

```
IQueuedOven asyncOven = (IQueuedOven)Marshal.BindToMoniker(
   "queue:ComputerName=WHITERABBIT/new:FourthCoffeeOven.Oven");

// Set the temperature, but don't wait for the oven before continuing
asyncOven.SetTemperature((short)300);
```

Supporting Loosely Coupled Events

As mentioned earlier, the natural companion to a queued method is an LCE. In our example, it would be useful to know when the oven has reached the correct temperature. The *System.EnterpriseServices* namespace provides attributes that you can use to define event classes. The first step is to create an interface that contains the various event methods. The *Oven* class will invoke these methods when it wants to raise events. In this example, there's only one method, *TemperatureReached*, and it takes a single parameter that indicates the new temperature of the oven. Like all event methods, it does not return a value:

```
public interface IOvenEvents
{
   public void TemperatureReached(short temperature);
}
```

Next, you create a serviced component that implements this interface, as shown in the following code. This is the event class (described earlier in this chapter), and you tag it *System.EnterpriseServices.EventClassAttribute*. The implementation of the *TemperatureReached* method should be empty. (The event sink supplied by the client will provide the real implementation.)

```
/** @attribute EventClassAttribute() */
public class OvenEventsClass extends ServicedComponent
   implements IOvenEvents
{
   // Method implementations must be empty
   public void TemperatureReached(short temperature) {}
}
```

Finally, to raise the *TemperatureReached* event, you create an instance of the *OvenEventsClass* and invoke the *TemperatureReached* method. The following code shows the body of the *SetTemperature* method of the *Oven* class:

```
// Set the temperature of the oven
public void SetTemperature(short temperature)
{
   // Wait for the correct temperature to be reached
   // The higher the temperature, the longer the wait
   System.Threading.Thread.Sleep(temperature * 100);

   // Raise the TemperatureReached event
   OvenEventsClass evt = new OvenEventsClass();
   evt.TemperatureReached(temperature);
}
```

The completed *Oven* class, event class, and interfaces are available in Oven.jsl in the Oven project:

A client that wants to sink the *TemperatureReached* event must create an event sink class and register it in the COM+ catalog. The event sink must be a serviced component and must implement the *IOvenEvents* interface, as shown by the *EventSink* class below. (This class is available in EventSink.jsl in the OvenEventSink project.)

```
public class EventSink extends ServicedComponent implements IOvenEvents
{
   public void TemperatureReached(short temperature)
   {
      MessageBox.Show("The oven is ready. The temperature is " +
         temperature + " degrees", "Oven ready");
   }
}
```

The *EventSink* component must be added to a COM+ application; you can either create a new one or add it to the application used by the *Oven* component. (If you export the *Oven* component, you'll also export the event sink.)

Once the *EventSink* component has been installed, you can follow the procedure described earlier in this chapter to attach the *IOvenEvents* implementation to *FourthCoffeeOven.OvenEventsClass* and subscribe to the event. If you then execute the OvenClient application, you'll see two message boxes. The first will appear after 20 seconds (when the oven reaches 200 degrees), and the second will appear 30 seconds later (when the oven reaches 300 degrees). In the meantime, the OvenClient program should have finished because the second call to *SetTemperature* uses the asynchronous interface.

Note We've provided another project called OvenInstaller that you can execute to create the COM+ application for the oven component if you don't want to do it by hand. The *main* method of the *OvenInstaller* class creates a *RegistrationHelper* object and invokes the *InstallAssembly* method, installing the FourthCoffeeOven.dll assembly (which contains the Oven components). Depending on where you've located the OvenInstaller and the Oven projects, you might need to change the relative path name indicated by the *OvenAssemblyPath* variable.

Best Practices for Serviced Component Design

The following list briefly summarizes best practices for designing serviced components.

- Define interfaces and set the *ClassInterfaceAttribute* of a serviced component to *ClassInterfaceType.None*.
- Supply values for *ApplicationNameAttribute*, *ApplicationIDAttribute*, and *ApplicationActivationAttribute* for an assembly that implements a serviced component.
- Use JIT activation with *AutoCompleteAttribute* wherever possible.
- Minimize the amount of client-specific state information that a serviced component holds.
- If a component can be called by multiple threads concurrently, choose an appropriate synchronization setting to ensure thread safety.

- If you're using pooling, implement *CanBePooled*, *Activate*, and *Deactivate*. Do not place initialization code in the constructor unless it needs to be performed only once.
- Implement and expose the *Dispose* method if a client needs to be able to destroy a serviced component. Do not use a finalizer.
- Use short-lived transactions to reduce contention in a resource manager. (Never wait for user input during a transaction.) Use an appropriate isolation level to maximize throughput while maintaining consistency.
- Do not mix declarative and imperative transactions. (Ideally, do not use imperative transactions at all.)
- Implement COM+ security. Define security roles using *SecurityRoleAttribute*.

Summary

In this chapter, you learned how to create and consume serviced components using J#. You should now have a reasonable understanding of how COM+ and .NET can be used together to build scalable components. You also learned how to use the features of the *System.EnterpriseServices* namespace to implement features such as JIT activation, object pooling, transactions, security, queued components, and LCEs.

15

Implementing Windows Services

A Windows service is a process that executes in the background, frequently implementing an operating system task. Services are a fundamental part of the Microsoft Windows operating system and are often used to provide protected access to sensitive resources. One example is the Event Log service, which writes records to the Windows event logs on behalf of applications. Another example is the World Wide Web Publishing Service, which controls Microsoft Internet Information Services (IIS) and allows your computer to act as a Web server. If you've used other operating systems such as UNIX, you might be familiar with *daemon* processes, which fulfill a similar role. (Do not confuse daemon processes with Java *daemon* threads, because they belong to an ordinary user process and are not started by the operating system.)

You can configure a Windows service to start automatically when the operating system boots. The background nature of a Windows service means that its options for input and output are very limited. For example, a Windows service should not attempt to write messages to the console or display message boxes, because there's no guarantee that a user will be logged in to acknowledge them. Instead, Windows services receive input from other applications through a set of APIs defined as part of the Windows operating system. Similarly, error information and other significant output is typically recorded in the Windows event logs.

You can create your own services using a variety of tools and techniques, ranging from the low-level Windows APIs available with the Platform SDK to simply configuring a COM+ application to execute as a service. Using the Windows APIs gives you a lot more control than the COM+ application option, but it requires that you write a lot more code. The .NET Framework Class Library provides a middle ground, allowing you to be in command of the operations performed by a Windows service but abstracting out many of the low-level details. The *System.ServiceProcess* namespace provides managed wrappers for the Windows service APIs, and Microsoft Visual Studio .NET provides the Windows Service template to use in creating your own service applications.

In this chapter, we'll examine how to interact with existing Windows services from Microsoft Visual J#. Then we'll look at how to create a new Windows service and examine such topics as service installation and service security with J#.

Controlling a Windows Service

Services are often configured to start automatically with the operating system, although an administrator can start and stop a service using the Services console in Control Panel. (In Control Panel, click Performance and Maintenance, click Administrative Tools, and then double-click Services.) You can also control services programmatically if you have the appropriate access rights—the assembly must be granted *System.ServiceProcess.ServiceControllerPermission*, which by default is denied to all assemblies other than those loaded from the local computer.

Displaying Service Information

The key to manipulating services with the Microsoft .NET Framework is to use the *System.ServiceProcess.ServiceController* class. A *ServiceController* object caches information about a particular service and makes this information available through a series of properties, which we'll examine in this section. The *ServiceController* class also provides methods that you can use to change the state of a service (start it, stop it, pause it, and so on).

Note You must add a reference to the System.ServiceProcess.dll assembly in order to use the *ServiceController* class.

The ServiceForm Windows Form (which is available in ControllerForm.jsl in the ServiceForm project) shows the *ServiceController* class in action. Its function mimics the Services console in Control Panel in that it lists all the services running on the local computer and allows you to start and stop services. (The data is displayed in a raw format, and you cannot change the properties of a service, unlike with the Services console). Figure 15-1 shows the application running.

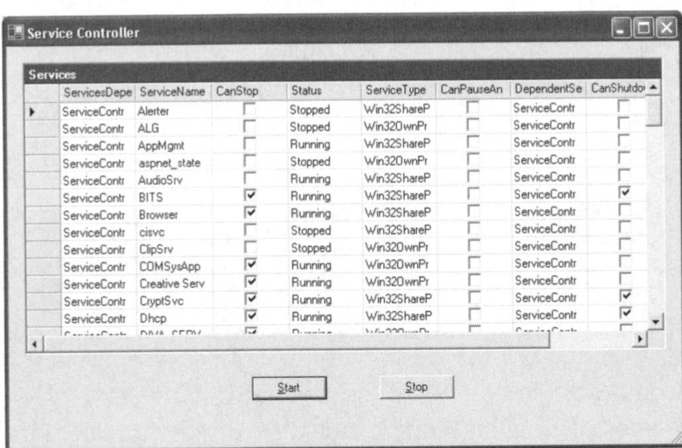

Figure 15-1 The ServiceForm application, showing the services executing on the local machine

The form comprises a *DataGrid* control called *serviceGrid* for displaying the services, two buttons for starting and stopping a selected service, and a status bar for reporting any errors as services are started and stopped.

If you examine the code in the *ControllerForm* class (this is the main form of the application), you'll see that we've declared an array of *ServiceController* objects:

```
:
import System.ServiceProcess.*;
:
public class ControllerForm extends System.Windows.Forms.Form
{
:
private ServiceController[] services;
```

The *ControllerForm* constructor populates the *services* array by calling the static *GetServices* method of the *ServiceController* class. *GetServices* is overloaded; the version used here retrieves the services installed on the local computer, but you can also supply the name of a machine as a *String*, and *GetServices* will return the services installed on that computer instead (assuming you have the appropriate access rights). The service information is displayed in the data grid using the *SetDataBinding* method, as shown below. This is a convenient way of binding the data in any data source to a data grid, and will render each item in the array or collection as rows in the grid. Each row will comprise one or more columns, derived from the fields of the data source. The data in the individual columns of the data grid is generated by executing the *ToString* method over each field in the data source.

```
public ControllerForm()
{
    ⋮
    services = ServiceController.GetServices();
    serviceGrid.SetDataBinding(services, null);
}
```

Note A data source can comprise several data members. The second parameter of *SetDataBinding* indicates which specific data member should be used. In the case of a simple collection or array, you can specify a *null* value for this parameter. If you want more information about the *DataGrid* control, look up the *System.Windows.Forms.DataGrid* class in the Visual Studio .NET documentation.

There are actually two classes of service available under Windows—those that implement device drivers (modems, CD-ROM, hard disks, network cards, and so on) and those that don't. The *GetServices* method returns a list of non–device driver services. If you want to retrieve a list of device driver services, execute the *GetDevices* method instead.

The properties of the *ServiceController* class displayed in the data grid are (in order of importance):

- **ServiceName** This *String* property identifies the service in the Windows Registry. No two services on the same computer can have the same service name.

Note The *ServiceName* property has *get* and *set* accessors. If you change the *ServiceName* property of a *ServiceController*, you will not actually change the name of the service. Instead, the *ServiceController* will be populated with the details for the specified service. (If you supply a name that doesn't exist, you'll get an exception). You can use this technique if you only want information about a single service. For example, the following fragment creates a *ServiceController* and fills it with information about the World Wide Web Publishing Service (W3SVC):

```
ServiceController controller = new ServiceController();
controller.set_ServiceName("W3SVC");
```

- **DisplayName** This is another *String* that contains an alternative name for the service. The *ServiceName* property is often short and meaningful only to the developer (and Registry hackers). On the other hand, the *DisplayName* property is sometimes referred to as the *friendly name* because it is often more meaningful and descriptive. Utilities such as the Services console use a service's *DisplayName* if it has one (it's optional); otherwise, it uses the *ServiceName*.

Note The *DisplayName* property acts in a similar manner to the *ServiceName* property if you change it—the *ServiceController* will be populated with the details of the matching service, or an exception will be thrown if there is no match.

- **Status** This property indicates the current state of the service. A service can be in one of a small set of states, and it can be asked to switch from one state to another by being sent requests or signals. Table 15-1 (in the next section) summarizes the states that are available.

- **CanStop** This Boolean property indicates whether the service can be asked to stop. If a service is critical to the operating system (such as the Security Accounts Manager service) it does not support stopping, and this property will be permanently set to *false*. Also, a service that does support stopping might be in a state in which it cannot currently be stopped (it might be starting up or already stopped, for example), so the value of this property also depends on the current state of the service.
- **CanPauseAndContinue** Some services can be paused. A paused service temporarily stops accepting requests but can quickly resume operations. You can resume a paused service by sending it a *Continue* request.
- **CanShutdown** This Boolean property is a slight misnomer because all services must shut down when the operating system shuts down. This property simply indicates whether the service should be notified when the operating system is shutting down.
- **ServiceType** This property indicates the type of the service, using values from the *System.ServiceProcess.ServiceType* enumeration. If the *ServiceType* property is *Adapter*, *FileSystemDriver*, *KernelDriver*, or *RecognizerDriver*, the service is actually a device driver. (You won't see any of these unless you populate the data grid with an array filled by using *ServiceController.GetDevices*.) Non–device driver services will have a *ServiceType* of *Win32OwnProcess* or *Win32ShareProcess*—a service can be implemented by its own executable, or an executable can contain several services (as discussed later).
- **ServicesDependedOn** This is an array of *ServiceController* objects that contain the services that this service needs to run (it is rendered in the data grid as a *ServiceController[] Array*). If any of these services are not running when this service is started, they will be started. If any of the services in this list stop running, this service will also stop.
- **DependentServices** This is another array of *ServiceController* objects; it lists the services that depend on this service and that will stop if this service is stopped.

Although it is not displayed in the data grid, the *ServiceController* class also has a *MachineName* property. This is a *String* that specifies the machine the service is running on.

Starting and Stopping a Service

The Start and Stop buttons start and stop a selected service; the user selects a service in the data grid and then clicks the appropriate button. The *Click* event handlers behind each button contain the necessary code.

The *startButton_Click* method determines which service the user selected by retrieving the value of the *CurrentRowIndex* property of the data grid. (The data grid is zero-based—the first row in the grid being row 0.) The program then obtains the current state of the service by querying the *Status* property of the *ServiceController* object at the identified offset in the *services* array:

```
private void startButton_Click (System.Object sender, System.EventArgs e)
{
   ⋮
   int serviceNum = serviceGrid.get_CurrentRowIndex();
   ServiceControllerStatus status = services[serviceNum].get_Status();
   ⋮
```

The value returned will be a member of the *System.ServiceProcess.ServiceControllerStatus* enumeration. Table 15-1 describes the values in this enumeration. Note that a service can accept requests for work only when it is in the *Running* state.

Table 15-1 *ServiceControllerStatus* Values

Value	Description
Running	The service is running and accepting work requests.
Paused	The service has been paused. In this state, the service is no longer accepting work requests but can quickly resume execution when the service receives a *Continue* request. When a service is paused, it might release some system resources. Not all services support pausing.
Stopped	The service has stopped running and has released any resources it used.
StartPending	The service has been asked to start and is currently initializing itself. The service is not yet ready to accept work requests.
PausePending	The service has been asked to pause but is not yet in the *Paused* state.
ContinuePending	The service has been asked to continue after being paused. The service is currently acquiring any resources required and is not yet able to accept work requests.
StopPending	The service has been asked to stop but has not yet halted.

A service can be asked to start running only if it is in the *Stopped* state. The *startButton_Click* method therefore checks that this is the case before attempting to start the service; if the service is not in the *Stopped* state, this method will report a warning in the status bar at the bottom of the form:

```
if (status == ServiceControllerStatus.Stopped)
{
   // Start the service
   ⋮
}
else
{
   statusBar.set_Text("Service is already running");
}
```

Starting a service can take a little time (up to 30 seconds), so the *startButton_Click* method changes the cursor to an hourglass and then sends a *Start* request to the service using the *Start* method of the *ServiceController*:

```
Cursor curs = Cursor.get_Current();
Cursor.set_Current(Cursors.get_WaitCursor());

services[serviceNum].Start();
```

The *Start* method completes when the signal has been passed to the service, but it does not wait until the service has started. You can suspend execution while a service starts using the *WaitForStatus* method. (You can optionally specify a *TimeSpan* timeout value.) The *startButton_Click* method waits for the service to reach the *Running* state before continuing:

```
services[serviceNum].WaitForStatus(ServiceControllerStatus.Running);
```

When the *startButton_Click* method resumes, it updates the status bar, refreshes the data grid, and restores the cursor:

```
statusBar.set_Text("Service started successfully");
services = ServiceController.GetServices();
serviceGrid.SetDataBinding(services, null);
serviceGrid.set_CurrentRowIndex(serviceNum);

Cursor.set_Current(curs);
```

The *stopButton_Click* method is called when the user clicks the Stop button. The technique used to stop a service is similar to that used for starting it, with one subtle difference: You can stop a service that is in a variety of states, but not all services allow you to stop them. So, rather than checking that the service is in a particular state, the *stopButton_Click* method examines the *CanStop* property of the *ServiceController* and proceeds only if *CanStop* is true:

```
if (services[serviceNum].get_CanStop())
{
   // Stop the service
   ⋮
}
else
{
   statusBar.set_Text("Service is already stopped, or does not
      support stopping");
}
```

Writing a Windows Service

You can use the classes in the *System.ServiceProcess* namespace to create new non–device driver services. (If you want to create a device driver service, you must resort to the Microsoft Windows Driver Development Kit [DDK].) When you develop a service, you must also create a service installer that can be used to configure the service and create the appropriate Windows Registry keys. In this section, we'll create a simple service called CakeService. This service will act as a remoting server that hosts the *CakeUtils.CakeInfo* class that we developed in Chapter 11. The *CakeInfo* class exposes the *FeedsHowMany* method, and we'll test the service by creating a remoting client that invokes this method in the CakeService service.

The Structure of a Service Application

As we mentioned earlier, a Windows service can be hosted in its own executable program, or the same program can host a number of services. The host program is executed by the Service Control Manager (SCM). The SCM is a part of the Windows operating system that handles requests to start services. Such requests are made when Windows boots as well as through tools that exploit the Windows Service APIs (such as the Services console and the ServiceForm application shown earlier). The SCM also sends other signals (such as *Stop*, *Pause*, and *Continue*) to a service when directed by Windows Service API calls.

Using the same program to contain multiple services is useful if those services have a lot of common functionality and maybe need to share some information. For example, the World Wide Web Publishing Service and the IIS Admin service are obviously related, and are both implemented by the Inetinfo.exe program. In our example, the CakeService service will be hosted in its own executable.

Visual Studio .NET supplies a Windows Service template that you can use to get a running start. However, this template is not available in every edition of

Visual Studio .NET (it is omitted from the Standard edition, for example), so we'll show you how to create a new service from scratch.

The *CakeService* class (which is available in CakeService.jsl in the CakeService project) was created using the Console Application template in Visual Studio .NET. To make a class into a service, it must extend the *System.ServiceProcess.ServiceBase* class. (You must also add a reference to the System.ServiceProcess.dll assembly.) The *ServiceBase* class provides a default implementation of a Windows service, and all you have to do is override its methods and properties and provide your own functionality where needed. At an absolute minimum, you should provide a default constructor in which you initialize the properties of the service and an *OnStart* method that will be executed when the service is started. You must also provide a *main* method that creates and runs the service (as explained shortly).

The *CakeService* constructor is executed when the process hosting the service starts running and creates an instance of the *CakeService* class. You should always invoke the *ServiceBase* constructor and then set the *ServiceName* property of the service. You can set other properties that determine how the service will respond to various events (see Table 15-2), but you should not perform any service-specific application logic in the constructor. Instead, you should use the *OnStart* method, for a couple of reasons:

- If the service shares its host executable with other services, the host process will commence running when the first service that it hosts starts. The host process will invoke the constructor for every service it contains (as shown later). This might be useful if all the services need access to some shared data structures, but it can also waste resources. In contrast, the *OnStart* method is invoked only when the service is sent the *Start* signal.
- If the service is stopped, the host process will not be terminated if it contains other services that are still running. If the service is restarted, the constructor will therefore not be executed again—although *OnStart* will be.

Notice the corresponding implications for finalization. If your service relies on a finalizer to free resources, the finalizer will not be executed until after the last service hosted by the executable stops and the host process can terminate. If you need to release any resources when a service stops, you should override the *OnStop* method.

The properties that you can set for a service and the methods you should implement are listed in Table 15-2.

Table 15-2 *ServiceBase* Properties

Property	Description
ServiceName	This is the name of the service; it is used to identify the service to the SCM when the service starts running. It should be the same as that recorded in the Windows Registry.
CanPauseAndContinue	This is a Boolean property that indicates whether the service supports pausing and resuming. If you set this property to *true*, you should implement the *OnPause* and *OnContinue* methods. *OnPause* releases any non-critical resources used by the service, and *OnContinue* reacquires them.
CanStop	This is a Boolean property that specifies that the service can be stopped once it is running. If you set this property to *true* you should consider overriding the *OnStop* method to perform any tidying up required by the service.
CanShutdown	This is a Boolean property that indicates that the service should be notified if it is running when the operating system shuts down. You implement the processing to be performed in the *OnShutdown* method. The service will not be sent a *Stop* signal, so much of the processing specified by the *OnStop* method should be performed by *OnShutdown* as well.
CanHandlePowerEvent	This is a Boolean property that specifies whether the service should be alerted if the computer power status changes (if the computer goes into hibernation mode, for example). You should implement the *OnPowerEvent* method to handle the alert. *OnPowerEvent* takes a *System.ServiceProcess.PowerBroadcastStatus* parameter indicating the reason for the change of power state.

Table 15-2 *ServiceBase* Properties

Property	Description
AutoLog	This is a Boolean property. If you set it to *true*, every *Start*, *Stop*, *Pause*, and *Continue* signal sent to the service will be automatically recorded in the Windows Application event log. If you want to record events in a different event log, you should set *AutoLog* to false and programmatically write messages to your selected event log in the *OnStart*, *OnStop*, *OnPause*, and *OnContinue* methods.
EventLog	This is a read-only property that returns a handle to the Windows Application event log used for recording events when *AutoLog* is *true*. The value is returned as a *System.Diagnostics.EventLog* object. If you want to add messages to the log, you can call the *WriteEntry* method of the *EventLog* object that's returned.

The constructor for the *CakeService* class is shown below. It sets the *ServiceName* property to "*Cake Service*", indicates that the service can be stopped by an administrator, and enables auto-logging:

```
public class CakeService extends ServiceBase
{
   public CakeService()
   {
      // Call the ServiceBase constructor first
      super();

      // The name of the service that appears in the Registry
      this.set_ServiceName("Cake Service");

      // Allow an administrator to stop (and restart) the service
      this.set_CanStop(true);

      // Report Start and Stop events to the Windows event log
      this.set_AutoLog(true);
   }
   ⋮
}
```

The *OnStart* method registers a remoting channel listening at port 6000 and configures the *CakeInfo* class in the *CakeUtils* assembly as a server-activated, singleton object that's accessed through the URL "CakeInfo.rem". (If you need to refresh your memory about how this works, see Chapter 11.)

```
protected void OnStart(String [] args)
{
   // Register a channel
   ChannelServices.RegisterChannel(new TcpChannel(6000));

   // Register the CakeInfo class
   RemotingConfiguration.RegisterWellKnownServiceType(
   Type.GetType("CakeUtils.CakeInfo, CakeUtils"), "CakeInfo.rem",
      WellKnownObjectMode.Singleton);
}
```

You might be interested to observe that *OnStart* takes a *String* array as a parameter. When an administrator configures a service using its Properties dialog box from the Services console in Control Panel, she can specify a set of space-delimited strings to be passed to the service, as shown in Figure 15-2. Any values specified will be packaged up into a string array and passed to the *OnStart* method.

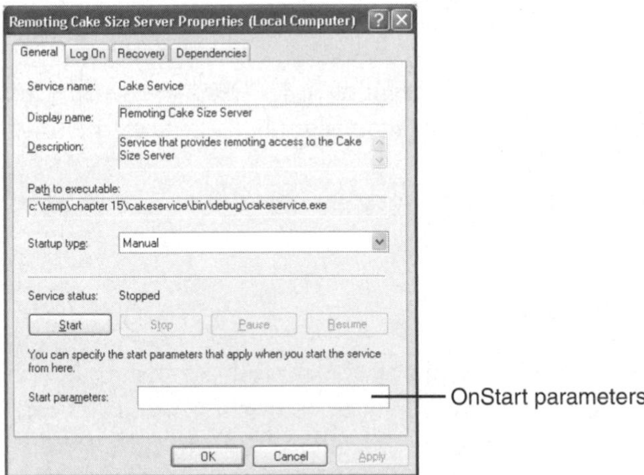

Figure 15-2 The Properties dialog box for a service

There is one major caveat with the *OnStart* method. The Windows operating system will allow your service up to 30 seconds to start. If the service has not started by the end of 30 seconds, Windows will assume that the service has frozen and will shut it down. Therefore, you must make sure that any processing you perform in *OnStart* will take less than 30 seconds to complete.

The *CakeService* can be stopped, but it has no *OnStopped* method because there is nothing for the *OnStopped* method to do in this example. (When the process running the service stops, all remote access will cease automatically because the remote objects will disappear.) Therefore, the default implementation will suffice!

The *main* method of the *CakeService* class is executed by the SCM when the first service in the host application is started. The *main* method should call the static *Run* method of the *ServiceBase* class to create and run the service:

```
ServiceBase.Run(new CakeService());
```

The *Run* method takes an object that implements a service and arranges for the *OnStart* method to be called. The *Run* method is overloaded. If the host program implements several services, they should all be instantiated and added to an array of *ServiceBase* objects. This array should then be passed as the parameter to run. For example

```
ServiceBase [] services = new ServiceBase[4];
services[0] = new CakeService();
services[1] = new AnotherService();
services[2] = new YetAnotherService();
services[3] = new AFinalService();
ServiceBase.Run(services);
```

Only the service being started will have its *OnStart* method invoked at this time, but as other services are sent Start signals their *OnStart* methods will be executed as well.

The complete *CakeService* class can be downloaded as a part of the CakeService project.

Understanding Installer Classes

Before you can use a service, it must be installed. To install a service, you can define an installer class. You can then use the *InstallUtil* utility supplied with the .NET Framework SDK to invoke the installer class and install your service. The *InstallUtil* tool takes an assembly and will attempt to install all components it contains that are tagged with *System.ComponentModel.RunInstallerAttribute*. You can use the *CakeServiceInstaller* class (shown later) to install the CakeService service. (It is supplied as part of the CakeService project.)

An installer class extends the *System.Configuration.Install.Installer* class. (You must add a reference to the System.Configuration.Install.dll assembly.) The *Installer* class provides a basic installation framework, and you override properties, methods, and events as required. An *Installer* object is associated with a single component. (The term component is used very loosely here; in the CakeService example, the CakeService itself is one component and the host process that executes it is actually another. This is because each of these items has its own set of properties that can be configured independently, as you'll see.) Each component to be installed will need an associated *Installer* object. If a component comprises many subcomponents, each will have its own associated *Installer* object. The *Installer* class contains the *Installers* property, which is a collection that you populate with *Installer* objects for configuring these subcomponents. (You can think of the data structure defined by the *Installer* class and the *Installers* property as a tree of installers.) The *InstallUtil* tool invokes the *Install* method of the top-level *Installer* object, which installs the component and recursively installs each of the subcomponents by iterating through the *Installers* property and executing the *Install* method of each item found.

You can subscribe to various events (such as *BeforeInstall* and *AfterInstall*) that are fired as installation progresses if you need to monitor progress. If an exception occurs during installation, the install process might roll back (firing *BeforeRollback* and *AfterRollback* events). If the installation is successful, it can be committed, and the *Committing* and *Committed* events will be fired. The *Installer* class also provides the *Uninstall* method together with the *BeforeUninstall* and *AfterUninstall* events.

Creating a New Installer

Much of the time, the default installation methods defined by the *Installer* class will be adequate; all you need to do for the *CakeServiceInstaller* class is to populate the *Installers* property with installers for the service and its host executable, and you can let *InstallUtil* get on with it. The best place to set the *Installers* property is the default constructor. (*InstallUtil* will instantiate your installer class using the default constructor.)

The *System.ServiceProcess* namespace contains two specialized *Installer* subclasses for installing services and their host processes. These classes are *System.ServiceProcess.ServiceInstaller* and *System.ServiceProcess.ServiceProcessInstaller*, respectively. To install a service, you typically create a single *ServiceProcessInstaller* object (that describes the service host executable) and as many *ServiceInstallers* as there are services in the host executable. You should set the properties of the *ServiceInstaller* object as required by your service. Table 15-3 describes the available properties.

Table 15-3 *ServiceInstaller* Properties

Property	Description
ServiceName	This is the name of the service. It *must* be the same as the *ServiceName* property that was specified when the service was created.
DisplayName	This is the friendly name of the service.

Table 15-3 *ServiceInstaller* Properties

Property	Description
StartType	This is a value from the *System.ServiceProcess.ServiceStartMode* enumeration. The possible values you can specify are *Automatic* (which indicates that the service should be started when Windows boots), *Manual* (which indicates that the service must be started manually by an administrator), and *Disabled* (which indicates that the services cannot be started at all).
ServicesDependedOn	This is a *String* array containing the *ServiceName* values for each service that this service depends on. When this service starts, the SCM will start any services in this list that are not already running.

The CakeService example includes only a single service, so the installer will require only a single *ServiceInstaller* object. The following code (which is taken from the constructor of the *CakeServiceInstaller* class) creates a *ServiceInstaller* object and populates the *StartType*, *ServiceName*, and *DisplayName* properties. The CakeService service does not depend on any other services. At the end of the constructor, the *ServiceInstaller* object is added to the *Installers* property.

```
private ServiceInstaller serviceInstaller = null;
⋮
public CakeServiceInstaller()
{
⋮
   serviceInstaller = new ServiceInstaller();
   serviceInstaller.set_StartType(ServiceStartMode.Manual);
   serviceInstaller.set_ServiceName("Cake Service");
   serviceInstaller.set_DisplayName("Remoting Cake Size Server");
   ⋮
   this.get_Installers().Add(serviceInstaller);
}
```

In a similar vein, you should also create and set the properties of a *ServiceProcessInstaller* object. This object defines security information that describes the security account the service should use to execute. Table 15-4 describes the available properties.

Table 15-4 *ServiceProcessInstaller* Properties

Property	Description
Account	The type of account the service should run as. You specify a value from the *System.ServiceProcess.ServiceAccount* enumeration. The values in this enumeration are *LocalService*, *LocalSystem*, *NetworkService*, and *User*. (These options will be described in detail later.) If the Account type is set to *User*, you can also supply values for the *Username* and *Password* properties to identify the account to use. (If you don't, you'll be prompted for this information when the service is installed by *InstallUtil*.)
Username	The name of the account the service should run as when the *Account* property is set to *User*.
Password	The password of the account the service should run as when the *Account* property is set to *User*.
HelpText	A text description of the requirements for any user account that executes the service.

The following code shows the parts of the *CakeServiceInstaller* constructor that relate to the *ServiceProcessInstaller* for the CakeService service:

```
private ServiceProcessInstaller processInstaller = null;
⋮
public CakeServiceInstaller()
{
   ⋮
   processInstaller = new  ServiceProcessInstaller();
   processInstaller.set_Account(ServiceAccount.LocalService);
   ⋮
   this.get_Installers().Add(processInstaller);
   ⋮
}
```

Selecting an Appropriate Security Account

The *Account* property of the *ServiceProcessInstaller* class determines security context and hence the privileges that are available to your service. (When a client uses a service, the code executed by the service runs using the security context specified for the service and does not impersonate the client.) It is important that you select the appropriate type of account for your service. If you select an ordinary user account and your service requires access to privileged system resources, the service will not execute correctly. However, it is also unwise—for security reasons—to run a service using an account that has too many privileges. For example, if you configure a service to run using an administrator account (or LocalSystem) and the service opens a command window (to execute a command file, for example), a user could abort the command file (by pressing Ctrl+C) and then have access to a command window that has Administrator privileges.

Each of the options in the *System.ServiceProcess.ServiceAccount* enumeration provides a different level of security.

- **LocalSystem** This is arguably the most powerful option (with the exception of certain user accounts). The LocalSystem account is a member of the Administrators group on the host computer, so it has access to the entire system. However, it does not have privileged network or domain access—it can use only those remote resources that permit anonymous access.
- **LocalService** This option causes the service to execute as the NT AUTHORITY\LocalService account. This account is available only on Windows XP and later. (InstallUtil cannot install the service if you use this option on Windows 2000.) The account has minimal privileges on the local machine by default—it can only access resources on the local machine that it has been granted access to or to which members of the Everyone and Authenticated Users groups have been granted access. It can use only the network resources that allow anonymous access.
- **NetworkService** This option causes the service to execute as the NT AUTHORITY\NetworkService account. This is also available only on Windows XP and later. Like LocalService, the NetworkService account has no local special privileges. The NetworkService account is typically used by services that require network access—it is configured to present the computer's credentials when it attempts to use a remote resource. As long as the computer has been granted access, the NetworkService account will be able to use the remote resource.
- **User** This option allows you to run the service in the security context of a specific user account. You supply the identity of the account

in the *Username* and *Password* properties of the *ServiceProcessInstaller* object. You can use any valid account, and the service will be able to access all the resources available to that account. This might not be wise—a user account can be disabled or removed, which will prevent the service from starting, or the account might be granted additional privileges (by being added to the Administrators group, for example). This can open a potential hole in your system security.

Adding a Service Description

If you examine a service using the Services console, you'll see that a service can have a text description. For some reason, neither the *ServiceBase* class nor the *ServiceInstaller* class actually provides the description as a property. The *System.ServiceProcess* namespace does contain the *ServiceProcessDescriptionAttribute* class, which looks promising at first glance. But unfortunately, it supplies a description for a service only when it is deployed as a component and used in a visual designer (such as the Windows Forms editor in Visual Studio .NET, when the description appears in the Properties window).

You can still set the description for a service, but you must insert it directly into the Windows Registry when the component is installed. The service description should be inserted in the Registry at the key *HKEY_LOCAL_MACHINE\System\CurrentControlSet\Services\<ServiceName>*, where *<ServiceName>* is the name of the service. You can add a text value labeled as *Description* to the service key. It would be inconvenient to expect an administrator to perform this task manually after the service has been installed, so you should instead override the *Install* method of the *Installer* class and perform the operation there. The *Install* method for the *CakeServiceInstaller* class is shown here:

```
import Microsoft.Win32.*;
⋮
public void Install(IDictionary stateSaver)
{
   super.Install(stateSaver);
   RegistryKey service = Registry.LocalMachine.OpenSubKey
      ("System").OpenSubKey("CurrentControlSet").OpenSubKey
      ("Services").OpenSubKey(serviceInstaller.get_ServiceName(), true);
      service.SetValue("Description",
      "Service that provides remoting access to the Cake Size Server");
}
```

Invoke the *Install* method of the parent class (which will cause the *Install* method of all the *Installer* objects in the *Installers* collection to be called) and add any other functionality you require. In this case, the *Install* method opens the key for the CakeService and sets the *Description* value. The *RegistryKey* and *Registry* classes are available in the *Microsoft.Win32* namespace.

Installing and Testing the Service

If you build the CakeService project (which comprises the *CakeService* and *CakeServiceInstaller* classes), the compiler will generate the assembly CakeService.exe. You can then execute InstallUtil to install the service as shown here:

```
C:\>InstallUtil CakeService.exe

Microsoft (R) .NET Framework Installation utility Version 1.0.3705.0
Copyright (C) Microsoft Corporation 1998-2001. All rights reserved.


Running a transacted installation.

Beginning the Install phase of the installation.
See the contents of the log file for the c:\temp\chapter 15\cakeservice\
bin\debug\cakeservice.exe assembly's progress.
The file is located at c:\temp\chapter 15\cakeservice\bin\debug\
cakeservice.InstallLog.
Installing assembly 'c:\temp\chapter 15\cakeservice\bin\debug\
cakeservice.exe'.
Affected parameters are:
   assemblypath = c:\temp\chapter 15\cakeservice\bin\debug\cakeservice.exe
   logfile = c:\temp\chapter 15\cakeservice\bin\debug\
cakeservice.InstallLog
Installing service Cake Service...
Service Cake Service has been successfully installed.
Creating EventLog source Cake Service in log Application...

The Install phase completed successfully, and the Commit phase is
beginning.
See the contents of the log file for the c:\temp\chapter 15\cakeservice\
bin\debug\cakeservice.exe assembly's progress.
The file is located at c:\temp\chapter 15\cakeservice\bin\debug\cakeservice.Ins
tallLog.
Committing assembly 'c:\temp\chapter 15\cakeservice\bin\debug\cakeservice.exe'.
Affected parameters are:
   assemblypath = c:\temp\chapter 15\cakeservice\bin\debug\cakeservice.exe
   logfile = c:\temp\chapter 15\cakeservice\bin\debug\
cakeservice.InstallLog

The Commit phase completed successfully.

The transacted install has completed.
```

A record of the installation progress will be written to the log files cakeservice.InstallLog and cakeservice.InstallState. The service will appear in the Services console (see Figure 15-3), and you can start and stop the service in the same way you would any other service.

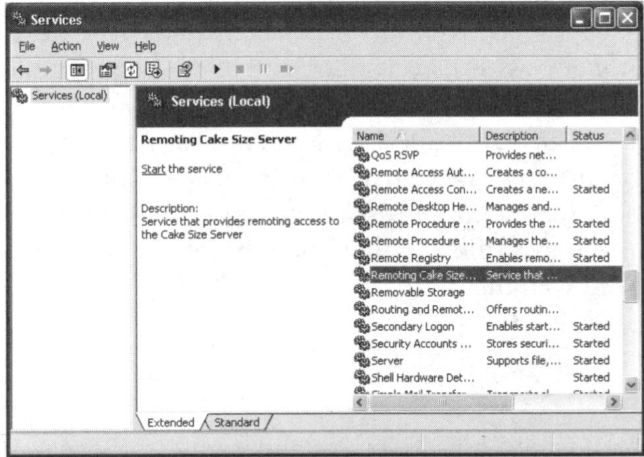

Figure 15-3 The Remoting Cake Size Server in the Services console

To test the service, start it and then execute the CakeClient program supplied in the CakeClient project. (This is a copy of the server-activated cake client program from Chapter 11.) The *main* method of the *CakeClient* class calls on the CakeService service to create a *CakeInfo* object, and then it invokes the *FeedsHowMany* method, passing details describing a 14-inch hexagonal fruit cake. If all is well, you should be informed that the cake will feed 31 people, as shown in Figure 15-4.

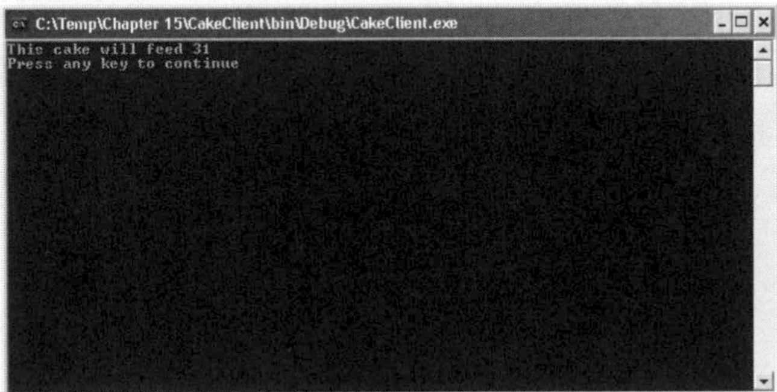

Figure 15-4 The output of the CakeClient program

Uninstalling a Service

You can uninstall a service using InstallUtil, specifying the */u* flag:

```
C:\>InstallUtil /u CakeService.exe
```

The InstallUtil program will call the *Uninstall* method of all classes in the specified assembly that are tagged with *RunInstallerAttribute*. The default *Uninstall* method of the *Installer* class is usually adequate and will arrange for the *Uninstall* method of all the installers held in the *Installers* property to be run. If you've overridden the *Install* method, you might also need to override *Uninstall* and undo any custom changes made during installation. In the case of the CakeService service, this is not necessary because the CakeService keys are automatically removed from the Registry when the service is uninstalled, taking the *Description* value with them.

Summary

In this chapter, you learned how to query and control services using the *ServiceController* class. You also learned how to create a new service application, taking the *ServiceBase* class as a framework and overriding methods, properties, and events as needed by your service. You saw how to install a service by creating a custom *Installer* class and populating its Installers property. Finally, you learned how to use the InstallUtil utility to install and uninstall a service through its custom installer class.

Part V

Building Applications for the Web

16

ASP.NET: A Better ASP

As noted in Chapter 1, the dominant application model in use today is a multi-tiered application with a Web-based interface. This model enjoys widespread acceptance in both the Microsoft .NET and Java 2 Enterprise Edition (J2EE) camps. Any framework that provides a foundation for such development must offer good support for developers of the Web-facing parts of the application. At the very least, it must provide abstractions of the low-level interaction between a client and a Web server.

Server-side Web components such as Microsoft Active Server Pages (ASP) running under Microsoft Windows and Java servlets in J2EE provide life-cycle management and object-based interfaces for interacting with the underlying HTTP messages being sent and received. These server-side frameworks also provide easy access to application functionality such as data access, security services, and other custom components written for the application.

However, the expectations surrounding Web-oriented applications are constantly increasing. For example, Web developers are expected to produce rich and powerful browser-based applications in a shorter and shorter time. This means that they need a much more standard infrastructure to help speed up the development of Web-based user interfaces. Another expectation is that an application's functionality should be easily adaptable to new channels and new types of client application and hardware. The clients might include specialist browsers running on handheld, mobile devices as well as Web services that allow other applications to exploit the functionality of your application.

The ASP.NET framework provides support for Web-oriented development in this demanding environment. ASP.NET supports two main types of applications: Web Forms applications, which produce HTML to be rendered in a browser, and Web service applications, which exchange data in XML format.

This chapter describes how the ASP.NET model works and explains the structure of a typical ASP.NET application. We'll concentrate on Web Forms applications and the delivery of content to a Web browser. Web service applications under ASP.NET will be covered in the next two chapters. In examining Web Forms, we'll look at essential aspects of ASP.NET that provide a good foundation for both Web Forms and Web services, such as the ASP.NET life cycle, application-level code, application configuration, and session management. All of the code shown in this chapter is from sample files that are part of the FourthCoffee and ErrorHandling sample projects.

Introducing ASP.NET

The creation of Web-based interfaces and their associated functionality accounts for a major part of most application development. One reason that HTML became so popular was its simplicity—anyone with a text editor could create their own Web pages. HTML works fine for static Web content, but in an application that will use Web pages for its user interface, the Web pages must interact with the application functionality and their content must change to display application data to the user. Such Web pages must contain some executable content to interact with the main application code, in addition to fixed HTML. Few people can create such Web pages using just a text editor—and even fewer would choose to do so.

A Web-based application runs in a specific context:

- The client interacts with the server using a request-response protocol.
- The client typically sends request information in text format, such as name/value pairs or tagged data.
- The server typically sends response information in text format, such as tagged data.

This description is intentionally generic—the Web means different things to different people. However, for most people the Web is synonymous with browser-based applications and content.

Browser-Based Web Applications

This chapter focuses on developing systems in which the client is assumed to be a Web browser. (The next two chapters will cover Web services, in which client applications can be almost any type of executable program.)

The context in which a browser-based application operates has the following characteristics:

- The client sends HTTP requests to the server. The HTTP request header contains some standard information that might be of use to the application developer. Other information from the client can be encoded as part of the URL used to access the server component (using HTTP *GET* requests), or it can be sent in the body of the request (using HTTP *POST* requests).
- The server processes the client request and generates output consisting mainly of HTML. Information can also be sent by embedding some XML in the output and by setting certain fields in the HTTP response header.

Although these two characteristics are required, many variables remain. The browser might be Microsoft Internet Explorer, Netscape Navigator, or Opera, for example. Even if your application is targeted at an intranet environment in which only Internet Explorer is used, you must still address the issue of handling the different levels of functionality available in different versions. As a Web application developer, you must typically make a decision about reach versus richness. In other words, should you develop a very functional application that can run only in Internet Explorer 5.5 and later, or should you create an application with a simpler interface and less functionality that can run on almost any browser? It's difficult to create an application that can adapt to the type of client and provide an appropriate level of richness. However, as you'll see, ASP.NET Web controls can help an application adapt to different clients and still deliver a rich user interface.

The ASP.NET Environment

An ASP.NET application, like its ASP predecessor, runs using Microsoft Internet Information Services (IIS). The files that make up an ASP.NET application reside in a virtual directory configured under IIS. An example of such a virtual directory is *http://www.fourthcoffee.com/FourthCoffee*. Typically, this directory is mapped to a folder under the Inetpub\wwwroot folder. Requests for files that reside below the virtual directory are handled by IIS.

IIS can implement some of the security required by the application (as discussed later) and can deliver requested HTML and media files to the client. IIS also maintains a list of filename extensions that are associated with particular server-side functionality. You can view these settings by starting the Internet Information Services management snap-in. In Control Panel, select Performance and Maintenance. In the pane that appears, select Administrative Tools and double-click on Internet Information Services. Open the entry for your computer (or the server on which you'll deploy your Web applications) and open the Web Sites folder. Right-click Default Web Site and choose Properties from the shortcut menu to display the Default Web Site Properties dialog box. Click on the Home Directory tab, and under Application Settings click the Configuration button.

The resulting Application Configuration dialog box is shown in Figure 16-1. Here you specify how files with different extensions are mapped to associated server-side functionality. The main functionality of ASP.NET Web applications is contained in ASP.NET pages, which have an .aspx filename extension. If you examine the line in the Application Mappings table for ASPX files, you'll see that these files are mapped to \Windows\Microsoft.NET\Framework\.NET-Version\aspnet_isapi.dll. This means that when a client requests an ASPX file, the request is delegated to the ASP.NET runtime (found in aspnet_isapi.dll), which executes the server-side functionality contained in such files.

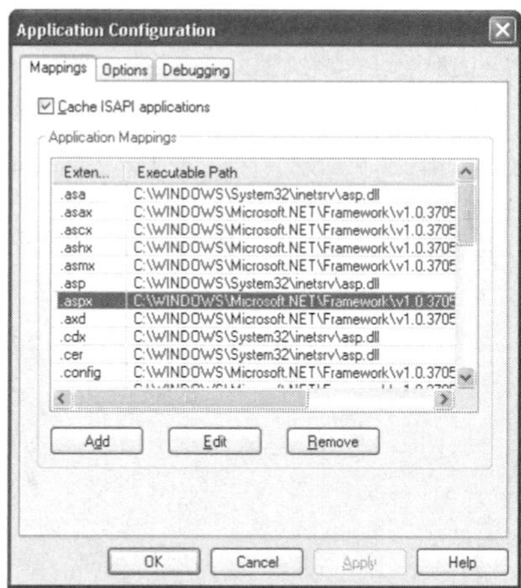

Figure 16-1 The IIS Application Configuration dialog box, which shows the mapping of file types to server-side functionality

So far, so good. However, this is not really any different from the way an ASP application works. ASP.NET gets its additional power from hosting the .NET common language runtime. Consequently, any ASP.NET page has access to the features and functionality of the .NET Framework. For example

- In ASP, developers often use COM to access system functionality. In ASP.NET, developers have seamless access to all of the functionality in the .NET Framework class libraries.

- In ASP, server-side code can be developed only in a limited number of scripting languages. In ASP.NET, server-side code can be developed in any language that supports .NET. Different parts of an ASP.NET application can use different languages if required.
- The code in an ASP page is interpreted by scripting engines every time the page is accessed. Under ASP.NET, the page and its associated code are converted into one executable assembly. This assembly is cached and used each time the page is accessed, which speeds up the application execution by three to five times.

Fortunately, such benefits come without ASP developers having to sacrifice the model they're familiar with.

The Basic ASP.NET Programming Model

The basic ASP.NET programming model is essentially the same as that of ASP. The URL of the client request identifies a particular ASP.NET page, the functionality on the page is run, and any output generated is delivered back to the client. The format of an ASP.NET page will look familiar to an ASP developer. Consider the code shown in Welcome.aspx, which is provided as a sample file in the FourthCoffee solution.

Welcome.aspx

```
<%@ Page language="VJ#" %>
<HTML>
<%
System.String ourName = "Fourth Coffee";
System.String optimalBrowser = "IE";
System.String thisBrowserName = get_Request().get_Browser().get_Browser();
%>
   <body>
      <P align="center"><FONT size="5"><STRONG>Welcome to <%= ourName %>
         </STRONG></FONT></P>
      <%
         if (thisBrowserName.Equals(optimalBrowser))
         {
      %>
         <P><% get_Response().Write(ourName); %> are happy to welcome users
             of Internet Explorer.</P>
      <%
         }
         else
         {
      %>
```

```
            <P>By employing ASP.NET Web controls,
                <% get_Response().Write(ourName); %> can also easily welcome
                users of <%= thisBrowserName %> browsers.</P>
        <%
            }
        %>
    </body>
</HTML>
```

As you can see, you can embed code within the HTML contained in an ASP.NET page by using code render blocks that start with <% and end with %>. These blocks will be familiar to ASP developers, as will the ability to evaluate expressions using the syntax <%= *expression* %>. The code in Welcome.aspx uses code render blocks to wrap J# code around HTML statements. The *if* statement checks to see what browser the user is running and displays a message based on that browser, as shown in Figure 16-2.

Figure 16-2 You can embed J# code in an ASPX page to perform many tasks, including determining which browser a user is running.

The page shows several features of ASP.NET:

- The *Page* directive <%@ *Page* %> defines attributes relating to this ASP.NET page. The only attribute defined for this page is *language*, which indicates that the default language for code on this page is "VJ#" (note that it is not just "J#", which will not be recognized). This will also be reasonably familiar to ASP developers—ASP directives are defined in a single delimiting block at the start of the page. We'll look at other directives and attributes later.

- Code render blocks are used to embed code within static HTML. The HTML sent back to the client will depend on the result of the *if* statement surrounding it. Variables can be declared in the code, and such variables obey the standard scoping rules for their language—in this case J#. By default, a variable declared inside a code render block is scoped to the page (that is, it is visible in all code render blocks on that page only). If a variable is declared inside a code block delimited by parentheses—{}—then this variable is visible only to code inside these parentheses.
- Certain functionality is available automatically to the developer. As you'll see later, each ASP.NET page is actually an instance of a subclass of *System.Web.UI.Page*. This class exposes properties that represent abstractions of the underlying HTTP functionality. For example, the information sent by the client can be accessed through the *Request* property, which is an instance of *System.Web.HttpRequest*. In Welcome.aspx, this object is retrieved using the *get_Request* method. (Remember that an unqualified method is implicitly invoked on *this*.) The *HttpRequest* instance has a *Browser* property that is an instance of *System.Web.HttpBrowserCapabilities*. You can retrieve the name of the client browser from the *HttpBrowserCapabilities* instance by using the *get_Browser* property accessor method.
- You can generate dynamic output from code in several ways. One way is to use a code render evaluation block, delimited by <%= %>, to evaluate the J# code within the block. The result of this evaluation is placed in the output stream in place of the code render evaluation block. Alternatively, you can use the *Write* method of the current *System.Web.HttpResponse* instance to output any text. The current *HttpResponse* is available through the *Response* property of the current page. Both of these output mechanisms are used in Welcome.aspx.

Just to prove that there's nothing up our sleeves, you can see the result of running the page in another browser in Figure 16-3.

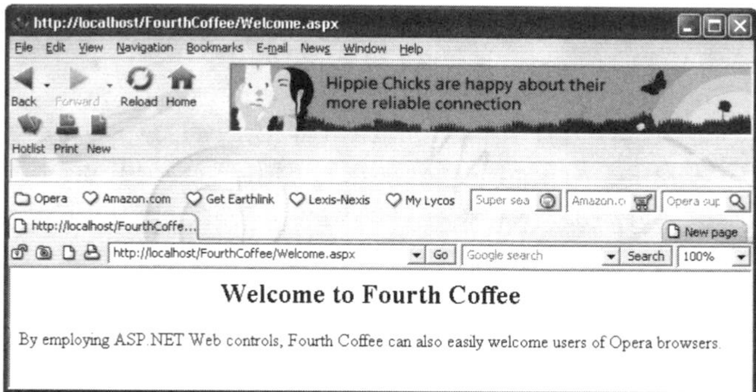

Figure 16-3 The server-side J# code can generate different output for different types of client Web browser.

One difference between ASP.NET and ASP is that in ASP.NET you can no longer define functions or subroutines in code render blocks. Instead, you must use method declarations enclosed in *script* tags:

```
<script runat="server">
   System.Web.HttpBrowserCapabilities thisBrowser;
   System.String thisBrowserName;

   private void SetBrowserInfo(System.Web.HttpRequest req)
   {
      thisBrowser = req.get_Browser();
      thisBrowserName = thisBrowser.get_Browser();
   }
</script>
```

It's important to remember the *runat="server"* attribute—otherwise, the code will be interpreted as client-side script and you'll get errors when the page is processed. Also note that the *script* tag is not a direct replacement for code render blocks. You cannot use it to delimit inline code—you can use it only to declare functions and variables. An example of the use of the *<script>* tag is provided in the Welcome2.aspx sample file.

By default, the language for code in a script element is assumed to be that defined in the *<%@ Page %>* directive. If you haven't defined a page-wide language, the application default will be used. Each Web application will have a default language defined in the *compilation* element of its Web.config file:

```
<configuration>
  <system.web>
    <compilation
        defaultLanguage="VJ#"
        debug="true"
```

```
    />
    ⋮
  </system.web>
</configuration>
```

This default definition is overridden by a page-level language declaration. All code in code render blocks must be written in the language defined either by the *language* attribute of the *<%@ Page %>* directive or the Web.config *compilation* element. We'll look at the syntax and content of the Web.config file in more detail later. The sample file Welcome3.aspx uses the *<%@Page %>* directive to override the default language defined in Web.config (J#) and use Visual Basic .NET instead.

If you haven't set the language for the page, you can override the application-level default language using the *language* attribute of the *script* element:

```
<script runat="server" language="C#">
  ⋮
</script>
```

Be careful with this feature: You can use only one language per page, so if you declare the language in multiple places, the declarations must match. If you try running the sample file Welcome4.aspx, which contains a mixture of J# and Visual Basic .NET code, you'll get a compilation error.

You might wonder why the default language is defined in an element called *compilation*. There's a good reason for this. As mentioned earlier, when an ASPX page is first accessed, the text and code are converted into a new class that will contain any code defined in the ASPX page along with code commands to output the static HTML content at the appropriate place. This new class is then compiled into MSIL and executed. The precise mechanism is described later in the chapter.

To do any real work in your Web application, you must access the .NET Framework or classes that you've written yourself or obtained from third parties. To use a class in your page, you can specify its fully qualified name:

```
<% System.Xml.XmlDocument doc = new System.Xml.XmlDocument(); %>
```

However, this can soon become tiresome, so you can import the whole namespace (as you can in J#) by using the *<%@ Import %>* directive:

```
<%@ Import namespace="System.Xml" %>
⋮
<% XmlDocument doc = new XmlDocument(); %>
```

You can see this example of importing a namespace in the sample file Welcome2.aspx. By default, the following namespaces are imported into an ASP.NET page:

- System
- System.Collections
- System.Collections.Specialized
- System.Configuration
- System.IO
- System.Text
- System.Text.RegularExpressions
- System.Web
- System.Web.Caching
- System.Web.Security
- System.Web.SessionState
- System.Web.UI
- System.Web.UI.HtmlControls
- System.Web.UI.WebControls

You must ensure that the assemblies containing the classes you're importing are available to the page both at compile time and run time. If you place the assemblies in the bin directory under the Web application's virtual directory, they'll be automatically linked to the application. You must link any other assemblies explicitly by using the *<%@ Assembly %>* directive to link the assembly to the current page.

HTML Forms and ASP Forms

HTML forms are at the heart of any Web-based application—they provide the standard way of gathering input from users. Figure 16-4 shows a simple HTML form. This form is part of an online cake ordering service and allows the user to determine how many people a cake of a certain size with a particular type of filling will serve.

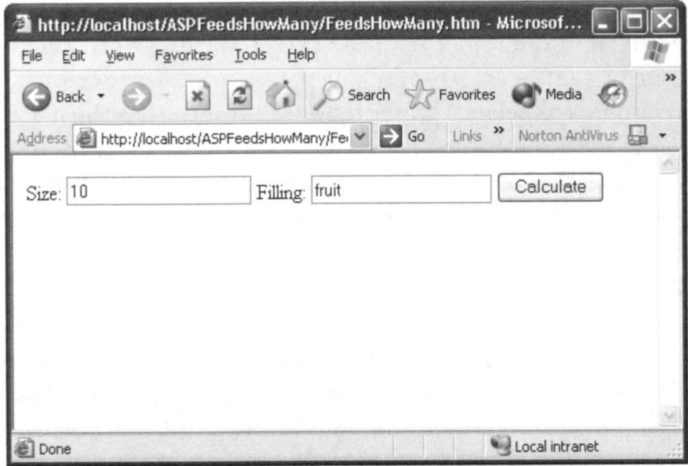

Figure 16-4 A simple HTML form

The HTML required to generate this form is fairly simple; it is shown in the FeedsHowMany.htm sample file listed below. As you can see, the form consists of three user input controls: two text boxes and a Submit button. These controls allow the user to specify a cake size and a type of filling. When the user clicks the Calculate button, the information in the two text boxes is sent to the URL specified by the *action* attribute. The *method* attribute defines whether the form data is appended to the URL (*method="get"*) or sent in the body of the HTTP request (*method="post"*). In this case, the action is just an example and is set to *someURL*, which will cause an error if you click the submit button.

FeedsHowMany.htm

```
<HTML>
   <BODY>
      <form method="post" action="someURL">
         Size: <input type="text" name="size">
         Filling: <input type="text" name="filling">
         <input type="submit" value="Calculate">
      </form>
   </BODY>
</HTML>
```

In the pre-ASP environment, this form would have been paired with some server-side functionality, such as a CGI script written in Perl, an ISAPI DLL, or a Java servlet. This is not an ideal style of development because the resulting application will consist of disparate components that must be kept in sync. Also, the server-side programming model and languages might be quite different from those used for the client development.

ASP and the equivalent JavaServer Pages (JSP) introduced a simpler model of server-side development in which the HTML for the Web page can be combined with script that is interpreted on the server. The script has access to server-side resources as well as any form data posted from the client, and it can use these resources and information to generate HTML dynamically as the page is delivered back to the client. This allows the static HTML of the page and the dynamic processing to be kept together, and it provides a more consistent development environment.

An ASP version of the entry form for cake information is shown in the listing of the FeedsHowMany.asp sample file. In this version, the page contains a *calculate* function written in JScript that is run on the server side to determine the number of people the cake will serve. (This calculation can also be written in JavaScript running on the client side, but because this information is a closely guarded secret, precise details of the calculation should not be sent to the client!)

FeedsHowMany.asp

```
<%@ Language=JScript %>
<HTML>
   <BODY>
      <form method="post" action="FeedsHowMany.asp">
         Size: <input type="text" name="size">
         Filling: <input type="text" name="filling">
         <input type="submit" value="Calculate"">
         <p>This will feed <% calculate() %> people</p>
      </form>
   </BODY>
</HTML>
<script language="jscript" runat="server">
function calculate()
{
   var filling = Request.Form("filling")();
   var size = Request.Form("size")();
   var numConsumers = 0;

   if (filling != null && filling != "" && size != null && size != "")
   {
      fruitFilling = (filling == "fruit") ? true : false;

      munchSizeFactor = (fruitFilling ? 3 : 1);

      numConsumers = size * munchSizeFactor;
   }

   Response.Write(numConsumers);
```

```
}

</script>
```

When the ASP page is accessed, it generates HTML that produces the form shown earlier in Figure 16-4. When the user fills out the form and clicks the Calculate button, the information is posted back to the URL of the ASP as defined by the form's *action* attribute. This causes the page to be processed again, but this time code in the ASP page can access the values submitted by the user through the intrinsic ASP *Request* object.

As part of the page processing, the *calculate* function is called. This function retrieves the size of cake and type of filling from the form and performs the calculation. Note that the *calculate* function is tagged as *runat="server"*, which indicates that it is a server-side script and that the function uses server-side objects made available by the ASP runtime, such as the intrinsic *Request* object. After the ASP has been processed, another version of the page is generated that contains the form, the message below it, and the correct number of cake eaters. This new page is then sent back to the client.

The result of asking how many people a 10-inch fruit cake will feed is shown in Figure 16-5.

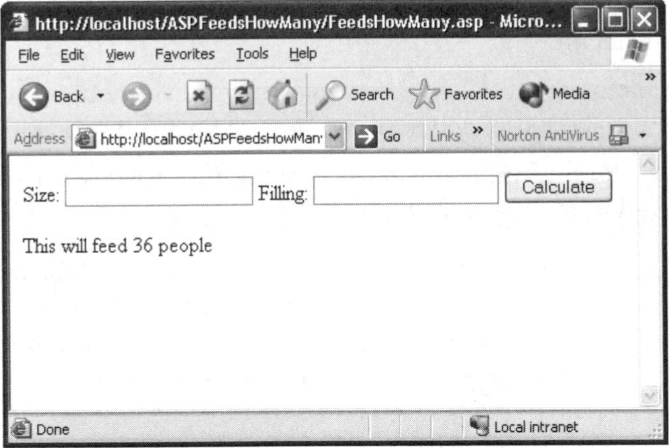

Figure 16-5 An ASP page can change what is displayed based on user input, such as the size and filling of a cake.

As you can see, the correct result is displayed, but the data entered into the form has been lost. To rectify this, you could add more code to the ASP page that would set the *value* attributes of the text boxes to match those sent by the client every time the form is generated. However, this would add to the complexity of the ASP page. As the application became more complex, other functionality would be needed, such as different actions to be performed based on different button clicks. All of this would require more code in the ASP to handle the different requirements. This approach has several problems:

- You end up continually reinventing the wheel because many people have already implemented the type of function that you want to perform. A lot of developer time is spent fiddling with code that processes the HTTP request and less time is spent writing business-oriented code.
- The code in the page can become quite complex because you must keep track of when form submissions are made and smooth the transition between client and server. An example of this is the need to repopulate the text fields in a form every time the page is refreshed.
- You have to connect parts of the application manually. For example, if a button click is to call a server-side function, you must hook up this client-side event to the server-side code yourself.

As you can see, ASP development is not without its problems. The main problems with ASP-based applications are as follows:

- The mixed pages of script and HTML can become complex and difficult to maintain.
- The programming model is somewhat awkward and requires considerable specialized knowledge of the underlying Web protocols.
- ASP pages tend to run relatively slowly because their script is interpreted every time they're called.

Trying to solve these problems using existing technologies can lead to other problems. For example, you could migrate large amounts of server-side script code into COM components that could be called from the ASP page. This would improve the maintainability of the ASP page, but you'd have a different maintenance headache because the server-side functionality would be separate from the ASP page. This brings us back to the earlier situation in which a static HTML page containing a form is separate from the Perl page that provides its functionality. The parts of the application begin to drift apart again.

What you need is an approach that provides one logical unit for the code and HTML that form this part of the application while also providing a simple and familiar development model. ASP.NET Web Forms provide this functionality.

ASP.NET Web Forms

To see how Web Forms work, let's create an ASP.NET version of the HTML form you saw earlier. To create an ASP.NET Web Form, you select the ASP.NET Web Application template from the Visual J# Projects in the New Project dialog box, as shown in Figure 16-6.

The ASP.NET application will need to run under the ASP.NET runtime, which in turn will need the facilities of a Web server such as that provided by IIS. Therefore, the application files (including the Visual Studio .NET project files) will be created in a new virtual directory under IIS. The name of the directory will be the name of the project, and you can define which server you want to create the directory on. As you create the ASP.NET project, Visual Studio .NET will contact the given server and arrange for an appropriate virtual directory to be created. This virtual directory will be set up with the correct IIS settings to allow the executable parts of the Web application to run.

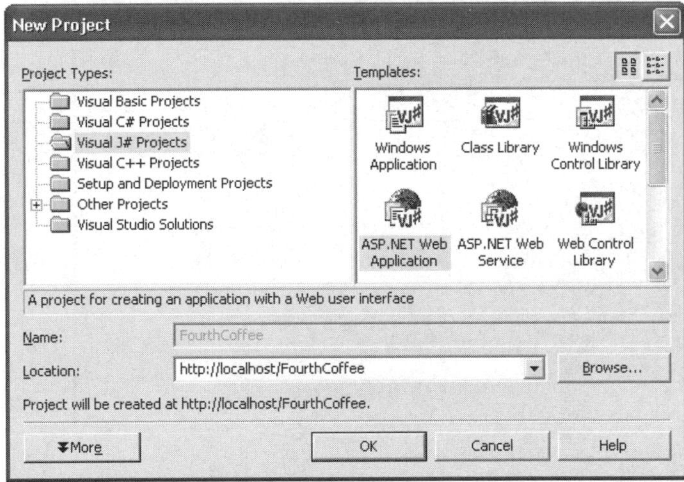

Figure 16-6 Selecting an ASP.NET Web application in the Visual Studio .NET New Project dialog box

As with any Web-based project in Visual Studio .NET, this application will be created on a Web server at the given URL. By default, the project will already contain a Web Form called *WebForm1*. You can rename this Web Form or delete it and then add a new Web Form to the project with the required name.

Note As you'll soon see, a Web Form consists of two parts: an ASPX file containing HTML and controls, and an associated JSL file containing the J# code. If you choose to rename WebForm1.aspx under Visual Studio .NET, this will also rename the associated WebForm1.aspx.jsl file. But be aware that the class name in the JSL file will remain as *WebForm1* unless you explicitly change it. You might also need to change the Start Page defined within the Debugging Configuration Properties of the project to ensure that it points to your new file.

The resulting project is shown in Figure 16-7. This figure also shows the Toolbox containing controls that you can use to populate the Web Form.

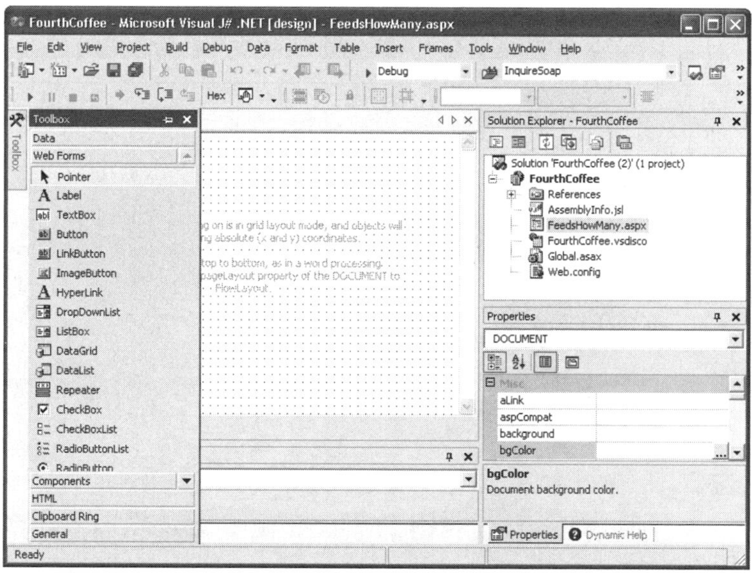

Figure 16-7 You can drag controls from the Toolbox onto the design view of an ASP.NET Web application.

To re-create the form you saw in FeedsHowMany.htm, you can use two *TextBox* controls, two *Label* controls, and a *Button* control. (Be sure to select these from the Web Forms list in the Toolbox.) You'll end up with something similar to Figure 16-8.

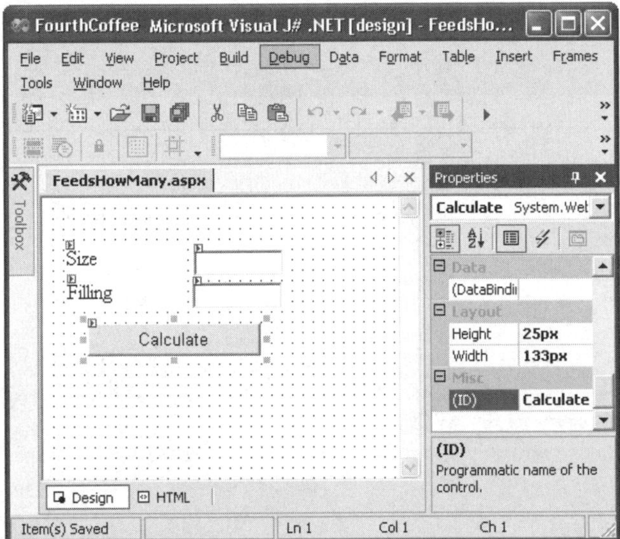

Figure 16-8 The basic cake consumer form as an ASP.NET Web Form

At this stage, it's worth looking at what was produced before we proceed further. The HTML generated as part of this Web Form is shown in FeedsHowMany.aspx (version 1). This Web Form is an early snapshot of code that will evolve into the FeedsHowMany.aspx page provided as a sample file in the FourthCoffee project. You should note two things about this Web page:

- The contents of the form have changed. The form now uses server-side controls instead of HTML tags.
- There is no explicit server-side code in this form except for the *Page* directive at the top of the page.

We'll examine both of these mysteries in turn.

FeedsHowMany.aspx (version 1)

```
<%@ Page language="VJ#" Codebehind="FeedsHowMany.aspx.jsl"
   AutoEventWireup="false" Inherits="FourthCoffee.FeedsHowMany" %>
<!DOCTYPE HTML PUBLIC "-//W3C//DTD HTML 4.0 Transitional//EN" >
<HTML>
   <HEAD>
      <meta name="GENERATOR" Content="Microsoft Visual Studio 7.0">
      <meta name="CODE_LANGUAGE" Content="VJ#">
      <meta name="vs_defaultClientScript"
       content="JavaScript (ECMAScript)">
      <meta name="vs_targetSchema"
       content="http://schemas.microsoft.com/intellisense/ie5">
```

```
    </HEAD>
    <body MS_POSITIONING="GridLayout">
        <form id="FeedsHowMany" method="post" runat="server">
            <asp:TextBox id="Size" style="Z-INDEX: 101; LEFT: 117px;
             POSITION: absolute; TOP: 40px" runat="server" Width="69px"
             Height="20px"></asp:TextBox>
            <asp:TextBox id="Filling" style="Z-INDEX: 104; LEFT: 116px;
             POSITION: absolute; TOP: 65px" runat="server" Width="69px"
             Height="20px"></asp:TextBox>
            <asp:Label id="Label2" style="Z-INDEX: 103; LEFT: 19px;
             POSITION: absolute; TOP: 63px" runat="server" Width="86px"
             Height="25px">Filling</asp:Label>
            <asp:Label id="Label1" style="Z-INDEX: 102; LEFT: 18px;
             POSITION: absolute; TOP: 37px" runat="server" Width="86px"
             Height="25px">Size</asp:Label>
            <asp:Button id="Calculate" style="Z-INDEX: 105; LEFT: 35px;
             POSITION: absolute; TOP: 97px" runat="server" Width="133px"
             Height="25px" Text="Calculate"></asp:Button>
        </form>
    </body>
</HTML>
```

The Server-Side Controls

Instead of traditional HTML *<INPUT>* tags, the text boxes and button for the form are represented by *<asp:TextBox>* and *<asp:Button>* tags, respectively. The text labels also have ASP tags (*<asp:Label>*) rather than ordinary HTML. All of these tags have the attribute *runat="server"* to indicate that they're processed on the server. Indeed, the whole form is labeled as *runat="server"*. Controls marked in this way are called *server-side controls*. The .NET Framework provides a variety of server-side controls, which are defined in the *System.Web.UI.WebControls* namespace.

A server-side control provides an ASP.NET developer with the same type of functionality as the equivalent control you'd use when building a Windows-based application, including design-time functionality. In Visual Studio .NET, you can drag and drop server-side Web controls onto a Web Form, change their properties, and hook up events just as you would if the controls were controls housed in a Windows Form. Later, you'll see how this simplifies event handling and interaction with the user.

One thing to note about server-side controls is that they do not require any special libraries installed on the client. A server-side control is responsible for representing itself in the client browser by generating standard HTML (and possibly script code) that can be downloaded to the client and rendered there. For example, consider what happens when a client browser accesses the Feeds-

HowMany.aspx page. The actual HTML sent to the client is shown in FeedsHowMany.htm (version 1 client side). As you can see, the server-side *TextBox*, *Label*, and *Buttons* controls have presented themselves as standard HTML *<INPUT>* and *<SPAN>* tags, and there are no *runat="server"* attributes anywhere to be seen. The server-side controls detect the client browser capabilities and generate output appropriate to that browser (in this case, Internet Explorer 6). This representation can be HTML 3.2 for a "down-level" browser or Dynamic HTML for Internet Explorer 5.5 or later.

The browser detection and adaptation of the server-side controls offers a great benefit. It means that you don't have to maintain multiple versions of your page for different browsers, nor do you have to create a "lowest common denominator" page that can be represented in all browsers.

FeedsHowMany.htm (version 1 client side)

```
<!DOCTYPE HTML PUBLIC "-//W3C//DTD HTML 4.0 Transitional//EN" >
<HTML>
   <HEAD>
      <meta name="GENERATOR" Content="Microsoft Visual Studio 7.0">
      <meta name="CODE_LANGUAGE" Content="VJ#">
      <meta name="vs_defaultClientScript"
       content="JavaScript (ECMAScript)">
      <meta name="vs_targetSchema"
       content="http://schemas.microsoft.com/intellisense/ie5">
   </HEAD>
   <body MS_POSITIONING="GridLayout">
      <form name="FeedsHowMany" method="post" action="FeedsHowMany.aspx"
       id="FeedsHowMany">
         <input type="hidden" name="__VIEWSTATE"
          value="dDwtMTE2MDIxNDc1NTs7PrwNYdg2U4LNokc3ysIeaWJtZ2/B" />

         <input name="Size" type="text" id="Size"
          style="height:20px;width:69px;Z-INDEX: 101; LEFT: 117px;
          POSITION: absolute; TOP: 40px" />
         <input name="Filling" type="text" id="Filling"
          style="height:20px;width:69px;Z-INDEX: 104; LEFT: 116px;
          POSITION: absolute; TOP: 65px" />
         <span id="Label2" style="height:25px;width:86px;Z-INDEX: 103;
          LEFT: 19px; POSITION: absolute; TOP: 63px">Filling</span>
         <span id="Label1" style="height:25px;width:86px;Z-INDEX: 102;
          LEFT: 18px; POSITION: absolute; TOP: 37px">Size</span>
         <input type="submit" name="Calculate" value="Calculate"
          id="Calculate" style="height:25px;width:133px;Z-INDEX: 105;
          LEFT: 35px; POSITION: absolute; TOP: 97px" />
      </form>
```

```
   </body>
</HTML>
```

The Code Behind the Page

The other aspect of the Web Form is the code to be run on the server. In this case, the server-side code associated with the Web Form is held in a separate file. The name and contents of this file are defined in the <%@ *Page* %> directive in the ASPX page:

```
<%@ Page language="VJ#" Codebehind="FeedsHowMany.aspx.jsl"
 AutoEventWireup="false" Inherits="FourthCoffee.FeedsHowMany" %>
```

The notable parts of this directive are the *language* attribute, which specifies that the code for the page is written in Visual J# (VJ#), and the *Codebehind* attribute, which indicates an associated JSL file that contains all of the code used in this page. The code in the J# file is referred to as the *code behind the page*, or simply the *code-behind*. The contents of this code-behind file are shown in FeedsHowMany.aspx.jsl (version 1). This file contains a standard J# class that inherits from a Web Forms–specific superclass, *System.Web.UI.Page*, which represents the environment and events required by an ASP.NET page. All of the controls that were added in the design view are represented in the J# class as protected member variables:

```
protected System.Web.UI.WebControls.TextBox Size;
protected System.Web.UI.WebControls.Label Label1;
protected System.Web.UI.WebControls.Label Label2;
protected System.Web.UI.WebControls.Button Calculate;
protected System.Web.UI.WebControls.TextBox Filling;
```

An event handler method, *Page_Load*, is provided for the page load event. You can use this to initialize any dynamic parts of the page. This method is specified as a handler for the *Load* event for this *Page* in the *InitializeComponent* method:

```
private void InitializeComponent()
{
   this.add_Load( new System.EventHandler(this.Page_Load) );
}
```

Other events that can be handled include initialization, rendering, and error conditions.

FeedsHowMany.aspx.jsl (version 1)

```
package FourthCoffee;

import System.Collections.*;
import System.ComponentModel.*;
import System.Data.*;
import System.Drawing.*;
import System.Web.*;
import System.Web.SessionState.*;
import System.Web.UI.*;
import System.Web.UI.WebControls.*;
import System.Web.UI.HtmlControls.*;

/**
 * Summary description for FeedsHowMany.
 */
public class FeedsHowMany extends System.Web.UI.Page
{
   protected System.Web.UI.WebControls.TextBox Size;
   protected System.Web.UI.WebControls.Label Label1;
   protected System.Web.UI.WebControls.Label Label2;
   protected System.Web.UI.WebControls.Button Calculate;
   protected System.Web.UI.WebControls.TextBox Filling;

   private void Page_Load(System.Object sender, System.EventArgs e)
   {
      // Put user code to initialize the page here
   }

   protected void OnInit(System.EventArgs e)
   {
      //
      // CODEGEN: This call is required by the ASP.NET Web Form Designer.
      // Do not remove this.
      //
      InitializeComponent();
      super.OnInit(e);
   }

   #region Web Form Designer generated code
   /**
    * Required method for Designer support - do not modify
    * the contents of this method with the code editor.
    */
   private void InitializeComponent()
   {
      this.add_Load( new System.EventHandler(this.Page_Load) );
```

```
    }
    #endregion
}
```

By default, Visual Studio .NET will create an assembly containing your code-behind classes and will store it in the bin directory below your Web application's directory. The *Inherits* attribute of the <%@ *Page* %> directive indicates the name of the class that contains the code-behind for this ASPX file. The class must inherit from the *System.Web.UI.Page* class, as shown in FeedsHowMany.aspx.jsl (version 1). When the runtime needs to load this class, it will search initially for an assembly in the *bin* directory. ASP.NET does *not* follow the default probing rules listed in Chapter 2, so if it does not find the required class in the bin directory, it will search the Global Assembly Cache (GAC) before giving up. If you want to include additional locations in which to search for assemblies, you must add this to your Web.config file using a *probing* element.

The following example searches for assemblies in the bin and myAssemblies directories under the virtual directory:

```
<configuration>
   <runtime>
      <assemblyBinding xmlns="urn:schemas-microsoft-com:asm.v1">
         <probing privatePath="bin;myAssemblies"/>
      </assemblyBinding>
   </runtime>
   ⋮
</configuration>
```

If you're using an alternative search path, you'll also need to specify the name of any assembly you want to include. One option is to use the <%@ *Assembly* %> directive in the appropriate page:

```
<%@ Assembly Name="FourthCoffee" %>
```

Alternatively, you can link it into the whole application using the *assemblies* element in the Web.config file:

```
    <compilation
        defaultLanguage="VJ#"
        debug="true">
        <assemblies>
         <add assembly="FourthCoffee"/>
      </assemblies>
    </compilation>
```

When an ASPX page is first accessed, its code-behind is located. The ASP.NET runtime then combines the class from the code-behind with the contents of the ASPX file to create a new J# class that inherits from the code-behind class. All of the text-based content of the ASPX page is represented in J# code, which includes the generation of the plain HTML text and tags from the ASPX file. As a result, the whole page becomes a single J# class that can be compiled into Microsoft Intermediate Language (MSIL) and stored in a new assembly. This sequence of events is shown in Figure 16-9. This new class and assembly are used by the ASP.NET runtime to service subsequent requests for the page. This eliminates the need to interpret script or even open extra files when servicing a client request.

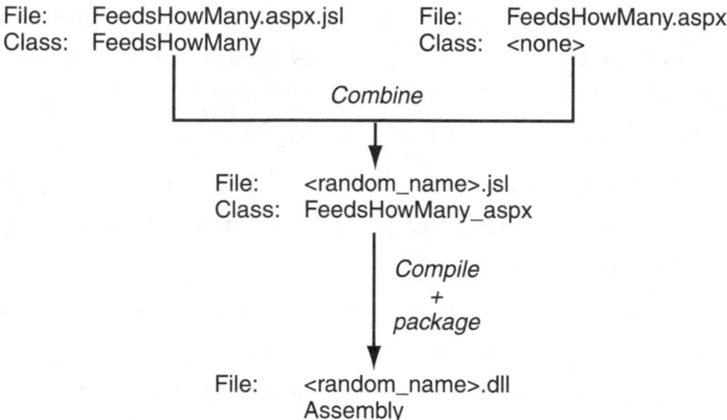

Figure 16-9 Combining parts of a Web Form to create an ASP.NET class to service client requests

The files for the generated class and its assembly are stored in the folder \Windows\Microsoft.NET\Framework\.NETVersion\Temporary ASP.NET Files. If you examine this folder, you should find a subfolder with the same name as the folder in which your ASP.NET application resides. If the ASP.NET runtime detects any change in the ASPX files in your application or in their code-behind assembly, it will regenerate the appropriate derived class and recompile it to create a new assembly. All of this happens without you having to do anything!

> **Caution** Be careful if you decide to rely on automatic compilation. By default, the dependency is on the ASPX file itself and the assembly in which the code-behind resides rather than the source file (the JSL file). This means that changes to the source file will not trigger a recompilation of the assembly by the ASP.NET runtime. To make the automatic compilation dependent on the source file, you must set the *Src* attribute in the *<%@ Page %>* directive to point to the source file.

This changes the dependency target and means that both the original assembly and the derived assembly will be regenerated if the source file changes.

At this stage, some readers who have an ASP background (and even some who don't) might be wondering what benefit all this offers. Well, the answer is simple:

- Separating the code and the HTML makes the application more maintainable. The code can be maintained by programmers and the HTML by Web designers, without too many worries about interfering with each other's work. However, the code and the HTML still form one logical unit for development and deployment.
- The compilation and caching model considerably improves the performance of ASP.NET pages compared to equivalent ASP pages that are interpreted.
- The use of server-side controls simplifies the creation of sophisticated user interfaces in Web browsers, including not only the display and positioning of controls, but also handling events generated by them (as you'll see in the next section).

Handling Events

You now have a Web Form that displays an HTML form in the Web browser. The next step is to make it do something! As discussed previously, this would be rather tortuous in the pre-ASP.NET model. ASP.NET server-side controls make this much easier. If you're using Visual Studio .NET, it's as simple as double-clicking on the Calculate button shown earlier in Figure 16-8. This will switch you to the code view and generate a *Calculate_Click* event handler for you to populate. Under the covers, the Forms Designer will add code in the *InitializeComponent* method to hook up this event handler method to the *Calculate* button's *Click* event:

```
this.Calculate.add_Click( new System.EventHandler(this.Calculate_Click) );
```

In Visual Studio .NET, the *InitializeComponent* method is hidden in a region of the JSL file marked "Web Form Designer generated code." Expand the code and examine it, but remember: Look but don't touch!

The *Calculate_Click* method is wrapped in a *System.EventHandler* delegate before being added to the *Button* control's *Click* event. You can do this sort of thing yourself if you need to subscribe to events manually. Once the event is hooked up, you can populate the *Calculate_Click* method with a simplified version of the "feeds how many" calculation:

```
private void Calculate_Click (System.Object sender, System.EventArgs e)
{
   boolean fruitFilling =
      (Filling.get_Text().Equals("fruit")) ? true : false;

   double munchSizeFactor = (fruitFilling ? 2.5 : 1);

   int numConsumers =
      (int)(Integer.parseInt(Size.get_Text()) * munchSizeFactor);
}
```

Recall from FeedsHowMany.aspx.jsl (version 1) that the Web Form has two *TextBox* controls, one called *size* and one called *filling*. The contents of these controls are retrieved by using the *Text* property. The contents of the *Size TextBox* are converted into an integer to be used as part of the calculation. At the end of the method, you have the number of consumers, but the question is how to get this back to the user.

One option, as with original ASP, is to use *Response.Write* at the end of the method:

```
this.get_Response().Write("This cake feeds " + numConsumers + " people");
```

Although this is serviceable, it is not very user friendly. The question arises of where this message will be written. Figure 16-10 shows that this message will appear at the top of the page.

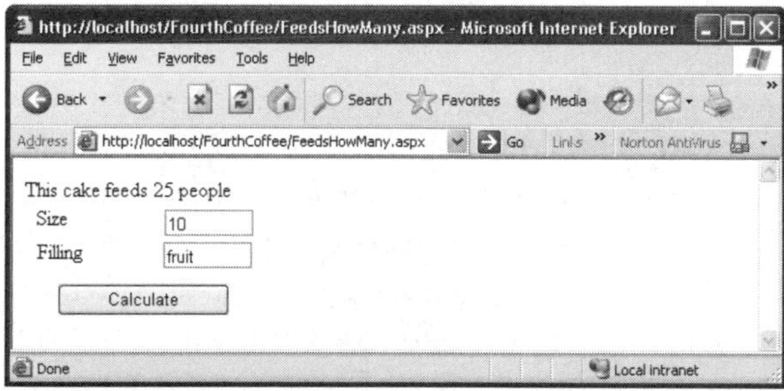

Figure 16-10 Sending information to the user using *Response.Write*

If you were to use a simple text-writing mechanism, you'd have to do any necessary text formatting by adding HTML tags into the string returned. To gain more control over the location and style of the message, you can take advantage of a *Label* server-side control to display the message. If you add another

Label to your Web Form called *Output*, you can set the text in this control once you've performed your calculation:

```
Output.set_Text("This cake feeds " + numConsumers + " people");
```

Because the *Label* is an ordinary control in Visual Studio, you can set its properties—the foreground and background colors, the text size, and so on—all without generating a single HTML tag yourself. Indeed, you don't even have to write any code to change these properties. You can just alter them by using the Properties pane of Visual Studio .NET. The example uses this mechanism to set the foreground and background color of the *Output Label*. The result is shown in Figure 16-11.

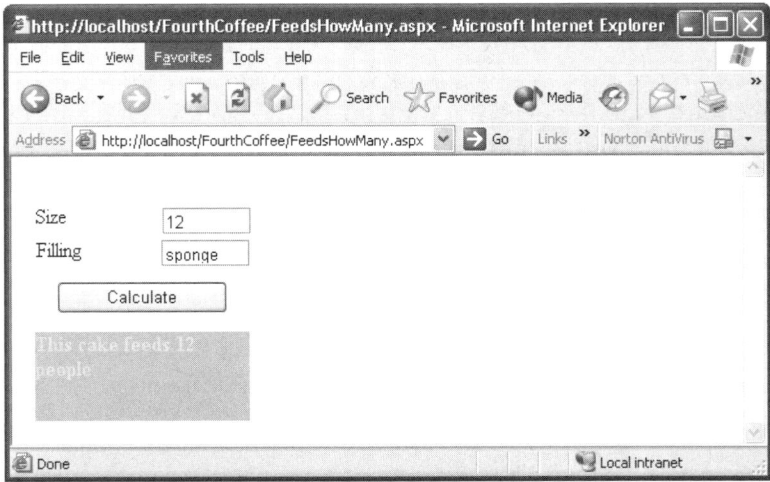

Figure 16-11 Using a label control to display messages

You should have noticed in the previous two figures that the values entered into the *filing* and *size* fields retained their contents even though the page went through a round-trip to the server to perform the calculation. No extra code was added to do this—the *TextBox* control took care of it. Each control has an *EnableViewState* property, and when it is set to *true* (the default), the form containing the controls will send down a hidden form field called *__VIEWSTATE* that contains a unique value. The state of each control is cached on the server and associated with this value so that each control's last known state can be retrieved automatically when it is rendered. The full code for this Web Form is shown in FeedsHowMany.aspx.jsl (version 2). This is the version provided as part of the sample page FeedsHowMany.aspx in the FourthCoffee project.

FeedsHowMany.aspx.jsl (version 2)

```
package FourthCoffee;

import System.Collections.*;
import System.ComponentModel.*;
import System.Data.*;
import System.Drawing.*;
import System.Web.*;
import System.Web.SessionState.*;
import System.Web.UI.*;
import System.Web.UI.WebControls.*;
import System.Web.UI.HtmlControls.*;

/**
 * Summary description for FeedsHowMany.
 */
public class FeedsHowMany extends System.Web.UI.Page
{
   protected System.Web.UI.WebControls.TextBox Size;
   protected System.Web.UI.WebControls.Label Label1;
   protected System.Web.UI.WebControls.Label Label2;
   protected System.Web.UI.WebControls.Button Calculate;
   protected System.Web.UI.WebControls.Label Output;
   protected System.Web.UI.WebControls.TextBox Filling;

   private void Page_Load(System.Object sender, System.EventArgs e)
   {
   }

   protected void OnInit(System.EventArgs e)
   {
      //
      // CODEGEN: This call is required by the ASP.NET Web Form Designer.
      // Do not remove this.
      //
      InitializeComponent();
      super.OnInit(e);
   }

   #region Web Form Designer generated code
   /**
    * Required method for Designer support - do not modify
    * the contents of this method with the code editor.
    */
   private void InitializeComponent()
   {
      this.Calculate.add_Click(
        new System.EventHandler(this.Calculate_Click) );
```

```
            this.add_Load( new System.EventHandler(this.Page_Load) );

        }
        #endregion

        private void Calculate_Click (System.Object sender, System.EventArgs e)
        {
            boolean fruitFilling =
              (Filling.get_Text().Equals("fruit")) ? true : false;

            double munchSizeFactor = (fruitFilling ? 2.5 : 1);

            int numConsumers =
              (int)(Integer.parseInt(Size.get_Text()) * munchSizeFactor);

            Output.set_Text("This cake feeds " + numConsumers + " people");
        }

    }
```

Client-Side Validation

As you've seen, ASP.NET provides a powerful server-based model for client interaction that makes developing Web applications quicker and easier. However, developer convenience is not the only consideration. Sending data back and forth between client and server is an expensive operation compared with local processing, especially if the client and server communicate over the Internet. Consequently, data should be processed on the client if possible rather than sent back to the server each time processing is needed. Naturally, it is not possible or even desirable to migrate a lot of application logic to the client. But there might be some functionality that can be safely and easily migrated to the client, thereby improving the performance of the application.

An example of such functionality is validating the contents of the fields in an HTML form. If you want, you can write client-side script to validate the contents of your form fields, but ASP.NET provides several server-side controls that can simplify this task. The most straightforward technique is to use a validator. You select a *RequiredFieldValidator* on the Web controls tab of the Visual Studio .NET Toolbox and associate it with a *TextBox*. You drag and drop the *RequiredFieldValidator* from the Toolbox onto the design surface of the Web Form. You position the *RequiredFieldValidator* where appropriate and set its *ErrorMessage* property to the message you want displayed using the Properties window.

The *RequiredFieldValidator* is transparent, so when it is not displaying an error message, the user won't see it. The error message is shown in the

RequiredFieldValidator when validation fails, so be sure to allow enough room for it to be displayed. To associate the *RequiredFieldValidator* with the *TextBox*, you locate the *ControlToValidate* property in the Properties window and set it to the name of the associated *TextBox*. (Visual Studio .NET will provide a drop-down list of controls that you can validate.)

The following HTML was generated by Visual Studio .NET as part of the FeedsHowManyWithValidation.aspx page after we associated a *RequiredField-Validator* with a *TextBox* by manipulating them graphically on the design surface:

```
<asp:TextBox id="Filling" style="Z-INDEX: 108; LEFT: 117px; POSITION:
 absolute; TOP: 40px" runat="server" Width="69px" Height="20px">
</asp:TextBox>
<asp:RequiredFieldValidator id="RequiredFieldValidator2" style="Z-INDEX:
 107; LEFT: 214px; POSITION: absolute; TOP: 69px" runat="server"
 Width="173px" Height="20px" ControlToValidate="Filling"
 ErrorMessage="Please enter cake filling" Visible="True">
</asp:RequiredFieldValidator>
```

In the preceding example, the *RequiredFieldValidator* is associated with the *TextBox* whose *id* is "*Filling*". The *RequiredFieldValidator* checks whether the *TextBox* is empty. If the *TextBox* is empty, the *RequiredFieldValidator* will display its error message and the form will not be submitted to the server. The result of running this ASPX page is shown in Figure 16-12.

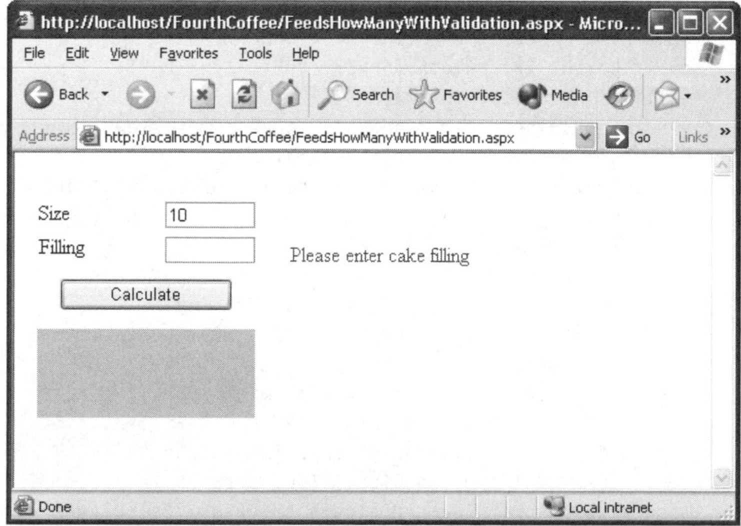

Figure 16-12 You can use validators to set individual validation error messages for particular fields in a Web Form.

There's no magic involved in client-side validation—an ASP.NET page containing validator controls generates client-side script to perform the validation, much as you could write yourself if you so desired. The generated code is shown in the listing FeedsHowManyWithValidation Generated HTML.

FeedsHowManyWithValidation Generated HTML

```
<!DOCTYPE HTML PUBLIC "-//W3C//DTD HTML 4.0 Transitional//EN" >
<HTML>
   <HEAD>
      <meta name="GENERATOR" Content="Microsoft Visual Studio 7.0">
      <meta name="CODE_LANGUAGE" Content="VJ#">
      <meta name="vs_defaultClientScript" content="JavaScript
      (ECMAScript)">
      <meta name="vs_targetSchema"
       content="http://schemas.microsoft.com/intellisense/ie5">
   </HEAD>
   <body MS_POSITIONING="GridLayout">
      <form name="FeedsHowMany" method="post"
         action="FeedsHowManyWithValidation.aspx"
       language="javascript" onsubmit="ValidatorOnSubmit();"
       id="FeedsHowManyWithValidation">
<input type="hidden" name="__VIEWSTATE"
   value="dDwtMjEwMTcyNjU1Ozs+LtpMd81aKMttUkt3FmSaFMPWsKA=" />

<script language="javascript"
 src="/aspnet_client/system_web/1_0_3705_0/WebUIValidation.js"></script>

         <input name="Size" type="text" id="Size"
          style="height:20px;width:69px;Z-INDEX: 109; LEFT: 117px;
          POSITION: absolute; TOP: 40px" />
         <span id="RequiredFieldValidator2" controltovalidate="Filling"
          errormessage="Please enter cake filling"
          evaluationfunction="RequiredFieldValidatorEvaluateIsValid"
          initialvalue="" style="color:Red;height:20px;width:173px;
          Z-INDEX:108;LEFT:214px;POSITION:absolute;TOP:69px;
          visibility:hidden;">Please enter cake filling</span>
         <input name="Filling" type="text" id="Filling"
          style="height:20px;width:69px;Z-INDEX: 103; LEFT: 116px;
          POSITION: absolute; TOP: 65px" />
         <span id="Label2" style="height:25px;width:86px;Z-INDEX: 102;
          LEFT: 19px; POSITION: absolute; TOP: 63px">Filling</span>
         <span id="Label1" style="height:25px;width:86px;Z-INDEX: 101;
          LEFT: 18px; POSITION: absolute; TOP: 37px">Size</span>
         <input type="submit" name="Calculate" value="Calculate"
          onclick="if (typeof(Page_ClientValidate) == 'function')
          Page_ClientValidate(); " language="javascript" id="Calculate"
          style="height:25px;width:133px;Z-INDEX: 104; LEFT: 35px;
          POSITION: absolute; TOP: 97px" />
         <span id="Output" style="color:Yellow;background-color:#C0C0FF;
```

```
        font-weight:bold;height:69px;width:167px;Z-INDEX: 105;
        LEFT: 18px; POSITION: absolute; TOP: 136px"></span>
       <span id="RequiredFieldValidator1" controltovalidate="Size"
        errormessage="Please enter cake diameter"
        evaluationfunction="RequiredFieldValidatorEvaluateIsValid"
        initialvalue="" style="color:Red;height:20px;width:172px;
        Z-INDEX:107;LEFT:212px;POSITION:absolute;TOP:42px;
        visibility:hidden;">Please enter cake diameter</span>

<script language="javascript">
<!--
   var Page_Validators =
      new Array(document.all["RequiredFieldValidator2"],
      document.all["RequiredFieldValidator1"]);
      // -->
</script>


<script language="javascript">
<!--
var Page_ValidationActive = false;
if (typeof(clientInformation) != "undefined" &&
 clientInformation.appName.indexOf("Explorer") != -1) {
    if (typeof(Page_ValidationVer) == "undefined")
       alert("Unable to find script library
       '/aspnet_client/system_web/1_0_3705_0/WebUIValidation.js'.
       Try placing this file manually, or reinstall by running
       'aspnet_regiis -c'.");
    else if (Page_ValidationVer != "125")
        alert("This page uses an incorrect version of WebUIValidation.js.
        The page expects version 125. The script library is " +
        Page_ValidationVer + ".");
    else
        ValidatorOnLoad();
}

function ValidatorOnSubmit() {
    if (Page_ValidationActive) {
        ValidatorCommonOnSubmit();
    }
}
// -->
</script>


      </form>
   </body>
</HTML>
```

We won't dwell on the precise syntactic details of the generated page, but the client-side code essentially works as follows:

- It contains a script tag that downloads a common ASP.NET JavaScript file, WebUIValidation.js, which contains a script to perform client-side validation. This file can be found in the folder \Inetpub\wwwroot\aspnet_client\system_web\.NETVersion\.
- The form containing the controls has its *onsubmit* event mapped to the *ValidatorOnSubmit* method that's defined in the client-side script. This method checks whether validation is required and then calls a standard validation function defined in WebUIValidation.js.
- Each validator is transformed into a hidden *<span>* element with attributes defining its associated control, the type of validation required (as defined by which standard JavaScript function to call), and its error message.
- All of the validators on the page are defined in an array, *Page_Validators*, so the client-side script can find them easily.

If you leave either of the text fields on the form blank, this client-side code will display a screen similar to the one shown earlier in Figure 16-12.

The types of validation controls are as follows:

- **RequiredFieldValidator** Makes sure the user does not leave a value unset.
- **RangeValidator** Ensures that a value is between set limits.
- **CompareValidator** Compares the value to a constant value or the value of another field. For example, you can use this control to ensure that a start time is less than a finish time.
- **RegularExpressionValidator** Ensures that a value matches a fixed pattern, such as an e-mail address (*name@host*).

If none of the available validators meet your requirements, you can implement your own validation by creating a *CustomValidator* and implementing client-side and server-side validation routines. Note that the standard validation controls can operate on both the client side and the server side. Usually, validation errors are caught early on the client side using the JavaScript-based mechanisms shown previously. If the client-side validation fails, the contents of the form will not be sent to the server. However, it is not always possible to use client-side validation.

The main objective of validation is to catch validation errors as early as possible. Ideally, all validation problems will have been fixed before the form is submitted to the server. However, the server-side part of the validation control will always perform its own validation when the form is received, to ensure that no accidental or malicious submission of invalid fields occurs. The server-side validation is especially important if client-side JavaScript is disabled in the browser. There is no way of knowing this without performing multiple round-trips, so the use of server-side validation acts as a failsafe mechanism. Note also that the HTML Document Object Model (DOM) of some browsers might be different from that expected by the validation control, in which case the validation control might not generate any client-side validation script and might simply rely on the server-side validation.

You can display all of your validation error messages in one place using the *ValidationSummary* control. This will poll all of the validators on the page to see whether their validation has failed. (Remember the *Page_Validators* array mentioned earlier?) If it has, the *ValidationSummary* will display the validator's failure message as part of its own output. The *ValidationSummary* can display its output in the main HTML page, in a message box, or both.

Figure 16-13 shows the output from the sample file FeedsHowManyWithValidationSummary.aspx. This page contains a *ValidationSummary* that displays the error information for both the size and filling validators. To achieve this result, you can drag and drop a *ValidationSummary* onto the Web Form design surface in an appropriate location. When the form is submitted, the *ValidationSummary* will poll all of the validators on the page to determine whether any validation errors occurred.

By default, the *ValidationSummary* displays a set of bullet points, each showing the *ErrorMessage* property of any validator on the page that has flagged an error. You can specify a meaningful message to display before this bulleted list by setting the *ValidationSummary* control's *HeaderText* property using the Visual Studio .NET Properties window. To ensure that the same information is not displayed twice, the *Text* property of the validators has been set to a single asterisk (*) so that the offending fields are just highlighted. (It can be blank if you want.) The *ValidationSummary* can also display its content as a list or as a single paragraph.

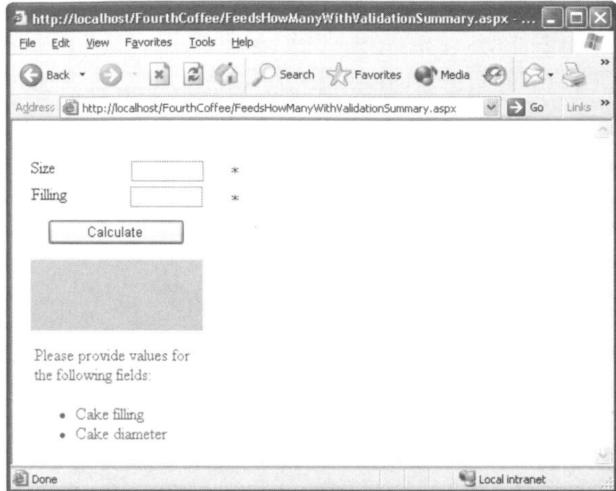

Figure 16-13 Using a *ValidationSummary* to display a validation error message

ASP.NET controls generally use client-side script where appropriate to reduce network round-trips and thus improve application performance. You can also use many other approaches for client-side scripting in your application, but an in-depth discussion of these approaches is beyond the scope of this chapter.

Migrating from ASP Pages

Chances are, you'll want any new projects that you start on a Windows platform to take advantage of the new features in the .NET Framework. But you might also need to migrate existing ASP-based application into ASP.NET. The first thing to note here is that you don't have to migrate everything immediately: ASP pages and ASP.NET pages can quite happily coexist on the same Web server or even in the same application, if this suits your purposes.

Language and Code

One main issue with migration is the language barrier. Most ASP applications are written using Visual Basic as the server-side language. If you want to recast these as J# (or C#), you'll obviously need to port the code. However, you've seen that you can use different languages in different pages, so you can migrate your code gradually on a page-by-page basis. You've seen the new *<%@ Page %>* directive for defining the language for the page that allows you to do this. Even if you decide to leave the code on some pages in Visual Basic, you'll still need to update them slightly due to language changes between ASP and ASP.NET. (See the .NET Framework documentation on Visual Basic for more details.) You also need to be aware of some other issues (some of which we've already covered), such as the need to enclose function definitions in their own *<script>* tag.

Because most ASP pages contain their functionality inline, you'll probably want to move a lot of this code to code-behind classes. Again, this is not obligatory and your newly migrated ASP.NET pages will work just fine. However, as discussed previously, placing your code in code-behind classes greatly improves the maintainability of your code. In fact, if you convert the filename extension of an ASP page to ASPX and then load it into a Visual Studio .NET project, you'll be prompted to create a code-behind class for the page in which its code can live.

Beyond the language issues, you'll need to ensure that your application continues to function as it always did. The major area of concern here is probably data access. However, you need not worry too much. All ADO code will still work under ASP.NET, but you should see better performance if you port your code to ADO.NET. This is particularly true if you use disconnected recordsets in ADO because the ADO.NET *DataSet* handles the disconnected scenario far better. You'll also still be able to instantiate and use any COM components from your ASP pages. The main caveat here is if you have COM components that expect to run in a single-threaded apartment (STA). Such components can be loaded only into an ASP.NET page that is itself single threaded. (ASP.NET pages are multithreaded by default.)

To set a page as an STA, you set the *AspCompat* attribute of the *<%@ Page %>* directive to *true*, as shown in this example:

```
<%@ Page language="VJ#" AspCompat="true" Codebehind="FeedsHowMany.aspx.jsl"
 AutoEventWireup="false" Inherits="FourthCoffee.FeedsHowMany" %>
```

The User Interface

In addition to application functionality, the other major area to consider when you migrate to ASP.NET is the user interface. Design-time controls are no longer supported, so if your application uses them, you must change them to Web controls. If your ASP pages use regular HTML controls, you must change these as well, although the changes will be minor because ASP.NET provides its own library of HTML controls. You can convert an ASP HTML control into an ASP.NET server-side HTML control by adding a *runat="server"* attribute. As long as the control has an *id* attribute, it will be accessible to server-side script, in much the same way as a server-side Web control.

The sample file MigratedFeedsHowMany.aspx that follows is a migrated version of the FeedsHowMany.asp ASP page shown earlier. The script code has been migrated to J# and the *<form>* and *<input>* HTML controls have all had the *runat="server"* attribute added. The text boxes can be directly accessed from server-side script using the names defined in their *id* attributes. Migrating this page took only a few minutes, most of it taken up with porting the code from JavaScript to J#.

MigratedFeedsHowMany.aspx

```
<%@ Page Language="VJ#" %>
<HTML>
   <BODY>
      <form runat="server" method="post"
         action="MigratedFeedsHowMany.aspx">
         Size: <input runat="server" id="SizeField" type="text"
            name="size">
         Filling: <input runat="server" id="FillingField" type="text"
            name="filling">
         <input runat="server" type="submit" value="Calculate">
         <p>This will feed <%= calculate() %> people</p>
      </form>
   </BODY>
</HTML>
<script language="VJ#" runat="server">
int calculate()
{
   String filling = FillingField.get_Value();
   String size = SizeField.get_Value();
   int numConsumers = 0;

   if (filling != null && filling.length() != 0 && size != null &&
      size.length() != 0)
   {
      boolean fruitFilling = (filling.Equals("fruit")) ? true : false;
      int munchSizeFactor = (fruitFilling ? 3 : 1);
      numConsumers = Integer.parseInt(size) * munchSizeFactor;
   }

   return numConsumers;
}

</script>
```

Although server-side HTML controls provide a useful mechanism when you convert from ASP to ASP.NET, bear in mind that they're not as powerful as server-side Web controls. Migration is their main purpose, so if you're designing new functionality, you should use Web controls rather than HTML controls.

Caution Be careful if your migration strategy involves using both server-side HTML controls and code-behind classes. The *id* attributes defined on the HTML controls are visible to code placed directly in the ASPX page, but Visual Studio .NET does not automatically insert a reference to them in the code-behind, as it does for Web controls. This means that if you want to access your HTML controls from your code-behind class, you must locate them programmatically. This involves writing code that iterates through the components that your page contains to locate controls of the correct type and *id*.

Pages, Controls, and Data

Now that you've learned how to create Web Forms and other ASP.NET pages, let's look in more detail at the *Page* class, its life cycle, and how to use controls in conjunction with a *Page*.

The *Page* Class

Every ASP.NET page has an associated *Page* class. This class can be created from an ASPX page that contains a mixture of HTML and code, or it can be formed from the merger of automatically generated code and a code-behind class (as described earlier). In either case, the attributes of the *<%@ Page %>* directive provide some key information when this class is created, as shown in Table 16-1.

Table 16-1 Important Attributes of the *<%@ Page %>* Directive

Page Attribute	Description
Language	The default language for the page.
Inherits	Defines the class that this page should extend—usually the code-behind class associated with the page. The runtime will search for this class in local assemblies stored in the bin directory under the directory in which the page resides, and then in any assemblies in the search path that are explicitly included in this page, and finally in assemblies in the GAC. If this search proves fruitless, the file defined with the *Src* attribute will be located and compiled.

Table 16-1 Important Attributes of the *<%@ Page %>* Directive

Page Attribute	Description
Src	Defines the name of the source file that holds the code-behind class for this page. Because .NET provides for cross-language inheritance, the code that makes up the page can be defined in any language supported by the common language runtime.
Transaction	Indicates whether the page is transactional and, if so, how transactions should be handled (as described later).
ErrorPage	Defines a page that will be displayed if an unhandled exception occurs (as described later).
ContentType	Sets the content type to be returned to the client in the HTTP response header. If you're generating XML rather than HTML, you should set this to *"text/xml"*.
EnableSessionState	Indicates whether the page is part of a session and has session state available to it (as described later).
EnableViewState	Indicates that the user interface state should be maintained between round-trips to the server when the same page is displayed multiple times (typically using a hidden field called *__VIEWSTATE* to maintain the association between the page and its state, as described earlier).

Each page can have only one *<%@ Page %>* directive, but it can appear anywhere on the page. This differs from ASP, where all directives must be on the first line.

Intrinsic Objects and Properties

As in ASP, certain HTTP-related functionality is available through the properties and methods of the *Page* class in ASP.NET. ASP employs the concept of *intrinsic objects* that are abstractions of important underlying concepts, including

- ***Request*** A *System.Web.HttpRequest* object that contains the HTTP information for the current request, including the fields from the HTTP header, such as the cookies, client browser, and type of request (*GET* or *POST*). If the request is a *GET*, parameters passed in are available as name/value pairs in the collection retrieved from the *QueryString* property. Alternatively, if the request is a *POST*, you can retrieve a *System.IO.InputStream* from the *InputStream* property and then read the data from the *POST* body. If the information sent by the client is form data, you can retrieve a collection of contents of the forms on the page as the name/value pairs from the *Form* property. Server-side information is also available, such as whether the user is authenticated (*IsAuthenticated* property) and information about the virtual and physical path associated with this request.

- ***Response*** A *System.Web.HttpResponse* object through which you can send information back to the client. You can use this object to access the HTTP header fields in the response to set cookies on the client and manipulate other HTTP headers such as the *StatusCode*. You can write data to the client using the *Write* or *WriteFile* methods, or you can obtain the *TextWriter* stored in the *Output* property and use that directly (or wrap it in another form of stream). When you've finished writing, you should call the *Flush* and *Close* methods on the *Response*. Output from an ASP page can be cached, ensuring that all of the output is sent to the client. You can also use the *Redirect* method to inform the client application (the browser) that it should go to another page.
- ***Server*** An instance of the *System.Web.HttpServerUtility* class through which you can access server-related functionality. This includes methods to retrieve the last error message (*GetLastError*), encode and decode HTML-encoded or URL-encoded strings (*Html-Encode*, *HtmlDecode*, *UrlEncode*, *UrlDecode*), and map a raw file-name to one relative to the current virtual directory (*MapPath*). You can use *Transfer* to redirect the current request directly to another page (rather than using *Response.Redirect*), or you can *Execute* another page and capture its output.
- **Session-scope and application-scope storage** You can access the session-scope and application-scope storage for this *Page* instance using its *Session* and *Application* properties (as discussed later).

The *Page* class also provides a *Controls* collection property that allows programmatic access to the child controls of the page. Some of the information set using the *<%@ Page %>* directive is also accessible programmatically, such as the *ErrorPage* property. You can change such properties as the context of your application changes.

Note If you're not subclassing the *Page* class, you can access the intrinsic objects using the *HttpContext* object. Simply call the static *HttpContext.get_Current* method to retrieve your *HttpContext*.

Events and Life Cycle

The *Page* class has certain events that fire during its life cycle. All of the events generated by a *Page* are inherited from the *Control* or *TemplateControl* classes. (The *Page* is just a specialized form of *Control*.) The most commonly used ones are the *Load* and *Unload* events. In FeedsHowMany.aspx.jsl (version 2), you might have noticed the *InitializeComponent* method:

```
private void InitializeComponent()
{
   this.Calculate.add_Click(
      new System.EventHandler(this.Calculate_Click) );
   this.add_Load( new System.EventHandler(this.Page_Load) );
}
```

Visual Studio .NET uses the *InitializeComponent* method to connect events to event handlers for the page (the same technique and method used for Windows Forms applications). As you can see, in this example two event handlers are hooked up, one for the *Load* event on *this* (the current *Page* instance) and one for the *Click* event on the *Calculate Button*. A *System.EventHandler* delegate is added to the list of delegates stored in the *Load* event through the *add_Load* call. This *EventHandler* refers to the *Page_Load* method, which you can use to perform page-specific initialization:

```
private void Page_Load(System.Object sender, System.EventArgs e)
{
   // Initialization here...
}
```

In this case, the event handlers are programmatically associated with events. ASP.NET also supports a feature called *automatic event wire-up*. This takes the form of a property on the *<%@ Page %>* directive called *AutoEventWireup*. If *AutoEventWireup* is set to *true* (the default, if not explicitly defined), the ASP.NET runtime will look for standard method names (such as *Page_Load* or *Page_Init*) that match the events for this page and automatically invoke them when that event occurs, regardless of any event hookups. This is convenient if you can use the standard method names, but don't use it in conjunction with manual hookups of the same events to the same handlers because this will cause the handler to be invoked twice.

Note By default, Visual J# .NET sets *AutoEventWireup* to *false* and connects events to event handlers in the *InitializeComponent* method, as previously shown.

The *Load* event is triggered every time the page is loaded. Note that an instance of the page is loaded and unloaded for every client request. The *Page* instance is used for the duration of that request and is then discarded. This means that instance data will not be retained between invocations. For example, if you wanted to keep a count of the number of times a page has been visited by a client, you could add a counter that's displayed using a *Label*:

```
protected System.Web.UI.WebControls.Label Count;
private int count = 0;

private void Page_Load(System.Object sender, System.EventArgs e)
{
   Count.set_Text("Count: " + ++count);
}
```

Unfortunately, this would display 1 every time you accessed it because the value of the *count* variable would be thrown away every time the page was unloaded. If you want to maintain state between client requests, you should use the instance of *System.Web.SessionState.HttpSessionState* provided through the *Page* object's *Session* property. This is discussed in detail later in the chapter.

The life-cycle events on an ASP.NET page exhibit a minor side-effect when you work with Web Forms. Web Forms pages post their data back to themselves, and some of the processing of this data might be performed in the *Load* event handler. But this handler is called every time the page is loaded—even the first time, before the user has had a chance to fill out the form. Any tasks that are based on the content of the form should not be performed until the user has submitted some information. To get around this, the *Page* class has an *IsPostBack* property that tells you whether the current page is being loaded and processed as the result of a form being posted to it or whether this is the initial display of the form. You can use this property to prevent form-based code from being executed the first time a Web Form is called:

```
private void Page_Load(System.Object sender, System.EventArgs e)
{
```

```
    if (this.get_IsPostBack())
    {
        // Event called as the result of a postback.
        // Process the contents of the form
        ⋮
    }
}
```

Common Controls

When you use Web Forms to create user interfaces, you need various types of controls that the user can interact with. You've seen that two types of server-side controls are available for building interfaces—HTML controls and Web controls. Web controls are the more powerful mechanism and are the standard type of control used in most ASP.NET applications. In Visual Studio .NET, you can drag Web controls from the Toolbox onto the design area for your page, set their properties, and set handlers for any events that they might raise. The Web controls can be found in the *System.Web.UI.WebControls* namespace.

You've already learned how to build a simple user interface using *Button*, *TextBox*, and *Label* controls. This section takes a brief tour of some of the other common controls you might want to use. (This is by no means an exhaustive list!)

Forms and Selection

You can use various server-side controls as part of a form to allow a user to enter information, select options, or indicate actions, including:

- **TextBox** A field in which a user can type text. A text box can be multiline or read-only or can display password-style asterisks instead of echoing the text typed. This can be hooked up to a server-side event that is triggered when text is entered.
- **Button** A standard button that can be connected to a server-side event that's triggered when the button is clicked.
- **ImageButton** A button represented by an image. This can be hooked up to a server-side event that's triggered when the button is clicked.
- **CheckBox** A standard single selectable check box that can be hooked up to a server-side event that's triggered when the box is selected.

- **CheckBoxList** A set of selectable check boxes that can be connected to a server-side event that's triggered when any of the boxes are selected.
- **DropDownList** A standard drop-down list containing a set of elements. This can be hooked up to a server-side event that's triggered each time the user selects a different element from the list.
- **ListBox** A multiple-item display that can allow one or more items to be selected. This can be hooked up to a server-side event that is triggered when the selection changes.
- **RadioButton** A single, selectable radio-style button that can be connected to a server-side event that's triggered when the button is selected.
- **RadioButtonList** A group of selectable radio buttons that are mutually exclusive so that only one can be selected at any time. This can be hooked up to a server-side event that's triggered each time the user selects a different button in the list.
- **HyperLink** A regular hyperlink with an associated URL.

For more information about these controls, see the .NET Framework documentation.

Displaying Information

You can choose from a selection of controls for displaying information to the user. They include

- **Label** A placeholder that can contain text and can be positioned in any location on the form. Use *Label* controls to display text to the user instead of the *Response.Write* method—it provides greater control over the positioning and format of the result.

Tip As a general rule, when you use Web Forms, avoid using the *Response.Write* method.

- **Literal** A placeholder for the display of text. This cannot be positioned in the way that a *Label* can.

- **Image** An image with alternative text for browsers that have image display disabled.
- **Table** A control for generating an HTML table. You use *TableCell* and *TableRow* controls in conjunction with the *Table* control.
- **Repeater** A control that repeats a provided output template and populates it based on a data source.
- **DataList** Similar to, but more powerful than, the *Repeater* control. It allows you to repeat a template, populating it with data from an ADO.NET data source, and edit the data.
- **DataGrid** A control for displaying data from an ADO.NET data source in a table that can be selected, sorted, and edited.
- **XmlControl** A control for displaying some or all of an XML document. Its primary purpose is to allow you to display the result of an XSLT transformation of the XML.

For more information about these controls, see the .NET Framework documentation.

Controlling Layout

When you define an ASP.NET page, you can choose between relative and absolute positioning of controls. Relative positioning uses something called *flow layout*, which places the controls next to each other across the page. If the combined width of the controls is greater than the width of the page, the layout will "flow" to a new row underneath, until all of the controls are visible. If the user resizes the form at run time, the positions of the controls will be adjusted automatically so none of them is truncated or hidden. This layout works on the same principle as the *FlowLayout* in the Abstract Window Toolkit (AWT).

The alternative is to use a *grid layout*, which is the default for Web Forms. This layout allows you to position controls in a precise location, but if a user resizes the form at run time, controls might disappear from view. You can set the type of layout used by changing the *pageLayout* property associated with that page in Visual Studio .NET.

Note that some controls, such as *Literal* controls, will not position themselves in a grid layout. In this case, you can add a *Panel* control to the grid and then place the offending controls within the *Panel*. This mechanism is also useful for user controls (described next).

Creating Your Own Controls

The standard functionality of ASP.NET Web Forms is powerful, but it doesn't always meet application-specific requirements. If necessary, you can create your own controls for use in your ASP.NET application. You can create your own server-side controls that you can use in the same way as those provided with the .NET Framework, but the details (although not rocket science) are beyond the scope of this chapter. If you have an application requirement for a slightly specialized version of an existing control, however, or for a common group of controls that can be used in multiple places (such as a navigation bar with multiple buttons, images, and labels), a user control might be the answer.

Creating a User Control

A user control consists of one or more Web controls placed in an instance of the *System.Web.UI.UserControl* class. You can create a user control in Visual Studio .NET by selecting Web User Control in the Add New Item dialog box. (There are other ways to create user controls, which you can pursue by referring to the .NET Framework documentation.) You'll see a design area similar to that for a Web Form. You can add controls as needed to create your user control. If you want to add custom code to your user control, you can access the code-behind and add methods as appropriate.

For example, suppose you want to create a navigation bar for the Fourth Coffee online store. It will contain a label for the Fourth Coffee Web site and several navigation buttons for Home, Back, and so forth. You can start by creating a user control in Visual Studio .NET. Choose the Add Web User Control option from the Project menu. By default, the user control uses a flow layout, so to obtain more precise positioning, you can drag and drop a *GridLayoutPanel* from the HTML section of the ToolBox onto the design surface of your user control and then resize it as appropriate. You can then drag and drop your Web controls, such as buttons, labels, and images, onto the *GridLayoutPanel* and add their event-handling code as appropriate. One of these buttons can be a Help button that takes the user to a page containing context-sensitive help. The target URL for this button would have to change from page to page because the context would change. The easiest way to do this is to provide a property, such as *HelpUrl*, on your user control class, as shown in the sample file Navigation.ascx.jsl listed here.

Navigation.ascx.jsl

```
package FourthCoffee;

import System.*;
import System.Data.*;
```

```
import System.Drawing.*;
import System.Web.*;
import System.Web.UI.WebControls.*;
import System.Web.UI.HtmlControls.*;

/**
 * Summary description for Navigation.
 */
public abstract class Navigation extends System.Web.UI.UserControl
{
   protected System.Web.UI.WebControls.Label Label1;
   protected System.Web.UI.WebControls.Button HomeButton;
   protected System.Web.UI.WebControls.Label Label2;
   protected System.Web.UI.WebControls.Button HelpButton;

   private System.String homeUrl = "default.htm";
   private System.String helpUrl = null;

   /** @property */
   public void set_HelpUrl(System.String url)
   {
      if (url != null && url.get_Length() != 0)
      {
         helpUrl = url;
         HelpButton.set_Enabled(true);
      }
   }

   /** @property */
   public System.String get_HelpUrl()
   {
      return helpUrl;
   }

   private void Page_Load(System.Object sender, System.EventArgs e)
   {
      // Put user code to initialize the page here
      if (helpUrl == null)
      {
         HelpButton.set_Enabled(false);
      }
   }

   #region Web Form Designer generated code
   protected void OnInit(System.EventArgs e)
   {
      //
      // CODEGEN: This call is required by the ASP.NET Web Form Designer.
```

```
        //
        InitializeComponent();
        super.OnInit(e);
    }

    /**
     * Required method for Designer support - do not modify
     * the contents of this method with the code editor.
     */
    private void InitializeComponent()
    {
        this.HomeButton.add_Click(
            new System.EventHandler(this.HomeButton_Click) );
        this.HelpButton.add_Click(
            new System.EventHandler(this.HelpButton_Click) );
        this.add_Load( new System.EventHandler(this.Page_Load) );

    }
    #endregion

    private void HomeButton_Click (System.Object sender, System.EventArgs e)
    {
        GoToPage(homeUrl);
    }

    private void HelpButton_Click (System.Object sender, System.EventArgs e)
    {
        GoToPage(helpUrl);
    }

    private void GoToPage(System.String page)
    {
        if (page.EndsWith(".aspx"))
        {
            get_Server().Transfer(page);
        }
        else
        {
            get_Response().Redirect(page);
        }
    }
}
```

Using a User Control

Once you've defined a user control, you can add it to other pages by registering it in the ASPX file of each host page. The following registration directive, used in the sample file Login.aspx, indicates that the tag *Navigation*, prefixed by *FourthCoffee*, refers to the class contained in the user control sample file Navigation.ascx:

```
<%@ Register TagPrefix="FourthCoffee" TagName="Navigation"
 Src="Navigation.ascx" %>
```

Within the host page, you can use the registered tag to indicate where the control should be positioned. The control declaration itself must be placed within the form for the page *(<form runat="Server">)*. Because the user control does not automatically work with grid layouts, if you're using a grid layout and you want to position the control in a precise location, you can place the control in a *Panel* Web control and then place the *Panel* within the form:

```
<asp:Panel id="Panel1" style="Z-INDEX: 105; LEFT: 21px; POSITION: absolute;
 TOP: 271px" runat="server" Height="81px" Width="572px">
   <FourthCoffee:Navigation id="navBar" runat="server">
   </FourthCoffee:Navigation>
</asp:Panel>
```

The user control will be displayed within the host page, just like any other Web control. You can see this in Figure 16-14, which shows the Login.aspx page with the Navigation user control visible at the bottom. (It contains the Home and Help buttons together with the logo "Welcome to Fourth Coffee, Your handy cake supplier.")

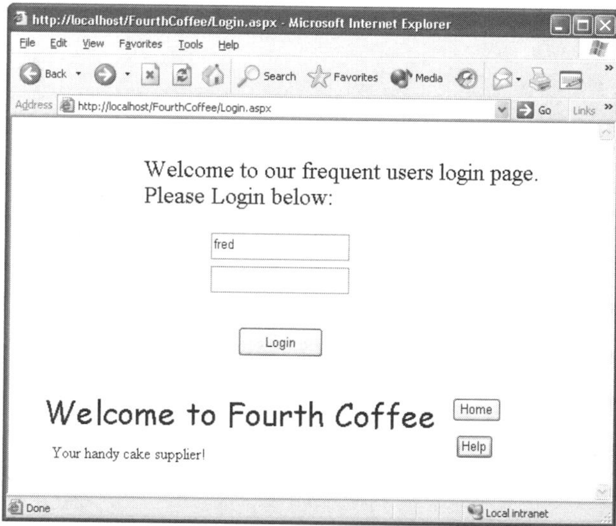

Figure 16-14 An ASP.NET User Control can be used to group common controls in a single entity.

If your user control contains custom functionality, such as the *HelpUrl* property discussed previously, you'll want to access this programmatically.

Within the host page, you can add code to find the user control within the *Panel* and set its property, as shown here:

```
Navigation navBar = null;
IEnumerator enumerator = Panel1.get_Controls().GetEnumerator();
while (enumerator.MoveNext())
{
   Control ctrl = (Control)enumerator.get_Current();
   System.String controlName = ctrl.GetType().get_Name();
   System.String controlName1 = ctrl.GetType().get_FullName();

   if (controlName.CompareTo("Navigation_ascx") == 0)
   {
      navBar = (Navigation)ctrl;
      break;
   }
}

navBar.set_HelpURL("LoginHelpPage.htm");
```

You can find this code in the *PageLoad* method of the sample file Login.aspx. This sample file also contains session and cookie manipulation (covered later).

Binding to Data

As mentioned in the previous section, some of the Web controls are intended for use with ADO.NET data sources. These controls are associated with, or *bound to*, a data source so that when they're rendered they reflect the contents of that data source. Again, an exhaustive examination of data binding to Web controls is outside the scope of this chapter, but we'll give you an idea of what you can do and how to perform simple data binding in J#. You can do many more things, such as paging through large amounts of data and handling events generated by user interaction.

Binding XML

As an example of data binding, consider the use of a *DataGrid* as a means of displaying the contents of the Fourth Coffee cake catalog. Given the catalog data in an ADO.NET *DataSet*, the *DataGrid* can generate a representation of one of the tables in the *DataSet*. The *DataGrid* will infer column names based on the columns in the underlying table. By default, the *DataGrid* will display the first table in the *DataSet*. To display another table, you can set the *DataMember* property of the *DataGrid* to that table.

A simple way to create an ADO.NET *DataSet* to which you can bind a *DataGrid* is to base one on an XML document. Recall from Chapter 5 and Chapter 7 that an ADO.NET *DataSet* leads a secret double life as an *XmlDataDocument*. Use this fact by loading XML into the *DataSet* and then binding the *DataSet* to a control. Consider the XML document in the CakeCatalog.xml sample file, shown below. This document maps to a *DataSet* comprising three tables, whose names are inferred from the schema of the XML document:

- *CakeType*, which maps to the *<CakeType>* element and contains the message, style, filling, shape, and description
- *Option,* which maps to the *<Option>* element and contains a list of the possible sizes
- *Sizes*, which maps to the *<Sizes>* element and is basically a key mapping table between the *CakeType* table and the *Option* table.

CakeCatalog.xml

```
<?xml version="1.0" encoding="utf-8" ?>
<CakeCatalog>
   <CakeType style="Celebration" filling="sponge" shape="round">
      <Message>Happy Birthday</Message>
      <Description>One of our most popular cakes</Description>
      <Sizes>
         <Option value="10 inch" />
         <Option value="12 inch" />
         <Option value="14 inch" />
      </Sizes>
   </CakeType>
   <CakeType style="Wedding" filling="sponge" shape="square">
      <Message />
      <Description>A 3-tier creation to grace any ceremony</Descrip-
tion>
   </CakeType>
   <CakeType style="Wedding" filling="fruit" shape="round">
      <Message />
      <Description>A heavier cake for hungrier guests</Description>
   </CakeType>
   <CakeType style="Christmas" filling="fruit" shape="square">
      <Message>Season's Greetings</Message>
      <Description>Spicy fruitcake for cold evenings</Description>
      <Sizes>
         <Option value="12 inch" />
         <Option value="14 inch" />
      </Sizes>
   </CakeType>
</CakeCatalog>
```

To display this data, we created a simple Web Form called ShowXmlCatalog.aspx in the FourthCoffee project, which contains two *DataGrid* controls. In the code-behind file ShowXmlCatalog.aspx.jsl, the XML document in the file CakeCatalog.xml is loaded into the *DataSet* called *xmlCatalog*. The application uses the *MapPath* method of the *HttpServerUtils* object to ensure that the filename is correct relative to the current virtual directory. The *DataSet* is then assigned to the *DataSource* property of two *DataGrid* controls. One *DataGrid* will display the cake type information, and the other will display the size options. To do this, the *DataMember* property is set to the appropriate inferred table name (*CakeType* and *Option*, respectively) and then the *DataBind* method is called. You will find the complete ShowXmlCatalog.aspx.jsl file in the FourthCoffee sample project.

The result of this data binding is shown in Figure 16-15.

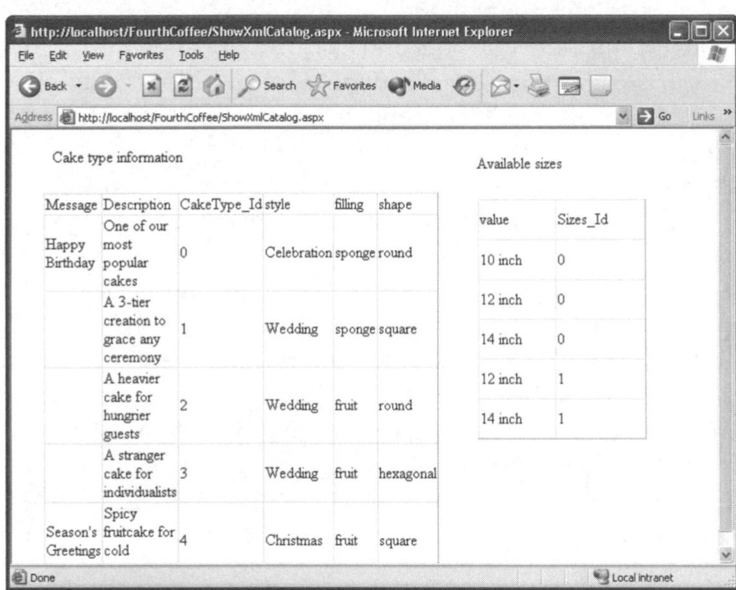

Message	Description	CakeType_Id	style	filling	shape
Happy Birthday	One of our most popular cakes	0	Celebration	sponge	round
	A 3-tier creation to grace any ceremony	1	Wedding	sponge	square
	A heavier cake for hungrier guests	2	Wedding	fruit	round
	A stranger cake for individualists	3	Wedding	fruit	hexagonal
Season's Greetings	Spicy fruitcake for cold	4	Christmas	fruit	square

value	Sizes_Id
10 inch	0
12 inch	0
14 inch	0
12 inch	1
14 inch	1

Figure 16-15 Simple data binding using a *DataGrid* and an XML document

All of this binding code is performed in the *Page_Load* method. If you've cached the *DataSet* when the page is first loaded or if you're binding different data based on user feedback, you might want to check the *IsPostBack* property before performing data loading or binding.

Binding SQL Data

As you've seen, the *DataSet* representation of the *XmlDataDocument* allows an XML document to be bound to a control. Hence, any binding you saw in the previous section can be performed equally well with a *DataSet* populated with data obtained from any other form of underlying data source.

You can also use a *DataReader* as a data source for the data binding of Web controls. This can be more efficient than using a *DataSet* when the data in question is read-only and cannot be cached and therefore must be retrieved every time.

Building ASP.NET Web Applications

Like ASP, ASP.NET automatically associates all executable pages and components under a particular virtual directory into a single Web application. In a Web application, certain state and functionality is often shared between all of those components. We'll look at the handling of application-wide state in the next section; in this section, we'll concentrate on application-wide functionality and configuration.

When people talk about a "Web application," they generally mean an instance of a particular application executing in the context of a Web server—analogous to an instance of a desktop application. You can have multiple instances of the same Web application running on different Web servers or even, given the appropriate configuration, running on the same Web server at the same time. The application-wide settings discussed here relate to a single instance of the Web application and can be changed between instances.

Two files are used to configure a Web application: Web.config and Global.asax. We'll look at these in turn.

Web.config

The Web.config file contains information such as authorization settings, the default language, and how errors are handled. We'll look at these settings in detail shortly, but in general terms the Web.config file is a standard XML-based .NET application configuration file with some Web-specific elements. The overall structure of the file is contained in an XML *configuration* element, which in turn houses a *system.web* element:

```
<?xml version="1.0" encoding="utf-8" ?>
<configuration>
  <system.web>
   <!-- Web application configuration in here -->
  </system.web>
<configuration>
```

To change the configuration for an application, you simply edit the file using a suitable editor. The ASP.NET runtime will build and cache the configuration for an application on first invocation. The configuration will be automatically reloaded when the runtime detects that the file has changed.

If necessary, you can have different Web.config files located in different directories in your application. This can be useful when different Web pages require different handling and configuration. By default, each child directory inherits the settings of the application's top-level virtual directory. You can use a directory-specific Web.config file to override the default settings if needed. You can also use the *location* element to set different settings for different parts of your application, as you'll see later when we discuss security.

Global.asax

The Global.asax file is the place to initialize application-wide objects and event handlers. This file is a special instance of an ASP.NET page, and as such it has an HTML part and an associated code-behind file. (In the case of J#, this is Global.asax.jsl.) The *Global* class is a subclass of *System.Web.HttpApplication*, whose primary purpose is to handle application life-cycle events. By default, the Global.asax file doesn't have a great deal in it—just one line similar to the following:

```
<%@ Application Codebehind="Global.asax.jsl" Inherits="FourthCoffee.Global"
%>
```

Note In Visual Studio, double-clicking on the Global.asax file will display a [Design] screen. To view and edit the actual file, right-click on the file. From the shortcut menu, choose Open With and then select Source Code (Text) Editor.

Events are generated throughout the application life cycle. You can define event handlers in the Global.asax.jsl code-behind file to handle these and other events, as shown in the code listing for a default Global.asax.jsl.

Global.asax.jsl

```
package FourthCoffee;

import System.Collections.*;
import System.ComponentModel.*;
import System.Web.*;
```

```
import System.Web.SessionState.*;
import System.IO.*;

/**
 * Summary description for Global.
 */
public class Global extends System.Web.HttpApplication
{
   public Global()
   {
      InitializeComponent();
   }

   protected void Application_Start(System.Object sender,
      System.EventArgs e)
   {
   }

   protected void Session_Start(System.Object sender,
      System.EventArgs e)
   {
   }

   protected void Application_BeginRequest(System.Object sender,
      System.EventArgs e)
   {
   }

   protected void Application_EndRequest(System.Object sender,
      System.EventArgs e)
   {
   }
   protected void Application_AuthenticateRequest(System.Object sender,
      System.EventArgs e)
   {
   }

   protected void Application_Error(System.Object sender,
      System.EventArgs e)
   {
   }

   protected void Session_End(System.Object sender, System.EventArgs e)
   {
   }

   protected void Application_End(System.Object sender,
      System.EventArgs e)
```

```
    {
    }

    #region Web Form Designer generated code
    /**
     * Required method for Designer support - do not modify
     * the contents of this method with the code editor.
     */
    private void InitializeComponent()
    {
    }
    #endregion
}
```

From an application standpoint, the events of interest are the application start and end events and the request start and end events. We'll discuss the events raised for errors, security, and session handling later. Because the *Global* class defined in Global.asax inherits from *System.Web.HttpApplication*, in each event handler you have access to methods, properties, and events defined in this class. These include the intrinsic objects you'd find on a typical ASP.NET page, such as the *Request*, *Response*, *Server*, *Application* state, and *Session* state objects.

Deploying an ASP.NET Application

As with any .NET Framework application, you can deploy an ASP.NET application by simply using *xcopy* to copy the files to an appropriate directory on the target server. However, this does not configure the appropriate settings required by IIS, such as indicating that the virtual directory being created contains a Web application. Instead, you should use Visual Studio .NET to create a Web Setup project. This project will build a Windows Installer (MSI) file that contains functionality to set up the correct IIS settings as the application is deployed.

To do this, select Web Setup project from under the Setup and Deployment Projects folder in the New Project dialog box. Add this project to the solution that contains the files you want to deploy. The Web Setup project presents you with various views of the deployment information. In the File System view, you can change the properties of the Web Application Folder that represents the virtual directory into which your application will be deployed. In the Properties window, you can set the name of the virtual directory, default document, and so forth. You should add the Content Files and Primary Output from your Web application project (for example, the *FourthCoffee* project) to the Web Application Folder of the Web deployment project so that these are bundled into the installer file. You can then build the installer file by building the Web deployment project.

You can use the installer to deploy the Web application on your own system or on another target server. An example of a Web Setup project is provided in the CakeDeployment sample project. This sample project creates an installer file for the FourthCoffee Web application.

Managing State

In most applications, you'll want to maintain information, or state. You might need to pass this information between pages in various scenarios:

1. When you need to pass information between two or more pages of an application as the user navigates between them. An example is a Web-based shopping cart in which order information is accumulated over many page views (and hence many client requests).
2. When you need to store information on the server between repeated requests to the same page, such as when you use a Web Form (as described earlier).
3. When you need to pass information between two pages of an application that are used to handle a single client request. Your application might invoke an ASP.NET page that performs some calculation, data retrieval, or routing before forwarding the request to another ASP.NET page that generates the HTML output.

ASP.NET provides three state management mechanisms that let you store state in the scope of a request, a session, or the whole application. These mechanisms can help manage state in the scenarios just described.

Session Scope

As noted previously, the lifetime of a page instance is tied to the request that it services. This means that you cannot use instance data—the traditional bastion of state in object-oriented applications—to save state in the first two scenarios listed above. To overcome this, ASP.NET continues and extends the concept of a *Session* object that was introduced in ASP. This *Session* object provides a persistent collection on the server side that can be associated with a particular user. There's no magic to this—the ASP.NET runtime simply uses cookies or URL rewriting to keep track of a particular user. When the user first accesses a page that is indicated to be part of a session, a new session is created and assigned a 128-bit number to identify it. This number is passed back and forth between the client and the server to identify multiple requests that constitute part of the same session.

Pages in a Web application are automatically provided with session state access unless they explicitly indicate that they do not want to be part of a session by setting the attribute *EnableSessionState="false"* in the *<%@ Page %>* directive. If a page is part of a session, you can store session state in the *Session* property of the *Page*. You use the *Add* method to add a data item and give it a name (or key):

```
protected System.Web.UI.WebControls.TextBox Name;
⋮
get_Session().Add("customer", Name.get_Text());
```

Later, you can then retrieve this information using the key as the parameter of the *get_Item* property accessor method of the *Session* object:

```
protected System.Web.UI.WebControls.Label Welcome;
⋮
System.String name = (System.String)get_Session().get_Item("customer");
if (name != null && name.get_Length() != 0)
{
   Welcome.set_Text("Welcome " + name);
}
```

You can see this in action in the code of the sample files FeedsHowManyWithSession.aspx and Login.aspx. In FeedsHowManyWithSession.aspx, you're presented with a hyperlink in the upper right corner that offers you the chance to re-login. This takes you to the Login.aspx page you saw earlier in Figure 16-14. The Click event handler for the Login button stores the login name supplied in the *Session* object before returning you to FeedsHowManyWithSession.aspx. The *Page_Load* method of FeedsHowManyWithSession.aspx sets a greeting using the name retrieved from the *Session* object, as shown in Figure 16-16.

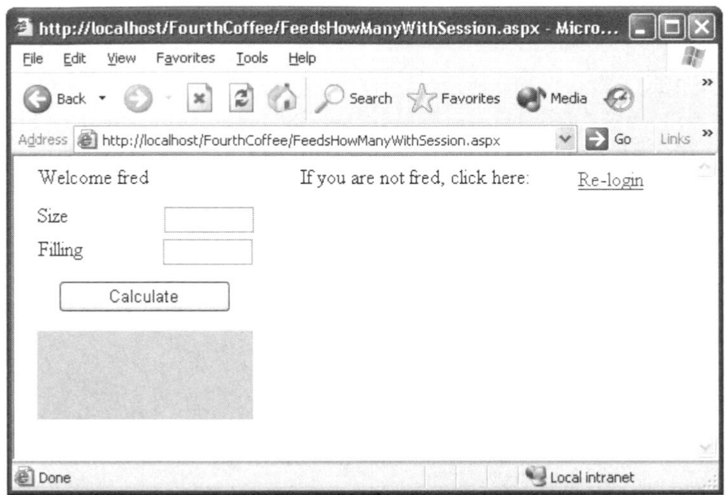

Figure 16-16 The *Session* object provides a way of sharing information between pages.

Caution Be careful when you retrieve data from a session. The type returned by the *get_Item* method is an *Object*, so you must know which type you expect and cast it appropriately.

Only objects can be stored in a session, not primitive types such as integers. If you need to store a primitive type, you should encapsulate it in an instance of its .NET Framework wrapper class. If you need to reset a value stored in the session, you simply use the *Add* method again with a different value. To remove a value, you use the *Remove* method:

```
get_Session().Remove("customer");
```

Caution The keys used by the *Session* are not case sensitive, so do not try to store multiple variables differentiated by case alone. If you do so, you might get an unwanted surprise when you remove one of them!

You can use the *RemoveAll* method or *Clear* method to clear out all of the values stored in a session:

```
get_Session().Clear();
```

In addition to storing objects in the session dynamically, you can also define static objects in the Global.asax file. A static object is instantiated automatically by the ASP.NET runtime. You can define a static object by adding an element to the Global.asax file (not its code-behind):

```
<%@ Application Codebehind="Global.asax.jsl" Inherits="FourthCoffee.Global" %>
<object id="catalog" runat="server" scope="session"
 class="System.Xml.XmlDataDocument" />
```

The line containing the *<object>* element defines a static object called *"catalog"* that is an instance of *System.Xml.XmlDataDocument*. Because the scope attribute is set to *"session"*, every session will have one of these objects created for it. The *HttpSessionState* object has a *StaticObjects* property that contains an instance of *HttpStaticObjectsCollection*. You can use the *GetObject* method of the *HttpStaticObjectsCollection* to retrieve a static object defined in this way:

```
System.Xml.XmlDataDocument doc = (System.Xml.XmlDataDocument)get_Session().
get_StaticObjects().GetObject("catalog");
```

If you need to perform any once-only session initialization, you can place the code in the *Session_Start* method that's defined in the code section of Global.asax. There's also a matching *Session_End* event into which you can add code to perform tasks such as persisting some of the contents of the *Session* object. (Again, consider a shopping cart—when the user quits the application, you might want to preserve the cart.)

Remote Session State

In ASP, you can store session state only in memory. This means that in ASP, session state is localized on the server to which the client connects. This is fine for a single-server solution, but as soon as you start operating in a multiserver environment, such as a Web farm, you have no guarantee that the client will connect to the same server each time. Therefore, you must store any session state in a location where it is accessible to every server in the farm.

You can define different ways of storing session state in the *system.web* section of the Web.config file using the *sessionState* element. You can use attributes of this element to define whether to use cookies to keep track of a session and to set a timeout for the session. The *mode* attribute defines the location in which the state is to be held. This location can be

- **InProc** In-process storage of session state is the default, out-of-the-box mechanism used for state management. It is compatible with ASP. State is stored in memory on the server instance that's handling the call. As stated earlier, this is fine if your application runs on only one server, but it is not robust in the face of failure and is unsuitable for an application that uses multiple Web servers. A typical Web.config entry for in-process state management is

  ```
  <sessionState mode="InProc" cookieless="false" timeout="20" />
  ```

- **StateServer** Out-of-process storage uses the ASP.NET State Service. This is a process that runs as a Windows Service and can be started and stopped using the Services applet in the Administrative Tools window in Control Panel. The ASP.NET State Service ensures that state is maintained should the Web application, or even IIS itself, terminate unexpectedly. It also operates in a Web Farm environment, permitting multiple servers to share the same state information. The ASP.NET State Service is installed as part of .NET Framework. You indicate which server and port the state service will run on using the *stateConnectionString* attribute. By default, the ASP.NET State Service listens on port 42424:

  ```
  <sessionState mode="StateServer"
     stateConnectionString="tcpip=192.168.0.4:42424"
     cookieless="false" timeout="20" />
  ```

- **SQLServer** This mode persists user state to a SQL Server database between page accesses. This mode is tolerant to machine failure because state information is preserved across machine shutdown and reboot. You should create a SQL Server database and populate it with the tables needed by the ASP.NET runtime using the SQL script InstallSqlState.sql located under "\Windows\Microsoft.NET\Framework\.NETVersion\". You can then set the *sqlConnectionString* attribute of the *sessionState* element to a SQL connection string that defines server and security information for the target instance of SQL Server:

  ```
  <sessionState mode="SQLServer"
     sqlConnectionString="data source=ALICE;user id=sa;password="
     cookieless="false" timeout="20" />
  ```

Tip If this is the first time you've accessed SQL Server from ASP.NET, you might encounter authorization issues. To overcome these, you can explicitly grant access to the database using the osql command-line tool supplied with the .NET Framework. First, grant permission to the ASPNET user so it can access the database:

```
C:\>osql -E -SSQLServerHostName
1> exec sp_grantlogin N'ASPApplicationHostName\ASPNET'
2> go
```

You then need to grant access to every database that ASPNET needs, in this case the ASPState database. To do this, execute the following osql commands:

```
3> exec sp_defaultdb N' ASPApplicationHostName \ASPNET', N'ASPState'
4> go
5> exit
```

Caution The contents of the *mode* attribute are case sensitive.

To try the state server or SQL Server state mechanisms, follow the appropriate instructions for installing them in the previous list and uncomment the appropriate part of the FourthCoffee sample project Web.config file. (Two prepared forms are provided—you'll need to edit the addresses and data-source information and comment out the *InProc* entry.) You can use either the *StateServer* mode or *SQLServer* mode for applications that are installed across Web farms. Also note that despite its resilience, the *SQLServer* mode comes at a price—each time you access cached data you're accessing a database, and this can be a slow operation, especially if the database is remote. Earlier, we noted that you can store any type of object in your session state. However, if you use either type of remote state storage, the objects must be serializable because they will be passed across a process boundary.

Application Scope

Some of the state that you want to cache will be used across multiple sessions (multiple users) running the application rather than on a per-session basis. To avoid having to load the same information into each session, you can use an application-scope state storage mechanism to store such state so that it is accessible from all sessions within the application.

Application-scope state is stored for the duration of the application, so it is removed only when the application shuts down. An example of state that you might want to cache across the application is a configurable set of values that are displayed in a drop-down list box. In this case, you can retrieve these values from a data source (perhaps an XML file or a database table) and store them in the *Application* object so that they can be quickly and easily accessed from every session.

Each *Page* has an *Application* property, which is an instance of *System.Web.HttpApplicationState* that represents application-scope state. This class provides the same set of accessor methods we discussed in the last section on session state—namely, *Add*, *Clear*, *Remove*, and *RemoveAll*. The class also has *Item* and *StaticObject* properties through which you can access the contents of the object. Static objects are defined in the same way for application scope as they are for session scope. The only difference is that the object element in Web.config has the *scope="application"* attribute value. There are also *Application_Start* and *Application_End* event handler methods defined in Global.asax, as mentioned earlier, in which you can place per-application initialization and shutdown code.

The *HttpApplicationState* class also has *Get* and *Set* methods that provide access to its contents. The *Get* method simply provides a more intuitive way of accessing the contents of the application object than accessing through the *Item* property. You should use the *Set* method to change the value of an existing entry rather than just using *Add* multiple times, as you would when you change the value of an entry in the session object.

One major difference between session-scope and application-scope state storage is that application-scope storage can be accessed concurrently by multiple threads from different sessions. This means you must guard the contents of the application when you manipulate them. The *HttpApplicationState* class provides *Lock* and *Unlock* methods to assist with this:

```
get_Application().Lock();
get_Application().Add("catalog", doc);
get_Application().UnLock();
```

Application state is particular to the current instance of the application and is not shared across multiple instances in a Web farm.

You can use the *System.Web.Caching.Cache* instance associated with the page as an alternative to the *Application* object for storing application-wide state. The *Cache* class is discussed in more detail later in the chapter.

Request Scope

If you recall our original list of scenarios in which state must be stored, scenario 3 required state to be shared by two pages executing as part of the same request. This is the case if one page transfers a client request to another page using the *Server.Transfer* method (not the *Response.Redirect* method—this would cause the client to start a whole new request). Obviously, you can use the session-scope or application-scope state storage mechanisms, but you can also pass data directly between pages in the same request. Essentially, you do this by adding a reference to the sending page to the receiving page and making the shared data available through property accessors on the sending page.

Cookies

If you want to keep track of your own user information, you can set your own cookies independently of ASP.NET. Consider a situation in which you want to cache the user's name to use it as the default value next time that person logs in. To achieve this, you can create an instance of the *System.Web.HttpCookie* class containing the user's name and then add it to the cookie collection stored in the *Response* object. The following code is from the Login.aspx.jsl sample file:

```
private System.String fcCookieName = "FourthCoffeeUserID";
⋮
private void LoginButton_Click (System.Object sender, System.EventArgs e)
{
// Do other work
⋮
// Store user name in a cookie to use next time
HttpCookie fcCookie = new HttpCookie(fcCookieName, Name.get_Text());
System.DateTime now = System.DateTime.get_Now();
System.TimeSpan duration = new System.TimeSpan(0,0,20,0);

fcCookie.set_Expires(now.Add(duration));

get_Response().get_Cookies().Add(colCookie);
}
```

The *Response* has a *Cookies* property that is a collection of *HttpCookies* to which you can add your new *HttpCookie* instance. The *HttpCookie* constructor has two forms—one just takes a cookie name and the other takes a name and a string value. (Cookies can store only strings, not objects.) Note that if you do not set an expiration time, the cookie will be held in memory in the Web browser and will disappear when the browser instance is closed. The code shown above persists the cookie for 20 minutes.

You can retrieve a cookie that you previously set by accessing the cookie collection of the *Request* object. The *Request* object has a *Cookies* property that contains a collection representing the cookies received from the client. You can retrieve an *HttpCookie* object containing your required cookie by passing its name to the *Get* method of the collection. This code, again from the Login.aspx.jsl sample file, shows how the cookie stored earlier can be retrieved and used. The overall effect is to provide any previously supplied user name as the default value in the User Name text box on the login page:

```
private void Page_Load(System.Object sender, System.EventArgs e)
{
   // Do other work
   ⋮

   // Base the suggested name in the Name field on the cookie
   // if there is one set
   HttpCookie fcCookie = get_Request().get_Cookies().Get(fcCookieName);
   if (fcCookie != null)
   {
      System.String cookieName = fcCookie.get_Value();
      if (cookieName != null && cookieName.get_Length() != 0)
      {
         Name.set_Text(cookieName);
      }
   }
}
```

Note The use of cookies here is fairly simplistic. If you were to do this for real, you would generate a GUID to represent the user and store this as the cookie. You could then use this GUID as the primary key in a database table in which you store the user's information.

Error Handling

The standard .NET error handling mechanism is based on exceptions. When your ASP.NET code uses other classes and components, exceptions might be generated if something goes wrong. As an application developer, you must detect and handle these exceptions appropriately.

An exception usually contains a message and other information to help you figure out the cause of the exception. Generally, this information is useful to the application developer and administrator but not the end user, so you generally won't want to display the exception to the user. Instead, you'll want to log the exception type and message in some persistent way, such as writing to the application error facility on your server or logging the message through Windows Management Instrumentation (WMI). You can then handle the exception in an elegant manner using a combination of the following mechanisms:

- Trying to recover from the error—for example, by retrying a failed database access and then proceeding normally.
- Performing graceful degradation, such as providing only part of the functionality for the user. This process is useful if the error is not critical and useful work can still be done.
- Displaying a user-friendly message to the user so the user understands what is going on and has the option to rectify the problem or return to a previous screen in the application.

The next question is where you handle your errors. You can handle them in three possible ways:

- On an application-wide basis
- On a per-page basis
- Locally, within the method executing at that time

We'll consider each of these in turn.

Application-Wide Error Handling

You can set an overall error handler for your application in the Global.asax file. To do this, you define a method body for the *Application_Error* method in the associated Global.asax.jsl file:

```
protected void Application_Error(System.Object sender, System.EventArgs e)
{
   // Log the error, and then do something about it...
   this.get_Server().Transfer("HandledError.aspx");
}
```

The method shown is from the Global.asax.jsl file in the ErrorHandling sample project. In this case, the error is passed to a specific custom error-handling page, HandledError.aspx, which is also in the ErrorHandling sample project. When the custom error page is loaded, it can retrieve the unhandled error that caused the application-level error handler to be invoked:

```
private void Page_Load(System.Object sender, System.EventArgs e)
{
```

```
    // Write a user-friendly message to the user Label
    UserMessage.set_Text("Please try later");

    System.Exception ex = this.get_Server().GetLastError();

    // Write a detailed message to the developer TextBoxes
    if (ex != null)
    {
        DevMessage.set_Text(ex.get_Message() + "\n\n" +
            ex.get_StackTrace());

        System.Exception nested = ex.get_InnerException();
        if (nested != null)
        {
            NestedMessage.set_Text(nested.get_Message() + "\n\n" +
                nested.get_StackTrace());
        }
    }
    else
    {
        DevMessage.set_Text("No exception information available");
    }
}
```

This error page displays a user-friendly message in the *UserMessage Label* control. Typically, this message is retrieved from a resource file based on the type of error and the circumstances under which it occurred. The two *TextBox* controls, *DevMessage* and *NestedMessage*, display the information that you would typically want to record in an application log file. You can invoke this functionality from the default.htm page in the ErrorHandling sample project. Select the hyperlink for application-wide error handling, and you'll be directed to the ApplicationErrorHandling.aspx page that contains a single button. Clicking this button will generate an exception. Because the exception is not handled in the page, the application-level error handler will catch it and display the HandledError.aspx page.

As you can see from the previous code, the exception that caused this page to be displayed is available from the *GetLastError* method on the *Server* property of the page. Because no specific error handling has been set on the page, the exception reported is an *HttpUnhandledException* that has been used to wrap the real exception. The underlying cause, an *ApplicationException*, is retrieved from the outer exception's *InnerException* property.

The message passed to the exception when it was created, and the stack trace indicating where the exception was generated, are both available for error recording. An example of this information is shown in Figure 16-17.

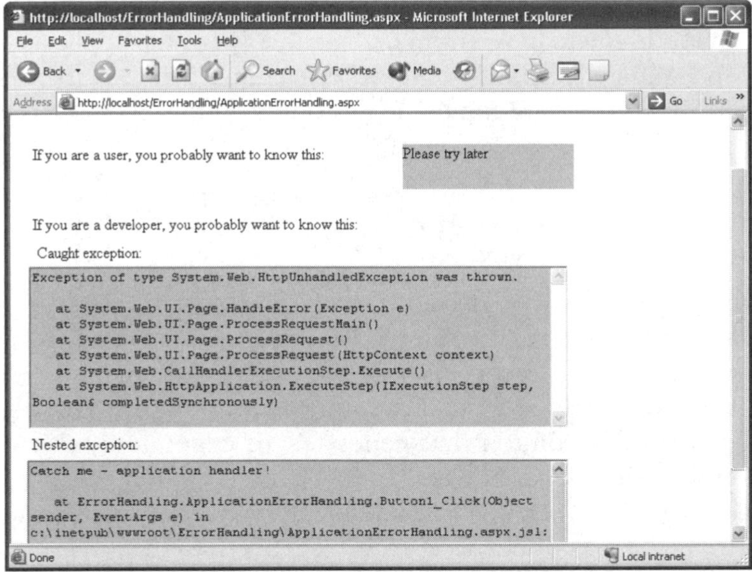

Figure 16-17 Using an error page to display a user-friendly message and log exception information

How you handle the exception will depend on your application, but for an ASP.NET Web application, you might want to redirect the user to an error page that displays an appropriate message. You can do this using the *Transfer* method of the *HttpServerUtility* for the current page:

```
this.get_Server().Transfer("HandledError.aspx");
```

Note There is no simple equivalent of the Windows Forms *MessageBox* class. This form of modal dialog box is available only when you use client-side script to display a JavaScript *Alert*.

You can also specify an error page for HTTP-level errors in the Web.config file. You can set this so remote users see friendly custom error messages and local developers and administrators see the full error details:

```
<customErrors defaultRedirect="defaulterror.aspx" mode="On">
  <error statusCode="404" redirect="filenotfound.htm" />
</customErrors>
```

Page-Specific Error Handling

Although it is useful to have error handling that spans the application, you'll frequently need more location-specific error handling. You can associate a custom error page with each ASPX page in your application by using the *ErrorPage* attribute of the *<%@ Page %>* directive:

```
<%@ Page language="VJ#" Codebehind="FeedsHowMany.aspx.jsl"
 ErrorPage="HandledErrorFromPage.aspx" AutoEventWireup="false"
 Inherits="FourthCoffee.FeedsHowMany" %>
```

This page-specific error handling will take precedence over the application-level error handling. The sample file ErrorPageErrorHandling.aspx defines an error page; you can access it from the page ErrorHandling/default.htm by selecting the per-page error handling using an error page hyperlink. Again, this page has one large button that generates an exception, which causes the defined error page to be shown.

Although the *ErrorPage* attribute is convenient and easy to implement, it suffers from one major drawback—the exception information is not propagated to the error page. To get hold of the exception information on a per-page basis, you must set an error handler when the page loads:

```
private void Page_Load(System.Object sender, System.EventArgs e)
{
   System.EventHandler errorHandler =
      new System.EventHandler(this.Page_Error);
   this.add_Error(errorHandler);
}

private void Page_Error(System.Object sender, System.EventArgs e)
{
   // Error handling code in here...
}
```

To connect the event handler, you add an *EventHandler* delegate to the *Error* property of the *Page*. When your target method is called, you have access to the underlying exception using the *Server.GetLastError* method. The exception returned from this is the exception that caused the problem—it is *not* wrapped in an *HttpUnhandledException*. An example of per-page error handling can be seen in the sample file PageErrorHandling.aspx. You can access this page from the page ErrorHandling/default.htm by selecting the per-page error handling using the Page Error event hyperlink. Again, this page has one large button that generates an exception. This exception is caught in the page and a specific error page is shown.

Note The interaction between page-level, application-level, and global error handling can be quite involved, especially if you do not clear the error. If you plan to use a combined approach in your application, you'd be well advised to experiment a little!

Local Error Handling

In addition to your overall application-level or page-level error handling strategy, you can also handle exceptions in-line in your ASP.NET code. To handle an exception in a method of an ASP.NET application, you can use a try/catch block as you would with any other J# application:

```
private void Calculate_Click (System.Object sender, System.EventArgs e)
{
   try
{
      // Perform business logic
}
catch(Exception ex)
{
      // Handle exception
}
}
```

As before, the action you take will be specific to your application. The sample file TryCatchErrorHandling.aspx shows this type of local exception handling; you can access it from the page ErrorHandling/default.htm by selecting the using try/catch to handle errors hyperlink. Again, this page has one large button that generates an exception, which is caught in a try/catch block.

Generating Exceptions

As an application developer, you might have defined your own set of exceptions based on *System.ApplicationException* that you use to signal application-specific errors:

```
// This should have been cleared on load, so complain if it hasn't
if (get_Session().get_Item("customer") != null)
{
   throw new MultipleLoginException("Multiple login problem");
}
```

You'll want to throw these exceptions where appropriate, including from your ASP.NET pages. If you catch these exceptions using a try/catch block in the method in which they are generated, there will be no problem. But what if you want to take advantage of page-level or application-level error handling? In this case, if you do not catch the exception, it will be caught by the page-level or application-level error handling. This is fine, but there is one thing you must do to make this work in J#. The methods defined as part of the classes in the .NET Framework do not have an attached attribute indicating which exceptions they can throw. However, if you throw any exceptions in your J# code, you must add a *throws* clause to the signature of the method in which you throw them. If you do not do this, the compiler will complain.

The following example shows how you can throw an exception in response to a button click:

```
private void LoginButton_Click (System.Object sender, System.EventArgs e)
   throws System.ApplicationException
{
   // This should have been cleared on load, so complain if it hasn't
   if (get_Session().get_Item("customer") != null)
   {
      throw new MultipleLoginException("Multiple login problem");
   }

   // We don't have any authentication system set up,
   // so just capture the user name and use this to be
   // friendly!
   get_Session().Add("customer", Name.get_Text());
   get_Server().Transfer("FeedsHowMany.aspx");
}
```

Security

If you're developing a professional application, security will likely be an important issue. Parts of your application might need to be restricted to authorized administrators, you might need to keep the contents of an exchange between client and server private, or you might simply need to identify your user to implement personalization features. ASP.NET has automatic security features that cater to different types of authentication and provide flexible authorization.

Authentication

ASP.NET uses the same type of declarative security configuration that you encountered with HTTP Remoting in Chapter 11. You can configure different parts of your application to require different levels of security. A user who navigates to a secure part of the application must be authenticated to determine whether he or she has the appropriate access rights.

You can indicate the type of authentication required by the application in the Web.config file, using the *authentication* element within the *system.web* element:

```
<authentication mode="Windows" />
```

The *mode* attribute defines the type of security to be used. In the example shown, it is set to use the underlying Windows security system, which will be based on the principals set up on your machine or domain. While this might be suitable for an intranet application, it won't be too useful if you're setting up your Web application for use by external users around the globe. In this case, you can set the authentication mode to Passport or Forms.

Passport-based authentication takes advantage of the Microsoft Passport system to authenticate users from either inside or outside the organization who have Passport accounts. Microsoft supplies the Passport SDK (available from *http://www.microsoft.com/myservices/passport/default.asp*), which you can use to authenticate a user. You can create an ASP.NET page that prompts the user for the details and verifies those details using the Passport SDK. The ASP.NET configuration file should specify the URL of this page, which will be invoked automatically whenever an unauthenticated user attempts to access your application:

```
<authentication mode="Passport">
   <passport redirectURL="FourthCoffeePassportAuth.aspx">
   </passport>
</authentication>
```

Using Forms authentication, you can also set up your own custom authentication system based on credentials supplied by the user in an HTML form (a traditional Web login page). Your application can then authenticate the user in its own way using the credentials entered.

The following example shows how forms-based authentication is configured. The *name* attribute specifies a cookie that will be used to hold user information when the user has been authenticated. (Additional attributes are available for specifying that the cookie should be encrypted or have a limited life.) This cookie is sent back to the server on every subsequent page access, and it ensures that the user is not reprompted for credentials every time he or she accesses a restricted resource. The *loginUrl* attribute is the name of the ASP.NET page that will be displayed if an unauthenticated user attempts to access the system. This is the page that should perform the necessary user validation and create the authentication cookie:

```
<authentication mode="Forms">
   <forms name="FourthCoffee" loginUrl="Login.aspx">
```

```
   </forms>
</authentication>
```

In both cases, if a user is redirected to an authentication page, the location of the original page that was requested will be cached until an authentication decision is made. A user who is authenticated can be transferred to the page originally requested using the static *RedirectFromLoginPage* method of the *System.Web.Security.FormsAuthentication* class (which contains a variety of static helper methods that are useful for building pages designed to authenticate users).

If you're using forms-based authentication, it's up to you how users are verified. User details can be held in a database, held in Active Directory, or even specified using the *credentials* child element of the *forms* element in the Web.config file, as shown below. You should supply a username and password pair for each valid user. Ideally, you should also encrypt the password, specifying the algorithm used with the *passwordFormat* attribute. (MD5 and SHA1 are currently supported.)

```
<authentication mode="Forms">
   <forms name="FourthCoffee" loginUrl="Login.aspx">
      <credentials passwordFormat="SHA1">
         <user name="ALongshaw"
            password="ADBF56F784AB63287CDF5F8092ACF5EF47139FD4"/>
         <user name="JSharp"
            password="75229FDA6812B5F9A3E6FCD12950F3CA5471EE75"/>
      </credentials>
   </forms>
</authentication>
```

The ASP.NET Web Form that performs the authentication can then execute *FormsAuthentication.Authenticate*, passing in the name and password entered by the user. The *Authenticate* method checks the name and password against each pair of credentials stored in the Web.config file until a match is found or the list is exhausted, and it returns a Boolean value indicating whether authentication was successful, as shown in the following example. (*Name* and *Password* are the names of *Text* fields on the authentication form.)

```
if (FormsAuthentication.Authenticate(Name.get_Text(), Password.get_Text()))
{
   FormsAuthentication.RedirectFromLoginPage(Name.get_Text(), false);
}
```

Authorization

For an authenticated user, you can use that person's principal information to assign access rights to particular resources. Again, you can use declarative security in the Web.config file with the *authorization* element:

```
<?xml version="1.0" encoding="utf-8" ?>
<configuration>
  <system.web>
    <authorization>
      <deny users="?"/>
    </authorization>
    ⋮
  </system.web>
</configuration>
```

The example denies anonymous users (denoted by the question mark) access to all application resources. An anonymous user is any user who is not authenticated. Many Web applications, especially those used over the Internet, provide some or all of their functionality to anonymous users. The setting shown means that users who try to access the Web application must be authenticated before they can use it. You can selectively allow access to an application by combining the *deny* element with the *allow* element:

```
<authorization>
   <deny users="*"/>
   <allow users="fred,joe,sue"/>
</authorization>
```

This allows only *fred*, *joe*, and *sue* access to the application and denies access to all other users (denoted by the asterisk). If your underlying security provider understands the concept of roles, you can also perform the authorization based on roles. If you're using Windows security, a role corresponds to a Windows group. The following example allows access to all members of the Administrators group:

```
<authorization>
   <deny users="*"/>
   <allow roles="Administrators"/>
</authorization>
```

While application-wide limitations are useful, most applications require more fine-grained control over access to resources so that some resources are accessible to all (such as a home page) and other resources have more stringent access restrictions. To implement this, you can specify location-specific authorization settings in the configuration element. The following example allows all users to view the Search.aspx page but limits access to any resources (such as ASPX pages) in the Admin subdirectory to members of the Administrators role:

```
<configuration>
  ⋮
  <system.web>
    <authorization>
      <deny users="?"/>
    </authorization>
  </system.web>

  <location path="Search.aspx">
    <system.web>
      <authorization>
        <allow users="*"/>
      </authorization>
    </system.web>
  </location>

  <location path="Admin">
    <system.web>
      <authorization>
        <allow roles="Administrators"/>
      </authorization>
    </system.web>
  </location>
</configuration>
```

Note The authorization defined in the Web.config file applies only to ASP.NET components such as ASPX files and not to plain HTML (HTM) files.

Caching

Two forms of caching are provided in ASP.NET:

- The caching of data to be used by the application logic
- The caching of generated page output so that it can be sent as part of subsequent responses without having to be regenerated

We'll examine both of these types of caching next.

Caching Application Data

The ASP.NET *System.Web.Caching.Cache* class provides an application-wide cache for data. Although it is similar to the *System.Web.HttpApplicationState* class in scope and intent, the *Cache* class provides a more sophisticated caching model. One instance of the *Cache* class is created automatically in each application domain, and it remains valid the entire time the application domain is active. It disappears only when the application domain is destroyed. It is accessible through the *Cache* property (*get_Cache*) of the current ASP.NET page. As with the *HttpApplicationState* class, you can store any type of object in a *Cache*, and the object is referenced by means of a *String* key. However, you can provide the *Add* method of the *Cache* with more information:

- **A timeout** You can set a timeout in absolute or relative terms, after which the entry will expire. When an entry expires, it is removed from the cache. One parameter to *Add* represents an absolute time, as a *DateTime* instance, at which the cache entry will expire. Alternatively, or in addition, you can pass in another parameter that a represents a relative, or sliding, timeout as a *TimeSpan* instance. If the cache entry has not been accessed for the given relative timeout, it will expire and be discarded. The timer associated with the relative timeout will be reset every time that entry is accessed. If you do not want your data to time out, you can pass *null* for these parameters.
- **A dependency** You can associate the cache entry with one or more files or directories by using the *CacheDependency* class. If any of the specified files or directories changes, the cache entry will expire and be discarded. You can also make one cache entry dependent on another so that it will expire when the other entry expires. Each cache entry can be dependent on multiple files, directories, and cache entries. Although the *Add* method takes only one *CacheDependency* class, you can choose from various constructors and you can construct nested *CacheDependencies* if required.
- **A callback** You can pass in an instance of the *CacheItemRemovedCallback* that specifies a method to be called when the cache entry expires. This can potentially update the contents of the entry if appropriate, or it can persist the last value of the entry to underlying storage. The callback is provided with the entry's key and value, together with a reason for its removal.
- **A priority** If ASP.NET starts to run low on memory, it will start removing items from the cache. You can set the priority of cache entries, which the cache manager will use when deciding which

entries to evict first. The priority value can be one of the entries in the *CacheItemPriority* enumeration.

Here's an example of adding and retrieving a cache entry:

```
DataSet catalog = null;
if (get_Cache().Get("CakeCatalog") != null)
{
   catalog = (DataSet)get_Cache().Get("CakeCatalog");
}
else
{
   System.String xmlFile = get_Server().MapPath("CakeCatalog.xml");
   catalog = new DataSet("catalog");
   catalog.ReadXml(xmlFile);

   System.DateTime now = System.DateTime.get_Now();
   System.DateTime midnight = new System.DateTime(now.get_Year(),
      now.get_Month(),
      now.get_Day(),
      23, 59, 59);

   get_Cache().Add("CakeCatalog",
      catalog,
      new CacheDependency(xmlFile),
      midnight,
      Cache.NoSlidingExpiration,
      CacheItemPriority.AboveNormal,
      null);
}
```

To retrieve an entry from the *Cache*, you call the *Get* method, passing in the key used to store it. As with the *Session* and *Application* objects, *Cache* values are stored as *System.Object*, so you must cast the return value appropriately.

In the example code, if no *Cache* entry is found for the given key, a new entry of the appropriate type (in this case, a *DataSet*) will be created. When the new entry is added, no callback is provided. If the callback or dependency is not required, it can be set to null. The example sets the absolute timeout to midnight on the day that the entry is stored, but no sliding timeout is set. You can specify one timeout or the other (or no timeout), but not both. To pass in an empty timeout value, you use the fixed values *NoSlidingExpiration* and *NoAbsoluteExpiration*, which are exposed as properties of the *Cache* class. The example code then sets a dependency on the file that contains the XML, using the *CacheDependency* constructor that takes the name of a single file. This code is used by the sample file ShowXmlCatalog.aspx.jsl in the FourthCoffee project to store the XML information for the cake catalog in the *Cache* object.

To overwrite an existing entry, you use the *Insert* method. Various overloaded forms of the *Insert* method allow you to reset the timeouts, dependencies, and callback, as well as the value. Otherwise, you can just refresh the value while retaining the rest of the information for the entry:

```
get_Cache().Insert("CakeCatalog", catalog);
```

Finally, you can remove a cache entry by using the *Remove* method:

```
get_Cache().Remove("CakeCatalog");
```

Note The *Cache* operates in conjunction with the session state management features of ASP.NET, and it can be retained using the ASP.NET State Server service or even retained in a SQL Server database, depending on the setting of the *<sessionState>* element in the Web.config file.

Output Caching

Although it is useful to be able to dynamically generate output to send to a browser, it can also cause overhead. If the information generated does not change for every client request, you can cache the output and serve the same page multiple times without having to regenerate it. This can significantly improve performance when you generate pages based on slowly changing data. Output caching depends on both the client and the server (and any intermediate proxies) supporting HTTP 1.1.

The simplest way to enable output caching is to use the *<%@ Output %>* directive in your ASPX page. This tag defines a caching time as follows:

```
<%@ OutputCache Duration="180" VaryByParam="None" %>
```

The *Duration* attribute defines the amount of time, in seconds, for which the generated page will be cached. When the duration expires, the page will be regenerated and then cached again for the same amount of time.

You can use the *VaryByParam* attribute to cache multiple versions of a page based on the parameters passed back in a *GET* or *POST* request. To create multiple cached versions based on the value of a particular parameter, you set the value of the *VaryByParam* attribute to the name of the parameter. You can define multiple attributes as the basis on which a version of the page will be cached by providing a semicolon-separated list:

```
<%@ OutputCache Duration="180" VaryByParam="Size;Filling" %>
```

To vary the page by any parameter, you use an asterisk as the attribute value. The *VaryByParam* attribute must be there even if, as in the earlier example, it is set to *None*. You can also cache multiple versions of a page based on HTTP header values or the requesting browser.

Sometimes only parts of a page will be constant while other parts will vary for every request. You can cache the constant parts by creating user controls that represent the parts that do not change often. You can then set the output caching for that control by using the <%@ *OutputCache* %> directive in its ASPX file. Alternatively, you can attach the *PartialCaching* attribute to the class in the code-behind for the user control. Again, multiple versions of these cached user controls can be maintained based on parameters and other factors.

You can also set all of the caching properties and behavior for a page programmatically.

Summary

This chapter described how the ASP programming model has been rolled forward into ASP.NET and made more powerful. Web Forms simplify much of the user interface code required for a Web application, and they make it as easy to develop a Web-based user interface as one based on the Windows user interface. You learned how a Web Form consists of an HTML file and associated code-behind and how each Web Form inherits from the *Page* class, which provides the intrinsic objects required to process the user request. You also learned that you can use the various types of validator Web controls so that client-generated events are handled on the server while validation remains on the client.

You learned that ASP.NET provides a wide range of server-side controls but that you can also create your own custom user controls. The chapter explained how data in a *DataSet* can be bound to data-oriented controls such as *DataGrid* controls. You saw how Web applications are configured and deployed and how security is configured. You learned about different scopes and types of state management, from request scope to session scope and application scope. Finally, you learned how ASP.NET's output caching can help to speed up requests for Web pages.

17

Building a Web Service

Web services are among the hottest topics in the software industry because they promise interoperability between heterogeneous systems through a commonly accepted set of standards that govern the layout and transportation of data. Web services also provide the foundation for the Global XML Web Services Architecture (GXA), which was discussed briefly at the end of Chapter 13. This chapter will describe the Web services architecture and show how you can exploit it to make services and components easily available over the Web. It will show how to create a Web service and how SOAP, XML, and HTTP interoperate to provide a generic transport mechanism for data. You'll also learn techniques for using Web services as facades for COM and other components. This chapter assumes that you're familiar with Web-oriented development, including ASP.NET as covered in Chapter 16.

An Overview of Web Services

Before we look at how to build and use Web services with Microsoft Visual J# .NET, let's briefly examine the technologies and principles that Web services are built on.

What Is a Web Service?

Generally speaking, the term *Web service* can have one of two related but distinct definitions:

- A set of standards and technologies that simplify integration of applications within and between organizations.

- The application of these standards and technologies to create a dynamic, online environment in which services can be discovered when they are required.

Much of the hype surrounding Web services is about the latter definition—the grand vision of Web services. For example, suppose your car's computer system detects that the engine needs its 12,000-mile service and then looks up the nearest car dealerships in some form of online registry. The car's computer can then use Web services to contact these dealerships, get the most competitive quote, determine the available time slots, and then give you this information. If you accept a quote and agree to get your car serviced, the car's onboard computer can then book you some movie tickets, through the Web services offered by the nearest theater, so you can watch a film while you wait for the car to be serviced. All of this can happen without human intervention (although you do have to watch the film yourself—you can't get Web services to do that for you).

The standards and technologies underlying Web services make this scenario possible, but you'd need to sort out many technical and business issues before this sort of interaction would be practical. As you'll see, even though Web services provide a useful integration mechanism, several key parts of the overall puzzle are missing, such as end-to-end security and transaction propagation. To address this, Microsoft and IBM have proposed a comprehensive architecture to enable the overall vision. This architecture, the GXA, will address such issues as security, transactions, value-added messaging, and business process flow.

While you're waiting for this brave new world of global Web services to emerge, you can use the Web service technologies available today to integrate existing applications. Web service interfaces are based on common standards, so you can integrate components with other Web service–based applications with far less effort than you would expend using many older mechanisms. This chapter and the next one will show you what you can do using the available Web service technologies delivered with Visual J# .NET.

Web Service Technologies

Chapter 1 provided a brief overview of Web services. Here, we'll take a whistle-stop tour of the technologies that underlie Web services.

HTTP

Most Web service traffic is propagated by the standard Web transport protocol Hypertext Transfer Protocol (HTTP). The advantage of using a common Web protocol such as HTTP is that it is already widely used. HTTP is often called "firewall friendly" because most firewalls will let HTTP pass through, although some will limit it to common HTTP ports such as 80, 8080, and 443. This is a great boon for the adoption of Web services, although some security issues remain unresolved.

At the protocol level, HTTP is a request/response protocol that carries a byte-encoded payload. The most common type of data that HTTP carries is text, such as an HTML document. The rest of the HTTP message consists of a header that defines, among other things, the type of content carried in the rest of the message. When a client sends an HTTP message, it is delivered to the server (which is usually listening on port 80), which processes the message and sends back a response over the same channel.

XML

We discussed XML and many of its uses in Chapter 5 and Chapter 6. In terms of Web services, XML is used for encoding the payload of Web service messages. The SOAP protocol specification defines a schema for XML messages that contains parameters and return values for Web service calls. The XML Schema standard provides type information in Web service calls. It defines a set of common types, such as strings and integers, and offers the ability to define your own compound or complex types. You can use XML to describe the operations offered by a Web service along with the types and numbers of parameters and return values. Using XML means that such a description will be independent of any particular platform or language.

MIME

XML is used to encode Web service requests and responses, but not everything can be described easily by using XML. In some cases, you might want to send binary data as part of a message, and mapping this into and out of XML can be a major undertaking. (The message would end up being very large, too.) In these cases, you can use Multipurpose Internet Mail Extensions (MIME) to attach binary data to an XML-based SOAP message. This makes transmitting and processing the data a lot more efficient.

MIME originated as a way of transmitting multimedia e-mail messages. You can use it with any text-based protocol that has a header, such as HTTP. To use MIME, you split a document into parts, each with its own section header. The section header defines the type of content held in that section, and the overall message is defined as having a content type of *multipart/mime*.

SOAP

SOAP originated from an effort to provide a Web-friendly transport mechanism for object-based remote procedure calls (RPCs). SOAP defines an XML message structure for encoding calls and their responses. A SOAP message can then be sent across any protocol that can carry XML. The most common protocol used is HTTP, although you can use other protocols as needed, such as Simple Mail Transfer Protocol (SMTP) for connectionless message exchange. The SOAP protocol employs MIME to attach non-XML data to SOAP messages. (This is sometimes called *SOAP with attachments*).

A SOAP message is contained in a SOAP envelope. The SOAP envelope contains a SOAP header and a SOAP body. The header contains metainformation for the message, and the body contains details of the operation to be performed. Figure 17-1 shows the format of a SOAP message. We'll look more closely at the contents of a SOAP message later in the chapter.

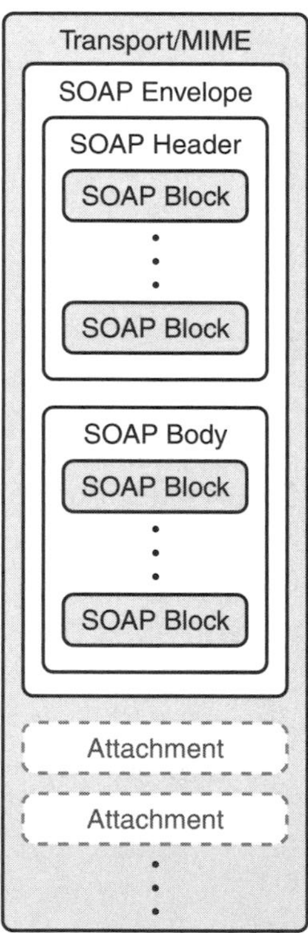

Figure 17-1 A SOAP message, which consists of a SOAP header, a SOAP body, and optionally some non-XML attachments

WSDL

Web Service Description Language (WSDL) provides an XML description of a Web service. Conceptually, WSDL is similar to the Interface Definition Languages (IDLs) used by COM and CORBA to define the methods, parameters, and return values of RPCs. However, WSDL can contain additional information relating to the location of the service.

A WSDL document consists of three basic parts:

- The definition of the interface, which comprises a list of messages that can be sent and the responses to be expected. Each message definition includes the number and types of the parameters and return values. These messages are grouped into *portType* elements, which define a logical grouping of operations. (An operation is based on a message.) A *portType* is similar to a COM or CORBA interface.
- Data type definitions. The XML Schema definition and the SOAP specification provide a set of standard data types, but you might need specific complex types to describe parameters passed by the Web service. We'll discuss these in more detail later in the chapter.
- Transport and endpoint information, including how to pass messages over a specific transport, such as SOAP. A *port* defines the location of a "live" service that implements the interface defined in a *portType*. A *service* is a group of ports that are offered as part of a logical service.

The specifics of WSDL documents are discussed later in the chapter.

UDDI

Once you've created your Web service, you have to figure out how potential users will locate it. If the number of users is limited, you can let them know the location of your service through e-mail or a similar mechanism and send them the WSDL description. However, this process is not scalable or feasible for a large number of users.

Universal Description, Discovery, and Integration (UDDI) defines a way of registering Web service information so that it can be dynamically discovered. UDDI provides a business-oriented registry and technical descriptions of the services (such as WSDL). A Web service user can look up services and their descriptions in a UDDI registry and use them to contact the Web service and make requests. Some public UDDI registries are accessible via the Internet, whereas internal UDDI registries can be run within organizations. UDDI is discussed in more detail in Chapter 18.

New Technologies in the GXA

As mentioned previously, solutions to some of the outstanding issues relating to Web services will be addressed in the GXA. Various proposals might form part of the GXA:

- **Web Service Flow Language (WSFL) and XLANG** These two proposals define a multiple message exchange between a client and a Web service.
- **Web Service Inspection Language (WSIL)** This proposal addresses the need to examine the Web service capabilities of a particular site. (This is covered in more detail in Chapter 18, which covers the DISCO discovery protocol.)
- **Web Services Referral Protocol (WS-Referral)** This is a simple SOAP-based protocol for configuring instructions about the routing of SOAP messages.
- **Web Services Routing Protocol (WS-Routing)** This is a simple, stateless, SOAP-based protocol for routing SOAP messages in an asynchronous manner over a variety of transports such as TCP, UDP, and HTTP.
- **Web Services Security (WS-Security)** This defines a set of security measures to provide end-to-end security for SOAP messages.
- **XML Digital Signature** This provides the ability to sign an XML document to authenticate its origin.
- **XML Encryption** This defines how an XML document should be encrypted and decrypted for end-to-end privacy.

For more details about the GXA and how it is evolving, see the protocol overview at *http://msdn.microsoft.com/ library/en-us/dnglobspec/html/wsspecs-over.asp*.

Web Services in .NET

Web services are a core part of the Microsoft .NET platform. You can deliver a Web service under the .NET platform in two ways:

- By creating a Web service based on ASP.NET. This Web service will live in a virtual directory under the control of Microsoft Internet Information Services (IIS). Visual Studio .NET allows you to create an ASP.NET Web service in all supported languages, including J#. The creation of Web service clients under Visual Studio .NET is covered in Chapter 18.

- By providing a .NET Remoting server that uses the HTTP transport and the XML serializer. Such a server can expose its methods as an XML Web service. The creation of this type of server was covered in Chapter 11. The creation of clients for this type of Web service is covered in Chapter 18.

As mentioned, Web services created under Visual Studio .NET can be written in any supported language and will run as managed code under the common language runtime. As such, they'll have access to all of the functionality in the .NET Framework Class Library. Specific classes for Web service creation are defined under the *System.Web.Services* namespace.

Creating a Web Service

So much for all the theory. How does this work in practice? The obvious thing to do next is to create a simple Web service and see how it works.

A Simple Web Service

An ASP.NET-based Web service is defined in an ASMX file. This file is similar to the ASPX files found in ASP.NET Web applications in that it can contain a mixture of ASP.NET directives (embedded in <%@ %> tags) and executable code. The main difference between an ASMX file and an ASPX file is that the ASMX file is not intended to contain any static markup. (An ASPX file will usually contain HTML as well as code.) This means that the whole ASMX file, excluding the directives, will be treated as executable code, so you do not have to enclose it in code render blocks or script tags.

Defining the Web Service

Let's say we want to create a Web service based on the simple form of the *FeedsHowMany* method. The first thing we need to do is create a file with the ASMX extension. This file must contain a Web service directive (<%@ *WebService* %>) that provides information about the Web service:

```
<%@ WebService Language="VJ#" Class="SimpleEnquiry" %>
```

As with the ASP.NET <%@ *Page* %> directive, the <%@ *WebService* %> directive defines the language in which the code on the page is written. It also defines a class to be used to service requests. This brings up another difference between Web services and other ASP.NET Web applications. ASP.NET Web applications that use the <%@ *Page* %> directive define a class from which they inherit. (The runtime creates a new class based on this inherited functionality and the various controls and tags defined in the ASPX file.) In the case of Web services, the code you supply is all that's needed to define and implement the service, so no new class is created. The class that handles requests for the Web service can be defined in the current file or can be held in a separate assembly in the bin directory of the virtual directory containing the Web service, or in the Global Assembly Cache (GAC). As you'll see later, you can use code-behind for Web services as well.

Implementing the Web Service

Your Web service must send and receive SOAP messages encoded in XML, so you might expect to have to write a lot of "plumbing" code to implement a Web service. However, to create a simple XML Web service based on ASP.NET, all you do is write a class in J# that implements the methods you want to expose as part of your Web service. You then tag each method you want to expose with the *WebMethod* attribute (*System.Web.Services.WebMethodAttribute*), as shown here:

```
/** @attribute WebMethodAttribute() */
public int FeedsHowMany(int diameter,
   System.String shape, System.String filling)
```

This attribute tells the ASP.NET runtime that you want to make this method visible as part of your Web service. Any methods that you want to expose must have *public* visibility, but the opposite is not true—*public* methods are not automatically exposed as part of your Web service; only those labeled with the *WebMethod* attribute are.

The parameters of this version of the method are a little different from before. Earlier versions of this method, described in the previous chapters, used *int* values for the shape and filling. These values were defined as constants in two other J# classes. This *FeedsHowMany* method will be exposed using WSDL, so it uses strings (such as *"square"*) to transmit this information because it is simpler than exposing the two other classes. The mapping of types and passing of nonstandard types are discussed later in the chapter. The complete *SimpleEnquiry* class is shown in the SimpleEnquiry.asmx sample file.

SimpleEnquiry.asmx

```
<%@ WebService Language="VJ#" Class="SimpleEnquiry" %>

import System.Web.Services.*;

public class SimpleEnquiry
```

```
{
   /** @attribute WebMethodAttribute() */
   public int FeedsHowMany(int diameter,
String shape, String filling)
   {
      Boolean fruitFilling = (filling.Equals("fruit")) ? true : false;
      double munchSizeFactor = (fruitFilling ? 2.5 : 1);
      int numConsumers = (int)(diameter * munchSizeFactor);

      return numConsumers;
   }
}
```

Testing the Web Service

You can place this ASMX file into any IIS virtual directory that allows scripts to be executed, and it will be identified and interpreted correctly. As with ASPX files, the .asmx suffix is defined as being associated with Windows\Microsoft.NET\Framework\<*.NETVersion*>\aspnet_isapi.dll, so files with this suffix will be passed to the ASP.NET runtime to be processed. Once the file has been placed in a suitable directory, you can access it directly from a browser using its standard URL. If you have installed the sample RawWebServices project on your local machine, you can access the XML Web service using the URL *http://localhost/RawWebServices/SimpleEnquiry.asmx*. This will display the page shown in Figure 17-2.

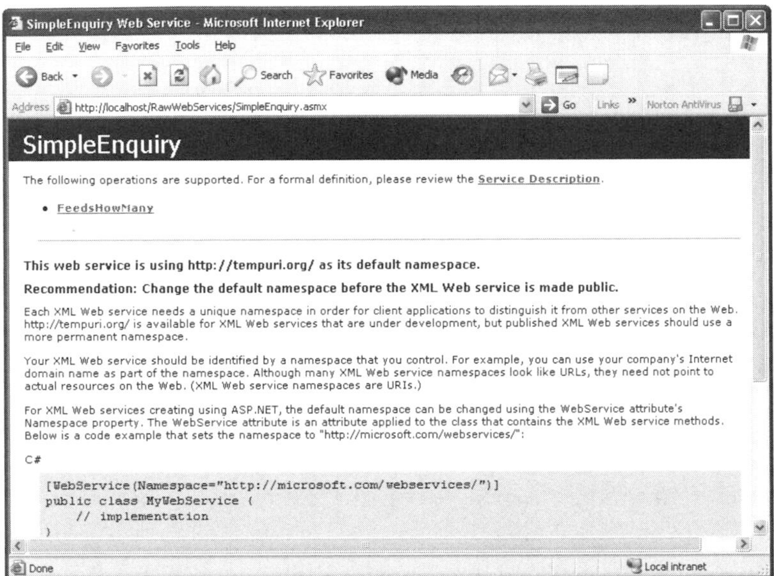

Figure 17-2 Using the default URL for an ASP.NET-based Web service in a Web browser to display information about the service

What's happening here is that the ASP.NET runtime is working out that this is not really a request to use the service. Using the basic page URL will issue a simple HTTP *GET* request for the page. This request contains no Web service information, so it will be interpreted as a browser-based request for information about the service. In response to such a browser-based request, ASP.NET will generate the HTML page shown in Figure 17-2. Most of this Web page tells you to use a valid namespace in your XML Web service description, but we'll ignore this for now and discuss it later. For the time being, concentrate on the *FeedsHowMany* bulleted hyperlink on the left side., When you click this hyperlink, it will take you to the test page for the *FeedsHowMany* method, as shown in Figure 17-3.

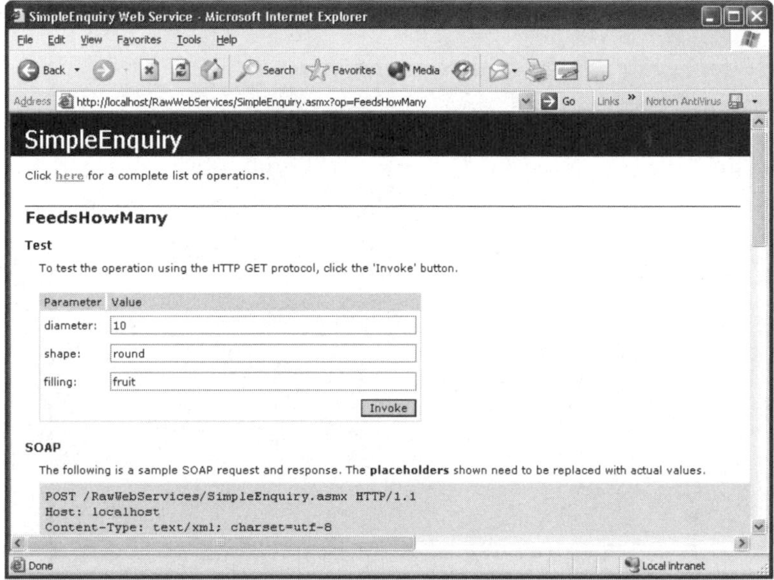

Figure 17-3 Testing your Web services using a Web browser

There's more to the test page than you can see in the figure—namely, protocol descriptions for the method. The protocol exchanges are discussed later—for now, you just need to know that the ASP.NET runtime makes this service accessible over raw HTTP (using either *POST* or *GET* methods) as well as SOAP. As you can see, this test page allows you to enter values for the three parameters. We filled these out with typical values (for a 10-inch round fruit cake). When you click the Submit button, the values will be sent to the Web service using the HTTP *GET* method, as you can see if you examine the HTML that defines the form containing the three parameter input fields:

```
<form target="_blank" action=
'http://localhost/RawWebServices/SimpleEnquiry.asmx/FeedsHowMany'
 method="GET">
```

In the case of requests that use HTTP *GET* or *POST*, you encode the target method by appending it to the Web service URL. The submission in this case uses *GET*, so the parameter values are simply encoded and appended to the URL. The result of sending these values to the Web service is shown in Figure 17-4.

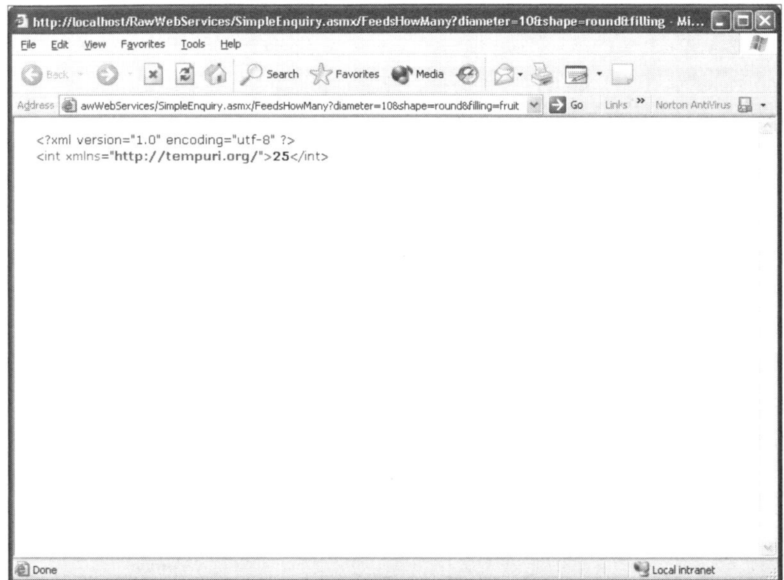

Figure 17-4 The result of submitting a test through the SimpleEnquiry Web service test page

Compilation and Dependencies

You've probably noticed that we haven't touched a compiler yet. Chapter 16 described ASP.NET's automatic compilation mechanism. If you create an XML Web service based on ASP.NET, this automatic compilation will also be performed on ASMX files. You can find the compiled version of SimpleEnquiry.asmx in a subdirectory named after the host virtual directory, under the folder \Windows\Microsoft.NET\Framework\<*.NETVersion*>\Temporary ASP.NET Files. If you look, you'll find two pairs of XML files and DLL assemblies. One of the DLL assemblies is the compiled version of the *SimpleEnquiry* class. The associated XML file (SimpleEnquiry.asmx.<*a number*>.xml) specifies the name of the assembly containing *SimpleEnquiry*, plus the source code file on which it depends:

```
<preserve assem="2szhq2zu" type="SimpleEnquiry" hash="14e3044cee7">
   <filedep name="c:\inetpub\wwwroot\RawWebServices\SimpleEnquiry.asmx" />
</preserve>
```

The other assembly and its associated XML file relate to the generation of WSDL for this service (as discussed later in the chapter).

The Web service shown is simple, with many loose ends and unanswered questions (which we'll cover in the rest of the chapter). The first question to answer is how you can create such a Web service using Visual Studio .NET.

Creating a Web Service Using Visual Studio .NET

Visual Studio .NET is intended to simplify the creation of all types of .NET applications, including XML Web services. When you create an XML Web service in Visual Studio .NET, you're essentially creating an ASP.NET application with a few variations. To create an XML Web service in Visual Studio .NET, select the Visual J# ASP.NET Web Service template in the New Project dialog box, as shown in Figure 17-5.

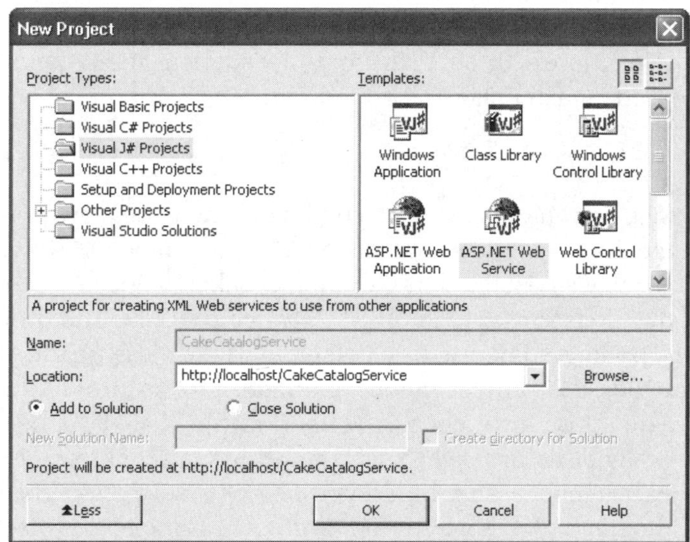

Figure 17-5 Selecting an ASP.NET Web service in the Visual Studio .NET New Project dialog box

The project wizard will create a skeleton XML Web service that contains the following items:

- All of the artifacts you would associate with a standard ASP.NET Web application, including Global.asax, Web.config, AssemblyInfo.jsl, references to standard libraries, and a new virtual directory under IIS in which to house the files.
- A Web service ASMX file. By default, this file is called Service1.asmx.
- A discovery (VSDISCO) file. This is a skeleton file to be used as part of the DISCO Web service discovery protocol.

You've already seen the ASP.NET application files, and discovery is covered in Chapter 18, so we'll focus now on the Web service file itself. The contents of Service1.asmx are similar to those of SimpleEnquiry.asmx (shown earlier), except Service1.asmx is set up automatically to use the code-behind model:

```
<%@ WebService Language="VJ#" Codebehind="Service1.asmx.jsl"
 Class="CakeEnquiryService.Service1" %>
```

Tip In Visual Studio, if you double-click on the Service1.asmx file, you'll see a design screen. To view and edit the actual file, right-click on the file, choose Open With from the shortcut menu, and select Source Code (Text) Editor.

The design screen offers you a hyperlink to the code view of the Web service. The default code provided is contained in the sample file Service1.asmx.jsl (shown below) that's contained in the sample CakeCatalogService project. The structure of the file is similar to an ASP.NET *Page* subclass. The project has various standard packages imported by default, and the class is placed in a package that matches the project name. A constructor is provided, and some initialization and closedown code is defined in the *#region* generated by the component designer. At first sight, this last part might seem strange. A Web service has no user interface, so why do you need the services of the component designer? Although a Web service class will have no need for visual controls, such as buttons and text boxes, you can still drop nongraphical controls onto the Web Forms designer surface for an ASMX file. These controls are accessible in the code-behind, and you can set their properties using the Property sheet in Visual Studio .NET.

Service1.asmx.jsl

```
package CakeEnquiryService;

import System.* ;
import System.Collections.*;
import System.ComponentModel.*;
import System.Data.*;
import System.Diagnostics.*;
import System.Web.*;
import System.Web.Services.*;

/**
 * Summary description for Service1.
 */
```

```
public class Service1 extends System.Web.Services.WebService
{
   public Service1()
   {
      //CODEGEN: This call is required by the ASP.NET Web Services Designer
      InitializeComponent();
   }

   #region Component Designer generated code

   /**
    * Required by the Web Services Designer
    */
   private IContainer components = null;

   /**
    * Required method for Designer support - do not modify
    * the contents of this method with the code editor.
    */
   private void InitializeComponent()
   {

   }

   /**
    * Clean up any resources being used.
    */
   protected void Dispose(boolean disposing )
   {
      if(disposing && components != null)
      {
         components.Dispose();
      }
      super.Dispose(disposing);
   }

   #endregion


   /**
    * WEB SERVICE EXAMPLE
    * The HelloWorld() example service returns the string Hello World
    * To build, uncomment the following lines then save and build the project
    * To test this web service, press F5
    */

//    /** @attribute WebMethod() */
//    public System.String HelloWorld()
```

```
//   {
//      return "Hello World";
//   }
}
```

From the standpoint of Web services, two points are of primary interest:

- The class inherits from *System.Web.Services.WebService*. As you saw earlier, this is not a prerequisite for a Web service class, but using *WebService* as your superclass gives you direct access to ASP.NET intrinsic objects such as *Server*, *Session*, *Application*, and *Context*. All other intrinsic objects, namely *Cache*, *Error*, *Request*, and *Response*, are available through the *Context* object (as are *Server*, *Session*, and *Application*). If you choose to not inherit from *WebService*, you can still get hold of the *Context* object using the static *HttpContext.get_Current* method.
- Because Web services have largely been developed by users of curly bracket languages (Java, C++, C#), the obligatory *HelloWorld* method is predefined, complete with the *WebMethod* attribute. In the true spirit of developers across the world, you can uncomment this method and adapt it to your own purposes!

Note The need to work your way through the *Context* object to obtain the *Request* and *Response* objects is intentional. You should not access the *Request* and *Response* data directly because it forms part of the underlying Web service interaction. You can generally retrieve any information you need without having to access the *Request*. Similarly, you return data to the client by using method return values rather than the *Response* object.

Web Service Description and Data Types

You've seen that creating a Web service involves writing a simple J# class and that the ASP.NET runtime does the rest. The ASP.NET runtime does a lot of work on your behalf, but sometimes you need more control over how your Web service appears to clients and the style of service it provides. One way you can do this is by adapting the description of your service. This effort might involve changing names and URIs, mapping types, and configuring the handling for custom types. Let's look at what you can do to customize service description and data type handling.

Exposing a Web Service Interface

When you tested out the simple Web service, you saw the screen shown earlier in Figure 17-2. Clicking the Service Description hyperlink on the right side of the screen displays the WSDL description of the service. This WSDL document is generated by the HTTP pipeline (part of ASP.NET), which recognizes the ASMX file extension and uses reflection to examine the class in search of Web service attributes. You've already seen how you can use the *WebMethod* attribute to annotate methods and have them exposed as part of your Web service.

This WSDL description is important because it provides the only source of information from which a client can determine the functionality provided by a Web service and how to access it. To control the contents of this document, you can apply various additional Web service attributes to classes, methods, and variables. All of these attributes are identified as part of the reflection process, and the generated WSDL is altered appropriately. We'll examine and tweak the WSDL document generated from the Web service class to suit our purposes.

Namespaces in WSDL

The root element of the WSDL document, *definitions*, contains various namespace definitions:

```
<definitions xmlns:http="http://schemas.xmlsoap.org/wsdl/http/"
 xmlns:soap="http://schemas.xmlsoap.org/wsdl/soap/"
 xmlns:s="http://www.w3.org/2001/XMLSchema" xmlns:s0="http://tempuri.org/"
 xmlns:soapenc="http://schemas.xmlsoap.org/soap/encoding/"
 xmlns:tm="http://microsoft.com/wsdl/mime/textMatching/"
 xmlns:mime="http://schemas.xmlsoap.org/wsdl/mime/"
 targetNamespace="http://tempuri.org/"
 xmlns="http://schemas.xmlsoap.org/wsdl/">
```

Because WSDL is an XML grammar, it has a schema that defines the structure of a WSDL document. This schema is defined at *http://schemas.xmlsoap.org/wsdl/*, and this URL is used as the default namespace for the document. Namespace prefixes are also defined for various standard encodings and structural information that might be required in the WSDL document, namely:

- A schema that defines how to describe SOAP message structures in WSDL documents. (An association between this schema and the namespace prefix *soap* is specified by the definition starting with *xmlns:soap*.)

- The encoding of complex types in SOAP messages (*xmlns:soapenc*)
- A schema that defines how to describe HTTP message structures in a WSDL document (*xmlns:http*)
- The MIME message structure/encoding for WSDL documents (*xmlns:mime*)
- A reference to the XML Schema type definitions (*xmlns:s*) that are used to define parameter types and complex types.

Finally, two namespaces relate to the Web service itself:

- *xmlns:s0*, which is used as a marker for complex type mappings within the document
- *targetNamespace*, which specifies that all of the names declared in this definition belong to the given namespace

By default, these last two namespaces are set to *http://tempuri.org/*, which is a dummy URL registered specifically for use as a temporary marker in generated XML Web service documents. It is usually acceptable to use *http://tempuri.org/* while you're developing your Web service in the safety of your own project group, but you must change this URI before you publish your Web service more widely. If you read the warning contained in the description screen for SimpleEnquiry.asmx (shown in Figure 17-2), you already know that it is important to assign a unique identity to your Web service so clients can differentiate your Web service from those of other Web service creators. The identity used for a Web service is typically based on the Web address of the organization or person creating the service. Because domain names are unique across the Web, they guarantee the uniqueness of identities based on them (assuming that your company has a policy to ensure that two service creators within the company do not use the same path in addition to the base URL).

You can use the *WebService* attribute to define the namespace associated with a particular Web service class. You can see this in the sample file Enquiry.asmx (part of the CakeCatalogService project), which contains the same *FeedsHowMany* method as the SimpleEnquiry.asmx sample file but was created using Visual Studio .NET. The following code changes the namespace associated with the Enquiry class from *http://tempuri.org/* to *http://fourthcoffee.com/CakeCatalog/*:

```
/** @attribute WebServiceAttribute(Namespace=
   "http://fourthcoffee.com/CakeCatalog/") */
public class Enquiry extends System.Web.Services.WebService
{
   ⋮
}
```

This action changes the generated WSDL document as shown here:

```
<definitions xmlns:http="http://schemas.xmlsoap.org/wsdl/http/"
 xmlns:soap="http://schemas.xmlsoap.org/wsdl/soap/"
 xmlns:s="http://www.w3.org/2001/XMLSchema"
 xmlns:s0="http://fourthcoffee.com/CakeCatalog/"
 xmlns:soapenc="http://schemas.xmlsoap.org/soap/encoding/"
 xmlns:tm="http://microsoft.com/wsdl/mime/textMatching/"
 xmlns:mime="http://schemas.xmlsoap.org/wsdl/mime/"
 targetNamespace="http://fourthcoffee.com/CakeCatalog/"
 xmlns="http://schemas.xmlsoap.org/wsdl/">
```

If you access the Enquiry service through a Web browser, you'll also see that the namespace warning is not displayed.

Type Definitions

WSDL documents build up to the service definition in a bottom-up manner. The first definitions in the document are for any complex data types used in the Web service messages passed between the client and the service.

The XML Schema standard defines a set of basic types, such as strings and integers. You can use these basic types to define more complex types by combining them, in much the same way that you would create an object or data structure by combining a group of basic types. WSDL uses complex types to define the sets of parameters and return values that are passed as part of a method call. Recall the signature for *FeedsHowMany*:

```
public int FeedsHowMany(int diameter, String shape,
   String filling)
```

Given this signature, the WSDL generator in ASP.NET will create two WSDL complex types, as defined by the *schema* element within the *types* element:

```
<types>
  <s:schema elementFormDefault="qualified" targetNamespace=
    "http://fourthcoffee.com/CakeCatalog">
    <s:element name="FeedsHowMany">
      <s:complexType>
        <s:sequence>
          <s:element minOccurs="1" maxOccurs="1" name="diameter"
             type="s:int" />
```

```
          <s:element minOccurs="0" maxOccurs="1" name="shape"
             type="s:string" />
          <s:element minOccurs="0" maxOccurs="1" name="filling"
             type="s:string" />
        </s:sequence>
      </s:complexType>
    </s:element>
    <s:element name="FeedsHowManyResponse">
      <s:complexType>
        <s:sequence>
          <s:element minOccurs="1" maxOccurs="1" name="FeedsHowManyResult"
             type="s:int" />
        </s:sequence>
      </s:complexType>
    </s:element>
    <s:element name="int" type="s:int" />
  </s:schema>
</types>
```

The complex type named *FeedsHowMany* represents the parameters passed into the method call—the diameter (an integer), shape (a string), and filling (another string). The complex type named *FeedsHowManyResponse* represents the return values from the method call, in this case a single integer. Notice that the target namespace for these type definitions is the same as the target namespace for the overall document. These complex types are used as part of the SOAP message definitions later in the WSDL document.

Later in the chapter, you'll see how more complex data types, such as object types, are mapped into WSDL.

Messages, Parameters, and Parts

The set of data types defined for describing parameters and return values are used in WSDL to build up descriptions of the messages passed between client and server. In SOAP terms, this means defining two messages, a request and a response:

```
<message name="FeedsHowManySoapIn">
  <part name="parameters" element="s0:FeedsHowMany" />
</message>
<message name="FeedsHowManySoapOut">
  <part name="parameters" element="s0:FeedsHowManyResponse" />
</message>
```

The *FeedsHowManySoapIn* message has a single SOAP part that carries a *FeedsHowMany* type, which contains the parameter values sent by the client. The *FeedsHowManySoapOut* message also contains a single SOAP part. In this case, it carries a *FeedsHowManyResponse* type containing the return value from the method.

As noted earlier, two HTTP bindings are provided by default in addition to the SOAP binding. These bindings do not use the complex type definitions from the *types* element but specify them as part of the message definition, as shown in the following *POST* message definitions:

```
<message name="FeedsHowManyHttpPostIn">
  <part name="diameter" type="s:string" />
  <part name="shape" type="s:string" />
  <part name="filling" type="s:string" />
</message>
<message name="FeedsHowManyHttpPostOut">
  <part name="Body" element="s0:int" />
</message>
```

The names of the SOAP and HTTP messages are based on the Web method name. If the exposed name needs to be different (for example, if you want to disambiguate overloaded methods, as discussed later), you can alter it using the *WebMethod* attribute, as shown in the following code fragment taken from the EnquiryWithRenaming.asmx.jsl sample file:

```
/** @attribute WebMethodAttribute(MessageName="CakeCapacity",
   Description="Tells you how many people a given cake feeds")
 */
   public int FeedsHowMany(int diameter, System.String shape,
      System.String filling)
```

Tip You can spread attribute declarations across multiple lines as shown in preceding code, but do not insert extra asterisks (*) at the start of continuation lines—this will cause compilation problems.

Defining the *MessageName* property for the *WebMethod* attribute changes the names of the SOAP and HTTP messages and of the complex types in the WSDL that is generated, as shown here:

```
<types>
   <s:schema elementFormDefault="qualified"
      targetNamespace="http://fourthcoffee.com/CakeCatalog/">
      <s:element name="CakeCapacity">
        <s:complexType>
          <s:sequence>
            <s:element minOccurs="1" maxOccurs="1" name="diameter"
```

```
             type="s:int" />
          <s:element minOccurs="0" maxOccurs="1" name="shape"
             type="s:string" />
          <s:element minOccurs="0" maxOccurs="1" name="filling"
             type="s:string" />
        </s:sequence>
      </s:complexType>
    </s:element>
    <s:element name="CakeCapacityResponse">
      <s:complexType>
        <s:sequence>
          <s:element minOccurs="1" maxOccurs="1"
             name="CakeCapacityResult" type="s:int" />
        </s:sequence>
      </s:complexType>
    </s:element>
    <s:element name="int" type="s:int" />
  </s:schema>
</types>
<message name="CakeCapacitySoapIn">
  <part name="parameters" element="s0:CakeCapacity" />
</message>
<message name="CakeCapacitySoapOut">
  <part name="parameters" element="s0:CakeCapacityResponse" />
</message>
```

You might have noticed that a description is also defined for the *FeedsHowMany* method in EnquiryWithRenaming.asmx.jsl. This description does not form any part of the WSDL associated with the message, but it shows up in the *PortType* (as discussed later). It also forms part of the service description HTML page that is displayed when you access the basic URL for this Web service, as shown in Figure 17-6.

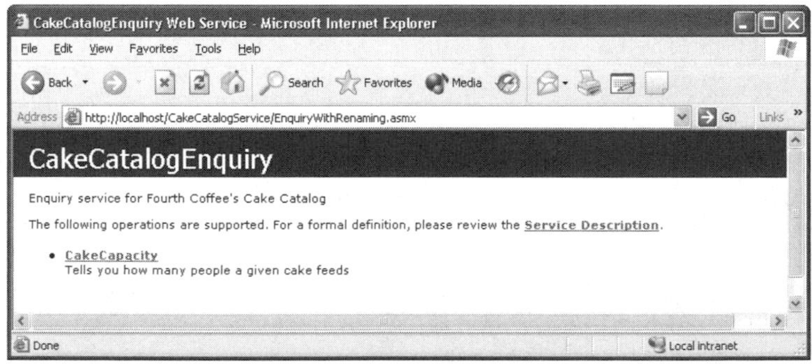

Figure 17-6 The Web service HTML description can contain textual method descriptions.

WSDL syntax does not allow for overloaded methods. This will not stop you from implementing overloaded methods on a class, but only one of them can be tagged with the *WebMethod* attribute. If you try to apply the *WebMethod* attribute to more than one overloaded method, as shown in the sample file EnquiryWithOverloading.asmx.jsl, your class will compile but you'll get the following runtime exception:

Tip *System.InvalidOperationException*: Both *Int32 FeedsHowMany* (*Int32*, *System.String*, *System.String*) and *Void FeedsHowMany* (*Int32*, *System.String*) use the message name *'FeedsHowMany'*. Use the *MessageName* property of the *WebMethod* custom attribute to specify unique message names for the methods.

If you really need to expose overloaded methods, you can use the *MessageName* of the *WebMethod* attribute to change the names of the overloaded methods.

Naming Parameters and Return Values

For SOAP messages, you use an *XmlSerializer* to convert the J# data types into XML. This means that in addition to the Web service-specific attributes you've seen so far, you can also use the XML serialization attributes contained in the *System.Xml.Serialization* namespace to alter the results of the conversion. You can use these XML-related attributes to change the name of a parameter or return value. (You'll see other uses later when we discuss type conversion.)

Caution Be careful when you change the names of parameters. SOAP messages are text-based, so the mapping of parameters in the message to parameters of the method is performed based on the name of the parameter. If you change the name of the parameter on the server but do not make a matching change on the client, the call won't fail, but the "missing" parameter will be assigned a default value when the Web service runtime invokes the method call.

To change the name of the *shape* parameter to *FeedsHowMany*, use the *XmlElementAttribute*, as shown in the EnquiryWithRenaming.asmx.jsl sample file:

```
public
int FeedsHowMany(int diameter,
   /** @attribute XmlElementAttribute("style") */ String shape,
   String filling)
```

This code causes the *shape* parameter to appear with the name *style* in the WSDL complex type description:

```
<s:element name="CakeCapacity">
 <s:complexType>
  <s:sequence>
   <s:element minOccurs="1" maxOccurs="1" name="diameter" type="s:int" />
   <s:element minOccurs="0" maxOccurs="1" name="style" type="s:string" />
   <s:element minOccurs="0" maxOccurs="1" name="filling" type="s:string" />
  </s:sequence>
 </s:complexType>
</s:element>
```

Note The *XmlElement* attribute will not change the name exposed in the HTTP *POST* and *GET* message definitions because the XML formatter is not used to process the message contents in these cases.

You can also change the name associated with the return value from the method using the *@attribute.return* directive (again, taken from the sample file EnquiryWithRenaming.asmx.jsl), as shown here:

```
/** @attribute.return XmlElementAttribute(ElementName="NumberOfPeople")
 */
/** @attribute WebMethodAttribute(MessageName="CakeCapacity",
   Description="Tells you how many people a given cake feeds")
 */
public
int FeedsHowMany(int diameter,
   /** @attribute XmlElementAttribute("style") */ String shape,
   String filling)
```

This changes the definition of the response complex type:

```
<s:element name="CakeCapacityResponse">
 <s:complexType>
  <s:sequence>
   <s:element minOccurs="1" maxOccurs="1" name="NumberOfPeople"
      type="s:int" />
  </s:sequence>
```

```
  </s:complexType>
</s:element>
```

You can also change the type mapping of the return value, as you'll see later.

Operations, Port Types, and Bindings

Once you've defined the set of messages that a Web service will use, you can group them into *portType* elements. You can think of a *portType* element as equivalent to an interface definition in the Java language. It provides a way to assign a set of messages into a cohesive, logical group. The following *portType* indicates that the *CakeCapacitySoapIn* and *CakeCapacitySoapOut* messages are the input and output of one logical operation. This operation represents a SOAP request and response.

```
<portType name="EnquiryWithRenamingSoap">
  <operation name="FeedsHowMany">
    <documentation>Tells you how many people a given cake
       feeds</documentation>
    <input name="CakeCapacity" message="s0:CakeCapacitySoapIn" />
    <output name="CakeCapacity" message="s0:CakeCapacitySoapOut" />
  </operation>
</portType>
```

Note that the operation name is *FeedsHowMany* rather than *CakeCapacity*. To change the operation name, you must use the SOAP-specific attributes discussed later. Also notice that the method description defined earlier using the *WebMethod* attribute appears here.

This is the point at which traditional IDLs such as COM IDL and CORBA IDL stop. However, because this is an XML Web service, you also need to know where to find the particular instance of the service and which protocols you can use to communicate with it. WSDL lets you associate a protocol with a *portType* to create a *binding* element:

```
<binding name=" EnquiryWithRenamingSoap" type="s0: EnquiryWithRenamingSoap">
  <soap:binding transport="http://schemas.xmlsoap.org/soap/http"
     style="document" />
  <operation name="FeedsHowMany">
    <soap:operation
       soapAction="http://fourthcoffee.com/CakeCatalog/CakeCapacity"
       style="document" />
    <input name="CakeCapacity">
      <soap:body use="literal" />
```

```
      </input>
      <output name="CakeCapacity">
        <soap:body use="literal" />
      </output>
    </operation>
  </binding>
```

The *type* attribute of the *binding* element indicates that the binding is associated with the *EnquiryWithRenamingSoap portType*. The contents of the binding element are similar to those of the *portType*, but they provide SOAP-specific information:

- The *transport* attribute in the *soap:binding* element indicates that this binding defines how to pass the given messages over HTTP. The URI *http://schemas.xmlsoap.org/soap/http* is used for HTTP bindings; other URIs can be used to bind messages to alternative transports such as FTP or SMTP.
- The *soapAction* attribute of the *soap:operation* element is a value that should be assigned to the HTTP *SOAPAction* header when the client is creating this SOAP call. This value can be used by the server to route the call to the correct method. However, this information is used only for HTTP bindings and is somewhat redundant because the name of the method also occurs as the name of the outermost element in the SOAP body.
- The remaining attributes (*use* on *soap:body*, and *style* on *soap:operation* and *soap:binding*) all relate to the way in which the parameters and return values are encoded. This is discussed in the following sidebar.

Document Literal vs. SOAP Encoding and RPC

You can look at a SOAP message in two ways. One approach is to continue the RPC-style analogy and say that each parameter and return value should be treated as an individual item to be defined in your call. Each item has its own separate part of the SOAP message in which it is defined. This is known as an "RPC-style" SOAP message, as defined in Section 7 of the SOAP specification. In conjunction with this RPC-style way of structuring a message, you also need a way of encoding particular data types in XML that you can use when you convert the parameter and return values into and out of XML. In the absence of any formal standard, you have to invent your own. This was the main approach taken by the original SOAP specification. When the specification was written, there was no standard XML Schema definition to provide a core set of XML-based data types, so the specification writers defined their own data encoding rules in Section 5 of the SOAP specification. (Hence this style of encoding is referred to as "SOAP encoding.")

When the XML Schema standard and its associated data types (the Information Set, or InfoSet for short) were defined, it became clear that they offered a much more flexible way of encoding information passed in SOAP messages. You can define a schema that describes the data to be passed in your SOAP call. One complex type can be defined to describe the set of parameters passed in and another can describe the return value(s). Your SOAP call will then become the exchange of two XML documents. This is known as "document-style" SOAP messaging. The contents of these XML documents are defined by a schema, so they can be validated, and their potential contents are as flexible as XML itself. The use of schemas and XML documents to define the contents of SOAP messages is referred to as *literal encoding*.

Nothing is intrinsically wrong with the SOAP encoding and RPC approach, but the document/literal approach is considered a more powerful way of exchanging SOAP messages. Newer SOAP-related products and specifications tend to default to the document/literal approach—including Visual Studio .NET and the .NET Framework. This might cause some short-term interoperability issues (discussed briefly later), but the adoption of document-style and literal encoding brings with it far more flexibility and extensibility.

Services and Ports

The final part of the WSDL document is the service definition itself. This consists of a set of ports that make up the service. A port specifies the endpoint at which a server implementing a particular binding can be found. In the case of our simple service, there are three *port* elements, one for the SOAP binding, one for the HTTP *POST* binding, and one for the HTTP *GET* binding:

```
<service name="EnquiryWithRenaming">
  <port name="EnquiryWithRenamingSoap"
     binding="s0:EnquiryWithRenamingSoap">
    <soap:addresslocation=
      "http://localhost/CakeCatalogService/EnquiryWithRenaming.asmx" />
  </port>
  <port name="EnquiryWithRenamingHttpGet"
     binding="s0:EnquiryWithRenamingHttpGet">
```

```
      <http:address location=
        "http://localhost/CakeCatalogService/EnquiryWithRenaming.asmx" />
    </port>
    <port name="EnquiryWithRenamingHttpPost"
       binding="s0:EnquiryWithRenamingHttpPost">
      <http:addresslocation=
         "http://localhost/CakeCatalogService/EnquiryWithRenaming.asmx" />
    </port>
  </service>
```

The *binding* attribute of the first *port* element associates it with the *EnquiryWithRenamingSoap* binding. The *location* attribute of the *soap:address* element indicates that you'll find a server at *http://localhost/CakeCatalogService/EnquiryWithRenaming.asmx* that implements this binding.

The *service* element has a *name* attribute that you can change using the *WebService* attribute you saw earlier. By default, the name of an XML Web service based on ASP.NET is the name of the code-behind class—in this case, *EnquiryWithRenaming*. The following example changes the name of the service to *CakeCatalogEnquiry*:

```
/** @attribute WebServiceAttribute(Namespace=
    "http://fourthcoffee.com/CakeCatalog/",
    Name="CakeCatalogEnquiry",
    Description="Enquiry service for Fourth Coffee's Cake Catalog") */
public class Enquiry extends System.Web.Services.WebService
{
   ⋮
}
```

This action results in changes to the names used throughout the WSDL document for *service*, *binding*, and *portType* elements, as shown here:

```
<portType name="CakeCatalogEnquirySoap">
  <operation name="FeedsHowMany">
    <documentation>Tells you how many people a given cake
       feeds</documentation>
    <input name="CakeCapacity" message="s0:CakeCapacitySoapIn" />
    <output name="CakeCapacity" message="s0:CakeCapacitySoapOut" />
  </operation>
</portType>
⋮
<binding name="CakeCatalogEnquirySoap" type="s0:CakeCatalogEnquirySoap">
  <soap:binding transport="http://schemas.xmlsoap.org/soap/http"
     style="document" />
  <operation name="FeedsHowMany">
    <soap:operation
```

```
        soapAction="http://fourthcoffee.com/CakeCatalog/CakeCapacity"
          style="document" />
      <input name="CakeCapacity">
        <soap:body use="literal" />
      </input>
      <output name="CakeCapacity">
        <soap:body use="literal" />
      </output>
    </operation>
  </binding>
  ⋮
  <service name="CakeCatalogEnquiry">
    <documentation>Enquiry service for Fourth Coffee's Cake Catalog
    </documentation>
    <port name="CakeCatalogEnquirySoap" binding="s0:CakeCatalogEnquirySoap">
      <soap:address location=
        "http://localhost/CakeCatalogService/EnquiryWithRenaming.asmx" />
    </port>
    ⋮
  </service>
```

The description string defined in the *WebService* attribute becomes a *documentation* element inside the *service* element. Again, this is shown as part of the HTML description generated by ASP.NET, as shown in Figure 17-7.

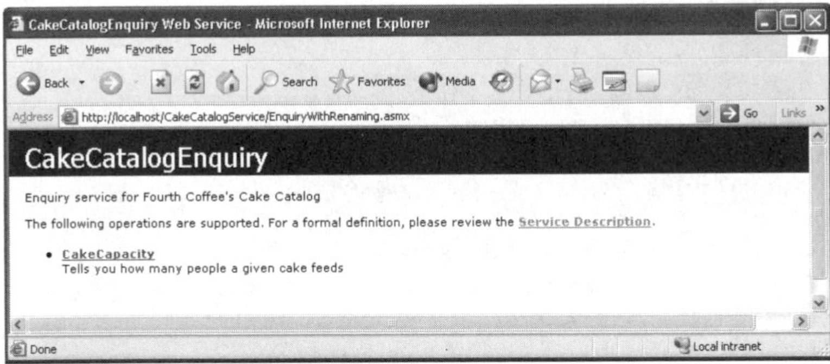

Figure 17-7 You can set the Web service HTML description using the *WebService* attribute.

Invoking the Service

Once the service has been defined, clients can access it. Given the description so far of the *CakeCatalogService*, a client can formulate a SOAP call as shown here and send it to the Web server on *localhost*:

```
POST /CakeCatalogService/EnquiryWithRenaming.asmx HTTP/1.1
User-Agent: Mozilla/
4.0 (compatible; MSIE 6.0; MS Web Services Client Protocol 1.0.3705.0)
Content-Type: text/xml; charset=utf-8
SOAPAction: "http://fourthcoffee.com/CakeCatalog/CakeCapacity"
Content-Length: 400
Expect: 100-continue
Connection: Keep-Alive
Host: localhost

<?xml version="1.0" encoding="utf-8"?>
<soap:Envelope xmlns:soap=http://schemas.xmlsoap.org/soap/envelope/
   xmlns:xsi=http://www.w3.org/2001/XMLSchema-instance
   xmlns:xsd="http://www.w3.org/2001/XMLSchema">
  <soap:Body>
    <CakeCapacity xmlns="http://fourthcoffee.com/CakeCatalog/">
      <diameter>10</diameter>
      <style>square</style>
      <filling>fruit</filling>
    </CakeCapacity>
  </soap:Body>
</soap:Envelope>
```

As long as the service is running on *localhost*, this request should elicit the following response:

```
HTTP/1.1 200 OK
Server: Microsoft-IIS/5.1
Date: Tue, 23 Apr 2002 11:27:52 GMT
Cache-Control: private, max-age=0
Content-Type: text/xml; charset=utf-8
Content-Length: 371

<?xml version="1.0" encoding="utf-8"?>
<soap:Envelope xmlns:soap=http://schemas.xmlsoap.org/soap/envelope/
   xmlns:xsi=http://www.w3.org/2001/XMLSchema-instance
   xmlns:xsd="http://www.w3.org/2001/XMLSchema">
  <soap:Body>
    <CakeCapacityResponse xmlns="http://fourthcoffee.com/CakeCatalog/">
      <NumberOfPeople>25</NumberOfPeople>
    </CakeCapacityResponse>
  </soap:Body>
</soap:Envelope>
```

Note These SOAP calls have been tidied up for readability. Please don't count the characters—the added linefeeds will make them add up to more than 400 and 371 characters, respectively!

Obviously, you don't want to have to write the low-level socket or HTTP code. Fortunately, Visual Studio .NET provides a way to import a WSDL description for a service and generate a Web service proxy that hides these details, making a Web service appear like a local method call to a client. The creation and use of proxies is discussed in the next chapter.

Passing Complex Data Types

The types used so far by the example XML Web service have been simple types. But in many cases, providing information as a set of simple, individual parameters might be inefficient or difficult to maintain. Many designs require that complex types be passed across component boundaries. These types generally represent complex domain concepts such as a customer or an order. They provide a central point of change for these descriptions and make the system easier to maintain. (If you add a customer ID to the customer type, all uses of the customer type will instantly have this modification—you won't have to add a new parameter to a whole bunch of methods.)

How do such domain objects map into WSDL and Web services? If you're developing a cake ordering system to be written in J#, at some point in your design you'll undoubtedly define an *Order* class that contains the data and probably some business logic related to the creation and manipulation of the order. You can implement this concept in various ways. You can create a full-blown class with properties and methods, or you can define a simple data-only class to hold the data and rely on other components for the business logic. (You might implement this as a *struct* in C#.) Alternatively, you can create a typed ADO.NET *DataSet* to hold many orders and provide manipulation functions based on it. Any of these options are fine in the .NET world. The best choice will depend on the context of your application and how that type fits in the application.

As you saw in Chapter 11, you can use .NET Remoting to distribute the components of such applications and pass complex types back and forth using serialization. However, if you intend to offer the functionality of your application as an XML Web service, different rules will apply. We'll talk about passing

DataSet objects across Web service boundaries shortly, but for now, consider passing domain-specific objects across a Web service interface.

Representing Objects in WSDL

As an example, look at the *SimpleOrder* class defined in the SimpleOrder.jsl sample file that is part of the CakeCatalogService project. This class contains:

- Four properties: a customer name, an order ID, an item description, and the number of those items requested. These are defined using private member variables and public property accessors (getters and setters).
- A default constructor and a constructor that allows you to create a fully populated object.
- A method containing some simple data validation that can be invoked to check that the order meets the constraints on its data.

In a typical object-oriented system, you can pass instances of this object to a hypothetical *SubmitSimpleOrder* method. This method will probably return another complex type called *Receipt* that contains:

- Three read-only properties for the customer name, the order ID, and a timestamp
- A single, all-at-once constructor for populating the receipt

This class is defined in the Receipt.jsl sample file. The *SubmitSimpleOrder* method would probably look something like this:

```
/** @attribute WebMethodAttribute() */
public Receipt SubmitSimpleOrder(SimpleOrder order)
{
   // Should probably have some database stuff here...

   Receipt receipt = new Receipt(order.get_CustomerName(),
   order.get_OrderId(),
   DateTime.get_Now());
   return receipt;
}
```

So, how does this map to an XML Web service operation? You can use the reflection capabilities of ASP.NET to find out.

If you define the *SubmitSimpleOrder* method shown above in a Web service called *SimpleOrdering*, for example, and then point your browser at *http://localhost/CakeCatalogService/SimpleOrdering.asmx*, the first thing you would find is that an exception is thrown because the *Receipt* class does not have a default constructor. It therefore cannot be serialized and passed across a network boundary. This is the same restriction placed on classes that are transmitted using .NET Remoting. A version of the *Receipt* class with a default constructor can be found in the sample file SerializableReceipt.jsl.

Using the updated form of the receipt, you'll get the following type definitions in your WSDL description of the Ordering service. (You can see this by viewing the WSDL for the SimpleOrderingWithBadReceipt sample Web service.)

```
<types>
  <s:schema elementFormDefault="qualified"
    targetNamespace="http://fourthcoffee.com/CakeCatalog/">
    <s:element name="SubmitSimpleOrder">
      <s:complexType>
        <s:sequence>
          <s:element minOccurs="0" maxOccurs="1" name="order"
             type="s0:SimpleOrder" />
        </s:sequence>
      </s:complexType>
    </s:element>
    <s:complexType name="SimpleOrder">
      <s:sequence>
        <s:element minOccurs="0" maxOccurs="1" name="CustomerName"
           type="s:string" />
        <s:element minOccurs="0" maxOccurs="1" name="ItemDescription"
           type="s:string" />
        <s:element minOccurs="1" maxOccurs="1" name="ItemQuantity"
           type="s:int" />
        <s:element minOccurs="1" maxOccurs="1" name="OrderId"
           type="s:int" />
      </s:sequence>
    </s:complexType>
    <s:element name="SubmitSimpleOrderResponse">
      <s:complexType>
        <s:sequence>
          <s:element minOccurs="0" maxOccurs="1"
             name="SubmitSimpleOrderResult"
             type="s0:SerializableReceipt" />
        </s:sequence>
      </s:complexType>
    </s:element>
    <s:complexType name="SerializableReceipt" />
  </s:schema>
</types>
```

The first thing to note here is that the *SubmitSimpleOrder* element is defined as containing a complex type, called *SimpleOrder*. The definition for

SimpleOrder contains type information indicating that a *SimpleOrder* element will contain *CustomerName* and *ItemDescription* strings (which can be *null*, hence the attributes *minOccurs="0"* and *maxOccurs="1")* and integer values for *ItemQuantity* and *OrderId*. However, if you examine the information generated for the *SerializableReceipt* class, you'll see that no information is defined for it in the WSDL except to say that it is a complex type. What's going on here?

ASP.NET Web services use the *XmlSerializer* (described in Chapter 10) to export .NET data into XML. This means that the data to be exported must follow the rules of the *XmlSerializer*—namely, it must be publicly visible outside the class. To appear in the WSDL type definitions, data must be declared in one of the following ways:

- As an instance variable with *public* visibility. This is generally accessible but leaves the data open to abuse by external classes—for example, external classes can set an object variable to *null* even if this is an invalid value.
- As a writable property. If your intention is to create an immutable object, such as a receipt, you might be tempted to create only *get* accessors for the data. However, if you do not provide *set* accessors, the values will not be generated in the WSDL and so will not be visible on the client. In other words, using a read-only property will not generate anything in XML. The property must be writable.

If you examine the *SimpleOrder* class, you'll see that its instance data is made visible through properties:

```
public class SimpleOrder
{
   private String customerName;

   /** @property */
   public void set_CustomerName(String name)
   {
      if (name != null && name.get_Length() != 0)
      {
         customerName = name;
      }
   }

   /** @property */
   public String get_CustomerName()
   {
      return customerName;
   }
```

```
    private int orderId;

    /** @property */
    public void set_OrderId(int id)
    {
       orderId = id;
    }

    /** @property */
    public int get_OrderId()
    {
       return orderId;
    }
    ...}
```

However, the variables in the *SerializableReceipt* class are read-only and are accessible through *get* accessors:

```
public class SerializableReceipt
{
   private String customerName;

   /** @property */
   public String get_CustomerName()
   {
      return customerName;
   }
   ⋮
```

The *XmlSerializer* will not expose the properties of the *SerializableReceipt* class to the client, so they do not appear in the WSDL description of the Web service. To make the fields in the *SerializableReceipt* class visible in the WSDL document, you should create property accessors for them, as shown in the SimpleWsReceipt.jsl sample file:

```
public class SimpleWsReceipt
{
  private String customerName;

  /** @property */
  public String get_CustomerName()
  {
    return customerName;
  }

  /** @property */
  public void set_CustomerName(String name)
```

```
  {
    customerName = name;
  }
  ⋮
```

The resulting WSDL looks like this:

```
<types>
  <s:schema elementFormDefault="qualified"
   targetNamespace="http://fourthcoffee.com/CakeCatalog/">
    ⋮
    <s:element name="SubmitSimpleOrderResponse">
      <s:complexType>
        <s:sequence>
          <s:element minOccurs="0" maxOccurs="1"
             name="SubmitSimpleOrderResult" type="s0:SimpleWsReceipt" />
        </s:sequence>
      </s:complexType>
    </s:element>
    <s:complexType name="SimpleWsReceipt">
      <s:sequence>
        <s:element minOccurs="0" maxOccurs="1" name="CustomerName"
           type="s:string" />
        <s:element minOccurs="1" maxOccurs="1" name="OrderId"
           type="s:int" />
        <s:element minOccurs="1" maxOccurs="1" name="Timestamp"
           type="s:dateTime" />
      </s:sequence>
    </s:complexType>
  </s:schema>
</types>
```

The description of the receipt in *SimpleWsReceipt* includes all of the receipt data, and this data will be marshaled and unmarshaled correctly between XML and the J# class. You can see this by examining the WSDL generated by the SimpleOrdering.asmx sample file.

Consequences of XML Serialization

As you've seen, to automatically export and import complex types between .NET and XML, you might have to greatly simplify your classes, effectively down to the level of a data structure. All of the data must be publicly visible and writable.

Although this might be initially disappointing, if you step back and think about it, it does make sense. When you call a method in a Web service or implement a Web service called by others, part of your system is outside of the .NET platform. The client for your Web service might be written in J#, C#, or Visual Basic .NET—or in the Java language, Perl, C++, or even Cobol. The type information described in the WSDL document must make sense in all of those languages and environments. You cannot export your .NET class in its native form to these environments. All you can really send is the data it contains. If this data needs functionality to manipulate or protect it at the receiving end, this functionality must be implemented on that platform and in that language.

At the simplest level, you can take the simple data-oriented class exposed through the Web service and manipulate the data members directly on the client. If it is important to you to reassociate the functionality with the data, you can reimplement your class on the receiving platform (in a suitable language). You can then perform custom deserialization of this part of the SOAP message so that it populates one of these native classes on the receiving platform. Similarly, you would have to perform the equivalent serialization when you pass one of these classes as part of your method call on the Web service. Such custom serialization is quite possible using popular Web service environments such as the .NET Framework and the Apache Axis toolkit, but these topics are beyond the scope of this chapter. For more information, look up the *<soapInterop>* element in the "Remoting Settings Schema" section of the .NET Framework documentation.

One main point to take from this discussion is that even if you're using the .NET Framework at both ends of your Web service method call, doing so will not automatically serialize and reconstitute native .NET objects at both ends. An added complication is that you must make sure that the appropriate type information is available at both ends. For example, if you're serializing an object of type *com.FourthCoffee.CakeCatalog.Order* into XML as part of the Web service and you want to reconstitute it on the client, the assembly containing *com.FourthCoffee.CakeCatalog.Order* must be available to the client (either locally, in the GAC, or downloadable from a URL). The bottom line is that if you want complex types, such as objects, to appear the same at both ends, you need to do some work to make it happen.

Nested Complex Types

If you need to model nested objects, such as an order and a list of items in that order, nested serialization will take place automatically, as long as the nested class also has its data available as publicly accessible member variables. You can modify the *SimpleOrder* class to create a new class called *Order* that contains an array of line items (as shown in the sample files Order.jsl and Item.jsl). You can use this *Order* class to submit an order containing several line items. The sample file Ordering.asmx is an evolved form of the SimpleOrdering.asmx file that uses this *Order* class. The *Order* class is represented in WSDL as follows:

```
<s:element name="SubmitOrder">
  <s:complexType>
    <s:sequence>
      <s:element minOccurs="0" maxOccurs="1" name="order"
         type="s0:Order" />
    </s:sequence>
  </s:complexType>
</s:element>
<s:complexType name="Order">
  <s:sequence>
    <s:element minOccurs="0" maxOccurs="1" name="customerName"
       type="s:string" />
    <s:element minOccurs="1" maxOccurs="1" name="orderId" type="s:int" />
    <s:element minOccurs="0" maxOccurs="1" name="items"
       type="s0:ArrayOfItem" />
  </s:sequence>
</s:complexType>
<s:complexType name="ArrayOfItem">
  <s:sequence>
    <s:element minOccurs="0" maxOccurs="unbounded" name="Item"
       nillable="true" type="s0:Item" />
  </s:sequence>
</s:complexType>
<s:complexType name="Item">
  <s:sequence>
    <s:element minOccurs="0" maxOccurs="1" name="itemDescription"
       type="s:string" />
    <s:element minOccurs="1" maxOccurs="1" name="quantity" type="s:int" />
  </s:sequence>
</s:complexType>
```

The WSDL defines the *Order* complex type, which includes an element called *items* (the name of the *Item[]* variable in the *Order* class), which has the type *ArrayOfItem*. The *ArrayOfItem* complex type definition indicates that it is a sequence of zero or more *Item* complex types, each of which contains a string *description* and an integer *quantity*. A client using an *XmlSerializer* will generate the following SOAP request using this WSDL description:

```
POST /CakeCatalogService/Ordering.asmx HTTP/1.1
User-Agent: Mozilla/
4.0 (compatible; MSIE 6.0; MS Web Services Client Protocol 1.0.3705.0)
Content-Type: text/xml; charset=utf-8
SOAPAction: "http://fourthcoffee.com/CakeCatalog/SubmitOrder"
Content-Length: 576
Expect: 100-continue
Connection: Keep-Alive
Host: localhost
```

```
<?xml version="1.0" encoding="utf-8"?>
<soap:Envelope xmlns:soap="http://schemas.xmlsoap.org/soap/envelope/"
xmlns:xsi="http://www.w3.org/2001/XMLSchema-instance" xmlns:xsd="http://
www.w3.org/2001/XMLSchema">
  <soap:Body>
    <SubmitOrder xmlns="http://fourthcoffee.com/CakeCatalog/">
      <order>
        <customerName>Peter Waxman</customerName>
        <orderId>12345</orderId>
        <items>
          <Item>
            <itemDescription>Birthday Cake</itemDescription>
            <quantity>7</quantity>
          </Item>
          <Item>
            <itemDescription>Party Cake</itemDescription>
            <quantity>3</quantity>
          </Item>
        </items>
      </order>
    </SubmitOrder>
  </soap:Body>
</soap:Envelope>
```

As you can see, the *XmlSerializer* will convert the array of *Item* classes into the XML element *items*. The *items* element is then nested inside the *order* element.

At first sight, you might be tempted to replace the array of *Items* with some form of collection available in the *System.Collections* namespace in the .NET Framework Class Library. This would certainly reduce the amount of effort involved in processing the array, particularly if you're dynamically adding and removing items. However, certain caveats apply here. First, some collection types cannot be passed to a Web service. For example, if you try to use a *Hashtable* as part of a Web service type, you'll get an exception at run time because of the way in which its elements are accessed. (You might recall the discussion in Chapter 10 about the difficulties that arise when you try to serialize a *Hashtable* using XML serialization.) Alternatively, you can use an *ArrayList* to hold your set of order items. The *WsReceipt* class shown below is an updated version of *SimpleWsReceipt* that holds a list of the items ordered (this can be checked by the client) in an *ArrayList*:

```
package CakeCatalogService;

import System.Collections.ArrayList;

public class WsReceipt
```

```
{
   ⋮
   private ArrayList orderContents;

   /** @property */
   public ArrayList get_OrderContents()
   {
      return orderContents;
   }

   /** @property */
   public void set_OrderContents(ArrayList items)
   {
      orderContents = items;
   }
⋮
}
```

The *orderContents* instance variable is exposed through the *OrderContents* property. Consider how this is represented in WSDL:

```
<s:complexType name="WsReceipt">
  <s:sequence>
    <s:element minOccurs="0" maxOccurs="1" name="CustomerName"
       type="s:string" />
    <s:element minOccurs="0" maxOccurs="1" name="OrderContents"
       type="s0:ArrayOfAnyType" />
    <s:element minOccurs="1" maxOccurs="1" name="OrderId" type="s:int" />
    <s:element minOccurs="1" maxOccurs="1" name="Timestamp"
       type="s:dateTime" />
  </s:sequence>
</s:complexType>
```

The collection is translated into WSDL as an *ArrayOfAnyType* that does not contain any detailed type information. This causes a problem for the client because it does not receive information about the *item* data that was previously marshaled when it used an array of *Items*. However, the information is not lost. Examination of the SOAP request shows that this information is still in there—you just need to do a little work to get at it:

```
HTTP/1.1 200 OK
Server: Microsoft-IIS/5.1
Date: Tue, 07 May 2002 11:56:09 GMT
Cache-Control: private, max-age=0
Content-Type: text/xml; charset=utf-8
Content-Length: 761

<?xml version="1.0" encoding="utf-8"?>
```

```
<soap:Envelope xmlns:soap=http://schemas.xmlsoap.org/soap/envelope/
   xmlns:xsi=http://www.w3.org/2001/XMLSchema-instance
   xmlns:xsd="http://www.w3.org/2001/XMLSchema">
  <soap:Body>
    <SubmitBuiltUpOrderResponse
       xmlns="http://fourthcoffee.com/CakeCatalog/">
      <SubmitBuiltUpOrderResult>
        <customerName>Peter Waxman</customerName>
        <orderId>987098</orderId>
        <timestamp>2002-05-07T12:56:09.1712500+01:00</timestamp>
        <orderContents>
          <anyType xsi:type="Item">
            <itemDescription>Party Cake</itemDescription>
            <quantity>12</quantity>
          </anyType>
          <anyType xsi:type="Item">
            <itemDescription>Wedding Cake</itemDescription>
            <quantity>3</quantity>
          </anyType>
        </orderContents>
      </SubmitBuiltUpOrderResult>
    </SubmitBuiltUpOrderResponse>
  </soap:Body>
</soap:Envelope>
```

Chapter 18 will discuss how a client can retrieve this information from the SOAP response.

Polymorphism and Generic Object Conversion

Another way to approach the generic data issue is to use the *XmlElement* and *XmlInclude* attributes. Using these attributes, you can define a set of types that can be found in a given *ArrayOfAnyType*. When the contents of the array are marshaled as XML, the XML serializer will substitute the appropriate type into the SOAP document. For example, consider the following C# Web method that manipulates a C# version of the *Order* class:

```
 [WebMethodAttribute]
 [XmlInclude(typeof(Order))]
public ArrayList GetMyOrder()
{
   ArrayList orders = new ArrayList();

   Order order = new Order();
   order.CustomerName = "Peter Waxman";
   order.OrderId = 12345678;

   Item[] items = new Item[2];
```

```
    items[0] = new Item();
    items[0].ItemDescription = "Wedding Cake";
    items[0].Quantity = 2;

    items[1] = new Item();
    items[1].ItemDescription = "Birthday Cake";
    items[1].Quantity = 7;
    order.OrderContents = items;

    orders.Add(order);

    return orders;
}
```

The return type of the method is completely generic. Again, this means that the WSDL generator does not know precisely what types to expect. You can help the WSDL generator out here by using the *XmlInclude* attribute to indicate the types you expect to be passed. The WSDL generated by this Web service defines the method's return type as an *ArrayOfAnyType*, but it also includes descriptions for the *Order* and *Item* types. If you access the Web service using Visual Studio .NET and call the *GetMyOrder* method through the test page, the XML response will be as follows:

```
<?xml version="1.0" encoding="utf-8" ?>
<ArrayOfAnyType xmlns:xsd=http://www.w3.org/2001/XMLSchema
   xmlns:xsi=http://www.w3.org/2001/XMLSchema-instance
   xmlns="http://tempuri.org/">
  <anyType xsi:type="Order">
    <CustomerName>Peter Waxman</CustomerName>
    <OrderId>12345678</OrderId>
    <OrderContents>
      <Item>
      <ItemDescription>Wedding Cake</ItemDescription>
      <Quantity>2</Quantity>
    </Item>
    <Item>
       <ItemDescription>Birthday Cake</ItemDescription>
       <Quantity>7</Quantity>
      </Item>
    </OrderContents>
  </anyType>
</ArrayOfAnyType>
```

The *anyType* element is now correctly tagged as being of type *Order*, which makes it easier to unmarshal on the client side.

So, the only question left is, "Why is the example in C# and not J#?" The reason is that the specification of these attributes requires a statement that can be evaluated at compile time to generate a .NET Framework *System.Type* instance. In C#, you can use the *typeof* operator to obtain one of these. However, the equivalent operator in J# returns a *java.lang.Class* instance, which is not altogether helpful and cannot be processed in the same way by the .NET Framework. The code that shows this example in operation is in the sample project CSTestWebService.

Passing *DataSet* Objects

As stated earlier, the conversion of complex types into XML and back again is a nontrivial task. Someone must take responsibility for identifying the complex type in transit and then perform the necessary marshaling and unmarshaling. An ADO.NET *DataSet* provides a high level of functionality in terms of its data-carrying capabilities and the relationships and constraints between the data. This potentially complex structure would be quite challenging to express in terms of a WSDL complex type. You might therefore conclude that it would be difficult to pass a *DataSet* across a Web service, but this is not the case.

DataSet objects can be serialized by the *XmlSerializer* to create an on-the-wire representation. This is not really surprising because you learned in Chapter 5 that *DataSet* objects lead a double life—as both relational data holders and XML documents. The pleasant surprise is that given an XML representation of a *DataSet*, the .NET Framework can reconstitute the *DataSet* at the receiving end.

The following code from the Catalog.asmx.jsl sample file shows the creation of a *DataSet* in response to a request:

```
/** @attribute WebMethodAttribute() */
public DataSet RetrieveCatalog()
{
   DataSet ds = new DataSet("Fourth Coffee Catalog");
   ds.ReadXml(get_Server().MapPath("CakeCatalog.xml"));
   return ds;
}
```

The SOAP response from this request takes the following form:

```
HTTP/1.1 200 OK
Server: Microsoft-IIS/5.1
Date: Wed, 24 Apr 2002 13:59:17 GMT
Cache-Control: private, max-age=0
Content-Type: text/xml; charset=utf-8
Content-Length: 3710

<?xml version="1.0" encoding="utf-8"?>
<soap:Envelope xmlns:soap="http://schemas.xmlsoap.org/soap/envelope/"
xmlns:xsi="http://www.w3.org/2001/XMLSchema-instance" xmlns:xsd="http://
```

```
www.w3.org/2001/XMLSchema">
  <soap:Body>
    <RetrieveCatalogResponse xmlns="http://fourthcoffee.com/CakeCatalog/">
      <RetrieveCatalogResult>
        <xs:schema id="CakeCatalog" xmlns=""
        xmlns:xs="http://www.w3.org/2001/XMLSchema"
        xmlns:msdata="urn:schemas-microsoft-com:xml-msdata">
        <xs:element name="CakeCatalog" msdata:IsDataSet="true"
         msdata:Locale="en-GB">
  <xs:complexType>
    <xs:choice maxOccurs="unbounded">
<xs:element name="CakeType">
  <xs:complexType>
    <xs:sequence>
<xs:element name="Message" type="xs:string" minOccurs="0"
 msdata:Ordinal="0" />
<xs:element name="Description" type="xs:string" minOccurs="0"
 msdata:Ordinal="1" />
<xs:element name="Sizes" minOccurs="0" maxOccurs="unbounded">
  <xs:complexType>
    <xs:sequence>
<xs:element name="Option" minOccurs="0" maxOccurs="unbounded">
  <xs:complexType>
    <xs:attribute name="value" type="xs:string" />
  </xs:complexType>
    </xs:element>
  </xs:sequence>
   </xs:complexType>
    </xs:element>
  </xs:sequence>
  <xs:attribute name="style" type="xs:string" />
  <xs:attribute name="filling" type="xs:string" />
  <xs:attribute name="shape" type="xs:string" />
</xs:complexType>
    </xs:element>
  </xs:choice>
</xs:complexType>
       </xs:element>
        </xs:schema>
  <diffgr:diffgram xmlns:msdata="urn:schemas-microsoft-com:xml-msdata"
   xmlns:diffgr="urn:schemas-microsoft-com:xml-diffgram-v1">
         <CakeCatalog xmlns="">
   <CakeType diffgr:id="CakeType1" msdata:rowOrder="0"
    diffgr:hasChanges="inserted" msdata:hiddenCakeType_Id="0"
    style="Celebration" filling="sponge" shape="round">
  <Message>Happy Birthday</Message>
  <Description>One of our most popular cakes</Description>
  <Sizes diffgr:id="Sizes1" msdata:rowOrder="0"
```

```
    diffgr:hasChanges="inserted" msdata:hiddenSizes_Id="0"
    msdata:hiddenCakeType_Id="0">
     <Option diffgr:id="Option1" msdata:rowOrder="0"
      diffgr:hasChanges="inserted" value="10 inch"
      msdata:hiddenSizes_Id="0" />
     <Option diffgr:id="Option2" msdata:rowOrder="1"
      diffgr:hasChanges="inserted" value="12 inch"
      msdata:hiddenSizes_Id="0" />
     <Option diffgr:id="Option3" msdata:rowOrder="2"
      diffgr:hasChanges="inserted" value="14 inch"
      msdata:hiddenSizes_Id="0" />
  </Sizes>
     </CakeType>
     ⋮
           </CakeCatalog>
         </diffgr:diffgram>
       </RetrieveCatalogResult>
     </RetrieveCatalogResponse>
  </soap:Body>
</soap:Envelope>
```

Although this listing was simplified to save space, it is still quite complex. The main points to extract from it are:

- The SOAP message contains an XML schema that defines the format of the data.
- The definition for the *CakeCatalog* element declares that it is a *DataSet*, using the *msdata:IsDataSet="true"* attribute.
- The data is contained in a *DiffGram*. (See Chapter 5 for more information on *DiffGram* elements).
- If the .NET Framework receives this message, it will have enough information to reconstitute the *DataSet*.
- If any other platform receives the message, it can use the schema definition to understand the data contained in the message and manipulate it accordingly.

Returning to the topic of designing XML Web services, you might need to retrieve data from a database, such as a list of customers, and return this to the client. One solution is to create a set of domain objects based on this data, such as an array of instances of a *Customer* class, and then pass these domain objects back from your Web service call. This will generate “clean” XML descriptions that can be consumed equally well by clients on any platform. However, if you use a *DataSet* (or, even better, a typed *DataSet*) to hold your list of customers, the *XmlSerializer* will generate the XML description for you. This description can be reconstituted into the typed *DataSet* on a .NET client or handled based on its schema in a non-.NET client. Given that you'll frequently retrieve database data in a *DataSet*, you should consider whether you really want to convert this data into domain object types or whether you should just pass back the *DataSet* and let the *XmlSerializer* generate the XML for you.

Passing XML Documents

One decision you must make when you design a Web service is what style of calls should be made between the client and server. As noted previously, the fact that SOAP originates from an initiative to run RPC over HTTP means that most of the focus is on RPC-style interaction. The alternative is to pass XML documents. However, you must consider whether you want to abandon language-specific types altogether and just pass a single XML document as a parameter to a Web method. This type of message-oriented exchange offers several advantages over the RPC-style interaction:

- You can define a schema for the document to verify the precise structure of its contents.
- You won't encounter any issues regarding the mapping of domain types to XML because the data is already represented as XML.
- You won't need to build and maintain ongoing state between client and server. (RPC-style calls tend to imply a certain amount of state.) All the information required to process the document can be carried with it.
- The interface of your service is far more flexible in the face of change. Because the signature of the call between client and server consists of a single parameter (the XML document) in which all the data is encoded, changes to that data will affect only the schema of the document passed. The signature of the method on your service will remain the same.

However, message-oriented exchanges also have some disadvantages:

- The validation of the document using a schema requires an extra step.
- You must use XML mechanisms, such as DOM, to manipulate your data rather than language-level mechanisms such as typed variables.

- If the processing of the document fails early, a lot of unnecessary data will have been passed.
- By having a single, generic parameter rather than multiple, specific parameters, you lose a lot of the type safety associated with interface-based remote interaction.
- Document-oriented interactions are more difficult to describe in WSDL.

If you define a method that returns an *XmlDocument* and attach the *WebMethod* attribute to this method, the generated WSDL will allow almost any content. The following is the WSDL generated for the *RetrieveXmlCatalog* method defined in the sample file Catalog.asmx.jsl. This method returns an *XmlDocument*. The *any* type in WSDL indicates any XML-compliant content.

```
<s:element name="RetrieveXmlCatalogResponse">
  <s:complexType>
    <s:sequence>
      <s:element minOccurs="0" maxOccurs="1"
         name="RetrieveXmlCatalogResult">
        <s:complexType mixed="true">
          <s:sequence>
            <s:any />
          </s:sequence>
        </s:complexType>
      </s:element>
    </s:sequence>
  </s:complexType>
</s:element>
```

The return value from the *RetrieveXmlCatalog* method will appear on the client as an *XMLNode* object that can be manipulated as appropriate, as you'll see in Chapter 18.

Creating an XML Web Service Application

So far, this chapter has focused on describing a Web service and defining the types passed between client and server. However, this is only one consideration when you create a Web service application. Let's look at some of the other issues you'll commonly deal with when you create distributed applications—such as security, transactions, and exposing existing (heritage) functionality.

Web Services as ASP.NET Applications

Most Web service implementations under .NET will be ASP.NET Web services, which means that they'll have all the underlying capabilities of an ASP.NET Web application. As noted earlier, you'll have access to all of the intrinsic objects available to an ASP.NET Web application, such as *Context*, *Server*, and *Application*. The model of invocation is also the same, in that the page is instantiated to service the request and is then discarded once the method has been completed. This means that many of the same principles apply in terms of component lifecycle.

State Management

The state management model for an ASP.NET Web service is exactly the same as for an ASP.NET Web application—it uses the *Session* and *Application* objects as described in Chapter 16. You might recall that the *Session* object is created on a per-client basis, normally based on cookies passed between the client and server. The *Application* object is shared globally between all clients of an application and does not rely on the passing of state information.

As you might expect, access to the *Application* object does not require any special processing or decoration in an XML Web service. The following code shows how you can maintain a Web service–wide counter by storing it in the *Application* object:

```
/** @attribute WebMethodAttribute() */
public int Increment() throws System.ApplicationException
{
   int count = 0;

   if (get_Application() == null)
   {
      throw new ApplicationException("Application was null");
   }

   System.Object obj = get_Application().get_Item("count");
   if (obj == null)
   {
      get_Application().Add("count", new Integer(0));
   }

   obj = get_Application().get_Item("count");
   Integer objCount = (Integer)obj;
   count = objCount.intValue();
   count++;
   objCount = new Integer(count);
   get_Application().set_Item("count", objCount);
```

```
    return count;
}
```

If a client calls this method repeatedly, it will see that the returned count increments.

On the other hand, you do not get a per-client session by default. You must set the *EnableSession* property of the *WebMethod* attribute to *true* for each method that needs to maintain state information. If you want to allow clients to build up an order over multiple calls to the service, you must start by initializing a new order, as shown in the following code:

```
/** @attribute WebMethodAttribute(EnableSession=true) */
public void StartBuiltUpOrder(String name, int id)
{
    Order order = new Order();
    order.customerName = name;
    order.orderId = id;
    get_Session().Add("Order", order);
}
```

After the customer informs the client application of the items he wants to order, the client can call a method to add each item in turn to the order maintained by the service on the client's behalf:

```
/** @attribute WebMethodAttribute(EnableSession=true) */
public void AddToOrder(String description, int quantity)
    throws System.ApplicationException
{
    Item item = new Item();
    item.itemDescription = description;
    item.quantity = quantity;

    Order order = (Order)get_Session().get_Item("Order");

    if (order == null)
    {
        throw new ApplicationException("Order was null");
    }

    int length = 0;
    Item[] newItems = null;
    if (order.items == null)
    {
        length = 1;
        newItems = new Item[length];
    }
    else
```

```
    {
        length = order.items.length + 1;
        newItems = new Item[length];
        Array.Copy(order.items, newItems, length - 1);
    }
    // Replace the items
    order.items = newItems;

    // Add the new item
    order.items[length - 1] = item;

}
```

This approach involves a certain amount of processing overhead. The method first checks to see that there is currently an order for this client; if not, an exception is thrown. The new item is then added to the array of items held in the order. This array manipulation comes about because we're using the same *Order* object to hold the state as it is passed between client and server for simple orders. Given that this object is accessed only on the server side when you build up the order dynamically, you can, for convenience, rewrite the *Order* class so that it uses one of the *System.Collection* types rather than an array. All of the preceding code showing examples of application and session state is contained in the Ordering.asmx.jsl sample file.

One obvious requirement for the session-based state management to work is that the client must support and allow cookies. This support is not enabled by default on client-side XML Web service proxies generated under .NET, so you must enable it explicitly. (This topic is covered in Chapter 18.) XML Web services cannot easily use the cookieless support for sessions. The cookieless support relies on the use of URL rewriting (mangling) and redirection of the client to a mangled URL (an HTTP 302 Found response that tells the client to go to another page). An example is shown here:

```
HTTP/1.1 302 Found
Server: Microsoft-IIS/5.1
Date: Tue, 07 May 2002 12:58:15 GMT
Location: /CakeCatalogService/(a55ctz55y2oyq0mnsenwv555)/Ordering.asmx
Cache-Control: private
Content-Type: text/html; charset=utf-8
Content-Length: 177

<html><head><title>Object moved</title></head><body>
<h2>Object moved to <a href='/CakeCatalogService/(a55ctz55y2oyq0mnsenwv555)/
Ordering.asmx'>here
```

```
</a>.</h2>
</body></html>
```

A standard Web service proxy generated under the .NET Framework will not handle this response because it expects an HTTP 200 OK response containing a SOAP envelope. You can potentially provide your own proxies or roll your own sessions by passing a customer SOAP header, but a discussion of such strategies is beyond the scope of this chapter.

Signaling Errors

When you create classes and interfaces for use under the .NET Framework, you generally signal error conditions using exceptions. You can subclass the *ApplicationException* class and define your own application-specific exceptions. But what happens when you need to indicate an error across a Web service interface?

Consider the scenario in which a client calls the Web method *GetCustomer*. If the code used by the method cannot access the database it needs, an *SqlException* will be generated. Unless you catch the exception, it will ripple all the way down the stack until it reaches the point at which the *GetCustomer* call arrived at the server. This exception must somehow be propagated back to the client. However, SOAP does not support the concept of an exception. Instead, a SOAP response can include a SOAP Fault to indicate that an error occurred on the server.

The format of a .NET exception includes a stack trace and possibly nested exceptions. This does not map easily into a SOAP Fault, so the .NET Framework Class Library defines the *System.Web.Services.Protocols.SoapException* class, which contains a set of properties that map to a SOAP Fault, including

- The message detailing the error.
- A fault code indicating an error with the call (not an internal application error). The *SoapException* class contains some fixed values you can use for this, such as *SoapException.ClientFaultCode*.
- The name of the Web service method.
- Additional error details supplied as XML in an *XmlNode* object.

In the case of an unhandled exception, the message is taken from the original exception, such as the *SqlException* in the example, and copied to the generated *SoapException*. The name of the originating Web method is set on the *SoapException*, and the *SoapException* is then converted into a SOAP Fault and sent back to the client.

The benefit of encapsulating error information in a SOAP Fault is that any type of client can take this information and interpret it. In the case of a client built using the .NET Framework, the *SoapException* is regenerated based on the SOAP Fault. All of the usual .NET Framework exception information, such as the stack trace, is added at this point. The exception is then thrown on the client side and hopefully caught by the client code!

The default error handling provided in a .NET Framework XML Web service is a useful fallback for propagating errors. However, it is not ideal because the message from the underlying exception might not have much meaning to the client. Therefore, it is best to catch exceptions that occur during a Web method call and then explicitly generate *SoapExceptions* containing the appropriate information. The advantage of this approach is that not only do you get to set a meaningful message, but you can also include more information using the *Detail* property.

To use the *Detail* property, you must create an appropriate XML document that can be used as part of the SOAP Fault. This document must contain a predefined root element named *detail* to fit with the SOAP specification. The correct name and namespace are provided by the read-only *DetailElementName* and *DetailElementNamespace* properties of the *SoapException* class. The following code, taken from the EnquiryWithException.asmx.jsl sample file, shows how to use these properties:

```
XmlDocument doc = new XmlDocument();

// Create a SOAP-compliant detail element that can be
// used as part of the SOAP Fault.
XmlElement root =
   doc.CreateElement(SoapException.DetailElementName.get_Name(),
   SoapException.DetailElementName.get_Namespace());
doc.AppendChild(root);
```

You can then populate the detail element with your own error information. The following example shows a version of the *FeedsHowMany* method that throws a *SoapException* if either of its string parameters is *null*:

```
public
int FeedsHowMany(int diameter,
    String shape,
    String filling) throws SoapException
{
  if (filling == null || shape == null)
  {
    String detailNamespace = "http://fourthcoffee.com";
    String prefix = "coffee";
```

```
    XmlDocument doc = new XmlDocument();

    // Create a SOAP-compliant detail element that can be
    // used as part of the SOAP Fault.
    XmlElement root =
      doc.CreateElement(SoapException.DetailElementName.get_Name(),
      SoapException.DetailElementName.get_Namespace());
    doc.AppendChild(root);

    // Add our own content to the detail message
    XmlElement params = doc.CreateElement(prefix, "Params", detailNamespace);
    root.AppendChild(params);

    XmlElement xmlShape = doc.CreateElement(prefix, "Shape",
       detailNamespace);
    xmlShape.AppendChild(doc.CreateTextNode(shape));
    params.AppendChild(xmlShape);

    XmlElement xmlFilling = doc.CreateElement(prefix, "Filling",
      detailNamespace);
    xmlFilling.AppendChild(doc.CreateTextNode(filling));
    params.AppendChild(xmlFilling);

    throw new SoapException("You passed in a null argument",
      SoapException.ClientFaultCode,
      "FeedsHowManyWithException",
      doc);
  }
 ⋮
}
```

A *Params* element is created below the *details* element. This *Params* element contains two other elements, each of which represents the value of one of the two string parameters passed into the method. By examining this information, the client can determine which parameter was incorrect. These child elements are defined in a namespace specific to the example company (Fourth Coffee); this is good practice whenever you create documents to be passed across Web service boundaries.

The *SoapException* is created using the generated detail document. The use of the *ClientFaultCode* flag indicates that the processing difficulty was due to a problem with the parameters sent from the client. Note that the method must declare that it throws a *SoapException*. The *SoapException* can be caught on the client in a *try/catch* block. The SOAP Fault generated by passing a null *Shape* argument is shown here:

```
HTTP/1.1 500 Internal Server Error.
Server: Microsoft-IIS/5.1
Date: Tue, 07 May 2002 13:40:32 GMT
Cache-Control: private
Content-Type: text/xml; charset=utf-8
Content-Length: 816

<?xml version="1.0" encoding="utf-8"?>
<soap:Envelope xmlns:soap="http://schemas.xmlsoap.org/soap/envelope/">
  <soap:Body>
    <soap:Fault>
      <faultcode>soap:Client</faultcode>
      <faultstring>System.Web.Services.Protocols.SoapException: You passed
       in a null argument at
       CakeCatalogService.EnquiryWithException.FeedsHowMany(Int32 diameter,
       String shape, String filling) in
       c:\inetpub\wwwroot\CakeCatalogService\EnquiryWithException.asmx.jsl:line
       86</faultstring>
      <faultactor>FeedsHowManyWithException</faultactor>
      <detail>
        <coffee:Params xmlns:coffee="http://fourthcoffee.com">
          <coffee:Shape>
          </coffee:Shape>
          <coffee:Filling>fruit</coffee:Filling>
        </coffee:Params>
      </detail>
    </soap:Fault>
  </soap:Body>
</soap:Envelope>
```

Securing a Web Service

XML Web services based on ASP.NET use the same security mechanisms as ASP.NET Web applications (discussed in Chapter 16). Given the nature of Web services, some security options such as forms-based authentication are redundant. However, new options are also available, such as the use of SOAP headers to carry authentication information. You could write a whole chapter (if not a whole book) on Web services and security, so this section will employ the Pareto Principle (otherwise known as the 80/20 rule) and concentrate on the three main options:

- Windows-based authentication
- Windows-based authentication over SSL
- Certificate-based authentication (which includes SSL by default)

The type of security you use will depend on your requirements for authentication and privacy. If you need privacy for data in transit, you must select one of the SSL options. If you do not need privacy, it is quicker and easier to use Windows-based authentication. Be sure that you have Windows authentication specified in the Web.Config file for your Web service:

```
<configuration>
  <system.web>
    <authentication mode="Windows" />
    ⋮
  </system.web>
</configuration>
```

In the context of the online cake store, you might want to provide access to certain additional services that are restricted to business partners. For example, consider an XML Web service called PartnerServices.asmx that contains the following method to give partners access to the secret Fourth Coffee cake recipe (which is not fully listed here due to commercial confidentiality):

```
/** @attribute WebMethodAttribute() */
public String GetRecipe()
{
   return "Eye of newt and toe of bat...";
}
```

By default, Web services built using Visual Studio .NET are configured to allow anonymous access. This means that the client does not need to take any special measures to propagate their security information. Such unlimited access might be fine in an intranet environment, but it's not suitable for interorganization or cross-department Web services in which security is important. The need for authentication will also vary depending on the sensitivity of the functionality being exposed. (You would not want to allow everyone to increase their salary by using the HR Web service, for example!).

To protect a Web service, you can use IIS security to indicate the type of authentication required, as follows:

- From the Start menu, choose Control Panel and then select Performance And Maintenance.
- Select Administrative Tools and double-click on Internet Information Services.
- Open the entry for your computer (or the server on which you deploy your Web services), and then open the Web Sites folder.

- Locate the virtual directory containing your Web service file and select the Web services file to be secured (in this case, the PartnerServices.asmx sample file under the CakeCatalogService folder), as shown in Figure 17-8.

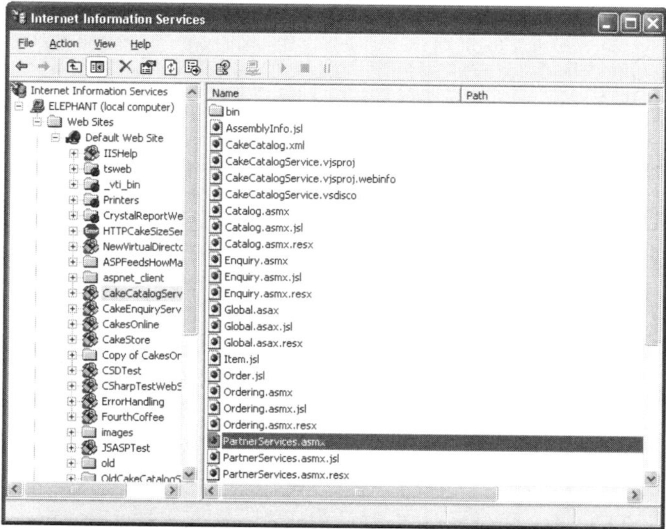

Figure 17-8 You can set security permissions down to the individual Web-service level.

- Choose Properties from the shortcut menu for this file to display the PartnerServices.asmx Properties dialog box.
- Click on the File Security tab and click the Edit button. The resulting Authentication Methods dialog box is shown in Figure 17-9.
- Clear Anonymous Access and select the type of Windows authentication required.

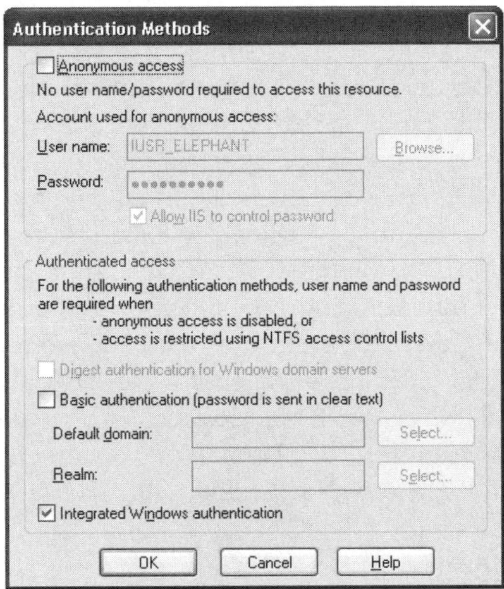

Figure 17-9 Selecting an appropriate form of Windows authentication for your Web service

If a client now tries to access the service without authentication, it will receive this error message:

```
The request failed with HTTP status 401: Access denied.
```

To access the Web service, the client must provide credentials to authenticate itself. These credentials can be a combination of username, password, and domain name. If the client is part of the same domain or workgroup as the Web service host computer, you can also use integrated security. Details on passing credentials from a client to a .NET Framework Web service are provided in Chapter 18.

You can grant or deny access to a specific Web service for a particular user or set of users by using the *<authorization>* element in the Web.Config file. This is the same mechanism employed by APS.NET Web applications. Chapter 16 discussed the use of the *<authorization>* element in detail.

You've now added authentication to your Web service. To protect data in transit you can employ SSL. To use SSL, you must obtain and install a server certificate. Clients will then access your Web service through a URL starting with *https://* in place of *http://*. You can make this happen by editing the WSDL generated by the Web service to use *https* in its service URL or by changing the URL used by the client at run time. Details about setting the target URL for a Web service client at run time are discussed in Chapter 18.

For a more flexible security solution across organizational boundaries, you can use client certificates. As before, you should use Windows authentication, but you should also associate specific client certificates with identities defined on your server. This configuration is performed under the Internet Information Services administration tool used earlier by using the Properties dialog box of the specific Web service files or over the whole virtual directory containing your Web services. On the File Security or Directory Security tab of the Properties dialog box, you'll find a section labeled Secure Communications that allows you to configure client certificates. For more details, see the product documentation. Once you've configured the certificates to use, you can pass them as part of the SOAP message sent by the client. Again, for more details, see Chapter 18.

You can find details on using SOAP Headers as a means of transporting authentication information in the .NET Framework documentation in the section titled "Securing XML Web Services Created Using ASP.NET."

Transactions and Web Services

Many business applications require updating of multiple databases as part of one business operation. To do this in a controlled and consistent way, you generally need to employ transactions. You can write code that controls transactions on a per-connection basis, or you can interact with the Distributed Transaction Coordinator (DTC) to take part in transactions that span multiple databases. As you saw in Chapter 14, serviced components, such as those provided by COM+, can take part in transactions without your having to write transaction-specific code. The component is tagged with *TransactionAttribute*, indicating to its container the type of transaction support it requires. Even if a transaction does not span multiple databases, you might find it convenient to use declarative transactions to simplify development.

Just as transactions are important to components, they are also important to Web services. A Web service will typically occupy the same role in an application as a serviced component—as a repository of business logic to be called by a client as necessary. Hence, you want to obtain the same level of transactional control. As before, you can control transactions on a per-connection basis if you're communicating with a single database. Methods for controlling such transactions are provided through the ADO.NET connection classes. However, you can also use declarative transactions with ASP.NET-based Web services by taking advantage of the transaction support in the *System.EnterpriseServices* namespace. To do this, you must specify the *TransactionOption* property of the *WebMethod* attribute. You assign this property a value from the *TransactionOption* enumeration to indicate what type of transaction support you need for the method. (The *TransactionOption* enumeration lives in the *System.EnterpriseSer-*

vices namespace, so remember to import this into the Web service JSL file and to add the System.EnterpriseServices.dll assembly as a reference into the project.)

The following code shows an updated form of the *SubmitOrder* method that uses a transaction attribute:

```
/** @attribute WebMethodAttribute(TransactionOption=
   TransactionOption.RequiresNew) */
public WsReceipt SubmitOrder (Order order,
   boolean shouldFail)
{
   // Should probably have some database stuff here...
   if (shouldFail)
   {
      throw new SoapException("Because you asked for this..." +
         msg, SoapException.ClientFaultCode);
   }

   WsReceipt receipt = new WsReceipt(order.get_CustomerName(),
        order.get_OrderId(), DateTime.get_Now());
   return receipt;
}
```

When a client calls this form of the *SubmitOrder* method, a new transaction will be started in which the method will run. An exception will cause the transaction to roll back. If no exceptions are thrown, ASP.NET will try to commit the transaction. You can access the current transaction context through the *ContextUtil* class and use the static methods *SetAbort* and *SetComplete* to control the outcome of the transaction.

It is important to understand that a Web method can act only as the root of a transaction. There is currently no standard way of propagating transaction information over SOAP calls (at least not until the GXA arrives), so a transaction started in a Web service client will be suspended while the Web service call is made. If a transaction is started by ASP.NET in response to a Web service method call, the transaction will propagate through calls to other .NET objects and COM+ components. Any updates to transactional resources, such as a database, made by these objects or components will become part of the transaction. These objects or components can affect the outcome of the transaction by throwing exceptions or setting the transaction state in the transaction context (through such methods as *SetAbort*).

In the same way that a client cannot propagate a transaction to a Web service, one Web service cannot propagate its transaction onto another Web service—the same issue of crossing a SOAP boundary applies. If a Web service method calls another Web service method that is denoted as transactional, it will suspend any existing transaction and start a new transaction for the new method.

Exposing Existing Applications as Web Services

In some cases, you'll create Web service-based applications from scratch. But in other cases, you might want to incorporate existing functionality into new Web service applications or provide Web service wrappers for existing functionality. We'll discuss this topic next.

What Do You Have Already?

Existing functionality can come in a variety of forms:

- If you've been pursuing a component-based strategy, much of your business logic might already be encapsulated in COM or COM+ components. In this case, you can use these components from ASP.NET managed code as described in Chapter 13 and Chapter 14.
- The code might exist as discrete methods in an existing DLL. In this case, you can access this functionality through the P/Invoke mechanism discussed in Chapter 13.
- You might have business code encapsulated in a Web-oriented application, such as ASP pages. In this case, you must factor out the existing code into methods that can be used as part of an ASP.NET-based Web service or a supporting class.
- The existing functionality might belong to a GUI-based application. As with the Web-oriented application, if the business logic is embedded in the GUI code, you must separate it out into discrete methods.

When you're looking to reuse existing functionality as part of a Web service, you should take some time to think about whether it actually fits into the Web service model. Considerations include:

- If the functionality was not previously distributed, will the functionality work with multiple users and with the anticipated number of users of the Web service?
- Are specific data types being passed around that will be difficult to expose through a Web service?

- Is the granularity appropriate for a Web service? If the functionality needs the client to make many method calls to achieve its aims, a lot of overhead and network traffic will result.

If you anticipate serious issues with the functionality you want to expose, you might want to use an alternative strategy, as described next.

Strategies for Exposing Functionality

To expose existing functionality as a Web service, you can choose from a few different approaches, depending on your requirements:

- If the functionality already exists as a DLL or COM/COM+ component, you might want to simply create a Web service server-side proxy for it. This involves creating a Web service containing a set of methods that match those of the DLL or component; the Web service simply delegates the calls to the DLL or component.
- If you have issues with data types or granularity, you can design a Web service-oriented interface for the functionality. You can then create a Web service facade based on this interface that will call the existing functionality as needed. This will also allow you to reduce network traffic or make interaction easier compared to using a simple server-side proxy.
- If you're not sure about the best distribution strategy to use, you can wrap the functionality as ordinary .NET classes that are deployed in regular assemblies. These classes can then be called from ASP.NET-based Web services or from .NET Remoting remote objects. If you're exposing functionality through .NET Remoting, you can use this approach to deliver the functionality across raw TCP/IP or over HTTP channels. If you're using a .NET Remoting server that's configured to use the HTTP transport and XML serialization, a client can access the server as a Web service using the SoapSuds utility, as discussed in Chapter 18.

Ultimately, Web services are a very flexible form of distribution. But as with any form of distribution, you must be careful about what you distribute and consider the consequences of doing so.'

Summary

In this chapter, we examined the purpose of Web services and the technologies they use. You learned how to create Web services simply and quickly using Visual Studio .NET and J#. You can create Web services as ASP.NET components with an ASMX file extension. You can expose Web methods from which ASP.NET will generate a service description in WSDL. Visual Studio .NET allows you to examine and test a Web service through a Web browser.

You learned that complex data types can be passed between a client and a Web service and that object parameters are automatically converted into such complex types defined in WSDL. You can pass *DataSet* objects and XML documents as parameters or return values to Web service operations. You learned that ASP.NET-based Web services use the same security mechanisms as ASP.NET Web applications and learned how to use ASP.NET state management to keep server-side state on behalf of a Web service client. The chapter also discussed error handling and how to apply an automatic transaction to an ASP.NET Web method. Finally, you learned strategies for exposing existing functionality as Web services.

18

Creating a Web Service Client

In Chapter 17, you learned how to create Web services and we used a Web browser to examine and test them manually. However, the whole point of Web services is that you access them programmatically, not through a Web browser. Web service clients can take many forms and can be written in a variety of languages on different platforms. Ideally, you should not need to be a SOAP expert to invoke a Web service; the mechanism for Web services should fit with the development paradigm of your environment and language.

The Web services examples you've seen so far have been used synchronously—that is, you wait for a response before proceeding. However, this is not always the best way of working. If an operation can take a relatively long time, at least in programming terms, you might want your application to get on with other tasks while the Web service is executing. Again, the model for doing this should fit seamlessly into your environment of choice.

Another notable aspect of the Web services you've encountered so far is that you've always known what functionality they offer because you've been privy to their creation. You've also known where to find them, assuming that you installed the sample files on your server. You won't always have this knowledge about the Web services you want to use. Sometimes you'll know where the service lives but not what it can do. In other cases, you might not even know where it lives—you might only know something about the type of service you need. As a Web service client developer, you need standard mechanisms for finding and interrogating Web services so you can build applications based on them.

This chapter will explain how to build a client for a Web service. It will describe how to create a Web proxy class and a Web reference, both manually and by using Microsoft Visual Studio .NET. The chapter will also show you how to call Web methods synchronously and asynchronously. Finally, it will discuss dynamic Web service discovery and the use of Universal Description, Discovery, and Integration (UDDI).

Web Service Clients

When you consume a Web service, you're presented with a lot of complex information about the available operations and how the service expects to be called. This section will look at how Visual Studio .NET and the Microsoft .NET Framework can take this information and present it in a developer-friendly way.

Note This chapter uses the URL *http://fourthcoffee.com* as the base URL for all Web services so the namespaces appear realistic. However, the Web services mentioned do not actually exist at fourthcoffee.com—this is a dummy URL provided by Microsoft for documentation purposes. We achieved the realistic effect by adding a line to our \Windows\System32\drivers\etc\hosts file to map fourthcoffee.com to 127.0.0.1 (*localhost*), so you must perform a similar mapping if you want to try out the samples without reimporting the Web references and recompiling them. However, all of the examples will work perfectly well with *localhost*—you'll simply have to do some mental mapping of the names as you go through the examples in the chapter.

The Client View of a Web Service

The publisher of a Web service will provide potential clients with information about the capabilities and location of the service. As you saw in Chapter 17, this usually takes the form of a Web Services Description Language (WSDL) document that contains a list of the operations provided by the service and the input and output parameters of these operations. A WSDL document uses XML Schema syntax to describe any complex types used as parameters. The operations are grouped into *portType* elements, which are combined with particular transport mechanisms to create ports. The WSDL document brings together one or more ports to create a service description that maps to a running instance of the service.

Given this information, you can construct your own SOAP calls using a *System.Net.WebClient*, *System.Net.HttpWebRequest*, *System.Net.Sockets.TcpClient*, or even a *System.Net.Sockets.Socket* object. However, this is messy work and requires that you have intimate knowledge of the SOAP specification and XML Schemas. Most of us have homes to go to and lives to lead outside of work, however, so the .NET Framework provides tools to help you quickly and easily create a client-side proxy to represent the Web service. These tools are integrated into Visual Studio .NET. Using these tools, you can create a proxy that represents the Web service as a .NET class and exposes the SOAP operations as methods of this class. This scenario is shown in Figure 18-1. The server shown is based on ASP.NET, but the same proxy pattern applies to all Web services no matter how they're implemented. (This is the beauty of Web services.)

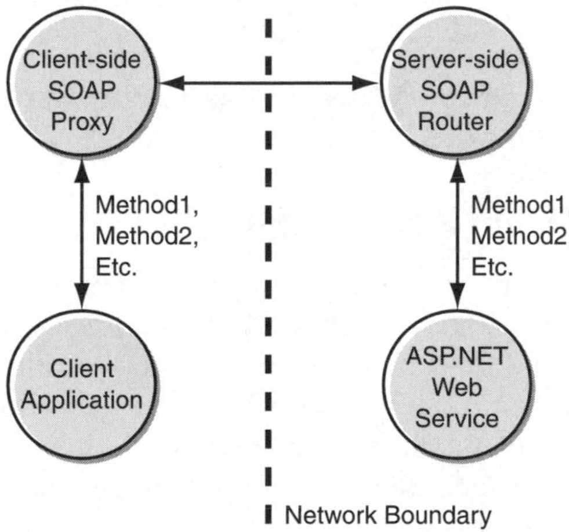

Figure 18-1 The client-side proxy represents the Web service for .NET clients.

You can invoke the proxy from any supported .NET language. In fact, you can generate it in the main .NET languages, including Microsoft Visual J#. To invoke a SOAP operation, the client calls a method of the proxy. The Web service proxy blends in with .NET programming paradigm, so it can be used from any type of .NET application, including ASP.NET pages, console applications, and Windows Forms, or from another Web service, as shown in Figure 18-2.

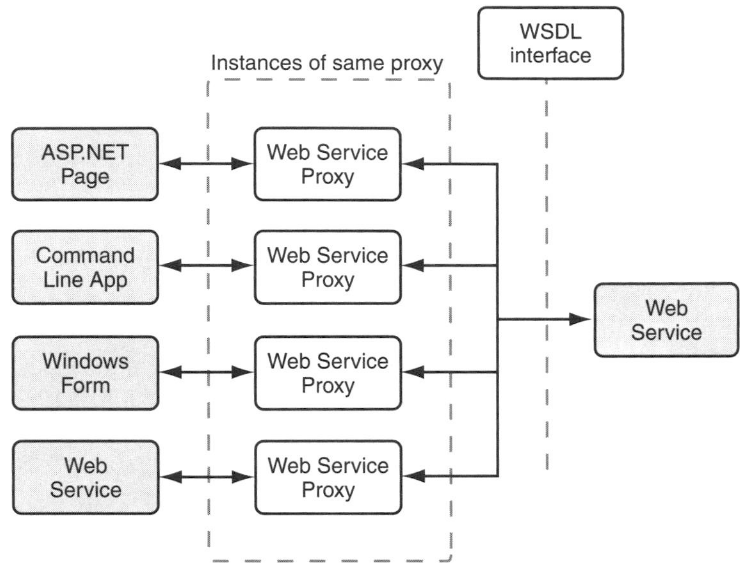

Figure 18-2 The same Web service proxy class can be used from any type of .NET application.

Creating a Web Service Client Using Visual Studio .NET

As an initial example, consider creating a client for the Fourth Coffee cake enquiry service as defined in Chapter 17. This is a Web service version of the familiar *FeedsHowMany* method. As a customer of the Fourth Coffee company, you need to obtain information about the service from which to create your proxy. We'll discuss some more automated and scalable mechanisms later, but for now assume that you've engaged in an e-mail exchange with the company and that they've provided you with the URL where you can locate the service: *http://fourthcoffee.com/CakeCatalogService/Enquiry.asmx.*

Note The Fourth Coffee company Web services are provided as sample files for this chapter. When you unpack the sample files, you'll find a Windows Installer file, CakeCatalogServiceInstaller.msi, at the top level. If you've already installed and run the sample files for Chapter 17, you do not need this installer. However, if you haven't installed the CakeCatalogService project from Chapter 17, this installer gives you a quick and easy way to do so. To install CakeCatalogService, double-click on the installer file and select all the defaults. (Click the Next buttons until you get to Finish, and then click that.) The Visual

Studio .NET solution file associated with these services can be found in the sample files in the CakeCatalogService folder. Once you've installed the installer file, you can examine and change the Web service code by loading the CakeCatalogService.sln solution file from this folder.

The client is a Console application called SimpleCakeEnquiry (contained in the file SimpleCakeEnquiry.jsl in the SimpleCakeEnquiry project). To generate the Web service proxy, you simply add a Web reference to the Enquiry Web service. You can do this by choosing Add Web Reference from the Project menu. In the Add Web Reference dialog box, type the URL of the Web service description (the WSDL file). Figure 18-3 shows what happens when you enter the enquiry service URL (*http://fourthcoffee.com/CakeCatalogService/Enquiry.asmx*). Visual Studio engages in a conversation with the Web service and obtains the same information we retrieved when we tested the Web service in Chapter 17. It uses the *?wsdl* suffix to obtain the WSDL for the service (referred to in the dialog box as the Contract) and displays the HTML documentation available from the Web service, as shown in Figure 18-3.

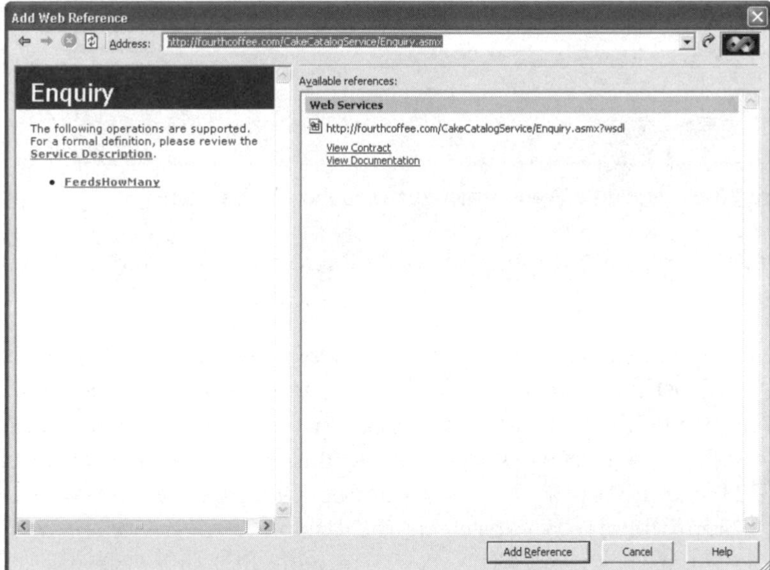

Figure 18-3 The Add Web Reference dialog box allows you to view Web service information.

To create the client-side proxy, click Add Reference. This imports the Web service description and builds the proxy in the language of the current project. The imported reference consists of the WSDL document, a DISCO document and a reference map. The latter two items are discussed later, but if you choose Show All Files from the Project menu, you can see the proxy itself (Reference.jsl) in Solution Explorer under the Reference.map folder below com.fourthcoffee in the list of Web references. You can view the code for this proxy, as shown in Figure 18-4.

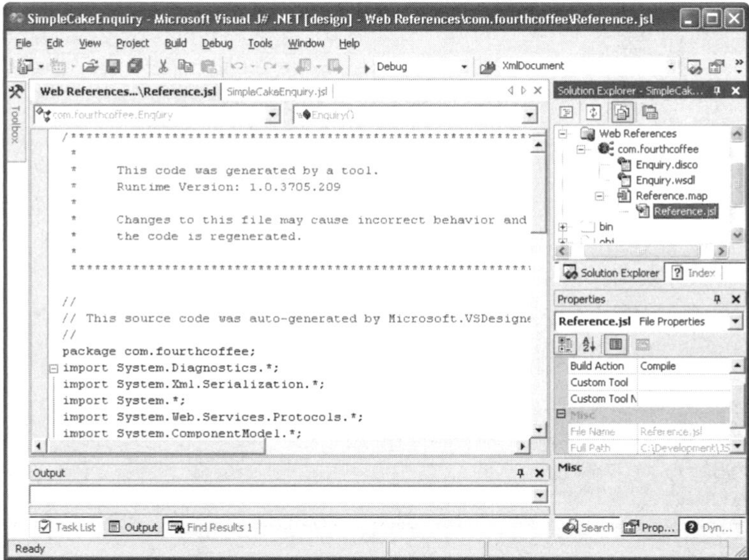

Figure 18-4 Adding a Web service reference to an application

We won't walk through the code line by line, but here are the main points to note:

- The package in which the proxy classes are generated is the same as the host name from the WSDL document—in this case, *fourthcoffee.com*. The package name used for the proxy should be unique or as distinctive as possible to avoid name clashes with other classes. (This is generally a good practice.) The use of the Web service domain name (reversed) as the basis for the package name will avoid clashes with Web services provided by other servers:

```
package com.fourthcoffee;
```

- The class name is the name of the service as defined in the *<service>* element of the WSDL document—in this case, *Enquiry*. This class extends *System.Web.Services.Protocols.SoapHttpClientProtocol*, which provides the basic connectivity and marshaling support for an HTTP-based SOAP exchange.

- The proxy class has a default constructor that sets the target URL of the service. The default value for this URL is obtained from the *<soap:address>* element contained in the *<service>* element in the WSDL document:

```
public Enquiry() {
  this.set_Url("http://fourthcoffee.com/CakeCatalogService/
Enquiry.asmx");
}
```

- Each method exposed by the Web service is represented by a method of the proxy. These methods are decorated with some of the XML serialization and Web service attributes you learned about in Chapter 17. These attributes define the element names and namespaces to be used in the request message and to be expected in the response. All of this information is automatically gathered from the appropriate part of the WSDL document:

```
/
** @attribute System.Web.Services.Protocols.SoapDocumentMethodAttrib
ute
("http://fourthcoffee.com/CakeCatalog/FeedsHowMany",
RequestNamespace="http://fourthcoffee.com/CakeCatalog/",
ResponseNamespace="http://fourthcoffee.com/CakeCatalog/",
Use=System.Web.Services.Description.SoapBindingUse.Literal,
ParameterStyle=System.Web.Services.Protocols.SoapParameter-
Style.Wrapped)*/
public int FeedsHowMany(int diameter, String shape, String filling)
{
```

- The methods themselves use the protected *Invoke* method of the *SoapHttpClientProtocol* class to send the SOAP message and wait for the response. You'll see three methods for every SOAP operation: one for synchronous operation and two for asynchronous operation. We'll discuss the asynchronous methods later. At this stage, we're considering only synchronous exchanges.

```
public int FeedsHowMany(int diameter, String shape, String filling)
{
   Object[] results = this.Invoke("FeedsHowMany", new Object[] {
      (System.Int32)diameter,
      shape,
      filling}
```

```
            );
        return ((int)(System.Int32)(results[0]));
    }
```

To use the proxy, you should import the package and instantiate the proxy. You can then call the methods of the proxy as you would methods of any other .NET Framework class. The complete code for the *SimpleCakeEnquiry* class, which calls the Enquiry Web service and displays the result, is shown here:

```
package SimpleCakeEnquiry;

import com.fourthcoffee.*;

public class SimpleCakeEnquiry
{
   /** @attribute System.STAThread() */
   public static void main(String[] args)
   {
      Enquiry enq = new Enquiry();

      int feeds = enq.FeedsHowMany(10, "square", "fruit");

      System.Console.WriteLine("That cake feeds " + feeds + " people");
   }
}
```

The Web service will inform you that this cake feeds 25 people.

Going Beyond the Simple Client Scenario

At this point, using Web services might seem easy. To an extent, this is true. If the service you need to communicate with is simple, like the Enquiry service used so far, you'll have few problems. However, in a commercial application, you need to consider what might happen in the following scenarios:

- An error occurs during a Web service call.
- The Web service moves to a different URL.
- The Web methods take complex types as parameters and return values.
- You need to use multiple Web services in a client application.
- A Web method takes a long time to complete.

Security is also a major concern, especially when a Web service is used across the Internet. Web service client developers will want to take advantage of other functionality (such as state management) that was covered from the server perspective in Chapter 17. Here, we'll discuss several issues related to creating Web service proxies in the "real world."

Handling Errors

When you define the interfaces between components in an application, you must define the set of exceptions or error conditions that can occur. The same is true with Web services. Web methods can throw application-defined exceptions. However, as you saw in Chapter 17, these exceptions are converted to *SoapException* instances as they cross the Web service boundary, so they can be converted into SOAP Faults that can be passed back to the client. Thus, from the client point of view, you must be prepared to encounter three types of exception:

- An underlying exception related to transporting information back and forth. For example, the server might not be able to respond to your request because it has crashed. In this case, you'll receive a low-level exception such as a *RuntimeException* raised by one of the underlying network classes. This type of exception comes with the territory when you develop distributed applications, and you cannot ignore it—you should catch such exceptions and try to handle them gracefully.
- A *SoapException* that's generated because of a problem in the underlying SOAP protocol exchange. A *SoapException* can be generated by a SOAP class used by the proxy to send and receive the SOAP messages. If the *Code* property is anything other than *SoapException.ServerFaultCode*, the problem is not due to an error on the server. (We'll discuss the codes shortly.)
- A *SoapException* that acts as a wrapper for an application-level error. When a Web service operation generates a SOAP Fault, the client-side .NET proxy will convert this into a *SoapException* and throw the exception for your client to catch. If the SOAP Fault is the result of an exception generated in a .NET-based Web service, the *Message* property of the *SoapException* will be a copy of the *Message* from the underlying exception.

The moral here is that you should always surround Web service calls with an exception handler.

One consideration here is how to determine what type of error has occurred on the server. Some parts of an exception that you might find useful, such as the stack trace, will relate to the client side rather than the server. Other parts, such as the inner exception, will not be set. However, extra information is available in a *SoapException* that you might find useful:

- The *Code* property indicates why the call failed. This property can be set to one of four values defined in the *SoapException* class. A value of *ClientFaultCode* indicates that the client sent something that was not correct, either in content or in formatting. *ServerFaultCode* indicates that the error occurred during server-side processing but was not due to bad information supplied by the client. *VersionMismatchFaultCode* indicates that incompatible versions of SOAP are in use (a rare occurrence). Finally, *MustUnderstandFaultCode* indicates that one of the SOAP headers labeled as *MustUnderstand* was not understood by the server. Again, this condition is unlikely to occur unless you've set your own SOAP headers.
- The *Actor* property indicates where the exception occurred. This is typically the URL of the Web service that was processing the request.
- The *Detail* property can contain more information if the Web service has explicitly generated the SOAP Fault. An example of this is shown in the *FeedsHowMany* method that is part of the proxy generated for the EnquiryWithException Web service. (The creation of the detail on the server side was shown in Chapter 17.)

The following code fragment shows SOAP exception handling from the *ExceptionCakeEnquiry* sample class:

```
public static void main(String[] args)
{
   try
   {
      CakeCatalogEnquiry enq = new CakeCatalogEnquiry();
      int feeds = enq.FeedsHowMany(10, null, "fruit");
      System.Console.WriteLine("That cake feeds " + feeds + " people");
   }
   catch (SoapException ex)
   {
      System.Console.WriteLine("SOAP Exception: " + ex.get_Message());
      System.Console.WriteLine("Code: " + ex.get_Code());
      System.Console.WriteLine("Actor: " + ex.get_Actor());
      System.Console.WriteLine("Detail: " +
         ex.get_Detail().get_OuterXml());
```

```
        }
        catch (Exception ex)
        {
            System.Console.WriteLine("Unexpected Exception: " +
                ex.getMessage());
        }
    }
```

The result of running this code is shown in Figure 18-5.

```
C:\Development\JSharp-non-network\WebServicesCh18\ExceptionCakeEnquiry\bin\Debug\E...
SOAP Exception: System.Web.Services.Protocols.SoapException: You passed in a nul
l argument
   at CakeCatalogService.EnquiryWithException.FeedsHowMany(Int32 diameter, Strin
g shape, String filling) in c:\inetpub\wwwroot\CakeCatalogService\EnquiryWithExc
eption.asmx.jsl:line 86
Code: http://schemas.xmlsoap.org/soap/envelope/:Client
Actor: FeedsHowManyWithException
Detail: <detail>
        <coffee:Params xmlns:coffee="http://fourthcoffee.com">
          <coffee:Shape>
          </coffee:Shape>
          <coffee:Filling>fruit</coffee:Filling>
        </coffee:Params>
      </detail>
Press any key to continue_
```

Figure 18-5 The *SoapException* class, which contains SOAP-specific information

Retargeting the Proxy

In the initial client application, we accepted the default location for the service obtained from the WSDL document. However, the service might move—the service provider might make a duplicate or updated service available at another URL, for example. Alternatively, if you're developing your own Web services as part of a distributed application, you'll have to move your development Web services to a testing environment and then on to the live servers. Because your Web reference will have been created based on the WSDL generated from the development Web service, it will contain the host name of the server on which that development Web service ran. As you move from development to test to live deployment, your client will need to be retargeted at a new server.

The most direct way to retarget the proxy is to change its *Url* property:

```
CakeCatalogEnquiry enq = new CakeCatalogEnquiry();
enq.set_Url("http://otherserver/CakeCatalogService/Enquiry.asmx");
```

If the client is a Console application, you could supply the replacement URL as a command-line argument. But a better solution that works for other types of clients is to put the URL in a configuration file, such as an ASP.NET application's web.config file. Visual Studio .NET provides an easy way of doing this. If you select a Web reference in Solution Explorer and look at the Properties for it, you'll see that one of these properties is URL Behavior. By default, this is set to *Static*. If you change this property to *Dynamic*, the generated proxy will be altered so that it looks in the configuration file for the Web service URL before using the URL provided in the WSDL document:

```
public CakeCatalogEnquiry() {
  String urlSetting =
  System.Configuration.ConfigurationSettings.get_AppSettings().get_Item(
  "ExceptionCakeEnquiry.com.fourthcoffee.CakeCatalogEnquiry");
  if ((urlSetting != null)) {
    this.set_Url(String.Concat(urlSetting, ""));
  }
  else {
   this.set_Url(
   "http://fourthcoffee.com/CakeCatalogService/EnquiryWithException.asmx");
   }
}
```

If you use this mechanism, you should define the value of the URL in the *<appSettings>* section of the application configuration file. This section consists of name/value pairs. Taking the sample code shown as an example, the name in the pair would be *ExceptionCakeEnquiry.com.fourthcoffee.CakeCatalogEnquiry* and the value would be the appropriate URL for the Web service:

```
<configuration>
   ⋮
   <appSettings>
      <add key="ExceptionCakeEnquiry.com.fourthcoffee.CakeCatalogEnquiry"
   value="http://test01/CakeCatalogService/EnquiryWithException.asmx" />
      ⋮
   </appSettings>
</configuration>
```

You might also want to change the target URL of the Web service client when you need to debug your services. When problems occur, it can be useful to capture SOAP messages going back and forth. You can do this using a tool such as TcpTrace (from *http://www.pocketsoap.com*), which will capture traffic between your client and the Web service. To do this, it listens on a given port (usually port 8080 on the local machine), logs all the traffic it receives, and then passes it on to the real destination. To use this tool, you must retarget your Web service proxy to the port and machine on which TcpTrace is running by setting its *Url* property. If TcpTrace is running on your local machine, you use a URL starting with *http://localhost:8080*.

Handling Complex Types

The *FeedsHowMany* method uses simple types for its parameters and return value. However, as discussed in Chapter 17, many applications will need to pass across more complex types. The Ordering Web service (in the Ordering.asmx file in the CakeCatalogService sample project) defines the *SubmitOrder* method, which takes an instance of a *CakeCatalogService.Order* as a parameter and returns an instance of *CakeCatalogService.WsReceipt*. The *Order* class itself contains an array of *CakeCatalogService.Item* instances and hence forms a nested complex type. (The WSDL generated for this service was discussed in Chapter 17.) The question from the client perspective is, "What sort of proxy methods are generated from this WSDL?"

A client for the Ordering Web service is provided in the OrderCakeClient project (in the file OrderCakeClient.jsl). This project includes a Web reference for the Web service at *http://fourthcoffee.com/CakeCatalogService/Ordering.asmx*, which generates the Reference.jsl file in the *com.fourthcoffee* namespace. The proxy file contains the proxy class itself—which is called *Ordering*—and also contains mappings for the complex data types it has found in the WSDL, as shown here:

```
/** @attribute System.Xml.Serialization.XmlTypeAttribute
(Namespace="http://fourthcoffee.com/CakeCatalog/")*/
public class Order {

    /** <remarks/> */
    public System.String CustomerName;

    /** <remarks/> */
    public Item[] OrderContents;

    /** <remarks/> */
    public int OrderId;
}

/** <remarks/> */
/** @attribute System.Xml.Serialization.XmlTypeAttribute
(Namespace="http://fourthcoffee.com/CakeCatalog/")*/
public class Item {

    /** <remarks/> */
    public System.String ItemDescription;

    /** <remarks/> */
    public int Quantity;
}

/** <remarks/> */
/** @attribute System.Xml.Serialization.XmlTypeAttribute
(Namespace="http://fourthcoffee.com/CakeCatalog/")*/
```

```
public class WsReceipt {

    /** <remarks/> */
    public System.String CustomerName;

    /** <remarks/> */
    public System.Object[] OrderContents;

    /** <remarks/> */
    public int OrderId;

    /** <remarks/> */
    public System.DateTime Timestamp;
}
```

The *Order*, *Item*, and *WsReceipt* classes are client-side representations of the classes with the same names that are used on the server side. On the client side, these classes become simple data structures that expose data through public data members. (See the section titled "Consequences of XML Serialization" in Chapter 17.) These classes are defined in the same package as the *Ordering* class (*com.fourthcoffee*); their associated XML elements appear in SOAP messages under the XML namespace *http://fourthcoffee.com/CakeCatalog/*.

The following code fragment from OrderCakeClient.jsl builds up an order by directly accessing the public member variables defined in the *Order* and *Item* classes and submits it using the *SubmitOrder* method:

```
Order order = new Order();
order.CustomerName = "Peter Waxman";
order.OrderId = 12345;

Item item1 = new Item();
item1.ItemDescription = "Birthday Cake";
item1.Quantity = 7;

Item item2 = new Item();
item2.ItemDescription = "Party Cake";
item2.Quantity = 3;

Item[] items = { item1, item2 };
order.OrderContents = items;

WsReceipt receipt = orders.SubmitOrder(order);
```

The contents of the receipt can be accessed through the public member variables defined in the *WsReceipt* class.

Handling Bulk Data

In the previous section, the *Order* class contained an array of *Item* instances. It is straightforward to pass an array comprising elements of a fixed type between a Web service client and server (as long as that type is serializable and its data is publicly accessible). However, this might not always be the most convenient way. As discussed in the section titled "Passing *DataSet* Objects" in Chapter 17, you might want to transmit data that has been retrieved from a database. Ideally, you shouldn't convert all of this into application-specific types solely to pass it across the Web service interface.

The *RetrieveCatalog* method of the sample file Catalog.asmx.jsl (in the CakeCatalogService project) returns a *DataSet*. The WSDL produced by this was discussed in the section titled "Passing *DataSet* Objects" in Chapter 17. This WSDL has been imported into the sample project DataSetCakeCatalog, which contains a client class called *DataSetCakeCatalog*. The *main* method of the *DataSetCakeCatalog* class invokes the *RetrieveCatalog* method of the Catalog Web service. The *DataSetCakeCatalog* class lists the contents of the retrieved *DataSet* as if it were any other *DataSet* obtained from an ordinary data source:

```
Catalog catalog = new Catalog();

DataSet ds = catalog.RetrieveCatalog();

DataTable table = ds.get_Tables().get_Item(0);
DataRowCollection rows = ds.get_Tables().get_Item(0).get_Rows();

DataColumnCollection columns = table.get_Columns();
for (int i = 0; i < columns.get_Count(); i++)
{
   if (i != 0) Console.Write(", ");
   Console.Write("" + columns.get_Item(i).get_ColumnName());
}
Console.WriteLine();

System.Collections.IEnumerator enumerator = rows.GetEnumerator();

while (enumerator.MoveNext())
{
   DataRow row = (DataRow)enumerator.get_Current();

   for (int i = 0; i < columns.get_Count(); i++)
   {
      if (i != 0) Console.Write(", ");
      if (row.get_Item(i) == null ||
         (row.get_Item(i) instanceof System.String &&
          row.get_Item(i).ToString().get_Length() == 0))
```

```
        {
            Console.Write("<empty>");
        }
        else
        {
            Console.Write("" + row.get_Item(i));
        }
    }
    Console.WriteLine();
```

The result of running this program is shown in Figure 18-6.

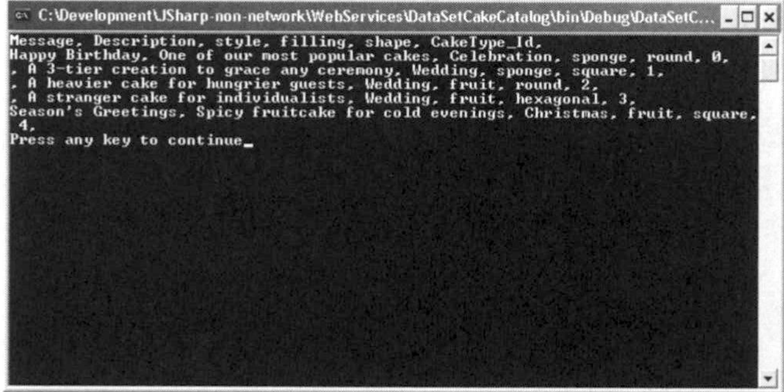

Figure 18-6 The DataSetCakeClient program lists the contents of the *DataSet* received.

Tip If the use of *DataSet* objects to transport bulk data appeals to you but the clunky syntax puts you off (calls such as *get_Item(0)* are not very descriptive or type-safe), consider using typed *DataSet* objects. A typed *DataSet* class lets you access data by using meaningful table, row, and column names. For more information on typed *DataSet* objects, see Chapter 7.

Passing XML Documents

As you might expect, sending and receiving XML documents through Web service interfaces is quite simple. Again, we dealt with the server-side aspects in Chapter 17, and you saw an example of this when we created the method *RetrieveXmlCatalog* in the sample file Catalog.asmx.jsl (in the CakeCatalogService project). From the client side, all you need to do is make the call, as shown here:

```
Catalog catalog = new Catalog();
```

```
XmlNode node = catalog.RetrieveXmlCatalog();

Console.WriteLine("Node is " + node.get_OuterXml());

Console.WriteLine("Namespace for CakeCatalog is " +
    node.get_NamespaceURI());
```

The code calls the method *RetrieveXmlCatalog*, which returns a *System.Xml.XmlNode*. Once you've received the *XmlNode*, you can manipulate it in the same way that you would any other XML document. For more information on manipulating XML, see Chapter 5. The full client can be found in the sample project XmlDocumentCakeClient. When you run this program, you'll see the output shown in Figure 18-7.

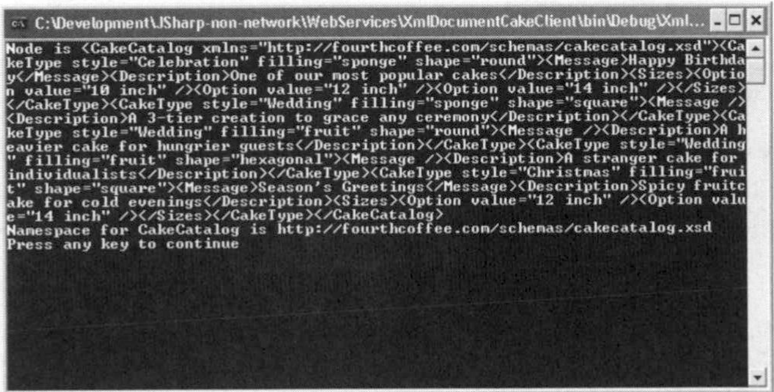

Figure 18-7 XML documents and their namespace information pass easily through Web service interfaces.

One interesting point is that the namespace specified in the original file (*http://fourthcoffee.com/schemas/cakecatalog.xsd*) is not affected by being encapsulated in various other XML documents on its passage back from the server.

Maintaining State

In Chapter 17, you saw how a Web service based on ASP.NET can maintain state on behalf of a client using the server-side *Session* object. For this to work, any client must be able to send and receive cookies. By default, the proxies generated from the WSDL description of the service do not use cookies. However, you can change this behavior by creating a new *System.Net.CookieContainer* object and passing it to the proxy through its *CookieContainer* property, as shown here:

```
import com.fourthcoffee.Ordering;
:
```

```
Ordering orders = new Ordering();
orders.set_CookieContainer(new System.Net.CookieContainer());
```

Caution This state management mechanism, available only when you communicate with Web services, is based on ASP.NET. It might be available on other Web services, such as those based on JavaServer Pages (JSPs) or servlets, but you should check the documentation for those services to ensure compatibility.

In this case, the proxy is for the Fourth Coffee ordering service defined in the CakeCatalogService project. This service provides a sequence of methods that can be used to build up an order on the client. It also exposes an *Increment* method that increments an application-scope count. The following code fragment from the SessionCakeClient.jsl sample file in the SessionCakeClient project shows a client using these calls. It calls the *Increment* method multiple times to illustrate how the application value can be updated and then builds up an order:

```
Console.WriteLine("Incrementing: " + orders.Increment());
Console.WriteLine("Incrementing: " + orders.Increment());
Console.WriteLine("Incrementing: " + orders.Increment());
Console.WriteLine("Incrementing: " + orders.Increment());
Console.WriteLine("Incrementing: " + orders.Increment());

orders.StartBuiltUpOrder("Peter Waxman", 987098);
orders.AddToOrder("Party Cake", 12);
orders.AddToOrder("Wedding Cake", 3);
WsReceipt receipt = orders.SubmitBuiltUpOrder();

Console.WriteLine("Receipt has " +
    receipt.OrderContents.length + " items");
```

The result of this code is shown in Figure 18-8. Note that this was the second run of the client code, so the application-wide value started from 5.

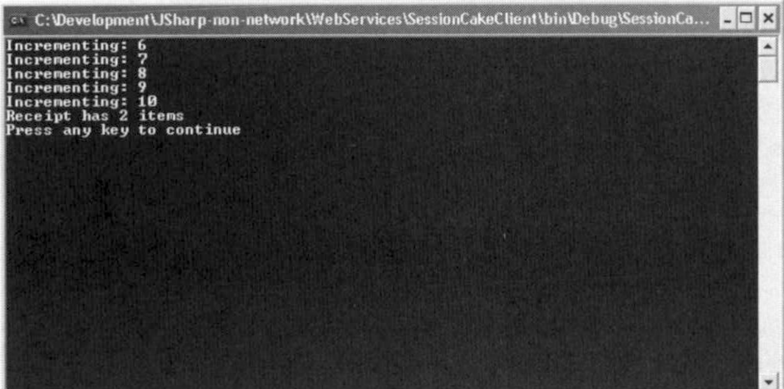

Figure 18-8 Cookies allow the server to maintain state on behalf of the client.

Note If you're familiar with ASP.NET, you might be wondering whether Web service proxies can work with cookieless mode. The simple answer is that they cannot. Cookieless mode uses URL rewriting (or mangling), which involves ASP.NET generating a different URL containing the state token and then telling the client to use this new URL. ASP.NET then intercepts this second request and retrieves the state token before forwarding the request to the real destination. This sequence relies on redirecting the client to the new URL by sending it an HTTP 302 object moved message. The Web service proxy does not handle redirection in this way, and so you'll get an exception.

A Brief Note on Polymorphism

The *WsReceipt* object returned from *SubmitBuiltUpOrder* contains a list of the items ordered. This list takes the form of an *ArrayList* containing *Item* objects. The declaration of this instance variable in the server-side *WsReceipt* class looks like this:

```
private ArrayList orderContents;
```

This instance variable is exposed through a property called *OrderContents*. Given that an *ArrayList* can contain any type of .NET object, in the WSDL description it looks like this:

```
<s:element minOccurs="0" maxOccurs="1" name="OrderContents"
 type="s0:ArrayOfAnyType" />
```

In the transmitted SOAP document, this WSDL description leads to the following XML elements:

```
<orderContents>
  <anyType xsi:type="Item">
    <itemDescription>Party Cake</itemDescription>
    <quantity>12</quantity>
  </anyType>
  <anyType xsi:type="Item">
    <itemDescription>Wedding Cake</itemDescription>
    <quantity>3</quantity>
  </anyType>
</orderContents>
```

As you can see, even though the basic element containing the serialized *OrderContents* is *<anyType>*, it has an *xsi:type* attribute that indicates a type of *Item*. The type attribute is added as the class is marshaled into XML; the *XmlSerializer* detects the type of the object it is serializing and adds the *xsi:type* attribute to each *anyType* element.

On the client side, the *OrderContents* property of the *WsReceipt* class is defined in the Reference.jsl file, as follows:

```
public class WsReceipt {
    /** <remarks/> */
    public Object[] OrderContents;
    ⋮
}
```

The *anyType* array has become an array of *Object* (which seems fairly reasonable in marshaling terms). How do you then get back your *Item* information? The key here lies in the fact that the *anyType* elements are denoted in the SOAP message as actually being of type *Item*. The *XmlSerializer* on the client side has access to this information. It also knows from the WSDL that there's a class definition in the same XML namespace for an *Item* class. Therefore, under the covers it actually unmarshals the contents of the *anyType* element into an instance of the *Item* class. These instances are then used to populate the array of *Objects*. Because the objects in the *OrderContents* array are really *Item* objects, all you need to do to use them is to cast each one to an *Item* type as you retrieve it. The following code fragment, from the main method of the *AnyTypeCakeClient* class (in the project AnyTypeCakeClient), shows how to do this:

```
for (int i = 0; i < receipt.OrderContents.length; i++)
{
   Item item = (Item)receipt.OrderContents[i];
   Console.WriteLine("Order item " + i + " is a " +
      item.ItemDescription + ", (" +
      item.Quantity + " unit(s))");
}
```

Making Secure Calls

In Chapter 17, we secured the Fourth Coffee PartnerServices Web service using Windows-based authentication. Anyone who wants to access this service must provide security credentials as part of the interaction with the server, as shown in this code fragment from the SecureCakeClient.jsl example file in the SecureCakeClient project:

```
import com.fourthcoffee.PartnerServices;
⋮
PartnerServices ps = new PartnerServices();

NetworkCredential credentials =
   new NetworkCredential("Peter Waxman",
   "ILoveCakes");

CredentialCache credentialCache = new CredentialCache();
ps.set_Credentials(credentialCache);

credentialCache.Add(new System.Uri(ps.get_Url()), "Basic", credentials);

String recipe = ps.GetRecipe();

Console.WriteLine("The secret recipe is: " + recipe);
```

This code creates an instance of the *System.Net.NetworkCredential* class. (You might recall the *NetworkCredential* class and some of the other classes and concepts discussed here from Chapter 9.) A username (Peter Waxman) and password (ILoveCakes) are supplied to the *NetworkCredential* constructor. This set of credentials must then be registered with the Web service proxy. You can add one or more sets of credentials to the credential cache held by the proxy. By default, the proxy has no cache set. (It uses anonymous authentication.)

To use a credential cache, you must create an instance of *System.Net.CredentialCache* and assign it to the *Credentials* property of the proxy (using the *set_Credentials* method in J#). You can then add the credentials you created earlier to the cache, specifying the target URL for which they are to be used (encapsulated in a *System.Net.Uri* object) and the type of authentication. The authentication type can be Basic, Digest, or NTLM. In this case, the credentials supplied will be used for Basic authentication. When the client makes the *GetRecipe* call on the Web service proxy, the proxy will provide the given credentials to authenticate the user and complete the SOAP operation.

An alternative is to supply the credentials of the current user as follows:

```
ps.set_Credentials(System.Net.CredentialCache.get_DefaultCredentials());
```

Using credentials in this way relies on Integrated Windows authentication being configured.

Note If you're importing Web service information from an ASP.NET-based Web service using the standard Visual Studio Web reference mechanism, you should be aware of one security issue: If the identity under which you're developing the code doesn't have access to the secure service (your code might be passing the credentials programmatically, for example), you won't be able to access the Web service to obtain its WSDL by using *?wsdl* unless you provide the appropriate credentials. If you're also the Web service developer, you might want to configure the security after you've imported the Web reference.

If you're using Secure Sockets Layer (SSL), you must access the Web service using a URL beginning with *https*. If this URL was not set in the original WSDL file, you can update the target URL by using the proxy's *Url* property.

If you want to use certificates, you can add them through the *ClientCertificates* property of the Web service proxy. You create instances of *System.Security.Cryptography.X509Certificates.X509Certificate* and add them to the collection as follows:

```
X509Certificate certificate =
   X509Certificate.CreateFromCertFile("c:\\certificates\\PeterW.cert");

ps.ClientCertificates.Add(certificates);

String recipe = ps.GetRecipe();
```

Making Transactional Calls

Chapter 17 showed how to use the WebMethodAttribute to make an ASP.NET-based Web service method transactional. This requires no special processing from the client side. The transaction is scoped to the WebMethod associated with a particular Web service operation and completes or aborts at the end of the method. There is currently no way of propagating transaction context between a Web service client and the Web service itself, so if the client is executing in the context of an existing transaction, it cannot make the server-side transaction part of this existing transaction. This problem should eventually be solved by the Global XML Web Services Architecture (GXA), as discussed at the end of Chapter 17.

Making Asynchronous Calls

Every Web service proxy created by Visual Studio .NET provides three method calls for each SOAP operation. For example, consider the *SubmitOrder* Web method from the Ordering.asmx.jsl sample Web service provided as part of the CakeCatalogService sample project. Open the Ordering.asmx.jsl file and find the *SubmitOrder* method. To simulate heavy server-side processing, add a 5-second wait into the implementation, as shown here:

```
/** @attribute WebMethod() */
public WsReceipt SubmitOrder(Order order)
{
   // Should probably have some database stuff here...
   // ... simulate this by waiting for a time :^)
   System.Threading.Thread.Sleep(5000);

   WsReceipt receipt = new WsReceipt(order.get_CustomerName(),
      order.get_OrderId(), DateTime.get_Now());
   return receipt;
}
```

Based on the WSDL description for this one method, three distinct methods are created in the Web service proxy. (The attributes have been removed for clarity.)

```
public WsReceipt SubmitOrder(Order order) {
   Object[] results = this.Invoke("SubmitOrder", new Object[] {
      order}
   );
   return ((WsReceipt)(results[0]));
}

public System.IAsyncResult BeginSubmitOrder(Order order, System.AsyncCallback c
allback, Object asyncState) {
   return this.BeginInvoke("SubmitOrder", new Object[] {
      order} , callback, asyncState);
}
```

```
public WsReceipt EndSubmitOrder(System.IAsyncResult asyncResult) {
   Object[] results = this.EndInvoke(asyncResult);
   return ((WsReceipt)(results[0]));
}
```

The *BeginSubmitOrder* and *EndSubmitOrder* methods represent an asynchronous invocation of the *SubmitOrder* operation defined in the WSDL. The asynchronous mechanism does not rely on the availability of an underlying asynchronous SOAP transport (such as SMTP). Instead, it uses a thread from the application domain's thread pool, which calls the synchronous form of the SOAP operation. The *BeginSubmitOrder* call will start the new thread and return quickly, so the caller can continue. Some of the types in the asynchronous method signatures might look familiar because Web service asynchronous calls use the same pattern and some of the same classes as asynchronous I/O (as discussed in Chapter 8).

As with any asynchronous operation, the main challenge is to retrieve the return value from the method—in this case, the receipt. Continually polling to see whether the asynchronous operation has completed defeats the purpose of invoking the method asynchronously. Instead, you can register a delegate that will be called when the operation completes. The following code fragment is from the sample file AsyncCakeClient.jsl and shows how you can register for notification:

```
boolean stillWaiting = true;
public void Callback(System.IAsyncResult result)
{
   stillWaiting = false;
}

public void AsynchronousCall(Order order)
{
   Ordering orders = new Ordering();

   IAsyncResult result = orders.BeginSubmitOrder(order,
      new AsyncCallback(Callback),
      null);

   while (stillWaiting)
   {
      System.Threading.Thread.Sleep(500);
      Console.WriteLine("Doing useful work (honest!)");
   }

   WsReceipt receipt = orders.EndSubmitOrder(result);

   Console.WriteLine("Receipt: ");
```

```
    Console.Write(receipt.CustomerName + "'s order number ");
    Console.Write(receipt.OrderId + " was received on ");
    Console.WriteLine("" + receipt.Timestamp);
}
```

The *AsynchronousCall* method takes an instance of *Order* and uses the *BeginSubmitOrder* method to start the asynchronous operation. In addition to the order, it passes in an instance of the *AsyncCallback* delegate. This delegate wraps the *Callback* method that sets the *boolean* instance variable *stillWaiting* to *false*. The *stillWaiting* variable is used as the condition of the *while* loop following the call to *BeginSubmitOrder*. The program will then loop. In each loop, it will sleep for half a second, write out a message, and then test the value of *stillWaiting*. (In a commercial application, the client would do some useful work rather than simply sleeping.) If the value of *stillWaiting* is *true*, the program will sleep again. Once the asynchronous operation has completed, the program will exit the loop.

Once you know that the asynchronous operation has completed, you can retrieve the return value by calling *EndSubmitOrder*. However, because a call to *BeginSubmitOrder* returns very quickly, you might have multiple asynchronous calls ongoing at any one time on the same proxy. When you call *EndSubmitOrder*, how will the proxy know which call you're referring to? The answer lies in the return value from *BeginSubmitOrder*, which is an object that implements *System.IAsyncResult*. The *IAsyncResult* implementation acts as an identifier for the asynchronous call, so you pass this object to *EndSubmitOrder* to retrieve the correct return value. The output from the *AsyncCakeClient* class is shown in Figure 18-9.

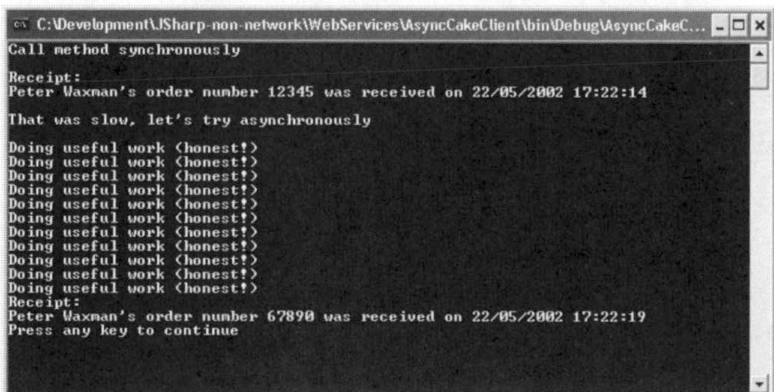

Figure 18-9 You can perform useful work while a Web service operation executes asynchronously.

The example code allows you to do some useful work while the asynchronous call is made. However, there is no need to have your main body of code call *EndSubmitOrder*. You can make this call in the delegate and store the return value in an instance variable. When you access such an instance variable, the usual caveats about multithreaded variable access apply, so you should synchronize access to the variable. (See Chapter 8 for details.)

Namespaces, WSDL, and Manual Proxy Generation

Visual Studio's ability to import WSDL documents and automatically generate proxies is very useful and is a great aid to developer productivity. However, it comes with one slight drawback. You might have noticed that when you import a Web reference into a project, the reference appears under the name of the host given in the WSDL *service* element (*com.fourthcoffee* in our example). So far, the clients have been targeted at one particular service on the Fourth Coffee site. What happens if you refactor your clients so they use more than one service?

For example, you can add a Web reference to the SimpleOrdering service (or any Fourth Coffee service). This will appear under the name *com.fourthcoffee* in the Web references. The classes defined in References.jsl for this Web reference are all placed in the package *com.fourthcoffee*. If you then add another Web reference, this time to the Catalog service, you might expect it to be added to the information under *com.fourthcoffee*. However, what actually happens is that a new Web reference, *com.fourthcoffee1*, is created, as shown in Figure 18-10. All of the classes in the Reference.jsl file for this Web reference are defined in the package *com.fourthcoffee1*.

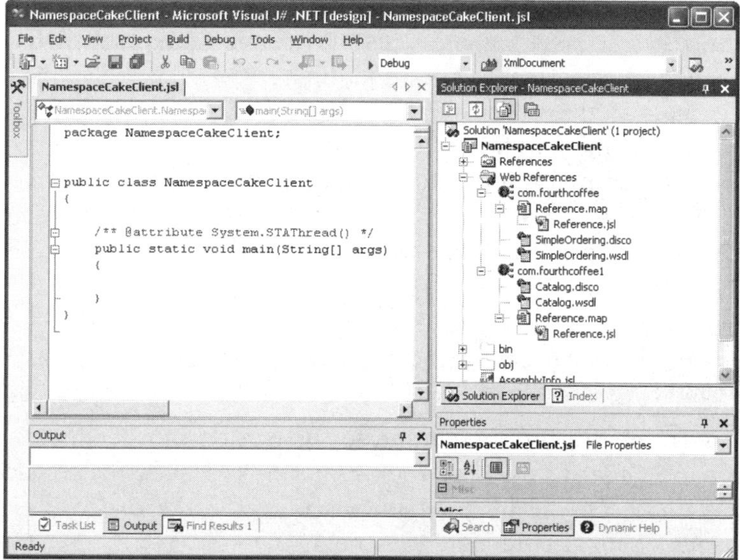

Figure 18-10 Multiple entries are created for Web services on the same server.

You might be wondering what the problem is. Consider an enhanced catalog service that returns instances of a *CatalogEntry* class. In the project shown in Figure 18-10, this class would be *com.fourthcoffee1.CatalogEntry*. You could modify the SimpleOrdering service so it will take instances of *CatalogEntry* when the contents of an order are specified. This would make life a lot easier for the client-side developer—or so you might think. In fact, when the Reference.jsl is created for this new SimpleOrdering service, it will create a new definition for *CatalogEntry* in the package *com.fourthcoffee1*. The compiler will, with some justification, deem that the types are different and that you therefore cannot use a *CatalogEntry* retrieved from the Catalog service as a parameter to the SimpleOrdering service. To get around this, you can do one of two things:

- Define schemas for your shared types and import them into your WSDL documents. This is the cleanest approach, although it does mean that you cannot import the Web service information into your application using the automatic WSDL generation capability (by appending *?wsdl* to your service URLs).
- Use the wsdl.exe command-line tool to generate the proxies manually so they're in the same namespace. Each file will contain its own definition of the *CatalogEntry* class, but they'll both be in the same package, so you must edit these files to remove one of the duplicate *CatalogEntry* definitions.

Manual proxy generation can also be convenient if you want to build your Web service clients as a batch process. To examine manual proxy generation, consider the Ordering Web service and the TestOrder Web service contained in the CakeCatalogService project. The TestOrder Web service contains a copy of the *SubmitOrder* method from the Ordering service, which uses the same complex types as parameters and return values. Adding separate Web references to each of these services would cause the issues described above. You can use wsdl.exe from the command line to generate your proxies manually as follows:

```
wsdl.exe /n:com.fourthcoffee.ordering
/l:"Microsoft.VJSharp.VJSharpCodeProvider, VJSharpCodeProvider,
Version=7.0.3300.0, Culture=neutral, PublicKeyToken=b03f5f7f11d50a3a"
http://fourthcoffee.com/CakeCatalogService/Ordering.asmx?wsdl
```

This command will generate the file Ordering.jsl, which contains the proxy for the Ordering service. The */n* flag indicates the namespace to be created for the classes—in this case, the *com.fourthcoffee.ordering* package. You can execute a similar command to generate a proxy for the TestOrder service. To use these manually generated proxies, follow this sequence of steps:

1. Generate the required proxies using wsdl.exe, as described above. The project ManualProxyCakeClient contains the file GenerateProxies.bat, which manually generates proxies for the Ordering Web service and for the TestOrder Web service. (You must run this batch file manually before building the project.)
2. Import the proxies into your client project by choosing Add Existing Item from the Project menu.
3. Add a reference to .NET assembly System.Web.Services.dll. This is normally done for you when you use Visual Studio .NET to generate a Web reference, but in this case you must add it manually.
4. If you compile at this point, you'll get a message about multiply-defined classes. The simplest way to solve this is to edit the TestOrder.jsl file and remove the definitions for *Order*, *Item*, and *WsReceipt*. The project will then compile and run correctly.

If the Web service definitions change, you must repeat these steps to regenerate the proxies.

Versioning and Updates

You should be sure to use the correct WSDL descriptions when you write Web service clients. This is particularly important in a development environment, in which service definitions can evolve rapidly. Visual Studio .NET will not automatically reimport a Web service description and regenerate the proxy because it does not know when the Web service description has changed. To ensure that a Web reference is up-to-date, you can choose Update Web Reference from the Web reference's shortcut menu, as shown in Figure 18-11.

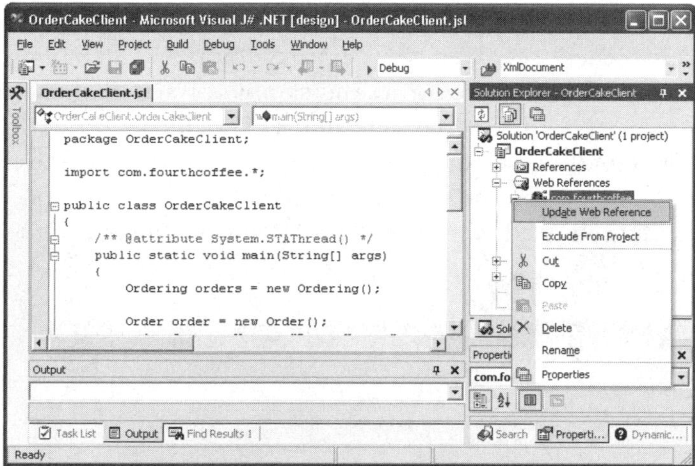

Figure 18-11 You should be sure that your Web references are up-to-date.

It is important to ensure that references are kept up-to-date because no version checking is performed on Web method calls. For example, if you add a parameter to a Web method and invoke this new version of the method from a client built using the old method, the SOAP infrastructure will not generate an error. All parameter matching is performed using names, so when the call is unmarshaled, ASP.NET will attempt to match the parameter names in the call to the parameters in the method. Any unknown names will be given default values, such as 0 for an integer. This means that the call will not break but might well misbehave. The same issue arises when you change parameter names.

Other Client Types

So far, we've examined the use of clients for SOAP-based, document-centric Web services, which are the default type of Web service created when you use ASP.NET. However, there are other types of services and other types of clients. We'll briefly examine some of them.

Web Service Clients for .NET Remoting Services

One question commonly seen in newsgroups and e-mail lists is about how to decide when to use Web services rather than .NET Remoting to build a distributed application. Each mechanism has its benefits, but it is possible to tread a middle path. If a .NET Remoting server uses the HTTP protocol and XML serialization, you can use the Web reference mechanism in Visual Studio .NET (or wsdl.exe) to create a Web service proxy for it. With a little care in the specification of namespaces, you can easily substitute a service based on .NET Remoting for one based on ASP.NET without having to change the client code.

To create a client-side Web service proxy for a .NET Remoting server, you simply create a Web reference for it. The sample project RemotingProxyCakeClient uses a proxy for the ServerActivatedHTTPCakeSizeServer from Chapter 11. The .NET Remoting server listens on port 7000 and advertises its URL as *CakeInfo.soap*. If you start the server, you can add a Web reference for this service by providing the URL *http://localhost:7000/CakeInfo.soap?wsdl*, as shown in Figure 18-12.

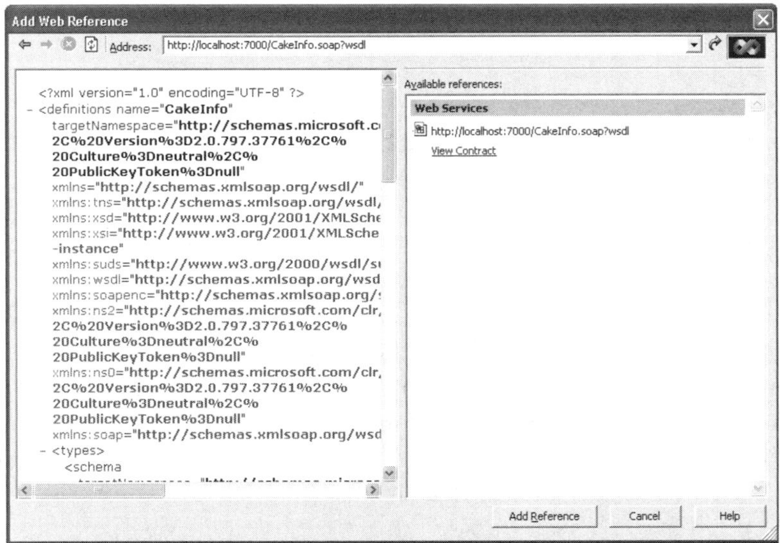

Figure 18-12 You can create Web service proxies for SOAP-based .NET Remoting servers in the same way you would for an ASP.NET Web service.

The Web reference provides a proxy class called *CakeInfoService* in the *localhost* package. You can import and use this class just as you would any other Web service proxy:

```
import localhost.CakeInfoService;
:
CakeInfoService info = new CakeInfoService();

// Ask about a 15", square, fruit cake...
```

```
int eaters = info.FeedsHowMany(15, 0, 1);

Console.WriteLine("This cake will feed " + eaters + " people");
```

.NET Remoting Clients for Web Services

Looking at things from the other direction, you might want to employ .NET Remoting to access a Web service. The soapsuds.exe tool that's provided as part of the .NET Framework allows you to do this. Basically, you feed soapsuds the WSDL describing the service and it will output source code or an assembly that contains a .NET Remoting–based proxy class for the service. Note that the SOAP messages used with .NET Remoting pass RPC-style messages with SOAP encoding (see the sidebar titled "Document Literal vs. SOAP Encoding and RPC" in Chapter 17), so the service must expose SOAP operations that can be accessed using RPC-style method calls. By default, all Web services based on ASP.NET use document-style and literal encoding.

To make ASP.NET Web methods RPC-friendly, you can apply the attributes *System.Web.Services.Protocols.SoapRpcServiceAttribute* and *System.Web.Services.Protocols.SoapRpcMethodAttribute*. For example, consider a form of the Enquiry Web service that's intended for RPC-style interaction:

```
/** @attribute WebServiceAttribute(Namespace="http://fourthcoffee.com/CakeCata-
log/RpcEnquiry",
  Description="RPC-style enquiry service for Fourth Coffee's Cake Catalog")
  */
/** @attribute SoapRpcServiceAttribute() */
public class RpcEnquiry extends System.Web.Services.WebService
{
   ⋮
   /** @attribute WebMethodAttribute() */
   public int FeedsHowMany(int diameter, String shape,
     String filling)
   {
      ⋮
   }
}
```

This *RpcEnquiry* class is provided as part of the CakeCatalogService sample project. You can use soapsuds.exe to generate an assembly containing a .NET Remoting–based proxy for this service, as shown here:

```
Soapsuds -pn:com.fourthcoffee.cakecatalog url:http://fourthcoffee.com/
CakeCatalogService/RpcEnquiry.asmx?wsdl -oa:SoapSudsCakeProxies.dll
```

By default, any source code is generated in Visual C#. The command shown above uses the *–oa* flag to instruct soapsuds to build an assembly called soapsudscakeproxies.dll rather than emit source code. The *–pn* flag changes the namespace (package) in which the proxy class is defined, in this case *com.fourthcoffee.cakecatalog*. After you've built the assembly, you can reference it from your project using the Add Reference command on the Project menu. To see what has been generated, you use the Object Browser. (Choose Other Windows from the View menu and then choose Object Browser.) You'll see an entry for *soapsudscakeproxies*, below which you will find the package *com.fourthcoffee.cakecatalog*, which is the namespace (package) name passed to soapsuds using the *–pn* flag. This package contains the class *RpcEnquirySoap*, which implements the *FeedsHowMany* method.

The *RpcEnquirySoap* class extends the *System.Runtime.Remoting.Services.RemotingClientProxy* class. This base class supplies useful helper functionality (cookies, authentication, and so on) that's similar to that provided by *SoapHttpClientProtocol* for document-oriented Web service proxies. Figure 18-13 shows the contents of the *soapsudscakeproxies* assembly. To use the proxy, import the *com.fourthcoffee.cakecatalog* package, instantiate the proxy, and call the *FeedsHowMany* method.

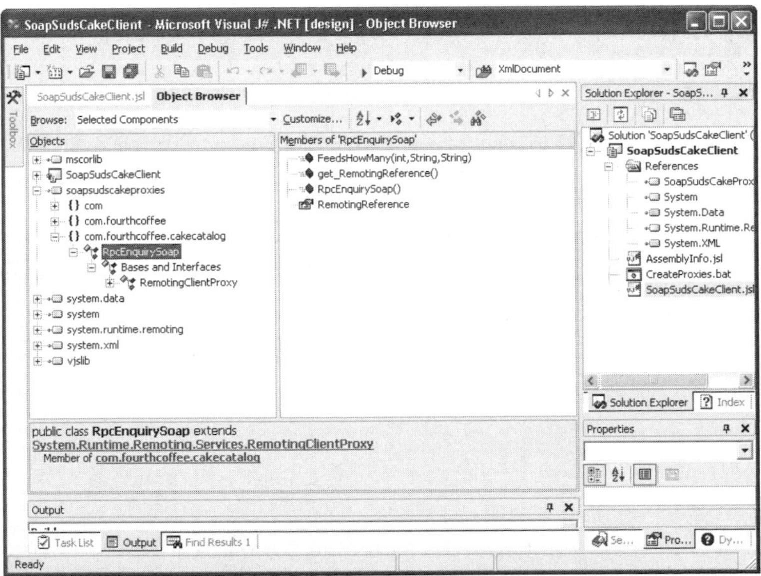

Figure 18-13 Soapsuds will create an assembly containing a .NET Remoting proxy for an RPC-style Web service.

Although this example uses a separate Web service to provide the RPC-style functionality, you can expose multiple sets of methods on the same service—some for RPC clients and some for document clients. This technique is beyond the scope of this chapter but is explained in the .NET Framework documentation.

Non-.NET Clients

It is quite possible to create a non-.NET client for a Web service based on ASP.NET or .NET Remoting. This, after all, is a primary objective of Web services. Several vendors and open source projects are currently working on various Java-based Web service toolkits, such as Apache Axis, so you can build Web service clients and servers that target the Java 2 platform. Interoperability is quite good now between different Web service toolkits, and there are even sites on the Web dedicated to publishing the results of interoperability tests.

Dynamic Discovery of Web Services

The ability to locate Web services is important—you won't always be able to contact a Web service developer by e-mail or phone to obtain Web service URLs and WSDL files. What you need is a way to obtain service description and location information based on one or more pieces of information about the service. We'll look at two mechanisms—one for discovering the Web services installed on a specific server (discovery) and another that provides a more global search for Web services (UDDI).

Discovering Services on a Server

Web Services Discovery protocol (also known as DISCO) defines a way to provide a Web service client with information about the Web services installed on a given server. DISCO comes in two forms: static and dynamic. A particular Web service can provide either a dynamic discovery (VSDISCO) file or a static discovery (DISCO) file to publish information about its Web service.

The information provided by DISCO can be used in two ways. At development time, you can add a Web reference to a source of DISCO information. This will create a proxy representing all the services on a server. Alternatively, at run time your application can programmatically access and use discovery information.

We'll examine how ASP.NET supports DISCO and also briefly look at where Web service discovery might lead in the future.

Static Discovery

In the case of static discovery, the client can consult a DISCO file that lists the Web services to be exposed. If you want to use a DISCO file to describe your Web services, you must create one from scratch and place it in an appropriate folder. In the case of the Web services we've used so far, an appropriate location would be the CakeCatalogService virtual directory. Here's an example of a simple static discovery file for a subset of the Web services provided by the CakeCatalogService:

```
<?xml version="1.0" encoding="utf-8" ?>
<disco:discovery xmlns:disco="http://schemas.xmlsoap.org/disco/">
<contractRef ref="http://fourthcoffee.com/CakeCatalogService/Catalog.asmx?WSDL"
   xmlns="http://schemas.xmlsoap.org/disco/scl/"/>
<contractRef ref="http://fourthcoffee.com/CakeCatalogService/Enquiry.asmx?WSDL"
   xmlns="http://schemas.xmlsoap.org/disco/scl/"/>
<contractRef ref="http://fourthcoffee.com/CakeCatalogService/Order-
ing.asmx?WSDL"
   xmlns="http://schemas.xmlsoap.org/disco/scl/"/>
</disco:discovery>
```

As you might expect, the discovery information is encoded as XML. Each Web service is advertised by a *contractRef* element. Once the client has retrieved this file, it can obtain the WSDL documents listed and use them to build a client-side proxy. When a client adds a Web reference to the DISCO file shown above, by providing the URL to it (*http://fourthcoffee.com/CakeCatalogService/CakeCatalog.disco*), the result will be a list of Web services available at that site, as Figure 18-14 shows.

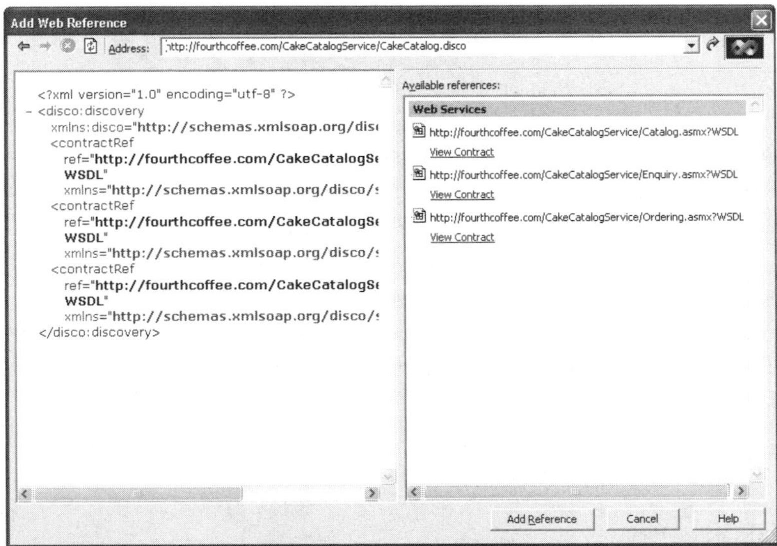

Figure 18-14 You target a static DISCO file directly to obtain Web service information for a server.

Note Discovery requires slightly different XML namespaces for the Web services you've seen so far. This will be explained shortly. If you try importing the DISCO file without making these namespace changes, you won't get the results discussed in this section.

One notable aspect of importing Web service information through a discovery document is that a single proxy file is created for all of the discovered Web services, as shown in Figure 18-15. This proxy file contains all of the individual proxy classes in a single package (namespace).

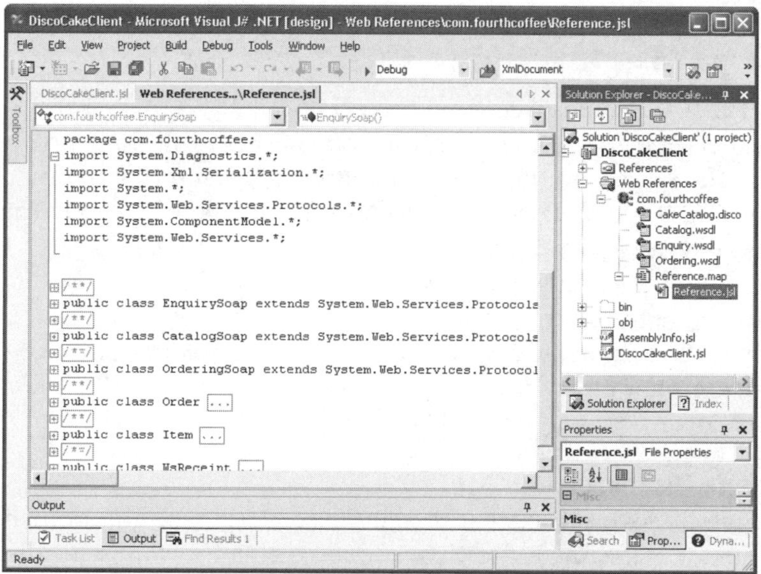

Figure 18-15 All the services defined in a DISCO file are exposed through a single proxy.

This approach can offer a definite advantage because it avoids some of the package conflicts that can arise when you import multiple Web services from one server, as described earlier. However, the single proxy can become cluttered and will need updating whenever any of the services change. The single proxy is also very sensitive to the use of XML namespaces. Each of the Web services must be defined with its own individual XML namespace using the *WebServiceAttribute*. (See Chapter 17 for details.) To use the sample Web services with the static DISCO file provided, you must edit them to specialize the *Namespace* property of the *WebService* attribute. Each class listed in the static

DISCO file has a commented version of the *WebService* attribute with the required namespace extension. Simply replace the default namespace in the service with the one in the comment. An example of such a comment is shown here:

```
//
// **** When you need to use DISCO, you should replace
// **** the WebServiceAttribute with this one:
//
// @attribute WebServiceAttribute(Namespace=
// "http://fourthcoffee.com/CakeCatalog/Enquiry")
//

/** @attribute WebServiceAttribute(Namespace="http://fourthcoffee.com/CakeCata-
log/ ")
  */
public class Enquiry extends System.Web.Services.WebService
```

The XML namespace property is important because if the Web services share the same XML namespace, only one of them will show up in a combined proxy. The reasons for this are quite tortuous, but suffice it to say that you must define distinct XML namespaces to take advantage of DISCO. This applies as much to dynamic discovery as it does to static discovery.

Under the covers, Visual Studio .NET uses the disco.exe command-line tool to obtain the discovery files from a server. You can use this tool yourself to retrieve the documents and use them to build proxies manually or for visual inspection. (For more information on disco.exe, see the .NET Framework documentation.)

Dynamic Discovery

Dynamic discovery is similar to static discovery, with the primary difference being the way that the list of Web services is built up. With static discovery, only information on the Web services listed in the DISCO file stored on the server are fetched. In contrast, dynamic discovery tries to list all Web services below the specified virtual directory unless it is specifically instructed not to.

To initiate dynamic discovery, the client requests a document with a *.vsdisco* extension. All of the Web services you've seen in this book have a VSDISCO file automatically created for them by Visual Studio .NET. Here's an example of a typical VSDISCO file:

```
<?xml version="1.0" ?>
<dynamicDiscovery xmlns="urn:schemas-dynamicdiscovery:disco.2000-03-17">
<exclude path="_vti_cnf" />
<exclude path="_vti_pvt" />
<exclude path="_vti_log" />
```

```
<exclude path="_vti_script" />
<exclude path="_vti_txt" />
</dynamicDiscovery>
```

This file is as unexciting as it looks. When a client requests a VSDISCO file, the request is processed by an instance of the *System.Web.Services.Discovery.DiscoveryRequestHandler* class. The *DiscoveryRequestHandler* object recursively searches the directory containing the VSDISCO file and all of its subdirectories for Web service (ASMX) files. The *DiscoveryRequestHandler* object will publish information about each ASMX file that it finds.

The primary function of the VSDISCO file is to limit the scope of the search by specifying subdirectories that should not be searched. Each *exclude* element removes the specified directory from the list of those to be searched. The *DiscoveryRequestHandler* will search each subdirectory for another VSDISCO file or a static DISCO file. If it discovers a VSDISCO file, it will use the file to determine which subdirectories of the subdirectory it should search. If it finds a DISCO file, it will consider this a definitive statement of what should be exposed for this point in the hierarchy, so the services contained in the file will be added to the *DiscoveryRequestHandler* object's list of services and no further subdirectories will be searched below that point. Similarly, if no ASMX files or VSDISCO files are found in a directory, its subdirectories will not be searched.

Tip If you intend to implement a dynamic discovery hierarchy, you should not place a DISCO and a VSDISCO file in same directory.

You can use dynamic discovery to create a proxy for the Web services on a server in the same way that you used static discovery—by adding a Web reference. The result of specifying the CakeCatalogService.vsdisco file in the Add Web Reference dialog box is shown in Figure 18-16. The contents of CakeCatalogService.vsdisco are the same as those in the example VSDISCO file shown previously. Again, a single file (Reference.jsl) is created that contains proxies for the discovered Web services. All of these proxies are defined in the same package. The XML namespace caveat discussed in the previous section on static discovery applies here also—if two or more services share the same XML namespace, only one of them will have a proxy generated for it and the others will be ignored. The sample project VsDiscoCakeClient shows this in action.

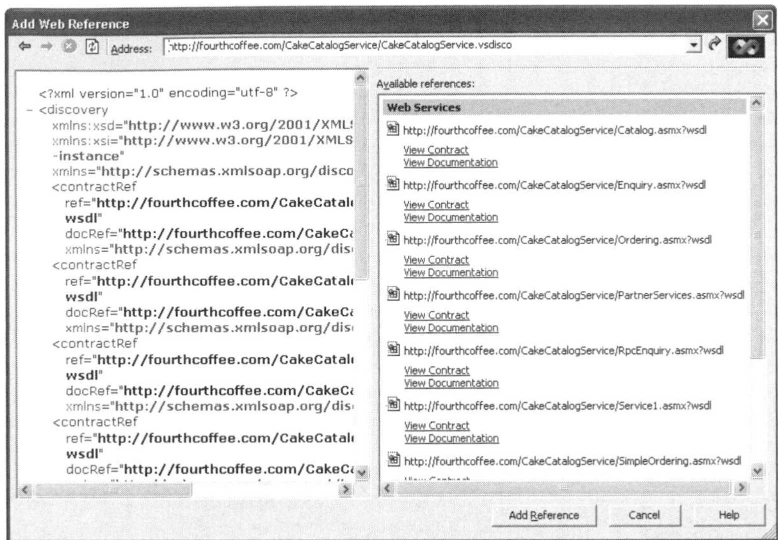

Figure 18-16 You target a dynamic DISCO file to obtain Web service information for a server.

You'll find a dynamic discovery file, Default.vsdisco, in the IIS root directory. If you query this file when you add a Web reference, you might discover all of the Web services deployed on the Web server (depending on how the Web server and its virtual directories have been configured). In a development environment, this can be a great advantage. However, this does have security implications if the server is visible from a nontrusted network. Therefore, the dynamic discovery protocol is not enabled by default. To enable it, you must uncomment the following line in your machine.config file (which resides in the \Windows\Microsoft.NET\Framework*.NETVersion*\CONFIG folder):

```
⋮
<httpHandlers>
  <add verb="*" path="*.vsdisco"
  type="System.Web.Services.Discovery.DiscoveryRequestHandler,
  System.Web.Services, Version=1.0.3300.0, Culture=neutral,
  PublicKeyToken=b03f5f7f11d50a3a" validate="false"/>
⋮
```

In a similar vein, you should make sure that any potential users (anonymous or otherwise) have permission to access all the directories that the *DiscoveryRequestHandler* is instructed to search. Failure to do this will lead to security problems when you add a Web reference to the VSDISCO file.

Note In our humble opinion, dynamic discovery should be used only in a development environment. You should always use static discovery files on production servers.

Programmatic Discovery

You can access discovery information programmatically by creating an instance of the *System.Web.Services.Discovery.DiscoveryClientProtocol* class and instructing it to search for discovery information at a given URL. The following code fragment, from the sample project DiscoExaminer, shows a simple search:

```
DiscoveryClientProtocol dcp = new DiscoveryClientProtocol();
DiscoveryDocument dd = dcp.DiscoverAny
   ("http://fourthcoffee.com/CakeCatalogService/CakeCatalog.disco");

dcp.ResolveOneLevel();

DiscoveryClientDocumentCollection docs = dcp.get_Documents();
IDictionaryEnumerator enumerator = docs.GetEnumerator();
while (enumerator.MoveNext())
{
   DictionaryEntry entry = (DictionaryEntry)enumerator.get_Current();
   Console.WriteLine("\n" + "*******************\n" + entry.get_Key()
      + "\n*******************");

   if (entry.get_Value() instanceof DiscoveryDocument)
   {
      DiscoveryDocument doc = (DiscoveryDocument)entry.get_Value();
      doc.Write(Console.get_Out());
   }
}
```

The *DiscoveryClientProtocol* object maintains a collection of discovery documents. You can populate this collection by calling the *ResolveOneLevel* or *ResolveAll* method. (*ResolveAll* tries to resolve everything recursively.) You can then examine the documents in the collection and act on them as required. The result of running this code is shown in Figure 18-17.

```
C:\Development\JSharp-non-network\WebServices\DiscoExaminer\bin\Debug\DiscoExamine...
********************
http://fourthcoffee.com/CakeCatalogService/Enquiry.asmx?WSDL
********************

********************
http://fourthcoffee.com/CakeCatalogService/CakeCatalog.disco
********************
<?xml version="1.0" encoding="IBM437"?>
<discovery xmlns:xsd="http://www.w3.org/2001/XMLSchema" xmlns:xsi="http://www.w3
.org/2001/XMLSchema-instance" xmlns="http://schemas.xmlsoap.org/disco/">
  <contractRef ref="http://fourthcoffee.com/CakeCatalogService/Catalog.asmx?WSDL
" xmlns="http://schemas.xmlsoap.org/disco/scl/" />
  <contractRef ref="http://fourthcoffee.com/CakeCatalogService/Enquiry.asmx?WSDL
" xmlns="http://schemas.xmlsoap.org/disco/scl/" />
  <contractRef ref="http://fourthcoffee.com/CakeCatalogService/Ordering.asmx?WSD
L" xmlns="http://schemas.xmlsoap.org/disco/scl/" />
</discovery>
********************
http://fourthcoffee.com/CakeCatalogService/Catalog.asmx?WSDL
********************

********************
http://fourthcoffee.com/CakeCatalogService/Ordering.asmx?WSDL
********************
Press any key to continue_
```

Figure 18-17 Using the *DiscoveryClientProtocol* object to programmatically discover Web service information

The Future of Discovery

The DISCO protocol is a first-generation Web service discovery protocol. Work is ongoing as part of the GXA to create a second-generation discovery language called Web Services Inspection Language (WS-Inspection). WS-Inspection is a joint effort between Microsoft and IBM to consolidate their previous, proprietary discovery protocols (DISCO and ADS, respectively) to provide a lightweight, standard Web services discovery protocol. For more information on WS-Inspection, see *http://msdn.microsoft.com/library/en-us/dnglobspec/html/wsinspecspecindex.asp*.

Discovering Services Through UDDI

UDDI provides a mechanism that allows an organization or an application to discover information about services offered by other organizations. UDDI data is held in a database called the UDDI registry. A UDDI registry contains essentially two types of information:

- Business information, including contact information and the categories under which the business should be listed. Categorization of businesses helps users find the right business more easily. Various categorization schemes are available.
- Service information, including the type of service and how to use it. A service can be anything from a consultancy service (whose interface would be a telephone number or a Web site) to a Web service that's described using WSDL. The rest of this section will concentrate on Web services.

You can search the UDDI registry in three ways. If you know the name of the organization you're looking for, you can search based on the name. This is called a *white pages search* (after that type of telephone directory). If you know only the type of business you're looking for, such as financial services, you can perform a search based on this type. This is termed a *yellow pages search*, again after that type of telephone directory. Finally, you can search based on the type of service, such as a particular interface description. This is known as a *green pages search*. Once you've found one or more organizations that match your requirements, you can obtain that service information, typically a WSDL description, and plug this information into your applications. There are many wider issues surrounding this style of Web service interaction, such as the need to agree on commercial terms. However, for the purposes of this chapter, we'll focus just on the technical side of things.

UDDI Registry Information

This chapter is not meant to provide a comprehensive description of UDDI, but the following information should help you to understand better what's going on.

You've seen that WSDL documents contain both the description of a service (*portType* elements and *binding* elements) and the location information (*service* and *port* elements). The UDDI standard defines two structures for these purposes. The *tModel* structure describes the service; in WSDL terms, this includes the complex type schema, in and out message definitions, *portType* elements, and *binding* elements. This forms a location-independent "interface" that can be shared by multiple service implementations that offer the same "interface." The UDDI *bindingTemplate* structure contains location information for a particular service. This equates to information defined in the WSDL *port* and *service* elements.

UDDI defines additional structures. A UDDI *businessService* structure combines a set of *bindingTemplate* structures into a logical service group. These, in turn, are contained in a *businessEntity* structure, where the contact information and description of the organization also reside.

You can use UDDI registries in several ways. There are a few global UDDI registries in which any registered company can store information. Examples include the public UDDI registries run by Microsoft, IBM, and XMethods. You can find information about accessing these registries at *http://*

uddi.microsoft.com, *http://www-3.ibm.com/services/uddi/*, and *http://services.xmethods.net/*, respectively. Microsoft and IBM provide both a test registry and a live registry.

As UDDI matures, local and private registries (on intranets, for example), are being put in place to store information about the services offered by specific organizations. An intranet version of UDDI will be available in .NET Server. Whether public or private, a UDDI registry can be used at design time to locate services and integrate them into an application or at run time to check that the service location is up-to-date.

To use service information located in a UDDI registry, you add a Web reference to your application. This generates a proxy for that service that you can use in your application. For example, the Microsoft entry in the company's public UDDI registry contains a description of how to access a UDDI registry. You can import this description into your application and use it. To start the import process, choose Add Web Reference from the Project menu and select the UDDI Registry link in the Add Web Reference dialog box (as shown in Figure 18-18) to use the Microsoft UDDI registry. Alternatively, you can type the URL of another UDDI registry and import service descriptions from there.

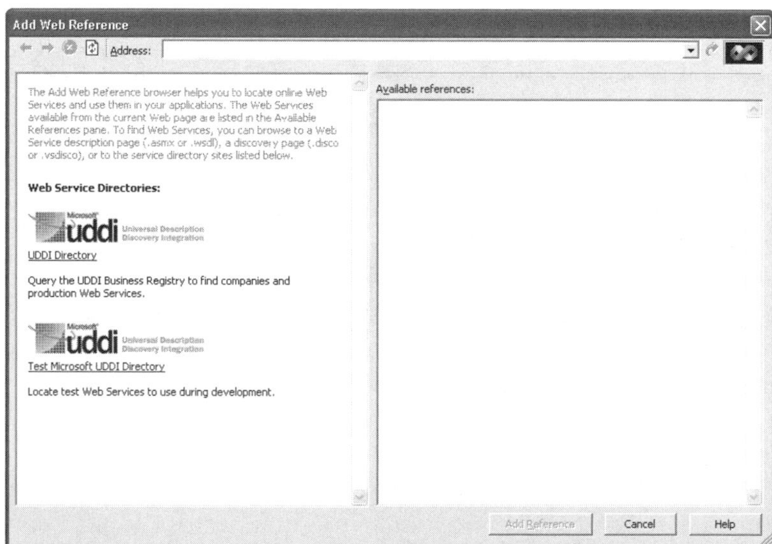

Figure 18-18 You select the UDDI Registry link to search the public UDDI registry.

Next, you enter the business name to search for—Microsoft in this case, as shown in Figure 18-19.

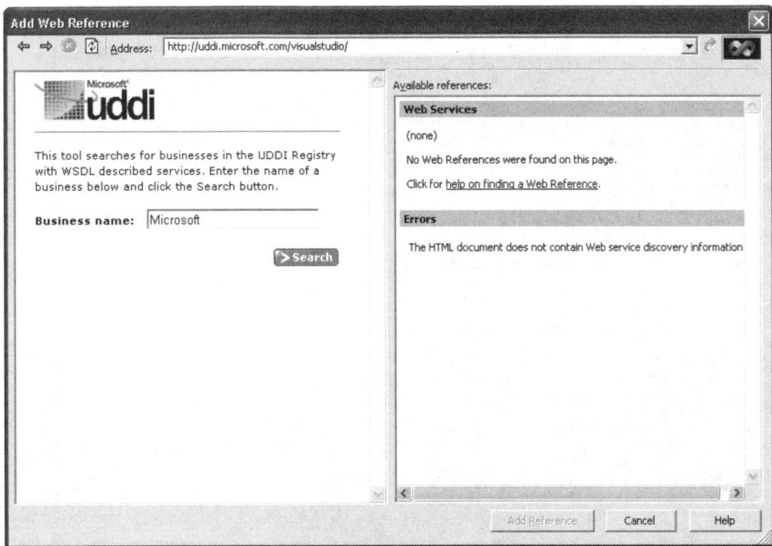

Figure 18-19 Searching for a business in the public UDDI registry

The next page lists the services offered by this company. One service is currently offered—UDDI itself, as shown in Figure 18-20.

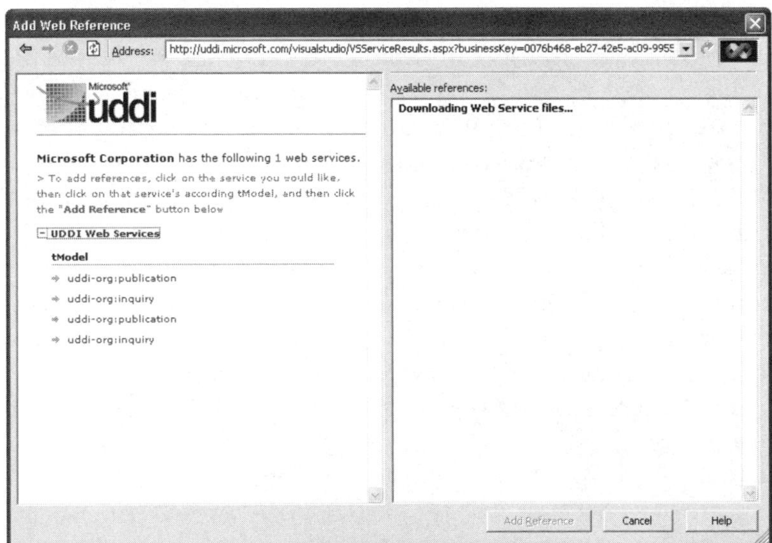

Figure 18-20 The one service offered is UDDI.

If you select uddi-org:inquiry, you'll see the WSDL description, as shown in Figure 18-21.

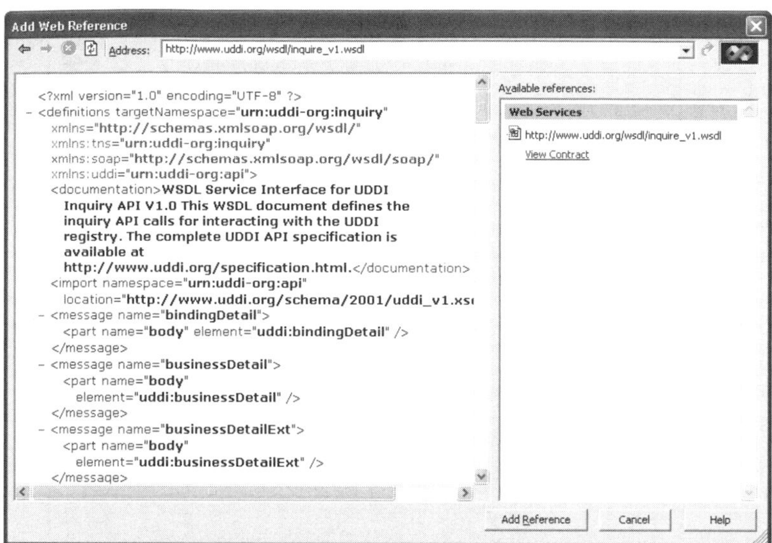

Figure 18-21 The UDDI service is described in WSDL.

Selecting Add Reference will create a proxy for this service in your project. The proxy classes are created in the *org.uddi.www* package. The main class is called *InquireSoap*, which provides a method for all of the SOAP messages in the UDDI specification that relate to enquiry. This is quite a complex API, and it is not possible to discuss it in detail here. Suffice it to say that if you want to obtain information from a UDDI registry, this proxy class will allow you to send those messages. One thing worth noting is that no default URL is associated with the proxy class. You have to decide which UDDI registry you want to query and then set the *Url* property appropriately. An example of the result of importing this UDDI proxy can be found in the sample project UDDIClient.

If you want to develop applications that register entries in a UDDI registry or submit queries to one, you can use the Web service interfaces you've just seen. Alternatively, you can download the Microsoft Universal Description Discovery and Integration .NET Software Development Kit (UDDI .NET SDK). This SDK provides a set of components that allow a .NET developer to interact with a UDDI registry.

Summary

In this chapter, you learned how to build a client for a Web service using Visual Studio .NET. You learned how to import a WSDL document and generate a Web service proxy from this client. You also learned some ways of handling error conditions and how to pass complex data types, ADO.NET *DataSet* objects, and XML documents.

The chapter also covered the client requirements for accessing secure, stateful, and transactional Web services. You learned how the client-side proxy enables asynchronous calls to be made to any Web service and how to directly use the wsdl.exe utility to set specific namespaces for proxy classes. We examined the interaction between Web services and .NET Remoting clients and servers based on XML and HTTP. We also looked at how to create a Web service client to talk to a .NET Remoting server and a .NET Remoting client to talk to an ASP.NET Web service.

Finally, the chapter examined the use of the DISCO protocol to expose specific groups of Web services and to import multiple Web services into a client application. We also covered the use of UDDI as a central repository of Web service information, and we created a skeleton UDDI client.

Index

Symbols and Numbers

& (ampersands), in URIs and streams posted to Web servers, 400
* (asterisks), in attribute declarations, 789
@ (at symbols)
  array class names and, 114
  placeholders in parameterized statements and, 276–277
: (colons), 207, 212
{} (curly brackets)
  using in Web services, 784
  variables declared within code render blocks using, 697
/ (forward slashes), match attribute and, 242
> and < (greater-than and less-than characters), 186
- (minus signs), inserting separators into menus, 164
+ (plus signs), in URIs and streams posted to Web servers, 400
? (question marks), placeholders in parameterized statements and, 276–277
; (semicolons), multiple paths specified using, 63
[(single brackets), array class names and, 114
_ (underscores), prefixing COM+ component interface names, 610
2PC (Two-Phase Commit) protocol, 651

A

Abstract Window Toolkit. *See* AWT
access control lists, 521
access rights. *See* permissions and permission sets
accessor methods
  overview, 98–100
  setting column properties, 293–294
  SQL statements and data sets, 286
acknowledgments, 530–532
activation
  configuration files and, 463–464, 469–471
  CORBA providing, 17
  just-in-time, 638–639
  in .NET Remoting model, 452–453
  server-activated object remoting, 465–467
Activator, 69–70, 71, 453–454, 469–470
Active Directory
  accessing service providers, 141
  certificates registered in, 537–538
  message queues querying, 496–497
  obtaining message queue information from, 523–525
  resolving paths for message queues, 503
ActiveX Data Objects. *See* ADO
ActiveX Data Objects for the .NET Framework. *See* ADO.NET
activities and synchronization, 633–637
administration queues, 530–532
ADO (ActiveX Data Objects)
  architecture, 22–23
  migrating from, 725
ADO.NET (ActiveX Data Objects for the .NET Framework)
  architecture
    components, 266–268
    data adapters, 269–270
    DataSet objects, 268–269
    disconnected access, 266
    history of, 23
    managing data from multiple sources, 265–266
  data stores
    building commands, 274–276
    connecting to, 270–274
    executing commands against, 274–285
    invoking stored procedures, 282–283
    JDBC compared to, 266–267
    retrieving single record from data source, 283
    using *DataReader* objects for read-only data retrieval, 283–285
    using parameters in statements, 276–282
  DataSet objects. *See DataSet* objects
  JDBC compared to, 139, 266–267
  migrating from ADO to, 725
  transaction management, 299–300
  XML and
    binding, 739–741
    inferring *DataSet* structure from XML, 304–306
    writing *DataRelation* objects as XML, 304
    writing *DataSet* objects as XML, 301–303
AL.exe (Assembly Linker tool), 52–53
aliases
  hard-coding, 564
  System Restore API methods, 563
  for virtual directories, 483, 485
alignment and field packing, 549–551, 558–559
ampersand (&)
  in URIs and streams posted to Web servers, 400
  in XML documents, 212
anonymous access to Web services, 823

ANSI arguments, 563–564
apartment state, message queue transactions and, 536
apartments
  COM objects executing in, 575–576
  migrating from ADO to ADO.NET, 725
  overview, 323–324
APIs. *See also* ADO.NET
  accessing data and metadata in XML documents, 191
  ODBC, 21–23
  threads and, 310
applets, 121
Application Center, 26
application configuration files. *See* configuration files
application domains
  divided into contexts, 339
  overview, 74–76
  threads, 312
application scope
  of ASP.NET pages, 751–752
  caching, 764–767
  error handling, 755–757
  HTTP forms storage, 729
architecture of .NET. *See N*-tier development; *specific components*
arrays
  of bytes
    converting strings into, 384, 385, 397
    deserialization and, 416
  of constructor values, 454, 469–470
  cross-language development and CLS, 44
  J/Direct and, 559
  Java and, 114–115
  queues array, 523–524
  services array, 669–670
  Web services using, 807, 845
  XML serialization and, 436
ASMX files
  compilation, 780
  overview, 775
  URLs accessing, 777–778
ASP (Active Server Pages)
  ASP.NET compared to, 698
  history of, 71–72
  HTML forms and, 700–704
  migrating from, 724–727
ASP.NET (Active Server Pages for the .NET Framework)
  associating error pages with ASPX pages using, 758
  attributes of, 727–728
  authentication provider, 405
  binding to data, 739–742
  browser-based applications, 692–693
  caching
    application data, 764–767
    output caching, 767–768
    storing application-wide state using, 752
  classes containing code-behind for ASPX files, 712
  compile-and-cache technique, 137
  controls
    creating, 735–739
    displaying information, 733–734
    forms and selection, 732–733
    layout, 734
    migrating to, 725–727
    Page class, 727–732
    Web controls, 739–742
    Web Forms server-side controls, 708–710
  dependency targets, 713–714
  deploying, 745–746
  environment, 693–695
  error handling
    application-wide, 755–757
    automatic event wire-up, 730–731
    generating exceptions, 759–760
    local, 759
    page specific, 757–758
  Global.asax, 743–745, 749, 755–757
  JSP compared to, 140–141
  language defined in, 699
  managing state
    application scope, 751–752
    cookies, 753–754
    remote session state, 749–751
    request scope, 753
    session scope, 746–749
  migrating from ASP pages, 724–727
  overview, 71–72
  programming model, 695–700
  security, 760–764
  server-side code defined in, 710
  state management and, 752
  threading, 323–324
  Web Forms. *See also* HTML forms
    ASP.NET and, 72
    client-side validation, 718–724
    code behind forms, 710–714
    creating, 705–708
    event handling, 714–718
    message queues and, 512–514
    server-side controls, 708–710
  Web services
    compilation and dependencies, 780
    defining, 775–776

implementing, 776–777
security, 822–826
signaling errors, 819–822
state management, 816–819
support for, 72–73
testing, 777–780
Web.config, 742–743
ASPX files
ASMX files compared to, 775
associating custom error pages with, 758
mapping, 694
output caching and, 767, 768
text-based content of, 712–713
assemblies. *See also specific types of assemblies*
adding to GAC, 59–60
application domains and, 76
binding, 55, 61–62
compiling Java classes into, 96–98
configuration files and, 464
configuring applications, 60–65
defined, 32
downloading, 62–63, 314, 373
GAC, 56–60
modules compared to, 53
namespaces and, 67
overview, 52–54
remote objects using, 479, 483
search paths, 63–64, 712
security and, 81–86
strongly named, 57–58, 616, 617
unsigned, 420
versioning, 52, 58–59, 61–62
viewing using ILDASM, 32–33
Web applications and, 399, 700
Web Forms and, 712
Assembly Linker tool (AL.exe), 52–53
assembly registration utility, 595
asterisks (*), in attribute declarations, 789
asynchronous operations
COM+ component interfaces to support, 609–611
connectionless sockets compared to, 383
J2EE and, 138
message queues, 525–532
processing requests, 401–402
serviced components, 661–664
sockets and, 383, 389–392
thread pooling and, 357–359, 391–392
Web service clients making, 853–856
atomic transactions
defined, 299
synchronizing threads and, 327–328, 334–335
transactional message queues and, 535
attributes
adding, 228
of ASP.NET, 727–728
assemblies and strong names, 58
context, 339
DataSet, looking for XML elements with, 305
declarations, multiline, 789
declarative security using, 78
defined, 33
deleting from DOM documents, 227
in DOM tree, 219
finding and processing, 198–202
metadata and, 131–133, 187
namespaces and, 188
navigating, 205–206
reflection and, 58
retrieving from DOM documents, 222–223
in XML documents, writing out, 209–211
audio data, transmitting, 382
authentication
application domains and, 78
ASP.NET, 760–762
authorization and, 405–408
credentials and user identification, 406–407, 851–852
HTTP remoting and, 485
message queues and, 537–539
preauthentication, 406
TCP remoting and, 474–475
XML Web services and, 822–826
authentication modules, 405–408
authentication (public key) tokens and unsigned serialized classes, 420
authorization
ASP.NET, 751, 762–764
authentication and, 405–408
SQL Server and, 751
authorization tokens, 408
automatic event wire-up, 730–731
AWT (Abstract Window Toolkit)
adding dialog boxes compared to Windows Forms library, 174
click event, 172
clipboard events, 179
compiling and running applications under .NET, 157–159
history of, 145
menus and menu items, 166, 167
overview, 146–148
Swing and, 90, 149
Windows Forms library compared to, 166, 167, 172, 179

B

background and foreground threads, 322–323, 356
Background Intelligent Transfer Service (BITS), 576
backward compatibility (legacy components), 12, 543–544
Basic authentication, 406–407
batch processes, 134, 858
BDK BeanBox, 92, 93
Bean Development Kit (BDK), 92
Bean-Managed Persistence (BMP), 136
big endian processor architecture
  cross-platform compatibility, 18
  overview, 13
  sockets and, 380, 381
binary data
  deserialization, 419–421, 431–432
  HTTP connections and, 397
  serialization, 412, 503
  sockets and, 381
binary encoding, 451
binding
  assemblies, 55, 61–62
  COM objects and, 580–589
  delegates, 172–173
  early, serviced components and, 623
  endpoints and sockets, 367, 386
  late binding, 580–585
  manual binding, 585–589
  serialization and, 421–422
  SQL binding, 741–742
  versioning and, 418
  Web services and, 793–795
  XML binding, 739–741
BITS (Background Intelligent Transfer Service), 576
BizTalk Server, 26
blocking
  designing out of message queuing operations, 525
  methods until messages are available, 508
  sockets
    Close method, 372–373
    Receive method, 387–389
    ReceiveFrom method, 385
    server responses, 378–379
  threads
    asynchronous I/O, 358–359
    event classes and, 347–353
    Monitor objects and sync blocks, 331–333
    Wait method and thread notification, 353
BMP (Bean-Managed Persistence), 136
Bond, Martin, 133
boxing and unboxing
  Java and, 504, 510
  overview, 111
bridges, 601
browsers. *See* Web services
buffering, 371–372, 378
Build Solution option (Visual Studio .NET), 180–181
bundling. *See* serialization
business services
  in J2EE, 135–136, 140
  JavaBeans and, 93–96
  presentation logic and, 72
  roles performed by, 6
  UDDI registry and, 870
  XML and, 185
byte ordering, 13, 381
bytecodes, 26, 39–40

C

C and C++
  external functionality, 261–263
  flashing title bars and taskbar buttons, 549
  memory management, 45–46
  polymorphic parameters, 569–570
  remoting and, 476–479
caching. *See also* GAC
  ASP.NET and
    application data, 764–767
    output caching, 764–768
    storing application-wide state using, 752
  ASPX files and output caching, 767, 768
  compile-and-cache technique, 137
  credentials, 407, 851–852
  HTTP connections, 403–404
  message queue connections, 521
  messages, 497, 528
  native image cache, 40
  schemas, 218
  shared state COM+ components, 645–650
callbacks
  ASP.NET and caching, 765
  COM+ components and SCP, 649
  P/Invoke and, 567–568
  receiving messages asynchronously and, 525
calling
  COM components
    calling COM+ components compared to, 608
    creating and using RCW, 572–577
    publishing events, 577–580
    using COM objects without type libraries, 580–589
  conventions for cross-language development, 568–569
  external functions from within XSLT stylesheets, 254, 257–263

RCWs (Runtime Callable Wrappers)
creating RCWs from command line, 576–577
handling *HRESULT* values, 574–575
marshaling and apartments, 575–576
RCW implementation, 573–574
stopped and suspended threads, 317
System Restore API, 551–571
CCWs (COM Callable Wrappers)
COM Interop and, 589–594
creating, 594–598
overview, 50, 589
RCWs referencing, 629
serviced components and, 650
testing, 598–600
Cdecl calling convention, 568
certificates
client certificates, 24, 401, 826
message queues and, 537–538
challenge/response mechanism, 405
channel sink providers, 493
channel sinks, 458–460, 492–494
channels
configuration files and, 461–463, 464, 481
custom, 492–494
defined, 70
registering, 451–452
security and, 474
characters forbidden in XML, 207, 212
class files (Java), migrating, 122–123
class libraries. *See also* .NET Framework Class Library
building, 329
core base class libraries, 32
Java, 68, 90–91
classes
ASP.NET pages using, 699–700
code access security and, 78, 85–86
components compared to, 91
cross-language development and CLS, 43, 44
DataSet structure and, 287–288
defining interfaces for, 585–588
descended from *System.Object*, 109
designing for COM Interop and, 589–594
JavaBeans as, 92
marshaling *struct* objects and unmanaged components, 548–551
names of
in J# compared to JDK, 162
Web services, 836–837
packaging and locating, 106–108
as reference types, 46
representing data adapters, 269
serializable, 414, 415, 420
services made from, 676
specifying GUIDs of, 585–586
synchronization and context attributes applied to, 339–341
Web Forms and, 712
Web services
defining, 776
names of, 836–837, 844
for XML manipulation, 192–193
XSLT and transformations, 246
click event
adding to forms using Visual Studio, 171–172
clipboards and, 179
of Open menu item, 176–177
starting and stopping services using, 673–675
Web Forms and ASP.NET, 714–715
client-activated object remoting
configuration files and, 464–465, 468, 469
lifecycles, 471, 473
overview, 452, 469–471
well-known objects, 457
client certificates, 24, 826
client/server (two-tier) architecture, 3–6
client-side validation, 718–724
clients. *See also* Web service clients
access to servers, restricting, 368
connection-oriented, 374–376
JavaBeans, accessing properties from, 99–100
Message Queuing 3.0 Clients, 496–497
in .NET Remoting model, 451–455
TCP remoting and, 464–465
ClipboardOwner interface, 150
clipboards, 178–180
CLR. *See* common language runtime
CLS (Common Language Specification), 43–45, 265
CMP (Container-Managed Persistence), 136
code access security
assemblies, 76
COM+ components, 655
evidence, 81–82, 85
permissions and permission sets, 82–85
policy information location, 81
requesting and refusing permissions, 85–86
security policy and code groups, 85
sockets and, 373
code behind
HTML controls and, 727
migrating from ASP pages to ASP.NET, 725
overview, 72
Web Forms, 710–714
Web services and, 782–784
code render blocks
language defined in, 698, 699
overview, 696
variables declared in, 697

Code View window (Visual Studio .NET)
  overview, 160–162, 163
  viewing menu and menu item code in, 167
  viewing *TextBox* controls in, 171
collections of objects. *See* graphs (object collections)
  graphs, 427–432, 435–436
  Web services using, 807–808
colons (:), 207, 212
COM
  interfaces, 587
  interoperatibility and bridges, 601
  tagging interfaces with IIDs, 590
COM+
  history of, 17
  integrity and transactions, 25
  J2EE compared to, 140
  overview, 605–607
  scalability and availability, 25
COM Callable Wrappers (CCWs). *See* CCWs
COM+ catalog, 613, 632
COM components
  calling
    calling COM+ components compared to, 608
    creating and using RCW, 572–577
    publishing events, 577–580
    using COM objects without type libraries, 580–589
  integrating into .NET applications, 50–51
  integrating .NET components into
    creating CCWs, 594–598
    designing .NET components for COM Interop, 589–594
    testing CCWs, 598–600
  migrating to J#, 122
COM+ components
  attaching to events, 618–620
  calling, 609
  consuming from J#, 607–621
  queued components, 661–662
  security
    code access, 655
    declarative, 656–657
    imperative, 660–661
    implementing, 657–659
  serviced components
    activation, 638–645
    asynchronous, 661–664
    building, 621–633
    caching shared state, 645–650
    designing, 664–665
    overview, 140
    registering and using, 629–633
    static methods, 637
    synchronization, 633–637
    transactions, 650–655
  subscribing to loosely coupled events, 613–621
  supporting loosely coupled events, 662–664
COM Interop
  apartments and, 575
  designing components for, 589–594
  late binding and, 580
  threads and managed code, 325
  unmanaged code and, 589
COM+ New Subscription Wizard, 618–620
command classes, building, 274–276
command line
  compiling Web applications from, 400
  creating RCWs from, 576–577
  generating strongly typed *DataSet* objects from, 290–291
  proxy generation using, 857–858
  retargeting Web service client proxies, 841
  running applications from, 180–181
  running tools from, 31
  working with discovery files, 865
command objects
  ADO.NET and, 270
  building, 275–276
  data store queries and, 275–276
  transactions associated with, 300
commands
  executing against data stores, 274–285
  invoking stored procedures, 282–283
comments
  attributes added using, 58
  ignoring in XML documents, 203–204
Commerce Server, 26
common language runtime, 30–40
Common Language Specification (CLS), 43–45, 265
Common Object Request Broker Architecture. *See* CORBA
communication
  asynchronous, 383, 389–392
  interthread, 343–355
compilation
  ASP.NET and, 699, 713
  assemblies created during, 53–54
  bytecodes, 39–40
  classes into assemblies, 96–98
  DLLs, 40, 43
  just-in-time, 30
  searching using XPath, 252
  XML Web services, 780
compile-and-cache technique, 137
compilers
  common language runtime, 30–40

cross-language development, 40–45
DataSet objects into libraries, 290–291
defining native methods, 546
J# compiler (vjc), 31, 96, 98
Java compiler, 39–40
javac compiler, 96–98
JavaScript compiler (jsc), 31
jc compiler, 121–122
jsc (JavaScript compiler), 31
memory management, 45–50
synchronization and, 338
unmanaged code integrated into .NET applications, 50–51
complex types, Web service clients handling, 808, 842–844
Component Designer (Visual Studio .NET), 288–291
component object model. *See* COM
Component Services console (Visual Studio .NET)
configuring COM+ security, 656–659
creating and configuring COM+ applications, 608–612, 618
enabling and disabling subscriptions, 620
installing applications, 614
tying subscribing clients to event classes, 613
components in *N*-tier systems, 7–8, 11. *See also specific types of components*
computer dead-letter queues, 500–501, 516
computer journal queues, 501, 519
Computer Management console (Visual Studio .NET)
certificates registered in Active Directory using, 537–538
enabling message authentication using, 539
finding GUIDs of message queues using, 527–528
making message queues transactional, 532
managing queues using, 498–499
message queue privileges, 522–523
viewing Queue Messages folders in, 507–508
COM sink event interface, 578, 590, 591–594, 618–619
concurrency
of COM+ components, 634
of message queues, 515–516
.config extension, 60
configuration elements, 742–743
configuration files
assembly download information in, 62
assembly information in, 60–61
clients using, 464–465, 469
editing, 64–65, 492
HTTP remoting and, 481, 483
IIS hosting remote objects and, 483–486
interface information in, 468
lease properties in, 474
registering request classes using, 395
retargeting Web service client proxies, 841–842
server-activated objects and, 474, 492
TCP remoting and, 461–464
templates and, 462–463
configuration information, storing, 190
connection-oriented sockets
accepting and rejecting client requests, 368–369
clients, 374–376
creating, 365
disabling sending and receiving data over, 371–373
establishing endpoints, 365–367
handling multiple clients and requests, 369–371
in listening mode, 367–368
overview, 363–364
reading data from, 369–371
TcpListener and *TcpClient* classes, 376–379
thread pooling and streams, 391–392
Web servers and, 394
connectionless sockets
overview, 382–387
thread pooling and streams, 392
Web servers and, 393
connections. *See also* JDBC
ADO.NET and, 269–270
caching, 403–404, 521
data adapters and, 268
events fired by, 273–274
HTTP connections and, 396–398, 403–404
pooling, 134, 273
settings defined in strings, 270–272
consistent bit (happy bit), 654–655
Console applications, 324
console I/O, 118–119
constants, P/Invoke defining, 556–557
constructors
client-activated objects, 469–470
command classes, 275
Java creating, 35, 131
RemotingServices class and, 487
server-activated objects, 467, 487
setting column properties, 293
Windows services and, 676–680
XML serialization and, 433–435, 436
consumer interface (OLE DB), 22–23
consumers and thread notification, 343–347
Container-Managed Persistence (CMP), 136
containers
managing EJBs, 136
SOAP messages, 772
XML serialization and, 435
context
remote objects and, 457
starting applications in specified, 164
static data and, 342–343
stream-based processing of XML data, 191
synchronization and, 339–341
synchronization and COM+ components, 634–637

transactional Web service methods, 853
of variables, serialization and, 423
Web-based applications, 692, 693
context-bound and context-agile objects
overview, 339
remote objects and, 448, 458
serviced components and, 624–625
controls
ASP.NET and
creating, 735–739
displaying information, 733–734
forms and selection, 732–733
layout, 734
migrating to, 725–727
Page class, 727–732
Web controls, 739–742
Web Forms server-side controls, 708–710
code-behind, 710, 782
HTML forms and
creating user controls on, 735–739
layout and positioning of, 734
overview of common controls, 732–734
HTTP forms and, 729
naming, 165
relative positioning of, 734
retrieving states of, 716
Swing, 168
TextBox controls
adding to Web Forms, 706–708
client-side validation, 718–719
clipboards and, 179–180
contents of, 715–716
designing, 168–171
server-side controls, 709–710, 732, 756
Web Forms and, 710
Web services, 782
Windows Forms, 164, 165–171
conversion. *See also* serialization; transformation
deserialization and, 418
Java objects into XML, 433
polymorphism, 809–811, 849–851
XML into .NET types, 207
cookieless support for sessions, 818–819, 849
cookies
forms-based authentication, 761–762
session-based state management and, 818–819
setting, 753–754
Web service clients and, 847–848, 849
CORBA (Common Object Request Broker Architecture), 16–17, 601
core base class libraries, 32
correlating messages, 517–519
Corvars.bat, 31
Create Code Group Wizard, 85
credentials
caching, 407, 851–852
passing, 825, 851–852
cross-language development. *See also* CLS
calling conventions, 568–569
consuming components, 104–106
JavaBeans, 100, 104–106
MSIL, 30
.NET Framework Class Library, 65–66
non-Microsoft technologies, 602
ORBs, 16–17
overview, 40–45
Visual Basic and, 41–43
Web services and, 19
cross-platform compatibility. *See also* interoperability
big endian and little endian, 18
message queuing and, 496
.NET Framework Class Library, 65–66
PLAF scheme, 148
RMI, 18
RPCs and, 16
serialization and, 382
XML and, 186
cross-process calls
mutexes, 353–354
RPCs and, 74, 75
cryptographic keys (encryption)
message queuing, 538
strong name utility generating, 57
support for, 408
curly brackets ({})
using in Web services, 784
variables declared using, 697

D

data adapters
in ADO.NET architecture, 268, 269–270
manipulating and updating data stores from, 292–296
populating *DataSet* tables from, 285–288
Data Link Properties dialog box (Visual Studio), 270, 272
data services
in J2EE, 134–135, 139–140
roles performed by, 6
XML and, 185
data sets. *See DataSet* objects
data slots, synchronizing threads, 342
data sources (ADO.NET). *See also specific sources*
architecture, 265–266, 268
comprising several data members, 670
connecting to, 270–272
data readers and, 283–285
managing data from multiple sources, 265–266

retrieving data from multiple sources, 269
retrieving single record from, 283
data stores (ADO.NET)
building commands, 274–276
connecting to, 270–274
executing commands against, 274–285
JDBC compared to, 266–267
manipulating and updating from data adapters, 292–296
retrieving single record from data source, 283
using *DataReader* objects for read-only data retrieval, 283–285
using parameters in statements, 276–282
data structures, P/Invoke mapping, 557–562
data types. *See also specific types*
on clipboard, 179–180
command objects and, 277–280
cross-language development and CLS, 43, 44
data readers and, 284
hierarchy of types, 108–117
interfaces and queued operations, 611
MSIL, 30
Web services. *See* Web services, data types
WSDL and, 787–793
XML and, 303, 438
Data view (XML Designer), 194
database management systems. *See* DBMS
datagrams, 383–385
DataSet objects
in ADO.NET architecture, 268–269
binding to *DataGrid* , 739–741
defining relationships and constraints, 296–299
manipulating and updating data stores from data adapters, 292–296
marshal-by-value objects and, 449
navigating typed, 288–291
navigating untyped, 291–292
passing across Web services, 811–814, 845–846
populating tables from data adapters, 285–288
serializing, 811
transforming, 250
typed, 846
using for data access, 285–299
writing as XML, 301–303
XML and, 191, 192, 231–233, 304–306
DBMS (database management systems). *See also specific systems*
architecture of, 4–6
connectivity and data formats, 12–21
data access, 21–23
integrity and transactions, 25
resource contention, 627
scalability and availability, 24–25
security, 23–24
serviced components and, 624
transmitting data, 21–23
DCOM (Distributed COM)
COM+ serviced components and, 650
overview, 17
periodic pinging, 471
reference counting, 471
dead-letter queues, 500–501, 516
deadlock, 333
declarations
in code render blocks, 697
control declarations on ASP.NET pages, 738
delegates, 100–101
multiline, 789
namespace, 216, 242
native methods, 548
in WSDL documents, 802
in XML documents, 210
XSLT parameters, 254–258
declarative security, 78–79
declarative transactions, 651
delegates
binding, 172–173
callbacks using, 567–568
declaring, 100–101
defined by RCWs, 578–580
multicasting supported by, 173
remoting and, 476, 478–479
SOAP and asynchronous calls, 854–855
dependencies, caches, 765
deployment. *See also* installing and uninstalling
assemblies as unit of, 52
of classes with Web servers, 137
in COM+ applications, 616
deploying to GAC, 59–60
just-in-time (JIT), 140
Web applications, 745–746
deployment packages, creating, 611–612
Description element, 211–212
description files for Web services. *See* WSDL
deserialization
binary deserialization, 419–421, 431–432
defined, 411
message bodies, 509
overview, 416–417
remoting and, 459
selective serialization, 422
versioning, 417–422
Design Patterns: Elements of Reusable Object-Oriented Software, 11
design patterns of *N*-tier systems, 11
Design View window (Visual Studio .NET), 160
adding controls to forms, 165–171
adding dialog boxes, 176–178

changing filenames and form names, 162–163
creating event handler methods, 171–172
designing distributed systems. *See* *N*-tier development
desktop GUIs, 146–150
device drivers, 22, 672
dialog boxes, adding to applications, 174–178
digital signatures, 408, 537–538
directory services and J2EE, 137–138
DISCO (Web Services Discovery) protocol, 863–866, 867
disco.exe, 865
disconnected operations. *See* asynchronous operations
Distributed COM. *See* DCOM
distributed systems. *See* *N*-tier development
.dll extension, omitting from filenames, 548
DLL hell, 51
DLLs, 122
compiling J# packages into, 41–43
configuration files, 60
converting files into, 104, 122
disadvantages of, 51–52
manifests containing information about, 32
MSIL and, 30
Ngen.exe used to compile, 40
placing in GAC, 595
references to EXE files wrapped inside, 479
strongly named, 57
unmanaged, invoking methods in
J/Direct, 546–551
P/Invoke, 50, 551–571
DNS (Domain Name System), 365–366, 378, 383
document object model. *See* DOM
document-style SOAP messages, 795
DOM. *See also* XML
extracting information from, 222–226
loading XML documents into, 220, 221
writing and manipulating XML documents, 227–230
DOM-based transformations, 249
DOM Node interface, 220
DOM trees
altering content in, 227–228
navigating, 222, 224–225
persisting changes to, 230
searching, 225–226
treating fragments as streams, 227
domain controllers, 497
Domain Name System (DNS), 365–366, 378, 383
done bit, 639–642, 654
downloading
assemblies, 62–63, 314, 373
exposing methods for, 402
drivers, 22, 672
DTC (Distributed Transaction Coordinator), 826
DTD (Document Type Definition)
attaching to XML documents, 215–216
history of, 213
overview, 188–189
dynamic discovery of Web service clients, 866–869
dynamic link libraries. *See* DLLs
dynamic output generated from ASP.NET code, 697
dynamic registration of serviced components, 630

E

early binding, 623
EIS (Enterprise Information Systems), 134–135, 139
EJBs (Enterprise JavaBeans)
client-activated objects compared to, 471
COM+ compared to, 140
overview, 135–136
empty objects, 417, 418
encapsulating functions, 261
encoding
converting strings into arrays, 384
strings submitted to Web servers, 400
target methods of HTTP requests, 779
Web services requests, 771
XML and, 188, 189, 190, 210
encryption
HTTP remoting and, 485
message queues and, 539–540
overview, 408
TCP remoting and, 474–475
end elements, explicitly writing, 211
endpoints. *See also* sockets
connection-oriented clients and, 365–367, 374
connectionless sockets and, 383, 384, 387
IP address element, 363–366
overview, 362
port number element, 363–366
TcpClient class and sockets, 378
TcpListener objects and, 376, 378
enterprise features of .NET. *See specific features*
Enterprise Information Systems (EIS), 134–135, 139
Enterprise JavaBeans (EJBs)
client-activated objects compared to, 471
COM+ compared to, 140
overview, 135–136
Enterprise Services, 25–26. *See also specific services*
entities
handling, 221
overview, 189
resolution, XML documents, 218
Entity EJBs, 135–136, 471

enumeration
callbacks and, 567–568
message queues, 523–525
messages and, 514–515
overview, 113
environment
ASP.NET, 693–695
Web Forms and, 710
Envoy MQ Client, 496
error handling. *See also* exception handling
application-wide, 743–745
ASP.NET and
application-wide, 755–757
automatic event wire-up, 730–731
generating exceptions, 759–760
local, 759
page specific, 757–758
client-side validation, 718–719, 723
reporting errors using *HRESULT*, 574–575
unmanaged functions setting error codes, 571
Web Forms and, 710
Web service clients, 839–841
XML validation errors, 216–217
error messages
displaying for users, 757
SOAP and, 820
errors, signaling conditions for, 819–822
event handling
clipboards and, 179–180
dialog boxes and, 176–178
sinking COM events, 577–580
Web Forms and, 714–718
Windows Forms and, 171–174
writing code for in Visual Studio, 172–174
XML deserialization and, 444
Event Log service, 667
event sinks
adding, 663–664
method and event names matching, 593–594
overview, 591–592
EventListener interface, 92, 96
events
attaching COM+ components, 618–620
COM components publishing, 577–580
defining, 100–102
fired during installation, 681
JavaBeans and, 92, 93–96
LCEs (loosely coupled events), 613–621, 662–664
parameters, 102–103
remote, 476–480
subscribing and unsubscribing to, 101–102, 444, 591
evidence and code access security, 81–82, 85
exception handling. *See also* error handling
monitors and, 332
P/Invoke and, 570–571
threads, 319, 320
Web service clients and, 839–841
XML documents, 208–209
exceptions. *See also specific causes of*
dialog boxes and, 178
overview, 115–116
remoting and, 455
security, 76–77
Exchange Server, 26
exclusive locks, 652
Execute Around pattern, 333
execute methods, 276, 283
express messages, 501, 506
eXtensible Markup Language (XML). *See* XML
Extensible Stylesheets Language Transformations. *See* XSLT
extension objects, 258–260
external entities, 218
external functions, calling from within XSLT stylesheets, 254, 257–263

F

field packing, 549–551, 558–559
file dialog boxes, adding to applications, 174–178
file streams, 414–415, 422
filename extensions
IIS list of, 693–694. *See specific extensions*
MSIL and, 30
filenames, changing, 162–163
files
saving DOMs as, 230
System Restore API saving, 552
writing *DataSet* objects as XML, 301–303
filters
applications acting as, 212
message properties, 518
subscribing components, 621
finalizers
overview, 48
serviced components and, 644
Windows services and, 676
"fire and forget" methods, 486
flashing title bars and taskbar buttons, 549–551
floating point values, 207
flow layout of controls on ASP.NET pages, 734, 735
flow of control, interrupting, 317
foreground and background threads, 322–323
format names used in message queues, 527–530
formatter sinks, 459

formatters
  changing, 483
  deserialization and, 416, 417, 420–421, 509
  HTTP remoting and, 481
  message queues and, 505
  overview, 412–415
  private data and, 482
  serialization and, 412–415
forms
  adding controls to, 167–171
  adding menus and menu items to, 165–167
  changing properties, 164
  closing and hiding, 173–174
  code behind, 72, 725, 727
  HTML forms
    ASP forms and, 700–704
    creating user controls on, 735–739
    layout and positioning of controls, 734
    overview of common controls, 732–734
  HTTP, 729
  login forms, 24
  names of, 162–163, 164
  overloaded, 221
  Web Forms (ASP.NET)
    ASP.NET and, 72
    client-side validation, 718–724
    code behind forms, 710–714
    creating, 705–708
    event handling, 714–718
    message queues and, 512–514
    server-side controls, 708–710
  Windows Forms
    controls, 164, 165–171
    creating, 160–164
    event model used by, 171–174
    message queues and, 512–514
  Windows Forms library, 145, 149–150
forms-based authentication, 761–762
forms-based security, 24
Forms Designer (Visual Studio .NET), 714

G

GAC (Global Assembly Cache)
  classes placed in, 594
  deploying to, 59–60
  DLLs placed in, 595
  RCWs placed in, 617
  strong names, 57–58, 468
  version numbers, 58–59
GAC Viewer, 56–57, 59–60
Gacutil tool, 60
Gamma, Erich, 11
garbage collection
  finalizers, 48, 644, 676
  IDisposable interface, through, 48–50
  primitive types, 109–110
  reference types and, 46
  remoting and, 472
  safe points, 317, 318
Generate Dataset dialog box (Visual Studio .NET), 289
generic host server application, 464
generic object conversion, 809–811, 849–851
Generic Principals, role-based security using, 77
Global Assembly Cache. *See* GAC
global scope
  objects and sync blocks, 332–333
  properties for lease managers, 473–474
  proxy settings, 398
  UDDI registries, 871–872
  XSLT parameter declarations, 255
Global XML Web Service Architecture (GXA)
  future of, 24
  overview, 602
  underlying Web services, 774
Global.asax
  defining static objects in, 749
  error handling and, 755–757
  overview, 743–745
globally unique identifiers. *See* GUIDs
graphical user interfaces. *See* GUIs
graphs (object collections), 427–432, 435–436
greater-than characters (>), XML using, 186
green pages search, 871
grid layout of ASP.NET pages, 734, 738
GUI libraries. *See* AWT; Swing
GuidGen utility (Visual Studio .NET), 590
GUIDs (globally unique identifiers)
  cookies and, 754
  correlating messages and, 517
  designing for COM Interop and, 590, 591
  disconnected message queues and, 527–528
  production and development versions of components, 632
  specifying, 585
GUIs (graphical user interfaces)
  adding controls to the Windows Form, 165–171
  compiling and running, 180–181
  creating the Windows Form, 160–164
  desktop GUIs, 146–150
  displaying dialog boxes, 174–178
  event handling, 171–174
  overview, 145
  porting existing Java applications, 150–159
  Swing, 90
  system clipboard and, 178–180

Gulliver's Travels, 13
GXA (Global XML Web Service Architecture)
 future of, 24
 overview, 602
 underlying Web services, 774

H

happy bit (consistent bit), 654–655
hard-coding
 aliases, 564
 IP addresses, 365
 type information in configuration files, 470
hashing
 Java serialization and versioning, 419
 overview, 408
 serializing hash tables, 429–430, 432, 435
Haywood, Dan, 133
heaps
 managed and unmanaged code, 545
 primitive types created on, 109
Helm, Richard, 11
hierarchies, traversing in XML documents, 202–205
Home interface, 136
host applications, 75–76
host servers, in .NET Remoting model, 451–455
HRESULT, 574–575
HTML forms. *See also* Web Forms (ASP.NET)
 ASP forms and, 700–704
 creating user controls on, 735–739
 layout and positioning of controls, 734
 overview of common controls, 732–734
HTML (Hypertext Markup Language)
 ASP compared to, 708
 ASP.NET code embedded in, 696, 697
 J2EE and, 136–137
HTTP forms, 729
HTTP (Hypertext Transfer Protocol)
 channels based on
  channel sinks and, 459
  HTTP remoting using, 481, 482–483
  SOAP used for, 451
 connection management and pooling, 403–404
 design principles, 19
 J2EE and, 136–137
 messaging over, 540
 remoting
  IIS hosting, 483–485
  remoting server hosting, 481–483
  security, 485–486
  TCP remoting compared to, 480
 request/response model
  data types and streams, 399–400
  overview, 394, 396–398
  persistent connections and, 403
  pipelining, 403
  pooling connections, 403–404
  WebRequest and *WebResponse* classes compared to, 401
 requesting and receiving data using, 396–399
 SOAP, 20–21
 underlying Web services, 770–771
Hypertext Transfer Protocol. *See* HTTP

I

I/O
 asynchronous, 357–359, 391–392
 console, 118–119
 interactive with users, 324
 reading and writing to files, 177–178
 synchronous, 378
IAuthenticationModule interface, 405
IChannel, *IChannelSender* and *IChannelReceiver* interfaces, 493
IClientChannelSink and *IServerChannelSink* interfaces, 492–493
IClientChannelSinkProvider and *IServerChannelSink-Provider* interfaces, 492–493
ICollection interface, 435
IConvertible interface, 418
IDataAdapter interface, 268, 269
IDataObject interface, 180
IDataReader interface, 283–285
IDbCommand interface, 270, 275–276
IDbConnection interface, 269
IDbTransaction interface, 300
IDE, advantages of, 157. *See also* Visual Studio .NET
identifiers. *See also* GUIDs
 for asynchronous calls, 855
 correlating messages and, 517–518
 cross-language development and CLS, 44
IDeserializationCallback interface, 432
IDispatch interface
 late binding and, 580, 583–584
 manual binding and marshaling, 585
 pointers to, 588
IDisposable interface
 deterministic garbage collection through, 48–50
 pooling and, 644
 security and, 659
IDL (Interface Definition Language). *See also* MIDL
 CORBA, 16–17
 Java, 90
 RPCs, 15
idle objects, 471–474. *See also* lifecycles

IEnumerator interface, 225
IErrorInfo interface, 575
if loops, 202, 208
IFormatter interface, 412–423, 414, 431
IIDs (interface IDs), 590, 615–616
IIOP (Internet Inter-ORB Protocol), 17
IIS (Microsoft Internet Information Services)
  ASP.NET and, 693–694, 745
  HTTP remoting, 483–486
  SSL support, 408
  Web services security and, 823–825
ILDASM (Intermediate Language Disassembler tool)
  metadata and, 124
  viewing manifests using, 58–59
  viewing MSIL code, 31–38
ILease interface, 473
IList interfaces, 390
IManagedObject interface, 595–596, 659
IMessage interface, 457, 458
IMessageFormatter interface, 505
imperative security, 660–661
imperative transactions, 651
in-memory processing of XML data
  extracting information from DOM documents, 222–226
  loading XML into *XmlDocument* class, 221
  overview, 219–220
  standards, 192
  treating DOM fragments as streams, 227
  writing and manipulating XML documents, 227–230
  writing *DataSet* objects as XML, 301
infinite loops, 317
inheritance
  class representing dialog boxes, 175
  classes inheriting methods from *System.Object*, 35–36
  .NET components deployed in COM+ applications and, 616
  Web service classes, 784
Inside the Java 2 Virtual Machine, 40
install-on-demand Windows Installer (MSI) files, 64
installing and uninstalling. *See also* deployment packages, creating
  applications using Visual Studio, 614
  building installer files when deploying ASP.NET applications, 746
  Windows services, 680–688
  xcopy deployment, 55
instance constructor, default in Java, 131
integration. *See* cross-platform compatibility
Intel processors, byte ordering, 13
Interface Definition Language. *See* IDL
interface IDs, 590, 615–616
interfaces. *See also* GUIs; IDL; user interfaces; *specific interfaces*
  ADO.NET and, 139, 265, 269–270
  defining for classes, 585–586
  designing for COM Interop and, 590–593
  DOM, 220–221
  exceptions defined for, 839
  externally implemented, 585, 587–588
  importance of, 623
  Java and
    getting list of, 125–126
    overview, 116–117
  Java Naming and Directory Interface (JNDI), 137–138, 141
  Java Native Interface (JNI)
    overview, 27, 545–546
    replaced by J/Direct and Platform Invoke Service, 121
  LCEs and, 662–663
  MS DTC and, 651
  naming schemes, 585, 587
  queued, 609–613, 661–662
  for remote objects, 467–468
  serializable, 18
  serviced components and, 623
  sinks and, 492–493
  specifying GUIDs of, 585–586
  tagging as visible to COM, 623
  TAPI coclass implementing, 573–574
  Web services, 773, 785–797
Intermediate Language Disassembler tool. *See* ILDASM
Internet Explorer, creating and managing, 577–580
Internet Information Services. *See* IIS
Internet Inter-ORB Protocol (IIOP), 17
Internet Network Information Center (NIC), 364
Internet Protocol addresses. *See* IP addresses
Internet security, 405–408. *See also* HTTP
Internet service providers (ISPs), 364
InternetExplorer interface, 578–579
InterNIC (Internet Network Information Center), 364
interoperability. *See also* cross-language development
  CCWs and, 589
  history of, 543–544
  HTTP remoting, 481
  JDK sockets and .NET sockets, 380
  non-Microsoft technologies, 600–602
  non-.NET clients for Web services, 863
  SOAP encoding and, 795
  XML Web services, 602
interthread communication, 343–355
intrinsic objects and properties in ASP.NET, 728–730
IObjectContext interface, 627
IObjectControl interface, 622, 643, 644

IP addresses
disconnected message queues and, 528–529
endpoints and, 363–366
obtaining, 364, 374, 383
overview, 363
IPrincipal interface, 77
ISerializable interface
marshal-by-value objects and, 450
overview, 423–425
SerializableAttribute compared to, 413–414
ISerializationSurrogate interface, 425–426
isolation levels for transactions, 300, 651–654
isomorphic (blittable) types, 546–548
ISponsor interface, 472
ISPs (Internet service providers), 364
ISurrogateSelector interface, 426
iteration. *See* looping
ITrackingHandler interface, 489
IUnknown interface, 588, 589
IXPathNavigable interface, 248, 250, 252

J

J# compiler (vjc), 31, 96, 98
J# .NET. *See* Visual J# .NET
J2EE (Java 2 Enterprise Edition)
application example (Java Pet Store), 142–144
business services in, 135–136
client-activated objects compared to stateful session beans, 471
COM/J2EE bridge, 601
data services in, 134–135
infrastructure, 137–138
.NET compared to, 139–142
.NET/J2EE bridge, 601
overview, 27, 133
server-activated objects compared to entity beans, 471
transaction management, 138
user services in, 136–137
jagged arrays, 115
Java
bytecodes, 39–40
class libraries, 68, 90–91. *See also* JavaBeans
classes, 96–98
compiling and running applications under .NET, 150–159
console I/O, 118–119
constructors created automatically, 35, 131
GUI libraries, 146–149
hierarchy of types, 108–117. *See also specific types*
history of, 26–27, 89–90
inherited methods, 35
menus and menu items compared to .NET, 167
methods with variable numbers and arguments, 118
MSIL, transforming into, 30–38
overview, 26–27
packaging and locating classes, 106–108
primitive types, 345
RMI, 17–19
security, 86
serialization, 411, 417, 419
threads, 119–121
XML, converting into, 433
Java 2 Enterprise Edition. *See* J2EE
Java APIs, 135, 433
Java Architecture for XML Binding (JAXB), 135, 433
Java Binary Converter tool (jbimp), 122–123
Java Connector Architecture, 134
Java Database Connectivity. *See* JDBC
Java Development Kit. *See* JDK
Java EJBs
client-activated objects compared to, 471
COM+ compared to, 140
overview, 135–136
Java Messaging Service (JMS), 138, 601
Java Naming and Directory Interface (JNDI), 137–138, 141
Java Native Interface (JNI)
overview, 27, 545–546
replaced by J/Direct and Platform Invoke Service, 121
Java shorts, 511
Java Transaction API (JTA), 138
Java Virtual Machine. *See* JVM
JavaBeans
business components created using, 93–96
consuming components, 104–106
defining properties, 98–100
instantiating, 137
J# compiler and, 96, 98
javac compiler and, 96–98
overview, 91–93
javac compiler, 96–98
javap tool, 39
JavaScript compiler (jsc), 31
JavaServer Pages (JSP), 137, 140–141
JAX-RPC (Java API for XML-based RPC), 135, 433
JAXB (Java Architecture for XML Binding), 135, 433
JAXM (Java API for XML Messaging), 135, 433
JAXP (Java API for XML Processing), 135
JAXR (Java API for XML Registries), 135
jbimp (Microsoft Java Binary Converter tool), 122–123
jc compiler, 121–122
JDBC (Java Database Connectivity)
ADO.NET compared to, 139, 266–267
architecture, 22
J2EE and, 134

J/Direct
  declaring native methods, 548
  isomorphic and nonisomorphic types, 546–548
  marshalling *struct* objects, 548–551
  P/Invoke compared to, 551
JDK (Java Development Kit)
  history of, 89–90
  Java compiler, 39–40
  migrating to .NET, 121–123
  names of classes and forms, 162
  omissions from, 121
  RMI registry (name service), 18
  sockets, 363, 376, 380
  threads, 120–121, 313
  versioning, 418
JIT (just-in-time) activation, 638–639
JIT (just-in-time) compilation, 30, 317
JIT (just-in-time) deployment, 140
JMS (Java Messaging Service), 138, 601
JNDI (Java Naming and Directory Interface), 137–138, 141
JNI (Java Native Interface)
  overview, 27, 545–546
  replaced by J/Direct and Platform Invoke Service, 121
Johnson, Ralph, 11
join operations, 316
journal queues, 501, 519
jsc (JavaScript compiler), 31
JSP (JavaServer Pages), 137, 140–141
JTA (Java Transaction API), 138
just-in-time (JIT) activation, 638–639
just-in-time (JIT) compilation, 30, 317
just-in-time (JIT) deployment, 140
JVM (Java Virtual Machine)
  common language runtime compared to, 30, 89
  overview, 26

K

Kay, Michael, 241
Kerberos authentication, 407, 485
key encryption
  strong name utility generating, 57–58
  support for, 408
keyboard input, 119

L

labels for messages, 507, 715–716
language. *See also* cross-language development; *specific languages*
  defining, 698–699
  migrating from ASP, 724–725
  native language adapters, 545–546
late binding, 580–585
layout managers, 146
LCEs (loosely coupled events)
  COM+ supporting, 662–664
  subscribing to, 613–621
leases and lease managers, 472–474
legacy components, 12, 543–544. *See also* interoperability
less-than characters (<), 186
Lib suffix, 572
library of classes. *See* .NET Framework Class Library
lifecycles
  ASP.NET and Web forms, 730, 731–732
  message aging and, 516–517
  property groups and, 647
  of remote objects, 470, 471–474, 487
  session scope of ASP.NET pages and, 746–749
  of threads, 315–318
Lilliputians, 13
Linux machines and DCOM, 17
listening state of sockets, 367–368, 374
literal encoding, 795
little endian processor architecture
  cross-platform compatibility, 18
  overview, 13
  sockets and, 380
loading data
  alternatives to *Load* and *LoadXml* methods, 232–233
  ASP.NET and Web forms, 730, 731–732
  load balancing, 493
  passing XSLT stylesheets, 248, 252
  XML data into *XmlDocument* class, 221
LocalService and LocalSystem accounts, Windows services executing as, 684
locking
  deadlock, 333
  isolation and, 652
  message queues, 516
  property groups and, 646–647
  synchronization and, 634
  using *Interlocked* class and, 334–335
  using *Monitor* objects and, 330–334, 344–347
  using *ReaderWriterLock* class and, 335–337
log files, information recorded in, 756
login forms, 24
looping
  asynchronous calls, 855
  connectionless sockets and, 383, 384, 385
  infinite, JIT compiling interrupting, 317
  printing out nodes using, 201
  SQL queries and, 233–234
  thread notification and *Wait* method, 345–346
loosely coupled events, 613–621, 662–664

M

machine names
  disconnected message queues and, 528–529
  specifying in *ServiceController* class, 672
managed classes, 630–631
managed code, 544
managed space, transitioning to unmanaged space, 588
manifests
  defined, 32
  overview, 53
  strong names and version numbers in, 58–59
  viewing using ILDASM, 32–33
manual binding, 585–589
manual proxy generation, 856–858
manual synchronization, 329–337
marshal-by-reference objects
  delegated methods and, 479
  leases and, 473
  overview, 450–451
  RemotingServices class extending, 487
marshal-by-value objects
  delegates as, 476
  in .NET Remoting architecture, 449–450
  serialization, 479
marshal-by-value parameters, 487
marshaling and unmarshaling
  across context boundaries, 339
  COM and apartments, 575–576
  COM objects and, 585, 588
  J/Direct and unmanaged space, 559
  JIT activation of COM+ components and, 638–639
  nonisomorphic data, 552
  overview, 15, 16
  remote method parameters, 475
  in Remoting architecture, 70–71
  RMI, 17
  serialization and, 411
  serviced components and cross-context transactions, 625
  struct objects, 548–551
  tracking handlers and, 489–492
memory, common language runtime managing, 45–50
menus and menu items, adding to forms, 165–167
message boxes, 617–618
message identifiers, 517–518
message queue triggers, 502
message queues. *See also* messages
  asynchronous operations
    disconnected queues, 527–530
    message peeking, 526–527
    receiving messages, 525–527
    requesting acknowledgement, 530–532
  attaching messages to, 504–506
  authentication, 537–539
  capacity of, 520
  changing properties of, 522–523, 524
  configuring interfaces to support, 609–611
  connection caching, 521
  emptying, 520
  encryption, 539–540
  enumerating, 523–525
  handling messages, 514–525
  HTTP and, 540
  length of, 377
  monikers, 612–613
  monitor containing, 346
  overview, 495–496
  pooled threads and, 356, 357
  posting messages, 507–508
  receiving messages, 508–512, 519
  reliability and transactions, 532–537
  response queues, 506–507, 510–511, 517–519
  security, 497, 521–523, 537–540
  for sent messages, 500
  serialization, 503, 505, 509
  transactional, 532–537
  for undelivered messages, 500–501
Message Queuing 3.0. *See also* message queues
  managing, 498–500
  message delivery, 501
  message queuing triggers, 502
  servers and Active Directory, 496–497
  system queues, 500–501
  transactional message queues, 498
Message Queuing API, 503–504
messages
  acknowledging delivery of, 531–532
  aging, 516–517
  channels and channel sinks, 458–460
  concurrency of message queues, 515–516
  correlating, 517–519
  enumerating, 514–515
  JMS (Java Messaging Service), 138, 601
  journaling, 519
  message peeking
    access rights, 522
    acknowledgments and, 532
    asynchronously, 526–527
    concurrent access by multiple queues, 515
    correlating messages, 519
    overview, 514
    transactional message queues and, 535–536
  posting, 507–508, 533
  receiving
    acknowledging receipt of, 531–532

asynchronous, 526–527
correlating messages, 519
overview, 508–512
in Remoting architecture, 70
retrieving from databases, 273–274
serialization and, 503, 505, 509
transformations, 459–460
WSDL and, 788–791, 793–795
messages to users, Web Forms and, 715–716
metadata
attributes and, 131–133
defining manually, 585–589
generated when JavaBean classes compiled, 100
overview, 123–124
in PE files, 53
reflection and, 124–131
remoting and, 464, 467
XML attributes and, 187
Metal PLAF, 148
methods
accessing properties using, 98–100
code access security and, 86
cross-language development, 44, 568–569
data readers and, 284–285
event sinks and, 591–592
invoking in unmanaged DLLs
J/Direct used for, 546–551
P/Invoke, 551–571
JavaBeans and, 92
late binding and, 580–585
LCEs and, 613
native, declaring, 548
primitive data accessed using, 111–112
of queued interfaces, 610
role-based security, 78
subscribing and unsubscribing to events, 101–102
synchronization, 338
variable numbers and arguments, 118
Web services and, 837–838
Microsoft Distributed Transaction Coordinator (MS DTC), 25, 651
Microsoft Interface Definition Language. *See* MIDL
Microsoft Intermediate Language. *See* MSIL
Microsoft Internet Explorer, creating and managing, 577–580
Microsoft Internet Information Services. *See* IIS
Microsoft Java Binary Converter tool (jbimp), 122–123
Microsoft Message Queuing 3.0. *See* Message Queuing 3.0
Microsoft .NET Framework Class Library. *See* .NET Framework Class Library
Microsoft Passport, 24
Microsoft TAPI 3.0 Type Library, 572–574
Microsoft Visual J# .NET. *See* Visual J# .NET
Microsoft Visual J++. *See* Visual J++
Microsoft Visual SourceSafe (VSS) settings, 122
Microsoft Visual Studio .NET. *See* Visual Studio .NET
Microsoft Windows 2000 thread priorities, 321–322
Microsoft Windows XP
System Restore API, 551–556
thread priorities and, 321–322
MIDL (Microsoft Interface Definition Language), 15, 576. *See also* IDL
migration
from ASP pages to ASP.NET, 724–727
from JDK and Visual J++, 121–123
MIME (Multipurpose Internet Mail Extensions), 771, 772
minus signs (-), inserting separators into menus, 164
modal and modeless dialog boxes, 175
modules. *See also* MSIL
compiling, 53
MSIL and, 30
monikers, 612–613
monitors
event classes signaling threads compared to, 349–350
queues and, 346
synchronization and, 330–334, 344–347
MS DTC (Microsoft Distributed Transaction Coordinator), 25, 651
Mscorcfg.msc, 64–65
mscorlib assembly, 32
MSI (Windows Installer) files
assemblies packaged as, 64
deploying ASP.NET applications and, 745
MSIL (Microsoft Intermediate Language). *See also* modules
ASPX files and, 713
compiling applications into, 30–38
compiling into native code, 40
data types, 112
directives, 36, 37
overview, 29
verification, 38–39
MSIL assembler (ILASM.exe), 38–39
MSMQ (Microsoft Message Queue). *See also* message queues
JMS and, 601
Message Queuing 3.0 compared to, 496
overview, 141
msxsl script, 260–263
multi-environment development. *See* cross-platform compatibility
multicasting, 173
multithreading
COM objects and apartments, 575
Java and, 120–121

message peeking and, 527
overview, 309
processes described, 12
synchronization
automatic, 338–341
interrupting threads and, 318
manual, 329–337
overview, 325–328
static and thread data, 341–343
synchronization and COM+ components, 633–637
thread notification, 343–354
thread pooling, 355–359
timers, 354–355
multitier development. *See N*-tier development
mutexes, 353–354

N

N-tier development
architecture, 6–8
connectivity and data formats, 12–21
data access, 21–23
integrity and transactions, 25
Java and, 26–27
.NET Enterprise Services, 25–26
scalability and availability, 24–25
security, 23–24
two-tier (client/server) architecture, 3–6
Nagle coalescing, 372, 381
name service, 15, 18
named templates, 254–255
names
of array classes, 114
classes and forms in J#, 162
of classes in ASP.NET pages, 699–700
of computers, 365–366, 367
cross-language development and CLS, 44
friendly names, 289–290
of messages in WSDL documents, 789–790
of operations in WSDL documents, 793
searching UDDI registry for, 871
of services, 670–671
strong names, 57–58
namespaces
ADO.NET and, 267
external functionality, 260–263
importing into ASP.NET pages, 699–700
importing into Visual Studio, 163
Java and, 121
in .NET Framework Class Library, 67–69
resolution, 107
SOAP Faults using, 820
validating against XML documents using, 216
in WSDL, 785–787, 858
XML documents and, 188, 192, 207, 229
XML serialization, 436–437
XSLT and, 242, 246
naming
forms, 162–163, 164
interfaces, 585, 587
JavaBeans, 92, 93–96
RCW performing transformations, 573–574
Web Forms, 706
native code, MSIL compiled into, 40
Native Image Generator (Ngen.exe), 40
native methods, declaring, 548
native types, 545–547
navigating
DOM trees, 222, 224–225
elements and attributes, 205–206
XML documents, 192, 251–252
nested data types, 805–809
nesting
DataSet objects, 304
reader and writer locks and, 336
transactions, 534
.NET. *See* Visual J# .NET
.NET Compact Framework, 66
.NET Enterprise Services, 25–26. *See also specific services*
.NET Framework Class Library
API for interacting with Message Queuing 3.0, 502
authentication support, 405–408
byte ordering, 381
channels in, 451
creating and managing threads using, 311–312
definitions of standard COM interfaces, 587
endpoints and, 365
IP address lookup, 365
Java and
arrays, 114–115
console I/O, 118–119
exceptions, 115–116
interfaces, 116–117
J# objects, 109
methods with variable numbers and arguments, 118
packaging and locating classes, 106–108
primitive types, 109–112
strings, 113–114
threads, 119–121
ubyte data type, 119
value types, 113
JNDI compared to, 141
namespaces, 67–69
overview, 65–69

pluggable protocols, 394–396
Visual J++ class libraries and, 90–91
.NET Framework Configuration tool
configuring code groups, 85
defining code access permission sets, 83–84
editing configuration files, 64–65
granting access to individual Web sites, 399
.NET Framework SDK, 31
.NET interop marshaler, 546, 575–576
.NET Remoting. *See also* remoting
architecture, 69–71, 449–451, 460
remoting model, 451–455
Web service clients, 859–863
network programming. *See N*-tier development; programming basics
NetworkService account, 684
Ngen.exe (Native Image Generator), 40
nodes in XML documents
associating with XML documents, 228
creating, 227–228
DOM Node interface, 220
navigating, 202–205, 224–225, 251–252
reading, 198–202
searching, 226, 251–252
testing type of, 201
nonblocking and blocking sockets, 387–389
nontransactional messages, 501
notifications
asynchronous calls and, 854–855
subscribing components receiving, 621
thread notification, 343–354
NTLM authentication, 407

O

Object Management Group (OMG), 16
object references. *See also* marshal-by-reference objects; reference objects
deserialization status, 431–432
proxies and, 457–458
remoting, 487
object request brokers (ORBs), 16–17
Object RPCs, 16–17
objects. *See also specific objects and types of objects*
application-wide, initializing in Global.asax, 743–745
deserialization, 416–417, 431–432
graphs (object collections), 427–432, 435–436
in Java class hierarchy, 109
lifecycles and leases, 471–474
representing in WSDL, 800–804
serializable, 413–414
synchronization, 339–341
ODBC (Open Database Connectivity), 21–22
old code integrated into .NET applications, 50–51
OLE DB
ADO.NET, 268, 269, 270–272
history of, 22–23
parameterized statements, data type mappings, 276–282
OMG (Object Management Group), 16
once-only session initialization, 749
one-way remoting, 486–487
Open Database Connectivity (ODBC), 21–22
Open File dialog box, adding to applications, 174
Open menu item, adding to applications, 176–178
ORBs (object request brokers), 16–17
ORPCs (Object RPCs), 16–17
outgoing queues, 497, 501
output caching, 767–768
overloading
cross-language development and CLS, 44
handling polymorphic parameters using, 570
WSDL and, 791

P

packages
importing multiple Web services from one server, 865
Java and, 106–107
names of, 836
parameters
ADO.NET support, 276–282
invoking stored procedures, 283
naming, 791–793
passing to threads, 314–315
polymorphic, 569–570
remote methods and, 475
transformations, 254–263
Web services and, 791–793, 859
WSDL documents and, 788–793
XSLT parameter declarations, 254–258
Pareto principle, 244, 254, 822
parsing
XML documents, 196–197
XML strings, 190
XPath strings, 252
passing
complex data types
nested, 805–809
passing *DataSet* objects, 811–814
polymorphism and generic object conversion, 809–811
representing objects in WSDL, 800–804
XML serialization, 804–805
credentials, 825, 851–852
parameters to threads, 314–315

stylesheets to *Load* method, 248
XML documents, 814–815, 846–847
XSLT stylesheets, 248, 252
Passport, 24
passport-based authentication, 761
pattern matching, 242
PE (Portable Executable) file format
compiling MSIL into, 38
metadata in, 53
overview, 30
permissions and permission sets. *See also* access rights
code access security and, 82–85
dynamic discovery and, 868
message queues and, 521–523
for programming Windows services, 668
SQL Server and ASP.NET, 751
PERMVIEW.exe tool, 86
persistence
of ASP.NET pages, 746–749
of connections, 403
to DOM trees, 230
J2EE and, 136
of objects, 411
XML used for, 190
PEVerify tool, 39
pinging, 471
P/Invoke (Platform Invoke Service)
callbacks, 567–568
calling conventions, 568–569
calling System Restore API, 551–571
compiling and running programs, 566–567
defining constants, 556–557
exception handling, 570–571
J/Direct compared to, 551
mapping data structures, 557–562
overview, 551
polymorphic parameters, 569–570
security, 571
System Restore API, 551–556, 562–564
Visual Basic compared to, 50
pipelining, 403
placeholders in parameterized statements, 276–277
PLAF (Pluggable Look and Feel) feature of Swing, 148–149
Platform Invoke Service. *See* P/Invoke
Pluggable Look and Feel (PLAF), 148–149
plus signs (+), in URIs and streams posted to Web servers, 400
pointers (C++), in common language runtime, 45–46, 46–47
polymorphism
object conversion, 809–811, 849–851
P/Invoke and, 569–570
pooling
COM+ serviced components, 627, 642–645
connection handles, 521
data store connections, 273
HTTP connection management and, 403–404
J2EE connections, 134
SOAP and asynchronous calls, 854
state variables and, 643–644
threads, 355–359, 391–392, 401, 854
port numbers
associating with service names, 367
client channels and, 464, 475, 479, 481
connection-oriented sockets, 363–367
HTTP and, 393, 481, 484
sockets comprised of, 12
TCP channels and, 453
TcpListener and *TcpClient* classes, 376–377, 378
UdpClient class, 386
portability. *See* cross-platform compatibility
Portable Executable (PE) file format
compiling MSIL into, 38
metadata in, 53
overview, 30
porting existing code. *See* migration
ports
multiple TCP channels and, 451
overview, 364
private message queues and, 506
State Service and, 750
TcpTrace, 842
WSDL and, 773, 793–797
prefixes
for COM+ component interface names, 610
namespace associations in XML documents, 188
for namespaces in WSDL documents, 785–786
namespaces in XML documents, 437
registering *http*, *https*, and *file*, 395
presentation logic, 72
primitive types
interfaces and queued operations, 611
Java and, 109–112
objects setting values using, 281
sending and receiving, 503–504
storage, 748
value types in common runtime language, 46
principals, 77, 80–81
priorities
ASP.NET and caching, 765
assigned to threads, 321–322
of pooled threads, 356
of queued messages, 501, 506
private assemblies
overview, 55–56

RCWs as, 577
search paths, 63–64
serviced components, 631
strongly named, 59
private connectors, creating, 627
private data serialization
binary serialization, 482
deserialization and, 425
inaccessible, 417
properties, 434–435
private-key encryption
message queuing, 538
strong name utility generating, 57
support for, 408
private objects, server-activated, 71, 452
private ports for server replies, 506
private queues
accessing, 497
asynchronous communication, 529–530
COM+ creating, 610
obtaining lists of, 525
for server replies, 506–507
private sockets, creating, 368
private types, 124, 126
private UDDI registries, 872
privileges. *See* permissions and permission sets
probing, 63–64
producer-consumer system architecture, 343–347
ProgIDs, 583, 585, 592
programmatic discovery of Web service clients, 869–870
programming basics. *See also N*-tier development
overview, 361
security over the Internet, 405–408
web network programming, 393–404
properties
data readers exposing, 284
defining, 98–100
of message queues, changing, 522–523, 524
of messages, filtering, 518
of parameter objects, 281
of *TextBox* and *TextBox* control, 169–171
viewing in Visual Studio, 170
Properties window (Visual Studio .NET)
alphabetizing properties listed in, 170
changing filenames and form names using, 163–164
click events in, 171–172, 176
code behind updated using, 164
protocols. *See also specific protocols*
associating with *portType* elements, 793–794
pluggable, 394–396
provider interface (OLE DB), 22
proxies. *See also specific proxies*
accessing objects across context boundaries, 339, 624–625
creating Web service client for .NET Remoting using, 860–861
global settings and, 398
JIT activation of COM+ components and, 638–639
marshal-by-reference objects and, 449, 450
in .NET Remoting model, 453,–458, 860–861
remoting using, 447
Web services
cookies, 818–819
creating, 835–836
creating clients, 833–834, 836–838
methods and, 837
retargeting, 841–842
WSDL documents generating, 856–858
public data
HTTP remoting and, 482
in WSDL documents, 802–803, 805
XML serialization and, 434–435
public-key encryption
strong name utility generating, 57–58
support for, 408
public key tokens and unsigned serialized classes, 420
public queues
attaching to, 504–506
disconnected message queues and, 529
overview, 496–497
syntax of, 504
publisher policy files, 62, 64–65

Q

QFE (Quick Fix Engineering) files, 62, 64–65
queries. *See* XPath
question marks (?), placeholders in parameterized statements and, 276–277
queued components, 661–662
queued types, 345
queued values, 344–347
queues. *See* message queues
Quick Fix Engineering (QFE) files, 62, 64–65

R

race conditions
aborting threads and, 319
synchronizing threads and, 326–327, 329
thread notification, 347, 350
ragged arrays, 115
raw sockets, 415
RCWs (Runtime Callable Wrappers)
calling

creating RCWs from command line, 576–577
handling *HRESULT* values, 574–575
marshaling and apartments, 575–576
RCW implementation, 573–574
delegate classes defined by, 578–580
late binding and, 580, 583, 584
overview, 50–51
references to CCWs, 629
strongly named, 616–617
read-locked message queues, 516
read-only data
DataReader objects and, 283–285
in WSDL documents, 802, 803
XML serialization and, 435
read operations
DataTables and, 233–234
reading bytes from keyboards, 119
reading from text input streams, 177
server responses, 378–379, 397
from sockets, 369–370
validation errors and, 217
XML documents using, 198–202, 204–206
reader locks, threads writing to resources, 335–337
recoverable messages, 501, 506
rectangular arrays, 115
reference objects, 450. *See also* marshal-by-reference objects
reference types, 45–46
references. *See also* object references; Web references
to assemblies, COM+ and, 616, 617
circular, 615
to columns in tables, 289–290
to current application domains, 312
to currently running threads, 321
to EXE files, wrapped inside DLLs, 479
to message queues, 529
unqualified, 121, 180, 313
reflection
configuration files and assemblies and classes, 464
JavaBeans and, 92
late binding and, 580–585
metadata and, 124–131, 464
overview, 92
Regasm.exe, 595
registering
object types, 461, 474
requests, 395
serviced components, 630–632
tracking handlers, 490–491
in UDDI registry, 773, 870–874
in Windows Registry
assemblies registered in, 630–632
service descriptions in, 685
services identified in, 670–671
Type objects created based on information found in, 583
viewing list of COM components and type libraries in, 572
relational data, 230–234
relational databases and ADO.NET, 265, 287–288
relations, 296–299, 306
relative positioning of controls on ASP.NET pages, 734
remote events, 476–480
Remote interface, 136
Remote Method Invocation. *See* RMI
Remote Procedure Calls. *See* RPCs
remote references. *See* marshal-by-reference objects
remoting
ASP.NET, 71–72, 749–751
channels and channel sinks, 458–460, 492–494
client-activated object remoting
configuration files and, 464–465, 468, 469
lifecycles, 471, 473
overview, 452, 469–471
well-known objects, 457
COM+ serviced components and, 649–650
exceptions thrown during, 455
HTTP, 480–486
interfaces, 467–468
.NET Remoting
architecture, 69–71, 449–451, 460
remoting model, 451–455
Web service clients, 859–863
ObjRef object and proxies, 457–458
one-way remoting, 486–487
registering object types, 461, 474
remote object activation, 71
remote objects, 448–451
RemotingServices class, 487–489
server-activated object remoting
activation modes, 465–467
configuration files, 474, 492
CORBA and, 17
IIS and, 483
lifecycles, 471
overview, 452, 461–468
well-known objects, 457
TCP remoting
client-activated, 469–471
HTTP remoting compared to, 480
object lifecycles and leases, 471–474
remote events, 476–480
remote method parameters, 475
security, 474–475
server-activated, 461–468
tracking handlers, 489–492
Web services, 72–73

remoting model, 451–455
request scope of ASP.NET pages, 753
requests
  asynchronous, 401–402
  HTTP forms and, 728–729
  registering, 395
  WSDL documents and, 788–793
responses
  fragmented, 397
  HTTP forms and, 729
  HTTP request/response model
    data types and streams, 399–400
    overview, 394, 396–398
    persistent connections and, 403
    pipelining, 403
    pooling connections, 403–404
    WebRequest and *WebResponse* classes compared to, 401
  queues, 506–507, 510–511, 517–519
  SOAP, 811–813
  WSDL documents and, 788–793
restore points, 552, 565
restoring systems. *See* System Restore API
RMI (Remote Method Invocation)
  alternatives to using, 121
  COM/J2EE bridge, 601
  Java serialization and, 411
  .NET/J2EE bridge, 601
  overview, 17
  reference and value objects, 18–19
  serialization, 18
role-based security, 763
root element
  of DOM, 222, 243
  of XML documents, 438
root node (XSLT), 243
RowSet interface, 134
Roxburgh, Peter, 133
RPC-style SOAP messages, 794–795, 814–815, 861
RPCs (Remote Procedure Calls)
  connectivity and data formats, 14–16
  defined, 448
  HTTP and, 19
  Java and, 135
  ORPCs (Object RPCs), 16–17
Running state of threads, 315, 321
runtime
  checking objects cast as interfaces during, 588
  MSIL code verification, 39
Runtime Callable Wrappers. *See* RCWs
runtime hosts, 75
runtime types, 207

S

safe points, 317, 318
Save menu item, adding to applications, 177–178
SAX API, 196, 209
scalability
  application domains affecting, 75
  DBMS, 24–25
  JIT activation, 638–639
  pooling, 273, 642–645
  state management, 639–642, 645
schema. *See* XML schema
SCM (Service Control Manager), 675, 680
scope
  of ASP.NET pages
    application scope, 751–752
    request scope, 753
    session scope, 746–750
  HTTP forms and, 729
  of XSLT parameter declarations, 255
SCP (serviced components proxy), 648–650
scripts and scripting
  functions and subroutines defined in, 698
  migrating from ASP pages to ASP.NET, 725
  transformations, 260–263
searching
  for assemblies, 712
  DOM trees, 225–226
  nodes in XML documents, 251–252
  paths, 63–64
  through UDDI registry, 871
security
  application domains, 74–76
  ASP.NET, 760–764
  code access security, 76, 81–86, 373, 655
  COM+ components
    code access, 655
    declarative, 656–657
    imperative, 660–661
    implementing, 657–659
  DBMS, 23–24
  declarative, 78–79
  dynamic discovery and, 868
  HTTP remoting, 485–486, 771
  imperative, 77, 80–81
  message queues, 497, 521–523, 537–540
  operating system security and, 77
  over the Internet, 405–408
  P/Invoke and, 571
  role-based, 76–81
  sockets and, 373
  strong names, 57–58
  TCP remoting, 474–475

threads and, 314
Web classes and, 399
Web service clients, 851–852
Web services and, 771, 822–826, 852
Windows services and, 682–685
Security Adjustment Wizard, 82
SEH (structured exception handling), 570–571
selective serialization, 422
self-contained (single-file) assemblies, 54
semicolons (;), multiple paths specified using, 63
separators inserted into menus, 166
serial version unique ID, 419
Serializable interface (Java), 18
serialization
custom, 419, 423–427
deserialization
binary deserialization, 419–421, 431–432
defined, 411
message bodies, 509
overview, 416–417
remoting and, 459
selective serialization, 422
versioning, 417–422
formatting data, 412–415
graphs (object collections), 427–432
HTTP remoting and, 481, 482
interfaces, 18
Java objects to XML files, 135
message queues and, 505
messages and, 503, 505, 509
method parameters, 611
overview, 411–412
remoting and
channel sinks, 459
marshal-by-value objects and, 450, 476, 479
ObjRef objects, 457
security, 474–475
state storage and, 751
RMI, 18
selective, 422
sockets and, 381–382
versioning, 417–422
XML. *See* XML serialization
serialization binders, 421–422
serialization surrogates, 425–426
serialver utility (JDK), 419
server-activated object remoting
activation modes, 465–467
configuration files, 474, 492
CORBA and, 17
IIS, 483–485
lifecycles, 471
overview, 452, 461–468
well-known objects, 457
server-side programming in ASP.NET
advantages of, 714
client-side validation and, 718–719
converting ASP into, 725–727
creating controls, 735–739
displaying information, 733–734
filename extensions associated with, 693–694
HTML forms and, 701–704
languages supported by .NET, 695, 702
message labels, 715
overview, 140–141, 708–710
services provided by, 691
user interaction, 732–733
server-side validation, 722, 723
server skeletons, 17
servers
connection-oriented, 364–373
HTTP remoting, 481–483
Message Queuing 3.0 Servers, 496–497
restricting access to, 368
TCP remoting and, 461–468
Service Control Manager (SCM), 675, 680
service description files for Web services. *See* WSDL
serviced components. *See* COM+ components, serviced components
serviced components proxy (SCP), 648–650
ServiceForm Windows Form, 668–669
services. *See* Web services; Windows services; *specific services*
Services console, 668–669, 684
servlets, 136–137
Session EJBs, 135–136
session scope
of ASP.NET pages, 746–750
of HTTP form storage, 729
shared assemblies, serviced components as, 631
shared locking, 652
Shared Property Manager (SPM), 646–647
shared resources, mutexes, 353–354
shared state of COM+ components, 645–650
shared types, importing schemas into WSDL documents, 857
short variables and serialization, 511
signaled state of threads, 347–353
signing
digital signatures, 408, 537–538
RCWs, 577
Simple Object Access Protocol. *See* SOAP
single-file (self-contained) assemblies, 54
single-pass processing. *See* stream-based processing of XML data
single-threaded apartments (STA), 725

SingleCall mode, 71, 465, 466
Singleton mode, 71, 465, 466
singleton transactions, 535–536
sink event interface, 578, 590, 591–594, 618–619
sinks
  channel sinks, 458–460, 492–494
  COM events, 577–580
  custom, 488, 492–494
  event sinks
    adding, 663–664
    method and event names matching, 593–594
    overview, 591–592
  formatter sinks, 459
  HTTP remoting and, 481
  overview, 459–460
  security and TCP remoting, 474–475
slots, synchronizing threads, 342
sn.exe (strong name utility), 57–58
SNK extension, 57
SOAP Faults, 819–822, 839, 840
SOAP (Simple Object Access Protocol). *See also* WSDL
  asynchronous calls and, 854
  authentication information and, 826
  binding elements in WSDL documents and, 794–795
  capturing messages, 842
  containers, 772
  data type definitions and, 788
  DataSet objects, 811–813
  design principles, 20–21
  error handling and, 819–822
  HTTP and, 451, 481, 540
  Java and, 135, 433
  messages, 788–791
  naming parameters and return values, 791–793
  .NET Remoting using, 861
  port types, 793–794
  sending messages, 837–838
  transactions and, 827
  Web service client proxies, 833–834
  Web services and, 72–73, 772
SOAP with attachments, 772
SOAPSUDS tool, 481
sockets
  asynchronous communication, 389–392
  blocking
    Close method, 372–373
    Receive method, 387–389
    ReceiveFrom method, 385
    server responses, 378–379
  buffering data, 371–372
  connection-oriented
    accepting and rejecting client requests, 368–369
    clients, 374–376
    creating, 365
    disabling sending and receiving data over, 371–373
    establishing endpoints, 365–367
    handling multiple clients and requests, 369–371
    in listening mode, 367–368
    overview, 363–364
    reading data from, 369–371
    TcpListener and *TcpClient* classes, 376–379
    thread pooling and streams, 391–392
    Web servers and, 394
  connectionless
    overview, 382–387
    thread pooling and streams, 392
    Web servers and, 393
  data transmission issues, 380–382
  determining conditions of, 390
  disadvantages of, 13
  interoperatibility with non-Microsoft technologies, 602
  overview, 12–14, 362–363
  ports and, 364
  security, 373
  serialization and, 381–382
  status queries, 389–390
  variable-length data and, 388
  Web network programming, 393–404
Sockets API, 362, 416
sources, transformation, 248–250
spaces in URIs and streams posted to Web servers, 400
SPM (Shared Property Manager), 646–647
sponsors and leases, 472–474
SQL
  binding Web controls, 741–742
  disadvantages of, 21
  ODBC, 21–23
SQL Server
  ADO.NET data adapters and, 268, 269
  architecture of, 5–6
  connecting to data sources, 270–272
  session state storage, 750–751
SQL statements
  accessor methods, 286
  command objects containing, 275
  data adapters, 286–288
  parameterized, data type mappings, 276–282
  reading content of *DataTables*, 233–234
SSL (Secure Sockets Layer)
  HTTP and, 485, 540
  overview, 408
  Web services and, 825, 852
STA (single-threaded apartments), 725
stack builder sink, 459–460

stack builders, 70
stacks
  MSIL and, 37–38
  security checking through, 79
  value types created on, 113
state management
  ASP.NET, 746–754
    application scope, 751–752
    cookies, 753–754
    remote session state, 749–751
    request scope, 753
    session scope, 746–749, 751–752
  COM+ serviced components, 639–642
  of threads, 315–318
  Web service clients, 847–849
  Web services, 816–819
state objects and JavaBeans, 93–96
State Server service (ASP.NET), 767
State Service (ASP.NET), 750
state variables, pooling, 643–644
stateful session bean (J2EE), 471
stateless and stateful objects, 645
states. *See also specific states*
  of connections, changed, 274
  of controls, retrieving, 716
  of services, 671, 673–674
  of threads, 315–318
static data
  remoting and, 466–467
  synchronization and threads, 329, 341–343
static discovery of Web service clients, 863–866
static fields and cross-language development, 44
static methods, 329, 637
static objects
  defining in Global.asax file, 749
  defining in Web.config, 752
static values and port numbers, 366–367
Stopped state of threads, 316
StoppedRequested state of threads, 319
storage
  of HTTP forms, 729
  of objects in sessions, 747–749
  persistent, J2EE and, 136
  of primitive types, 748
  of queues, 520
  of session state, 749–750
  TLS (thread local storage), 341–342
  of XML documents, 192
stored procedures, invoking, 282–283
stream-based processing of XML data
  classes supporting XML documents, 192
  escaping and copying when writing, 212
  exception handling, 208–209
  overview, 190–191
  parsing using *XMLReader* class, 196–197
  processing model of, 202
  processing using an *XMLTextReader* instance, 197–205
  reading and navigation options, 205–206
  traversing hierarchies and reading content, 202–205
  types and namespaces, 207–208
  writing using *XmlWriter* class, 209–212
streams
  asynchronous I/O and thread pooling, 358–359, 391–392
  binary, 397
  characters forbidden in, 400
  custom formatting of serialization streams, 423–425
  defining for socket architecture, 14
  deserializing data on, 416
  DOMs as, 227, 230
  reading one-at-a-time, 177–178
  sending to Web servers, 399–400
  serialization and, 414–415, 440
  synchronous I/O, 378
  text-based, 397
  XML
    deserializing, 441–444
    serialization and, 440
    writing *DataSet* objects as, 301–303
strings
  array of bytes, 384, 385
  Java and, 113–114
  XML, 190, 207–208
strong names
  assemblies, 57–58, 616, 617
  binding policies applied to, 61
  RCWs and, 616–617
  stored in GAC, 468
struct objects, marshalling, 548–551
structure definitions, 213–214
structured exception handling (SEH), 570–571
structures, primitive types as, 110
stubs
  CORBA, 17
  JIT activation of COM+ components and, 638–639
  RPCs and, 14–15
stylesheets, templates for XSLT and transformations, 240–244, 246–250
subroutines defined in ASP.NET, 698
subscribers and LCEs, 613
subscriptions, 618–620, 621
suffixes. *See also specific suffixes*
  ASMX files, 777
  for RCWs, 572
  remote object URIs, 452, 481

suspended server applications, 453. *See also* lifecycles
suspending threads, 316–318
Swift, Jonathan, 13
Swing
 adding dialog boxes, 174, 177
 adding dialog boxes using .NET Framework Class library, 178
 AWT and, 149
 click events, 172
 clipboards, 178
 controls, 168
 menus and menu items, 166, 167
 overview, 90, 148–149
 redeveloping the GUI, 159–181
switch-case statement, 201
sync blocks, 330, 331–333
synchronization
 activities and COM+ components, 633–637
 automatic, 338–341
 creating and managing threads, 311
 interchangeable threads, 120, 121
 interrupting threads and, 318
 manual, 329–337
 overview, 325–328
 serviced components, 625
 static and thread data, 341–343
 writing *DataRelation* objects as XML, 304
synchronizer wrapper objects, 333
synchronous I/O, 378
system contracts, adapters in J2EE, 134–135
system queues, 500–501
System Restore API
 calling, 551–556
 defining methods in, 562–564
 invoking, 565–566
 running, 566–567
System.Web.dll assembly, 400

T

tables within *DataSet* objects. *See DataTable* objects
tags
 serializable objects, 413–414
 XML using, 186–188, 194
TAPI3 (Microsoft Type Library), 572–574
targets
 Web service proxies, 837
 XML documents and transformation, 248–250
TCP/IP, 362, 363
TCP remoting
 client-activated, 469–471
 HTTP remoting compared to, 480
 object lifecycles and leases, 471–474
 remote events, 476–480
 remote method parameters, 475
 security, 474–475
 server-activated, 461–468
TCP (Transmission Control Protocol)
 channels based on, 451–452, 453, 459
 connection-oriented clients' sockets based on, 374
 connection-oriented sockets using, 362
TcpTrace, 842
Teach Yourself J2EE in 21 Days, 133
templates
 application configuration files and, 462–463
 named templates, 254–255
 for Windows services, 675–676
 for XSLT stylesheets, 240–244, 246–250
temporary files, recoverable messages as, 501
terminated servers in .NET Remoting model, 453
terminating threads
 aborting, 319–320, 322
 background and foreground threads, 322–323
 interrupting, 318
 mutexes and, 353
text documents, XSLT output format, 240–241, 249–250
text input streams, reading data from, 177–178
text strings, reading content of elements with, 205–206
TextBox controls
 adding to Web Forms, 706–708
 client-side validation, 718–719
 clipboards and, 179–180
 contents of, 715–716
 designing, 168–171
 server-side controls, 709–710, 732, 756
thread local storage (TLS), 341–342
thread-relative static fields, 341
thread-safe methods, 466
threads. *See also* multithreading
 aborting, 319–320, 322
 application domains and, 76, 312
 background and foreground threads, 322–323
 blocking
  asynchronous I/O, 358–359
  event classes and, 347–353
  Monitor objects and sync blocks, 331–333
  Wait method and thread notification, 353
 creating, 312–314
 defined, 309
 interthread communication, 343–355
 Java and, 119–121
 multiplex, 389–390
 notification, 343–354
 overview, 310–312
 passing parameters to, 314–315
 pooling, 355–359, 391–392, 401, 854

priorities assigned to, 321–322
references to currently running, 321
running order of, 325
scheduling, 321–323
security and, 314
single-threaded apartments, 575
states of, 315–318
suspending, 317–318, 327
terminating
aborting, 319–320, 322
background and foreground threads, 322–323
interrupting, 318
mutexes and, 353
unmanaged code and, 323–325
timeout parameters
ASP.NET and caching, 765
HTTP connections and, 396–397, 404
output caching and, 767
pooling, 642–643
ReaderWriterLock class and threads, 336
for receiving messages, 508–509
for sockets, 372, 388–390
WaitOne and thread notification, 347
Windows services startup and, 679
timers, interthread communication and, 354–355
Tlbexp.exe, 595
Tlbimp (Type Library Importer), 576–577, 616–617
TLS (thread local storage), 341–342
TLS (Transport Layer Security), 408
tracking handlers, 489–492
transactional message queues
delivery modes for, 501
overview, 498
reliability and, 532–537
transactional resource managers, 624, 625–626
transactions
COM+ components
duration of transaction, 654–655
isolation levels, 651–654
serviced components, 640
managing
ADO.NET, 299–300
J2EE and, 138, 141–142
rolling back, 626–627
Web service clients, 852–853
Web services and, 826–828
transformation. *See also* XSLT
advantages of, 238–240
applying stylesheets to XML documents, 246–250
applying transformations, 244–245
channel sinks and, 459–460
classes supporting, 192
external functionality, 254, 257–263
optimization, 250–254
overview, 237–238
parameterization, 254–263
partial, 253–254
RCW performing, 573–574
support for, 246
XML and XSLT, 191
XSLT processing model, 240–244
Transmission Control Protocol. *See* TCP
transparent proxies
COM+ serviced components and, 648, 650
object references and, 457, 458
sink chains, 460
static methods calls, 467
transport information in WSDL, 794
transport sinks, 459
trees
DOM, 219, 219–220
XSLT, 243–244, 253
try/catch blocks, 209, 759
Two-Phase Commit (2PC) protocol, 651
two-tier (client/server) architecture, 3–6
type libraries
accessing when creating RCWs from command line, 576–577
using COM objects without, 580–589
type library export utility, creating CCWs, 595
Type Library Importer, 576–577, 616–617
types. *See also* data types
host server applications exposing, 463–464
of messages, examining upon receipt, 510
of objects, configuration files containing information about, 468, 469, 470
XML
converting into .NET Framework types, 207–208
obtaining information from objects, 434–435
serialization and changing names of types, 437–438
serialization and collections, 435, 436

U

UDA (Universal Data Access), 22
UDDI (Universal Description, Discovery, and Integration), 773
UDDI registry, 773, 870–874
UDP (User Datagram Protocol)
deserialization and, 416
handling sockets, 385–386
overview, 382, 383
waiting for messages, 384
underscores (_), prefixing COM+ component interface names, 610

Unicode
J/Direct and, 563–564
XML documents and, 188, 210
Uniform Resource Identifiers. *See* URIs
Uniform Resource Locators. *See* URLs
uninstalling. *See* installing and uninstalling
unique identifiers, 517
unique serial numbers, 431–432
Universal Data Access (UDA), 22
Universal Description, Discovery, and Integration (UDDI), 773
UNIX
byte ordering, 13, 380–381
J2EE vs .NET, 139
port numbers, 367
unmanaged code. *See also* P/Invoke
callbacks, 567–568
calling COM components, 571–589
calling conventions for cross-language development, 568–569
defined, 544
exception handling, 570–571
integrated into .NET applications, 50–51
polymorphic parameters, 569–570
security, 571
threads and, 320–321, 323–325
unmanaged DLLs, invoking methods in
J/Direct, 546–551
P/Invoke, 551–571
unmanaged space, transitioning to managed space, 588
unmanaged types, 559–562
unmapped exceptions, 575
unmarshaling. *See* marshaling and unmarshaling
unsigned types, 548, 558
updates, Web service clients, 858–859
URIs (Uniform Resource Identifiers)
characters forbidden in, 400
encryption and, 408
overview, 393
remote objects, 452–453, 481, 487
temporary, in WSDL files, 786
tracking handlers and, 490, 492
URLs (uniform resource locators)
accessing ASMX files using, 777–778
associating with UDDI-created proxy classes, 874
disconnected message queues and, 529
programmatic discovery using, 869–870
retargeting Web service client proxies, 841–842
rewriting (mangling), 818–819
User Datagram Protocol. *See* UDP
user interaction, server-side controls on Web Forms, 732–733
user interfaces. *See also* interfaces; Swing
ASP.NET and, 69, 692
creating controls, 735–739
displaying information, 733–734
forms and selection, 732–733
J2EE and, 136–137
JMS and, 138
layout, 734
migrating from ASP pages, 725–727
user services
in J2EE, 136–137, 140–141
roles performed by, 6
XML and, 185
users
authenticating, 406–407
error messages displayed for, 757
resizing forms, 734

V

validation
HTML forms, 718–724
remote object URIs, 453
XML documents, 189, 190, 192, 213–218, 221
value objects compared to reference objects, 450
value types
in common language runtime, 46
Java and, 113
varargs, 568
Venner, Bill, 40
verification
of MSIL code, 39
overview, 47
of unmanaged code, 571
versioning
assemblies, 58–59, 61–62
scheme used by .NET, 58–59
serialization and, 417–422
serviced components and, 632–633
Web service clients, 858–859
virtual directories of Web applications
ASMX files in, 777
assemblies placed in bin directory, 700, 712
changing properties of, 745
child directories inheriting settings from, 743
creating, 705
placing service description files in, 863
security and, 824, 826
Visual Basic, 41–43
Visual J++
class libraries, 90–91
migrating to .NET, 121–123
Visual J# compiler (vjc), 31, 96, 98

Visual J# .NET
  class libraries, 90–91. *See also* .NET Framework Class Library
  deploying to, 59–60
  history of, 27
  migrating to, 121–123
  Visual J# and JDK, 90
Visual J# Upgrade Wizard, 122
Visual Studio IntelliSense, 289, 290
Visual Studio .NET
  adding controls to Windows Forms, 165–171
  ADO.NET support, 270, 272
  apartment threading and, 324
  clipboard and, 178–180
  compiling and running applications, 180–181, 400
  creating and configuring COM+ applications using, 608–612
  creating Web Forms using, 705–707
  creating Windows Forms, 160–164
  displaying dialog boxes, 174–178
  event handling, 171–174
  generating XSD schema, 441–442
  manipulating XML files using, 193–195
  message queues and, 499–500, 512–514, 532–533
  porting AWT applications to .NET, 157–159
  RCWs created using, 572–576
  Web service clients created using, 834–838
  Web services created using, 781–784, 823
  Web Setup projects created using, 745–746
vjc (J# compiler), 31, 96, 98
vjscor and vjslib assemblies, 32–33
Vlissides, John, 11
VSDISCO (Web Services Discovery) protocol, 866–869
VSS (Microsoft Visual SourceSafe), 122

W

WAR (Web Archive) files, 137
Web
  applications as ASP.NET applications, 816–826
  HTTP, 19
  request/response model
    asynchronous requests and, 401–402
    authentication and, 405, 406, 407
    creating requests, 396–398
    data types and streams, 399–400
    encryption and, 408
    overview, 394–396
    WebClient classes exposing methods, 402
  security and, 399
  SOAP, 20–21
  Web services, 19–20
Web applications
  adapting to different versions of browsers, 709
  HTTP and, 396–399, 403–404
  pluggable protocols, 394–396
  posting data, 399–401
  processing requests asynchronously, 401–402
  using *WebClient* objects, 402
Web Archive (WAR) files, 137
Web Controls, 72, 739–742
Web Forms (ASP.NET). *See also* HTML forms
  ASP.NET and, 72
  client-side validation, 718–724
  code behind forms, 710–714
  creating, 705–708
  event handling, 714–718
  message queues and, 512–514
  server-side controls, 708–710
Web methods, 72–73, 861–862
Web references
  DISCO files using, 864
  multiple services referenced, 856, 858
  .NET Remoting using, 860
  security, 852
  UDDI registries using, 872, 874
  updating, 858–859
  VSDISCO files using, 867, 868
  Web service client proxies, 836
  Web service proxies, 835–836, 841
Web servers, deploying classes with, 137
Web service clients
  asynchronous calls, 853–856
  client types, 859–862
  client view of Web service, 832–834
  creating, 834–838
  dynamic discovery of services, 866–874
  error handling, 839–841
  handling bulk data, 845–846
  handling complex types, 808, 842–844
  maintaining state, 847–849
  namespaces, WSDL, and manual proxy generation, 856–858
  passing XML documents, 846–847
  per-client sessions, 817–818
  programmatic discovery of services, 869–870
  retargeting the proxy, 841–842
  security, 851–852
  static discovery of services, 863–866
  transactional calls, 852–853
  versioning and updates, 858–859
Web Service Description Language. *See* WSDL
Web services. *See also* XML; *specific services*
  creating
    compilation, 780
    defining, 775–776

exposing existing applications as Web services, 828–829
implementing, 776–777
security, 822–826
signaling errors, 819–822
state management, 816–819
testing, 777–780
transactions, 826–828
Visual Studio used for, 781–784
data types
complex, handling, 842–844
complex, passing, 799–811
nested, complex, 805–809
polymorphism and generic object conversion, of complex 809–811
representing objects in WSDL, 800–804
XML serialization, 804–805
HTTP, 399–400
invoking services, 797–799
passing *DataSet* objects, 811–814
passing XML documents, 814–815
WSDL defining, 773
defined, 769–770
delivering under .NET, 774–775
descriptions, 790, 863–866, 867
design principles, 19–20
exposing interface
messages, parameters, and parts, 788–791
naming parameters and return values, 791–793
type definitions, 787–788
HTTP remoting and, 481
importing multiple from one server, 865
interoperability and, 602
J2EE and, 135
security, 822–826, 852
support for, 72–73
technologies underlying, 770–774
writing *DataSet* objects as XML, 301
XML and, 185
Web Services Discovery protocol, 863–866, 867
Web Services Inspection Language, 870
Web Setup projects, 745–746
Web.config
authentication in, 761–762, 763, 764
authentication specified in, 823, 825
defining static objects in, 752
error handling and, 757
language defined in, 699
overview, 742–743
retargeting Web service client proxies, 841–842
searching for assemblies, 712
well-known service types
client-activated objects, 452, 453
configuration files and, 464, 465, 468, 469
server-activated objects, 457
while loops
printing out nodes using, 201
thread notification and *Wait* method, 345–346
white pages search, 871
white spaces, ignoring in XML documents, 202–205
Winapi calling convention, 569
Windows Forms
controls, 164, 165–171
creating, 160–164
event model used by, 171–174
message queues and, 512–514
Windows Forms library, 145, 149–150
Windows Installer (MSI) files, 64, 745
Windows native type mappings, 546–547
Windows Principals
declarative security, 77
role-based security, 78
Windows Registry
assemblies registered in, 630–632
service descriptions in, 685
services identified in, 670–671
Type objects created based on information found in, 583
viewing list of COM components and type libraries in, 572
Windows SDK, 310
Windows Service template (Visual Studio .NET), 675–676
Windows services. *See also specific services*
controlling, 668–675
displaying information about, 668–672
overview, 667–668
security, 682–685
starting and stopping, 671–675, 676
writing
adding descriptions, 685–686
installer classes, 680–685
installing and testing, 686–687
structure of applications, 675–680
uninstalling, 688
WinHelp, invoking using P/Invoke, 569–570
worker threads
asynchronous I/O, 358–359
overview, 355
queue requests, 356–357
wrappers. *See also* CCWs; RCWs
creating, 556–557
J# classes acting as, 552
primitive types in, 110–111, 748
queueing Java primitive types, 345
synchronizer wrapper objects, 333
thread-safe, 330

writer locks, threads writing to resources, 335–337
WS-Inspection, 870
WSDL (Web Service Description Language). *See also* SOAP
  client view of documents, 832–834
  complex data types found by Web service clients in, 842–844
  importing into Visual Studio, 835–836
  namespaces in, 785–787, 856–858
  overloaded methods in, 791
  ports in, 795–797
  representing objects in, 800–804
  type definitions, 787–788
  UDDI and, 871, 873–874
  underlying Web services, 773
  versioning and, 858–859
wsdl.exe command-line tool, 857–858

X

xcopy deployment, 55, 745
XDR (XML Data Reduced), 214
XML Data standard, 213
XML designer (Visual Studio .NET), 193–195
XML (eXtensible Markup Language). *See also* DOM; Web services
  ADO.NET and
    binding and, 739–741
    inferring *DataSet* structure from XML, 304–306
    writing *DataRelation* objects as XML, 304
    writing *DataSet* objects as XML, 301–303
  advantages of, 185
  application configuration information specified using, 60
  creating documents, 229–230
  as a data format, 186–190
  disadvantages of, 189
  discovery information encoded in, 864, 865–866, 867
  elements of, 187
  in-memory processing
    extracting information from DOM documents, 222–226
    loading XML into *XmlDocument* class, 221
    overview, 219–220
    standards, 192
    treating DOM fragments as streams, 227
    writing and manipulating XML documents, 227–230
    writing *DataSet* objects as XML, 301
  inferring schema of documents, 304–306
  J2EE and, 135, 136–137
  Java objects converted into, 433
  namespaces, 865–866
  overview, 230–234
  roles performed by, 189–190
  SOAP, 20–21
  stream-based processing
    classes supporting for XML documents, 192
    escaping and copying when writing, 212
    exception handling, 208–209
    overview, 190–191
    parsing using *XMLReader* class, 196–197
    processing model of, 202
    processing using an *XMLTextReader* instance, 197–205
    reading and navigation options, 205–206
    traversing hierarchies and reading content, 202–205
    types and namespaces, 207–208
    writing using *XmlWriter* class, 209–212
  support for, 140, 190–192
  transformations. *See* transformations
  underlying Web services, 771
  validation and entity resolution, 213–218
  Web service clients passing documents, 814–815, 846–847
  Web services and, 19
XML formatter, 417
XML Registries, 135
XML Schema Definition tool, 214
XML schema documents (XSD), 193–195, 441–442
XML schemas
  attaching to documents, 215–216
  classes supporting, 192
  defining for document validations, 217–218
  defining multiple, 216, 217
  history of, 213–214
  inferring, 232, 304–306
  manipulating files using Visual Studio, 193–195
  overview, 188–189
  writing *DataSet* objects as XML, 301, 303
  XML document format and, 213–214
XML serialization
  controlling serialization, 438–440
  of *DataSet* objects, 811
  deserialization, 417, 441–444
  graphs and, 435–436
  HTTP remoting and, 481, 482
  messages and, 503
  namespace and type handling, 436–438
  overview, 412, 413
  Web services and, 804–805, 809–811
  WSDL and, 791–793
XML types, 303, 438
XmlNode interface, 226
XMLT processor, 240–241

XPath
classes supporting, 192
overview, 226
searching and navigating nodes in XML documents, 251–252
searching through DOM trees, 226
transformations, 250–254, 257–258
XSD files (XML schema documents), 193–195, 441–442
XSD.exe, 214
XSD.exe, 441–443
XSLT (Extensible Stylesheets Language Transformations)
advantages of, 244
processing model, 240–244
stylesheets for documents
importing data into, 254–258
output formats, 249–250
passing, 248, 252
templates for, 240–244, 246–250
transformations, 244–245, 252–253
XSLT Programmer's Reference 2nd Edition, 241

Y

yellow pages search, 871

Z

zones and code access security, 81–82

About the Authors

The authors of this book work for Content Master Ltd., a technical authoring and consultancy company in the United Kingdom that specializes in developing technical content.

John Sharp has developed MSDN Field Sessions and MOC courseware for Microsoft and has recently completed coauthoring *Visual C# .NET Step by Step* for Microsoft Press.

Andy Longshaw is a consultant, writer, and educator specializing in Web-based technologies and components, particularly in design and architecture.

Peter Roxburgh has authored a wide variety of courses and articles on Java and mobile computing topics and is an invited member of the WAP Group. He has recently coauthored *.NET Applications for Mobile Devices* for Microsoft Press.

Sheep Shears

How do sheep lose their wool? With sheep shears. And who wields them? Sheep shearers, of course. Shearing sheep is physically demanding. Good shearers check to see that their shears are clean and sharp, remove the sheep from a small catching pen, shear the fleece (wool) off in a set pattern of blows (shearing strokes), and release the sheared sheep into a counting-out pen. A good shearer can shear up to 300 sheep a day and charges about $2.50 per head, depending on what class of sheep (lambs, rams, ewes) are sheared.

At Microsoft Press, we use tools to illustrate our books for software developers and IT professionals. Tools very simply and powerfully symbolize human inventiveness. They're a metaphor for people extending their capabilities, precision, and reach. From simple calipers and pliers to digital micrometers and lasers, these stylized illustrations give each book a visual identity, and a personality to the series. With tools and knowledge, there's no limit to creativity and innovation. Our tagline says it all: the *tools you need to put technology to work.*

The manuscript for this book was prepared and galleyed using Microsoft Word. Pages were composed by Microsoft Press using Adobe FrameMaker+SGML for Windows, with text in Garamond and display type in Helvetica Condensed. Composed pages were delivered to the printer as electronic prepress files.

Cover Designer:	Methodologie, Inc.
Interior Graphic Designer:	James D. Kramer
Principal Compositor:	Kerri DeVault
Interior Artist:	James D. Kramer
Copy Editor:	Ina Chang
Indexer:	Kari J. Kells

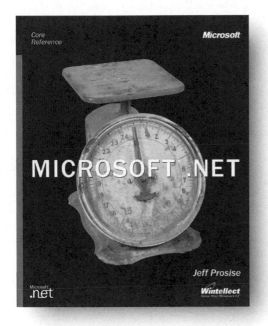

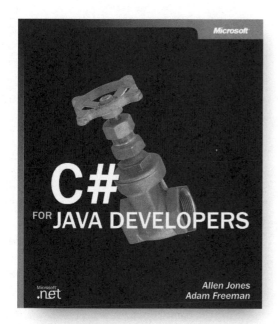

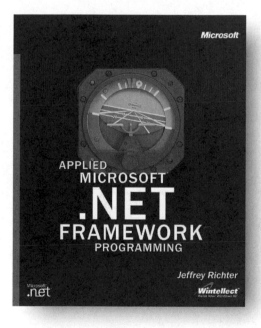

Get a **Free**
e-mail newsletter, updates, special offers, links to related books, and more when you

register on line!

Register your Microsoft Press® title on our Web site and you'll get a FREE subscription to our e-mail newsletter, *Microsoft Press Book Connections.* You'll find out about newly released and upcoming books and learning tools, online events, software downloads, special offers and coupons for Microsoft Press customers, and information about major Microsoft® product releases. You can also read useful additional information about all the titles we publish, such as detailed book descriptions, tables of contents and indexes, sample chapters, links to related books and book series, author biographies, and reviews by other customers.

Registration is easy. Just visit this Web page and fill in your information:

http://www.microsoft.com/mspress/register

Microsoft®

Proof of Purchase

Use this page as proof of purchase if participating in a promotion or rebate offer on this title. Proof of purchase must be used in conjunction with other proof(s) of payment such as your dated sales receipt—see offer details.

Microsoft® Visual J#™ .NET (Core Reference)

0-7356-1550-0

CUSTOMER NAME

Microsoft Press, PO Box 97017, Redmond, WA 98073-9830